W9-AHA-692

CICS Handbook

CICS Handbook

Yukihisa Kageyama

Intertext Publications
McGraw-Hill Book Company

New York St. Louis San Francisco Auckland Bogotá
Hamburg London Madrid Mexico Milan Montreal
New Delhi Panama Paris São Paolo
Singapore Sydney Tokyo Toronto

The views expressed herein are those of the author and do not necessarily reflect the view of the United Nations.

Library of Congress Catalog Card Number 89-85584

Copyright © 1989 by Multiscience Press, Inc. All rights reserved. Printed in the United States of America. Except as permitted under the United States Copyright Act of 1976, no part of this book may be reproduced or distributed in any form or by any means, or stored in a database or retrieval system without the prior written permission of the publisher.

10 9 8 7 6 5 4 3 2 1

ISBN 0-07-033637-7

Intertext Publications/Multiscience Press, Inc.
One Lincoln Plaza
New York, NY 10023

McGraw-Hill Book Company
1221 Avenue of the Americas
New York, NY 10020

Composed by Context, Inc., San Diego, CA

Contents

Preface

The Customer Information Control System (CICS) is one of the most popular Database/Data Communication (DB/DC) control systems. Because of its general acceptance by all industries for their wide variety of applications, CICS seems to have become a standard DB/DC control system in large mainframe computer installations. Therefore, every data processing professional should know about CICS to the same degree as a high-level language (COBOL, for example), Job Control Language (JCL), and Time Sharing Option (TSO). This book is about how to utilize CICS effectively and productively from an application development point of view.

Objective

The objective of this book is to serve readers as a comprehensive guide book to CICS application development.

From this book, one can learn a wide variety of CICS commands, because it describes virtually all CICS commands with the most commonly used options and their practical applications. Also, from this book one can learn a number of advanced and useful programming techniques which can be used immediately in the actual CICS application systems for the real business applications.

In addition, since writing CICS application programs itself is only a part of developing CICS application systems, this book goes beyond the conventional books of CICS application programming. That is, this book discusses various advanced topics and guidelines such as application-related entries of CICS control tables, system security considerations, recovery/restart considerations, tests and debugging techniques, intercommunication facilities, and system design considerations. All of these are required for developing effective CICS application systems.

Further, this book includes the most up-to-date topics such as CICS/MVS, VS COBOL II, DB2, Multi-Region Operation (MRO),

Intersystem Communication (ISC), LU6.2, Advanced Program-to-Program Communications (APPC), CICS OS/2, and Systems Application Architecture (SAA). Particularly, topics of distributed processing are extensively discussed. These are the topics of increasing importance today and for the future.

Therefore, after reading, understanding, and digesting this book, one should be able to develop complex CICS application systems based on the forward-looking system design approaches with a comfortable understanding of system activities behind CICS.

Expected Readers

This book is written for any data processing professionals who wish to learn CICS application development. However, since this book uses COBOL as a primary language, readers should have sufficient experience in COBOL programming in the batch system environment. Otherwise, no prior online experience is expected of the reader.

At the same time, this book is intended for those experienced systems analysts and CICS application programmers who wish to improve their knowledge and skills of CICS application development from the introductory level to the advanced level.

Structure

The chapters in this book are arranged in such a way that readers will be able to acquire knowledge of CICS application development gradually from the introductory level to the advanced level. The last chapter is a case study in which the readers can integrate all knowledge and skills acquired in this book.

Since one can learn programming only by practice, the exercises are important elements of this book. Therefore, most chapters have programming exercises at the end. Readers are encouraged to actually try these exercises.

Appendices provide a sample program, summary of CICS commands, BMS macros, etc. These should assist the reader to understand concretely the topics discussed in the main chapters. They should also serve as convenient references.

The glossary lists some significant CICS-related terms and acronyms to aid the reader in understanding technical terms and their abbreviations.

CICS Command Format

CICS commands with their exceptional conditions are summarized in Appendix B. As can be seen, many of them have many options, some of which are mutually exclusive or dependent on certain options. This implies that even if each command format is shown with the full options and each option is explained individually, it would not be very helpful in showing the reader how to use these commands in the actual programming situations.

Therefore, instead of showing all command formats with the full options, this book takes a different approach. That is, for certain complex commands, this book presents the actual coding examples of the CICS commands for the most common situations which the reader would face during actual programming. Based on these examples, the options of the commands are explained. The reader will find that this approach is more helpful than the conventional method.

Restrictions

This book is based on the current CICS/MVS Version 2 Release 1 and VS COBOL II. These two software products are by definition for the CICS command level. Therefore, by CICS application development, this book means developing CICS application systems based on the CICS command level.

However, at the time of this book's publication, many CICS installations are still using CICS/OS/VS Version 1 Release 7 and VS/COBOL. Therefore, an effort is made in this book to make sure that descriptions, examples of CICS commands and related topics are independent of the versions of CICS and COBOL. When a distinction is required among versions of CICS and COBOL, it will be specified as such.

Acknowledgments

This book was originally written as a classroom textbook for the CICS application development course which the author teaches at New York University. This textbook has been subsequently revised for general data processing professionals who wish to learn the subject.

The author wishes to express his gratitude to the students who participated in his CICS course at New York University. Their inspiring questions and debates in the class enriched the contents of this book.

References

This book uses the following IBM manuals from the CICS/MVS Version 2 Release 1 library and others as sources:

CICS/MVS Version 2 Release 1 Library

GC33-0155	General Information
SC33-0139	Application Programming Primer
SC33-0504	Facilities and Planning Guide
SC33-0506	Installation Guide
SC33-0507	Customization Guide
SC33-0509	Resource Definition (Macro)
SC33-0510	Operations Guide
SC33-0511	CICS-Supplied Transactions
SC33-0512	Application Programmer's Reference
SC33-0514	Messages and Codes
SC33-0516	Problem Determination Guide
SC33-0519	Intercommunication Guide
SC33-0520	Recovery and Restart Guide
SC33-0521	Performance Guide
SC33-0522	XRF Guide

Others

GC26-4042	VS COBOL II General Information
GC26-4135	MVS/XA Integrated Catalog Administration: Access Method Services Reference
SC26-4080	DB2 Application Programming Guide for CICS/OS/VS Users
SC26-4362	SAA; Writing Applications: A Design Guide
SC33-0616	CICS OS/2 System and Application Guide
90X7790	OS/2 E.E. Version 1.1 APPC Programming Reference

1

Introduction to CICS

1.1 Batch and Online Systems

Characteristics

There are two types of computer application systems. One is the batch application system and the other is the online application system. Because of the wide acceptance of time sharing software (for example, TSO), the distinction between these two types has become less clear. However, there still exist certain characteristics which distinguish these two types of application systems from each other.

Figure 1-1 summarizes these characteristics. If you are familiar with the batch system, these characteristics are self-explanatory except for a few online-related concepts, which we will discuss later in detail.

As these characteristics suggest, the batch system has a system environment where jobs run one by one in a conventional way, whereas the online system has a system environment where many transactions run concurrently.

Advantages of the Online System

These days, the online system is so common that virtually every large mainframe installation has at least one online application system. This is because the online system has advantages over the batch systems. Some of the advantages are as follows:

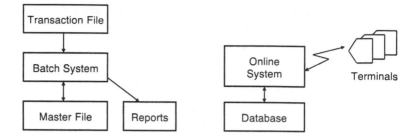

	Batch System	**Online System**
Input	Data from card, tape, disk. Batched, sequential, scheduled. Need preparation (e.g., keypunch, data coding).	Data from terminal. Random, concurrent. Can be entered as data arrive.
Update of file	Reserved during a job. Other jobs have to wait.	Concurrent. Instant.
File I/O	I/O must be in sequence.	I/O can be concurrent.
Output	Printed reports, output files. User must wait for batch jobs to produce reports (day, week, month).	Message to terminals. Updated files, system log. Reports printed in local printer. Instant feedback.
Start of job	Operator (or Operating System) initiates the job. Other jobs in the same region must wait.	Once CICS is initialized, entering transaction id triggers the transaction to start.
Processing mode	Single task. Single-thread. Priority in job scheduling.	Multitask. Multithread. Priority processing.
End of job	Each job.	Each transaction. Once CICS is terminated, no transactions can be entered.
Turnaround	Usually much longer.	Usually almost instantly.
Resource usage	Less.	More.
Example of application	Monthly sales report.	Airline reservation system.

Figure 1-1   Characteristics of batch and online systems.

- Up-to-date file (information) can be shared among many users simultaneously and instantly.
- Data validation and editing can be done at the data entry time.
- Users can use the computer facility whenever it is needed.

Advantages of the Batch System

On the other hand, in spite of the ever-increasing popularity of the online system, the batch system has not died out, and it still contributes to the large portion of data processing requirements. This is because the batch system has advantages over the online system. Some of the advantages of the batch system are as follows:

- Certain information does not have to be updated or displayed on a real-time base. Users can wait until the next day, the end of a week, or the end of a month. In this case, the batch system is sufficient for the purpose.
- If massive file updates or lengthy calculations are involved, the batch system should be used because the online processing in these areas tends to be very costly in terms of resource consumption.

Choice of Online or Batch System

There is no question of superiority or inferiority between the online system and the batch system, they are simply different. For certain applications, the online system may be more suitable than the batch system, while the batch system may be more suitable for other applications.

For example, airline reservation applications would be suitable for the online system, while complex mathmatical applications would be suitable for the batch system. Therefore, one must make a rational decision to choose either the online system or batch system based on the nature of the application.

Complementary Nature

Also, the online system is usually accompanied by the batch system. After a certain amount of online real-time operations, a series of batch jobs are run against the database which the online system updated. These batch jobs further process data in the database and produce periodical and ad hoc reports. In this sense, therefore, the online system and batch system are inseparable, and they are complementary.

1.2   Brief History of CICS

The advantages of the online system were first recognized in the late 1950s and early 1960s by such businesses as the airline and banking industries, which pioneered the development of the large-scale online systems. Since then, online systems have become explosively popular among all industries.

Prior to CICS

Until the late 1960s, all online systems were developed on a custom-made basis for each application for each installation. However, developing an online system is a complex project involving the operating system (OS), telecommunication access methods, data access methods, and application programs.

Therefore, instead of developing an online system from scratch each time, the database/data communication (DB/DC) control system was developed in order to provide the control functions of the online system environment. Under a DB/DC control system, an application program can concentrate on the application processing, being free from considerations of OS, hardware, etc., which are not really the interest of the application programs. Developing an online application system under the DB/DC control system as a result became significantly easier and faster.

Early CICS (Macro Level)

The Customer Information Control System (CICS) was developed by IBM in the late 1960s as a DB/DC control system. The initial version was the macro level CICS, under which, as the name "macro" suggests, the application programs used the Assembler-macro type CICS macros for requesting CICS services. Under the CICS macro level, application development became significantly easier. However, it was still cumbersome work which required special skills.

CICS Command Level

Over time, CICS was constantly upgraded and functionally enhanced. One significant upgrade was from the macro level to the command level. CICS commands are the high-level language version of CICS macros, in a sense that one CICS command achieves a CICS service which would have been achieved by a series of CICS macros. Therefore, under CICS command level, application development became much easier than under the CICS macro level.

Current CICS Family

There are currently five CICS products available, each of which is developed for a particular operating system. These products are as follows:

Product	Operating System
CICS/MVS Version 2 Release 1	MVS/XA, MVS/ESA
CICS/OS/VS Version 1 Release 7	MVS, MVS/XA
CICS/DOS/VS Version 1 Release 7	VSE
CICS/VM Release 2	VM/SP
CICS OS/2	OS/2

Functionally, all of these CICS products are compatible with each other, with certain exceptions caused by the differences among the corresponding operating systems. Therefore, if you learn one CICS product (e.g., CICS/MVS under MVS/XA), you can easily use other CICS products.

CICS/MVS

CICS/MVS Version 2 Release 1, upon which this book is based, is the current version of the mainstream CICS product, replacing its older version, CICS/OS/VS Version 1 Release 7. It runs under the Multiple Virtual Storage/Extended Architecture (MVS/XA) operating system and provides comprehensive services as a general purpose DB/DC control system in the virtual system environment.

Specifically, CICS/MVS takes advantage of the MVS/XA operating system for addressing above the 16-megabyte line. With VS COBOL II, which also takes advantage of the XA environment, CICS application programs (command level) under CICS/MVS can utilize 2 gigabytes (2,000 million bytes) of address space. Further, CICS/MVS offers a sophisticated recovery/restart capability through the Extended Recovery Facility (XRF).

In spite of its functional comprehensiveness and complexity, the current CICS/MVS is easy to use not only from an application programming point of view, but also from a system programming point of view. This is one of the reasons why CICS/MVS is one of the most widely used DB/DC control systems.

1.3   CICS System Concept

Objective

The primary objective of CICS is to provide the control and service functions of the database/data communication (DB/DC) system as a package. That way, CICS users can develop their own customized DB/DC system by concentrating on the application development based on their own needs, freed from detailed considerations for the operating system and computer hardware, including communication terminals.

CICS itself is not a DB/DC system unless applications accompany it, because CICS provides only the control environment for the DB/DC system. This is why CICS is categorized as a DB/DC control system.

CICS System Components

The CICS system concept is illustrated in Figure 1-2. As shown, CICS positions itself between the operating system and application programs. The essential role of CICS is, therefore, to interface between application programs and the operating system as the DB/DC control system. To this end, CICS consists of five major system components, each of which provides the various specialized CICS services as follows.

Data-Communication Functions The component of data-communication functions provides an interface between CICS and terminals or other systems. The following CICS services are offered:

- To interface to telecommunication access methods, such as VTAM, TCAM, BTAM.
- To free application programs from terminal hardware through Basic Mapping Support (BMS), which provides:

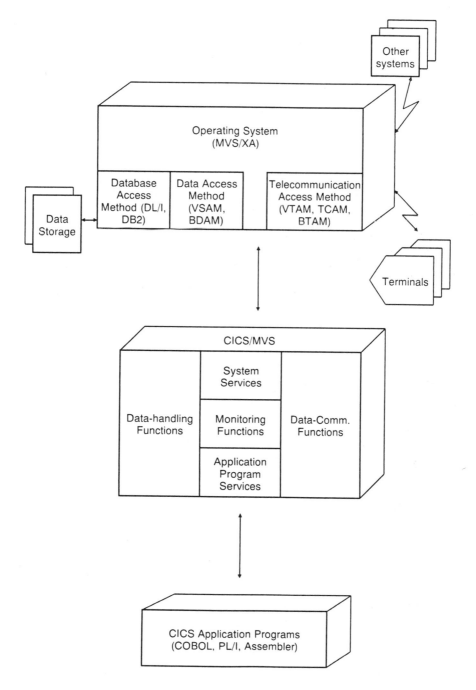

Figure 1-2 CICS system concept.

— device independence
— format independence
- To provide Multi-Region Operation (MRO), through which more than one CICS region in a system can communicate.
- To provide Intersystem Communication (ISC), through which a CICS region of a system can communicate with other CICS regions in other systems or other non-CICS systems.

Data-Handling Functions   The component of data-handling functions provides an interface between CICS and data. The following CICS services are offered:

- To interface with data access methods, such as VSAM and BDAM.
- To interface with database access methods, such as DB2, SQL/DS, and DL/I.
- To maintain data integrity by:
  — control of simultaneous record updates
  — protection of data at task ABENDs
  — protection of data at system (CICS or OS) failures

Application Program Services   The component of application program services provides an interface between CICS and application programs. The following CICS services are offered:

- To interface with COBOL, PL/I, Assembler programs
- Command level translator
- Excution diagnostic facility (EDF)
- Command interpretater (CECI)
- Screen definition facility
- Trace and dump facilities

System Services   The component of system services provides an interface between CICS and the operating system. The following CICS services are offered:

- Program control, such as load and release of application programs
- Storage control, such as acquiring and freeing of storage
- Task control, such as task scheduling based on the task priority

Monitoring Functions   The component of monitoring functions monitors various events within CICS and provides a series of statistics to be used for system tuning.

CICS Application Programs

CICS application programs do not come with the CICS product, and they must be developed by the CICS users using various CICS services. However, as discussed above, CICS offers all services and control functions required for the DB/DC system. This means that CICS users can spend most of their time in application programming instead of system programming.

Therefore, for the CICS users, CICS application programming is the major task required to develop their own DB/DC system. This is the most significant advantage of using CICS as the DB/BD control system.

CICS Application Development

Writing CICS application programs itself does not automatically create an effective CICS application system. In addition to application programming, one has to consider many other aspects, such as CICS control tables, system security, reliability, performance, user-friendliness. This book will discuss all of these aspects required for developing effective CICS application systems.

1.4   CICS Control Program and Tables

The CICS system components described in the previous section are the convenient grouping of CICS system programs, each of which performs its own specialized functions. Actually, the core portion of CICS (called the CICS nucleus) consists of IBM-supplied CICS control programs and corresponding user-specified CICS control tables. Figure 1-3 shows some of them, which are particularly related to the CICS application development.

In this book, all CICS control programs and the CICS control tables shown in Figure 1-3 will be discussed in conjunction with the CICS application development. However, it should be noted that in addition to these control programs and tables, CICS has other control programs and tables which are primarily related to system programming.

CICS Control Programs (IBM-Supplied)	CICS Control Tables (User-Specified)
FCP (File Control Program)	FCT (File Control Table)
JCP (Journal Control Program)	JCT (Journal Control Table)
KCP (Task Control Program)	PCT (Program Control Table)
PCP (Program Control Program)	PPT (Processing Program Table)
SCP (Storage Control Program)	-
TCP (Terminal Control Program)	TCT (Terminal Control Table)
TDP (Transient Data Program)	DCT (Destination Control Table)
TSP (Temporary Storage Program)	TST (Temporary Storage Table)
(Others)	(Others)

Figure 1-3 Some of the CICS control programs and tables.

Advantages

Constructing the CICS nucleus by the control programs and corresponding control tables provides unique advantages. CICS control programs achieve their primary tasks based on their corresponding tables. Once installed in the computer facility, CICS control programs can be kept as they are, while system programmers can keep adding or modifying the control table entries as hardware configuration changes or as application programs are added.

This approach makes the CICS system flexible and easy to maintain. From an application programming point of view, application programs are almost free from the considerations for hardware, and they can concentrate on the application specifications.

CICS Start-Up

Starting up a CICS system involves a series of complex tasks internally, while externally it appears relatively simple because of the concept of the CICS control programs and their corresponding control tables. The following are typical procedures for CICS start-up:

CICS itself is a job, whose JCL is executed just like any other batch job. The main job step in the CICS job is the CICS System Initialization Program (SIP). Usually, every day in the morning, the computer operator or the system automatically runs this CICS job. The CICS job, or SIP to be more precise, loads the corresponding System Initialization Table (SIT), based on which SIP further loads all control programs and tables, and performs initial housekeeping tasks. Then CICS is ready to execute CICS transactions within its own region.

CICS Shutdown

Similarly, shutting down the CICS system appears externally relatively simple in spite of its internal complexity. The following are the typical procedures for CICS shutdown:

Usually, at the end of a day, the computer operator terminates the CICS job by entering the Master Terminal transaction with the shutdown option. Then the CICS job produces various logs, statistics, dumps and other reports, and ends. After this, no CICS transaction could be executed in the region which has already disappeared.

1.5   Structure of CICS Application Program

Since a CICS application program (command level) is a program, it has a basic structure, and the program must be coded based on a set of rules similar to any other program. Since this book uses COBOL as the primary programming language, let us now discuss the structure of the CICS application program (command level) in COBOL.

Figure 1-4 summarizes the basic structure of the CICS application program in COBOL, while Appendix A shows a complete example of a CICS application program (command level) in COBOL. You can verify yourself that the sample program in Appendix A follows the basic structure summarized in Figure 1-4.

Requirements for COBOL Program

The requirements of each DIVISION of the COBOL program for the CICS command level are as follows:

Identification Division   The IDENTIFICATION DIVISION must satisfy the following requirements:

• Program-ID is required.
• Other comments, such as below, are optional, but recommended:
  — AUTHOR
  — DATE-WRITTEN
  — DATE-COMPILED
  — REMARKS

```
IDENTIFICATION DIVISION.
PROGRAM-ID.              xxxxxx.

ENVIRONMENT DIVISION.
DATA DIVISION.
WORKING-STORAGE SECTION.
77   ----------                     )
     :                              )    Specify Working Storage
01   ----------                     )       data.
     :
LINKAGE SECTION.                          Optional
     :
PROCEDURE DIVISION.
     :                              )
     (COBOL Statements)            )
     :                              )    Program logic
     (CICS Commands)               )
     :                              )
     GOBACK.
```

Figure 1-4 Basic structure of CICS application program in COBOL.

Environment Division   The ENVIRONMENT DIVISION must satisfy the following requirements:

• Only the header is required.
• No other entries, such as CONFIGURATION SECTION, INPUT-OUTPUT SECTION, FILE CONTROL, or SELECT, are needed.

Data Division   The DATA DIVISION must satisfy the following requirements:

• FILE SECTION (including FD, RD or SD) is not required.
• WORKING-STORAGE SECTION is required. Specify here your Working Storage data. The length of Working Storage plus the length of Task Global Table (TGT) must not exceed 64K bytes.
• LINKAGE SECTION is optional. Depending on the application program, this may have to be coded; otherwise it does not have to be coded. If this section is not coded, CICS Command Level Translator will automatically insert it for the minimum requirements.

Procedure Division   The PROCEDURE DIVISION must satisfy the following requirements:

• COBOL statements and CICS commands should be coded here.

- The following COBOL statements are prohibited because these basically trigger OS Supervisor Calls (SVCs), which cannot be issued in a CICS application program:
  — ACCEPT, CURRENT-DATE, DATE, DAY, DISPLAY, EXHIBIT, STOP RUN, TRACE
  — Any I/O statements (OPEN, CLOSE, READ, WRITE, REWRITE, DELETE, START)
  — REPORT WRITER feature
  — SORT feature
- Equivalent statements (except Report Writer and Sort) are prepared in the form of CICS commands.
- A CICS application program must end with the CICS RETURN command and/or GOBACK statement.
- The CALL statement is allowed if the called program does not issue any CICS commands or inhibited COBOL statements mentioned above and if it is written as a reentrant program (see Section 1.13). The CALL statement in this case can be issued as the following example:

```
CALL subprog USING  xxx yyy zzz
```

where "subprog" is the name of subprogram, and xxx, yyy, zzz are the names of parameters to be passed to the subprogram.

Improvements by VS COBOL II

VS COBOL II provides a much better interface to CICS than VS/COBOL. In results, some of the restrictions mentioned above have been removed under VS COBOL II. An application program written in VS COBOL II can issue the following statements:

GOBACK: Control will be returned to another VS COBOL II program or CICS itself.

STOP RUN: Control will be returned to CICS.

EXIT PROGRAM: Control will be returned from a VS COBOL II subprogram to a VS COBOL II main program.

CALL: A CICS application program written in VS COBOL II can CALL a subprogram written in VS COBOL II (reentrant by definition), regardless of whether the subprogram issues CICS commands or not.

Other improvements by VS COBOL II will be discussed later in this book as related subjects are discussed.

1.6   Command Format and Argument Values

General Command Format

Appendix B summarizes the most commonly used CICS commands. As can be seen, each command has its own options, based on the following general format:

```
EXEC CICS function
     [option (argument value)]
     [option (argument value)]
        :
```

The "function" is a CICS service request. The "option" is one of the options available to the command. The "argument value" determines the characteristics of the value to be placed for the option as detailed information.

End of Command Delimiter   The command delimiter indicates the end of a command, but it is dependent on language (COBOL, PL/I, or Assembler), as follows:

COBOL	PL/I	BAL
END-EXEC	;	End of continuation (at column 72)

Example   Taking the READ command as an example, the following is an actual command coding with the associated delimiter in three languages:

COBOL	PL/I	BAL	
EXEC CICS READ	EXEC CICS READ	EXEC CICS READ	*
DATASET('FILEA')	DATASET('FILEA')	DATASET('FILEA')	*
INTO(IOAREA)	INTO(IOAREA)	INTO(IOAREA)	*
RIDFLD(KEYNUM)	RIDFLD(KEYNUM)	RIDFLD(KEYNUM)	*
LENGTH(REC-LEN)	LENGTH(REC-LEN)	LENGTH(REC-LEN)	*
UPDATE	UPDATE;	UPDATE	
END-EXEC.			

COBOL as Primary Language   This book uses COBOL as the primary language for CICS application programming (command level). Therefore, hereafter, all commands and program examples will be discussed in terms of the COBOL program.

Argument Values

The argument values determine the characteristics of a value to be placed to an option as detailed information. Since these argument values are used for describing the command format, one must understand what they are. There are six types of argument values in COBOL, as follows:

Data Value   The data value is an actual value or the name of a field which contains that value, as shown in the example below. It could be a literal constant value or the field name in which the value is defined. It is used for specifying such values as the record length and key length.

```
        8
KEYLENG                    <=== 77 KEYLENG PIC S9(4) COMP VALUE 8.
```

Data Area   The data area is a data name or a field name which is defined in the Working Storage Section, as shown in the example below. It is used for specifying such names as the input/output area and key field.

```
RECORD-AREA                <=== 01 RECORD-AREA.
                                  05 FIELD1 PIC X(5).
                                  05 FIELD2 PIC X(20).
```

Pointer-Ref   The pointer-ref(erence) is the name of a Base Locator for Linkage (BLL) cell, which is defined as the full word binary field (PIC S9(8) COMP), as shown in the example below. It is used to establish addressability. We will discuss this subject in detail later (see Section 2.7).

```
LINKAGE SECTION.
01    PARMLIST.
      05   FILLER        PIC S9(8) COMP.
      05   A-POINTER     PIC S9(8) COMP.      <==  Pointer-ref
      05   B-POINTER     PIC S9(8) COMP.      <==  Pointer-ref
01    A-DATA-AREA.
      05   FIELD1    -----
      05   FIELD2    -----
01    B-DATA-AREA.
      05   FIELDA    -----
      05   FIELDB    -----
```

Name The name is a literal constant or the name of a data area defined in the Working Storage Section, as shown in the example below. It is used for such purposes as dataset name and map name.

```
'FILEA'
FILE-NAME       <=== 05 FILE-NAME PIC X(5) VALUE 'FILEA'.
```

Label The label is a COBOL paragraph or section name. It is used for passing control to the paragraph or the section of the Procedure Division.

HHMMSS The HHMMSS indicates a decimal constant (e.g., 120316) or the data name of S9(7) COMP-3 field (containing the value 0hhmmss+). It is used for the time expression.

1.7   Command Language Translator and Compiler

The CICS commands are not legal statements which a language compiler can recognize. Therefore, all CICS commands must be translated to the legal statements of the language on subject (i.e., Assembler, COBOL, or PL/I). For this purpose, there is one CICS command language translator for each of Assembler, COBOL, and PL/I.

Comparison of Program Compile

In order to understand the function of the CICS command language translator, let us compare the compilation process of a CICS application program with the conventional program (i.e., batch program).

- *Conventional batch programs*: The compiler directly compiles the source codes. The object from the compiler is then linkedited, creating a load module of the program.
- *CICS application programs (command level)*: The translator first translates CICS commands of the source codes into legal statements of the language on subject (e.g., COBOL). Using the output from the translator, the compiler compiles the program. The object from the compiler is then linkedited, creating a load module of the program. This process is illustrated in Figure 1-5.

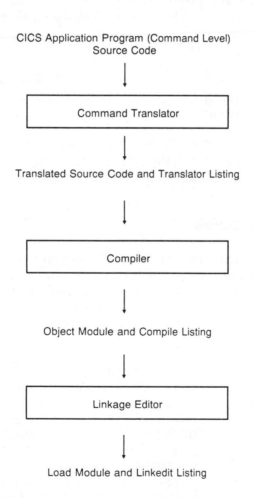

Figure 1-5 Program compile with CICS command language translator.

Example of Translation

Appendix A (Sample Program) shows a CICS application program (command level) in COBOL in the source code list (before translation) and in the compile list (after the translation). If you compare these two lists carefully, you will see what the translator actually does. The following are two major points to note:

- The translator comments out the original CICS commands and replaces them by the standard COBOL CALL statements.
- The translator also inserts necessary variables and statements in the application program for CICS housekeeping purposes.

Translator Options for COBOL

There are various options available in the CICS command language translator for COBOL. In general, the defaults are recommended, except for the following considerations:

- Specify LANGLVL(2) if VS/COBOL is to be used.
- Specify COBOL2 if VS COBOL II is to be used.
- Specify DLI if DL/I commands are to be used in the application program.

COBOL Compiler Options

The COBOL compiler options do not depend on whether the COBOL program to be compiled is a CICS application program with CICS commands or a batch application program without CICS commands. Therefore, you can specify the COBOL compiler options in the best suitable way for your application and your installation. However, the following options should be noted:

VS COBOL Options	Equivalent VS COBOL II Options	Function
LIB	LIB	Copy library
CLIST	OFFSET	Condensed list
DMAP	MAP	Data map
OPTIMIZE	OPTIMIZE	Optimization
SXREF	XREF	Sorted cross-reference
(n/a)	FDUMP	Formatted dump
(n/a)	RENT	Reentrant mode

The LIB option is required since BMS Symbolic Maps are to be copied from the COPY library. The DMAP and CLIST options gives the data map and condensed listing of COBOL statements, respectively, so that these options are very useful for the effective debugging. The OPTIMIZE option optimizes the program and reduces the program size significantly, so that it helps to conserve the system resources. The SXREF option provides the sorted cross-reference, so that this is always convenient for the program debugging.

If the VS COBOL II compiler is to be used, the equivalent options listed above should be specified. In addition, the FDUMP option should be specified since this gives a formatted dump when the program terminates abnormally. Also, the RENT option should be specified in order to make the application program reentrant (see Sections 1.13, 1.14).

JCL Example for COBOL

JCL is always installation dependent, and as such it is difficult to present a generalized example any reader can use. Figure 1-6 is one typical example of JCL, supplemented by a cataloged procedure in

```
//XXXXXXXX JOB ------- (JOB ACCOUNT INFORMATION, ETC) -------
//*
//*****************************************************************
//*                                                               *
//*    JCL EXAMPLE FOR CICS COBOL TRANS, COMP & LINK              *
//*                                                               *
//*****************************************************************
//*
//COBUCL  EXEC CICEITCL,REG=768K,OUTC='*',
//             INDEX='CICS.R210'
// PARM.TRN='NOSEQ,LANGLVL(2)',
// PARM.COB='NOTRUNC,LIB,SIZE=580K,BUF=40K,CLIST,SXREF,OPT,DMAP,NOSEQ'
//TRN.SYSIN    DD DSN=AAAAAAA.TEXT.COBOL(TXT1INQ1),DISP=SHR
//COB.SYSLIB   DD
//             DD DSN=AAAAAAA.TEXT.MAPSYMB,DISP=SHR
//LKED.SYSLMOD DD DSN=AAAAAAA.TEXT.LOADLIB(TXT1INQ1),DISP=SHR
//LKED.SYSIN   DD *
//
```

```
Notes:
=====
  (1)  This JCL is for IBM MVS Operating System.
  (2)  This JCL uses a cataloged procedure CICEITCL.
  (3)  In TRN.SYSIN, specify a source program library of CICS COBOL
       application programs with a module name (i.e., program name).
  (4)  In COB.SYSLIB, concatenate a BMS symbolic map library.
  (5)  In LKED.SYSLMOD, specify application LOADLIB or system
       LOADLIB with the load module name (i.e., program name).
  (6)  Since JCL is installation dependent, this JCL may not be
       suitable to your installation.
```

Figure 1-6 JCL example for translation, compile, and linkedit of CICS command level application program.

Figure 1-7 for translation, compile, and linkedit of a COBOL program under CICS.

1.8 Execution of a CICS Application Program

Basic Procedures

In order to execute a CICS application program under CICS, the application programmer should follow the following procedures:

1. Translate, compile, and linkedit a CICS application program (command level) into the CICS application program library (LOADLIB).
2. Define the transaction identifier into PCT with the associated program name.
3. Define the program into PPT.
4. Sign on to CICS.
5. Enter the transaction identifier.

Additional Preparation Required

Above are only the basic procedures for executing a CICS application program. In addition to the basic procedures, the detailed CICS system environment must be prepared properly by the system programmers or application programmers. The following are some examples:

• The terminal must be registered in TCT.
• The CICS user identifier must be registered in SNT.
• Other CICS tables (e.g., FCT, JCT, DCT) must be prepared for the application program, if required.

JCL

JCL is not required to run a CICS application program (or transaction), since JCL is prepared for the CICS job itself by the system programmer. Once the CICS job starts, this job is considered as one CICS region, under which more than one application transaction (or program) can be executed simultaneously.

```
//CICEITCL PROC SUFFIX=1$,
//               INDEX='CICS.R150',
//               OUTC=A,
//               REG=256K,
//               BUF=16K,
//               WORK=SYSDA
//*
//*****************************************************************
//*                                                              *
//*        CATALOGED PROCEDURE FOR                               *
//*            CICS COBOL PROGRAM TRANS, COMP AND LINK           *
//*                                                              *
//*****************************************************************
//*
//*
//*              *** TRANSLATION STEP ***
//*
//TRN       EXEC PGM=DFHECP&SUFFIX,
//               REGION=&REG
//STEPLIB   DD  DSN=&INDEX..LOADLIB,DISP=SHR
//SYSPRINT  DD  SYSOUT=&OUTC
//SYSPUNCH  DD  DSN=&&SYSCIN,
//               DISP=(,PASS),UNIT=&WORK,
//               DCB=BLKSIZE=400,
//               SPACE=(400,(400,100))
//*
//*              *** COMPILE STEP ***
//*
//COB       EXEC PGM=IKFCBL00,REGION=&REG,
//               PARM='NOTRUNC,LIB,SIZE=&REG,BUF=&BUF'
//SYSLIB    DD  DSN=&INDEX..COBLIB,DISP=SHR
//SYSPRINT  DD  SYSOUT=&OUTC
//SYSIN     DD  DSN=&&SYSCIN,DISP=(OLD,DELETE)
//SYSLIN    DD  DSN=&&LOADSET,DISP=(MOD,PASS),
//               UNIT=&WORK,SPACE=(80,(250,100))
//SYSUT1    DD  UNIT=&WORK,SPACE=(460,(350,100))
//SYSUT2    DD  UNIT=&WORK,SPACE=(460,(350,100))
//SYSUT3    DD  UNIT=&WORK,SPACE=(460,(350,100))
//SYSUT4    DD  UNIT=&WORK,SPACE=(460,(350,100))
//*
//*              *** LINK-EDIT STEP ***
//*
//LKED      EXEC PGM=IEWL,REGION=&REG,
//               PARM=XREF,COND=(5,LT,COB)
//SYSLIB    DD  DSN=&INDEX..LOADLIB,DISP=SHR
//          DD  DSN=SYS1.COBLIB,DISP=SHR
//SYSLMOD   DD  DSN=&INDEX..LOADLIB,DISP=SHR
//SYSUT1    DD  UNIT=&WORK,DCB=BLKSIZE=1024,
//               SPACE=(1024,(200,20))
//SYSPRINT  DD  SYSOUT=&OUTC
//SYSLIN    DD  DSN=&INDEX..COBLIB(DFHEILIC),
//               DISP=SHR
//          DD  DSN=&&LOADSET,DISP=(OLD,DELETE)
//          DD  DDNAME=SYSIN
```

```
NOTES:
=====
(1)  This cataloged procedure is for IBM MVS Operating System.
(2)  TRN step translates CICS/VS command level COBOL source code
     into the standard COBOL code.
(3)  COB step is a standard VS/COBOL compile step, using the output
     from the translation step (TRN).
(4)  LKED is a standard linkedit step, using the output from the
     compilation step (COB).
(5)  Since JCL is installation dependent, this cataloged procedure
     may not be suitable to your installation.
```

Figure 1-7 Cataloged procedure example for CICS command level application program.

Linkedit

At the linkedit time of a CICS application program, the load module name (i.e., the output from the linkedit step) must be the same name as the program name specified in PCT and PPT, as follows:

Name of load module = Program name in PPT
                     = Program name in PCT

If this convention is not kept, CICS would not be able to find or execute the program.

1.9 Sign-On/Off

Sign-on

The primary function of CICS sign-on is to associate your CICS user identifier with the CICS system in terms of security, priority, and other functions.

For signing on, you have to use the CICS-supplied transaction CESN or CSSN, which prompts the sign-on screen (Figure 1-8). In order to complete the sign-on, the correct user identifier (or name) and password must be typed on the screen. Unless you complete the sign-on to CICS successfully, you can not initiate your protected CICS transactions.

CSSN is the conventional sign-on transaction. The password for CSSN is constant, unless it is manually changed. CESN is the new sign-on transaction with the External Security Manager (ESM), which provides better security functions. The password for CESN expires automatically in the specified period through ESM (see Chapter 14).

```
CICS/VS SIGNON - ENTER USERID

USERID:
PASSWORD:
NEW PASSWORD:
```

Figure 1-8 CICS sign-on screen.

Sign-off

The primary function of CICS sign-off is to disassociate your CICS user identifier from CICS in terms of security. For signing off, you have to use CICS-supplied transaction CSSF. Once you complete the CSSF transaction, you can no longer execute protected CICS transactions.

1.10   Initiation of CICS Transaction

Transaction Initiation Process

How a CICS transaction is initiated in a CICS region is a complex process, involving CICS control programs and control tables. In order to understand the mechanism behind CICS, Figure 1-9 illustrates a simplified process of a typical transaction initiation in the CICS region.

A transaction identifier and data (e.g., TSK1 XXXXXX) are entered in a terminal (e.g., TRM1). TCP with TCT recognizes incoming data from the terminal. SCP acquires the storage for the Terminal Input-Output Area (TIOA). TCP places the data from the terminal into TIOA and sets the pointer into the TCT entry of the terminal. If there is no task associated with this terminal, TCP passes control to KCP, which realizes the transaction identifier in the data in TIOA. SCP acquires the storage for the Task Control Area (TCA), in which KCP prepares control data for this task. KCP, through PCT, tries to find the application program associated with the transaction. If PPT entry of the application program does not show the resident address of the program, KCP passes control to PCP, which fetches the application program from the load library and places it into the main storage. KCP passes control to the application program. The application program starts its processing — the transaction has been initiated.

This process also illustrates how well the CICS control programs and control tables achieve their functions, being complementary to each other.

Ways of Initiating CICS Transactions

The above is only one way of initiating a CICS transaction. Actually, there are several ways of initiating CICS transactions. The following are five ways of initiating CICS transactions:

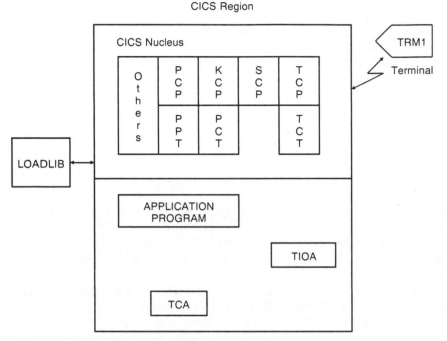

Figure 1-9 Initiation of CICS transaction.

1. By a transaction identifier entered in a terminal with ENTER key. This is the most common way of initiating a CICS transaction.
2. By a transaction identifier associated with a terminal for pseudo-conversation. This is a typical way of achieving a pseudo-conversation.
3. By the START command, which initiates a transaction specified in the parameter.
4. By the Automatic Task Initiation (ATI). The Destination Control Table (DCT) entry for an Intrapartition Transient Data Queue can have a trigger level parameter and the associated CICS transaction to be initiated if the trigger level is reached.
5. By a 3270 attention identifier. For the IBM 3270 type terminals, any of PF keys and PA keys could be defined in PCT to initiate a CICS transaction.

We will say more about these five methods of initiating CICS transactions later in this book.

1.11   Basic CICS Application Programming

Now that we have discussed the basic concepts of CICS, we are ready to discuss how the actual CICS application program (command level) looks. Appendix A shows a complete CICS application program (command level) as a sample program. However, the sample program in Appendix A is too complex at this point. Therefore, let us write a very simple CICS application program (command level) using only three basic commands, RECEIVE, SEND, and RETURN, without a formal introduction to these commands.

Basic CICS Commands

RECEIVE Command   The RECEIVE command is used to receive incoming data from the terminal to which this CICS transaction (program) is associated. A receiving area must be defined in the Working Storage Section, and it has to be specified in the INTO parameter. The length field must be defined in the Working Storage Section as a halfword binary field (S9(4) COMP), and it has to be specified in the LENGTH option with the proper value.

SEND Command   The SEND command is used to send outgoing data to the terminal. The data to be sent must be stored in a field defined in the Working Storage Section, and this field name has to be specified in the FROM parameter. The length must be specified the same as that of the RECEIVE command.

RETURN Command   One of the functions of the RETURN command is to terminate the transaction and return control to CICS. For basic use, it does not require any parameters.

Program Specifications

The specifications of this demonstration program, which uses these three basic CICS commands, are as follows:

• Read a message from a terminal.
• Send the message back with an acknowledge message to the same terminal.
• Terminate the transaction.

Coding Example

The following is a typical coding example of the demonstration program based on the specifications above:

```
IDENTIFICATION DIVISION.
PROGRAM-ID.    TESTPROG.
REMARKS.
      THIS IS A SAMPLE PROGRAM TO SHOW A BASIC STRUCTURE OF CICS
      APPLICATION PROGRAM (COMMAND LEVEL) IN COBOL.
*
ENVIRONMENT DIVISION.
DATA DIVISION.
WORKING-STORAGE SECTION.
77    MSG-LENGTH              PIC S9(4) COMP.
01    INPUT-MESSAGE.
      05   I-TRANS-ID         PIC X(4).
      05   FILLER             PIC X.
      05   I-MSG-DATA         PIC X(35).
01    OUTPUT-MESSAGE.
      05   O-MSG-ID           PIC X(30).
      05   FILLER             PIC X.
      05   O-MSG-DATA         PIC X(35).
*
PROCEDURE DIVISION.
*
* RECEIVE MESSAGE.
*
      MOVE 40 TO MSG-LENGTH.
      MOVE LOW-VALUES TO INPUT-MESSAGE.
      EXEC CICS RECEIVE
           INTO(INPUT-MESSAGE)
           LENGTH(MSG-LENGTH)
      END-EXEC.
*
* PREPARE OUTPUT MESSAGE FOR ACKNOWLEDGE.
*
      MOVE LOW-VALUES TO OUTPUT-MESSAGE.
      MOVE I-MSG-DATA TO O-MSG-DATA.
      MOVE 'FOLLOWOING MESSAGE RECEIVED:'
           TO O-MSG-ID.
      MOVE 66 TO MSG-LENGTH.
*
```

```
* SEND ACKNOWLEDGE MESSAGE.
*

      EXEC CICS SEND
            FROM(OUTPUT-MESSAGE)
            LENGTH(MSG-LENGTH)
            ERASE
      END-EXEC.
*
* TERMINATE TASK.
*

      EXEC CICS RETURN
      END-EXEC.
*

      GOBACK.
```

Execution Results   During the execution of this program logic, the following activities will occur:

- At the completion of the RECEIVE command, 40 bytes (specified in MSG-LENGTH) of data from the terminal will be placed into the field INPUT-MESSAGE.
- At the completion of the SEND command, 66 bytes of message (specified in MSG-LENGTH) which the terminal user sent will be redisplayed to the original terminal, preceded by the leading message "FOLLOWING MESSAGE RECEIVED:".
- At the completion of the RETURN command, the transaction will be terminated.

Discussion

The above is an actual CICS application program (command level). If the CICS environment for this program, such as PCT and PPT, has been established properly, and if this program has been translated, compiled, and linkedited successfully, this program will actually run.

The point we are trying to make here is that CICS command level application programming is easy. Later we will discuss more complex commands, but the basic programming concept remains the same as in this demonstration program.

1.12 Some Unique Concepts Under CICS

There are certain unique concepts under CICS. They are multitasking, multithreading, and quasi-reentrancy. Some of these are not necessarily unique to CICS, but CICS manages all of these quite efficiently. In order to understand the CICS application program (command level) further, let us discuss these concepts.

Multitasking

Multitasking means that the operating system (OS) allows more than one task to be executed concurrently, regardless of whether the tasks use the same program or different programs. Therefore, this is not a unique concept to CICS. But, CICS manages multitasking of CICS tasks within its own region. That is, CICS provides a multitasking environment where more than one CICS task run concurrently.

Multithreading

Multithreading is the system environment where the tasks are sharing the same program under the multitasking environment. Multithreading is a subset of multitasking, since it concerns tasks which use the same program.

Under the multithreading environment, a program is shared by several tasks concurrently. For each task, the program (i.e., instructions and data area) must work as if it were executing instructions exclusively for each task. Therefore, it requires special considerations such as reentrancy or serial reusability.

Contrary to the multithreading environment, under the single threading environment, a program is used by only one job (or task) at a time. A typical example is a batch job.

Although multithreading is not a unique concept to CICS, CICS manages multithreading of CICS tasks within its own region. That is, CICS provides the multithreading environment where more than one CICS task, which uses the same program, run concurrently.

Quasi-Reentrancy

In order to make multithreading possible, an application program must be "reentrant" (under OS) or "quasi-reentrant" (under CICS).

For an online system, it is important to understand accurately the concepts of reentrancy (under OS) and quasi-reentrancy (under CICS). Therefore, let us discuss these concepts in detail in independent sections under the titles of reentrant program and quasi-reentrant program (see Sections 1.13 and 1.14, respectively).

1.13   Reentrant Program

A reentrant program is a program which does not modify itself so that it can reenter to itself and continue processing after an interruption by the operating system (OS) which, during the interruption, excutes other OS tasks including OS tasks of the same program. It is also called a "reenterable" program or "serially reusable" program.

A nonreentrant program is a program which modifies itself so that it cannot reenter to itself. Therefore, it cannot be used in the multithreading environment. Batch programs are the typical examples of non-reentrant program.

Reentrant programs are used in the online system, and they make it possible for OS to establish the multithreading environment which the online system requires. Therefore, "reentrant program" is a term for the OS/multithreading environment.

Concept

How a reentrant program works can be described in the following way: Between two consecutive Supervisor Calls (SVCs), an OS task (A) which uses a program has exclusive use of the CPU resource. At an interruption time (i.e., SVC) in the program, the OS task (A) is suspended. OS saves the status of the OS task (A), and executes other tasks (e.g., B, C). When other OS tasks reach a SVC while the task A's wait status becomes complete, OS restores the status of the task A (i.e., "reenter" to the program) and continues to execute until the next SVC.

This process makes it possible for tasks A, B, and C to run concurrently. If tasks A, B, and C use the same program, data areas of the program will be destroyed unless the data area is kept unique to each task. Similarly, if task A, B, and C use the same program and if the program alters the program itself for a task, the program would not be the same among the tasks which use the same program. The reentrant program ensures the uniqueness of the data area and program logic to each task based on a certain programming convention.

Convention for Reentrant Program

In order to ensure the uniqueness of the data area and program logic to each task, the reentrant program must follow a set of programming conventions described below:

- *Constants in Working Storage*: The reentrant program defines only constants in its ordinary data area (e.g., Working Storage Section). These constants will never be modified and shared by the tasks.
- *Variables in Dynamic Working Storage*: The reentrant program acquires a unique storage area (called Dynamic Working Storage — DWS) dynamically for each task by issuing GETMAIN (OS macro). All variables will be placed in this DWS for a task. All counters would have to be initialized after the DWS has been acquired.
- *Restriction on Program Alteration*: The program must not alter the program itself. If it alters itself after a SVC, it must restore the alteration to the original before the next SVC.

1.14   Quasi-Reentrant Program

A quasi-reentrant program is a reentrant program under the CICS environment. That is, the quasi-reentrant program is a CICS program which does not modify itself. That way, it can reenter to itself and continue processing after an interruption by CICS which, during the interruption, excutes other CICS tasks including CICS tasks of the same program.

Under CICS, a program interruption and reentry occur not at an SVC time, but at the time of a CICS command which may consist of several SVCs or may not consist of any SVCs at all. Therefore, the quasi-reentrant program is a term under the CICS/multithreading environment. It is called "quasi" in order to distinguish this from the reentrant program, which is the term under OS/multithreading environment.

Concept

The concept of how the quasi-reentrant program works can be best described in conjunction with the reentrant program. In the description of the concept of reentrant program (Section 1.13), if the words "OS" and "SVC" are replaced with "CICS" and "CICS command," respectively, then that would describe the concept of the quasi-reentrant program.

Convention for Quasi-Reentrant Program

In order to maintain the quasi-reentrancy, a CICS application program must follow the similar convention of a reentrant program, as follows:

* *Constants in Working Storage*: The quasi-reentrant program defines only constants in its ordinary data area (e.g., Working Storage Section). These constants will never be modified and shared by the tasks.
* *Variables in Dynamic Working Storage*: The quasi-reentrant program acquires a unique storage area (called Dynamic Working Storage — DWS) dynamically for each task by issueing the CICS macro equivalent GETMAIN. All variables will be placed in this DWS for each task. All counters would have to be initialized after the DWS has been acquired.
* *Restriction on Program Alteration*: The program must not alter the program itself. If it alters itself after a CICS macro or command, it must restore the alteration before the subsequent CICS macro or command.

CICS Macro Level

In the earlier versions of CICS, the CICS application programs were written based on the CICS macros which were functionally primitive in comparison to the CICS commands. In order to establish the quasi-reentrancy, the CICS macro level application programs were required to follow the convention described above.

CICS Command Level

CICS command level is the new generation of CICS which replaced the CICS macro level. Under the CICS command level, when CICS executes a CICS command level COBOL application program, CICS automatically acquires a unique copy of the Working Storage Section of the application program for each task. Therefore, the application program does not have to acquire DWS for each task.

In case the application program is altered by the program itself during execution of the program for a task, the information for the program alteration will be kept in Task Global Table (TGT) which is a part of the program. Since CICS acquires TGT uniquely to each task (as it does for Working Storage Section), when another task which uses the same program is initiated, the task can use the original (i.e., not altered) program.

This implies that for all CICS command level COBOL application programs, the quasi-reentrancy is automatically ensured. Therefore, an application programmer can write COBOL programs for CICS without any consideration of the quasi-reentrancy.

The know-how of writing a quasi-reentrant program under the CICS macro level used to be considered a highly specialized skill. But the CICS command level makes even novice COBOL programmers able to write a quasi-reentrant program. This is the great achievement of the CICS command level.

VS COBOL II

VS COBOL II supports the CICS command level only; it does not support the CICS macro level. One of the significant improvements by VS COBOL II is that a program written in VS COBOL II can be reentrant if the RENT option is specified at the compile time. This has an important implication in the CICS application programs written in VS COBOL II (command level by definition). That is, if a CICS application program is written in VS COBOL II, this CICS application program becomes reentrant (not quasi-reentrant).

This reentrant nature of CICS application programs written in VS COBOL II removes many restrictions which ordinary CICS application programs (command level) written in VS COBOL faced. Some of them were described in Section 1.5.

The notable improvement is that, because of reentrancy, a CICS application program written in VS COBOL II can issue the CALL statement for executing a subprogram which has CICS commands as long as the subprogram is written in VS COBOL II. We will discuss this subject further in Section 3.2.

Exercise

Develop a CICS application program (command level) based on the following specifications:

1. Transaction identifier is INQ1 and Program identifier is TXT1INQ1.
2. The program starts with receiving the following message from a terminal:

```
INQ1 nnnnn
```

where nnnnn is an employee number.

3. Respond to the terminal user with the following message:

```
INQUIRY KEY RECEIVED FOR EMPLOYEE nnnnn.
```

where nnnnn is the employee number received.

4. Terminate the task.

5. The program must be a complete COBOL program for the CICS command level.

2

Application Program Housekeeping

2.1 Exceptional Conditions

An abnormal situation during execution of a CICS command is called an "exceptional condition." This is different from an abnormal situation during execution of COBOL statements (i.e., ordinary ABEND).

Checking exceptional conditions is similar to checking return codes after executing COBOL input/output statements in non-CICS programs. It is strongly recommended to check exceptional conditions after every CICS command.

Each CICS command has its own set of possible exceptional conditions. Appendix B summarizes CICS commands with their associated exceptional conditions. Common exceptional conditions and their meanings will be discussed in each command description in this book.

Some exceptional conditions are significant to the particular command, while others are less significant. Therefore, the application program does not have to check all exceptional conditions of the command. Only significant exceptional conditions of the command should be checked after the command execution.

Command Code and Response Code

The CICS command executed last is shown in a system field EIBFN (see Section 2.11), while the response code for the last CICS command is shown in another system field EIBRCODE (see Section 2.11). The exceptional condition is nothing but the interpretation of the response code in the EIBRCODE field based on the command code in the EIBFN field. This could be verified in Appendix E.

When an exceptional condition is detected in a CICS application program, therefore, it is a good practice to display the command code in the EIBFN field and the response code in the EIBRCODE field in the hexadecimal mode along with the exceptional error message, so that the exceptional condition can be precisely identified. This is especially useful when only significant exceptional conditions are checked and other minor ones are checked as the general error condition.

ABEND Codes

If an exceptional condition occurs during execution of a CICS application program, and if the program does not check the exceptional condition, CICS may continue executing the program or terminate abnormally the execution of the program, depending on the exceptional condition and the command involved. If the execution is abnormally terminated, CICS will issue the abnormal termination (ABEND) code, which is associated with the exceptional condition on subject. Appendix E lists the common ABEND codes and their related exceptional conditions.

2.2   HANDLE CONDITION Command

Function

The HANDLE CONDITION command is used to transfer control to the procedure label specified if the exceptional condition specified occurs.

Once a HANDLE CONDITION request has been made, it remains active until the end of the program or another HANDLE CONDITION request overrides it. In order to avoid the confusion over which HANDLE CONDITION request is active, it is strongly recommended that a HANDLE CONDITION request always be paired with a CICS command. It should be noted, however, that this command cannot detect ordinary program ABENDs such as data exception error (0C7) unrelated to CICS commands.

A HANDLE CONDITION request is effective only within the program which issues the HANDLE CONDITION command. That is, if the control is passed to another program, the HANDLE CONDITION request in the calling program will no longer be honored in the called program.

Format

The format of the HANDLE CONDITION command is as follows:

```
EXEC CICS HANDLE CONDITION
     condition(label)
     [condition(label)]
     [ERROR(label)]
END-EXEC.
```

The "condition" represents an exceptional condition. If a label is specified, control will be passed to the labeled paragraph of the program when the condition specified occurs. If no label is specified, it has the effect of canceling the previously set HANDLE CONDITION request, and default action will be taken.

The general error condition (ERROR) can be specified within the same list to specify that all other conditions cause control to be passed to the label specified.

Although more than one HANDLE CONDITION command can be issued in the program, no more than 12 conditions can be specified in a single HANDLE CONDITION command.

Example

Let us again use the RECEIVE and SEND commands as an example. The most significant exceptional condition to these basic commands is LENGERR.

For the RECEIVE commad, if the terminal user enters data longer than the length specified in the command, the command will encounter the LENGERR condition. In this case, the data will be truncated at the specified length, while the length field will contain the actual length of data entered.

For the SEND command, if an out-of-range value or negative value is specified as the length, the command will encounter the LENGERR condition.

Now, as an example, let us try to intercept the LENGERR condition and other conditions using the HANDLE CONDITION command with LENGERR and ERROR. The program should look as follows:

```
WORKING-STORAGE SECTION.
01   WK-TIOA.
     05   FILLER    PIC X(50)
77   WK-LEN        PIC S9(4) COMP.
     :
     :
PROCEDURE DIVISION.
     :
     :
     EXEC CICS HANDLE CONDITION
          ERROR(GENERAL-ERR-RTN)
          LENGERR(LENGERR-RTN)
     END-EXEC.
     MOVE 20 TO WK-LEN.
     EXEC CICS RECEIVE
          INTO(WK-TIOA)
          LENGTH(WK-LEN)
     END-EXEC.
     :
     :
LENGERR-RTN.
     MOVE 14 TO WK-LEN.
     MOVE 'TOO MUCH DATA' TO WK-TIOA.
     EXEC CICS SEND
          FROM(WK-TIOA)
          LENGTH(WK-LEN)
     END-EXEC.
     GO TO RET-RTN
GENERAL-ERR-RTN.
     MOVE 20 TO WK-LEN.
     MOVE 'OTHER ERROR OCCURRED' TO WK-TIOA.
     EXEC CICS SEND
          FROM(WK-TIOA)
          LENGTH(WK-LEN)
     END-EXEC.
RET-RTN.
     EXEC CICS RETURN
     END-EXEC.
```

Execution Results   During the execution of this program logic, the following activities will occur:

• During the execution of the RECEIVE command, if the LENGERR condition occurs, control will be passed to the paragraph LENGERR-RTN.
• If other exceptional conditions (i.e., general error: ERROR) occur, control will be passed to the paragraph GENERAL-ERR-RTN.

Standardization of Handle Condition

It is an established fact that an effective use of the HANDLE CONDITION command significantly reduces the likelihood of transaction ABENDs. For this reason, some installations have strict CICS application programming standards that all CICS commands must be paired with the HANDLE CONDITION command.

Therefore, in this book, let us establish our own programming standard for the HANDLE CONDITION command as follows:

• All CICS commands (except the RETURN command) must be paired with the HANDLE CONDITION command.
• Only critical conditions should be specified.
• Other noncritical conditions can be intercepted by the general error condition (i.e., ERROR).
• All exercises in this book must follow this standard.
• Alternatively, the RESP option approach (see Section 2.6) can be used.

The sample program in Appendix A of this book shows how all exceptional conditions are intercepted by the HANDLE CONDITION commands.

2.3   Loop on Exceptional Condition

An exceptional condition routine passed by a HANDLE CONDITION command can contain another CICS command, which may cause the same exceptional condition. In this case, there will be an infinite loop. This usually occurs when an exceptional condition handling routine passed by a CICS command issues the same CICS command.

Such loops should be avoided in the application program, by issuing the IGNORE command (see Section 2.4), by specifying NOHAN-

DLE option in the command in the exception handling routine (see Section 2.6), or by simply terminating the task.

Example

The SEND command is a very stable command which hardly causes exceptional conditions when it is used for the basic terminal operations. But if by mistake a negative value or an out-of-range value is specified in the length field, this will cause the LENGERR condition.

Using the exceptional condition LENGERR of the SEND command as an example, the following program demonstrates a loop on the exceptional condition:

```
WORKING-STORAGE SECTION.
77   MSG-LEN                      PIC S9(4) COMP.
77   OUT-MSG                      PIC X(20).
*
PROCEDURE DIVISION.
*
      MOVE -19 TO MSG-LEN.                      <=== Attention.
      MOVE 'TEST OUTPUT MESSAGE' TO OUT-MSG.
      EXEC CICS HANDLE CONDITION
          LENGERR(LENGERR-RTN)
      EXD-EXEC.
      EXEC CICS SEND
          FROM(OUT-MSG)
          LENGTH(MSG-LEN)
          ERASE
      END-EXEC.
          :
          : (some other processing)
          :
LENGERR-RTN.
      MOVE -16 TO MSG-LEN.                      <=== Attention.
      MOVE 'WRONG MSG LENGTH' TO OUT-MSG.
      EXEC CICS SEND
          FROM(OUT-MSG)
          LENGTH(MSG-LEN)
          ERASE
      END-EXEC.
      EXEC CICS RETURN
      END-EXEC.
```

Execution Results During the execution of this program logic, the following activities will occur:

• Since the first SEND command has the negative length value, it will encounter the LENGERR condition.
• The HANDLE CONDITION command will intercept the LENGERR condition and pass the control to LENGERR-RTN.
• Since the second SEND command in LENGERR-RTN also has the negative length value, it will encounter another LENGERR condition.
• At this point, the HANDLE CONDITION command is still effective for the LENGERR condition, so that it will intercept the LENGERR condition and pass control to LENGERR-RTN again.
• Here, an infinite loop will start.

A Solution In order to prevent this loop, specify the NOHANDLE option (see Section 2.6) in the SEND command in LENGERR-RTN.

2.4 IGNORE CONDITION Command

Function

The IGNORE CONDITION command causes no action to be taken if the condition specified (e.g., LENGERR) occurs in the program. That is, control will be returned to the next instruction following the command which encountered the exceptional condition. The request by the IGNORE CONDITION command is valid until the subsequent HANDLE CONDITION command for the same condition.

Format

The format of the IGNORE CONDITION is as follows:

```
EXEC CICS IGNORE CONDITION
     condition
     [condition]
END-EXEC.
```

The "condition" indicates an exceptional condition. No more than 12 conditions are allowed in the same command.

Example

The following is a simplified example of the IGNORE CONDITION
command with the LENGERR condition:

```
EXEC CICS IGNORE CONDITION
      LENGERR
END-EXEC.
EXEC CICS RECEIVE
      INTO(-----)
      LENGTH(-----)
END-EXEC.
```

Execution Results At the execution of the RECEIVE command, if the
LENGERR condition occurs, the condition will be ignored, and the
control will be passed to the next statement after the RECEIVE command.

Programming Considerations

Once the HANDLE CONDITION or IGNORE CONDITION com-
mand has been executed for a condition, the specification remains in
effect until the program ends or until another HANDLE CONDI-
TION or IGNORE CONDITION command is executed for the same
condition.
    If these commands are mixed up as shown in the example below, it
will be very confusing to find what would happen if the specified
condition occurs. Therefore, these commands should not be mixed up.
The simplest way to avoid the confusion is to specify the HANDLE
CONDITION command paired with each command.

```
EXEC CICS HANDLE CONDITION LENGERR(LENGERR-RTN1) ---- END-EXEC.
EXEC CICS RECEIVE INTO(---) NOHANDLE ---------------- END-EXEC.
EXEC CICS SEND FROM(---) ---------------------------- END-EXEC.
EXEC CICS HANDLE CONDITION LENGERR(LENGERR-RTN2) ---- END-EXEC.
EXEC CICS SEND FROM(---) ---------------------------- END-EXEC.
EXEC CICS HANDLE CONDITION LENGERR ------------------ END-EXEC.
EXEC CICS SEND FROM(---) ---------------------------- END-EXEC.
EXEC CICS IGNORE CONDITION LENGERR ------------------ END-EXEC.
EXEC CICS SEND FROM(---) ---------------------------- END-EXEC.
```

2.5   PUSH and POP Commands

Functions

The PUSH and POP commands are used to suspend and reactivate, respectively, all HANDLE CONDITION requests currently in effect. These are useful while performing a subroutine embedded in a main program. A called routine can use the PUSH command to suspend the existing HANDLE CONDITION requests, whereas, before returning control to the caller, the called routine can restore the original requests using the POP command.

Similarly, the PUSH and POP commands can be used to suspend and reactivate, respectively, the HANDLE AID command (see Section 7.7) and HANDLE ABEND command (see Section 16.2).

Format

The formats of the PUSH and POP commands are as simple as shown in the example below. The function code HANDLE must be explicitly specified.

Example

The following is a simplified example to illustrate the functions of the PUSH and POP commands:

```
      EXEC CICS HANDLE CONDITION                <==  Independent.
         ----------
      END-EXEC.
         :
      PERFORM  SUBRTN-A.
         :
      EXEC CICS HANDLE CONDITION
         ----------
      END-EXEC.
         :
         :
SUBRTN-A SECTION.
      EXEC CICS PUSH HANDLE                      <==  Attention.
      END-EXEC.
         :
      EXEC CICS HANDLE CONDITION                 <==  Independent.
         ----------
```

```
    END-EXEC.
        :
    EXEC CICS POP HANDLE                          <==  Attention.
    END-EXEC.
SUBRTN-A-EXIT.
    EXIT.
```

Execution Results   During the execution of this program logic, the following activities will occur:

- At the completion of the PUSH command in SUBRTN-A, all HANDLE CONDITION requests which have been in effect in the mainline routine will be suspended.
- At the completion of the POP command, all HANDLE CONDITION requests which have been suspended in SUBRTN-A will be reactivated.
- Between the PUSH and POP commands, any HANDLE CONDITION requests can be issued, independent of those in the mainline routine.
- In this way, the HANDLE CONDITION requests specified in the mainline routine are completely independent of those in the SUBRTN-A routine.

Technical Notes

Even if the PUSH and POP commands are issued in the subroutine, the conditions established in the HANDLE CONDITION command in the subroutine will be active in the mainline routine after control is returned to the mainline.

If this is not desirable, you should offset the conditions established by the HANDLE CONDITION command in the subroutine by specifying conditions without paragraph names in the HANDLE CONDITION command before returning to the mainline routine.

2.6   Alternatives to HANDLE CONDITION Command

There are two other alternatives to the HANDLE CONDITION command for dealing with the exceptional conditions. The NOHANDLE option should be specified for the special purpose only, while the RESP option can be used as the alternative approach to the HANDLE CONDITION command.

NOHANDLE Option

The NOHANDLE option can be specified in any CICS command, and it will cause no action to be taken for any exceptional condition occurring during execution of this command.

This option is very useful to prevent a loop on the exceptional condition. However, this option should be used for the special purpose only, because the excessive use of this option defeats the purpose of the exceptional conditions and the HANDLE CONDITION command.

A simplified example of the NOHANDLE option using the SEND command is as follows:

```
EXEC CICS SEND
      FROM(---)
      LENGTH(---)
      NOHANDLE                    <=== Attention
END-EXEC.
```

Execution Results   During the excution of the SEND command, even if some exceptional condition occurs, no action will be taken. The control will be returned to the next statement after the SEND command.

RESP Option

The RESP option can be specified in any CICS command. Its function is similar to the return code in the batch program. If the RESP option is specified in a command, CICS places a response code at a completion of the command. The application program can check this code, then proceed to the next processing. This approach has an advantage over the HANDLE CONDITION command approach, because this approach makes the program more structured.

If the RESP option is specified in a command, the NOHANDLE option is applied to this command. Therefore, the HANDLE CONDITION requests will have no effect in this case.

The following are the procedures to utilize the RESP option in a CICS command:

1. Define a fullword binary field (S9(8) COMP) in the Working Storage Section as the response field.
2. Place the RESP option with the response field in a command (any CICS command).

3. After command execution, check the response code in the response field with DFHRESP(xxxx), where xxxx is:
    • NORMAL for normal completion.
    • Any exceptional condition.

Example   The following is an example of the RESP option using the SEND command:

```
WORKING-STORAGE SECTION.
77 WS-RCODE     PIC S9(8) COMP.
      :
PROCEDURE DIVISION.
      :
      EXEC CICS SEND
            FROM(---)
            LENGTH(---)
            ERASE
            RESP(WS-RCODE)              <=== Attention.
      END-EXEC.
*
      IF WS-RCODE = DFHRESP(NORMAL)     <=== Normal completion.
            GO TO NORMAL-RTN.
      IF WS-RCODE = DFHRESP(LENGERR)    <=== Exceptional condition.
            GO TO LENGERR-RTN.
      GO TO GENERAL-ERR-RTN.
*
  NORMAL-RTN.
      :
      :
  LENGERR-RTN.
      :
      :
  GENERAL-ERR-RTN.
      :
      :
```

Execution Results   During the execution of this program logic, the following activities will occur:

• At the completion of the SEND command, the WS-CODE field (fullword binary) will have the response code of the command execution result.

- If the SEND command completes normally, control will be passed to NORMAL-RTN.
- If the SEND command encounters LENGERR, control will be passed to LENGERR-RTN.
- If the SEND command encounters other exceptional conditions, control will be passed to GENERAL-ERR-RTN.

2.7   Base Locator for Linkage (BLL)

The Base Locator for Linkage (BLL) is an addressing convention used to address storage outside the Working Storage Section of an application program. If BLL is used for the input commands (e.g., READ, RECEIVE), it will improve the performance, since the program would be accessing directly the input buffer outside of the program. Also, if BLL is used for the dynamic table loading, it will save the size of the application program, since the application program does not have to reserve the space for the table in the program.

Convention

BLL operates by addressing the storage as if it were a parameter to the program. Therefore, in order for BLL to work as intended, the program must construct BLL based on the following convention:

The parameter list must be defined by means of a 01 level data definition in the Linkage Section as the first area definition to the Linkage Section, unless a communication area is being passed to the program, in which case DFHCOMMAREA must be defined first.

The parameter list consists of a group of the address pointers, each of which is defined as the fullword binary field (S9(8) COMP). This is called the BLL cells. The parameter list is followed by a group of 01 level data definitions, which would be the actual data areas.

The first address pointer of the parameter list is set up by CICS for addressing the parameter list itself. From the second address pointer onward, there is a one-to-one correspondence between the address pointers of the parameter list and 01 level data definitions. That is, the second address pointer and third address pointer point the address of the first 01 level and the second 01 level fields, respectively, and so on.

Applications

In a CICS application program (command level), the BLL convention is used commonly for the following two applications:

- *CICS Command with SET Option*: BLL is commonly used by the SET option of certain CICS commands. See Section 4.5 for an example.
- *Accessing CICS System Areas*: Another common use of BLL is for accessing CICS system areas. See Section 2.9 for an example.

Programming Notes

When the BLL cells are established, it should be made sure that the areas defined by the 01 level field definition have the proper length. If the area defined is larger than the actual data size, the program might accidentally destroy some CICS system areas or protected areas, which might cause a storage violation.

If the area to be defined is greater than 4096 bytes, a special technique is required for concatinating more than one BLL cell for one 01 level data field.

Improvements by VS COBOL II

VS COBOL II provides CICS application programs with a significant improvements in the area of addressability through the special ADDRESS register. Therefore, if an application program is written in VS COBOL II, the program no longer requires building the BLL cells in the Linkage Section.

The program can directly specify the 01 level field definitions in the Linkage Section without defining the BLL cells. We will discuss more details of this subject in Section 4.5 and Section 2.9.

2.8   SERVICE RELOAD Statement

Function

The SERVICE RELOAD statement is used to ensure addressability to a particular area defined in the Linkage Section. Therefore, this statement must be used following whenever the content of BLL cell is changed in any way. This statement is valid only for for DOS/VS, OS/VS COBOL, or COBOL V4 compiler.

Format

The format of the SERVICE RELOAD statement is as follows:

```
SERVICE RELOAD field name
```

where "field name" is a symbolic name of the data area defined in 01 level of the Linkage Section. See the next section for an example.

Improvements by VS COBOL II

As discussed in the previous section, since VS COBOL II offers a much improved addressability through the special ADDRESS register, if an application program is written in VS COBOL II, it does not require one to establish the BLL cells. Consequently, it does not require one to issue the SERVICE RELOAD statement after the input/output operations associated with the fields defined in the Linkage Section.

2.9 ADDRESS Command

Function

The ADDRESS command is used to access information in the CICS system areas. For the ADDRESS command, the BLL cells must be properly defined based on the convention.

Format

The format of the ADDRESS command is as follows:

```
EXEC CICS ADDRESS
    option(pointer-ref)
    [option(pointer-ref)]
END-EXEC.
```

The pointer-reference is to be set by CICS to address the area which you wish to access. Therefore, the BLL cells must be constructed in the Linkage Section based on the convention discussed before.

Commonly Used Options

The following are the commonly used options of the ADDRESS command:

CSA: To access the Common System Area (CSA), which is a CICS system area defined by the system.

CWA: To access the Common Work Area (CWA), which is a CICS system work area defined by the system programmer in SIT.

TCTUA: To access the Terminal Control Table User Area (TCTUA), which is a work area associated with a terminal. TCTUA is defined as one per terminal in TCT.

TWA: To access the Transaction Work Area (TWA), which is a work area associated with a task. TWA is defined as one per task in PCT.

Example

The following is a simplified example of the ADDRESS command using the options of CSA, TCTUA, and TWA:

```
LINKAGE SECTION.
01    PARMLIST.                                <== BLL cells.
      05    FILLER       PIC S9(8) COMP.
      05    CSA-PTR      PIC S9(8) COMP.
      05    TCTUA-PTR    PIC S9(8) COMP.
      05    TWA-PTR      PIC S9(8) COMP.
01    CSA-LAYOUT.
      05    CSA-FIELD1   PIC X(5).
      :
01    TCTUA-LAYOUT.
      05    TCTUA-FIELD1   PIC X(10).
      :
```

```
01   TWA-LAYOUT.
     05   TWA-FIELD1      PIC X(20).
     :
*
PROCEDURE DIVISION.
*
     EXEC CICS ADDRESS
          CSA(CSA-PTR)
          TCTUA(TCTUA-PTR)
          TWA(TWA-PTR)
     EXD-EXEC.
     SERVICE RELOAD CSA-LAYOUT.              <==   Attention
     SERVICE RELOAD TCTUA-LAYOUT.            <==   Attention
     SERVICE RELOAD TWA-LAYOUT.              <==   Attention
        :
        : (more processing)
        :
```

Execution Results During the execution of the program logic, the following activities will occur:

- In the BLL cells, the pointer-references (i.e., address pointers) CSA-PTR, TCTUA-PTR, TWA-PTR are established to point the address of CSA-LAYOUT, TCTUA-LAYOUT, TWA-LAYOUT, respectively.
- At the completion of the ADDRESS command, the BLL cells will have the address of the system areas (CSA, TCTUA, and TWA, in this case).
- After the SERVICE RELOAD statement, the application program can use any field in CSA-LAYOUT, TCTUA-LAYOUT, and TWA-LAYOUT.

Improvements by VS COBOL II

If the application program is written in VS COBOL II, the above program becomes much simpler. In this case, the PARMLIST as the BLL cells is no longer required. In the ADDRESS command, the reserved word "ADDRESS " is used for each of 01 level field definitions. Further, the SERVICS RELOAD statements are no longer required. The following is an example of VS COBOL II coding to achieve exactly the same functions as the example above in VS COBOL:

```
LINKAGE SECTION.
01    CSA-LAYOUT.
      05    CSA-FIELD1      PIC X(5).
      :
01    TCTUA-LAYOUT.
      05    TCTUA-FIELD1    PIC X(10).
      :
01    TWA-LAYOUT.
      05    TWA-FIELD1      PIC X(20).
      :
*
PROCEDURE DIVISION.
*
      EXEC CICS ADDRESS
           CSA(ADDRESS OF CSA-LAYOUT)
           TCTUA(ADDRESS OF TCTUA-LAYOUT)
           TWA(ADDRESS OF TWA-LAYOUT)
      EXD-EXEC.
           :
           : (more processing)
           :
```

Execution Results   At the completion of the ADDRESS command, the special ADDRESS registers assigned to the fields of CSA-LAYOUT, TCTUA-LAYOUT, and TWA-LAYOUT will contain the address of these fields, respectively. Therefore, after the ADDRESS command, the fields CSA-LAYOUT, TCTUA-LAYOUT, and TWA-LAYOUT are directly pointing to the respective fields, so that the application program can freely use these fields.

2.10   ASSIGN Command

Function

The ASSIGN command is used to access the system value outside of the application program. Some information obtained from this command is very useful for application programming.

Format

The format of the ASSIGN command is as follows:

```
EXEC CICS ASSIGN
    option(data-area)
    [option(data-area)]
END-EXEC.
```

For the length option, the data area must be defined as the halfword binary field (S9(4) COMP).

Commonly Used Options

The following are the commonly used options of the ASSIGN command:

CWALENG: To access the length of CWA.
TCTUALENG: To access the length of TCTUA.
TWALENG: To access the length of TWA.
USERID: To access the user-id (8-character field).
ABCODE: To access the ABEND code (4-character field).

Example

The following is an example of ASSIGN command using the USERID option:

```
WORKING-STORAGE SECTION.
77   WK-USERID            PIC X(8).
     :
PROCEDURE DIVISION.
     :
     :
    EXEC CICS ASSIGN
         USERID(WK-USERID)
    END-EXEC.
```

Execution Results At the completion of the ASSIGN command, the CICS user identifier which initiated this transaction will be placed in WK-USERID.

2.11   EXEC Interface Block (EIB)

CICS automatically provides some system-related information to each task in a form of EXEC Interface Block (EIB), which is unique to the CICS command level. All fields of EIB are summarized in Appendix D. Since this information is automatically provided by CICS, the application programs can use them right away. The sample program in Appendix A shows an example of how to use EIB information.

Commonly Used EIB Information

The following is some commonly used EIB information:

EIBAID:	Attention-id (1 byte)
EIBCALEN:	Length of DFHCOMMAREA (S9(4) COMP)
EIBDATE:	Date when this task started (S9(7) COMP-3, 000yyddd+)
EIBFN:	Function code of the last command (2 bytes)
EIBRCODE:	Response code of the last command (6 bytes)
EIBTASKN:	Task number of this task (S9(7) COMP-3)
EIBTIME:	Time when this task started (S9(7) COMP-3, 0hhmmss+)
EIBTRMID:	Terminal-id (1 to 4 characters)
EIBTRNID:	Transaction-id (1 to 4 characters)

Example

The following is a typical example of using EIB information in an application program:

```
PROCEDURE DIVISION.
    IF EIBTRMID = 'CRT1'
        GO TO ROUTINE-CRT1.
    IF EIBTRNID = 'INQ1'
        GO TO ROUTINE-INQ1.
```

Execution Results   During the execution of the program logic, the following activities will occur:

- If the terminal identifier is 'CTR1', control will be passed to the paragraph ROUTINE-CRT1.
- If the transaction identifier is 'INQ1', control will be passed to the paragraph ROUTINE-INQ1.

Considerations for CICS System Information

Most CICS application programs (command level) can achieve their required tasks without referring to any CICS system information, except EIB. Since the most frequently required system information is in EIB, the application programs should take advantage of CICS command level, which automatically provides EIB.

Although it is up to the installation's policy decision, the use of CWA, TCTUA, or TWA should be discouraged, because whenever a programmer wishes to change the size or layout of CWA, TCTUA, or TWA, the CICS table (SIT, TCT or PCT, respectively) has to be re-established and all related programs must be recompiled, which reduces maintainability.

Consequently, you do not have to be concerned with the BLL cells too much. The BLL cells should be used only when definitely required (e.g., the SET option for high performance).

2.12 Storage Control

CICS Storage Control Program (SCP) controls requests for main storage by the application programs. There are two commands available: GETMAIN and FREEMAIN.

GETMAIN Command

Function The GETMAIN command is used to obtain a certain amount of storage.

Format The format of the GETMAIN command is as follows:

```
EXEC CICS GETMAIN
          SET(pointer-ref)
          LENGTH(data-value) | FLENGTH(data-value),
          [INITIMG(data-value)]
          [NOSUSPEND]
END-EXEC.
```

The pointer reference is set to the address of the acquired storage area by CICS. Therefore, the corresponding BLL cell must be established. The length of the storage which you wish to acquire should be specified in either the LENGTH or FLENGTH option. The maximum length of storage to be acquired is 65,520 bytes for the LENGTH option and 1,073,741,824 bytes for the FLENGTH option. The IN-ITIMG option determines the initial value to be filled in the storage to be acquired. The NOSUSPEND option, if specified, inhibits the NOSTG condition and returns to the next instruction.

Example   The following is an example of the GETMAIN command:

```
WORKING-STORAGE SECTION.
77   INIT-CHR        PIC X VALUE LOW-VALUE.
     :
LINKAGE SECTION.
01   PARM-LIST.
     02   FILLER      PIC S9(8) COMP.
     02   DWS-PTR     PIC S9(8) COMP.
01   DWS-AREA.
     02   FIELD1      PIC X(100).
     02   FIELD2      PIC X(200).
     :
PROCEDURE DIVISION
     :
     EXEC CICS GETMAIN
          SET(DWS-PTR)
          LENGTH(300)
          INITIMG(INIT-CHR)
     END-EXEC.
     SERVICE RELOAD DWS-AREA.            <==   Attention
     :
```

Execution Results   At the completion of the GETMAIN command, the storage of 300 bytes will be acquired for DWS-AREA, which would contain all null characters (i.e., LOW-VALUE).

Common Exceptional Conditions   The following are exceptional conditions common to the GETMAIN command:

LENGERR: The length specified exceeded the limit.
NOSTG: No storage is available for the specified amount. The default action is that the task will be suspended until storage become available.

Improvements by VS COBOL II

If the application program is written in VS COBOL II, the application program becomes much simpler. In this case, the PARMLIST in the Linkage Section and the SERVICE RELOAD statement are no longer required. Instead, the GETMAIN command requires the special word ADDRESS in the SET parameter to point the address of the field on subject. The following is an example of the GETMAIN command in VS COBOL II, which achieves the exact function as the example above in VS COBOL:

```
WORKING-STORAGE SECTION.
77   INIT-CHR      PIC X VALUE LOW-VALUE.
     :
LINKAGE SECTION.
01   DWS-AREA.
     02   FIELD1   PIC X(100).
     02   FIELD2   PIC X(200).
     :
PROCEDURE DIVISION
     :
     EXEC CICS GETMAIN
          SET(ADDRESS OF DWS-AREA)
          LENGTH(300)
          INITIMG(INIT-CHR)
     END-EXEC.
          :
```

Execution Results At the completion of the GETMAIN command, the storage of 300 bytes will be acquired for DWS-AREA, which would contain all null characters (i.e., LOW-VALUE).

FREEMAIN Command

Function The acquired storage area should be freed as soon as it is no longer required. The FREEMAIN command is used to release the storage which has been acquired. If the acquired storage area is not freed, it will be freed when the task terminates.

Format The format of the FREEMAIN command is as follows:

```
EXEC CICS FREEMAIN
    DATA(data-area)
END-EXEC.
```

The DATA parameter is used to specify the area name of the storage to be released.

Example The following is an example of the FREEMAIN command:

```
EXEC CICS FREEMAIN
    DATA(DWS-AREA)
END-EXEC.
```

Execution Results The storage acquired for DWS-AREA will be freed (i.e,. it will disappear).

Programming Considerations

In the CICS macro level, these storage control functions were always used in order to maintain the quasi-reentrancy of the application programs. However, in the CICS command level, since quasi-reentrancy is guaranteed for COBOL programs, these storage control functions are not very meaningful. Virtually all CICS application programs (command level) can be written without using the GETMAIN and FREEMAIN commands.

Exercise

Modify the Exercise for Chapter 1 as follows:

1. Transaction identifier is INQX, and Program identifier is TXT2INQX.
2. Specify the HANDLE CONDITION command to each CICS command (except HANDLE CONDITION and RETURN) to detect major exceptional conditions.
3. Minor exceptional conditions can be grouped under the general error condition (ERROR).
4. In each condition handling routine, send an appropriate error message and terminate the task.
5. Be sure there will be no loop in the exceptional conditions.

3

Program Control

3.1 Introduction

The CICS Program Control Program (PCP) governs a flow of control among CICS application programs and CICS itself. The name of a CICS application program must be registered in the Processing Program Table (PPT), otherwise the program will not be recognized by CICS.

Available Commands

The following commands are available for the Program Control services:

LINK:	To pass control to another program at the lower level, expecting to be returned.
XCTL:	To pass control to another program at the same level, not expecting to be returned.
RETURN:	To return to the next higher-level program or CICS.
LOAD:	To load a program.
RELEASE:	To release a loaded program.

Relationship Among Task, Transaction, and Program

Up to this point, we used the words "task," "transaction," and "program" without really defining their concepts. They are independent concepts, but they are closely related to each other. Since CICS Program Control services require the accurate understanding of these concepts, let us define these concepts clearly.

Task A task is a unit of work which is scheduled by Operating System (OS). CICS as a whole is one of many tasks under OS (other tasks: TSO, Batch jobs, IMS, etc). Similar to OS, CICS schedules a unit of work within CICS. This is called a CICS task. That is, a CICS task is a unit of work which CICS schedules. A CICS task may be accomplished by executing one or more CICS programs.

Transaction A transaction is an entity to initiate a task. Under CICS, a CICS transaction is a CICS task which is initiated though a transaction identifier (1 to 4 characters). This transaction identifier must be registered in the Program Control Table (PCT).

A CICS transaction can create more than one task concurrently if the same transaction is initiated more than once within a very short interval. Usually one CICS transaction is created for accomplishing some application processing.

While a task is a single execution of a transaction in terms of precise definition, both task and transaction mean the same in the single event environment. Therefore, both terms are often used interchangeably.

Program A program is a set of instructions to achieve some unit of work. Under OS, CICS is a set of programs which achieve some units of work.

Under CICS, a CICS application program (max. 524,152 bytes) is a set of instructions to perform some units of work (i.e., CICS task). CICS application programs must be registered in the Processing Program Table (PPT). A CICS application program may perform one CICS task or more than one CICS task.

Application Program Logical Levels

The application programs under CICS run at various logical levels, as illustrated in Figure 3-1. The first CICS application program to receive control from CICS within a task runs at the highest logical level 1. A LINKed program runs at the next lower logical level from the LINKing program, while a XCTL'ed prgram runs at the same logical level as the XCTL'ing program. The RETURN command always passes control back to the program at one logical level higher.

The concept of application program logical levels must be well understood, otherwise there will be a confusion in controlling the flow of programs. In Figure 3-1, program A is at the logical level 1, so that the RETURN command in program A will cause control to be returned to CICS itself at the level 0.

Since program A issues the XCTL command for program B, program B will be at the logical level 1 also. Therefore, the RETURN command in program B will also cause control to be returned to CICS itself at the level 0, not program A at the level 1.

Since program B issues the LINK command for program C, program C will be at the level 2. Therefore, the RETURN command in program C will cause control to be returned to program B at the level 1. Since program C issues the XCTL command for program D, program D will be at the level 2. Therefore, the RETURN command in program D will cause control to be returned to program B at the level 1, not program C at the level 2.

3.2 LINK and XCTL Commands

Function of LINK Command

The LINK command is used to pass control from an application program at one logical level to another application at the next lower logical level. The calling (LINKing) program expects control to be

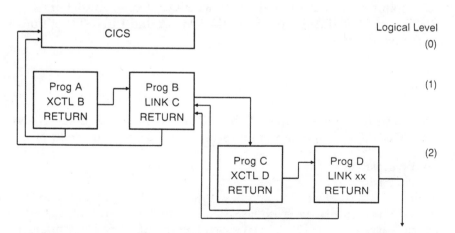

Figure 3-1 Application program logical levels.

returned to it. Data can be passed to the called program through a special communication area called COMMAREA. Since this command requires more overhead, performance is relatively poor in comparison to the XCTL command.

Function of XCTL Command

The XCTL command is used to pass control from one application program to another application program at the same logical level. The calling (XCTL'ing) program does not expect control to be returned. Data can be passed to the called program through a special communication area called COMMAREA. Since this command requires less overhead, performance is relatively better in comparison to the LINK command.

Format

The format of LINK and XCTL commands are very similar to each other, as shown below:

```
EXEC CICS LINK                    EXEC CICS XCTL
     PROGRAM(name)                     PROGRAM(name)
     [COMMAREA(data-name)]             [COMMAREA(data-name)]
     [LENGTH(data-value)]              [LENGTH(data-value)]
END-EXEC.                         END-EXEC.
```

The name of the called program to which control is passed must be specified in PROGRAM. For the COMMAREA and LENGTH options, see the next section.

Example

The following is an example of the XCTL command with the HANDLE CONDITION command to intercept the exceptional conditions:

```
WORKING-STORAGE SECTION.
01    WS-COMMAREA.
      05    WS-COM-FIELD1       PIC X(50).
      05    WS-COM-FIELD2       PIC X(50).
77    WS-CALEN                  PIC S9(4) COMP.
      :
```

```
PROCEDURE DIVISION.
    :
    (Prepare data in WS-COMMAREA)
    MOVE 100 TO WS-CALEN.
    EXEC CICS HANDLE CONDITION
        PGMIDERR(PGM-NOTFND-RTN)
        ERROR(GENERAL-ERR-RTN)
    END-EXEC.
    EXEC CICS XCTL
        PROGRAM('TESTPGM')
        COMMAREA(WS-COMMAREA)
        LENGTH(WS-CALEN)                    <== The length of COMMAREA.
    END-EXEC.
```

Execution Results   During the execution of the program logic, the following activities will occur:

• At the normal completion of the XCTL command, control will be passed to the program TESTPGM with 100 bytes of data in WS-COMMAREA.
• If the program TESTPGM is not found in PPT, control will be passed to PGM-NOTFND-RTN of this program through the HANDLE CONDITION command.
• If other errors occur during excution of XCTL command, control will be passed to GENERAL-ERR-RTN of this program through the HANDLE CONDITION command.

Common Exceptional Conditions

The following are the exceptional conditions common to both LINK and XCTL command:

NOTAUTH: A resource security check has failed.
PGMIDERR: The program specified is not found in PPT.

Applications

Instead of developing one big program, it is a good practice to develop several functional modules in order to achieve the functions which the big program would have achieved. This approach significantly improves program maintainability. The LINK and XCTL commands are commonly used for controlling the flow of these functional modules. One typical example is shown in the Case Study (Chapter 19).

Considerations for VS COBOL II

As described before, a CICS application program written in VS COBOL II (command level by definition) can be reentrant. Therefore, it can issue the CALL statement for executing a subprogram which may have CICS commands as long as the subprogram is written in VS COBOL II (i.e., reentrant).

Since the CALL statement can pass the parameters (or data) to the subprogram through the USING option, the CALL statement can achieve all of what the LINK or XCTL command achieves. Does this mean that all subprogram calls should be done by the CALL statement instead of the LINK or XCTL command?

The answer depends on the situation of the application program. If the CALL statement is used in the main program, the subprogram will be linkedited into the load module of each main program which uses this subprogram. This may improve performance, but this will increase the program size, thereby increasing the storage requirement of the CICS region. Further, if the subprogram is changed, all main programs which use this subprogram must be relinkedited.

If the LINK or XCTL command is used in the main program, only one copy of the subprogram will be shared among the main programs which use this subprogram in the same CICS region. This will reduce the storage requirement of the region. Also, in this case, when the subprogram is changed, the main programs do not have to be relinkedited.

As discussed above, both the CALL statement approach and the CICS command (LINK or XCTL) approach have advantages and disadvantages. Therefore, a careful evaluation should be done as to which approach should be taken. As a general guideline, if the subprogram is large and used by many programs, it would be better if the CICS command (LINK or XCTL) is used in the main program instead of the CALL statement.

3.3   Data Passing Through COMMAREA

Data can be passed to a called program using the COMMAREA option of the LINK or XCTL command in a calling program. The called program may alter the data content of COMMAREA and the changes will be available to the calling program after the RETURN command (see the next section) is issued in the called program. This implies that the called program does not have to specify the COMMAREA option in the RETURN command.

If the COMMAREA is used in the calling program, the area must be defined in the Working Storage Section of the program (calling), whereas, in the called program, the area must be defined as the first area in the Linkage Section (preceding the BLL cells), using the reserved name DFHCOMMAREA.

The length of the COMMAREA must be specified in the LENGTH parameter of the LINK or XCTL command in the calling program. The LENGTH parameter must be defined as a halfword binary field (S9(4) COMP). The maximum length which can be specified is 65,536 bytes.

EIBCALEN determines whether COMMAREA was sent by the calling program. If EIBCALEN is greater than 0, COMMAREA was sent. This should always be checked.

Example

Taking the example of Section 3.2, in order to receive the data passed through COMMAREA in the program of Section 3.2, the receiving program (TESTPGM) must have the following structure:

```
WORKING-STORAGE SECTION.
            :
            :
LINKAGE SECTION.
01    DFHCOMMAREA.
      05    LK-FIELD1       PIC X(50).
      05    LK-FIELD2       PIC X(50).
*
PROCEDURE DIVISION.
      IF EIBCALEN = 0
            GO TO ERR-RTN.
      MOVE LK-FIELD1 TO -----.
      (Hereafter, you can use the data in DFHCOMMAREA.)
```

Execution Results   If this program is called by the program in Section 3.2, DFHCOMMAREA will have the data of the WS-COMMAREA of the calling program in Section 3.2.

3.4   RETURN Command

Function

The RETURN command is used to return control to the next higher logical level, or CICS itself if this is the highest logical level.

Format

The format of the RETURN command is as follows:

```
EXEC CICS RETURN
    [TRANSID(name)
      [COMMAREA(data-area)
        [LENGTH(data-value)]]]
END-EXEC.
```

If none of TRANSID, COMMAREA, or LENGTH is specified, and if COMMAREA had been passed by a calling program, the RETURN command makes the data in COMMAREA available to the calling program. That is, the called program does not have to use the COMMAREA option in the RETURN command.

If the TRANSID option is used, the specified transaction identifier will be the transaction identifier for the next program to be associated with the terminal. This is allowed only in the program at the highest logical level. If the TRANSID option is specified, the COMMAREA and LENGTH option can be used to pass data to the next task in the same manner described in Section 3.3.

Example

The best examples are shown in Sections 3.12, 3.13, and 3.14.

Common Exceptional Conditions

The following are the exceptional conditions common to the RETURN command:

INVREQ: The RETURN command with the COM-
                  MAREA option is specified in a program
                  which is not at the highest level; or the RE-
                  TURN command with the TRANSID option is
                  specified in a task which is not associated
                  with a terminal.
NOTAUTH: Resource security check has failed.

3.5 LOAD Command

Function

The LOAD command is used to load a program or a table which is
independently compiled or assembled, linkedited and registered in
PPT. This command is useful for loading a table dynamically. That
is, as an application, a table can be coded in Assembler, assembled,
and linkedited. Then a COBOL program can load it as a table.

Format

The format of the LOAD command is as follows:

```
EXEC CICS LOAD
     PROGRAM(name)
     [SET(pointer-ref)]
     [LENGTH(data-area) | FLENGTH(data-area)]
     [ENTRY(pointer-ref)]
     [HOLD]
END-EXEC.
```

The address of the loaded program (or table) will be placed in the
pointer-reference specified in the SET parameter. Therefore, the corresponding BLL cell must be constructed based on the convention. If
the HOLD option is specified, the loaded program (or table) will be
permanently resident until explicitly released. If the HOLD option is
not specified, the loaded program (or table) will remain until the RE-
LEASE command is issued or the task is normally or abnormally
terminated. If the LENGTH or FLENGTH option is specified, at the
completion of loading, the length of the program (or table) will be
placed in the data area. LENGTH requires a halfword binary area

(S9(4) COMP) while FLENGTH requires a fullword binary area (S9(8) COMP). If the ENTRY option is specified, the entry point of the program will be placed in the pointer-reference.

Example

The following example illustrates that a table defined in an Assembler program (CNTRYTBL) is to be loaded into a CICS application program (PROG1) coded in COBOL. It assumes that both CNTRYTBL and PROG1 are registered in PPT.

Assembler Program   This program defines a table to be used by another program.

```
CNTRYTBL   CSECT
           DC     CL10'10U.S.A.'
           DC     CL10'11CANADA'
           DC     CL10'12U.K.'
           :
           :      (10 entries)
           END
```

COBOL Program   This program loads and uses the table outside of the program.

```
IDENTIFICATION DIVISION.
PROGRAM-ID        PROG1.
REMARKS.
          THIS IA AN EXAMPLE FOR TABLE LOADING.
ENVIRONMENT DIVISION.
DATA DIVISION.
WORKING-STORAGE SECTION.
77   TBL-LEN               PIC S9(4) COMP.
:
LINKAGE SECTION.
01   PARM-LIST.
     05   FILLER           PIC S9(8) COMP.
     05   CNTRYTBL-PTR     PIC S9(8) COMP.
01   CNTRYTBL-DATA.
     05   FILLER     OCCURS 10 TIMES.
          10   CNTRY-CODE     PIC 99.
          10   CNTRY-NAME     PIC X(8).
```

```
*
 PROCEDURE DIVISION.
*
* PLACE EXCEPTIONAL CONDITION HANDLING
*
      EXEC CICS HANDLE CONDITION
           PGMIDERR(PROG-NOT-FOUND)
      END-EXEC.
*
* LOAD A TABLE
*
      EXEC CICS LOAD
           PROGRAM('CNTRYTBL')
           SET(CNTRYTBL-PTR)
           LENGTH(TBL-LEN)                <== Length will be placed.
      END-EXEC.
      SERVICE RELOAD CNTRYTBL-DATA.       <== Required.
*
* REFER TABLE
*
      MOVE CNTRY-CODE(1) TO ----------.
      MOVE CNTRY-NAME(1) TO ----------.
           :
           :
```

Execution Results   During the execution of this program, the following activities will occur:

- After the completion of the LOAD command and the SERVICE RE-LOAD statement, the CNTRYTBL table will be loaded and the PROG1 program could refer the table.
- The length of the CNTRYTBL table will be placed in TBL-LEN.

Common Exceptional Conditions

The following are the exceptional conditions common to the LOAD command:

NOTAUTH:	Resource security check has failed.
PGMIDERR:	Program specified is not found.

Improvements by VS COBOL II

As mentioned repeatedly in Chapter 2 (Application Program House-keeping), VS COBOL II provides significant improvements in addressability. Therefore, if the application program is written in VS COBOL II, the above example of LOAD command becomes much simpler. The differences are as follows:

1. PARM-LIST in the Linkage Section is not required.
2. The LOAD command must have the special word ADDRESS for pointing the address of the field specified in the Linkage Section, as follows:

```
EXEC CICS LOAD
      PROGRAM('CNTRYTBL'),
      SET(ADDRESS OF CNTRYTBL-DATA)
      LENGTH(TBL-LEN)
END-EXEC.
```

3. The SERVICE RELOAD statement is not required.

3.6   RELEASE Command

Function

The RELEASE command is used to release a program (or table) which has been loaded previously.

Format

The format of the RELEASE command is as follows:

```
EXEC CICS RELEASE
      PROGRAM(name)
END-EXEC.
```

The name of the program to be released must be specified in the PROGRAM parameter.

Example

Taking the example of Section 3.5, the following is an example of the RELEASE command for releasing the CNTRYTBL table which has been loaded:

```
EXEC CICS RELEASE
     PROGRAM('CNTRYTBL')
END-EXEC.
```

Execution Results The loaded table "CNTRYTBL" in the example of Section 3.5 will be released.

Common Exceptional Conditions

The following are the exceptional conditions common to the RELEASE command:

NOTAUTH: Resource security check has failed.
PGMIDERR: Program specified is not found.

3.7 Processing Program Table (PPT)

Function

The primary function of the Processing Program Table (PPT) is to register all CICS application programs and BMS maps. The Program Control Program (PCP) uses this table for controlling the application programs. Unless a CICS application program is registered in PPT, the program is unrecognizable to CICS.

PPT Entry Definition

One PPT entry can be defined using an Assembler macro DFHPPT. The following are the commonly used options of the DFHPPT macro by the application programmers:

```
DFHPPT      TYPE=ENTRY,
            PROGRAM= name | MAPSET=name,
            [PGMLANG= ASSEMBLER | COBOL | PLI],
            [RES= NO | ALIGN | FIX | PGOUT | YES],
            :
            :  (other options)
            :
```

PROGRAM or MAPSET is used to specify the name of the application program (1 to 8 characters) or the mapset name (1 to 7 characters), respectively. PGMLANG is used to specify the programming language (COBOL, PL/I, or Assembler) of the application program. If this is not specified, Assembler is assumed. The BMS mapsets are considered as written in Assembler.

RES indicates the residency status of the program in the storage. If this is not specified, RES=NO is assumed, and the program will be fetched only at the first excution time. If RES=YES is specified, the program will be resident in (virtual) storage. If RES=FIX is specified, the program will be placed in real storage (i.e., not virtual storage).

Example

The following is an example of PPT entries:

```
DFHPPT      TYPE=ENTRY,PROGRAM=PROG1,PGMLANG=COBOL
DFHPPT      TYPE=ENTRY,PROGRAM=PROG2,PGMLANG=PLI
DFHPPT      TYPE=ENTRY,PROGRAM=PROG3
DFHPPT      TYPE=ENTRY,PROGRAM=MSBINQ2
DFHPPT      TYPE=ENTRY,MAPSET=MSBINQ3
DFHPPT      TYPE=ENTRY,MAPSET=MSBINQ4
```

Technical Notes

The program name to be registered in PPT must be the load module name of the program in the load library (LOADLIB), and this program name in PPT must be used in the PROGRAM parameter of the LINK, XCTL and LOAD commands. If these names are not identical, the PGMIDERR condition will occur.

3.8   Program Control Table (PCT)

Function

The primary function of the Program Control Table (PCT) is to register the control information of all CICS transactions. The CICS Task Control Program (KCP) uses this table for identifying and initializing the transactions. Unless a CICS transaction is registered in PCT, the transaction cannot be initiated under CICS.

PCT Entry Definition

One PCT entry can be defined using an Assembler macro DFHPCT. The following are the commonly used options of the DFHPCT macro by the application programmers:

```
DFHPCT     TYPE=ENTRY,
           TRANSID=name,
           TASKREQ=xxxx,
           PROGRAM=name,
           [DTIMOUT=mmss],
           [RTIMOUT=mmss],
           [RESTART= NO | YES],
           [TRANSEC= 1 | decimal],
           [DUMP= YES | NO],
           [TRNPRTY= 1 | decimal],
           [TWASIZE= 0 | decimal],
             :
             : (other options)
             :
```

TRANSID defines the transaction identifier (1 to 4 characters). TASKREQ indicates the Program Function key (PF1 to PF24) or Program Attention key (PA1 to PA3) to be used for the transaction initiation. PROGRAM must name the application program associated with this transaction. The program name specified must be registered in PPT. DTIMOUT indicates the length of the time out for the transaction deadlock case. If the specified length expires, the task will be cancelled. RTIMOUT indicates the length of the time out for the terminal response. If the operator does not respond within the specified time length, the task will be cancelled. RESTART indicates whether the automatic transaction restart is to be applied after the completion of the transaction recovery from the abnormal termination of the transaction. TRANSEC is used to specify the transaction security code (1 to 64). DUMP indicates whether the dump is to be taken after the abnormal termination of the transaction. TRNPRTY indicates the transaction priority (0 to 255). TWASIZE is used to specify the size of the Transaction Work Area (TWA). If this is specified, the specified size of TWA will be acquired for each task of this transaction, which can use the acquired TWA for its own purposes.

Example

The following example is a typical definition of one PCT entry for a transaction:

```
DFHPCT     TYPE=ENTRY,
           TRANSID=INQ1,
           PROGRAM=PROG1,
           DTIMOUT=0500,
           RTIMOUT=1500,
           RESTART=YES,
           TRANSEC=3
```

In this case, if INQ1 is typed in a terminal and the ENTER key is pressed, transaction INQ1 will be initiated (i.e., program PROG1 will be initiated).

Task Initiation by PF Key

In some cases, you might wish to initiate a task by pressing a PF key for operational convenience. For such a case, specify in PCT:

```
TASKREQ=PF6          (example for PF6)
```

Suppose that this option is inserted in the PCT entry example above: if the terminal user presses the PF6 key, transaction INQ1 will be initiated. Even in this case, INQ1 can also be initiated by typing INQ1 and pressing the ENTER key, since both the TASKREQ and TRANSID options are specified.

3.9   Terminal Conversation

As the nature of an online system, a CICS application program involves interactions with the terminal users. Sending a message (or screen) to the terminal user and receiving a response from the user is called a "conversation" with the terminal user.

The following is a typical example of conversing with the terminal user:

1. A terminal user enters a transaction with an employee number.
2. The system sends the personal profile of the employee.
3. The user updates the profile data (e.g., address) and presses the ENTER key.
4. The system receives the data and updates the record of this employee and sends a confirmation message to the user.

Under CICS, there are three modes of terminal conversation with the terminal user as follows:

Conversational Mode

In the conversational mode, the program accomplishes a conversation by simply sending a message to the terminal, waiting for the user to respond, and receiving the response from the terminal. A program or transaction written in this mode is called the conversational program or transaction, respectively. We will discuss the details of the conversational mode in Section 3.10.

Pseudo-Conversational Mode

In the pseudo-conversational mode, the conversation is accomplished by more than one task. But, from the user's point of view, it looks like a normal conversation. A program or transaction written in this mode is called the pseudo-conversational program or transaction, respectively. We will discuss the details of the pseudo-conversational mode in Sections 3.11 through 3.14.

Nonconversational Mode

The nonconversational mode does not involve any conversation (i.e., interaction) with the terminal user, because usually the transaction in this mode is a one-way transaction for output only, such as:

- Report printing
- Message switching

Since the nonconversational transaction does not involve the conversation with the terminal users, the transaction must be initiated in special ways. There are two ways of initiating the nonconversational transaction. They are:

- Automatic Task Initiation (see Section 11.6)
- The START command in another transaction (see Section 13.6)

3.10 Conversational Transaction

When a program (or transaction) attempts a conversation with a terminal user (i.e., sending a message, expecting a response from the user), it issues a pair of SEND and RECEIVE commands (or equivalent commands).

The program waits until the user responds, holding resources unnecessarily. Only after the completion of the user's response (i.e., pressing the ENTER key) does the program proceed to the next processing.

Since human response is incomparably slower than the CPU speed, a significant amount of resources will be wasted just waiting. Hence, this is a very inefficient way of conversing with the user.

Example

The conversational transaction is a case of one transaction identifier (1 PCT entry) and one program (1 PPT entry). Let us suppose that PCT entry is defined as:

```
TSK1      DFHPCT    TYPE=ENTRY,TRANSID=TSK1,PROGRAM=PROG1, -----
```

Then, the conversational program PROG1 should look like the following:

```
PROCEDURE DIVISION.                     Terminal Operations
   :
   :
FIRST-PROCESS.
   EXEC CICS RECEIVE ----        <==        TSK1,12345
   END-EXEC.
```

```
        :
     (Some process)
        :
     EXEC CICS SEND -------        ==>         EMP(12345) PROFILE
     END-EXEC.                     ))
*                                  )) (Program waits for response.)
  SECOND PROCESS.                  ))
     EXEC CICS RECEIVE ----        <==         (User enters data.)
     END-EXEC.
        :
     (Some process)
        :
     EXEC CICS SEND -------        ==>         PROFILE UPDATED
     END-EXEC.
```

Execution Results   During the execution of this program logic, the following activities will occur:

- At the first RECEIVE command, the program will receive some data from the terminal.
- After processing the data, at the first SEND command, the program will send the data to the terminal and wait for the response from the user at the second RECEIVE command.
- As soon as the user types some data and presses the ENTER key, the program will receive the data.
- After processing the data, at the second SEND command, the program will send the final message to the terminal.

3.11 Pseudo-Conversational Transaction

In the pseudo-conversational transaction, when a program (or transaction) attempts a conversation with a terminal user (i.e., sending a message, expecting a response from the user), it terminates the task after sending a message with a linkage for the next task (or program).

When the user completes the response (i.e., pressing the ENTER key), the next task (or program) is automatically initiated by CICS. This task (or program) receives the message from the terminal and processes it.

From the system's point of view, this is a multitask operation, whereas, from the user's point of view, this is a normal conversation. This is why it is called "pseudo-conversational."

Since the task is terminated and resources are freed while waiting for the user's response, this approach is much more efficient than the conversational approach.

Commonly Used Techniques

There are three commonly used techniques available in order to develop the pseudo-conversational transaction. They are:

Technique 1:   Multiple transaction identifiers and multiple programs.
Technique 2:   Multiple transaction identifiers but one program.
Technique 3:   One transaction identifier and one program.

We will discuss these approaches in Sections 3.12, 3.13, and 3.14, respectively.

3.12   Pseudo-Conversational Technique 1

Approach

Pseudo-conversational technique 1 uses the multiple transaction identifiers (PCT entries) and multiple programs (PCT entries). It performs the terminal conversation in the following way:
A conversational program is logically and physically divided into separate programs after sending a message and before receiving the message. For each separate program, a unique CICS transaction identifier is assigned. Before terminating the program, each program issues the RETURN command with the next transaction identifier which is associated with the next program, unless it is the last return to CICS itself. In this way, a series of terminal conversations can be carried out continuously.

Advantage and Disadvantage

An advantage of this approach is that it is relatively easy to develop. But, its disadvantage is that it increases a number of transaction identifiers (PCT entries) and programs (PPT entries). Also, there tends to be significant redundancy in programming. Therefore, this approach is not recommended.

Example

Let us take a case of two transaction identifiers (PCT entries) and two programs (PPT entries). In this case, the PCT entries would look like:

```
TSK1      DFHPCT     TYPE=ENTRY,TRANSID=TSK1,PROGRAM=PROG1,------
TSK2      DFHPCT     TYPE=ENTRY,TRANSID=TSK2,PROGRAM=PROG2,------
```

Then, the programs PROG1 and PROG2 should look like:

```
Transaction=TSK1
Program=PROG1

        PROCEDURE DIVISION.
                :
                EXEC CICS RECEIVE ---- END-EXEC.
                :
                EXEC CICS SEND ------- END-EXEC.
                EXEC CICS RETURN
                        TRANSID('TSK2')
                END-EXEC.
                :

Transaction=TSK2
Program=PROG2

        PROCEDURE DIVISION.
                :
                EXEC CICS RECEIVE ---- END-EXEC.
                :
                EXEC CICS SEND ------- END-EXEC.
                EXEC CICS RETURN
                END-EXEC.
```

Execution Results   During the execution of these program logics, the following activities will occur:

• After the the terminal user types transaction identifier TSK1 and presses the ENTER key, the associated program PROG1 will be initiated, since the PCT entry for transaction TSK1 points program PROG1.

- Program PROG1, after receiving and processing the data, will send some data to the terminal and terminate itself by the RETURN command with the TRANSID option, associating the terminal with transaction TSK2.
- As soon as the user types data and presses the ENTER key, transaction TSK2 will be initiated, and associated program PROG2 will be initiated, since the PCT entry for transaction TSK2 points program PROG2.
- Program PROG2 will receive the data from the terminal, process it, send the final message to the terminal, and terminate itself by the RETURN command.

3.13   Pseudo-Conversational Technique 2

Approach

Pseudo-conversational technique 2 uses the multiple transaction identifiers (PCT entries) but only one program (PPT entry). It performs the terminal conversation in the following way:

Similar to technique 1, but instead of dividing into logically and physically separated programs, these separate programs are combined into one physical program, which has two functional routines to achieve the same functions as the physically separate programs in technique 1. The other areas remain the same as technique 1.

Advantage and Disadvantage

This approach reduces the number of programs (PPT entries). But it still creates many transaction identifiers (PCT entries) as does technique 1. Therefore, this approach is not recommended either.

Example

Let us take a case of two transaction identifiers (PCT entries) but one program (PPT entry). In this case, the PCT entries should look like:

```
TSK1      DFHPCT     TYPE=ENTRY,TRANSID=TSK1,PROGRAM=PROG1,------
TSK2      DFHPCT     TYPE=ENTRY,TRANSID=TSK2,PROGRAM=PROG1,------
```

Then, program PROG1 should look like:

```
PROCEDURE DIVISION.
*
      IF EIBTRNID = 'TSK1'
            PERFORM TSK1-RTN.
      IF EIBTRNID = 'TSK2'
            PERFORM TSK2-RTN.
      GO TO ERR-RTN.
*
  TSK1-RTN.
      EXEC CICS RECEIVE ----------
      END-EXEC.
            :
            : (some process)
            :
      EXEC CICS SEND ----------
      END-EXEC.
      EXEC CICS RETURN
            TRANSID('TSK2')
      END-EXEC.
*
  TSK2-RTN.
      EXEC CICS RECEIVE ----------
      END-EXEC.
            :
            : (some process)
            :
      EXEC CICS SEND ----------
      END-EXEC.
      EXEC CICS RETURN
      END-EXEC.
*

            :
```

Execution Results   During the execution of this program logic, the following activities will occur:

- Similar events as with technique 1 will occur.
- However, in the case of technique 2, instead of activating the different programs, since PCT points the same program PROG1, CICS activates the same program PROG1 at the first transaction initiation for TSK1 as well as the second transaction initiation for TSK2.

- In the top of program PROG1, there is a housekeeping routine which passes control to the appropriate paragraph based on the transaction identifier in EIBTRNID.
- TSK1-RTN processes the first iteration for transaction TSK1, while TSK2-RTN processes the second iteration for transaction TSK2.
- Therefore, one program PROG1 of technique 2 will achieve the same functions achieved by two programs PROG1 and PROG2 of technique 1.

3.14 Pseudo-Conversational Technique 3

Approach

Pseudo-conversational technique 3 uses only one transaction identifier (PCT entry) and only one program (PPT entry). It performs the terminal conversation in the following way:

One physical program consists of multiple logical programs, each of which takes care of one conversation. When a logical program of the physical program terminates, it issues the RETURN command with the TRANSID option for the transaction identifier defined in PCT, but it also passes a piece of data (let us call it "Internal Transaction Identifier") through COMMAREA indicating which conversation it is expecting the next time control is returned to the same physical program for the next logical program path.

Advantages

Technique 3 has the same efficiency as technique 2 with the multiple transaction identifiers and one program. But, this technique requires only one transaction identifier (PCT entry). It is quite efficient if one transaction consists of several (pseudo) conversations, since you can save the number of PCT entries. Therefore, this technique is highly recommended.

Example

Technique 3 is the case of one transaction identifier (PCT entry) and one program (PPT entry). Therefore, the PCT entry should look like:

```
TSK1      DFHPCT     TYPE=ENTRY,TRANSID=TSK1,PROGRAM=PROG1,------
```

Then, the program PROG1 should look like:

```
IDENTIFICATION DIVISION.
PROGRAM-ID.      PROG1.
REMARKS.
           THIS IS AN EXAMPLE OF THE MOST EFFECTIVE
           PSEUDO-CONVERSATIONAL MODE PROGRAM.
ENVIRONMENT DIVISION.
DATA DIVISION.
WORKING-STORAGE SECTION.
01   WK-COMMAREA.
     05   WK-INT-TRANSID          PIC X(4).
LINKAGE SECTION.
01   DFHCOMMAREA.
     05   LK-INT-TRANSID          PIC X(4).
*
PROCEDURE DIVISION.
*
     IF EIBTRNID NOT = 'TSK1'
         GO TO LOGIC-ERR.
     IF EIBCALEN = 0
         GO TO TSK1-RTN.
     IF LK-INT-TRANSID = 'TSK2'
         GO TO TSK2-RTN.
     GO TO LOGIC-ERR.
*
TSK1-RTN.
     EXEC CICS RECEIVE ----------
     END EXEC.
         :
         : (some process)
         :
     EXEC-CICS SEND ----------
     END-EXEC.
     MOVE 'TSK2' TO WK-INT-TRANSID.
     EXEC CICS RETURN
         TRANSID('TSK1')
         COMMAREA(WK-COMMAREA)
         LENGTH(4)
     EXD-EXEC.
*
```

```
TSK2-RTN.
     EXEC CICS RECEIVE ----------
     END EXEC.
          :
          : (some process)
          :
     EXEC CICS SEND ----------
     END-EXEC.
     EXEC CICS RETURN
     END-EXEC.
```

Execution Results   During the execution of this program logic, the following activities will occur:

- Similar events as with technique 2 will occur.
- However, in the case of technique 3, instead of using different transaction identifiers, only one transaction identifier TSK1 is used, while a piece of data (TSK2) indicating the second iteration will be passed through the COMMAREA for the second iteration.
- At the top of program PROG1, there is a housekeeping routine which passes control to the appropriate paragraphs based on the information in EIBTRNID and the data passed through COMMAREA.
- If the data has not been passed through COMMAREA (i.e., EIBCALEN = 0), then this is the first iteration, so that the TSK1-RTN will be excuted.
- If the data has been passed (i.e., IEBCALEN > 0), and the data received is equal to the internal transaction identifier (TSK2), then this is the second iteration, so that the TSK2-RTN will be executed.
- Therefore, one transaction identifier (TSK1) and one program (PROG1) of technique 3 will achieve the same functions achieved by two transaction identifiers (TSK1 and TSK2) and two programs (PROG1 and PROG2) of technique 1.

Internal Transaction Identifier

The internal transaction identifier is a piece of data which indicates at which entry the program is under the pseudo-conversational mode. This could be simply a numeric value or alphabet character, such as "1," "2," "3," or "A," "B," "C."

However, if you associate this internal transaction identifier with a BMS map name (which will be discussed in Chapter 8) or its abbreviation, you would find it very convenient in terms of program maintainability. A typical example is shown in the sample program in Appendix A of this book.

Technique 3 is nothing but a simple application of data passing through COMMAREA. The additional data could be passed through the same COMMAREA at the same time, depending on the application requirements.

External Transaction Identifier

Since the term "internal transaction identifier" was created in this book, in order to avoid confusion, let us hereafter call the ordinary transaction identifier defined in PCT the "External Transaction Identifier."

Programming Standard

Since pseudo-conversational technique 3 offers a significant advantage over the other techniques, hereafter, this technique will be the programming standard for the pseudo-conversational programs in this book. Therefore, all exercises in this book should be resolved through technique 3.

Exercise

Develop a pseudo-conversational program, using technique 3 described in Section 3.14, based on the following specifications:

1. Transaction identifier (external) is ODR1 and Program identifier is TXT3ODR1.
2. The program starts with receiving the following message from the terminal:

   ODR1 nnnnn

   where nnnnn is an item number.
3. Prepare, in the program, the following product table:

Item #	Description	Unit Price($)
00001	PRODUCT-A	1.10
00010	PRODUCT-B	2.50
00115	PRODUCT-C	5.99

4. Check the item number received against this product table. If it is not in the table, send an error message "UNKNOWN ITEM. TRANSACTION CANCELED. TRY AGAIN." and terminate the task.

5. If the item number is in the table, send a message "ENTER QUANTITY IN QQQQQ:," then return with the external transaction identifier = ODR1 and the internal transaction identifier = ODR2. Pass the item number (nnnnn), corresponding description and unit price through COMMAREA.

6. Upon receiving control again, receive the quantity which the user entered.

7. Based on the information on hand, calculate the order amount. Then prepare and send the following message as one line message:

```
ITEM=nnnnn NAME=xxxxxxxxx QUANTITY=zz,zz9
ORDER AMOUNT=$zzz,zz9.99
```

8. Terminate the task.

9. As the programming standard, every major exceptional condition must be intercepted by the HANDLE CONDITION command, in which case, send an appropriate error message and terminate the task. Be sure to avoid looping in the exceptional conditions.

File Control (1): Random Access

4.1 Introduction

The CICS File Control Program (FCP) provides application programs with services to read, update, add, and delete records in a file. In addition, it makes application programs independent of the structure of the database, while it manages exclusive control over the records in order to maintain the data integrity during record updates.

Supported Access Methods

CICS File Control supports the VSAM and BDAM data access methods, of which VSAM is the primary data access method under CICS. There are three types of VSAM file, all of which are supported by CICS. These are as follows:

- VSAM/Key-Sequenced Dataset (VSAM/KSDS)
- VSAM/Entry-Sequenced Dataset (VSAM/ESDS)
- VSAM/Relative Record Dataset (VSAM/RRDS)

Available Commands

In this chapter, we will discuss the commands for ramdom access to VSAM/KSDS. In Chapter 5, we will discuss the command for sequential access to VSAM/KSDS. In chapter 6, we will discuss how to utilize these commands for VSAM/ESDS and VSAM/KSDS.

For random access to VSAM/KSDS, the following commands are available:

READ:	To read a record directly
WRITE:	To newly write a record
REWRITE:	To update an existing record
DELETE:	To delete a record
UNLOCK:	To release exclusive control acquired for update

4.2　Special Services of File Control

In the online system environment, the CICS File Control must provide more than just services of reading, writing, updating, and deleting records in a file. It must provide additional services unique to the online system environment. These special services are data independence, exclusive control over resources during updates, and file open/close.

Data Independence

Data independence is a concept of a program being independent of the structure of database or the data access methods. The CICS File Control provides data independence to application programs, so that the application programmer does not have to be concerned with such data-dependent COBOL parameters or JCL as:

• INPUT-OUTPUT SECTION
• SELECT statement
• FD statement
• OPEN/CLOSE
• JCL

The system programmer (or application programmer) defines the File Control Table (FCT) to specify the characteristics of files to be used under CICS, while the application programmer codes application programs using CICS commands. In this way, it is almost transparent to the application programmer which data access method is being used.

Exclusive Control During Updates

If a task is updating a record, the other tasks must be excluded from updating that record, otherwise data content will be updated incorrectly. This control is called exclusive control over the resources during updates. This is important because in the CICS environment, many tasks might be concurrently accessing the same file (possibly the same record).

In Figure 4-1, Case 1 illustrates how a record of a file is successfully updated with exclusive control over the record (resource), whereas Case 2 illustrates how the record is wrongly updated without exclusive control over the record (resource).

Prior to CICS, maintaining exclusive control over the resources was the application program's responsibility. However, now CICS automatically maintains exclusive control during updates for the CICS application program similar to Case 1. That is, CICS automatically arranges file updating among tasks in the manner of Case 1, so that Case 2 would never occur under CICS. Therefore, the application programs are mostly freed from the considerations for maintaining exclusive control over the resources.

File Open/Close

When an application program accesses a file, the file must be open under CICS. For this, FCT defines an initial file open/close status (see Section 6.6). If a file is closed, you must open the file using the Master Terminal transaction (CEMT) before you initiate an application transaction (program) which uses this file. CICS Ver. 1.7 (or later) loosened this restriction a little. But file open/close is still CICS's task, not application program's task. For the details, refer to Sections 16.10 through 16.16.

4.3   Review of VSAM Files

To utilize the File Control commands effectively, it is advantageous for you to understand the concept of the Virtual Storage Access Method (VSAM). Since the subject of VSAM is broad and complex and would require a complete book for itself, this section will only review and highlight the concept of VSAM.

VSAM is one of the most efficient and reliable data access methods available under the virtual storage system environment. There are

Assumptions For both Case 1 and Case 2, the following assumptions were made:

Inventory at Hand:	100 units
Order by Task A:	50 units
Order by Task B:	30 units

Case 1: Successful Updates with Exclusive Control

		Inventory Level		
Time	Events	Task A	Task B	Record/File
1	Task A reads	100		100
2	Task A reduces	100-50= 50		100
3	Task A rewrites	50		50
4	Task B reads		50	50
5	Task B reduces		50-30=20	50
6	Task B rewrites		20	20

Results As the time passes by from 1 to 6, the following activities will occur:

- As soon as task A (or B) reads the record of the file for update, the record is reserved for the task; that is, exclusive control over the record is maintained.
- Therefore, the order of record updates is controlled in such a way that task A completes its record update first to reduce the inventory by 50, and only then does task B start updating the record to reduce the inventory by 30.
- Since exclusive control over the record was maintained, the inventory level of the record in the file has been successfully updated and the new inventory level is now 20 units.

Case 2: Wrong Updates without Exclusive Control

		Inventory Level		
Time	Events	Task A	Task B	Record/File
1	Task A reads	100		100
2	Task B reads	100	100	100
3	Task A reduces	100-50=50	100	100
4	Task B reduces	50	100-30=70	100
5	Task A rewrites	50	70	50
6	Task B rewrites		70	70

Results As the time passes by from 1 to 6, the following activities will occur:

- Since exclusive control is not maintained over the record, the order of record updates are mixed between task A and task B.
- Therefore, the inventory level of the record in the file is wrongly updated, once by Task A to 50 units (100–50), then by Task B to 70 units (100–30). Although the total order amount by the Task A and B is 80 units, the new inventory level in the record shows 70 units. This is wrong.

Figure 4-1 Exclusive control during updates.

three types of VSAM file, any of which can be read directly as well as sequentially: VSAM/Entry Sequenced Dataset (VSAM/ESDS), Key-Sequenced Dataset (VSAM/KSDS), and Relative Record Dataset (VSAM/RRDS)

Each type of VSAM file has the origin of the conceptual evolution which represents the area of strength, as follows:

- Concept of QSAM ⟶ VSAM/ESDS: Effective in sequential access
- Concept of ISAM ⟶ VSAM/KSDS: Effective in random as well as sequential access
- Concept of BDAM ⟶ VSAM/RRDS: Effective in fast random access

VSAM/KSDS (Key-Sequenced Dataset)

The concept of VSAM/KSDS is illustrated in Figure 4-2. As can be seen, the VSAM/KSDS file consists of the Index portion and the Data portion.

```
Index Portion

    Highest Index Set        3600 | 5000 | ----

    Index Set    1210 | 2210 | 3600 | F/S        ------ | 5000 | F/S  ...

    Seq. Set     1010 | 1055 | 1210 | F/S     1350 | 1600 | 2210 | F/S  ...


Data Portion

CA 1    C  11    1001 | 1002 | 1005 | 1010 |       Free Space

        C  12    1020 | 1022 | 1030 | 1050 | 1055 |    Free Space

        C  13    1100 | 1102 | 1105 | 1150 | 1170 | 1200 | 1210 | F/S

        C  14              Free Space


CA 2    C  21    1300 | 1305 | 1310 | 1320 | 1350 |    Free Space

        C  22    1400 | 1410 | 1415 | 1500 | 1600 |    Free Space

        C  23    2000 | 2010 | 2071 | 2150 | 2180 | 2200 | 2210 | F/S

        C  24              Free Space

                            :
                            :
```

Figure 4-2 Concept of VSAM/KSDS.

Index Portion The Index portion consists of the three levels of index such as the Sequence Set (the lowest index), the Index Set (next higher index), and the Highest Index Set record (highest index).

Data Portion The Data portion also consists of three levels of data. The lowest level is the record. Each record is identified by means of a key which must be defined uniquely within the file. The next higher level of Data portion is the Control Interval (CI), whose length is a multiple of 256 bytes. CI is the unit of the physical input/output operation. One or more records can be stored in one CI, while within the CI, all records are arranged in a sequential order based on the key. All indexing is done in terms of CIs (not records). The highest level of the Data portion is the Control Area (CA), which is simply a group of CIs.

Identifying a Record In the example of Figure 4-2, there are two Control Areas (CA). CA 1 consists of four Control Intervals (CI 11, 12, 13, 14). CI 11 has four records, of which the highest record is 1010. The remaining of CI 11 is a free space of the CI. Within CA 1, CI 11, 12, and 13 have records, while CI 14 is a free space of the CA. CA 2 has the similar structure.

The Sequence Set (the lowest index) has several CIs. The first CI has three records, each of which points the highest record in the CI of the Data Portion (e.g., 1010 for CI 11). The Index Set (the middle index) has several CIs. The first CI has four records, each of which points the highest record in the Sequence Set (e.g., 1210 for the first CI of the Sequence Set). The Highest Index Set is one CI which has several records, each of which points the highest record of each CI in the Index Set.

Based on this concept, VSAM can identify each record within this VSAM/KSDS cluster, given the key of the record. Therefore, any record can be added or deleted randomly. Also, any record can be read randomly or sequentially (forward as well as backward).

Input/Output Operations Since CI is a unit of physical input/output operations, even if you wish to read one particular record directly, the entire CI which contains that record among other records will be read. Therefore, for better performance, the CI size should be smaller if the file is used mainly for direct access. On the other hand, if the file is mainly used for sequential access, the CI size should be larger for better performance.

Split Each CI and CA has free space which is used for record insertion. When the free space of a CI is exhausted and a new record is to be added, VSAM first splits the CI in half, placing the latter half of the records in the available CI. Then, VSAM inserts the new record in the appropriate position. This is called a "CI split."

Similarly, when all free CIs in a CA are exhausted, a split of the CA occurs in a similar manner to the CI split. This is called a "CA split." Since CI splits and CA splits not only degrade the performance but also decrease the efficient use of the VSAM space, the CI size should be determined so as to minimize the number of CI splits and CA splits.

VSAM/ESDS (Entry-Sequenced Dataset)

The concept of VSAM/ESDS is illustrated in Figure 4-3. As can be seen, in a VSAM/ESDS file, records are arranged in the entry order, so that new records are always added to the space after the last record in the file. This implies that no records can be deleted at any time.

Each record is identified by its Relative Byte Address (RBA). This means that ESDS does not require either key or index, but that each record can be accessed directly using RBA, if so desired. Usually, ESDS is used for sequential record access.

VSAM/RRDS (Relative Record Dataset)

The concept of VSAM/RRDS is illustrated in Figure 4-4. As can be seen, a VSAM/RRDS file consists of a series of fixed-length slots which have been predefined by VSAM. Therefore, by definition, RRDS is a fixed-length record file.

Each record is identified by its Relative Record Number (RRN). This means that neither key nor index is required. A new record can be added sequentially at the next available RRN, or at the specified RRN directly.

VSAM/RRDS provides better performance if it is used properly. But, managing RRN is left to the programmer.

RBA

00	10	25	35	55
Rec1	Rec2	Rec3	Rec4	(space)
(10 bytes)	(15 bytes)	(10 bytes)	(20 bytes)	Add

Figure 4-3 Concept of VSAM/ESDS.

RRN

1	2	3	4	5			
Rec1	Rec2	Rec3	Rec4	Rec5			

(Fixed-length records)

Figure 4-4 Concept of VSAM/RRDS.

Restrictions in This Book

In order to avoid confusion on the data access methods and CICS File Control commands in this book, let us establish a restriction that only VSAM files are used for File Control operations.

BDAM will be excluded from this book becase it is a somewhat outdated data access method, which does not facilitate the maximum advantage of CICS command level. Under the CICS command level, VSAM should be used as the primary data access method for the following reasons:

• VSAM is IBM's primary data access method.
• VSAM is highly reliable.
• VSAM provides high performance if it is used properly.

4.4   READ Command with INTO Option Using Full Key

Function

The READ command with the INTO option using the full key of a record is used to read a specific record specified by the full key. The data content of the record will be moved into the specified field defined in the Working Storage Section of the program.

Format

The format of the READ command with the INTO option using the full key for VSAM/KSDS is as follows:

```
EXEC CICS READ
     DATASET(name) | FILE(name)
     INTO(data-area)
     RIDFLD(data-area)
     LENGTH(data-value)
END-EXEC.
```

This is the basic format for the READ command. As the other options are introduced, the format will vary slightly. But the basic concept remains the same. The following points should be noted:

DATASET (or FILE) names the file which you wish to read. The
file name specified must be defined in FCT. FILE is the preferred
name under CICS/MVS, but it performs the same function as
DATASET.

INTO names the field in the Working Storage Section to which the
record content is to be placed. RIDFLD is used to specify the key
field which identifies the record to be read. LENGTH (halfword binary field: S9(4) COMP) indicates the maximum length of the record
to be read. This is optional. But, if it is specified, at the completion of
the command, CICS will place the actual length of the record into
the LENGTH field.

Example

The following is an example of the READ command with the INTO
option using the full key:

```
WORKING-STORAGE SECTION.
77    WK-LEN                             PIC S9(4) COMP.
01    FILE-IOAREA.
      05    REC-A.
            10    REC-A-KEY
                  15    REC-A-KEY-CITY     PIC XX.
                  15    REC-A-KEY-SEQ      PIC 999.
            10    REC-A-DETAIL             PIC X(30).
            :
PROCEDURE DIVISION.
*
      MOVE 35 TO WK-LEN.
      MOVE 'NY001' TO REC-A-KEY.
      EXEC CICS READ
```

```
            DATASET('FILEAAA')
            INTO(FILE-IOAREA)
            RIDFLD(REC-A-KEY)
            LENGTH(WK-LEN)
      END-EXEC.
```

Execution Results   At the completion of this program logic, the following actions will occur:

- CICS will read the record NY001 and place the data in the INTO field (FILE-IOAREA).
- The actual record length will be placed in WK-LEN.

Common Exceptional Conditions

The following are exceptional conditions common to the READ command with the INTO option using the full key:

DUPKEY:	A duplicate record is found in the specified key. The first record in the file which has that key will be read. If you wish to read other records of the same key, you have to use the Browse operation (see Chapter 5).
NOTFND:	No record with the key specified is found.
LENGERR:	The specified length is shorter than the actual record length. The record will be truncated at the length specified and moved into the INTO field. The actual length will be placed in the LENGTH field.

NOTOPEN Condition

The exceptional condition NOTOPEN originally meant that the file specified is not open, so that the file cannot be used. However, this condition has been removed from CICS Ver 1.7 (or later). That is, under CICS Ver. 1.7 (or later), if the file is not open at the time of a File Control command, CICS automatically opens the file and executes the command. Therefore, under CICS Ver. 1.7 (or later), it is meaningless to check the NOTOPEN condition.

4.5   READ Command with SET Option Using Full Key

Function

The READ command with the SET option using the full key is used to read a specific record specified in the full key. CICS sets the address pointer to the address of the record in the file input/output area within CICS, so that the application program can directly refer to the record without moving the record content into the Working Storage area defined in the program. Therefore, the SET option provides a better performance than the INTO option.

Format

The format of the READ command with the SET option using the full key for VSAM/KSDS is shown in the example below. For the SET option, the BLL cells must be constructed in the Linkage Section based on the convention. The address pointer (pointer-reference) to the file area in BLL must be specified in the SET parameter. The RIDFLD filed must be defined in the Working Storage Section (i.e., not in the Linkage Section). After the READ command, the SERVICE RELOAD statement must be issued in order to ensure the proper addressability. The format related to the other options or parameters remains the same as in the case of the READ command with the INTO option.

Example

The following is an example of the READ command with the SET option using the full key, in order to achieve the same objective of reading the record NY001 as Section 4.4:

```
WORKING-STORAGE SECTION.
77    WK-LEN                            PIC S9(4) COMP.
77    WK-REC-A-KEY                      PIC X(5).
      :
      :
LINKAGE SECTION.
01    PARM-LIST.
      05    FILLER                      PIC S9(8) COMP.
      05    FILE-PTR                    PIC S9(8) COMP.
```

```
01   LK-FILE-IOAREA.
     05   LK-REC-A.
          10   LK-REC-A-KEY.
               15   LK-REC-A-KEY-CITY      PIC XX.
               15   LK-REC-A-KEY-SEQ       PIC 999.
          10   LK-REC-A-DETAIL             PIC X(30).
          :
          :


PROCEDURE DIVISION.
*
     MOVE 35 TO WK-LEN.
     MOVE 'NY001' TO WK-REC-A-KEY.
     EXEC CICS READ
          DATASET('FILEAAA')
          SET(FILE-PTR)
          RIDFLD(WK-REC-A-KEY)
          LENGTH(WK-LEN)
     END-EXEC.
     SERVICE RELOAD LK-FILE-IOAREA.        <== Must be issued.
          :
          :
```

Execution Results   During the execution of this program logic, the following activities will occur:

- During the execution of the READ command, CICS will acquire the I/O area, place the record read, and place the address of the I/O area into the pointer-reference (FILE-PTR).
- Therefore, after the SERVICE RELOAD statement, the application program will be able to refer to any fields in LK-FILE-IOAREA.

Common Exceptional Conditions

The exceptional conditions common to the READ command with the SET option using full key are the same as in the case of the INTO option (see Section 4.4).

Programming Considerations

When you use the SET option, be sure that the data area defined by the 01 level has the proper length. If the area is too large, the program might accidentally destroy some of the CICS system areas, which might cause a storage violation.

This SET option is faster than the INTO option because CICS does not have to move the record content to the Working Storage of the program. But, for program simplicity and maintainability, the INTO option is recommended. The difference in performance is only moving the record data into the INTO field of the program and possible page faults, which may not be significant.

Improvements by VS COBOL II

If the application program is written in VS COBOL II, the above example becomes much simpler. In this case, PARM-LIST defined in the Linkage Section is no longer required. In the READ command, the reserved word "ADDRESS" must be used in the SET parameter in order to point the address of the field. The SERVICE RELOAD statement is no longer required either. The following is an example of the READ command with the SET option in VS COBOL II:

```
WORKING-STORAGE SECTION.
77    WK-LEN                                  PIC S9(4) COMP.
77    WK-REC-A-KEY                             PIC X(5).
       :
       :
LINKAGE SECTION.
01    LK-FILE-IOAREA.
       05   LK-REC-A.
             10   LK-REC-A-KEY.
                   15    LK-REC-A-KEY-CITY      PIC XX.
                   15    LK-REC-A-KEY-SEQ       PIC 999.
             10   LK-REC-A-DEATAIL             PIC X(30).
       :
       :
PROCEDURE DIVISION.
*
      MOVE 35 TO WK-LEN.
      MOVE 'NY001' TO WK-REC-A-KEY.
      EXEC CICS READ
            DATASET('FILEAAA')
            SET(ADDRESS OF LK-FILE-IOAREA)
            RIDFLD(WK-REC-A-KEY)
            LENGTH(WK-LEN)
      END-EXEC.
       :
       :
```

Execution Results During the execution of this program logic, the following activities will occur:

- During the execution of the READ command, CICS will acquire the I/O area, place the record read, and point this address to the I/O area (LK-FILE-IOAREA) defined in the Linkage Section.
- Therefore, after the completion of the READ command, the application program will be able to refer to any fields in LK-FILE-IOAREA.

4.6 READ Command with GENERIC Option

Function

The READ command with the GENERIC option is used to read a nonspecific record based on the generic key (i.e., a higher part of the key) specified, instead of the full key. This is useful when you do not know the complete information of the key.

In order to simplify the discussion, let us use the INTO option in the READ command, noting that the SET option also could be used as an alternative.

Format

The format of the READ command with the GENERIC option using the INTO option for VSAM/KSDS is shown in the example below. For this option, in addition to specifying explicitly GENERIC as the option, the length of the generic key must be specified in the KEY-LENGTH field, and the generic key data must be provided in the RIDFLD field. The format related to the other options or parameters remains the same as the case in the READ command with the INTO option.

Example

Assuming the same Working Storage Section in Section 4.4, the following is an example of the READ command with the GENERIC option based on the INTO option:

```
MOVE 35 TO WK-LEN.
MOVE 'NY' TO REC-A-KEY.          <== Generic read with the first 2
EXEC CICS READ                       bytes of the key.
     DATASET('FILEAAA')
     INTO(FILE-IOAREA)
     RIDFLD(REC-A-KEY)
     KEYLENGTH(2)                <== Length of generic key.
     GENERIC                     <== Must be specified.
     LENGTH(WK-LEN)
END-EXEC.
```

Execution Results Suppose that file FILEAAA has records in the following order:

```
BO001
DC001
DC002
NY000     <== Then, this record (NY000) will be read,
NY001         beacuse this is the first record of
NY002         the generic key "NY".
PH001
PH002
```

Common Exceptional Conditions

The following is the exceptional condition common to the READ command with the GENERIC option:

INVREQ: The keylength specified is greater than the actual keylength of the record.

4.7   READ Command with GTEQ Option

Function

The READ command with the GTEQ option is used to read a non-specific record whose key is equal to or greater than the full key data specified. This is useful when you know the full key, but you are not sure that the record with that key exists in the file.

In order to simplify the discussion, let us again use the INTO option in the READ command, noting that the SET option could be also used as an alternative.

Format

The format of the READ command with the GTEQ option using the INTO option for VSAM/KSDS is shown in the example below. For this option, GTEQ must be explicitly specified as the option. The format related to the other options or parameters remains the same as in the case of the READ command with the INTO option.

Example

Assuming the same Working Storage Section in Section 4.4, the following is an example of the READ command with the GTEQ option based on the INTO option:

```
MOVE 35 TO WK-LEN.
MOVE 'NY003' TO REC-A-KEY.   <== Must be full key.
EXEC CICS READ
     DATASET('FILEAAA')
     INTO(FILE-IOAREA)
     RIDFLD(REC-A-KEY)
     GTEQ                    <== Greater than or equal to search.
     LENGTH(WK-LEN)
END-EXEC.
```

Execution Results Suppose that file FILEAAA contains the same records as Section 4.6. Then, record PH001 will be read, since record NY003 does not exist.

4.8 READ/UPDATE and REWRITE Commands

Function

A combination of the READ command with the UPDATE option and the REWRITE command is used to update a record. Between these two commands, exclusive control over the record will be maintained

for this task, so that no other tasks can access this record for updates. Therefore, the interval between these two commands should
be as short as possible.

In order to simplify the discussion, let us again use the INTO option in the READ command, noting the SET option could also be
used as an alternative.

Format

The format of the READ command with the UPDATE option for
VSAM/KSDS is shown in the example below. For this option, UP-
DATE must be explicitly specified as the option. The format related
to the other options or parameters remains the same as in the case
of the READ command with the INTO option.

The format of the REWRITE command is also shown in the example below. DATASET (or FILE) must name the same file read by the
prior READ/UPDATE command. The FROM data area must be the
same record area used by the READ/UPDATE command. LENGTH
(halfword binary field) indicates the length of the new record. The
value in LENGTH could be changed if the record size is different for
update. But, changing the length is not recommended from the system design's point of view.

Example

Assuming the same Working Storage Section of Section 4.4, the following is an example of record update achieved by the combination
of the READ/UPDATE command and the REWRITE command:

```
MOVE 35 TO WK-LEN.
MOVE 'NY001' TO REC-A-KEY.
EXEC CICS READ
     DATASET('FILEAAA')
     INTO(FILE-IOAREA)
     RIDFLD(REC-A-KEY)
     LENGTH(WK-LEN)
     UPDATE                  <== Read for updating.
END-EXEC.
     :                    )
     :                    )   This interval should be
MOVE 'THIS IS TEST FOR UPDATE'  )   very short.
```

```
      TO REC-A-DESC.
EXEC  CICS REWRITE              <== Actual update.
      DATASET('FILEAAA')        <== Same file name as the READ.
      FROM(FILE-IOAREA)         <== Same data area as the READ.
      LENGTH(WK-LEN)            <== The length of the new record.
END-EXEC.
```

Execution Results   During the execution of this program logic, the following activities will occur:

- At the completion of the READ/UPDATE command, record NY001 will be read and reserved for the subsequent update. That is, exclusive control over the record is maintained for this task.
- At the completion of the REWRITE command, the same record NY001 will be rewritten and the record will be released from exclusive control.

Common Exceptional Condition

The following is the exceptional condition common to the REWRITE command:

INVREQ: The REWRITE command is issued without a prior READ command with the UPDATE option.

4.9   UNLOCK Command

Function

The READ command with the UPDATE option normally maintains exclusive control over the record read until:

- The record is updated by the REWRITE command.
- The transaction is normally or abnormally completed.

However, there are occasions when after reading a record through the READ command with the UPDATE option, it is found that the update is no longer required. In this case, the application program should release exclusive control from the record, so that other tasks can access the same record. For this purpose, the UNLOCK command is prepared. That is, the UNLOCK command is used to release the exclusive control from the record.

Format

The format of the UNLOCK command is shown in the example below. DATASET (or FILE) names the file from which exclusive control is to be released.

Example

Assuming the same Working Storage Section of Section 4.4, the following is an example of the UNLOCK command:

```
      :
(READ/UPDATE of Section 4.8)
      :
EXEC CICS UNLOCK
     DATASET('FILEAAA')
END-EXEC.
```

Results   During the execution of this program logic, the following activities will occur:

- At the completion of the READ/UPDATE command, the record NY001 will be read and reserved.
- At the completion of the UNLOCK command, the record NY001 will be released from exclusive control.

4.10   WRITE Command

Function

The WRITE command is used to write (add) a record directly into a file based on the key specified.

Format

The format of the WRITE command for VSAM/KSDS is as follows:

```
EXEC CICS WRITE
    DATASET(name) | FILE(name)
    FROM(data-area)
    LENGTH(data-value)
    RIDFLD(data-area)
END-EXEC.
```

DATASET (or FILE) names the file to which the record is to be written. FROM names the field where the record data exist. LENGTH indicates the length of the record to be written. It is required for a variable record. But even for a fixed length record, it should be specified.

Example

Assuming the same Working Storage Section of Section 4.4, the following is an example of the WRITE command:

```
MOVE 35 TO WK-LEN.
MOVE 'NY004' TO REC-A-KEY.
EXEC CICS WRITE
    DATASET('FILEAAA')
    FROM(FILE-IOAREA)
    RIDFLD(REC-A-KEY)
    LENGTH(WK-LEN)
END-EXEC.
```

Execution Results   The record whose key is NY004 will be written into file FILEAAA.

Common Exceptional Conditions

The following are the exceptional conditions common to the WRITE command:

DUPREC:	The duplicate record is found.
NOSPACE:	No disk space is available for the record addition.
LENGERR:	The length specified is greater than the maximum length specified in the VSAM cluster.

4.11   WRITE Command with MASSINSERT Option

Function

The WRITE command with the MASSINSERT option is used to add a group of records whose keys are in ascending order into a file. If there are many records to be added as a group, this option will provide high performance in writing these records.

Since the MASSINSERT option causes exclusive control over the file, the file must be released by the UNLOCK command after the completion of the WRITE command.

Procedures

The following are the procedures for the mass-insert operations using the WRITE command with the MASSINSERT option:

1. Establish the first record key.
2. Issue the WRITE command with the MASSINSERT option.
3. Increment the key in the ascending order.
4. Repeat steps 2 and 3 until all records have been written.
5. Issue the UNLOCK command to release the exclusive control over the file.

Format

The format of the WRITE command with the MASSINSERT option for VSAM/KSDS is shown in the example below. MASSINSERT must be explicitly specified as the option. The format related to the other options or parameters remains the same as the case of the WRITE command without the MASSINSERT option.

Example

Using the same Working Storage in Section 4.4, the following is an example of the mass-insert operations using the WRITE command with the MASSINSERT option:

```
PROCEDURE DIVISION.
    :
    MOVE 'TX000' TO REC-A-KEY.
MASS-INS-LOOP.
    Add 1 to REC-A-KEY-SEQ.
    :
    (prepare the record content)
    :
    MOVE 35 TO WK-LEN.
    EXEC CICS WRITE
        DATASET('FILEAAA')
        FROM(FILE-IOAREA)
        RIDFLD(REC-A-KEY)
        LENGTH(WK-LEN)
        MASSINSERT                    <== Attention.
    END-EXEC.
    IF REC-A-KEY-SEQ < 99
        GO TO MASS-INS-LOOP.
*
    EXEC CICS UNLOCK                  <== Required.
        DATASET('FILEAAA')
    END-EXEC.
```

Execution Results   During the execution of this program logic, the following activities will occur:

- Records TX001 through TX099 (total 99 records) will be written one by one at the completion of each WRITE/MASSINSERT command, during which the exclusive control will be maintained over file FILEAAA.
- At the completion of the UNLOCK command, the exclusive control over file FILEAAA will be released.

4.12   DELETE Commnd

Function

The DELETE command is used to delete one record or a group of records from a file. There are three approaches to using the DELETE command.

DELETE after READ/UPDATE Approach

In this approach, the DELETE command is issued without the record key information (i.e., RIDFLD) after the READ command with UPDATE option has been completed. The record which was read by the READ/UPDATE command will be deleted from the file.

Format The format of the DELETE command in this approach for VSAM/KSDS is shown in the example below. The only parameter required is DATASET (or FILE), which must name the same file used by the prior READ/UPDATE command.

Example The following is an example of the DELETE command after the prior READ/UPDATE command:

```
    :
(READ/UPDATE of Section 4.8)
    :
EXEC CICS DELETE
     DATASET('FILEAAA')
END-EXEC.
```

Execution Results Record NY001 which was read by the prior READ/UPDATE command will be deleted from file FILEAAA.

Common Exceptional Condition The following is the exceptional condition common to the DELETE command used in this approach:

INVREQ: The DELETE command without the RIDFLD
                  option is issued without a prior READ/UP-
                  DATE command.

Direct DELETE Approach

In this approach, the DELETE command is issued with the full key information in the RIDFLD field. The record specified will be directly deleted from the file.

Format The format of the DELETE command in this approach for VSAM/KSDS is shown in the example below. DATASET (or FILE) must name the file from which a record is to be deleted. In addition, the full key data must be provided in the RIDFLD field for the record to be deleted.

Example The following is an example of the DELETE command for
the direct record deletion:

```
      :
(without prior READ/UPDATE command)
MOVE 'NY001' to REC-A-KEY.
EXEC CICS DELETE
     DATASET('FILEAAA')
     RIDFLD(REC-A-KEY)                    <==== Required.
END-EXEC.
```

Execution Results Record NY001 will be directly deleted from file
FILEAAA.

Common Exceptional Conditions The following are the exceptional
conditions common to the DELETE command in this approach:

DUPKEY: There is more than one record with same key.
NOTFND: The record specified is not found.

Group Record DELETE Approach

In this approach, the DELETE command is issued with the GE-
NERIC option. A group of records which satisfy the generic key specified will be deleted from the file.

Format The format of the DELETE command in this approach for
VSAM/KSDS is shown in the example below. In addition to the required parameters for the direct delete, GENERIC must be explicitly
specified as the option. The KEYLENGTH indicates the length of the
generic key. The higher part of the key information must be supplied
in the RIDFLD field. A half-word binary field (S9(4) COMP) should
be provided to NUMREC, which will contain the number of the records deleted by this generic delete.

Example The following is an example of the DELETE command with
the GENERIC option:

```
WORKING-STORAGE SECTION.
     (Same as Section 4.4)
     :
77   WK-DEL-COUNT            PIC S9(4) COMP.
     :
```

```
PROCEDURE DIVISION.
     :
     MOVE 'NY' TO REC-A-KEY.          <=== Specify value of
     EXEC CICS DELETE                      generic key.
          DATASET('FILEAAA')
          RIDFLD(REC-A-KEY)
          KEYLENGTH(2)                <=== Specify generic
          GENERIC                          keylength.
          NUMREC(WK-DEL-COUNT)
     END-EXEC.
```

Execution Results   Suppose that file FILEAAA contains the same records as Section 4.6. Then, all of NY000, NY001, and NY002 will be
deleted. And the number of records deleted will be returned to the
NUMERIC field (WK-DEL-COUNT=3 in this case).

Common Exceptional Condition   The following is the exceptional condition common to the DELETE command in this approach:

INVREQ: The keylength specified is greater than the
                      actual keylength of the record.

4.13   Transaction Deadlocks

When one transaction needs exclusive use of some resource (e.g., a
record of a file) which is already held by a second transaction, the
first transaction waits for the resource to be released by the second.
However, if the second transaction cannot release the resource because it is waiting for some other resource held by the first, both
transactions will be interlocked. This is called "Transaction Deadlock." The only way of breaking the deadlock is to cancel one or both
transactions.

Causes of Transaction Deadlocks

There are three major causes of transaction deadlocks, as follows:

1. *Exclusive Control over Record*

    When a record is being modified (i.e., updated or deleted), the
    transaction has exclusive control over the record for the dura-

tion. This exclusive control over the record can cause the transaction deadlock.

Taking the example below, transaction A reserves the exclusive control over File1/Record1, while transaction B reserves the exclusive control over File2/Record2. Transaction A tries to read File2/Record2 for update, but it has to wait because File2/Record2 is held by transaction B. Meanwhile, transaction B tries to read File1/Record1 for update, but it has to wait because File1/Record1 is held by transaction A. Since both transactions A and B wait, neither transaction can complete the first update. Therefore, infinite wait occurs.

```
Transaction A :      READ UPDATE      File1/Record1
Transaction B :      READ UPDATE      File2/Record2
Transaction A :      READ UPDATE      File2/Record2
Transaction B :      READ UPDATE      File1/Record1
            <<<< Deadlock >>>>
```

2. *Exclusive Control over VSAM Control Interval (CI)*

When a record of a VSAM file, regardless of whether it is KSDS, ESDS, or RRDS, is being modified (i.e., updated or deleted), the transaction has exclusive control over not only the record but also the entire CI which contains the record on subject for the duration. This exclusive control over CI can cause the transaction deadlock.

Taking the example below, transaction A reserves exclusive control over CI of File1, which contains all of Record1 through Record5, although transaction A is updating only Record1. Meanwhile, transaction B reserves exclusive control over CI of File2, which contains all of Record1 through Record5 although transaction B is updating only Record2. This causes the similar situation to case 1 above, resulting in infinite wait by both transactions.

```
CI of File1 and File2
```

Record1	Record2	Record3	Record4	Record5

```
Transaction A :      READ UPDATE      File1/Record1
Transaction B :      READ UPDATE      File2/Record2
Transaction A :      READ UPDATE      File2/Record3
Transaction B :      READ UPDATE      File1/Record4
            <<<< Deadlock >>>>
```

3. *Exclusive Control over Logical Unit of Work (LUW)*

If a transaction has modified a recoverable record, and if the resource recovery is specified for the resource on subject, the record will still be locked even after the modification request (update, delete) has been completed. The same transaction may continue to access and modify the same record, but the other transactions are obliged to wait during this Logical Unit of Work (LUW) until the transaction releases the lock either by issuing a Sync Point request or by terminating the transaction itself. This causes a similar situation to case 1 above, resulting in infinite wait by both transactions.

This is related to Recovery/Restart. We will study the details of the Sync Point and LUW in Chapter 15.

Considerations for Avoiding Deadlocks

The transaction deadlock causes not only the deadlocked transactions to wait, but also other transactions, which try to use the same resources exclusively reserved for the deadlocked transactions, to wait. Therefore, in a CICS system, it is crucial to avoid transaction deadlocks. The following are some considerations for avoiding or reducing the likelihood of transaction deadlocks:

- If possible, online updates/deletes of records should be avoided. Instead, batch jobs should be used for the updates/deletes.
- The READ/UPDATE command should be paired with the RE-WRITE, DELETE, or UNLOCK command immediately after it is issued, before any other READ/UPDATE commands are issued.
- The WRITE/MASSINSERT requests must be completed with the UNLOCK command to release exclusive control over the file. No other operation on the file should be performed until the UNLOCK is completed.

4.14   Double Updating During Pseudo-Conversation

Double updating is a general term for wrong update of a resource (e.g., record) without exclusive control over the resource, resulting in a loss of data integrity over the resource.

In Section 4.2 we discussed exclusive control over the resources by File Control. Because of this capability of exclusive control, data integrity of record is automatically maintained during file updates, so that double updating of record by two independent tasks will never occur. However, this is not the case if file update is attempted during pseudo-conversation. In this case, double updates of the record may occur.

Cause

As we discussed in Chapter 3, pseudo-conversation is achieved by a series of independent tasks (or transactions). When a task sends a message to the terminal, the task terminates itself, thereby releasing the resources while waiting for a response from the terminal. When the terminal user responds by pressing the ENTER key, the next logical task is initialized and the task resumes processing using data from the terminal.

The problem is that exclusive control over the resource ends when the task is terminated. This means that even if the first task issues the READ/UPDATE command against a file, exclusive control over the record of the file ends at task completion. Therefore, the second task of the same pseudo-conversation has to issue the READ/UP-DATE command again before issuing the REWRITE command. That is, between the first task and the second task, the record is released from exclusive control. Meantime, if another pseudo-conversational task attempts updates of the same record, double updates of record could occur.

This can be well illustrated if we use Case 2 (Wrong Updates without Exclusive Control) in Figure 4-1 (Exclusive Control over Resources). In this example, let us suppose that the events of time 1 and 2 occur during the first tasks A1 and B1, and that the events of time 3 through 6 occur during the second tasks A2 and B2. During pseudo-conversation of A (by A1 and A2) and B (by B1 and B2), since exclusive control is lost, the record is wrongly updated. That is, double updating has been done against the record.

Solution by Programming Convention

Double updating during pseudo-conversation could occur as long as we insist on the pseudo-conversational mode. However, we can prevent it or make it less harmful by the programming convention as follows:

Programming Convention: All record updates should be done by combination of the READ/UPDATE command and REWRITE command in the same task. The update data should be applied to the record content obtained by the READ/UPDATE command before the REWRITE command. This is to say that the update data should not be applied to the record content which has been passed by the previous task through COMMAREA or any other mechanism.

If this programming convention is maintained, in the second task of pseudo-conversation, Case 2 will never occur and Case 1 will always be maintained. That is, data integrity always will be maintained and the record always will be successfully updated.

The only drawback to this approach is that the starting balance (or data content) of the record at the second task may be different from that of the first task during the pseudo-conversation. But this would be less harmful if the message to the terminal by the second task shows the starting balance as well as the ending balance (or data content) after update. Probably this would be acceptable in most applications. Therefore, the solution by programming convention is recommended.

Solution by Update Identifier

There are several complete solutions to the double updating problem during pseudo-conversation. Some are tedious to implement. Others slow down performance significantly. Among those, the solution by the update identifier may be the most effective solution.

The update identifier is the halfword binary (S9(4)COMP) field containing the update counter. This update identifier field is included in every record to be updated. Whenever a task intends to update a record, the task increments the value of the update identifier by 1. The record is rewritten during the same task, and the task passes the update identifier to the next task for pseudo-conversation through COMMAREA. In the next task, before updating the record, the task checks the update identifier of the record against the value of the update identifier passed through COMMAREA.

If the values are different, this means that another pseudo-conversational task is trying to update the same record. Therefore, this task cancels itself, sending a cancellation message informing the terminal user to reenter the transaction a little later.

If the values are the same, this means that no other task but this one is trying to update the same record. Therefore, this task can proceed to update the record normally.

This is one way of artificially maintaining exclusive control over the record between two consecutive tasks. It works effectively without slowing performance significantly, although every record to be updated must have the update identifier field.

Exercise

Develop the Personnel Data Maintainance (PER1) transaction, based on the following specifications:

1. Personnel Master File (PERVSPMS) is a VSAM/KSDS file whose key is an employee number. Each record has the following layout:

Field Name	PIC	Contents
		Record Key
PER-EMPNO	9(5)	Employee Number
		Record Detail
PER-NAME	X(25)	Name
PER-DEPT	X(10)	Department
PER-ROOM	X(10)	Room
PER-EXT	9(4)	Telephone Extension
PER-RANK	X(5)	Position Rank
PER-TITLE	X(10)	Position Title
PER-AGE	99	Age
PER-SEX	X	Sex (M/F)
PER-SALARY	S9(10)V99 COMP-3.	Annual Gross Salary
PER-INSPOLICY	9(7) COMP-3.	Insurance Policy Number
PER-INSPREM	S9(7)V99 COMP-3	Insurance Premium

2. Transaction id is PER1 and Program id is TXT4PER1.
3. The program starts with sending an instruction message as follows:

```
"ENTER FUNCTION AND KEY IN FORM OF FFF KKKKK"
```

where   FFF   :   DIS = Display an existing employee.
                  UPD = Update an existing employee.
                  ADD = Add a new employee.
                  DEL = Delete an existing employee.
        KKKKK :   Employee number.

4. Return with the external transaction id = PER1 and the internal transaction id = PER2.
5. Upon receiving control again, read the input message and validate the data. If the function requested is invalid, send an error message and return with the external transaction id = PER1 and the internal transaction id = PER2, so that the user can reenter the data.
6. If the function is DIS, UPD, or DEL, the employee number received must exist in the PMS file. If the function is ADD, the employee number received must not exist in the PMS file. If the data is invalid, send a proper error message and return with the external transaction id = PER1 and the internal transaction id = PER2, so that the user can reenter the data.
7. If DIS is requested, read the record of the employee and display the Employee number, Name, Dept., Room and Extension, and terminate the task.
8. If ADD is requested, write a dummy record of this new employee in the PMS file for later use. The record has the valid data in the key (i.e., employee number), but the rest of the record is space or null. Send the add completion message with this employee number and terminate the task.
9. If DEL is requested, delete the record of this employee. Send a delete completion message with this employee number and terminate the task.
10. If UPD is requested, do the same as step 7, but, instead of terminating the task, return with the external transaction id = PER1 and the internal transaction id = PER3. Also pass the employee number through COMMAREA. Assume that the user updates Dept., Room, and/or Extension. Upon receiving control again, receive the data. Based on the input data and the employee number from COMMAREA, update and rewrite the PMS record of this employee. Send the update completion message with this employee number and terminate the task.
11. During this processing, all major exceptional conditions must be intercepted and the proper message must be sent to the terminal. Then, forcefully terminate the task.

12. *Note:* The UPD option may be too advanced at this point. Therefore, you should code the program without the UPD option first. If time allows, you should modify the program to include the UPD option.

5

File Control (2): Sequential Access

5.1 Introduction

Under CICS, any of VSAM/KSDS, VSAM/ESDS, or VSAM/RRDS can be accessed randomly as well as sequentially. Since we discussed random access to the VSAM/KSDS files in the previous chapter, let us discuss now sequential access to the VSAM/KSDS files in this chapter.

Available Commands

Sequential access of VSAM file under CICS is called "browsing," for which the following commands are available:

STARTBR:	To establish a position for a browse (sequential read) operation
READNEXT:	To read a next record (forward)
READPREV:	To read a previous record (backward)
RESETBR:	To reestablish another position for a new browse
ENDBR:	To complete a browse operation

Order of Browse Operation

During a browse operation, you must follow the order of events, otherwise you would encounter the invalid request condition (INVREQ). The order of events must be as follows:

Events	Commands
1. Start.	
2. Establish a starting position.	STARTBR
3. Retrieve a next record.	READNEXT or READPREV
4. If processing of the record is required, then process and go to step 3.	
5. If more records are required, then go to step 3.	
6. If it is required to establish another position, then, reestablish the new position, and go to step 3.	RESETBR
7. Terminate the browse operation.	ENDBR
8. End.	

5.2   STARTBR Command

Function

The STARTBR command is used to establish a browse starting position for a file. This command is for establishing the position only. The actual record will be read by the next read command (READNEXT or READPREV).

Format

The format of the STARTBR command for VSAM/KSDS is as follows:

```
EXEC CICS STARTBR
     DATASET(name) | FILE(name)
     RIDFLD(data-area)
     GTEQ
END-EXEC.
```

DATASET (or FILE) names the file to which you wish to apply the browsing operation. The file name specified must be registered in FCT. FILE is the preferred name under CICS/MVS, but it performs the same function as DATASET.

RIDFLD indicates the starting key of the record for the browse operation. GTEQ (default option) indicates the starting position to be set at the record key which is equal to or greater than the starting key specified in the RIDFLD field.

Example

The following is an example of the STARTBR command:

```
WORKING-STORAGE SECTION.
77   WK-LEN                        PIC S9(4) COMP.
01   FILE-IOAREA.
     05   REC-A-KEY.
          10   REC-A-KEY-CITY       PIC XX.
          10   REC-A-KEY-SEQ        PIC 999.
     05   REC-A-DETAIL             PIC X(30).
PROCEDURE DIVISION.
     :
     MOVE 'NY000' TO REC-A-KEY.    <== Establish full key
     EXEC CICS STARTBR                  (could be in record area).
          DATASET('FILEAAA')
          RIDFLD(REC-A-KEY)
          GTEQ                     <== Default
     END-EXEC.
```

Execution Results   Suppose the file has the records in the following order:

```
BO001
DC001
DC002
NY001      <== Then, browse starting position is set here
NY002          (NY001). The actual record NY001 will be
NY003          read by the next READNEXT command.
PH001
PH002
```

Commonly Used Options

The following are the commonly used options for the START command:

GTEQ: If no record is found for the exact key, CICS places the position to the next available record.

EQUAL: If no record is found for the exact key, the exceptional condition NOTFND will occur.

GENERIC: The generic key could be used in the similar manner to the READ command with the GENERIC option (see Section 4.6).

Common Exceptional Conditions

The following are the exceptional conditions common to the STARTBR command:

DSIDERR: The file specified is not found in FCT.
NOTFND: The specified record is not found.

5.3   READNEXT Command for VSAM/KSDS

Function

The READNEXT command is used to read a record of a file sequentially forward. The STARTBR must have been successfully completed prior to issuing the READNEXT command.

Format

The format of the READNEXT command for VSAM/KSDS is as follows:

```
EXEC CICS READNEXT
     DATASET(name) | FILE(name)
     INTO(data-area)
     LENGTH(data-value)
     RIDFLD(data-area)
END-EXEC.
```

DATASET (or FILE) must name the same file name as the prior STARTBR command. INTO is used to specify the field in the Working Storage Section where the actual record data is to be placed. RIDFLD indicates the record key. LENGTH (a halfword binary field, S9(4) COMP) indicates the maximum length of the record to be read. At the completion of the command, CICS will place the actual record length here.

Alternative to the INTO option, the SET option can be used in a manner similar to the READ command (see Section 4.5).

It is recommended that the maximum record length be specified in the LENGTH field each time. If the file is a variable record file, the next record might be truncated by the next read if the same READNEXT command is used without specifying the maximum record length.

Example

Assuming the same Working Storage Section of Section 5.2, the following is an example of the READNEXT command for VSAM/KSDS:

```
(STARTBR as per Section 5.2)

MOVE 35 TO WK-LEN.              <== Establish the length.
EXEC CICS READNEXT
     DATASET('FILEAAA')
     INTO(FILE-IOAREA)
     RIDFLD(REC-A-KEY)          <== Required.
     LENGTH(WK-LEN)             <== Should be specified.
END-EXEC.
```

Execution Results   At the completion of this program logic, the following actions will occur:

- A record will actually be read into the INTO area. That is, the record NY001 will be placed in FILE-IOAREA.
- CICS will place the actual key into the RIDFLD area (REC-A-KEY).
- CICS will place the actual record length into the LENGTH area (WK-LEN).
- If the same READNEXT command is issued again, the record NY002 will be read; that is, the record will be read forward.

Common Exceptional Conditions

The following are the exceptional conditions common to the READNEXT command:

DUPKEY: The key of the record is a duplicate of the next record's key.

ENDFILE: The end of file is detected.

LENGERR: The actual record length is greater than the length specified.

5.4   READPREV Command

Function

The READPREV command is used to read a record of a file backward. The STARTBR command must have been successfully completed prior to issuing the READPREV command.

Format

The format of the READPREV command for VSAM/KSDS is shown in the example below. The options and parameters are the same as the READNEXT command.

Example

Assuming the same Working Storage Section of Section 5.2, the following is an example of the READPREV command:

```
(STARTBR for DC002)

MOVE 35 TO WK-LEN.              <== Establish the length.
EXEC CICS READPREV
     DATASET('FILEAAA')
     INTO(FILE-IOAREA)
     RIDFLD(REC-A-KEY)          <== Required.
     LENGTH(WK-LEN)             <== Should be specified.
END-EXEC.
```

Execution Results   At the completion of this program logic, the following actions will occur:

- Exactly the same results of READNEXT (Section 5.3) can be applied, except that the record will be read backward. In this case, the record DC002 will be read.
- If the same READPREV command is issued again, the record DC001 will be read; that is, the record will be read backward.

Common Exceptional Conditions

The exceptional condition common to the READPREV command includes the same conditions mentioned in the READNEXT command. In addition, the following conditions should be watched:

NOTFND: The record positioned by the STARTBR command or the RESETBR command (see Section 5.6) is not found. The STARTBR or RESETBR command prior to the READPREV command must specify an existing record as the start key. Otherwise, at the READPREV time, the NOTFND condition will occur, in which case the browse operation must be terminated by the ENDBR command or reset by the RESETBR command.

INVREQ: The GENERIC option must not be used in the STRATBR command prior to the READPREV command. If the READPREV command is issued after the Generic STARTBR command, the INVREQ condition will occur at the READPREV command excution time.

5.5 Special Techniques for Sequential Read

There are a few special techniques for sequential read. These are very useful, practical, and convenient techniques in the actual CICS application programming.

Skip Sequential Read

The technique of skip sequential read is used to skip records while continuing the browse operation established by the prior STARTBR command. For the READNEXT command, the new key for skipping must be in the forward direction from the current record. That is, you cannot skip the records backward when you use the READNEXT command. Similarly, for the READPREV command, the new key for skipping must be in the backward direction from the current record. That is, you can not skip the records forward when you use the READPREV command.

Example   Assuming the same Working Storage Section of Section 5.2, the following is an example of skip sequential read using the READNEXT command:

```
EXEC CICS STARTBR --------          (as per Section 5.2)
END-EXEC.
  :
MOVE 35 TO WK-LEN.
EXEC CICS READNEXT --------          (as per Section 5.3)
END-EXEC.                            (NY001 read)
  :
MOVE 35 TO WK-LEN.
EXEC CICS READNEXT --------          (as per Section 5.3)
END-EXEC.                            (NY002 read)
  :
MOVE 35 TO WK-LEN.
MOVE 'PH000' TO REC-A-KEY.      <== Place a skipping key.
EXEC CICS READNEXT --------          (as per Section 5.3)
END-EXEC.
```

Execution Results   Record PH001 of Section 5.2 will be read (that is, NY003 will be skipped), and sequential read can be continued from there.

Changing Direction of Browse

After the STARTBR command, the direction of browse can be changed from forward to backward by simply switching the READNEXT command to the READPREV command, or vice versa. However, the first READPREV (or READNEXT) command after the direction change will read the same record as the last READNEXT (or READPREV, respectively) command, as illustrated below:

```
STARTBR ==> READNEXT ==> READNEXT ==> READNEXT ==> READPREV ==> READPREV
             (rec1)        (rec2)       (rec3)       (rec3)       (rec2)

                                            ↑
                                    Change of Direction
```

5.6   RESETBR Command

Function

The RESETBR command is used to reestablish another starting point within the same browse operation against the same file. The RESETBR command performs exactly the same function as the STARTBR command, except that reposition is much faster because the file is already in the browse mode by the prior STARTBR command. That is, without issuing the ENDBR command (see the next section), the RESETBR command makes it possible to reposition the dataset for a new browse operation.

Similar to the STARTBR command, the RESETBR command does repositioning only. The actual record read will be done by the next READNEXT or READPREV command. The RESETBR command can also be used for changing the characteristics of browse, for example, from generic key positioning to full key positioning, or vice versa.

Format

The format of the RESETBR command for VSAM/KSDS is shown in the example below. The options and parameters are the same as the STARTBR command.

Example

Assuming the Working Storage Section of Section 5.2, the following is an example of the RESETBR command:

```
(Assuming:
     STARTBR as per Section 5.2 for NY000.
     READNEXT as per Section 5.3 for NY001.
     Skip-sequential as per Section 5.5 for PH000.)

     MOVE 'DC001' TO REC-A-KEY.
     EXEC CICS RESETBR
          DATASET('FILEAAA')
          RIDFLD(REC-A-KEY)
          GTEQ
     END-EXEC.
```

Execution Results At the completion of the program logic, the following activities will occur:

• The browsing position is reset to the record DC001.
• Therefore, after the next READNEXT, the record DC001 will be read.

Common Exceptional Conditions

The exceptional condition common to the RESETBR command includes the same conditions mentioned in the STARTBR command. In addition, the following condition should be watched:

> INVREQ: The RESETBR command is issued without the prior STARTBR command.

5.7 ENDBR Command

Function

At the physical end-of-file (no record exists physically further) or logical end-of-file (no relevant record exists further), the browse operation must be terminated. The ENDBR command performs this function. That is, the ENDBR command is used to terminate the browse operation which was initiated by the prior STARTBR command.

Format

The format of the ENDBR command is shown in the example below. The only required parameter is DATASET (or FILE), which must name the file to which you wish to terminate the browse operation.

Example

The following is an example of the ENDBR command:

```
EXEC CICS ENDBR
     DATASET('FILEAAA')
END-EXEC.
```

Execution Results   The browse operation will be terminated for file FILEAAA.

5.8 Multiple Browse Operations

The multiple browse operations are used to perform several concurrent browse operations against the same file. One browse operation is to be identified by the REQID parameter in the browse commands.

As shown in the example below, for multiple browse operations, all browse commands (STARTBR, READNEXT, READPREV, RESETBR, and ENDBR) must have the REQID parameter to identify to which browse operation group the command belongs. The other parameters and options of each browse command remain the same as the case of the single browse operation. Once REQID is established, within the same REQID group, the browse operation can be performed in any way as you wish, independently from the other REQID group.

Example

The following example illustrates three concurrent browse operations against the same file FILEAAA:

```
*
* OPERATION (1)
*
      MOVE 'NY000' TO REC-A-KEY1.
      EXEC CICS STARTBR
          DATASET('FILEAAA')
          REQID(1)                         <== Attention.
          RIDFLD(REC-A-KEY1)
          GTEQ
      END-EXEC.
*
* OPERATION (2)
*
      MOVE 'DC002' TO REC-A-KEY2.
      EXEC CICS STARTBR
          DATASET('FILEAAA')
          REQID(2)                         <== Attention.
          RIDFLD(REC-A-KEY2)
          GTEQ
```

```
        END-EXEC.
*
* OPERATION (3)
*
        MOVE 'BO000' TO REC-A-KEY3.
        EXEC CICS STARTBR
            DATASET('FILEAAA')
            REQID(3)                            <== Attention.
            RIDFLD(REC-A-KEY3)
            GTEQ
        END-EXEC.
*
* OPERATION (1)
*
        MOVE 35 TO WK-LEN1.
        EXEC CICS READNEXT
            DATASET('FILEAAA')
            REQID(1)                            <== Attention.
            INTO(FILE-IOAREA1)
            RIDFLD(REC-A-KEY1)
            LENGTH(WK-LEN1)
        END-EXEC.
*
* OPERATION (2)
*
        MOVE 35 TO WK-LEN2.
        EXEC CICS READPREV
            DATASET('FILEAAA')
            REQID(2)                            <== Attention.
            INTO(FILE-IOAREA2)
            RIDFLD(REC-A-KEY2)
            LENGTH(WK-LEN2)
        END-EXEC.
*
* OPERATION (3)
*
        MOVE 35 TO WK-LEN3.
        EXEC CICS READNEXT
            DATASET('FILEAAA')
            REQID(3)                            <== Attention.
            INTO(FILE-IOAREA3)
            RIDFLD(REC-A-KEY3)
            LENGTH(WK-LEN3)
        END-EXEC.
```

Execution Results   During the execution of this program logic, the following activities will occur:

- For Operation 1: NY001 will be read (forward read).
- For Operation 2: DC002 will be read (backward read).
- For Operation 3: BO001 will be read (forward read).

Programming Considerations

The multiple browse operations are the convenient operations, because the application program can browse the same file in more than one way independently and concurrently. However, one browse operation occupies one string of VSAM. If all VSAM strings are exhausted for one VSAM file, the other transaction will have to wait until one of the strings becomes free. In this respect, the multiple browse operations are the costly operations. Therefore, they should be used only when they are definitely required.

5.9   Updating During Browse Operations

During the browse operations against a file, you might encounter such a case that you wish to update a record in the same file while continuing the browsing operations. Since the browsing operations and the update operations are mutually exclusive against the same file at the same time, updating during browse operations requires a special technique.

Procedures

The following is a set of procedures to achieve the record update during the browse operation:

1. After the READNEXT command, issue the ENDBR command for temporarily suspending the browse operation.
2. Issue the READ command with the UPDATE option.
3. After manipulating the record, issue the REWRITE command for updating the record.
4. Issue the STARTBR command for resuming the browse operation.
5. Issue the READNEXT command to skip the record which has been updated.
6. Issue another READNEXT command and resume the browsing operation as before.

Example

Assuming the same Working Storage Section of Section 5.2, the following is an example of updating a record during the browse operations:

```
EXEC CICS STARTBR -----        (As per Section 5.2)
    :
MOVE 35 TO WK-LEN.
EXEC CICS READNEXT -----        (As per Section 5.3)
    :
    (Found that an update is required.)
    :
EXEC CICS ENDBR                 <== Suspend the browse.
    DATASET('FILEAAA')
END-EXEC.
EXEC CICS READ                  <== Read for update.
    DATASET('FILEAAA')
    INTO(FILE-IOAREA)
    RIDFLD(REC-A-KEY)
    LENGTH(WK-LEN)
    UPDATE
END-EXEC.
    :
(Some updating of record NY001)
    :
EXEC CICS REWRITE               <== Rewrite the record.
    DATASET('FILEAAA')
    FROM(FILE-IOAREA)
    LENGTH(WK-LEN)
END-EXEC.
EXEC CICS STARTBR
    DATASET('FILEAAA')
    RIDFLD(REC-A-KEY)
    GTEQ
END-EXEC.
EXEC CICS READNEXT -----        <== Dummy read to skip the record.
EXEC CICS READNEXT -----        <== Browse operation resumes.
    :
```

Execution Results   During the execution of this program logic, the following actions will occur:

- By the ENDBR command, the browse operation will be suspended.
- By the READ/UPDATE command, the same record NY001 will be read and reserved for the update.
- By the REWRITE command, record NY001 will be rewritten.
- By the STARTBR command, the browse position will be set for record NY001.
- By the first READNEXT command, the same record NY001, which has been updated, will be read.
- Then, by the second READNEXT command, the next record will be read and the browsing operation will resume.

Programming Considerations

In order to update a record during the browse operation, you must issue the ENDBR command first to suspend the browse operation, as in the example above. If you issue the READ command with the UPDATE option and subsequent REWRITE command without having issued the ENDBR command, a transaction deadlock might occur.

Exercise

Develop the Personnel Data Inquiry (PIQ1) transaction based on the following specifications:

1. Transaction id is PIQ1 and Program id is TXT5PIQ1.
2. This program uses the Personnel Master File (PERVSPMS) described in the Exercise for Chapter 4.
3. The program starts with sending an instruction message as follows:

```
"ENTER START-KEY, END-KEY, FUNCTION AND SELECTION CRI-
TERIA IN SSSSS EEEEE FFF NNN:"
```

where   SSSSS: Starting key of PMS.
           EEEEE: Ending key of PMS.
           FFF: AGE = Number of employees above or equal to the age specified.
                    SEX = Number of male and female.
                    SAL = Number of employees whose salary is greater than or equal to the value specified.
           NNN: Either age or annual salary in $1,000.

4. Return with the external transaction id = PIQ1 and the internal transaction id = PIQ2.
5. Upon receiving control again, read the input message and validate the data. If the function requested is invalid, or if the selection criteria value for AGE or SAL is invalid, send a proper error message and return with the external transaction id = PIQ1 and the internal transaction id = PIQ2, so that the user can reenter the data.
6. Input data is valid. Read the PMS file sequentially only between the keys SSSSS and EEEEE. Count the number of employees who meet the selection criteria. At EOF (either logical or physical), send the number with a proper response message, then terminate the task.
7. Maintain the program standard for exceptional conditions as usual.

6

File Control (3): Advanced Topics

6.1 Sequential Read for VSAM/ESDS

Function

Similar to a VSAM/KSDS file, a VSAM/ESDS file can be read sequentially forward or backward. This can be accomplished by the STARTBR command and the READNEXT or READPREV command, respectively, with the RBA option, which is the special option for the VSAM/ESDS file.

Approach

The following is a set of procedures to achieve a forward (or backward) sequential read of a VSAM/ESDS file from the beginning (or the end) of the file:

1. Define a fullword binary field (S9(8) COMP) for the Relative Byte Address (RBA) of the VSAM/ESDS file.
2. Place initially LOW-VALUES or HIGH-VALUE in the RBA field for the forward read or backward read, respectively.
3. Issue the STARTBR command with the RBA and EQUAL options. Note that the GTEQ option is not valid for the VSAM/ESDS file. The other options and parameters are the same as the case of the STARTBR command for VSAM/KSDS.

4. Issue the READNEXT or READPREV command with the RBA option for reading the record sequentially forward or backward, respectively. The other options and parameters are the same as the case of the READNEXT or READPREV command for VSAM/KSDS.

Format

The format of the STARTBR and READNEXT commands with the RBA option is shown in the example below. RBA must be explicitly specified as the option. A fullword binary field (S9(8) COMP) must be defined for RBA of the VSAM/ESDS file and placed in the RIDFLD parameter. The other options and parameters are the same as the case of the STARTBR and READNEXT commands for the VSAM/KSDS file.

Example

The following is an example of the forward sequential read of a VSAM/ESDS file from the beginning of the file:

```
WORKING-STORAGE SECTION.
77   ESDS-RBA              PIC S9(8) COMP.
77   WK-LEN                PIC S9(4) COMP.
01   FILE-IOAREA.
     05   REC-A.
          10   FIELD1      PIC X(5).
          10   FIELD2      PIC X(20).
     :
     :
PROCEDURE DIVISION.
     :
     :
     MOVE LOW-VALUES TO ESDS-RBA.    <== Attention.
     EXEC CICS STARTBR               <== Positions at the first
          DATASET('ESDSFILE')              record.
          RIDFLD(ESDS-RBA)
          RBA                        <== Required for VSAM/ESDS.
          EQUAL                      <== GTEQ is invalid for ESDS.
     END-EXEC.
*
```

```
MOVE 100 TO WK-LEN.
EXEC CICS READNEXT
     DATASET('ESDSFILE')
     INTO(FILE-IOAREA)
     RIDFLD(ESDS-RBA)
     LENGTH(WK-LEN)
     RBA                              <== Required for ESDS.
END-EXEC.
```

Execution Results   During the execution of this program logic, the following activities will occur:

- At the completion of the STARTBR command, the first record in file ESDSFILE will be positioned for the browse operations.
- At the completion of the READNEXT command, the first record will be read into FILE-IOAREA and the actual RBA of the record will be placed in ESDS-RBA.
- The actual length of the record will be placed in WK-LEN.

Similarly, backward sequential read can be accomplished by simply replacing LOW-VALUE and READNEXT command with HIGH-VALUE and READPREV command, respectively.

6.2   Sequential Write for VSAM/ESDS

Function

The WRITE command with the RBA option is used to write records sequentially into a VSAM/ESDS file. This process does not involve any browsing operations. The record will be always written after the last existing record.

Format

The format of the WRITE command with the RBA option is shown in the example below. RBA must be explicitly specified as the option. A fullword binary field (S9(8) COMP) must be defined for RBA of the VSAM/ESDS file, and placed in the RIDFLD parameter. At the completion of the WRITE command, CICS will place the actual RBA of the record in this fullword binary field. The other options and parameters are the same as the case of the WRITE command for the VSAM/KSDS file.

Example

The following is an example of the WRITE command with the RBA option for sequential writing of a record into a VSAM/ESDS file:

```
WORKING-STORAGE SECTION.
77    ESDS-RBA                          PIC S9(8) COMP.
77    WK-LEN                            PIC S9(4) COMP.
01    FILE-IOAREA.
      05    REC-A.
            10    FIELD1                PIC X(5).
            10    FIELD2                PIC X(20).
      :
      :
PROCEDURE DIVISION.
      :
      : (prepare a record in FILE-IOAREA)
      :
      MOVE 100 TO WK-LEN.
      EXEC CICS WRITE
            DATASET('ESDSFILE')
            RIDFLD(ESDS-RBA)                     <== Required.
            LENGTH(WK-LEN)
            RBA                                  <== Required.
      END-EXEC.
```

Execution Results The record will be added next to the last existing record, and the actual RBA will be placed in ESDS-BRA.

6.3 Random Access to VSAM/ESDS

In VSAM/ESDS, a new record is always added sequentially next to the last existing record. However, a record can be read sequentially as well as randomly. In the previous two sections, we discussed the sequential read and sequential write for VSAM/ESDS. Now, let us discuss how to read a record randomly from the VSAM/ESDS file.

Approach

The following is a set of procedures to read a record randomly from the VSAM/ESDS file.

1. Provide a fullword binary field (PIC S9(8) COMP) for the Relative Byte Address (RBA), and place this in the RIDFLD parameter.
2. Provide the proper value to this RIDFLD field, noting that you must know the exact value of RBA of the record you wish to read.
3. Place the RBA option explicitly in the READ command.

Example

The following is an example of the READ command with the RBA option for reading directly a record from a VSAM/ESDS file:

```
WORKING-STORAGE SECTION.
    :
77   ESDS-RBA              PIC S9(8) COMP.
77   WK-LEN                PIC S9(4) COMP.
01   FILE-IOAREA.
     05   REC-A.
          10   FIELD1    PIC X(5).
          10   FIELD2    PIC X(20).
     :
PROCEDURE DIVISION.
    :
     MOVE 100 TO WK-LEN.
     MOVE 200 TO ESDS-RBA.
     EXEC CICS READ
          DATASET('ESDSFILE')
          RIDFLD(ESDS-RBA)
          LENGTH(WK-LEN)
          RBA                                  <== Attention.
     END-EXEC.
```

Execution Results   The record (RBA=200) of file ESDSFILE will be read.

6.4   Input/Output Operations for VSAM/RRDS

In VSAM/RRDS, a record can be read or written randomly or sequentially. The input/output operations for VSAM/RRDS are very
similar to those for VSAM/ESDS.

Approach

The following is a set of the basic procedures for dealing with the
input/output operations against the VSAM/RRDS file:

1. Provide a fullword binary field (PIC S9(8) COMP) for the Relative Record Number (RRN) of the VSAM/RRDS file, and place
   this in the RIDFLD parameter.
2. Provide the proper value to this RIDFLD field for random access.
3. Place explicitly the RRN option in the input/output commands.

Example

The following is an example of the READ command with the RRN
option for reading a record directly from a VSAM/RRDS file:

```
WORKING-STORAGE SECTION.
        :
77    RRDS-RRN            PIC S9(8) COMP.
77    WK-LEN              PIC S9(4) COMP.
01    FILE-IOAREA.
      05    REC-A.
            10    FIELD1    PIC X(5).
            10    FIELD2    PIC X(20).
      :
PROCEDURE DIVISION.
      :
      MOVE 100 TO WK-LEN.
      MOVE 5 TO RRDS-RRN.
      EXEC CICS READ
            DATASET('RRDSFILE')
            RIDFLD(RRDS-RRN)
            LENGTH(WK-LEN)
            RRN                      <== Attention.
      END-EXEC.
```

Execution Results   The record (RRN=5) of file RRDSFILE will be read.

Generalization to Other Commands

This basic procedure can be applied to the other input/output operations, such as READ/UPDATE, REWRITE, WRITE, DELETE, and browse commands aginst the VSAM/RRDS file.

6.5   VSAM Alternate Index

The VSAM Alternate Index (AIX) feature allows one to uniquely locate a record using a different key structure on the same VSAM/KSDS or ESDS file. Since most applications of VSAM AIX involve VSAM/KSDS, for simplicity, let us discuss AIX using VSAM/KSDS.

For one VSAM/KSDS file, more than one AIX can be created. The original VSAM/KSDS file is called the Base Cluster. The relationship between the Base and Alternate is as follows:

Base	**Alternate**
Prime Key	Alternate Key
Base Index	Alternate Index (AIX)
Base Cluster	Alternate Index Cluster

Concept of Alternate Index

The concept of the Alternate Index is illustrated in Figure 6-1. In this example, the data component of Base Cluster has a series of records which consists of the employee number (Prime Key), last name, and other personal profile data. The Base Index is constructed based on the employee number (Prime Key) in the numeric order, and point to the corresponding record in the data component of Base Cluster. Note that the employee number (Prime Key) is unique so that there are no duplicate records in the Base Cluster.

The Alternate Index (AIX) is constructed based on the employee's last name (Alternate Key) in the alphabet order, and points to the corresponding record in the data portion of the AIX Cluster. Note that there are three KENNEDYs, which will cause the duplicate key

Alternate Index Cluster

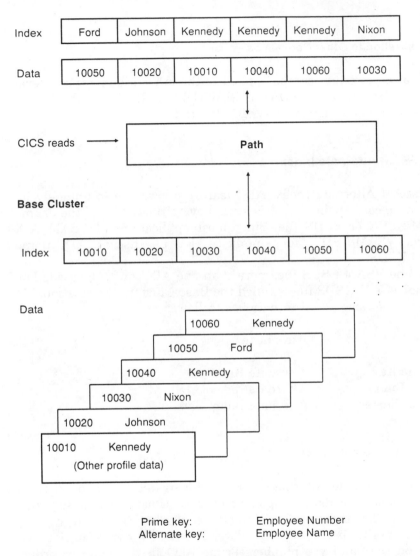

Prime key: Employee Number
Alternate key: Employee Name

Figure 6-1 Concept of VSAM alternate index.

condition. Each record in the data portion of the AIX Cluster has
only a pointer to the Base Index so that from the AIX the corresponding record in the Base Cluster can be accessed. This concept
makes one able to access the full information of the Base Cluster
from AIX, as well as from the Base Index.

Note that the illustration in Figure 6-1 is simplified in terms of relationship among records, Control Intervals (CIs), and index, in order to clearly show the concept of VSAM Alternate Index. Since a VSAM Alternate Index, in this case, is a VSAM/KSDS file, for the relationship among these records, CIs, and index, Section 4.3 should be referred to.

Path

Actually, reading a record in the AIX Cluster itself does not directly point to the corresponding record in the Base Cluster. Between the AIX Cluster and Base Cluster, there is a special linkage mechanism called "Path," through which the corresponding record in the Base Cluster can be read. Therefore, the Path must be defined and related to the AIX Cluster. Then, the CICS application program reads the Path (not AIX itself) in order to obtain the corresponding record in the Base Cluster.

Creating AIX

In order to create an Alternate Index, the VSAM utility program (IDCAMS) must be used, in the following way:

1. Create a Base Cluster using the DEFINE CLUSTER command.
2. Load data into the Base Cluster using the REPRO command or other commands.
3. Create an AIX Cluster using the DEFINE ALTERNATEINDEX command.
   • Define the Alternate Key.
   • Relate to the Base Cluster.
4. Build AIX using the BLDINDEX command.
   • At this point, the AIX Cluster will have the actual data loaded from the Base Cluster.
5. Define a Path using the DEFINE PATH command.
   • Specify the AIX Cluster as the path entry.

After this, the Path behaves as if it were a VSAM/KSDS with the Alternate Key and corresponding records in the Base Cluster.

Since AIX is simply another VSAM file from CICS's point of view, in order to access AIX from CICS, DDNAME of the corresponding Path (not AIX Cluster itself) must be registered in FCT with the BASE option (see Section 6.6).

Browsing Operations with AIX

Any Browsing operations can be performed against an AIX (actually against the corresponding Path) as if it were an ordinary VSAM/KSDS file. For this, the file name of this Path must be specified in the browsing commands. The rest of the operations are the same as those for the Base Cluster.

The DUPKEY condition (i.e., duplicate key is found) is quite common to the AIX browse operations. The application program must deal with this situation. Using the example in Figure 6-1, the DUPKEY condition in the AIX can be described in the following way: That is, there are three KENNEDYs (10010, 10040, 10060). When a READNEXT reads 10010, the DUPKEY condition occurs, implying that there are other records with same name (key). When the next READNEXT reads 10040, the DUPKEY condition again occurs, implying that there are still other records with same name (key). When the next READNEXT reads 10080 (i.e., last KENNEDY), no DUPKEY condition occurs, implying the end of the same name (key). The application program must handle this unique situation of DUPKEY condition.

Update Operations for AIX

Through the UPGRADE option and UPDATE option of the DEFINE ALTERNATEINDEX and DEFINE PATH commands, respectively, VSAM upgrades AIX through the Path when the corresponding Base Cluster is updated, added, or deleted. But, within the same key of AIX, the order of the records is not properly maintained based on the Prime Key if update occurs in the Base Cluster.

At the next file recreation time (i.e., usually, file reorganization time), these changes in the Base Cluster will be fully reflected to AIX. That is, within the same key of the AIX, the records will be placed in the Prime Key order.

This creates a minor synchronization problem between the Base Cluster and AIX between two file reorganizations. The best way to overcome this situation is to follow the following procedures:

1. All update should be done through the Base Cluster.
2. Perform the file reorganization periodically to reflect the changes to the AIX and Path.
3. If the synchronization is crucial, do the file reorganization every day.

Programming Considerations

A CICS application program does not have to be aware of whether the file is accessing AIX or Base Cluster, as long as the considerations are given for the DUPKEY condition and updating described above.

6.6   File Control Table (FCT)

Function

The primary function of the File Control Table (FCT) is to register control information of all files (VSAM, BDAM) which are used under CICS. CICS/FCP uses this table for identifying files and performing input/output operations against them.

FCT Entry Definition

One FCT entry can be defined using an Assembler macro DFHFCT. The following are the commonly used options and parameters of the DFHFCT macro:

```
DFHFCT     TYPE=DATASET | FILE,
           ACCMETH=BDAM | VSAM,
           DATASET=name | FILE=name,
           SERVREQ=(ADD, BROWSE, DELETE, READ, UPDATE),
           [FILSTAT=(ENABLED | DISABLED,
                     OPENED | CLOSED)],
           [BUFND=n+1],
           [BUFNI=n],
           [STRNO=n],
           [DSNAME=name],
           [DISP=OLD | SHR],
           [BASE=name]
```

ACCMETH defines the data access method (BDAM or VSAM of this file. DATASET (or FILE) names the file which you wish to access under CICS. The name in the DATASET (or FILE) parameter must correspond to the DDNAME of the file specified in the JCL of the CICS job itself (see also the DSNAME and DISP parameters below). FILE is the preferred name under CICS/MVS, but it performs the same function as DATASET.

SERVREQ is used to specify the authorized input/output operations against the file. The only specified services (ADD, BROWSE, DELETE, READ, or UPDATE) will be authorized during the File Control command execution. If other than the specified services is requested inFile Control command, the INVREQ condition will occur.

FILSTAT indicates the initial file status when CICS initially starts. When a CICS transaction accesses a file, the file must have been OPENED and ENABLED, regardless of the initial status. The file can be opened or closed through the Master Terminal (CEMT) transaction (see Section 16.10).

BUFND and BUFNI indicate the number of VSAM data buffers and VSAM index buffers, respectively. STRNO indicates the number of VSAM strings by which the concurrent access to the file is allowed. The numbers in BUFND, BUFNI, and STRNO should be optimal, taking into account performance (the large number is better) and resource consumption (the small number is better).

DSNAME and DISP options can be specified as ordinary JCL, in which case JCL of the CICS job itself must not include a DD card for this file. DSNAME names the actual name of the file. DISP specifies the disposition of the file. If OLD is specified, the file is to be used only in this CICS region. If SHR is requested, the file may be shared with other regions. This feature is very helpful for system programmers since all file related information can be placed in FCT.

If the file being registered is a Path for an AIX Cluster, BASE must be specified to name the Base Cluster of that AIX Cluster.

Example

The following example is a typical definition of one FCT entry for a Base Cluster (i.e., not a Path for AIX Cluster):

```
DFHFCT    TYPE=DATASET,
          ACCMETH=VSAM,
          DATASET=FILEAAA,
          SERVREQ=(ADD,BROWSE,DELETE,READ,UPDATE),
          FILSTAT=(DISABLED,CLOSED),         <== Recommended.
          BUFND=3,                      )
          BUFNI=2,                      )    <== Small number should
          STRNO=2,                      )       be specified.
          DSNAME=MKT.PRD.CMA.BASE,
          DISP=SHR
```

VSAM Alternate Index

For a VSAM Alternate Index (AIX), the FCT entry can be defined as if it were an ordinary VSAM file, except:

1. The name (DDNAME) of the Path for the AIX (not AIX Cluster itself) must be specified in the DATASET (or FILE) parameter.
2. The name (DDNAME) of the Base Cluster must be specified in the BASE parameter.

The following is an example of FCT entry for a VSAM Path for an AIX Cluster:

```
DFHFCT      TYPE=DATASET,
            ACCMETH=VSAM,
            DATASET=FILEALT,
            SERVREQ=(BROWSE,READ),
            FILSTAT=(DISABLED,CLOSED),
            BUFND=3,
            BUFNI=2,
            STRNO=2,
            DSNAME=MKT.PRD.CMA.PATH,
            DISP=SHR,
            BASE=FILEAAA
```

6.7 DL/I Database Access

Database Language/I (DL/I) is the database access method of Information Management System (IMS), which is another popular IBM DB/DC control system similar to CICS. The DL/I database is a hierarchical database constructed for the DL/I database access method.

CICS, as a DB/DC control system, provides an interface to DL/I, independent of IMS in addition to the File Control functions performed by the CICS File Control Program. Therefore, through this DL/I interface, all DL/I services can be used under CICS.

System Concept

As shown in Figure 6-2, within a CICS region, there is a built-in interface to DL/I (optional). This DL/I interface communicates with the DL/I database access method software included in CICS. In this way, CICS can have a direct control over the DL/I database, indepen-

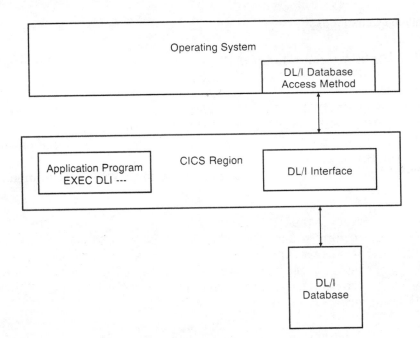

Figure 6-2 DL/I database access by CICS.

dent of IMS. That is, the CICS region itself can manage the DL/I accesses.

CICS application programs can issue a special set of commands for DL/I services. The DL/I interface interprets the service requests by the application program and pass control to the DL/I access method modules which actually access the DL/I database.

Command Format

Similar to the CICS commands, the DL/I commands have their own command format, as follows:

```
EXEC DLI function
        [options]
END-EXEC.
```

where "function" is a DL/I service, and "options" are the options of the DL/I service.

The CICS application programs can freely issue these DL/I commands as they are required. The CICS command translator translates these DL/I commands into the proper COBOL statement similar to the ordinary CICS commands.

Available Commands

Virtually all DL/I services are available in the form of corresponding DL/I commands in CICS. Therefore, if you know DL/I, you can use it under CICS.

Since DL/I itself would require one independent book, it is considered outside of this book's scope. Therefore, this book excludes how to use DLI commands under CICS.

DBD and PSB Generation

DL/I Database Description (DBD) defines the physical structure of a DL/I database, while Program Specification Block (PSB) defines the database elements an application (or a group of application programs) is authorized to use. Therefore, these could be many PSBs against one DBD. This concept provides the application programs with data independence. That is, the application programs can be written reasonably independently of the physical structure of the DL/I database, as long as PSB remains the same.

DBD and PSB are generated based on the DL/I statement (actually Assembler macros), which are assembled, linkedited and stored in the DL/I control libraries. These DBD and PSB generations are done completely outside of CICS as a part of DL/I database preparation.

Control Tables

Since CICS has the direct control over DL/I, in order to utilize DL/I services, CICS control tables must be defined for the directory of DBDs and PSBs through the control table definition macros DFHDLDBD and DFHDLPSB, respectively. Once these table entries have been defined, the CICS application programs can freely issue DL/I commands in the program for accessing the DL/I database.

6.8 DB/2 Database Access

DATABASE 2 (DB2) is IBM's Database Management System (DBMS), which has established its position as the industry standard for the relational database. The database access method for the DB2 database is called Structured Query Language (SQL).

CICS, as a DB/DC control system, provides an interface to DB/2, in addition to file control functions and DL/I services. However, since DB2 requires its own region independent of the CICS region, the way of interfacing to DB2 by CICS is different from that to DL/I.

System Concept

As shown in Figure 6-3, CICS and DB2 each requires its own region uniquely under the operating system (MVS/XA). The CICS region manages accesses to the VSAM files through the File Control and to the DL/I database through the DL/I interface. Independently, DB2 region manages accesses to the DB2 database. In order to make an interface between CICS and DB2, DB2 has a special facility called "CICS Attachment Facility," which connects DB2 to CICS.

CICS application programs can issue a special set of commands for SQL services in order to access the DB2 database. SQL requests by the CICS application programs are passed from the CICS region to the CICS attachment facility of the DB2 region through which the DB2 database is accessed. The results of DB2 database access are returned to the CICS region through the CICS attachment facility of the DB2 region.

At the same time, the CICS application program can issue the File Control commands and DL/I commands in order to access the VSAM files and DL/I databases, respectively, in the CICS region, if they are required.

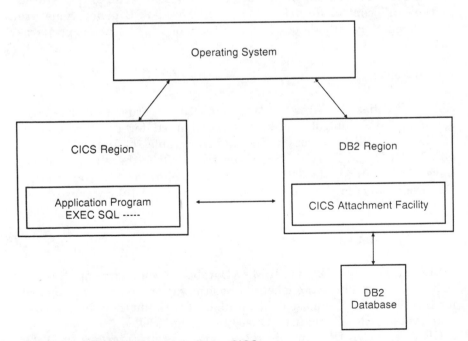

Figure 6-3 DB2 database access by CICS.

Command Format

Similar to the CICS command and DL/I commands, SQL commands have their own command format. CICS application programs can issue freely the SQL commands in the program. The format of SQL commands is:

```
EXEC SQL function
     [options]
END-EXEC.
```

where "function" is an SQL service and "options" are the options of the SQL service.

DB2 Pre-Compiler

In case of DL/I, the CICS command translator can directly translate the DL/I commands (i.e., EXEC DLI commands) in the CICS application program. However, for DB2, a separate pre-compile must be done in order to translate the SQL commands into the COBOL statements. Although the CICS command translator does not reject the SQL commands as the syntax error, the translation time is usually shorter if DB2 pre-compile is done prior to CICS command translation. Therefore, the order of pre-compile and linkedit should be as follows:

Source program   (includes EXEC SQL -----
| and EXEC CICS -----)

Translation by DB2 Pre-compiler
|

Translation by CICS Command Translator
|

Compile by COBOL
|

Linkedit by Linkage Editor
|

Load Module

Available Commands

Since the CICS application program with the SQL commands is translated by the DB2 pre-compiler itself (i.e., not the CICS command translator), the CICS application program is entitled to use all SQL commands available without translation errors or compile errors. However, the SQL commands to be used in a CICS application program are limited to the ones listed below:

SELECT
FETCH
UPDATE
DELETE
INSERT

These five SQL commands are all you need for developing DB2 applications under CICS. Therefore, if you know SQL, you can imbed these SQL commands in the CICS application program freely as you wish.

Similar to DL/I, DB2 itself would require one independent book for describing how DB2 works and how DB2 database can be accessed. Therefore, it is outside of this book's work scope.

7

Terminal Control

7.1 Introduction

The CICS Terminal Control Program (TCP) provides communication services between user-written application programs and terminals, using the information defined in the Terminal Control Table (TCT). Usually, unformatted screens are used for the Terminal Control operations. Therefore, the interpretation of the data stream is the application program's responsibility.

Terminals Supported by CICS

CICS supports many terminals for data communications. The following are some examples:

- General purpose terminals, such as IBM 3270 Information Display System.
- Specialized purpose terminals, such as IBM 3600 Finance Communication System.

Commonly Used Commands for 3270

The commands are available depending on the terminal type. The following are the commonly used commands for the IBM 3270 type terminals:

RECEIVE:	To receive data from the terminal.
SEND:	To send data to the terminal.
ISSUE PRINT:	To print a hard copy of the screen to a printer.
ISSUE COPY:	To copy a screen to another terminal.
HANDLE AID:	To control the program flow based on the attention id.

We have already used the RECEIVE and SEND commands. This chapter formally introduces these commands in detail. However, in actual business applications, unless you use the specialized purpose terminals, you would mostly use the formatted screens with the CICS Basic Mapping Support (BMS) which we will discuss in the next three chapters (8, 9, 10). Therefore, the actual applications of the Terminal Control commands are limited, unless CICS intercommunication (see Chapter 17) is involved.

For this reason, although there are other Terminal Control commands (e.g., CONVERSE), this chapter discusses only those basic commands listed above and their related topics, including the Terminal Control Table (TCT).

7.2   RECEIVE Command

Function

The RECEIVE command is used to receive the unformatted data from the terminal or logical unit (LU) of a communication network.

Format

The format of the RECEIVE command is shown in the example below. INTO is used to specify the area in the Working Storage Section to which the data from the terminal is to be placed. LENGTH (the halfword binary field, S9(4) COMP) indicates the length of the message to be received. The example shown uses the INTO option. Alternatively, you could use the SET option, similar to the READ command with the SET option.

Example

The following is an example of the the RECEIVE command:

```
WORKING-STORAGE SECTION.
77   MSG-LEN          PIC S9(4) COMP.
01   TERM-AREA.
     02   TRANSID    PIC X(4).
     02   FILLER     PIC X.
     02   EMP-NO     PIC 9(5).


PROCEDURE DIVISION.
     :
     MOVE 10 TO MSG-LEN.
     EXEC CICS RECEIVE
          INTO(TERM-AREA)
          LENGTH(MSG-LEN)
     END-EXEC.
```

Execution Results   At the completion of this program logic, the following activities will occur:

- The first 10 characters of the screen image will be read into the INTO field. It is left to the application program to interpret the message. The program must know the information contents, length, and location.
- The actual length of the message will be placed in the LENGTH field (i.e., MSG-LEN).

Common Exceptional Conditions

The following is the exceptional condition common to the basic use of the RECEIVE command:

LENGERR: Actual data entered from the terminal exceeds the length set by the program in the LENGTH parameter. The data in the INTO area will be truncated, but the LENGTH field will have the actual length of the data at the terminal.

7.3 Limiting Screen Conversations

The example of Section 7.2 is useful if a programmer intends to limit the number of screen conversations. That is, the example makes it possible to show an employee profile right away, for example, saving one conversation under the ordinary method.

Ordinary Approach

The following is an example of the ordinary screen conversation, which requires two input and two output operations:

First, a transaction id (INQ1) is typed. The program will display an instruction map asking for an employee number for the employee profile. The terminal user types the employee number (12345). The program receives the data, based upon which it displays the employee profile of 12345.

```
C    <----------- INQ1  (Transaction initiation)

I    -----------> TYPE EMPLOYEE NUMBER: xxxxx
     <-----------                       12345     (Response)
C
     -----------> EMPLOYEE PROFILE
S                     12345
```

Terminal Control Approach

The following is an example of the screen conversation using the Terminal Control command, which requires only one input and one output operation:

The terminal user types a transaction id with an employee number (INQ1,12345). The program receives the data, using the RECEIVE command. Knowing the first five characters are the transaction id and comma, the program takes the next five characters as the employee number, based on which it displays the employee profile.

```
C    <-------------- INQ1,12345
I
C
S    -------------> EMPLOYEE PROFILE
```

This approach saves one conversation for asking the employee number. Therefore, this approach is much preferred to the ordinary approach described above.

Since most of terminal operations are done through Basic Mapping Support (BMS), which will be discussed in the next three chapters, the actual applications of the Terminal Control commands are very few. Limiting the screen conversations described above is only one practical application of the Terminal Control commands.

7.4 SEND Command

Function

The SEND command is used to send the unformatted data to the terminal or logical unit (LU) in a communication network.

Format

The format of the SEND command is shown in the example below. FROM is used to specify the area in the Working Storage Section from which the data is to be sent to the terminal. LENGTH (halfword binary field, S9(4) COMP) indicates the length of the message to be sent.

Example

The following is an example of the the SEND command:

```
WORKING-STORAGE SECTION.
77   MSG-LEN          PIC S9(4) COMP.
01   TERM-AREA.
     02   MSG1        PIC X(10).
     02   FILLER      PIC X.
     02   MSG2        PIC X(20).

PROCEDURE DIVISION.
         :
     (prepare some message in TERM-AREA.)
         :
     MOVE 31 TO MSG-LEN.
     EXEC CICS SEND
         FROM(TERM-AREA)
         LENGTH(MSG-LEN)
     END-EXEC.
```

Execution Results   31 characters of data in TERM-AREA will be sent to the terminal.

Common Exceptional Condition

The following is the exceptional condition common to the basic use of the SEND command:

LENGERR: An out-of-range or negative length value is specified.

7.5   ISSUE Commands

CICS Terminal Control provides a group of ISSUE commands which perform advanced Terminal Control functions. The most commonly used ISSUE commands are as follows:

ISSUE PRINT Command

Function   The ISSUE PRINT command is used to make a hard copy print of a screen on a printer. Upon the completion of the command execution, the current screen image on the terminal (3270) will be printed on the first available printer attached to the same control unit which the current terminal is connected (VTAM only).

Format   The format of the ISSUE PRINT command is as follows:

```
EXEC CICS ISSUE
     PRINT
END-EXEC.
```

ISSUE COPY Command

Function   The ISSUE COPY command is used to copy a screen image of the terminal into another terminal. At the completion of the command execution, the current screen image will be copied into the specified terminal, which must be attached to the same control unit to which the original terminal is attached (VTAM only).

Format   The format of the ISSUE COPY is as follows:

```
EXEC CICS ISSUE
    COPY
    TERMID(name)
END-EXEC.
```

TERMID indicates the 1- to 4-character terminal id (e.g., TRM1) of the terminal to which the screen image is to be copied.

7.6   Attention Identifier (AID)

Attention Identifier (AID) indicates which method the terminal operator has used to initiate the transfer of information from the terminal device to CICS. Some examples of AIDs are: PF keys, PA keys, ENTER key, and CLEAR key.

Obtaining AID Information

The EIBAID field in EIB contains the AID code of the most recently used AID. Therefore, the EIBAID field can be tested after each Terminal Control (or BMS) input operation (i.e., the RECEIVE or RECEIVE MAP command). If a program is written in a pseudo-conversation mode, the AID information is available in the EIBAID field from the beginning of the program.

Standard AID List (DFHAID)

CICS provides the standard AID list in a form of copy library member (DFHAID), so that a program can use this list by specifying in the program:

```
COPY DFHAID
```

The DFHAID member contains such AID codes as:

DFHENTER: ENTER key
DFHCLEAR: CLEAR key
DFHPA1 - 3:   PA1 to PA3 keys
DFHPF1 - 24:   PF1 to PF24 keys

Program Example

The following is an example of using AID information in a program:

```
IF EIBAID = DFHPF3
    PERFORM END-ROUTINE.
IF EIBAID = DFHPA1
    PERFORM CANCEL-ROUTINE.
IF EIBAID = DFHENTER
    PERFORM NORMAL-ROUTINE.
GO TO WRONG-KEY-ROUTINE.
```

Execution Results   During the execution of this program logic, the following activities will occur:

* If the PF3 key is pressed, END-ROUTINE will be performed.
* If the PA1 key is pressed, CANCEL-ROUTINE will be performed.
* If the ENTER key is pressed, NORMAL-ROUTINE will be performed.
* If any other key is pressed, WRONG-KEY-ROUTINE will be performed.

7.7   HANDLE AID Command

Function

The HANDLE AID command is used to specify the label (i.e., paragraph name) to which control is to be passed when the specified AID is received. After the completion of any terminal input commands such as RECEIVE and RECEIVE MAP commands, control will be passed to the specified paragraph in the program. This is one way of substituting the EIBAID checking approach in the previous section.

Format

The format of the HANDLE AID command is as follows:

```
EXEC CICS HANDLE AID
    Option(lable)
END-EXEC.
```

where "label" is the paragraph name of the program to which control is to be passed.

Commonly Used Options

More than one option can be specified in one HANDLE AID command. The following are the commonly used options of the HANDLE AID command:

• Any key name (PA1 to PA3, PF1 to PF24, ENTER, CLEAR)
• ANYKEY (any of above except ENTER key)

Example

The following is an example of the HANDLE AID command:

```
EXEC CICS HANDLE AID
     PF3(END-ROUTINE)
     PA1(CANCEL-ROUTINE)
     ENTER(NORMAL-ROUTINE)
     ANYKEY(WRONG-KEY-ROUTINE)
END-EXEC.
*
EXEC CICS RECEIVE            <==  This could be RECEIVE MAP.
     INTO(TERM-AREA)
     LENGTH(MSG-LEN)
END-EXEC.
```

Execution Results At the completion of the RECEIVE command, control will be passed to the appropriate routine based on the key pressed, just the same as in Section 7.6.

7.8 Terminal Control Table

Function

The primary function of the Terminal Control Table (TCT) is to register all terminals which are to be under CICS's control. The CICS Terminal Control Program (TCP) uses this table for identifying the terminals and performing all input/output operations against these terminals.

Since TCT specification requires knowledge of telecommunication access methods and characteristics of terminal (hardware), preparation of TCT is usually left to the system programmer. Application programmers and systems analysts, however, should know the following parameters:

TCT Entry Definition

One entry of TCT can be defined using an Assembler macro DFHTCT. The followings are some options and parameters particularly related to application programming:

```
DFHTCT    TYPE=TERMINAL,
          ACCMETH=VTAM,
          TRMIDNT=name,
          TRMTYPE=type,
          FEATURE=(UCTRAN,----),
             :
```

TRMIDNT is used to specify the terminal id (1 to 4 characters). Unless the terminal is registered in TCT in this way, the terminal is not recognizable by CICS. TRMTYPE defines the type of terminal, such as IBM 3270 terminal or others. FEATURE indicates the terminal services CICS offers (see below).

UCTRAN Option

The FEATURE=UCTRAN option is used to translate all lower-case characters to upper-case characters for the 3270 terminals. Since most CICS application systems can be developed using only upper-case characters, it is very useful to specify this option in TCT. If this option is specified, the application programs do not have to be concerned with the upper/lower-case differences, since all characters are to be treated as the upper-case characters.

Chapter

8

BMS (1): Maps

8.1 Formatted Screen

So far, we have dealt with the unformatted screen. But in the real online system, the formatted screens are more commonly used. In order to display a formatted screen, a terminal such as IBM 3278 must receive a series of data stream called Native Mode Data Stream (NMDS) based on the hardware protocol.

NMDS is a mixture of Buffer Control Characters (BCCs) and text data. Therefore, in order to send or receive the formatted screen, the application program must format all BCCs and text for the output screen or must interpret all BCCs for the input screen, respectively, based on the hardware protocol of the terminal.

Example of Formatted Output Screen and NMDS

Suppose that we wish to display a formatted screen on an IBM 3270 type terminal. NMDS for 3270 must be constructed as shown in Figure 8-1 and sent to the terminal by the application program. NMDS shown in Figure 8-1 is for displaying the formatted screen shown in Figure 8-2, of Section 8.11, as an example.

Some Problems of NMDS

NMDS is designed for a particular hardware device (i.e., terminal). This implies that the protocol of NMDS is different for different

163

types of terminals. Therefore, NMDS is both device dependent and format dependent.

It is not impossible to code a program which uses NMDS, although it is very difficult. However, the program, if NMDS is used, would face the following serious problems:

• The terminal device might be changed.
• The screen format may be changed, although the field size may remain the same.
• On each of these occasions, the program will have to be changed, which reduces maintainability.

In order to free the application program from the above problems caused by NMDS, the application program should have device independence and format independence. For this purpose, CICS provides Basic Mapping Support (BMS).

8.2 Introduction to BMS

For the reasons described in the previous section, CICS has a standard facility, called Basic Mapping Support (BMS), to deal with the formatted screen operations.

S T X	E S C	E W	W C C	S B A	08	S F	A T R	Employee Name Change	S F	A T R	PNC2		E T X

Some BCCs for the 3270 terminals are denoted as follows:

STX:	Start Text	(X'02')
ESC:	Escape Command	(X'27')
EW:	Erase/Write Command	(X'F5')
WCC:	Write Control Character	
SBA:	Set Buffer Address	(X'11')
SF:	Start Field	(X'1D')
ATR:	Attribute Character	
IC:	Insert Cursor	(X'13')
ETX:	End Text	(X'03')

Figure 8-1 Example of 3270 Native Mode Data Stream.

Primary Functions

The fundamental objective of BMS is to free application programs from the burden of dealing with NMDS for the formatted screen operations. Toward this objective, BMS provides the following primary functions:

- To remove device dependent codes from an application program by placing all device dependent codes (e.g., 3270 BCCs) in maps.
- To remove constant information from an application program by placing the default constants (e.g., titles, headers, keywords) in maps.
- To construct NMDS required to produce the desired screen.
- To provide an access to data fields of NMDS using symbolic field names, which allows repositioning of field without modifying application programs.
- To provide a text handling capability.
- To provide the Terminal Paging facility, which allows combination of several small mapped data areas into one or more pages of output.
- To provide the Message Routing facility, which allows sending of messages to one or more terminals.

BMS Maps

A screen defined through BMS is called a "map." There are two types of maps: a physical map, which is primarily used by CICS, and a symbolic map, which is primarily used by the application programs.

BMS map is nothing but a program (or CSECT table) written in the Assembler language. However, you do not have to program the BMS map as such, because a set of Assembler macros (BMS macros) are provided by CICS for the BMS map coding.

Based on how a map or a group of maps is linkedited, there are two units of the map: map, which represent a BMS coding for a screen panel, and mapset, which represents a load module.

We will discuss these concepts more in detail in the next sections.

8.3   Physical Map and Symbolic Map

Physical Map

The primary objective of the physical map is to ensure the device independence in the application programs.

More concretely, for input operations, the physical map defines maximal data length and starting position of each field to be read and allows BMS to interpret an input NMDS.

For output operations, the physical map defines starting position, length, field characteristics (Attribute bytes) and default data for each field, and allows BMS to add BCCs and commands for output in order to construct an output NMDS.

Physical Map Generation   The physical map is a program in a form of load module. Therefore, the physical map is coded using BMS macros, assembled separately, and linkedited into the CICS load library, as follows:

BMS macro ⟶ Assembly ⟶ Linkedit ⟶
coding

Load module ⟶ LOADLIB ⟶ To be used by CICS

Symbolic Map

The primary objective of the BMS symbolic map is to ensure the device and format independence to the application programs. Therefore, through the symbolic map, a layout change in the formatted screen can be done independent of the application program coding as long as the field name and length remain the same.

The symbolic map serves as DSECT for referencing the Terminal Input/Output Area (TIOA). It is used by the application program which issues a COBOL COPY statement in order to include a symbolic map in the program.

Symbolic Map Generation   A symbolic map is a copy library member, which is to be included in the application program for defining the screen fields. Therefore, the symbolic map is coded using BMS macros, assembled separately, cataloged into a copy library (COPYLIB), and at the time of application program compile, it will be copied into the application program. This process is illustrated as follows:

BMS macro ⟶ Assembly ⟶ Symbolic map ⟶ COPYLIB
coding   definition

⟶ Copied (COPY) into CICS application program

8.4   Map and Mapset

Map

A representation of one screen format is called a map. One or a group of maps makes up a mapset.

Mapset

A group of maps which are linkedited together is called a mapset. Each mapset must be registered in PPT, since CICS considers the BMS mapset as a program coded in Assembler. The mapset name consists of two parts as follows:

Generic Name:	1 to 7 characters
Suffix:	1 character

Application program uses only the generic name. The suffix is required at the mapset definition time in order to distinguish the device types if the same mapset is used for different types of terminals. While the application program uses only the generic name of the mapset name, CICS automatically inserts the suffix depending on the terminal in use, thereby ensuring the device independence to the application program.

Original Intention of Map/Mapset

You can construct a screen (panel) with multiple maps dynamically at the execution time. This is called the multimap panel (see Chapter 10). For this type of panel, several maps can be defined separately but as one group (mapset) for constructing a screen (panel). Therefore, one mapset represents one screen image.

This was the original intention of map and mapset concepts. However, this original intention is now somewhat obsolete, regardless of whether or not the multimap panel is used.

Actual Usage

There are two cases of utilizing the concepts of map and mapset, as follows:

Case 1: A mapset consists of single map, for example:

MSBINQ2   MPBINQ2

Case 2: A mapset consists of several maps, for example:

MSBINQ2   MPBINQH
          MPBINQD
          MPBINQT

Whether you choose case 1 or 2 depends on the installation standards, but case 1 is recommended as long as one map represents one screen image (i.e., not the multimap panel), for the following reasons:

• It is simple.
• You can assemble and linkedit only one map/mapset to be changed.
• This is the original concept of mapset representing one screen image.

Case 2 is more meaningful if you are using the multimap panel (see Chapter 10). In some installations, however, it is encouraged that a group of maps used in the same transaction be put into the same mapset (i.e., case 2). Since this approach has an advantage of reducing a number of PPT entries, it is up to you which approach you choose.

8.5   Map Definition Macros

Available Macros

As a program must be coded using a programming language, a BMS map also must be coded. For this purpose, BMS provides Assembler macros as follows:

DFHMSD: To define a mapset.
DFHMDI: To define a map.
DFHMDF: To define a field.

General Format

The BMS map definition macros are purely Assembler macros. Therefore, the following coding convention must be maintained:

```
Col.                    Col.                          Col
1                       16                            72
-----------------------------------------------------------
Symbol     Operation    Operands (parameters          Cont.
                        separated by commas)
```

Example The following is an example of BMS macro coding using the DFHMSD macro, in order to show the format of the macro coding:

```
MSBINQ2    DFHMSD       TYPE=MAP,MODE=INOUT,                X
                        LANG=COBOL,TIOAPFX=YES
*
*    ANY COMMENTS
*
```

Order of Macros

There is a rule for the order of BMS macros which must be followed. That is, within one mapset definition, the map definition can be specified as many times as you wish. Within one map definition, the field definition can be specified as many times as you wish. This rule is illustrated as follows:

```
DFHMSD     TYPE=DSECT or MAP        <==  A mapset
DFHMDI     -------                  <==     A map
DFHMDF     -------                          A field
DFHMDF     -------                          A field
  :                                          :
DFHMDI     -------                  <==     A map
DFHMDF     -------                          A field
DFHMDF     -------                          A field
  :                                          :
DFHMDI     -------                  <==     A map
DFHMDF     -------                          A field
DFHMDF     -------                          A field
  :                                          :
DFHMSD     TYPE=FINAL
END
```

8.6   DFHMSD Macro

Function

The DFHMSD macro is used to define a mapset and its characteristics or to end a mapset definition. Only one mapset definition is allowed within one Assembly run.

Format

The full format of the DFHMSD macro is summarized in Appendix C, while the basic format of the DFHMSD macro is shown in the example below, followed by the description of the commonly used options.

The mapset name (1 to 7 characters) must be specified as the symbol to the DFHMSD macro.

Example

The following is a basic example of the DFHMSD macro:

```
MSBINQ2    DFHMSD    TYPE=&SYSPARM,                     X
                     MODE=INOUT,                        X
                     LANG=COBOL,                        X
                     STORAGE=AUTO,                      X
                     TIOAPFX=YES,                       X
                     CNTL=(FREEKB,FRSET,PRINT)
```

Commonly Used Options

The following are some of the commonly used options of the DFHMSD macro:

TYPE=	To define the map type.
DSECT:	For symbolic map.
MAP:	For physical map.
&SYSPARM:	For special assembly procedure (see Section 8.11).
FINAL:	To indicate the end of a mapset coding.
MODE=	To indicate input/output operation.
IN:	For the input map.
OUT:	For the output map. This is recommended for maps involving output only.

INOUT:	For the input/output map. This is recommended for maps involving both input and output.
LANG=	To define the language of the application program (COBOL, ASM, PLI, or RPG).
STORAGE=AUTO:	To acquire a separate symbolic map area for each mapset. This is recommended for the beginners. Advanced readers should use the BASE option discussed in Chapter 10.
TIOAPFX=YES:	To reserve the prefix space (12 bytes) for BMS commands to access TIOA properly. This is required for the CICS command level.
CNTL=	To define the device control requests.
FREEKB:	To unlock the keyboard.
FRSET:	To reset MDT to zero (i.e., not modified) status. See Section 8.10.
ALARM:	To set an alarm at screen display time.
PRINT:	To indicate the mapset to be sent to the printer.
TERM=type:	Required if other than the 3270 terminal is used. This ensures device independence by means of providing the suffix.
SUFFIX=nn:	To specify the user provided suffix number. This must correspond to the TCT parameter.

End of Mapset Definition

One mapset definition must be ended with another DFHMSD macro with the TYPE=FINAL option as follows:

DFHMSD   TYPE=FINAL

8.7   DFHMDI Macro

Function

The DFHMDI macro is used to define a map and its characteristics in a mapset. The DFHMDI macro can be issued as often as you wish within one DFHMSD macro.

Format

The full format of the DFHMDI macro is summarized in Appendix C, while the basic format of the DFHMDI macro is shown in the example below.

The map name must be specified as the symbol to the DFHMDI macro. SIZE(ll,cc) is used to define the size of the map by the line size (ll) and column size (cc). LINE and COLUNM indicates the starting position of the map in line and colums numbers, respectively. JUSTIFY is used to specify the map to be LEFT justified or RIGHT justified.

In addition, the DFHMDI macro has the same options used in the DFHMSD macro, such as CNTL and TIOAPFX. If the DFHMDI macro has the same options specified in the DFHMSD macro, the options specified in the DFHMDI macro override the ones specified in the DFHMSD macro.

In this chapter, we will deal with the basic options only. The options for the more sophisticated map definition will be discussed in Chapter 10.

Example

The following is a basic example of the DFHMDI macro:

```
MPBINQ2     DFHMDI     SIZE=(24,80),                   X
                       LINE=1,                         X
                       COLUMN=1,                       X
                       JUSTIFY=LEFT
```

The above DFHMDI macro coding defines the following screen format:

```
              80 columns
         ------------------------
         IX                    I      X: Starting position (1,1)
24       I      Map MPBINQ2    I         Left justified.
lines    I                     I
         I                     I
         ------------------------
```

Technical Notes

The combination of SIZE, LINE, COLUMN, and JUSTIFY makes a variety of maps, such as the following:

```
SIZE=(05,20),LINE=01,COLUMN=01,JUSTIFY=LEFT      .....     (a)
SIZE=(05,20),LINE=06,COLUMN=20,JUSTIFY=LEFT      .....     (b)
SIZE=(05,20),LINE=15,COLUMN=80,JUSTIFY=RIGHT     .....     (c)
```

```
      0          22         4                              8
      1          01         0                              0
      ----------------------------------//-----------------
01 I----------                                            I
   II   (a)   I                                           I
   II         I                                           I
05 I--------------------                                  I
   I          I   (b)   I                                 I
   I          I        I                                  I
10 I          ----------                                  I
   I                                                      I
   I                                                      I
15 I                                      -----------I
   I                                      I   (c)   II
   I                                      I         II
20 I                                      -----------I
   I                                                      I
```

8.8 DFHMDF Macro

Function

The DFHMDF macro is used to define a field in a map and its characteristics. The DFHMDF macro can be issued as many times as you wish within one DFHMDI macro.

Format

The full format of the DFHMDF macro is summarized in Appendix C, while the basic format of the DFHMDF macro is shown in the example below.

If the field name is required, the name of the field (1 to 7 characters) must be specified as the symbol to the DFHMDF macro. POS=(ll,cc) indicates the starting position of the field in the line number (ll) and column number (cc) including the attribute character (see Section 8.9). INITIAL defines the initial value of the field (if any). ATTRB defines the attribute character of the field which defines the characteristics of the field. LENGTH indicates the length of the field excluding the attribute character. JUSTIFY=RIGHT is used for the right justifying the field, which is useful for numeric field definition. JUSTIFY=LEFT is the default. PICIN and PICOUT defines the PICTURE clause of the symbolic map in COBOL, which is useful for numeric field editing (e.g., PICOUT='ZZZ,ZZ9.99-').

Example

The following is a basic example of the DFHMDF macro:

```
        DFHMDF    POS=(3,1),                              X
                  INITIAL='CUSTOMER NO. :',               X
                  ATTRB=ASKIP,                            X
                  LENGTH=14
CUSTNO  DFHMDF    POS=(3,16),                             X
                  ATTRB=(UNPROT,NUM,FSET,IC),             X
                  JUSTIFY=RIGHT,                          X
                  PICIN='9(8)',                           X
                  PICOUT='9(8)',                          X
                  LENGTH=8
```

The above example of the DFHMDF macro defines the following screen layout:

```
              1         2         3
     12345678901234567890123456789 0
     -----------------------------// ---
  1  I                              I     where,
  2  I                              I     &: Attribute character
  3  I&CUSTOMER NO. :&nnnnnnnn       I     n: Unprotected numeric
     I                              I     _: Cursor
     I                              I
```

8.9   Attribute Character

For constructing a screen format, you must understand the concept of a unique piece of information called "attribute character." The attribute character is an invisible 1-byte character which precedes a screen field and determines the characteristics of the field.

Commonly Used Attribute Options

The attribute character (or field attribute) for a screen field of a BMS map can be defined by the ATTRB parameter of the DFHMDF macro which defines the field. While Appendix C shows the full list of the ATTRB options, the following are some commonly used options of the ATTRB parameter of the DFHMDF macro:

ASKIP |:	Autoskip. The data cannot be entered into the field. The cursor skips to the next field.
PROT |:	Protected field. The data cannot be entered into the field. If data is entered, it will cause the input-inhibit status.
UNPROT :	Unprotected field. The data can be entered. This should be specified for all input fields.
NUM:	Numeric field. Only numeric (0 to 9) and special characters ("." and "-") are allowed. Alphabet input will cause the input-inhibit status.
BRT |:	Bright display (i.e., highlight).
NORM |:	Normal display.
DRK:	Dark display (invisible). This is useful for the password field.
IC:	Insert cursor. The cursor will be positioned in this field. If IC is specified in more than one field of a map, the cursor will be placed in the last field.
FSET:	Field set. MDT (see the next section) is set on so that the field data is to be sent from the terminal to the host computer regardless of whether the field is actually modified by the user.

8.10   Modified Data Tag (MDT)

In order to understand the concept of data transfer from a terminal to the application program, it is important to know the concept of "Modified Data Tag" (MDT).

MDT is one bit of the attribute character. If it is off (0), it indicates that this field has not been modified by the terminal operator. If it is on (1), it indicates that this field has been modified by the operator. Only when MDT is on, will the data of the field be sent by the terminal hardware to the host computer (i.e., to the application program, in the end).

An effective use of MDT drastically reduces the amount of data traffic in the communication line, thereby improving performance significantly. Therefore, BMS maps and CICS application programs should be developed based on careful considerations for MDT.

How to Set/Reset MDT

There are three ways of setting and resetting MDT, as follows:

1. When the terminal user modifies a field on a screen, MDT will be set to "1" (on) automatically by the terminal hardware.
2. If CNTL=FRSET is specified in the DFHMSD or DFHMDI macro, when the mapset or the map is sent to the terminal, MDT will be reset to "0" (off: i.e., not modified) for all fields of the mapset or the map, respectively.
3. Further, if FSET is specified in the ATTRB parameter of the DFHMDF macro for a field, when the map is sent to the terminal, MDT will be set to "1" (on, i.e., modified) for the field, regardless of whether the field has been modified by the terminal user.

Programming Techniques

You cannot assume that the terminal user will always type some data into all unprotected fields. He/she might forget to type some required field, or he/she might intentionally skip certain fields. In such cases, the program might not receive data in the field as the program expects. In order to overcome this troublesome situation, the following techniques should be used:

- Code CNTL=FRSET in DFHMSD or DFHMDI.
- Code ATTRB=(FSET,----) in all DFHMDF macros for the fields, from which the application program expects to receive data, regardless of whether they are input fields or output fields.

FRSET is very useful when the same map is repeatedly sent to the terminal for the data entry. By specifying FRSET, MDT will be always reset to zero whenever the map is redisplayed. This will prevent the MDT status of each field of the map from being carried over from the previous display of the same map. If the same map is redisplayed without the FRSET option, although each field of the screen may look initialized, the MDT status of the field is actually that of the previous map used.

It should also be noted that data can be received even from the output fields if MDT is set on. Therefore, FSET should not be placed in any title fields or unlabeled fields, since it will distort the data alignment in the corresponding symbolic map, and it will also increase the data traffic in the communication line.

MDT Problems

Many people forget to set or reset MDT in the fields and get into trouble later. The following scenario illustrates how troublesome MDT could be:

When you send a map, expecting the terminal user to type some data, it is always a good practice to specify default values in the applicable input fields, so that the user does not have to type every input field on the screen. In this case, since these default input fields already have values (set by the program), the user would not type the data unless he/she wishes to change it to another value. That is, MDT of these fields would not be set on (1) unless the user types some data in the field. Then, suppose that the user press the ENTER key without typing any new value in this field. The application program receives this map. But, in this case, since MDT is off (0) in these default input fields, the symbolic map would not have the data in these fields.

A *solution:* If you have a convention described in the programming technique above, you could avoid this problem, since MDT of all input fields have been set on (1) by the map itself. Otherwise, whenever you prepare default values in input fields, you have to dynamically allocate the attribute character which has MDT on (1) to these fields in your application program. This is a tedious task which you should avoid. Therefore, the programming technique described above is highly recommended.

8.11   BMS Map Generation

We have discussed each of three BMS map definition macros. In order to integrate the understanding of these macros, let us here actually code and generate a BMS map.

Map Coding

Figure 8-2 shows a simple model screen layout for the personnel name change application. The map name and the mapset name are MPBPNC2 and MSBPNC2, respectively. Based on this screen layout, Figure 8-3 shows an example of the actual BMS macro coding for the map.

```
        0    0   0         1                                    7
        1    6   8         6                          //        0
 1    I            &EMPLOYEE  NAME  CHANGE                &PNC2    I
 2    I                                                            I
 3    I       &EMP-NO     &NAME                                    I
 4    I&1.    &nnnnn      &xxxxxxxxxxxxxxxxxxxxxxxxx               I
 5    I&2.    &nnnnn      &xxxxxxxxxxxxxxxxxxxxxxxxx               I
      I                                                            I
      //                                                          //
      I                                                            I
21    I yyyyyyyyyyyyyyyyyyyyyyyyyyyyyyyyyyyyyyyyyyyyyyyyyyyyyyyyy I
22    I yyyyyyyyyyyyyyyyyyyyyyyyyyyyyyyyyyyyyyyyyyyyyyyyyyyyyyyyy I
23    I yyyyyyyyyyyyyyyyyyyyyyyyyyyyyyyyyyyyyyyyyyyyyyyyyyyyyyyyy I
24    I yyyyyyyyyyyyyyyyyyyyyyyyyyyyyyyyyyyyyyyyyyyyyyyyyyyyyyyyy I
      I                                                  //        I
```

where   &: Attribute character
          n: Unprotected numeric field
          x: Unprotected alphanumeric field
          _: Initial cursor position
          y: Autoskipped alphanumeric field

Let us assume a simple model screen layout, as the example shown above, for the personnel name change application. The terminal used is assumed to be a IBM 3270 type terminal. The BMS mapname and mapset name for this screen are MPBPNC2 and MSBPNC2, respectively.

Figure 8-2 Model screen layout.

```
0         1         2         3         4         5         6         7
1234567890123456789012345678901234567890123456789012345678901234567890123456789012
--------------------------------------------------------------------------
**************************************************************************
*                                                                        *
*                    SAMPLE BMS MAP CODING                               *
*                                                                        *
*                 (MAP/MAPSET=MPBPNC2/MSBPNC2)                           *
*                                                                        *
**************************************************************************
*
MSBPNC2 DFHMSD TYPE=&SYSPARM,                                              X
               MODE=INOUT,                                                X
               CTRL=(FREEKB,FRSET,PRINT),                                 X
               LANG=COBOL,                                                X
               STORAGE=AUTO,                                              X
               TIOAPFX=YES
MPBPNC2 DFHMDI SIZE=(24,80),                                              X
               LINE=1,                                                    X
               COLUMN=1
        DFHMDF POS=(01,08),                                               X
               LENGTH=20,                                                 X
               ATTRB=(ASKIP,BRT),                                         X
               INITIAL='EMPLOYEE NAME CHANGE'
        DFHMDF POS=(01,70),                                               X
               LENGTH=04,                                                 X
               ATTRB=(ASKIP),                                             X
               INITIAL='PNC2'
        DFHMDF POS=(03,06),                                               X
               LENGTH=14,                                                 X
               ATTRB=(ASKIP),                                             X
               INITIAL='EMP-NO    NAME'
        DFHMDF POS=(04,01),                                               X
               LENGTH=02,                                                 X
               ATTRB=(ASKIP),                                             X
               INITIAL='1.'
M2EMPN1 DFHMDF POS=(04,06),                                               X
               LENGTH=05,                                                 X
               JUSTIFY=RIGHT,                                             X
               ATTRB=(UNPROT,NUM,IC,FSET),                                X
               PICIN='9(5)',                                              X
               PICOUT='9(5)'
        DFHMDF POS=(04,12),                                               X
               LENGTH=01,                                                 X
               ATTRB=(ASKIP)
```

Based on the model screen layout of the map/mapset MPBPNC2/MSBPNC2 in Figure 8-2, the above is a typical BMS map coding.

Figure 8-3 Sample coding of BMS map.

```
M2NAME1 DFHMDF POS=(04,16),                              X
               LENGTH=25,                                X
               ATTRB=(UNPROT,FSET)
        DFHMDF POS=(04,42),                              X
               LENGTH=01,                                X
               ATTRB=(ASKIP)
        DFHMDF POS=(05,01),                              X
               LENGTH=02,                                X
               ATTRB=(ASKIP),                            X
               INITIAL='2.'
M2EMPN2 DFHMDF POS=(05,06),                              X
               LENGTH=05,                                X
               JUSTIFY=RIGHT,                            X
               ATTRB=(UNPROT,NUM,FSET),                  X
               PICIN='9(5)',                             X
               PICOUT='9(5)'
        DFHMDF POS=(05,12),                              X
               LENGTH=01,                                X
               ATTRB=(ASKIP)
M2NAME2 DFHMDF POS=(05,16),                              X
               LENGTH=25,                                X
               ATTRB=(UNPROT,FSET)
        DFHMDF POS=(05,42),                              X
               LENGTH=01,                                X
               ATTRB=(ASKIP)
M2ERR1  DFHMDF POS=(21,01),                              X
               LENGTH=79,                                X
               ATTRB=(ASKIP)
M2ERR2  DFHMDF POS=(22,01),                              X
               LENGTH=79,                                X
               ATTRB=(ASKIP)
M2ERR3  DFHMDF POS=(23,01),                              X
               LENGTH=79,                                X
               ATTRB=(ASKIP)
M2ERR4  DFHMDF POS=(24,01),                              X
               LENGTH=79,                                X
               ATTRB=(ASKIP)
        DFHMSD TYPE=FINAL
        END
```

Figure 8-3 (continued) Sample coding of BMS map.

Mapset Definition Since the mapset name is MSBPNC2, the mapset definition macro (DFHMSD) must have MSBPNC2 as the label at the column 1 of coding sheet. In this example TYPE=&SYSPARM is used for the convenience of assembling (see Assemblying Considerations below). The rest of options and parameters are very standard to such a conventional map as this example.

Map Definition Since the map name is MPBPNC2, the map definition macro (DFHMDI) must have MPBPNC2 as the label at column 1 of the coding sheet. Unless you have an intentional purpose, the size of the map should be defined for the full screen (e.g., 24 rows by 80 columns). If you define the smaller size than full screen (e.g., 10 rows by 40 columns), it would be difficult to find the actual field position on the screen, because the field position is defined relative to the size of the map. For this reason, the example has SIZE=(24,80) and the starting position at LINE=1 and COLUMN=1.

Field Definition A series of field definition macros (DFHMDF) are to follow. The position of the field defined in the POS parameter actually means the position of the attribute characters preceding the field, while the length of the field defined in the LENGTH parameter is the length of the field excluding the attribute character. You must define the values accurately to the POS and LENGTH parameters based on the screen layout. The order of field definition must be from the top to bottom and left to right of the screen. You do not need to define every field of the screen to cover the entire space of the screen. That is, you can define only those fields in which you are interested. Depending on the characteristics of the field, the following is a set of guidelines for effective field definition.

Field Title Definition The field title should be defined as the auto-skipped field without the field name since usually you do not wish to change dynamically. Therefore, ASKIP should be used for the attribute definition (ATTRB). You could brighten the title using the BRT attribute, but excessive use of bright title might make the terminal users a little uncomfortable. The title should be hard coded using the INITIAL parameters. Since you do not need to receive data from the title field, MDT should not be set on; that is, FSET should not be specified in the ATTRB parameter.

Alphanumeric Input Field Definition The alphanumeric input field should be defined as the unprotected field with MDT set on. Therefore, ATTRB=(UNPROT,FSET) is recommended. If you wish to place the cursor, IC should be specified in the ATTRB parameter.

Numeric Input Field Definition For the numeric input field, if you are not dealing with the numeric sign or decimal point (see Sections 8.13 and 8.14), the field should be defined as the unprotected numeric field with MDT set on. Therefore, ATTRB=(UNPROT,FSET,NUM) is recommended. If you wish to place the cursor, IC should be specified in the ATTRB parameter. In addition, if you specify JUS-TIFY=RIGHT and PICIN parameters, you could use the value in the field directly in the program after receiving the map without the detailed validation check. However, if you are dealing with the numeric sign or decimal point using a sophisticated money edit subroutine (see Section 8.14), it might be better if you simply define the field as the unprotected alphanumeric field, depending on the specifications of the money edit subroutine.

Output Field Definition   The output field should be defined simply as the auto-skipped field. Therefore, ATTRB=ASKIP is recommended. If you require an edited numeric value display, PICOUT (e.g., PICOUT='Z,ZZ9.99-') should be used, depending on the requirement. FSET (i.e., MDT on) should not be specified in the ATTRB parameter, unless you really wish to receive the data from this output field.

Skipper and Stopper   Skippers and Stoppers (see Section 8.15) should be properly defined, as required, since these increase user-friendliness. However, Stoppers should not be used excessively because they slow the speed of data entry operations by the terminal user.

End of Mapset Definition   A mapset coding must be concluded with the mapset definition macro (DFHMSD) with the TYPE=FINAL option. In addition, since this is the end of Assembler coding, the Assembler statement END should be coded as the last statement.

Assembling Considerations

Now that the BMS map coding has been completed, you have to assemble and linkedit this map. The basic rule is that you assemble and linkedit the map for the physical map once, then assemble the map coding again for the symbolic map.

However, it is a cumbersome task to assemble a mapset once for the physical map and again for the symbolic map. Therefore, usually a cataloged procedure is provided in your installation for you to be able to assemble both physical and symbolic maps in one run using the &SYSPARM option.

Figures 8-4 and 8-5 show an example of the typical JCL and cataloged procedures, respectively, for BMS map assemble and linkedit. It should be noted that the cataloged procedure CICSMAP in Figure 8-4 uses the SYSPARM option for jobsteps ASM1 and ASM2 of both the physical map and symbolic map, respectively. If TYPE=&SYSPARM is specified in the DFHMSD macro for defining a mapset, and if PARM='SYSPARM(MAP)' or PARM='SYSPARM(DSECT)' is specified in the assembly step (i.e., PGM=IFOX00), the Assembler program forcefully overrides the source code of TYPE=&SYSPARM to make TYPE=MAP or TYPE=DSECT, respectively. In this way, the same BMS map coding can be used for assembling both the physical map and the symbolic map.

If you execute the job for assembling and linkediting the map (represented in Figure 8-4 and 8-5), the physical map will be created and placed in the load module library, while the symbolic map will be created and placed in the copy library.

Including Symbolic Map in the Application Program

Since the symbolic map is a member of the copy library, you have to copy into your application program. This can be accomplished by simply using the COBOL COPY statement, as follows:

```
COPY mapsetname.
```

For example, if you wish to include the symbolic map you created by the sample coding (Figure 8-3), as it is done in the sample program of Appendix A, you specify in the Working Storage Section of the application program:

```
COPY MSBPNC2.
```

```
//XXXXXXXX JOB --------(JOB ACCOUNT INFORMATION, ETC) -------
//*
//*********************************************************************
//*                                                                  *
//*    JCL EXAMPLE FOR CICS BMS ASM & LINK                           *
//*                                                                  *
//*********************************************************************
//*
//CICSMAP EXEC CICSMAP,MAPSET=MSBPNC2,
//             SRCELIB='YYYYYYY.TEXT.MAPSRCE',
//             LOADLIB='YYYYYYY.TEXT.LOADLIB',
//             SYMBLIB='YYYYYYY.TEXT.MAPSYMB',
//             CICSIDX='CICS.R210'
//
```

```
Notes:
=====
(1)  This JCL is for IBM MVS Operating System.
(2)  This JCL uses a cataloged procedure CICSMAP.
(3)  In MAPSET, specify a mapset name.
(4)  In SRCELIB, specify a source library name for BMS macro
     coding.
(5)  In LOADLIB, specify a load library name to which a physical
     map is to be placed.
(6)  In SYMBLIB, specify a symbolic map library name.
(7)  Since JCL is installation dependent, this JCL may not be
     suitable to your installation.
```

Figure 8-4 JCL example for BMS map assemble and linkedit.

```
//*
//*********************************************************************
//*                                                                   *
//*      CATALOGED PROCEDURE FOR CICS BMS MAP ASM & LINK              *
//*           FOR BOTH PHYSICAL AND SYMBOLIC MAPS                     *
//*                                                                   *
//*********************************************************************
//*
//CICSMAP PROC SRCELIB=DUMMY,
//             LOADLIB=DUMMY,
//             SYMBLIB=DUMMY,
//             MAPSET=DUMMY,
//             CICSIDX='CICS.R161'
//*
//PRT1     EXEC PGM=IEBGENER
//SYSPRINT DD SYSOUT=*
//SYSIN    DD DUMMY
//SYSUT2   DD SYSOUT=*,DCB=(RECFM=F,LRECL=80,BLKSIZE=80)
//SYSUT1   DD DSN=&SRCELIB(&MAPSET),DISP=SHR
//*
//ASM1     EXEC PGM=IFOX00,REGION=320K,PARM='SYSPARM(MAP)'
//STEPLIB  DD DSN=&CICSIDX..LOADLIB,DISP=SHR
//SYSLIB   DD DSN=SYS1.MACLIB,DISP=SHR,DCB=BLKSIZE=19040
//         DD DSN=&CICSIDX..MACLIB,DISP=SHR
//*******  DD DSN=&CICSIDX..SOURCE,DISP=SHR
//SYSUT1   DD UNIT=SYSDA,SPACE=(CYL,(5,5))
//SYSUT2   DD UNIT=SYSDA,SPACE=(CYL,(5,5))
//SYSUT3   DD UNIT=SYSDA,SPACE=(CYL,(5,5))
//SYSPUNCH DD UNIT=SYSDA,SPACE=(CYL,(5,5)),DSN=&&TEMP,
//            DISP=(,PASS),DCB=(RECFM=FB,BLKSIZE=400)
//SYSPRINT DD SYSOUT=*
//SYSIN    DD DSN=&SRCELIB(&MAPSET),DISP=SHR
//*
//LKE1     EXEC PGM=LINKEDIT,PARM='LIST,LET,XREF'
//SYSUT1   DD UNIT=SYSDA,SPACE=(1024,(100,100))
//SYSPRINT DD SYSOUT=*
//SYSLIN   DD DSN=&&TEMP,DISP=(OLD,DELETE)
//SYSLMOD  DD DSN=&LOADLIB(&MAPSET),DISP=SHR
//*
//ASM2     EXEC PGM=IFOX00,REGION=320K,PARM='SYSPARM(DSECT)'
//STEPLIB  DD DSN=&CICSIDX..LOADLIB,DISP=SHR
//SYSLIB   DD DSN=SYS1.MACLIB,DISP=SHR,DCB=BLKSIZE=19040
//         DD DSN=&CICSIDX..MACLIB,DISP=SHR
//SYSUT1   DD UNIT=SYSDA,SPACE=(CYL,(5,5))
//SYSUT2   DD UNIT=SYSDA,SPACE=(CYL,(5,5))
//SYSUT3   DD UNIT=SYSDA,SPACE=(CYL,(5,5))
//SYSPUNCH DD DSN=&SYMBLIB(&MAPSET),DISP=SHR
//SYSIN    DD DSN=&SRCELIB(&MAPSET),DISP=SHR
//SYSPRINT DD SYSOUT=*
//*
```

Notes:
=====
(1)   This cataloged procedure is for IBM MVS Operating System.
(2)   PRT1 step prints the source BMS code.
(3)   ASM1 and LKE1 steps Assemble and Linkedit the physical map.
(4)   ASM2 assembles the symbolic map.
(5)   ASM1 and ASM2 steps have the SYSPARM option for MAP and DSECT,
      respectively, so that the same BMS source code can be used
      for the physical map and symbolic map, respectively.
(6)   Since JCL is installation dependent, this cataloged procedure
      may not be suitable to your installation.

Figure 8-5 Cataloged procedure for BMS map assemble and linkedit.

Format of Symbolic Map

By the procedure described above, the symbolic map is now copied into the application program. Figure 8-6 shows the actual symbolic map of the map MPBPNC2 and mapset MSBPNC2, created by the sample coding (Figure 8-3). The symbolic map starts with the 01 level definition of map name specified in the DFHMDI macro with the suffix of "I" for the input map or "O" for the output map. Next is the definition of FILLER PIC X(12), which is the TIOA prefix created by TIOAPFX=YES of the DFHMSD macro, and this is required by BMS under the CICS command level.

For each field name (1 to 7 characters) you specified in the DFHMDF macro, BMS creates three fields for inputs and another three fields for outputs, by placing one character suffix to the original field name. The meaning of these fields are as follows:

name+L:	The halfword binary (PIC S9(4) COMP) field. For the input field, the actual number of characters typed in the field will be placed by BMS when the map is received. For the output field, this is used for the dynamic cursor positioning (see Section 9.6).
name+F:	Flag byte. For an input field, it will be X'80' if field has been modified but no data is sent (i.e., the field is cleared). Otherwise, this field is X'00'.
name+A:	The attribute byte for both input and output fields.
name+I	The input data field. X'00' will be placed if no data is entered. Note that space X'40' is data. The application program should differentiate X'00' from space (X'40').
name+O:	The output data field.

Mapset and PPT

From CICS's point of view, a mapset is nothing but one program (or CSECT table) written in Assembler. Therefore, all mapsets must be registered in PPT as follows:

```
        DFHPPT      TYPE=ENTRY,MAPSET=name
or      DFHPPT      TYPE=ENTRY,PROGRAM=name
```

```
01  MPBPNC2I.
    02  FILLER PIC X(12).
    02  M2EMPN1L    COMP  PIC  S9(4).
    02  M2EMPN1F    PICTURE  X.
    02  FILLER REDEFINES M2EMPN1F.
     03 M2EMPN1A    PICTURE  X.
    02  M2EMPN1I  PIC 9(5).
    02  M2NAME1L    COMP  PIC  S9(4).
    02  M2NAME1F    PICTURE  X.
    02  FILLER REDEFINES M2NAME1F.
     03 M2NAME1A    PICTURE  X.
    02  M2NAME1I  PIC X(25).
    02  M2EMPN2L    COMP  PIC  S9(4).
    02  M2EMPN2F    PICTURE  X.
    02  FILLER REDEFINES M2EMPN2F.
     03 M2EMPN2A    PICTURE  X.
    02  M2EMPN2I  PIC 9(5).
    02  M2NAME2L    COMP  PIC  S9(4).
    02  M2NAME2F    PICTURE  X.
    02  FILLER REDEFINES M2NAME2F.
     03 M2NAME2A    PICTURE  X.
    02  M2NAME2I  PIC X(25).
    02  M2ERR1L     COMP  PIC  S9(4).
    02  M2ERR1F     PICTURE  X.
    02  FILLER REDEFINES M2ERR1F.
     03 M2ERR1A     PICTURE  X.
    02  M2ERR1I  PIC X(79).
    02  M2ERR2L     COMP  PIC  S9(4).
    02  M2ERR2F     PICTURE  X.
    02  FILLER REDEFINES M2ERR2F.
     03 M2ERR2A     PICTURE  X.
    02  M2ERR2I  PIC X(79).
    02  M2ERR3L     COMP  PIC  S9(4).
    02  M2ERR3F     PICTURE  X.
    02  FILLER REDEFINES M2ERR3F.
     03 M2ERR3A     PICTURE  X.
    02  M2ERR3I  PIC X(79).
    02  M2ERR4L     COMP  PIC  S9(4).
    02  M2ERR4F     PICTURE  X.
    02  FILLER REDEFINES M2ERR4F.
     03 M2ERR4A     PICTURE  X.
    02  M2ERR4I  PIC X(79).
```

After assembling the BMS source code in Figure 8-2, the above is the symbolic map of map/mapset MPBPNC2/MSBPNC2 produced.

Figure 8-6 Symbolic map of map/mapset MPBPNC2/MSBPNC2.

```
01   MPBPNC2O REDEFINES MPBPNC2I.
     02   FILLER PIC X(12).
     02   FILLER PICTURE X(3).
     02   M2EMPN1O PIC 9(5).
     02   FILLER PICTURE X(3).
     02   M2NAME1O  PIC X(25).
     02   FILLER PICTURE X(3).
     02   M2EMPN2O PIC 9(5).
     02   FILLER PICTURE X(3).
     02   M2NAME2O  PIC X(25).
     02   FILLER PICTURE X(3).
     02   M2ERR1O  PIC X(79).
     02   FILLER PICTURE X(3).
     02   M2ERR2O  PIC X(79).
     02   FILLER PICTURE X(3).
     02   M2ERR3O  PIC X(79).
     02   FILLER PICTURE X(3).
     02   M2ERR4O  PIC X(79).
```

Figure 8-6 (continued) Symbolic map of map/mapset MPBPNC2/MSBPNC2.

Example In order to actually use the mapset coded in the example (Figure 8-3), the following PPT entry must be made:

```
DFHPPT TYPE=ENTRY,MAPSET=MSBPNC2
```

8.12 Screen Definition Facility (SDF)

Screen Definition Facility (SDF) is an interactive screen definition software which works under CICS or TSO. This is a program product provided by IBM.

Advantages

SDF provides many advantages over the traditional BMS map coding using the BMS macros. Some of the SDF's advantages are:

• Through SDF, a programmer can define screens directly and interactively on the 3270 terminal.
• SDF produces BMS coding automatically, so that the programmer does not have to code BMS macros.

- SDF provides an excellent test facility. The screen layout can be checked interactively as the programmer defines the screen.
- In addition, SDF provides a variety of utilities, such as:
  — Map generation
  — Copy/delete/rename functions
  — Directory listing

Therefore, if your installation does not have it yet, SDF is highly recommended. However, this does not mean that you do not have to learn BMS map coding if you use SDF. On the contrary, if you understand BMS map coding, you can utilize SDF more easily and more effectively.

8.13   Numeric Sign Handling

In actual business applications, you would have to deal with a numeric sign in certain fields of a screen in many instances. However, except for output operations, BMS's function in this area is primitive. Therefore, some special techniques are required. The following are some of these techniques:

For Output Operations

It is easy to deal with a numeric sign in the BMS output operation. In the map, you simply define a field with the PICOUT parameter, which edit the numeric sign conveniently, as the following example:

```
CUSTBAL    DFHMDF    POS=(xx,xx),ATTRB=(ASKIP),
                     LENGTH=10,
                     PICOUT='ZZ,ZZ9.99-'
                or     'ZZ,ZZ9.99+'
```

In the application program, move a signed numeric value to the field in the symbolic map, as the following example:

```
MOVE CMA-A-CUSTBAL TO CUSTBALO.
```

where CMA-A-CUSTBAL is defined as PIC S9(5)V99 COMP-3, for example. Then the edited numeric value will be displayed with the sign on the screen.

For Input Operations

BMS does not (as COBOL does not) recognize a sign character (+ or -) as a part of numeric value. Therefore, special considerations must be made. The better solutions are by screen design, instead of programming tricks. There are basically three approaches, as follows:

1. *Separate Amount Field Approach*

   In this approach, you create both credit (+) and debit (-) fields, and instruct the terminal users to enter the value (absolute) in one of two fields, depending on the sign.
   As an example, let us assume the following screen layout:

   ```
                          CREDIT(+)   OR   DEBIT(-)
   ADJUSTMENT AMOUNT:     xxxxxxx          xxxxxxx
   ```

   Then, in the map, define the fields with the PICIN parameter, as in the following example:

   ```
           ADJCR       DFHMDF      POS=(--,--),LENGTH=7,
   and     ADJDR                   ATTRB=(UNPROT,NUM,FSET),
                                   JUSTIFY=RIGHT,
                                   PICIN='9(5)V99'
   ```

   In the program, move the credit field to a signed numeric field or move the debit field to the same field and invert the sign, as in the following example:

   ```
   IF ADJCRL > 0
        MOVE ADJCRI TO ADJ-AMT.
   IF ADJDRL > 0
        MOVE ADJDRI TO ADJ-AMT
        COMPUTE ADJ-AMT = ADJ-AMT * -1.00.
   ```

   where ADJ-AMT is defined as PIC S9(5)V99 COMP-3, for example.

2. *CR/DR Field Approach*

   In this approach, you create a CR(+)/DR(-) field next to the numeric field, and instruct the terminal users to enter either

CR or DR after entering the numeric value, depending on the sign.

As an example, let us assume the following screen layout:

```
                        AMOUNT    CR(+)/DR(-)
ADJUSTMENT AMOUNT:   xxxxxxx      xx
```

Then, in the map, define the two fields with the PICIN parameter, as in the following example:

```
ADJAMT      DFHMDF      POS=(xx,xx),LENGTH=7,
                        ATTRB=(UNPROT,NUM,FSET),
                        JUSTIFY=RIGHT,
                        PICIN='9(5)V99'
ADJSGN      DFHMDF      POS=(xx,xx),LENGTH=2,
                        ATTRB=(UNPROT,FSET),
```

In the program, move the numeric field to a signed numeric field. If the sign field is "DR," invert the sign, as in the following example:

```
MOVE ADJAMTI TO ADJ-AMT.
IF ADJSGNI = 'DR'
      COMPUTE ADJ-AMT = ADJ-AMT * (-1.00).
```

3. *Money Edit Subroutine Approach*

The most sophisticated approach is to develop a money edit subroutine to deal with the numeric sign. This will be discussed in detail in the next section.

8.14   Decimal Point Handling

Similar to the case of numeric sign handling, in actual business applications, you would have to deal with a decimal point in certain numeric fields for many occasions. In this case, too, BMS's function is primitive. Therefore, special techniques similar to numeric sign handling are required. The following are some of these techniques:

For Output Operations

It is easy to deal with a decimal point in the BMS output operations. The same technique used in numeric sign handling can be used to deal with a decimal point in the BMS output operations (see the previous section).

For Input Operations

BMS does not (as COBOL does not) recognize a decimal point as a part of a numeric value. Therefore, special considerations must be made. Reasonable solutions exist by the screen design as well as by the program logic.

1. *Virtual Decimal Point Approach*

   In this approach, you create a numeric field with a virtual decimal point, and instruct the terminal users to enter the numeric data as such.
   As an example, let us assume the following screen layout:

   ```
   REMITTANCE AMOUNT:                        xxxxxxx
   (IN 99999V99 WITHOUT DECIMAL POINT)
   ```

   Then, in the map, define the field with the PICIN parameter, as in the following example:

   ```
   REMAMT      DFHMDF      POS=(xx,xx),LENGTH=7,
                           ATTRB=(UNPROT,NUM,FSET),
                           JUSTIFY=RIGHT,
                           PICIN='9(5)V99'
   ```

   In the program, use the field directly, or move it to a signed numeric field (e.g., PIC S9(5)V99 COMP-3).

2. *Separate Dollar/Cents Field Approach*

   In this approach, you create both dollar and cents fields separately, and instruct the terminal users to enter in both fields.
   As an example, let us assume the following screen layout:

```
                        DOLLAR    CENTS
REMITTANCE AMOUNT:      xxxxx     xx
```

Then, in the map, define both fields with the PICIN parameter, as in the following example:

```
REMDOL:  with PICIN '9(5)'
REMCEN:  with PICIN '99'
```

In the program, merge these two fields into one signed numeric field, as in the following example:

```
COMPUTE REM-AMT = REMDOLI + REMCENI/100.
```

where REM-AMT is defined as PIC S9(5)V99 COMP-3, for example.

3. *Money Edit Subroutine Approach*

In this approach, you develop a subroutine to deal with a decimal point and a decimal sign in a character string.
As an example, let us assume the following screen layout:

```
ADJUSTMENT AMOUNT:    xxxxxxx      (WITH DECIMAL POINT
                                    AND SIGN)
```

Then, in the map, define the field (e.g., ADJAMT) as an alphanumeric field. In the program, use the money edit subroutine against the symbolic field of the map (ADJAMTI).

Usually, most installations have their own money edit subroutines. But, if your installation does not have one, it is relatively easy to develop one. The specifications of the money edit subroutine are as follows:

- Find the numeric sign (+ or -) in the field (ADJAMTI) backward, that is from right to left. If "-" is found, move "-" to the sign field (e.g., ADJ-SIGN).
- Find further the decimal point in the field (ADJAMTI) backward.
- Two numeric characters right to the decimal point is cents amount. Move to a numeric field (e.g., ADJ-CEN).
- Numeric characters left to the decimal point is dollar amount. Move to a numeric field (e.g., ADJ-DOL).

- Merge these two values, as in the following example:

```
COMPUTE ADJ-AMT = ADJ-DOL + ADJ-CEN/100.
```

where ADJ-AMT is defined as PIC S9(5)V99 COMP-3, for example.
- If the sign field (ADJ-SIGN) has the value "-," invert the sign of ADJ-AMT by multiplying -1.

8.15 Skipper/Stopper Techniques

For the BMS map coding, you code only required fields of a screen. In other words, you do not have to code every part of the screen including the gaps between two fields.

However, it is a good practice to always skip the cursor to the next unprotected field after one unprotected field. For this, you need the Skipper technique.

Also, for some important unprotected field, the cursor should be intentionally stopped after the field in order to prevent erroneous field overflow by the terminal users. For this, you need the Stopper technique.

Skipper Technique

The Skipper is an unlabeled 1-byte field with the autoskip attribute. Therefore, you can define the Skipper field as follows:

```
DFHMDF    POS=(xx,xx),ATTRB=ASKIP,LENGTH=1
```

You can place a Skipper after an unprotected field, as in the following screen layout example:

```
&xxxxx&$       &xx
```

where

&:	Attribute byte
x:	Unprotected field
$:	Skipper field

In this case, the cursor automatically skips after the first unprotected field to the second unprotected field in spite of a gap between. If the Skipper field was not placed, the cursor would stop after the first unprotected field, or invade the gap field. Accordingly, the Skipper makes fast and accurate data entry operations possible. Therefore, it is highly recommended to place the Skipper after every unprotected field.

Stopper Technique

The Stopper is an unlabeled 1-byte field with the protect attribute. Therefore, you can define the Stopper field as follows:

```
DFHMDF      POS=(xx,xx),ATTRB=PROT,LENGTH=1
```

You can place the Stopper after an unprotected field, as in the following screen layout example:

```
&xxxxxxxxxxxxxxxxxxx&#&$
&xxxxxxxxxxxxxxxxxxx&#&$
&xxxxxxxxxxxxxxxxxxx&#&$
```

where

    #:   Stopper field

Let us assume that the input field above (xxxxx...) is an address line, and that an address line must be less than 20 characters. If the user types more than 20 characters, the cursor will stop at the Stopper field after the unprotected field (i.e., the address line), and the input-inhibit status will occur. Unless the user presses the RESET key in the terminal, he/she could not proceed further. If the user completes the entry at the 15th column and presses the field-skip key, the cursor would stop at the Stopper field.

This is a practical way to make sure that the first address line does not overflow to the second address line. If the Stopper field were not placed and if the Skipper field was placed right after the unprotected field, the user might continue to write the first address line data in the second line, since the cursor would automatically move to the second line.

Since the Stopper ensures a proper data entry to the field, it is very helpful, if it is properly used. However, since the Stopper slows down the data entry operations, its excessive use should be avoided.

8.16   Screen Design Considerations

Good screen design is one of the primary considerations for a successful online system. Some can design highly efficient screens naturally without any training, while others design "difficult-to-use" screens even after training.

Your strategy should be:

• Place yourself into a position of the terminal user who would be using the screen.
• Make it easy to use.
• Use common sense.
• Be simple.

The following are some considerations for good screen design:

Functional Screen Design

• Design the screen layout similar to the source document according to which terminal users enter the data.
• Place the screen id (i.e., map name or its abbreviation) at the top right corner of a screen, because this helps at problem determination time.
• Make the screen and field title self-explanatory.
• Use concise instructions.
• Break a large field into subfunctional units. For example, the address field should be broken into Street/ Apt./ City/ State/ County/ ZIP.
• Place a sequence number in the repeated field or group of fields.
• Provide error message fields. Usually, the last few lines (e.g., four lines) should be reserved for the edit error messages.

User-Friendly Screen Design

• Use the default option if appropriate. If the terminal user does not enter any data in a field, the application program will assume the

default value, depending on the application subject. This reduces actual keystrokes by the user.
- Let the application program calculate the values as much as possible, not the user. For example, if product number and order quantity are given, the order value should be calculated by the program.
- Position the cursor at the most appropriate place.
- Highlight some important field or error field or use similar techniques (e.g., color, reverse image, blinking).
- Use an alarm in case of an entry error.
- Send an instructive message in case of entry error. The message should be instructive, but kind, even humorous with the non–data processing terms.

Artistic Screen Design

- Design a visually beautiful screen by using indentations and space lines/fields effectively.
- Design a simple screen layout. Do not make it too crowded.

Considerations for Human Factors

- Use effectively the fact that the cursor moves or skips from left to right and top to botton within the screen.
- Place the most frequently used fields at the top part of the screen.
- Group the related fields together.
- Use the Skipper/Stopper techniques at appropriate places.
- Minimize unnecessary manual field skips.
- Use the fact that data on the left side of a screen is easier to work with than data on the right side.

Exercise

Code a BMS map based on the following specifications:

1. Map characteristics:
   - Mapset name: MSBIPE2
   - Mapname: MPBIPE2
   - The map is used for both input and output to an IBM 3278 model 2 terminal.
2. Screen layout: The following is the screen layout of the map MPBIPE2/MSBIPE2:

```
              1           2           3
              0           0           3
 1   I                 INSURANCE POLICY ENTRY                    IPE2 I
 2   I                                                                I
 3   I      EMPLOYEE NO: nnnnn       NAME    : yyyyyyyyyyyyyyyyyyyyyy I
 4   I      POLICY NO  : nnnnnnn     ROOM    : yyyyyyyyyy             I
 5   I                               EXTENTION: 9999                  I
 6   I                                                                I
 7   I         COVERAGE CODE         PREMIUM                          I
 8   I      1.   xx                  zzz,zz9.99                       I
 9   I      2.   xx                  zzz,zz9.99                       I
10   I      3.   xx                  zzz,zz9.99                       I
11   I                                                                I
12   I         TOTAL                 z,zzz,zz9.99                     I
     I                                                                I
     I                                                                I
21   I  yyyyyyyyyyyyyyyyyyyyyyyyyyyyyyyyyyyyyyyyyyyyyyyyyyyyyyyyyyyyy  I
22   I  yyyyyyyyyyyyyyyyyyyyyyyyyyyyyyyyyyyyyyyyyyyyyyyyyyyyyyyyyyyyy  I
23   I  yyyyyyyyyyyyyyyyyyyyyyyyyyyyyyyyyyyyyyyyyyyyyyyyyyyyyyyyyyyyy  I
24   I  yyyyyyyyyyyyyyyyyyyyyyyyyyyyyyyyyyyyyyyyyyyyyyyyyyyyyyyyyyyyy  I
```

where,

n: Unprotected numeric field
x: Unprotected alphanumeric field
y: Autoskipped alphanumeric field
z or 9: Autoskipped, edited numeric field
_: Initial cursor position

3. Technical notes:
   - All title fields must be defined as ASKIP.
   - The cursor must automatically move to the next unprotected field, that is, the Skippers must be provided properly.
   - Last four lines are reserved for the edit error messages.
   - The field position shown above should be used as a guideline. The actual position can be shifted, as long as the layout makes sense. Design a pretty screen.
   - This map will be used in the Exercise for Chapter 9.

9

BMS (2): Input/Output Operations

9.1 Introduction

In the previous chapter, we discussed the BMS maps themselves. We are already familiar with what they are and how they are created through the BMS map definition macros. Now let us discuss how these BMS maps are used in the application programs for the actual terminal input/output operations, which are performed by a set of CICS commands for BMS.

Functions

The CICS commands for BMS perform the following three basic functions:

1. *Map Sending Function*
   Using the data in the symbolic map, BMS prepares the output Native Mode Data Stream (NMDS) the corresponding physical map, and sends to the terminal (or printer), as illustrated in Figure 9-1.
2. *Map Receiving Function*
   Using the input NMDS from the terminal, BMS prepares data in the symbolic map through the corresponding physical map, as illustrated in Figure 9-1.
3. *Text Handling Function*
   BMS prepares text without using a map and sends to the terminal.

In this chapter, we will discuss only these basic functions of BMS commands. In addition to these basic functions, BMS provides advanced functions (e.g., paging), which will be discussed in the next chapter.

Available Commands

The following commands are available for the basic BMS input/output operations:

RECEIVE MAP: To receive a map.
SEND MAP: To send a map.
SEND CONTROL: To send a control function to the terminal.
SEND TEXT: To send a text.
SEND PAGE: To send the accumulated text or maps as a logical message.

9.2   RECEIVE MAP Command

Function

The RECEIVE MAP command is used to receive a map from a terminal. At the completion of the command, the symbolic map of the specified map will contain the valid data from the terminal in the following three fields per each field defined by the DFHMDF macro:

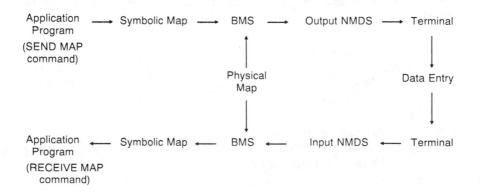

Figure 9-1 Concept of BMS operations.

fieldname+L:	The length field which contains actual number of characters typed in the screen field.
fieldname+F:	The flag byte field, which is normally X'00'. It will be X'80' if the screen field has been modified but cleared.
fieldname+I:	The actual input data field. If no data were typed in the screen field, X'00' will be filled.

Format

The basic format of the RECEIVE MAP command is as follows:

```
EXEC CICS RECEIVE
     MAP(name)
     MAPSET(name)
END-EXEC.
```

MAP defines the name of the map which was defined in the corresponding DFHMDI macro. MAPSET defines the name of the mapset which was defined in the corresponding DFHMSD macro. If nothing else is specified, the INTO option is assumed, and BMS automatically finds the symbolic map area to place the data from the terminal.

The format shown is the simplest way of issuing the RECEIVE MAP command, for which the map/mapset must be coded with the STORAGE=AUTO option in the corresponding DFHMSD macro. We will discuss an advanced use of the RECEIVE command in the next chapter.

Example

Assuming that the names of map and mapset are MPBINQ2 and MSBINQ2, respectively, and that STORAGE=AUTO is specified in the DFHMSD macro, the following is an example of the RECEIVE MAP command:

```
WORKING-STORAGE SECTION.
    :
    COPY MSBINQ2.              <== Symbolic map copy.
    :                          ( 01 MPBINQ2I.
    :                          (      :
PROCEDURE DIVISION.            ( 01 MPBINQ2O REDEFINE MPBINQ2I.
```

```
      :
      :
EXEC CICS RECEIVE
        MAP('MPBINQ2')              <== From DFHMDI macro.
        MAPSET('MSBINQ2')           <== From DFHMSD macro.
END-EXEC.
```

Execution Results CICS automatically finds the symbolic map area
(mapname+I) and places the mapped data. Therefore, the area
MPBINQ2I (in this case) will contain the mapped data from the terminal in the form of a symbolic map. The application program can
use the field names (+I) defined in DFHMDF macros.

Commonly Used Options

The following are the commonly used options for the basic use of the
RECEIVE MAP command:

TERMINAL ASIS: To override the upper-case translation speci-
                fied in TCT (FEATURE=UCTRAN).
SET: This option can be used in a manner similar
                to the READ command with the SET option.

Common Execptional Condition

The following is the exceptional condition common to the basic use of
the RECEIVE MAP command:

MAPFAIL: This occurs if the data to be mapped has the
                length of zero, or contains no SBA code. This
                usually happens when the user presses the
                ENTER key without typing data if no FSET
                is specified in DFHMDF macros.

9.3 Data Validity Checking

After the completion of the RECEIVE MAP command, the data from
the terminal are placed in the fields of the symbolic map. However,
you can not assume that all data in the symbolic map are valid,
since BMS has nothing to do with the quality of data contents in the
fields which were entered by the terminal user. Therefore, you must
validate the data in each field before you use it.

One of the online system's advantages is its capability of realtime (i.e., instant) data validation and feedback to the user. Therefore, you should take this advantage and perform data validity checking as thoroughly as possible right after the RECEIVE MAP command.

Procedures

The following is a set of procedures for the effective data validity checking after the completion of the RECEIVE MAP command:

1. Perform the data validity checking in detail as soon as the program receives data form the terminal.
2. Check the fieldname+L:
   • If it is zero, no data has been entered by the user. Therefore, take the default action, or consider an error if it is the required field.
   • If it is a positive value, some data of that length has been entered. Therefore, validate the field data in the fieldname+I.
3. Alternatively, check directly the fieldname+I:
   • If it is LOW-VALUES or SPACE, no data has been entered or space key has been pressed. Therefore, take the default action, or consider an error if it is the required field.
   • If it is not LOW-VALUE or space, some data has been entered. Therefore, validate the field data in the fieldname+I.
   • Note that CICS considers spaces as data. Therefore, space may be the valid data, depending on the application specifications.
4. If an error is detected, prepare an error message. For this, each map should have the error message fields (e.g., at the bottom four lines of the screen).
5. Do not stop the data validity checking at the first error detection. Go to the next field for another validation.
6. Repeat this until all data fields have been verified or all error message fields have been exhausted.
7. At completion of the data validation, if there are errors, send error message(s) to the terminal for the user to correct them and reenter.

Example

A simple example of data validity checking can be seen in the sample program in Appendix A.

Check List for Data Validation

Validating the data in a field itself is not unique to the online system. Even in the batch system, programs have to perform data validation. As a check list, the following points should be considered against each field:

- Valid data type such as character, integer, decimal
- Valid range of acceptable numeric values such as hhmmss, yymmdd
- Valid number of character or digit allowed
- Valid appearance in the list of "legal" values
- Valid logical relationship to other data item such as mutual exclusiveness

Error Field Highligting

If an error is detected in a field, you might wish to highlight this field. You can do so by placing a bright attribute character using dynamic attribute character assignment technique (see Section 9.7). Since this approach increases user-friendliness, many people use this technique.

However, this puts some burden on the application programming, thereby lowering program maintainability. If you display proper error messages, the terminal user would understand on which field he/she made an error. Therefore, error field highlighting is not necessarily the thing which you always have to do.

9.4   SEND MAP Command

Function

The SEND MAP command is used to send a map to a terminal. Before issuing this command, the application program must prepare the data in the symbolic map of the map to be sent, which has the following three fields per each field defined by the DFHMDF macro:

fieldname+L: The length field, to which the application program does not have to prepare the data except for the dynamic cursor positioning (see Section 9.6).

fieldname+A: The attribute character field, to which the application program does not have to prepare the data except for the dynamic attribute character assignment (see Section 9.7).

fieldname+O: The actual output data field, to which the application program must place the data.

Format

The basic format of SEND MAP command is as follows:

```
EXEC CICS SEND
     MAP(name)
     MAPSET(name)
     [CURSOR]
     [ERASE]
END-EXEC.
```

MAP defines the name of the map defined in the corresponding DFHMDI macro. MAPSET defines the name of the mapset defined in the corresponding DFHMSD macro. CURSOR makes the application program able to position the cursor dynamically on any part of the screen. ERASE erases the current screen before displaying the map to be sent.

If nothing else is specified, the FROM option is assumed, and BMS automatically finds the symbolic map area to take the data to the terminal.

The format shown is the simplest way of issuing the SEND MAP command, for which the map/mapset must be coded with the STORAGE=AUTO option in the corresponding DFHMSD macro. In addition, there are several commonly used options for the SEND MAP command which will be discussed later in this section. You could use these options as required.

In this chapter, we will discuss only basic BMS output operations, while in the next chapter, we will discuss a series of advanced ways of using the SEND MAP command.

Example

Assuming that the names of map and mapset are MPBINQ2 and MSBINQ2, respectively, and that STORAGE=AUTO is specified in the DFHMSD macro, the following is an example of the SEND MAP command:

```
WORKING-STORAGE SECTION.
        :
    COPY MSBINQ2.
        :
        :
PROCEDURE DIVISION.
        :
        :
    MOVE LOW-VALUES TO MPBINQ2O.              <== Recommended.
    (Edit symbolic map using fieldnames(+O).)
        :
    EXEC CICS SEND
        MAP('MPBINQ2')
        MAPSET('MSBINQ2')
        CURSOR                     <== Optional but recommended.
        ERASE
    END-EXEC.
```

Execution Results   CICS automatically finds the symbolic map area (mapname+O) and sends the mapped data to the terminal. Therefore, the data in the area MPBINQ2O will be sent to the terminal.

Commonly Used Options

The following are commonly used options for the basic use of the SEND MAP command:

ERASE: If this is specified, the current screen will be erased before the map specified appears on the screen. If this is not specified, the map specified will be overwritten onto the current screen. Therefore, a double image screen might appear, which may be useful for sending error messages into the current screen, because the current screen will be kept as it is.

ERASEAUP: To erase all unprotected fields. The protected fields or attribute fields remain as they are in the current screen. Therefore, if you have sent the error messages into the protected fields and if you wish to refresh the screen, this option should not be used. Instead, the SEND MAP command with the ERASE option should be used.

FREEKB: To free the keyboard.

ALARM: To make an alarm sound.

FRSET: To reset MDT to zero (i.e., not modified) for all unprotected fields of the screen.

DATAONLY: Only application program data in the symbolic map is to be sent to the terminal. The attribute character must be provided for each field. If the fieldname+A is X'00', the corresponding attribute byte in the screen will not be changed.

MAPONLY: Only the default data from the physical map is to be sent to the terminal. If this option is specified, FROM option must not be specified.

Programming Considerations

It is a good practice to clear (MOVE LOW-VALUES) the symbolic map area in the program before editing for the screen, because it ensures that the default physical map is used as the base.

If the device control options can be specified at the map definition time, do so. In the CICS SEND MAP commands, these options should be specified only when it is definitely required.

The proper use of the DATAONLY or MAPONLY option lightens the communications line traffic. Therefore, if you are using the low speed lines, these options improve the response time significantly. However, this makes programming logic complicated, thereby reducing the maintainability of the program. Therefore, if you are using local terminals or remote terminals through the high speed lines, the DATAONLY or MAPONLY option is not necessarily the option you always have to use. For further discussion, see Section 18.6.

9.5 SEND CONTROL Command

Function

The SEND CONTROL command is used by an application program to dynamically establish the device control options without actually sending a map.

Format

The basic format of the SEND CONTROL command is as follows:

```
CICS EXEC SEND
     CONTROL
     [CURSOR(data-value)]
     [ERASE | ERASEAUP]
     [FREEKB]
     [ALARM]
     [FRSET]
END-EXEC.
```

CURSOR defines the relative cursor position in the screen, start-ing from zero. Other options have the same functions as the options described in the SEND MAP command.

Example

The following is an example of the SEND CONTROL command:

```
CICS EXEC SEND
     CONTROL
     ERASE                    Screen will be cleared.
END-CICS.

CICS EXEC SEND
     MAP(----)
     MAPSET(----)             Map specified will be displayed.
END-EXEC.
```

Execution Results During the execution of this logic, the following activities will occur:

- At the completion of the SEND CONTROL command, the screen will be cleared.
- At the completion of the SEND MAP command, the map will be displayed on the clear screen.

Programming Consideration

If the device control options can be specified at the map definition time, you should do so. It is advisable that you should avoid device control dynamically in the program because of its low maintainability.

9.6   Cursor Positioning Techniques

Placing a cursor in a particular position of a screen is sometimes very useful in order to make the system more user-friendly. There are three approaches to cursor positioning.

Static Positioning

In this approach, you define a cursor position in a map by placing 'IC' in the ATTRB parameter of the DFHMDF macro for a particular field. When the map is sent, the cursor will appear in this field. If there is more than one field (DFHMDF macro) with IC specified in one map (DFHMDI macro), the last IC would be honored. The following is an example of the static cursor positioning:

```
DFHMDF     POS=(3,16),
           ATTRB=(UNPROT,FSET,IC)
           LENGTH=8
```

Dynamic/Symbolic Positioning

In this approach, you dynamically position a cursor through an application program using a symbolic name of the symbolic map by placing -1 into the field length field (i.e., fieldname+L) of the field where you wish to place the cursor. The SEND MAP command to be issued must have the CURSOR option (without value). Also, the mapset must be coded with MODE=INOUT in the DFHMSD macro.

Then, at the completion of the SEND MAP command, the map will be displayed with the cursor at the position dynamically specified in the application program (by -1), irrespective of the static cursor position defined in the map definition time. The following is an example of dynamic/symbolic cursor positioning:

```
       WORKING-STORAGE SECTION.
                   :
           COPY MSBINQ2
C      01  MPBINQ2I.
C          06   FILLER    PIC X(12).
```

```
C           06   FLD1L      PIC S9(4) COMP.
C           06   FLD1F      PIC X.
C           06   FLD1I      PIC X.
                 :
                 :
        PROCEDURE DIVISION.
                 :
            MOVE -1 to FLD1L.
            EXEC CICS SEND
                MAP('MPBINQ2')
                MAPSET('MSBINQ2')
                CURSOR                          <=== Required
                ERASE
            END-EXEC.
```

Execution Results   The cursor will be placed at the FLD1 field of map MPBINQ2.

   This approach provides the application program with complete device independence and format independence. Therefore, this approach is useful when you wish to place the cursor at the field which has data entry error detected by your data edit routine.

Dynamic/Relative Positioning

In this approach, you dynamically position a cursor through an application program using the CURSOR(data-value) option in the SEND MAP command with the value of the relative position (starting from zero) of the terminal. At the completion of the SEND MAP command, the map will be displayed with the cursor at the specified position, overriding the static cursor position defined at the map definition time. The following is an example of the dynamic/relative cursor positioning:

```
EXEC CICS SEND
    MAP(-----)
    MAPSET(-----)
    CURSOR(100)
    ERASE
END-EXEC.
```

Execution Results   The cursor will be placed at position 100 of the terminal, relative to zero at the beginning of the screen.

Although this approach makes the application program able to position the cursor dynamically, since the relative position of the terminal is device dependent, this approach is device dependent and format dependent. Whenever the terminal type is changed or the screen layout is changed, the application program will have to be modified to reflect the change. This lessens the program maintainability.

Programming Considerations

You should specify the default cursor position when you define a map using the static cursor positioning approach. When you need to position the cursor dynamically, you should use the dynamic/symbolic cursor positioning approach instead of the dynamic/relative cursor positioning approach for the better maintainability, since the dynamic/symbolic cursor positioning approach ensures the device and format independence.

Checking Cursor Position

You might wish to know where the cursor was when the data was transmitted from the terminal. This can be easily accomplished by checking EIBCPOSN, which is a halfword (S9(4) COMP) binary field in EIB, and contains offset position (relative to zero) of the cursor in the screen. It is available after the completion of the RECEIVE MAP command.

An application of cursor position checking is the following: You can establish a convention that when a terminal user needs instructions for entering one particular field, he/she positions the cursor at the field and press the PF1 key (for example). Then, the program sends some instruction screen (e.g., HELP screen). For this kind of application, the program must know the position of the cursor, for which EIBCPOSN gives the information required.

9.7 Attribute Character Assignment

An attribute character defines the characteristics of a field on the screen. The attribute character of each field must be defined at the map definition time in the ATTRB parameter of the DFHMDF macro. The attribute character defined in this way remains throughout the system as the default.

However, it is sometimes required to change the charcteristics of a field (e.g., form PROTect to UNPROTect) dynamically through an application program. This section discusses the detail of the attribute character and the technique of assigning it dynamically through an application program.

Attribute Character Format

The attribute character is 1 byte (i.e., 8 bits) of data consisting of the following bit pattern:

Bit	Function
0, 1	Value determined by the contents of bits 2 to 7.
2	0: Unprotected 1: Protected
3	0: Alphanumeric 1: Numeric
2,3	11: Autoskip
4,5	00: Normal Intensity/Nondetectable 01: Normal Intensity/Dectectable 10: High Intensity/Detectable 11: Dark/Nondetectable
6	0: Must be zero.
7	0: Not modified (MDT off) 1: Modified (MDT on)

Standard Attribute Character List

CICS provides the standard attribute character list (DFHBMSCA) in a form of a COPYLIB member (see Appendix D). This list covers most of the required attribute characters for an application program. You can use this list by copying into the Working Storage Section of the application program through the COPY statement as follows:

```
COPY DFHBMSCA
```

Appendix D shows the full content of DFHBMSCA, while the following are some useful standard attribute characters in DFHBMSCA:

DFHBMASK: Autoskip
DFHBMFSE: Unprotected, MDT on
DFHUNNUM: Unprotected, MDT on, numeric
DFHUNIMD: Unprotected, high intensity, MDT on
DFHUNINT: Unprotected, high intensity, MDT on, numeric

User Defined Attribute Character

Using the bit pattern format of the attribute character described above, you can define your own attribute character. As an example, let us construct an attribute character for:

```
Unprotected          )
Numeric              )              B'00011001'
High Intensity       )            = X'19'
Modified             )            = 25
```

The bit pattern and the decimal value for this attribute character will be the ones shown above. Therefore, in the Working Storage Section of the application program, you define:

```
77   ATTR-CHR                      PIC S9(4) COMP VALUE 25.
77   ATTR-FILLER REDEFINES ATTR-CHR.
     02    FILLER                  PIC X.
     02    ATTR-UP-NU-HI-MO        PIC X.    <== Use this.
```

Since the S9(4) COMP is a halfword binary (i.e., 2 bytes) field, in order to use the latter in byte, the above programing technique is required. The field ATTR-UP-NU-HI-MO is the attribute character we tried to create

It should be noted that the attribute character of the above example happens to be DFHUNINT of the standard attribute character list (DFHBMSCA). In Appendix D, the hexadecimal value of DFHUNINT is X'D9'. But, when a 3270 terminal receives an attribute character, only bits 2 to 7 will be used. Therefore, although the value of the above user defined attribute character is X'19', it will achieve the same function as DFHUNINT.

This implies that the DFHBMSCA list has most of the commonly used attribute characters, so that there will be virtually no need for you to define the attribute characters by yourself.

Dynamic Attribute Character Assignment

You can assign a default attribute character in a BMS map. But, in the cases like an edit error in a field, you might wish to highlight the field indicating an error. This can be accomplished by dynamically assigning a new attribute character for the field on subject.

For the dynamic attribute character assignment, you place the pre-defined attribute character (e.g., from the DFHBMSCA list) to the fieldname+A of the field to which you wish to dynamically assign the attribute character.

The attribute character to be dynamically assigned must be chosen very carefully based on the requirements (e.g., for brightening) and the characteristics of the field (e.g., alphanumeric or numeric).

When the map is sent through the SEND MAP command, the new attribute will be in effect on the field on subject, overriding the original attribute defined at the map definition time.

As an example, let us try to position the cursor at the FLD1 field and highlight it. Since the FLD1 field is an alphanumeric input field, we need the standard attribute character DFHUNIMD (unprot, MDT on, bright) for brightening the field. Note that MDT should be set on since this is an input field. Using DFHUNIMD, the following is an example of the dynamic attribute character assignment:

```
        WORKING-STORAGE SECTION
                    :

            COPY DFHBMSCA
            COPY MSBINQ2
C     01 MPBINQ2I.
C            06   FILLER    PIC X(12).
C            06   FLD1L     PIC S9(4) COMP.
C            06   FLD1F     PIC X.
C            06   FLD1I     PIC X(nn).

                    :
                    :

C     01 MPBINQ2O REDEFINES MPBINQ2I.
C            06   FILLER    PIC X(12).
C            06   FILLER    PIC X(2)
C            06   FLD1A     PIC X.
C            06   FLD1O     PIC X(nn).

                    :
                    :
        PROCEDURE DIVISION.
                    :
```

```
EXEC CICS RECEIVE
     MAP('MPBINQ2')
     MAPSET('MSBINQ2')
END-EXEC.
     :
(edit check)
(found FLD1I is wrong.)
(place an error message.)
     :
MOVE -1 TO FLD1L.              <=== Dynamic cursor assign.
MOVE DFHUNIMD to FLD1A.        <=== Dynamic attribute
EXEC CICS SEND                              character assign.
     MAP('MPBINQ2')
     MAPSET('MSBINQ2')
     CURSOR                    <=== Required.
     ERASE
END-EXEC.
```

Execution Results At the completion of this program logic, the following activities will occur:

- The cursor will be positioned at the FLD1 field by the dynamic/symbolic cursor positioning.
- The field will be highlighted by dynamic attribute character assignment.

9.8 Upper/Lower-Case Characters

System Design for Upper-Case Character Only

Most of CICS application systems can be designed using the upper-case characters only. In this case, as per Section 7.8, you can specify in TCT:

```
FEATURE=(UCTRAN,----)
```

Then, when an application program receives data from the terminal which has the specification for UCTRAN, CICS automatically translates all lower-case characters into upper-case characters, regardless of the original form of the input characters. This means that all lower-case characters will be treated as upper-case characters in the application program; that is: "a" is equal to "A," for example.

For the simplicity of the system, this approach is strongly recommended.

System Design for Both Upper/Lower-Case Characters

Some CICS application systems may require both upper-case and lower-case characters. For example, if correspondence is heavily involved between a company and customers, it would look better if you can automatically print the correspondence letter in both upper-case and lower-case characters.

In this case, you should not specify FEATURE=(UCTRAN, ---) in TCT. Then, the data will be sent to (or received from) the terminal as it is; that is: "a" is not equal to "A," for example. It is then the application program's responsibility to translate the upper-case characters to the lower-case characters, or vice versa, if required.

If you use this approach, the application programs will become difficult to maintain. For example, COBOL or PL/I coding must be done in upper-case characters only, while other text could be in upper-case or lower-case characters. Therefore, this approach should be chosen only when it is strongly justified.

Technique of Upper/Lower-Case Translation

If your terminal is not specified for the upper-case characters only (i.e., UCTRAN), and if you wish to treat all lower-case characters from the terminal as the upper-case characters in the program, you can translate all lower-case characters to the upper-case characters in the program using the COBOL TRANSFORM statement.

The following is an example of translation of the lower-case characters to the upper-case characters using the TRANSFORM statement:

```
WORKING-STORAGE SECTION.
      COPY MSBINQ2.
77    UPPER-CHR-SET  PIC X(26) VALUE
            'ABCDE--------XYZ'.                    )  There must be
77    LOWER-CHR-SET  PIC X(26) VALUE
            'abcde--------xyz'.                    )  one-to-one
      :                                            )  correspondence.
```

```
PROCEDURE DIVISION.
        :
      EXEC CICS RECEIVE
           MAP('MPBINQ2')
           MAPSET('MSBINQ2')
      END-EXEC.
      TRANSFORM MPBINQ2I
           CHARACTERS
           FROM LOWER-CHR-SET
           TO   UPPER-CHR-SET.
```

Execution Results   During the execution of this program logic, the following activities will occur:

- At the completion of the RECEIVE MAP command, map area MPBINQ2I will have the symbolic data from the terminal which may have both upper-case and lower-case characters.
- At the completion of the TRANSFORM statement, all lower-case characters in map area MPBINQ2I will be translated to upper-case characters.

TERMINAL ASIS Option

In the RECEIVE MAP command, there is one option called TERMINAL ASIS. If this option is specified, the program receives characters from the terminals as they are (i.e., "a" not = "A"), regardless of whether UCTRAN is specified in TCT entry for the terminal. In effect, therefore, this option neutralizes the UCTRAN specification in TCT.

If you are not sure that your terminal is under the effect of UCTRAN, and if you wish to receive the data always in both upper-case and lower-case characters, the TERMINAL ASIS option should be specified in the RECEIVE MAP command.

9.9   Print Operations through BMS

BMS makes it easy to print reports in the local printer. This can be accomplished by issuing the SEND MAP command with the PRINT option. Then, the map specified will be printed on the printer connected to the same controller to which the display terminal is connected. In this case, since the map is sent to the printer, the map will not be sent to the display terminal.

For the print operations through BMS, you must satisfy one prerequisite that the map specified must have the CTRL=(PRINT,----) parameter in the mapset definition macro (DFHMSD) or map definition macro (DFHMDI).

Format

The format of the SEND MAP command with the PRINT option is shown in the example below. PRINT indicates the map to be sent to the printer instead of the display terminal. For NLEOM, see the further description below.

Example

Taking the same map/mapset in Section 9.4, the following is an example of the BMS print operation using the SEND MAP command with the PRINT option:

```
EXEC CICS SEND
     MAP('MPBINQ2)
     MAPSET('MSBINQ2')
     PRINT
     NLEOM                          <=== Recommended.
END-EXEC.
```

Execution Results Map MPBINQ2/MSBINQ2 will be printed in the printer instead of the display terminal.

NLEOM Option

The NLEOM option is recommended when the PRINT option is specified in the SEND MAP command. If NLEOM is specified, BMS builds the data stream using the New Line characters and blank characters to position the fields on the printer page. The data stream is terminated by the EOM (end of message) which stops printing. Consequently the NLEOM option can manage the printer buffer more efficiently, and it may allow larger pages to be printed from the same buffer. Therefore, the printing speed would be much faster.

Programming Considerations

The printers involve a complex hardware mechanism which causes mechanical troubles frequently, such as paper jam, and print ribbon jam. Therefore, a transaction which involves file updates should not use the PRINT option.

The PRINT option should be used in the transaction which does not involve any file updates, because if the transaction only reads the files (without update or write), then the transaction can be simply reentered for printing in case of the mechanical failure of the printer.

9.10 Edit-Error Screen Approach

Usually the bottom few lines of a screen should be reserved for displaying the error messages. The best way to handle this situation is to define a body mapset and an error mapset and to send the latter without the ERASE option.

Example

As an example, let us assume that the body map/mapset and error map/mapset are defined as follows:

```
Body Mapset (MSBODR2):   20x80            --------------------
Error Mapset (MSBERR1):    4x80           I      MSBODR2       I
                                          I                    I
                                          --------------------
                                          I      MSBERR1       I
                                          --------------------
```

Then, the following is an example of the edit-error screen approach:

```
WORKING-STORAGE SECTION.
01   WK-COMMAREA.
     05   WK-INT-TRNID       PIC X(4).
     :
     COPY MSBODR2.
     COPY MSBERR1.
     :
*
```

```
LINKAGE SECTION.
01   DFHCOMMAREA.
     05   INT-TRNID          PIC X(4).
*
PROCEDURE DIVISION.
     IF EIBTRNID NOT = 'ODR1'
          GO TO LOGIC-ERR.
     IF EIBCALEN=0
          GO TO ODR1-RTN.
     IF INT-TRNID = 'ODR2'
          GO TO ODR2-RTN.
     GO TO LOGIC-ERR.
ODR1-RTN.
     :
     MOVE LOW-VALUES TO MPBODR2O.
     : (Prepare data for MSBODR2 for output)
     :
*
* SEND MAP MSBODR2 (BODY)
*
     EXEC CICS SEND
          MAP('MPBODR2')
          MAPSET('MSBODR2')
          ERASE
          CURSOR
     END-EXEC.
*
* RETURN FOR PSEUDO-CONVERSATIONAL MODE.
*
ODR1-RETURN.
     MOVE 'ODR2' TO WK-INT-TRNID.
     EXEC CICS RETURN
          TRANSID('ODR1')
          COMMAREA(WK-COMMAREA)
          LENGTH(4)
     END-EXEC.
*
* ODR2 LOGIC.
*
ODR2-RTN.
*
* RECEIVE MAP MSBODR2
*
     EXEC CICS RECEIVE
```

```
            MAP('MPBODR2')
            MAPSET('MSBODR2')
       EXD-EXEC.
       :
       : (Field editing)
       : (If no edit errors, go to EDIT-OK.)
   EDIT-ERR.
       MOVE LOW-VALUES TO MPBERR1O.
       :
       : (Prepare edit error messages onto MSBERR1 map)
       :
       EXEC CICS SEND
            MAP('MPBERR1')
            MAPSET('MSBERR1')
       END-EXEC.                    <== ERASE must not be specified.
       GO TO ODR1-RETURN.
*
   EDIT-OK.
       :
       : (Further processing)
       :
```

Execution Results   During the execution of this program logic, the following activities will occur:

- During the first iteration, the body map (MPBODR2/MSBODR2) will be sent to the terminal.
- During the second iteration, the error map (MPBERR1/MSBERR1) will be displayed, overriding the body map (MPBODR2/ MSBODR2), but without interfering with the body map (that is, the body map will be kept as is), because the ERASE option is not specified in the SEND MAP command.
- In effect, the error message will appear at the bottom of the original screen.

Advantages

This approach is easy to use and it reduces the data traffic in the communications line, thereby improving the terminal response time. If you use this approach, you do not have to be heavily concerned with the DATAONLY or MAPONLY option when you display the body screen. This improves maintainability.

Drawback

If you use this approach, you cannot dynamically assign cursor or attribute character on the body mapset when you send the error mapset. Therefore, it is not possible to highlight error fields or place cursor to the error field. But, if you carefully prepare the error messages, the terminal user understands where the errors are. Therefore, this is a minor drawback.

9.11   Text Building by BMS

BMS provides the function of text building which is used for the output operations. Through the BMS text building function, a text will be displayed within the margins determined by the device (i.e., display terminal or printer), without requiring the formatting by the program. This means that no BMS maps are required for the BMS text operations.

BMS automatically segments the text stream into lines, breaking the stream at a word boundary, that is, no words will be cut in the middle, while the new line character (X'15') and space (X'40') embedded in the text will be honored.

Type of Text Stream

There are two types of text stream, as shown below. The single text stream consists of only one text body (define in the Working Storage Section), whereas the multitext stream consists of more than one text body, each of which is defined in the Working Storage Section. The single text stream and the multitext stream could have either the header or trailer or both as the option.

```
Single text stream          Multitext stream

    ----------                  ----------
    I Header I                  I Header I

    ----------                  ----------
    I Body I                    I Body 1 I

    ----------                  ----------
    I Trailer I                 I Body 2 I

                                ----------
                                I Body 3 I

                                ----------
                                I Trailer I
```

Programmer's Task

If the BMS text building function is used, the programmer's task becomes as simple as follows:

1. Build a text stream in the Working Storage Section. There could be more than one text stream.
2. If required, prepare a header.
3. If required, prepare a trailer.
4. If it is a single text stream, issue the SEND TEXT command.
5. If it is a multitext stream, issue a series of SEND TEXT commands with the ACCUM option, then issue the SEND PAGE command.

In this chapter, we will discuss the basic BMS text building function. Therefore, we assume that the text will be displayed in one screen. A case which involves a multipage text will be discussed in the next chapter.

9.12   SEND TEXT Command (without ACCUM)

Function

The SEND TEXT command without the ACCUM option is used to send a single-stream text to a terminal. For this command, BMS maps are not required.

Format

The basic format of the SEND TEXT command without the ACCUM option is as follows:

```
EXEC CICS SEND TEXT
     FROM(data-value)
     LENGTH(data-value)
     [HEADER(data-value)]
     [TRAILER(data-value)]
     [ERASE]
END-EXEC.
```

FROM defines the text body field in the Working Storage Section. LENGTH (the halfword binary field, S9(4) COMP) indicates the length of the text to be sent, excluding the header or trailer (if any). HEADER (optional) and TRAILER (optional) names the header data and trailer data, respectively, which require the special format (see Section 9.14). ERASE indicates the screen to be cleared before the text is displayed.

Example

The following is an example of the SEND TEXT command without the ACCUM option:

```
WORKING-STORAGE SECTION.
01    TEXT-HEADER             -------               (see Section 9.14)
01    TEXT-TRAILER            -------               (see Section 9.14)
77    TEXT-BODY          PIC X(400).
77    TEXT-LENGTH.        PIC S9(4) COMP.
PROCEDURE DIVISION.
      :
      :
      MOVE '----(any text)----'           <== Edit the text
          TO TEXT-BODY.
      MOVE 364 TO TEXT-LENGTH.             <== Set actual length.
      EXEC CICS SEND TEXT
          FROM(TEXT-BODY)
          LENGTH(TEXT-LENGTH)
          HEADER(TEXT-HEADER)              <== Optional.
          TRAILER(TEXT-TRAILER)            <== Optional.
          ERASE
      EXD-EXEC.
```

Execution Results   The text will appear in the order of header, body, and trailer. The text line will be automatically broken at the word boundary.

Commonly Used Option

The following is the commonly used option of the SEND TEXT command without the ACCUM option:

PRINT: If you wish printing instead of displaying the text on the screen, specify the PRINT option. Also, the NLEOM option is recommended.

Programming Considerations

The SEND command without the ACCUM option should be used only for a single page screen. Therefore, you must make sure that the text will be displayed within one screen, taking into account the header and trailer. If the overflow occurs, BMS automatically splits the page and creates the next page. However, in the terminal, the split screen overrides the original screen. In effect, the terminal user will see only the split screen. We will discuss in the next chapter how to handle this kind of case.

9.13 Multitext Operations

Function

In many occasions, you might wish to send several paragraphs of text, each of which is defined separately in the Working Storage Section of the program, as one message to the terminal. In this case, since one message (one logical text) consists of several paragraphs (several text blocks), let us call this type of message a "multitext" message. The multitext operation is used to send this multitext message to the terminal as one logical text.

For the multitext operations, it is required to use two commands as follows:

1. Use the SEND TEXT command with the ACCUM option for accumulating the text blocks.
2. Then, issue the SEND PAGE command to send the entire text (i.e., logical message).

For simplicity, in this section, let us limit the amount of text in the multitext message so that the multitext message can be displayed in one screen (more accurately, one page of the screen). We will discuss the case of the multitext/multipage message in the next chapter.

Format

The format of the SEND TEXT command with the ACCUM option and the SEND PAGE command is shown in the example below. In the SEND TEXT command, ACCUM must be explicitly specified as the option. Other options and parameters are the same as the case of

the SEND TEXT command without the ACCUM option. In the
SEND PAGE command, the TRAILER (optional) indicates the trailer
to be sent after the last text block accumulation.

Example

The following is an example of multitext operations using the SEND
TEXT with the ACCUM option and the SEND PAGE command:

```
WORKING-STORAGE SECTION.
01    TEXT-HEADER        -------              (see Section 9.14)
01    TEXT-TRAILER       -------              (see Section 9.14)
77    TEXT-BODY1         PIC X(100) VALUE '---stream 1---'.
77    TEXT-BODY2         PIC X(200) VALUE '---stream 2---'.
77    TEXT-BODY3         PIC X(150) VALUE '---stream 3---'.
77    TEXT-LENGTH.       PIC S9(4) COMP.
        :
PROCEDURE DIVISION.
        :
*
* SEND BODY 1.
*
      MOVE 100 TO TEXT-LENGTH.          <== Set actual length.
      EXEC CICS SEND TEXT
          FROM(TEXT-BODY1)
          LENGTH(TEXT-LENGTH)
          HEADER(TEXT-HEADER)           <== Optional.
          ACCUM                         <== Accumulate.
          ERASE
      EXD-EXEC.
*
* SEND BODY 2.
*
      MOVE 200 TO TEXT-LENGTH.          <== Set actual length.
      EXEC CICS SEND TEXT
          FROM(TEXT-BODY2)
          LENGTH(TEXT-LENGTH)
          ACCUM                         <== Accumulate.
          ERASE
      EXD-EXEC.
*
* SEND BODY 3.
```

```
*
      MOVE 150 TO TEXT-LENGTH.            <== Set actual length.
      EXEC CICS SEND TEXT
           FROM(TEXT-BODY3)
           LENGTH(TEXT-LENGTH)
           ACCUM                          <== Accumulate.
           ERASE
      EXD-EXEC.
*
* SEND ENTIRE TEXT.
*
      EXEC CICS SEND PAGE
           TRAILER(TEXT-TRAILER)
      END-EXEC.
```

Execution Results During the execution of this program logic, the following activities will occur:

• At the completion of each SEND TEXT command with the ACCUM option, the text bodies (1, 2, and 3) will be accumulated.
• At the completion of the SEND PAGE command, the entire logical message will be sent to the terminal. The text will appear in the order of Header, Body1, Body2, Body3 and Trailer, each of which will be displayed as a paragraph (i.e., starting from column 1 of the next line).
• If the ERASE option is specified with the ACCUM option in the SEND TEXT command, only the first SEND TEXT command will honor the erase function. Therefore, in the above example, bodies 2 and 3 will appear in the same screen as body 1.

Programming Considerations

As per the restriction made in this section, the same programming considerations as in the previous section are applied. You should make sure that the text will fit in one screen.

9.14 Text Header and Trailer

The header and/or trailer can be attached to the text body during command execution, as has been shown in the examples in the previous two sections. For this, the header and/or trailer must be constructed based on the format convention.

Format

The format of the text header and trailer is as follows:

```
LLPCdata----------pppp--------data----------------------------
```

where,

LL:	The halfword binary field (S9(4) COMP) containing length of the data excluding the prefix expressed in LLPC.
P:	A character denoting the position of the page number if automatic paging is requested. If automatic paging is not requested, this one byte should be a space.
C:	One-byte control field used by BMS.
data:	The actual data of the header or trailer.
pppp:	The position and length of the automatic page number if the automatic paging is requested. The character must be the same one specified in P.

Example

As an example, let us assume the following header:

```
COMPANY PROFILE   - PAGE nn -
```

Then, the following is an example of a typical Working Storage Section coding for the header above:

```
01   TEXT-HEADER.
     05   FILLER   PIC S9(4) COMP VALUE 29.
     05   FILLER   PIC X VALUE '&'.
     05   FILLER   PIC X.
     05   FILLER   PIC X(29) VALUE
                   'COMPANY PROFILE   - PAGE && -'.
```

Execution Results CICS automatically place the page number in the page field (&&) when the header is displayed.

Exercise

Using the map (MPBIPE2/MSBIPE2) coded in the Exercise for Chapter 8, develop the Insurance Policy Entry (IPE1) transaction, based on the following specifications:

1. Transaction id is IPE1 and Program id is TXT9IPE1.
2. The program uses the Personnel Master File (PERVSPMS) described in the Exercise for Chapter 4.
3. Set up the premium table in the program as follows:

Coverage Code	Base Premium
A1	50.00
B1	100.00
C1	150.00

4. The program starts with sending map MPBIPE2/MSBIPE2 to the terminal. Return with the external transaction id = IPE1 and the internal transaction id = IPE2.
5. Upon receiving control again, receive the map. Validate the input data. The employee number received must exist in the PMS file, but he/she must not have the policy number already in the PMS record. The coverage codes received must exist in the premium table. If the data is invalid, position the cursor onto the error field, highlight the field, prepare the error message at the bottom of IPE2 map. Repeat this for all errors, then send IPE2 map. Return with the external transaction id = IPE1 and the internal transaction id = IPE2, so that the user can correct and reenter.
6. If the data is valid, calculate individual insurance premiums based on the coverage codes as follows:

$$Premium = Base\ Premium * (Sex\ Factor) * (100 + AGE)/100$$

   where Sex Factor = 1.00 for 'M'(ale) 1.20 for 'F'(emale).
7. Calculate the total premium. Update the PMS record of this employee for the policy number and total premium. Rewrite the record.
8. Edit the map for the name, room, extension, individual premium, and total premium. Send the map and terminate the task.
9. As usual, the programming standard for Handle Condition must be maintained.
10. During the entire operation, if the PF12 key is pressed, send a cancellation message and forcefully terminate the transaction.

10

BMS(3): Advanced Applications

10.1 Types of BMS Panel Operations

In the previous chapter, we discussed CICS commands for the simple BMS panel (screen) operations. Actually, BMS is able to deal with a variety of panel (screen) operations, such as:

1. *Single Map Panel*
   The single map panel is a panel consisting of one BMS map. This is the most common type of panel for BMS operations.
2. *Text Panel*
   The text panel is a panel consisting of one or more text blocks. This type of panel does not use BMS maps, but it is very useful for text operations.
3. *Multipage Message*
   The multipage message is a message consisting of a series of pages (panels). This is useful for displaying a large amount of information on the terminal at once. There are two cases:
   • Single map panel case
   • Text case
4. *Multimap Panel*
   The multimap panel is a single panel consisting of several BMS maps. This is useful for constructing a complex panel. There are two cases:
   • Static panel case
   • Dynamic panel case

5. *Multimap / Multipage Message*
   The multimap/multipage message is a message consisting of a series of panels, each of which consists of more than one map; that is, a combination of 3 and 4. There are two cases:
   • Static panel case
   • Dynamic panel case

   In the previous chapter, we discussed the basic BMS panel operations of single map panel and text panel. In this chapter, we will discuss the remaining BMS panel operations as well as other advanced topics related to BMS.

10.2   Multipage Message with Single Map Panel

Function

The operation of the multipage message with single map panel is used to send a logical message consisting of a series of single map panels (called pages), similar to the one in Figure 10-1.

Programming

For the operations of multipage message with single map panel, the application program must follow the following procedures:

1. Issue the SEND MAP command with the ACCUM and PAGING options, which accumulates the map as a multipage message.
2. Repeat step 1 until all maps have been accumulated.
3. Issue the SEND PAGE command, which actually sends the entire maps as one logical message (i.e., multipage message).

Command Format

The format of the SEND MAP command with the ACCUM and PAGING options and the SEND PAGE command is shown in the example below. In the SEND MAP command, ACCUM and PAGING must be explicitly specified for accumulating the maps as the multipage message. Other options and parameters of the SEND MAP command are the same as the case of Section 9.4. The options and parameters of the SEND PAGE command are the same as the case of Section 9.13, with the additional comments to be made later in this section.

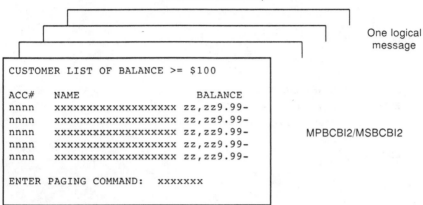

Figure 10-1 Example of multipage message with single map panel.

Example

As an example, let us assume an application with which you wish to display a list of all customers, whose balances are equal to or greater than $100, using the screen shown in Figure 10-1. There may be more than one screen required to display all of those customers, which implies that the application requires the multipage message.

The simplified program specifications for this application are as follows:

- Browse the Customer Master File.
- Select the customers who have a balance of no less than $100.00.
- Edit onto Map/Mapset MPBCBI2/MSBCBI2, which can contain data of up to five customers.
- If the map becomes full, send the map for accumulating into a logical message.
- Repeat until the EOF.
- Send the logical message, which consists of several MSBCBI2 maps.
- Terminate the transaction.

The following is an example of the multipage message with a single map panel, based on the program specifications above.

```
WORKING-STORAGE SECTION.
77   LINE-COUNTER        PIC S9(4) COMP.
     :
```

```
        COPY MSBCBI2.
        :
        :
  PROCEDURE DIVISION.
        :
        :
        MOVE 0 TO LINE-COUNTER.
        EXEC CICS STARTBR -------------- END-EXEC.
        EXEC CICS HANDLE CONDITION
            ENDFILE(EOF-RTN)
        END-EXEC.
*
* EDIT MAP MSBCBI2.
*
  LOOP1.
        (Establish Record length)
        EXEC CICS READNEXT ---------- END-EXEC.
        IF CUST-BAL < 100.00
            GO TO LOOP1.
        ADD 1 TO LINE-COUNTER.
        :
        : (Edit data in the proper line of MSBCBI2.)
        :
        IF LINE-COUNTER < 5
            GO TO LOOP1.
*
* ACCUMULATE A PAGE.
*
        EXEC CICS SEND
            MAP('MPBCBI2')
            MAPSET('MSBCBI2')
            ERASE
            ACCUM            )    <== Page accumulation.  (At this
            PAGING           )        point, CICS does not send
        END-EXEC.                     actual screen yet.)
            MOVE 0 TO LINE-COUNTER.
            GO TO LOOP1.
  EOF-RTN.
        EXEC CICS ENDBR ---------- END-EXEC.
        IF LINE-COUNTER = 0
            GO TO PAGE-RTN.
        EXEC CICS SEND
            MAP('MPBCBI2')
```

```
            MAPSET('MSBCBI2')
            ERASE
            ACCUM
            PAGING
       END-EXEC.
 *
 * SEND A LOGICAL MESSAGE (ENTIRE PAGES).
 *
  PAGE-RTN.
       EXEC CICS SEND              <== At this point, a series of
           PAGE                        screens are actually sent.
       END-EXEC.
 *
 * TERMINATE TASK.
 *
  RETURN-RTN.
       EXEC CICS RETURN
       END-EXEC.
```

Execution Results   During the execution of this program logic, the following activities will occur:

• At each SEND MAP/ACCUM/PAGING command, the map MPBCBI2/MSBCBI2 will be accumulated as a multipage message.
• At the completion of the SEND PAGE command, a series of maps MPBCBI2/MSBCBI2 will be sent to the terminal as one logical message (i.e., one multipage message).

SEND PAGE command

The function of the SEND PAGE command (see Appendix B) is to send a logical message which consists of more than one map or text block to the terminal. Usually, it is used without any options or parameters as shown in the example above.

There are a few options in the SEND PAGE command, in addition to the TRAILER option discussed in Section 8.13. However, the SEND PAGE command should be issued without other options. If you specify the other options, you should know the exact meaning of the options.

One unique option is OPERPURGE. If this is specified, the BMS logical message will be purged only when the operator types the Page Terminate command (T/A: see Section 10.3). If this option is not specified, the logical message will be kept in the Temporary Storage Queue (see Chapter 12), and will be purged when nonpaging command is entered (i.e., usually a transaction id for a new transaction). Therefore, unless you really need to specify OPERPURGE, it should not be specified.

For Printing

If you wish to print the multipage message in the printer instead of displaying to the display terminal, you can do so by specifying the PRINT option (with the NLEOM option recommended) in the first SEND MAP/ACCUM/PAGING command, and by specifying the AUTOPAGE option in the SEND PAGE command. This causes all panels to be automatically sent to the printer.

10.3 Paging Commands

The paging commands are used to retrieve one page of one multipage message (one logical message) which consists of more than one page of screen.

Suppose that one multipage message (a logical message) consists of 10 pages (panels). The first page will be automatically displayed at the terminal after the SEND PAGE command is executed in the program, while the other physical pages are stored in the Temporary Storage Queue by CICS. However, in order to get the next page (or other pages), the terminal user must type the paging commands on the existing panel on the terminal. Once a paging command is typed, the appropriate page will be displayed.

Therefore, every panel (screen) in the multipage message should have one unprotected field (e.g., 10 bytes field) for the paging commands to be typed, as in the following example:

```
----------------------------------------
I                                       I
I            (Body of Panel)            I
I                                       I
I                                       I
I   ENTER PAGING COMMAND: xxxxxxxxxx    I
----------------------------------------
```

Commonly Used Paging Command

The following are the commonly used paging commands (P/x) and their examples:

Format: P/x,

where x is:		Example
n:	n-th page	P/2
+n:	"n" page forward	P/+1
-n:	"n" page backword	P/-1
C:	Current page	P/C
N:	Next page	P/N
P:	Previous page	P/P
L:	Last page	P/L

Other Paging Commands

There are other paging commands for special purposes, and these commands should be used with care and attention. The following are some of these special paging commands:

- T/x: For terminating the page. (e.g., T/A, T/B, T/C)
- C/tttt: For copying the page to a terminal (tttt).
- X/yyyy: For chaining the message queue to a task (yyyy).
- P/Q: For displaying the title of the routed message (see Section 10.12).

Technical Notes

The paging commands mentioned above are actually the user-defined codes for the paging functions which are defined in the System Initialization Table (SIT). Usually, they are defined in SIT in the following way:

PGCHAIN=X/	for Page Chain
PGCOPY=C/	for Page Copy
PGPURGE=T/	for Page Purge
PGRET=P/	for Page Retrieval

But your installation may have different definitions. This means that the P/x command is not necessarily for page retrieval in your installation. You should check with your system programmer for the valid paging commands in your installation.

10.4   Single-Keystroke Retrieval (SKR)

If the terminal user has to type the paging commands each time the user wishes the next page (or other pages), the page retrieval operation may not be user-friendly. The Single-Keystroke Retrieval (SKR) operation provides the user with the same functions as the paging commands but by pressing only PF keys or PA keys, thereby simplifying the page retrieval operations.

Defining SKR Keys

The SKR keys are the user-defined keys. Therefore, you (or your system programmer) have to define them into CICS. The following two steps define the SKR keys:

1. In SIT (System Initialization Table) macro (DFHSIT), specify:

    ```
    SKRxxxx='Page retrieval command' parameter,
    ```

    where   xxxx is PF1 to PF24 or PA1 to PA3. For example:

    ```
    SKRPF8='P/N':   For page forward (next page)
    SKRPF7='P/P':   For page backward (previous page)
    SKRPF3='P/L':   For the last page
    SKRPF5='P/1':   For the first page
    ```

2. In PCT macro (DFHPCT), specify one entry per each SKRxxxx as follows:

    ```
    DFHPCT      TYPE=ENTRY,
                TASKREQ=PF8,        <== Change for all PF and PA
                PROGRAM=DFHTPR,         keys defined in SKRxxxx.
                CLASS=SHORT,
                DTIMOUT=0500,
                RTIMOUT=1500,
                SPURGE=YES,
                RESTART=YES,
                TWASIZE=800
    ```

Using SKR Keys

When a multipage message (a logical message) is sent to the terminal, just press the PF or PA keys assigned for the SKR operations (instead of typing paging commands). The PF keys or PA keys will trigger the same function performed by the paging command.

It should be noted that even if you define the SKR keys, the paging commands are still valid. You can use SKR keys as well as the paging command, if you wish.

10.5   PURGE MESSAGE Command

Function

When a multipage message (a logical message) is being built (i.e., pages are being accumulated), the application program might encounter some abnormal situation (e.g., an exceptional condition detected) and realize that it is no longer necessary to build the logical message. In this kind of case, the application program can issue the PURGE MESSAGE command. The command will purge the multipage message (a logical message) which has been built thus far in the Temporary Storage Queue by BMS.

Format

The format of the PURGE MESSAGE is as follows:

```
EXEC CICS PURGE
     MESSAGE
END-EXEC.
```

Example

The following is an example of the PURGE MESSAGE command:

```
        :
    EXEC CICS HANDLE CONDITION
        ENDFILE(EOF-RTN)            <== To detect EOF.
        ERROR(PURGE-RTN)            <== To detect abnormal error.
```

```
          END-EXEC.
LOOP-RTN.
     (Prepare for sequential read)
     EXEC CICS READNEXT ---------
     END-EXEC.
     (Edit a map)
     EXEC CICS SEND
          MAP(-------)
          MAPSET(-------)
          ACCUM                      <== Accumulate maps.
          PAGING                     <== Build pages.
     END-EXEC.
     GO TO LOOP-RTN.
EOF-RTN.
     EXEC CICS SEND
          PAGE                       <== Send the logical message.
     END-EXEC.                       (Normal case)
     GO TO RETURN-RTN.
PURGE-RTN.
     EXEC CICS PURGE
          MESSAGE                    <== Purge the logical message.
     END-EXEC.                       (Abnormal case)
RETURN-RTN.
     EXEC CICS RETURN
     END-EXEC.
```

Execution Results During the execution of this program logic, the following activities will occur:

- At each SEND MAP/ACCUM/PAGING command, the map will be accumulated as a multipage message (a logical message).
- If the general error condition (i.e., ERROR) is detected during the READNEXT command, the logical message will be purged by the PURGE MESSAGE command. Otherwise, the logical message will be built until the end of the file (i.e., ENDFILE), then the entire logical message will be sent to the terminal by the SEND PAGE command.
- If the PURGE MESSAGE command is not issued, the logical message built thus far in the form of the Temporary Storage Queue will remain until the next transaction is activated.

10.6 Multipage Message with Text

Function

Similar to the nontext case, the text can be sent in the form of multipage message. That is, the operation of the multipage message with the text is used to send a logical message consisting of a series of text pages (panels), similar to the one in Figure 10-2.

Programming

For the operations of multipage message with text, the application program must follow the following procedures:

1. Issue the SEND TEXT command with the ACCUM and PAGING options, which accumulates a text block as a multipage message.
2. Repeat step 1 until all text blocks have been sent.
3. Issue the SEND PAGE command, which actually sends the entire text as one logical message (i.e., multipage message).

Command Format

The format of the SEND TEXT command with the ACCUM and PAGING options and the SEND PAGE command is shown in the example below. The format is the same as in the case of Section 9.13, except that for the multipage message with text, the SEND TEXT command also requires the PAGING option.

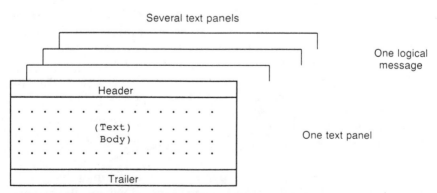

Figure 10-2 Example of multipage message with single map panel.

Example

The following is an example of the SEND TEXT command with the ACCUM and PAGING options and the SEND PAGE command for the multipage message with text:

```
LOOP-RTN.
      (Edit a text block in the body.)
      EXEC CICS SEND
            TEXT
            FROM(--------)
            LENGTH(-------)
            HEADER(-------)            <== Optional.
            TRAILER(-------)           <== Optional.
            ERASE                      <== Honors the first page only.
            ACCUM              )
            PAGING             )       <== Text page accumulation.
      END-EXEC.
             :
      (If more text to be built, go to LOOP-RTN.)
             :
SEND-PAGE-RTN.
      EXEC CICS SEND
            PAGE               <== Send a logical message of text.
            TRAILER(-------)   <== Optional.
END-EXEC.
```

Execution Results   During the execution of this program logic, the following activities will occur:

- At the completion of each SEND TEXT/ACCUM/PAGING command, the text blocks will be accumulated as a multipage message. If one text block (i.e., the contents of the FROM parameter) exceed one panel, BMS automatically splits into the next page.
- At the completion of the SEND PAGE command, the multipage message of the entire text stream will be sent to the terminal.

Technical Notes

The terminal user must use the paging commands in order to retrieve each page of the multipage text message. However, in the case of the BMS text operations, which are for output only, there is no input field in the screen to type any paging commands. Therefore, the SKR operations are the only ways of performing the paging commands for retrieving pages. If your installation does not have the SKR keys defined yet, you should define them by yourself.

The header and trailer texts can be attached as basic text operations. The header and trailer texts must be constructed based on the format convention in Section 9.14. If the TRAILER option is specified in the SEND TEXT command, the trailer text will appear at the bottom of each page. If the TRAILER option is specified in the SEND PAGE command, the trailer text will appear in the last paragraph of the last page only.

The PURGE MESSAGE command can be issued if you wish to purge the message after it has been built, before it is sent.

10.7   Multimap/Static Panel

Characteristics of Panel

A multimap/static panel is a panel which consists of more than one map, each of which has an absolute position in the entire panel. A typical example of this type of panel might consist of the header map, body map, and trailer map, as shown in Figure 10-3.

Map Coding

For coding the multimap/static panel, you code a mapset with several maps using the BMS macros (i.e., DFHMSD, DFHMDI, DFHMDF). In the DFHMDI macro, you specify the absolute position

	Mapset	MCBINQ2
Header Map	Map	MCBINQH
Body Map	Map	MCBINQB
Trailer Map	Map	MCBINQT

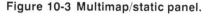

Figure 10-3 Multimap/static panel.

of each map in the parameters COLUMN and LINE. Also, you specify HEADER=YES or TRAILER=YES for the header or trailer, respectively, if required.

Using the panel layout shown above as an example, the following is an example of the BMS map coding for the multimap/static panel:

```
MSBINQ2   DFHMSD    TYPE=MAP,
                    MODE=INOUT,
                    LANG=COBOL,
                    STORAGE=AUTO,
                    TIOAPFX=YES,
                    CNTL=(FREEKB,FRSET,PRINT)
MPBINQH   DFHMDI    SIZE=(02,80),
                    LINE=1,                   <== Absolute position.
                    COLUMN=1,                 <== Absolute position.
                    HEADER=YES                <== Header map.
          DFHMDF    ----------                <== Field definitions.
                       :
MPBINQB   DFHMDI    SIZE=(17,80),
                    LINE=4,                   <== Absolute position.
                    COLUMN=1                  <== Absolute position.
          DFHMDF    ----------                <== Field definitions.
             :
MPBINQT   DFHMDI    SIZE=(02,80),
                    LINE=23,                  <== Absolute position.
                    COLUMN=1,                 <== Absolute position.
                    TRAILER=YES               <== Trailer map.
          DFHMDF    ----------                <== Field definitions.
             :
```

Programming

In order to send a multimap/static panel to a terminal, the application program must follow the following procedures:

1. Issue the SEND MAP command with the ACCUM option (without PAGING option), which accumulates the map for a logical panel.
2. Repeat step 1 above until all maps have been accumulated.
3. At the end of a "logical panel," issue the SEND PAGE command, which sends the entire logical panel.

Using the maps coded above, the following is an example of the SEND MAP command with the ACCUM option and the SEND PAGE command for the multimap/static panel operations:

```
    :
    EXEC CICS SEND                  <== Accumulate the header map.
         MAP('MPBINQH')
         MAPSET('MSBINQ2')
         ERASE
         ACCUM                      <== PAGING not required.
         CURSOR
    END-EXEC.
    :
    : (Edit the body map)
    :
    EXEC CICS SEND                  <== Accumulate the body map.
         MAP('MPBINQB')
         MAPSET('MSBINQ2')
         ERASE
         ACCUM                      <== PAGING not required.
         CURSOR
    END-EXEC.
    EXEC CICS SEND                  <== Accumulate the trailer map.
         MAP('MPBINQT')
         MAPSET('MSBINQ2')
         ERASE
         ACCUM                      <== PAGING not required.
         CURSOR
    END-EXEC.
*
    EXEC CICS SEND                  <== Send the logical panel.
         PAGE
    END-EXEC.
```

Execution Results   During the execution of this program logic, the following activities will occur:

- At the completion of each SEND MAP/ACCUM command, the header map, body map, and trailer map will be accumulated for a logical panel.
- At the completion of the SEND PAGE command, the multimap/static panel (one single panel of three maps) will appear on the terminal.

Technical Notes

The ERASE option in the SEND MAP command with the ACCUM option will be honored only the first time. That is, the ERASE option specified in the subsequent SEND MAP/ACCUM commands (for the body and trailer maps, in the case above) will be ignored.

Although the program issues the SEND PAGE command, since the multimap/static panel is one panel, it is not required that terminal users use the paging commands for retrieving the panels.

10.8 Multimap/Dynamic Panel

Characteristics of Panel

A multimap/dynamic panel is a panel which consists of more than one map, but each map's position is relative to other maps. BMS determines the actual map position at the execution time. A typical example of this type of panel might consist of the header map, one-line body map, and trailer map, as shown in Figure 10-4.

Map Coding

For creating the multimap/dynamic panel, you prepare BMS map coding similar to the case of the multimap/static panel. But, in the case of the multimap/dynamic panel, you specify in DFHMDI macro,

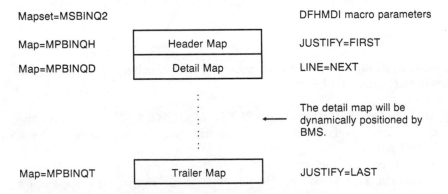

Figure 10-4 Example of multimap/dynamic panel.

the relative position of each map using the JUSTIFY, LINE, COL-UMN options, as shown in Figure 10-4.

Actually, the JUSTIFY, LINE, COLUMN options can be specified in any combination of below:

```
JUSTIFY=([LEFT | RIGHT],        Map to be left or right justified.
          [FIRST | LAST])        Map to be first or last of panel.


LINE=number | NEXT | SAME
```

where,

number:	Absolute line position in the panel.
NEXT:	Next line after the previous map sent.
SAME:	Same line as the previous map sent.

```
COLUMN=number | NEXT | SAME
```

where,

number:	Absolute column position in the panel.
NEXT:	Next column after the previous map sent.
SAME:	Same column as the previous map sent.

Also, the header map or trailer map can be identified by specifying in the DFHMDI macro:

```
HEADER=YES
```

or

```
TRAILER=YES
```

Using the panel layout shown above as an example, the following is an example of BMS map coding for the multimap/dynamic panel:

```
MSBINQ2   DFHMSD    TYPE=MAP,
                    MODE=INOUT,
                    LANG=COBOL,
                    STORAGE=AUTO,
                    TIOAPFX=YES,
                    CNTL=(FREEKB,FRSET,PRINT)
MPBINQH   DFHMDI    SIZE=(2,80),
```

```
                        JUSTIFY=FIRST,           <== First map
                        HEADER=YES               <== Header map
            DFHMDF      -------------
            :
MPBINQD     DFHMDI      SIZE=(1,80),             <== One line detail map
                        LINE=NEXT          <== Next line positioning
            DFHMDF      -------------
            :
MPBINQT     DFHMDI      SIZE=(2,80),
                        JUSTIFY=LAST,            <== Last map
                        TRAILER=YES              <== Trailer map
            DFHMDF      -------------
            :
```

Programming

The programming for sending a multimap/dynamic panel is the same as the case of the multimap/static panel. That is, you issue a series of the SEND MAP/ACCUM commands for accumulating the map as a logical panel, and issue the SEND PAGE command for sending the logical panel. The difference will appear in the terminal side. That is, the actual map position will be dynamically determined at the execution time.

Using the maps coded above, the following is an example of program coding for the multimap/dynamic panel:

```
:
EXEC CICS SEND                   <== Accumulate the header map.
     MAP('MPBINQH')
     MAPSET('MSBINQ2')
     ERASE
     ACCUM                       <== PAGING is not required.
     CURSOR
END-EXEC.

LOOP.
     :
     : (Edit one detail map)
     :
     EXEC CICS SEND                   <== Accumulate the detail map.
          MAP('MPBINQD')
          MAPSET('MSBINQ2')
```

```
            ERASE
            ACCUM                       <== PAGING is not required.
            CURSOR
       END-EXEC.
       (If more detail line required,  <== Programmer must know all
            GO TO LOOP.)                    detail maps will fit in
            :                               one screen.
       EXEC CICS SEND                   <== Accumulate the trailer map.
            MAP('MPBINQT')
            MAPSET('MSBINQ2')
            ERASE
            ACCUM                       <== PAGING is not required.
            CURSOR
       END-EXEC.
  *
       EXEC CICS SEND                   <== Send a logical panel.
            PAGE
       END-EXEC.
```

Execution Results   During the execution of this program logic, the following activities will occur:

- At the completion of each SEND MAP/ACCUM command, the header map, a series of detail maps, and the trailer map will be accumulated, occupying the proper position dynamically established by BMS based on the specifications of the BMS maps at the next line in this case.
- At the completion of the SEND PAGE command, the multimap panel (one single panel dynamically formatted with a series of maps) will appear on the terminal.

Technical Notes

As was the case for the multimap/static panel, for the multimap/dynamic panel, the terminal user does not have to use paging commands to retrieve the panel.

Since the multimap/dynamic panel is a panel (i.e., one page) by definition, you must make sure that all maps would fit into one panel, including the space for the trailer map (optional). During the map accumulation, if too many maps are accumulated, causing the overflow to the panel, CICS will detect it and return the OVER-FLOW exceptional condition to the SEND MAP/ACCUM command.

10.9   Multimap/Static/Multipage Message

Characteristics

A series of multimap/static panels can be sent to a terminal as a logical message (i.e., multipage message). Let us call this "Multimap/Static/Multipage" message. This is no more than a combination of the multipage message with single panel and multimap/static panel. A typical example of this type of message would be as shown in Figure 10-5.

Map Coding

Since the multimap/static/multipage message uses the multimap/static panels, the map coding for this message is the same as the case of the multimap/static panel (Section 10.7).

Programming

In order to send a multimap/static/multipage message to a terminal, the application program must follow the following procedures:

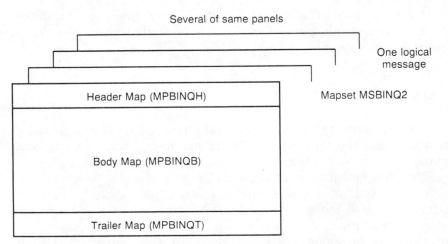

Figure 10-5 Example of multimap/static/multipage message

1. Issue the SEND MAP command with the ACCUM and PAG-
   ING options for accumulating maps as a multipage message.
2. Repeat step 1 above until all maps have been accumulated.
3. At the end of the logical message (i.e., multipage message),
   issue the SEND PAGE command.

Using the map coding of Section 10.7, the following is an example
of the SEND MAP command with the ACCUM and PAGING options
for the multimap/static/multipage message:

```
LOOP.
      EXEC CICS SEND              <== Accumulate the header map
          MAP('MPBINQH')               within a new page.
          MAPSET('MSBINQ2')
          ERASE
          ACCUM
          PAGING                  <== PAGING required.
          CURSOR
      END-EXEC.
      :
      : (Edit the body map)
      :
      EXEC CICS SEND              <== Accumulate the body map within
          MAP('MPBINQB')               the page.
          MAPSET('MSBINQ2')
          ERASE
          ACCUM
          PAGING                  <== PAGING required.
          CURSOR
      END-EXEC.
      EXEC CICS SEND              <== Accumulate the trailer map
          MAP('MPBINQT')               within the page.
          MAPSET('MSBINQ2')
          ERASE
          ACCUM
          PAGING                  <== PAGING required.
          CURSOR
      END-EXEC.
      (If there are more bodies to be sent,
          GO TO LOOP.)
*
      EXEC CICS SEND              <== Send a logical page
          PAGE                         (i.e., multipage message).
      END-EXEC.
```

Execution Results   During the execution of this program logic, the following activities will occur:

- At the completion of each SEND MAP/ACCUM/PAGING command, BMS will accumulate maps as the multimap/static panel.
- At the completion of the SEND MAP/ACCUM/PAGING command for the trailer map, BMS will automatically consider it as the end of one multimap/static panel, and accumulate the panel as one page of the multipage message.
- At the completion of the SEND PAGE command, a series of multimap/static panels will be displayed as a multipage message.

Technical Notes

Since the multimap/static/multipage message is the multipage message, the terminal user must use the paging commands to access the individual pages, except the first page.

10.10   Multimap/Dynamic/Multipage Massage

Characteristics

A series of multimap dynamic panels can be sent to a terminal as a logical message (i.e., multipage message). Let us call this "Multimap/Dynamic/Multipage Message." This is a combination of the multipage message with single panel and the multimap/dynamic panel. A typical example of this type of message would be as shown in Figure 10-6.

Map Coding

Since the multimap/dynamic/multipage message uses the multimap/dynamic panels, the map coding for this message is the same as the case of the multimap/dynamic panel (Section 10.8).

Programming

The programming for the multimap/dynamic/multipage message is similar to the case of the multimap/static/multipage message. You

Several of same panels

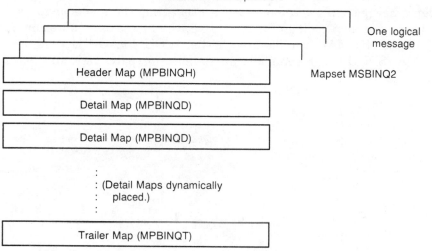

One logical
message

Header Map (MPBINQH)   Mapset MSBINQ2

Detail Map (MPBINQD)

Detail Map (MPBINQD)

: (Detail Maps dynamically
   placed.)

Trailer Map (MPBINQT)

Figure 10-6 Example of multimap/static/multipage message

issue the SEND MAP command with the ACCUM and PAGING options for accumulating maps as a multipage message, and issue the
SEND PAGE command for sending the logical message (i.e., multipage message).

However, since this logical message involves the multimap/dy-
namic panel, to which BMS automatically determines the actual position at the execution time, the page overflow becomes a crucial
issue. The program must deal with this exceptional condition from
the SEND MAP/ACCUM/PAGING command.

Page Overflow Processing

At map accumulation time (i.e., SEND MAP/ACCUM/PAGING command), if a panel becomes overflowed, counting on lines for the
trailer map, BMS will return an exceptional condition OVERFLOW.
When the OVERFLOW condition is detected, the program must take
the following actions:

1. Send the trailer map (optional).
2. Send the header map (optional).
3. Send the detail map which caused the OVERFLOW condition.
4. Then continue processing.

In this OVERFLOW handling routine, BMS will automatically assign a new page if the coming map is other than the trailer map.

Using the map coding of Section 10.8, the following is an example of the SEND MAP command with the ACCUM/PAGING command and the SEND PAGE command for the multimap/dynamic/multipage message:

```
        EXEC CICS HANDLE CONDITION
                OVERFLOW(OVF-RTN)           <== Establish OVERFLOW handling.
                ERROR(BMS-ERR-RTN)
        EXD-EXEC.
*
    PAGE-LOOP.
        EXEC CICS SEND                      <== Accumulate the header map
            MAP('MPBINQH')                      within the page.
            MAPSET('MSBINQ2')
            ERASE
            ACCUM
            PAGING                          <== PAGING required.
            CURSOR
        END-EXEC.
    DETAIL-LOOP.
        :
        : (Edit the detail map)
        :
        EXEC CICS SEND                      <== Accumulate the detail map
            MAP('MPBINQD')                      within the page.
            MAPSET('MSBINQ2')
            ERASE
            ACCUM
            PAGING                          <== PAGING required.
            CURSOR
        END-EXEC.
        (If there are more detail maps to be sent,
            GO TO DETAIL-LOOP.)
        EXEC CICS SEND                      <== Accumulate the trailer map
            MAP('MPBINQT')                      within the page.
            MAPSET('MSBINQ2')
            ERASE
            ACCUM
            PAGING                          <== PAGING required.
            CURSOR
```

```
        END-EXEC.
*

        EXEC CICS SEND              <== Send a logical page
            PAGE                        (i.e., a multipage message).
        END-EXEC.
        GO TO RETURN-RTN.
*
* PAGE OVERFLOW HANDLING ROUTINE.
*
    OVF-RTN.
        EXEC CICS SEND              <== Accumulate the trailer map
            MAP('MPBINQT')              within the same page, and
            MAPSET('MSBINQ2')           accumulate the page.
            ERASE
            ACCUM
            PAGING                  <== PAGING required.
            CURSOR
        END-EXEC.
        EXEC CICS SEND              <== Accumulate the header map in
            MAP('MPBINQH')              the new page.
            ERASE
            ACCUM
            PAGING                  <== PAGING required.
            CURSOR
        END-EXEC.
        EXEC CICS SEND              <== Accumulate the detail map in
            MAP('MPBINQD')              the page. This is the detail
            MAPSET('MSBINQ2')           map which caused the OVERFLOW.
            ERASE
            ACCUM
            PAGING                  <== PAGING required.
            CURSOR
        END-EXEC.
        GO TO DETAIL-LOOP.          <== To continue processing.
```

Execution Results   During the execution of this program logic, the following activities will occur:

- At the completion of each SEND MAP/ACCUM/PAGING in the main logic, the maps will be accumulated as the multimap/dynamic panel.
- When the overflow condition occurs, the control will be passed to the overflow handling routine, in which a trailer map will be sent.

This concludes a page (i.e., a panel). The next header map and detail map will be composed in the next page.
- In results, at the completion of the SEND PAGE command, a series of multimap/dynamic panels will be sent to the terminal as a multipage message.

Technical Notes

Since the multimap/dynamic/multipage message is the multipage message, the terminal user must use the paging commands to access the individual pages, except for the first page.

It should be noted that in order to send a multimap/dynamic/multipage message, the application program must issue many SEND MAP/ACCUM/PAGING commands: several times for a panel, multiplied by the number of pages (panels). This means that if a panel consists of 20 dynamic maps, and if there are 30 pages (panels) to send, the program must issue the SEND MAP/ACCUM/PAGING command 600 times (20x30). This is a very costly output operation in terms of resource consumption. If the multipage message with single map panel is used for this case, the number of SEND MAP/ACCUM/PAGING command will be reduced to only 30. Therefore, the multipage message with single map panel should be used as much as possible. The multimap/dynamic/multipage message should be used only when it is definitely advantageous.

10.11   Design Considerations for BMS Operations

When you decide what kind of BMS maps/commands should be used in your system, you should consider various aspects of the system as a whole. You might wish to use the multimap/dynamic/multipage message approach, because it is technically interesting and challenging. However, this is not necessarily the best approach to the given situation.

Suggestions

The multimap panel (single or multipage, static or dynamic panel) approach should be used only when it is definitely required, because of the high degree of resource usage, complex programming, low maintainability, and slower response time.

Instead, it is strongly recommended that the multipage message with single panel (map) approach be taken as much as possible, because of the contrary reasons to the above.

Free-Format Map Approach

If you create a free-format map (24x80), as shown below, for the multipage message with single panel (map), you can dynamically edit this free-format map within the program.

This is much faster than using the multimap panels in terms of performance. Then, you do not really need to pursue the multimap panel approach. We will discuss more about this free-format map approach (see Section 10.14 for the detail).

```
                    80 columns
              --------------------
              I                  I
     24       I                  I    Free-Format Map
     lines    I                  I
              I                  I
              --------------------
```

10.12 Message Routing

A message can be routed to one or more terminals other than the direct terminal with which the program has been communicating. The message eligible for routing is a message constructed by the SEND MAP command with the ACCUM option (with or without PAGING option). This implies that for message routing you must use the SEND MAP/ACCUM command (with or without PAGING option) even if you are using a single map panel.

Route List

In order to identify the destination for message routing, a Route List must be constructed. The Route List is a table consisting of a series of destination entries, each of which determines the destination of the message routing. One entry (16 bytes) of the Route List has the following format:

```
TTTTrrOOOsrrrrrr
```

where,

TTTT:	Terminal id (4 bytes) defined in TCT.
rr:	Reserved.
OOO:	Operator id (3 bytes) defined in SNT.
s:	Status flag.
rrrrrr:	Reserved (6 bytes space).

If the terminal id is specified, the message will be routed to the specified terminal as soon as the terminal becomes free. The terminal must have been signed-on.

If an operator id is specified, the message will be routed to the terminal which the specified operator is using as soon as the terminal becomes free. The terminal must have been signed on.

If both the terminal id and operator id are specified, the message will be routed to the designated terminal as soon as the designated operator signs on to the terminal and it becomes free. The terminal does not have to have been signed on.

It should be noted that the terminal id of the terminal to which the current transaction is associated should not be specified in the Route List, because this terminal will receive the message as the source (i.e., not destination) terminal of the message routing.

The end of the Route List must be coded with a halfword binary -1, as follows:

```
FILLER PIC S9(4) COMP VALUE -1.
```

Example Assuming two destinations for the message routing, the following is an example of the Route List coding:

```
01   WK-ROUTE-LIST.
     05   DEST1.
          10   TERM1    PIC X(4)          VALUE SPACES.
          10   FILLER   PIC XX            VALUE SPACES.
          10   OPID1    PIC X(3)          VALUE SPACES.
          10   FLAG1    PIC X.
          10   FILLER   PIC X(6)          VALUE SPACES.
     05   DEST2.
          10   TERM2    PIC X(4)          VALUE SPACES.
          10   FILLER   PIC XX            VALUE SPACES.
          10   OPID2    PIC X(3)          VALUE SPACES.
          10   FLAG2    PIC X.
          10   FILLER   PIC X(6)          VALUE SPACES.
     05   RLIST-END    PIC S9(4) COMP VALUE -1.
```

Operator Class Codes

In addition to the Route List, the message can be routed based on the operator class (1 to 24) which is defined in SNT (see Section 14.2). For this, a three-byte (i.e., 24 bits) field called "Operator Class Codes" should be constructed to represent each operator class in reverse order. A corresponding bit must be on (1) if the operator class is designated as the routing destination.

The message will be routed to every terminal at which users of the specified operator class are signed on. The terminal must have been signed on.

Example Suppose that we wish to send the message to the operator classes 1, 8 and 10, then the bit pattern and the corresponding decimal value will be as follows:

B'----001010000001'   = X'281' = 641

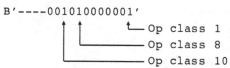

```
                    └── Op class 1
                   └──────── Op class 8
             └──────────── Op class 10
```

Then, define the Operator Class Codes field (3 bytes) in the Working Storage Section with the decimal value of the bit pattern. Since S9(8) COMP gives a fullword binary field (4 bytes), it requires a little trick to prepare the 3-byte field. The following is an example:

```
01   DUMMY0.
     05 DUMMY1 PIC S9(8) COMP VALUE 641.
     05 DUMMY2 REDEFINES DUMMY1.
        10 FILLER PIC X.
        10 WK-OP-CLASS PIC XXX.            <== Use this.
```

WK-OP-CLASS is the Operator Class Codes field to be used in the program.

Title of Message

A title of the message can be specified as an option. The terminal operator can see this title by typing the paging command (P/Q: see Section 10.3) to inquire whether some messages have been routed. The message title must be constructed in the following manner:

```
01    MSG-TITLE.
      05    TITLE-LENGTH    PIC S9(4) COMP VALUE nn.
      05    TITLE-DATA      PIC X(nn) VALUE '-------'.
```

where nn is the actual length of the title (up to 62).

ROUTE Command

Function The ROUTE command establishes the message routing environment but does not send the message yet. The next SEND PAGE command (after the ROUTE command) actually sends the message to the destinations.

Format The format of the ROUTE command is as follows:

```
EXEC CICS ROUTE
     [LIST(data-area)],
     [OPCLASS(data-area)],
     [INTERVAL(hhmmss)  |   TIME(hhmmss)],
     [TITLE(data-area)],
     [ERRTERM(name)]
END-EXEC.
```

LIST and OPCLASS name the Route List and Operator Class Codes, respectively, defined in the Working Storage Section. INTERVAL or TIME determines the actual timing of the message delivery in the time interval or the time, respectively. TITLE names the title field defined in the Working Storage Section. ERRTERM is used to specify the terminal id of the terminal to which error messages (if any) are to be sent.

Example Using the Route List, Operator Class Codes, and Message Title prepared above, the following is an example of the ROUTE command:

```
MOVE 'TRM1' TO TERM1.
MOVE 'TRM2' TO TERM2.
EXEC CICS ROUTE                       <== Establish the route
     LIST(WK-ROUTE-LIST)                   environment.
     OPCLASS(WK-OP-CLASS)
     TITLE(MSG-TITLE)
```

```
        ERRTERM('MST1')
END-EXEC.
    :
    :
EXEC CICS SEND MAP ACCUM (PAGING) ------- END-EXEC.
    :
EXEC CICS SEND PAGE END-EXEC.          <== Route the message.
    :
```

Execution Results During the execution of this program logic, the following activities will occur:

* At the completion of the ROUTE command, the routing environment will be established.
* At the completion of the SEND PAGE command, the message will be routed to the destinations, based on the combination of the specifications in the LIST and OPCLASS parameters.

Overflow Processing

If you are dealing with the multimap/dynamic/multipage message, the program must perform the overflow processing properly. As a suggestion, you should assume that all terminals are the same type. Then, you can use the same overflow processing described in Section 10.10. If there are various types of terminals in the destination, a more complex overflow processing will be required, in which case a proper IBM manual should be referred to.

Message Routing to Printer

The message routing can be done toward the printers connected to CICS. You can do this by taking the same approach as the message routing to the display terminals, except that you use the PRINT option in the SEND MAP/ACCUM(/PAGING) command, and the AUTOPAGE option in the SEND PAGE command. As a general rule for the BMS printing operations, the maps must have been coded with CTRL=(PRINT,---) in the mapset definition macro (DFHMSD).

Example The following is an example of the message routing to the printers:

```
      :
EXEC CICS ROUTE
     LIST(----)
     ERRTERM('----')
END-EXEC.
      :
EXEC CICS SEND
     MAP(-----)
     MAPSET(----)
     ACCUM
     PAGING
     PRINT                      <== Required.
     NLEOM                      <== Recommended.
END-EXEC.      :
     (SEND MAP can be repeated.)
      :
EXEC CICS SEND
     PAGE
     AUTOPAGE                   <== Recommended.
END-EXEC.
```

Execution Results During the execution of this program logic, the following activities will occur:

• At the completion of the ROUTE command, the routing environment will be established.
• At the completion of the SEND PAGE/AUTOPAGE command, the message will be routed to the printers, which automatically print all pages of the message.

10.13 Occurrence Handling in BMS Map

Taking an example of map MPBPNC2/MSBPNC2 in Section 8.11, in this kind of case, there are two fields in one line which is repeated two times. It is a tedious task if you define each of these fields (2x2=4) with a unique name as defined in Section 8.11. This would become problematic in the application program.

It would be useful if these repeated fields can be addressed with the same field name with subscript, like using OCCURS in the COBOL coding. The BMS field definition macro (DFHMDF) has the parameter OCCURS, which provides a very primitive function for occurrence handling. But how it works and how it should be used are

not made clear, unless you try to find them by trial and error. Therefore, a clearer approach should be sought.

Useful Technique

There is a useful technique for occurrence handling. The following is
a set of procedures for this technique:

1. Define all fields of a BMS map with the unique field names.
2. Assemble and linkedit the BMS map.
3. Forcefully modify the symbolic map for OCCURS.
4. In application program, use the modified field name with the
   subscript.

Example

Using map MPBPNC2/MSBPNC2 in Section 8.11, the following is an
example of the symbolic map intentionally modified for occurrence
handling:

```
        COPY MSBPNC2
C    01   MPBPNC2I.                          <== Same as original.
C         06   FILLER    X(12).
              :
              :
C    01   MPBPNC2O REDEFINES MPBPNC2I.       <== Same as original.
C         06   FILLER    X(12).
              :
              :

     01   MPBPNC2-DUMMY REDEFINES MPBPNC2I.       ))   <== Newly
          05   FILLER     PIC X(12).                ))        inserted.
          05   FILLER OCCURS 2 TIMES.               ))
               10   M2EMPNNL  PIC S9(4) COMP.       ))
               10   M2EMPNNA  PIC X.                ))
               10   M2EMPNNI  PIC 9(5).             ))
               10   FILLER REDEFINES M2EMPNNI.      ))
                    15   M2EMPNNO  PIC 9(5).        ))
               10   M2NAMENL  PIC S9(4) COMP.       ))
               10   M2NAMENA  PIC X.                ))
               10   M2NAMENI  PIC X(25).            ))
               10   FILLER REDEFINES M2NAMENI.      ))
                    15   M2NAMENO  PIC X(25).       ))
```

```
05   FILLER OCCURS 4 TIMES.           ))
     10   M2ERRNL   PIC S9(4) COMP.   ))
     10   M2ERRNA   PIC X.            ))
     10   M2ERRNO   PIC X(79).        ))
```

Then, in the application program, you can use the following redefined fieldnames with the subscripts:

```
M2EMPNNI (LINE)    or    M2EMPNNO (LINE)
M2NAMENI (LINE)    or    M2NAMENO (LINE)
M2ERRNO  (LINE)
```

where LINE is subscript (1 or 2 in this case).

This is exactly what the sample program in Appendix A does. For
better understanding, the sample program in Appendix A should be
carefully examined.

10.14   Free-Format Map Approach

The multimap panel approach and the multimap/multipage message
approach are useful for dealing with a very complex screen layout.
However, Section 10.11 discourages these approaches for highly jus-
tifiable reasons, and suggests using the multipage message with single map.

A "free-format map" is a plain full-screen map (e.g., 24x80) whose
entire space is defined as the free space based on the occurrence
handling technique. The free-format map approach offers advantages
of the multipage message with single map, while it can deal with a
very complex screen layout relatively easily.

Procedures

The following is a set of procedures for the free-format approach:

1. Define the free-format map, as the example shown in Figure
   10-7. This example has the map space of 24 lines by 80 columns. The first column of each line is reserved for the attribute character, the first 2 lines are reserved for the heading
   title, and the last 2 lines are reserved for the paging commands. Therefore, this map offers a free space of 20 lines by 79
   columns.

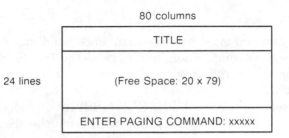

Figure 10-7 Example of free-format map.

2. In the application program, consider this free space as a report space (similar to the batch programs), and edit the free space as you wish.
3. When the free space is full (i.e., the map is filled with the data), issue the SEND MAP command with the ACCUM/PAGING option to accumulate the free-format map as the multipage message.
4. Repeat until all data have been sent.
5. Issue the SEND PAGE command to send the multipage message to the terminal.

Map Coding

The free-format map is nothing but an ordinary BMS map (single map panel). The following is an example of the free-format map coding based on the screen layout above:

```
MSBFREE    DFHMSD    TYPE=MAP,MODE=INOUT,STORAGE=AUTO,
                     TIOAPFX=YES,CNTL=(FREEKB,FRSET)
MPBFREE    DFHMDI    SIZE=(24,80),LINE=1,COLUMN=1
MFTITL     DFHMDF    POS=(01,01),LENGTH=79,ATTRB=ASKIP,
                     INITIAL='     ANY TITLE       '
MFLIN01    DFHMDF    POS=(03,01),LENGTH=79,ATTRB=ASKIP
MFLIN02    DFHMDF    POS=(04,01),LENGTH=79,ATTRB=ASKIP
   :          :         :
   :          :         :
MFLIN19    DFHMDF    POS=(21,01),LENGTH=79,ATTRB=ASKIP
MFLIN20    DFHMDF    POS=(22,01),LENGTH=79,ATTRB=ASKIP
           DFHMDF    POS=(24,01),LENGTH=21,ATTRB=ASKIP,
                     INITIAL='ENTER PAGING COMMAND:'
           DFHMDF    POS=(24,25),LENGTH=5,ATTRB=(UNPROT,IC,FSET)
```

Programming

The application program must use the occurrence-handling technique against the free-format map. Then, one page of the free-format map becomes one page of the report space. You can use this report space freely as you wish.

Using the free-format map (MPBFREE/MSBFREE) coded above, the following is an example of program coding for the free-format map approach:

```
WORKING-STORAGE SECTION.
77   LINE-CNT          PIC S9(4) COMP.
*
* LINE LAYOUT FOR FREE-FORMAT MAP.        <== An example line layout
01   LINE-LAYOUT.                              using Figure 10-1.
     05   FILLER        PIC X(5) VALUE SPACES.
     05   FFL-ACCNO     PIC 9(3).
     05   FILLER        PIC X(5) VALUE SPACES.
     05   FFL-NAME      PIC X(30).
     05   FILLER        PIC X(5) VALUE SPACES.
     05   FFL-BAL       PIC ZZZ,ZZ9.99-.
     05   FILLER        PIC X(20) VALUE SPACES.
*
     COPY MSBFREE
01   FREE-MAP-REDEF  REDEFINES MPBFREEI.    ))   <== Occurrence
     05   FILLER        PIC X(12).          ))        handling
     05   FILLER  OCCURS 20 TIMES.          ))
          10   LINENNL  PIC S9(4) COMP.     ))
          10   LINENNA  PIC X.              ))
          10   LINENNO  PIC X(79).          ))
     :
     :
PROCEDURE DIVISION.
     :
     MOVE ZERO TO LINE-CNT.
MAP-LOOP.
     ADD 1 TO LINE-CNT.
     :
     (Read a record from Master file.)
     (Let us assume HANDLE CONDITION with ENDFILE(EOF-RTN).)
     (Edit LINE-LAYOUT, e.g., FFL-ACCNO, FFL-NAME, FFL-BAL.)
     :
     MOVE LINE-LAYOUT TO LINENNO(LINE-CNT).
```

```
      IF LINE-CNT < 20
          GO TO MAP-LOOP.
      EXEC CICS SEND
          MAP('MPBFREE')
          MAPSET('MSBFREE')
          ACCUM
          PAGING
          ERASE
      END-EXEC.
      MOVE ZERO TO LINE-CNT.
      MOVE LOW-VALUES TO MPBFREEO
      GO TO MAP-LOOP.
EOF-RTN.
      EXEC CICS SEND
          PAGE
      EXD-EXEC.
```

Execution Results   During the execution of this program logic, the following activities will occur:

- In the MAP-LOOP logic, each line of the free-format map will be edited one by one after reading a record from the master file.
- When 20 lines are edited, the SEND MAP/ACCUM/PAGING command will be issued. At completion of this command, one page of the free-format map will be accumulated as a multipage message.
- This will be repeated until the ENDFILE condition of the master file is detected.
- At this point, the SEND PAGE command will be issued. At the completion of this command, a series of free-format maps will be sent to the terminal as the multipage message.
- The terminal user must use the paging commands to retrieve each page of the multipage message.

More Advanced Technique

You could use more than one line for certain displays. For example, two lines for the remittance display, five lines for the order display, one line for the refund display, etc. Then you can dynamically move to the free space in the free-format map by controlling the line counter properly. If the free space is exhausted, you can send the map as in the basic procedures above. In this way, you can display very complex screens easily.

Advantages

Since the free-format map approach offers many advantages over the complex BMS operations, it is highly recommended. The following are some advantages:
• This approach can deal with a complex screen layout, because it is just like preparing a report in a batch program.
• This approach makes an application program simple and easy if you are familiar with report writing in the batch programs.
• This approach requires low resource usage, because this approach issues significantly fewer SEND MAP/ACCUM/PAGING commands than the multimap panel approaches, regardless of whether it is a static or dynamic approach.
• Therefore, this approach provides better response time.

Restrictions

The free-format map approach is valid for the applications involving only output operations (e.g., inquiry applications). It cannot be used for applications involving input operations.

10.15   BASE Option Approach

So far, we have used the STORAGE=AUTO option in the mapset definition macro (DFHMSD). The STORAGE=AUTO option makes the symbolic map in the mapset occupy separate (i.e., not redefined) areas of storage in the Working Storage Section. Consequently, the BMS commands (SEND MAP and RECEIVE MAP) can be easily issued, without specifying the FROM, INTO, or LENGTH parameters.

However, if an application program uses many maps, which is quite common in real business applications, then the program requires a large storage size. Therefore, a more efficient approach should be sought for a reduction of required storage size. The BASE option is very suitable in this situation.

Concept

If the BASE option is specified (instead of STORAGE=AUTO) in the DFHMSD macro, the same storage base will be used for the symbolic maps from more than one mapset. In other words, one mapset will share the same storage area (base) with other mapsets in an application program. Also one map within one mapset will share the same storage area (base) with other maps (if any) of the same mapset. Consequently, the storage requirements for the symbolic maps will be significantly reduced within the application program.

Map Coding

In order to use the BASE option approach, the mapset must be defined differently from the STORAGE=AUTO approach through the DFHMSD macro. BASE names the 01 level common map input/output area, which must be defined in the Working Storage Section of the application program with a length large enough to cover all maps.

Using the example of the mapset defined in Section 8.6, the following is an example of the mapset definition for the BASE option approach:

```
MSBINQ2    DFHMSD    TYPE=&SYSPARM
                     MODE=INOUT,
                     LANG=COBOL,
                     BASE=MAP-IOAREA,    <== 01 level W/S area where BMS
                                             I/O area is shared with other
                                             maps.
                     TIOAPFX=YES,
                     CNTL=(FREEKB,FRSET,PRINT)
```

Programming

Using the map defined above, the following is an example of the program coding for the BASE option approach:

```
WORKING-STORAGE SECTION.
01   MAP-IOAREA.                         <== Required.
     05   FILLER    PIC X(1000).         <== Specify max. map length.
*
     COPY MSBINQ2.      )                <== Redefines 01 MAP-IOAREA.
     COPY MSBINQ3.      )
          :
          :
PROCEDURE DIVISION.
          :
          :
```

```
EXEC CICS RECEIVE
     MAP('MPBINQ2')
     MAPSET('MSBINQ2')
     END-EXEC.
     :
(Some processing using fieldnames(+I).)
     :
     :
MOVE LOW-VALUES TO MAP-IOAREA.            <== Clear MAP-IOAREA.
     :
(Edit symbolic map using fieldnames(+O).)
  :
EXEC CICS SEND
     MAP('MPBINQ3')
     MAPSET('MSBINQ3')
     CURSOR
     ERASE
END-EXEC.
```

Execution Results   Using the execution of this program logic, the following activities will occur:

- At the completion of the RECEIVE MAP command, MAP-IOAREA will contain the mapped data from the terminal in the form of symbolic map (MPBINQ2/MSBINQ2). After this, the program can use the fieldnames (+I) defined in the DFHMDF macros.
- At the completion of MOVE LOW-VALUE TO MAP-IOAREA, the area will be cleared for preparing the output data in the same area. The program can use the fieldnames(+O) for the output data preparation for map MPBINQ3/MSBINQ3.
- At the completion of the SEND MAP command, the contents of the symbolic map (MPBINQ3/MSPINQ3) in MAP-IOAREA will be sent to the terminal.

Restrictions

Since the same storage area is shared by many maps among mapsets, you must be careful that a map being used is not overwritten with other maps. In this respect, this approach is not convenient for application programs which use the multimap panels or multimap/multipage message, because these messages require more than one map at one panel operation.

But, if an application program uses the single map panel or multi-page message (with single map panel), and if the program is written strictly in the pseudo-conversational mode, it could deal with maps one by one. Therefore, in this case, the risk of map overwriting will be minimal.

10.16   CICS Command Subroutine Approach

The CICS command subroutine approach is a technique by which each CICS command is coded in a form of subroutine, placed at the back of the program, and performed from the main body of the program. An example is shown in the sample program in Appendix A.

The simple CICS command subroutine approach (as shown in Appendix A) can be used without difficulty, because each command could have the literal constants imbedded in each command if they are required. However, since the use of literal constants limits the general use of the command subroutine, the more generalized approach should be sought. Therefore, let us discuss the generalized CICS command subroutine approach using the SEND MAP and RECEIVE MAP commands as an example.

So far, we have used the literal constant in the map and mapset names in the BMS commands, as in the following example:

```
EXEC CICS SEND
     MAP('MPBINQ2')                <== Literal constant.
     MAPSET('MSBINQ2')             <== Literal constant.
END-EXEC.
```

But you might sometimes wish to use variable names in the CICS commands instead of the literal constants, so that the same command subroutine could be used for other maps, too. This can be accomplished easily by using the BASE option approach.

Procedures

The following is a set of procedures for the generalized CICS command subroutine approach using the SEND MAP and RECEIVE MAP commands:

1. Use the BASE option approach as described in the previous section.

2. Use the variable names for map name, mapset name, and map length in the SEND MAP and RECEIVE MAP commands.
3. Make the command subroutines for the SEND MAP and RECEIVE MAP commands, using the variable names established for map name, mapset name, and map length.
4. In the main logic, establish variables for the map name, mapset name, and length (if required), then PERFORM these command subroutines.

Example

Let us assume that maps MPBINQ2/MSBINQ2 and MPBINQ3/MSBINQ3 are coded with the BASE option using the common map area name MAP-IOAREA (as in Section 10.15). The following is an example of program coding for the generalized CICS command subroutines for the SEND MAP and RECEIVE MAP commands:

```
WORKING-STORAGE SECTION.
01   MAP-IOAREA.                       <== Required.
     05   FILLER     PIC X(1000).      <== Specify max. map length.
     COPY MSBINQ2.                     <== Redefines 01 MAP-IOAREA.
     COPY MSBINQ3.
*
01   MAP-VARIABLES.
     05   MAP-NAME      PIC X(7).      <== Map name variable.
     05   MAP-MAPSET    PIC X(7).      <== Mapset name variable.
     05   MAP-LENGTH    PIC S9(4) COMP.   <== Map length variable.
     :
     :
PROCEDURE DIVISION.
MAIN-RTN.
     :
     (Housekeeping)
     :
TASK1-RTN.
     :
     (Edit map MSBINQ2/MPBINQ2)
     :
     MOVE 'MSBINQ2' TO MAP-MAPSET.
     MOVE 'MPBINQ2' TO MAP-NAME.
     MOVE 200       TO MAP-LENGTH.    <== Establish map length.
```

```
        PERFORM MAP-SEND-RTN.
        :
TASK2-RTN.
        :
        MOVE 'MSBINQ2' TO MAP-MAPSET.
        MOVE 'MPBINQ2' TO MAP-NAME.
        PERFORM MAP-RECEIVE-RTN.
        :
        (Edit map MSBINQ3/MPBINQ3)
             :
        MOVE 'MSBINQ3' TO MAP-MAPSET.
        MOVE 'MPBINQ3' TO MAP-NAME.
        MOVE 300      TO MAP-LENGTH.      <== Establish map length.
        PERFORM MAP-SEND-RTN.
        :
TASK3-RTN.
        :
        MOVE 'MSBINQ3' TO MAP-MAPSET.
        MOVE 'MPBINQ3' TO MAP-NAME.
        PERFORM MAP-RECEIVE-RTN.
        :
        :
*
* CICS COMMAND SUBROUTINES
*
MAP-SEND-RTN SECTION.
        EXEC HANDLE CONDITION
            ERROR(MAP-SEN-ERR-RTN)
        END-EXEC.
        EXEC CICS SEND
            MAP(MAP-NAME)
            MAPSET(MAP-MAPSET)
            FROM(MAP-IOAREA)                    <==  Required.
            LENGTH(MAP-LENGTH)
            ERASE
            CURSOR
        END-EXEC.
        GO TO MAP-SEND-EXIT.
MAP-SEN-ERR-RTN.
        (Some error handling routine)
MAP-SEND-EXIT.
        EXIT.
```

```
*
MAP-RECEIVE-RTN SECTION.
      EXEC HANDLE CONDITION
            ERROR(MAP-REC-ERR-RTN)
      END-EXEC.
      EXEC CICS RECEIVE
            MAP(MAP-NAME)
            MAPSET(MAP-MAPSET)
            INTO(MAP-IOAREA)                      <==  Required.
      END-EXEC.
      GO TO MAP-RECEIVE-EXIT.
MAP-REC-ERR-RTN.
      (Some error handling routine)
MAP-RECEIVE-EXIT.
      EXIT.
```

Execution Results The subroutines MAP-SEND-RTN and MAP-RECEIVE-RTN will be used for both maps MPBINQ2/MSBINQ2 and MPBINQ3/MSBINQ3.

Advantages

You know by now that CICS translator comments out all CICS commands in the source program and shifts the indentation. This makes the COBOL compile list extremely difficult to read. If this CICS command subroutine approach is used, since the mainline logic would not use any CICS commands, the compile list would not be distorted. Therefore, the list would be easy to read.

In addition, all CICS commands can be written in the form of standardized subroutines, which can be shared many times within the same program or among different programs (if these subroutines are copied into each program). Since each subroutine is standardized, you would be sure that if there are abnormalities in the command execution, the cause would most likely be the wrong data in the variables for the command subroutine. Therefore, this approach improves maintainability significantly.

This is the very professional way of coding an efficient CICS application programm. Therefore, the CICS command subroutine approach is highly recommended.

Technical Notes

In the SEND MAP command subroutine, since the CICS command translator has no way of directly finding the length of the map due to the map name indirectly specified in the variable for the map name (MAP-NAME in the above example), the length of the symbolic map (i.e., not physical map) should be specified in the LENGTH parameter. The best way to obtain an accurate map length is to refer to DMAP (or MAP in case of VS COBOL II) in the compile list for the map on the subject. DMAP (or MAP) shows the total length of the symbolic map.

Exercise

This exercise is to develop four (4) Insurance Premium Report (IPRx) transactions, using different approaches to achieve the same objective, based on the following specifications:

Approach 1: Multipage/Single Map Panel Case

1. Transaction id is IPRA and Program id is TXTAIPRA.
2. The program uses the Personnel Master File (PERVSPMS) defined in the Exercise for Chapter 4.
3. Code 2 maps as follows:

```
Mapname = MPBIPR2, Mapset name = MSBIPR2
```

```
I               INSURANCE POLICY REPORT                    IPR2 I
I                                                               I
I    SPECIFY START KEY:              nnnnn                      I
I    SPECIFY DESTINATION TERMINAL: xxxx                        I
I                                                               I
I                                                               I
I                                                               I
I  yyyyyyyyyyyyyyyyyyyyyyyyyyyyyyyyyyyyyyyyyyyyyyyyyyyyyyyyyy I
I  yyyyyyyyyyyyyyyyyyyyyyyyyyyyyyyyyyyyyyyyyyyyyyyyyyyyyyyyyy I
```

Mapname = MPBIPR3, Mapset name = MSBIPR3

```
I                  INSURANCE POLICY REPORT                        IPR3 I
I                                                             PAGE: zz  I
I    EMP-NO  NAME                        POLICY-NO     PREMIUM        I
I 1. 99999  yyyyyyyyyyyyyyyyyyyyyyyyy    9999999    z,zzz,zz9.99  I
I 2. 99999  yyyyyyyyyyyyyyyyyyyyyyyyy    9999999    z,zzz,zz9.99  I
I 3. 99999  yyyyyyyyyyyyyyyyyyyyyyyyy    9999999    z,zzz,zz9.99  I
I 4. 99999  yyyyyyyyyyyyyyyyyyyyyyyyy    9999999    z,zzz,zz9.99  I
I 5. 99999  yyyyyyyyyyyyyyyyyyyyyyyyy    9999999    z,zzz,zz9.99  I
I                                                                    I
I                                                                    I
I    END OF DISPLAY                                                  I
I    ENTER PAGING COMMAND (EG. P/N, P/P, ETC): xxxxxxx              I
```

where,

n:	Unprotected numeric field
x:	Unprotected alphanumeric field
y:	Autoskipped alphanumeric field
z or 9:	Autoskipped, edited numeric field
_:	Initial cursor position

Technical Notes
- The screen layout shown should be considered as a basic guideline, so that the actual field position can be shifted a little. Define user-friendly maps.
- The cursor must be automatically skipped to the next unprotected field.
- The "END OF DISPLAY" field must be initially invisible.
4. The program starts with sending map MPBIPR2/MSBIPR2 to the terminal. Return with the external transaction id = IPRA and the internal transaction id = IPR2.
5. Upon receiving control again, receive the map. Validate the input data. The employee number received must exist in the PMS file. For this program, ignore the data in the destination terminal field. If the data in the start key field is invalid, place the cursor onto the field, highlight the field, prepare an error message at the bottom of the map, and send it. Return with the external transaction id = IPRA and the internal transaction id = IPR2, so that the user can correct and reenter.
6. If the data is valid, read the PMS file sequentially. If a record does not have the policy number (zero or space), skip the record. If a record has the policy number, edit the data in the

detail line of map MPBIPR3/MSBIPR3, by controlling the proper line counter.

7. Repeat step 6 for 50 eligible records or until EOF, whichever comes first. Every time the map becomes full, send the map as a multipage message. The page number on the top must be incremented accordingly. The last IPR3 screen must have the "END OF DISPLAY" field visible.
8. Send the page, and terminate the task.
9. At any time, if the PF12 key is pressed, forcefully cancel the transaction.
10. Although this is not required, if you can, try to use the free format approach and CICS command subroutine approach.

Approach 2: Message Routing Case

1. Modify the specifications of Approach 1 (i.e., Program TXTAIPRA) as follows:
2. Transaction id is IPRB and Program id is TXTAIPRB.
3. For this program, the data in the destination terminal field in MPBIPR2/MSBIPR2 must be validated.
4. You are to route the IPR3 screen to three terminals, all of which are known to be IBM 3278-2 or equivalent. These terminals are as follows:
   • Insurance Department Supervisor terminal (id = INS1)
   • Terminal whose id is given through the IPR2 screen
   • Master terminal (id = MST1)
5. The rest of the specifications remain the same as for Approach 1.

Approach 3: Multimap/Dynamic Panel Case

1. Modify the specifications of Approach 1 (i.e., program TXTAIPRA) as follows:
2. Transaction id is IPRC and Program id is TXTAIPRC.
3. Use the original map MPBIPR2/MSBIPR2, but code separately three substitute maps for MPBIPR3/MSBIPR3 as follows:
   a. Header Map (MPBIPRH/MSBIPRX): This consists of only the header portion (i.e., the first three lines) of MPBIPR3/MSBIPR3.
   b. Detail Map (MPBIPRD/MSBIPRX): This is one line detail map and consists of the one detail line of MPBIPR3/

MSBIPR3. Hence, the line number must be edited as a variable by the program.

c. Trailer map (MPBIPRT/MSBIPRX): This consists of only the trailer portion (i.e., "END OF DISPLAY" field and paging command field) of MPBIPR3/MSBIPR3.

4. Read sequentially only five eligible PMS records which have the insurance policy number, or until EOF, whichever comes first.

5. Construct a multimap/dynamic panel using the maps IPRH, IPRD and IPRT. Send the page.

6. The rest of the specifications remain the same as for Approach 1.

Approach 4: Multimap/Dynamic/Multipage Message Case

1. Modify the specifications of Approach 3 (i.e., program TXTAIPRC) as follows:

2. Transaction id is IPRD and Program id is TXTAIPRD.

3. Read sequentially 50 eligible PMS records which have the insurance policy number, or until EOF, whichever comes first.

4. Construct a multimap/dynamic/multipage message using the maps IPRH, IPRD, and IPRT. A proper page overflow processing must be done. The page number in the map IPRH must be incremented properly. The last screen must have "END OF DISPLAY" visible. Send the page.

5. The rest of the specifications remain the same as for Approach 3.

11

Transient Data Control

11.1 Introduction

The CICS Transient Data Control Program (TDP) allows a CICS transaction to deal with sequential data called Transient Data files. A Transient Data file can be used as either an input file (i.e., a transaction can read the records) or an output file (i.e., a transaction can write the records), but not both.

The Transient Data is sometimes called Transient Data Queue (TDQ), while other times it is called Transient Data Destination. The word "Queue" is used because the records in the Transient Data are put together in the sequential mode (i.e., "Queue"). The word "Destination" is used because this sequential data is directed to other transactions (i.e., "Destination"). Both terms are used interchangeably and they mean essentially the same.

There are two types of TDQ: Intrapartition TDQ and Extrapartition TDQ. Although the same CICS commands are used for both Intrapartition TDQ and Extrapartition TDQ, the applications of these two types of TDQ are very different.

Regardless of the type, each TDQ is identified by a 1- to 4-character identifier called "destination id." All destination ids must be registered in the Destination Control Table (DCT).

Intrapartition TDQ

An Intrapartition TDQ is a group of sequential records which are produced and processed by the same and/or different transactions within a CICS region. This is why the word "Intrapartition" is used.

All Intrapartition TDQs are stored in only one physical file (VSAM) in a CICS region, which is prepared by the system programmer. From an application program's point of view, however, only sequential access is allowed for a queue. Once a record is read from a queue, the record will be logically removed from the queue; that is, the record cannot be read again.

The Intrapartition TDQ is used for the various applications such as:

- Interface among CICS transactions
  Appl. Prog. 1 ⟶ TDQ ⟶ Appl. Prog. 2 ⟶ Report
- Automatic Task Initiation (ATI)
- Message routing
- Message broadcast

Extrapartition TDQ

An Extrapartition TDQ is a group of sequential records which interfaces between the transactions of the CICS region and the systems (or batch jobs) outside of the CICS region. This is why the word "Extrapartition" is used.

In the input Extrapartition TDQ, records are produced by the programs outside of the CICS region (e.g., batch jobs, TSO, PC) to be processed by the CICS transaction as input, whereas in the output Intrapartition TDQ, records are produced by the CICS transactions as output to be processed outside of CICS.

Each Extrapartition TDQ is a separate physical file, and it may be on the disk, tape, printer, or plotter. This implies that each file (i.e., Extrapartition TDQ) must be open within the CICS region when it is used by the CICS transaction. DCT determines the initial OPEN/CLOSE status of a file, while the file can be opened or closed through the Master Terminal transaction (CEMT: see Section 16.10) during a CICS session.

The Extrapartition TDQ is typically used for the following two applications:

- Interface to batch (or TSO, or PC) jobs.
  CICS Appl. Prog. ⟶ TDQ ⟶ File ⟶ Batch Prog.
- Interface from batch (or TSO, or PC) jobs.
  Batch Prog. ⟶ File ⟶ TDQ ⟶ CICS Appl. Prog.

Available Commands

The following commands are available for the Transient Data Control:

WRITEQ TD: To sequentially write a record in a TDQ. Valid for both Intrapartition and Extrapartition TDQ.

READQ TD: To sequentially read a record in a TDQ. Valid for both Intrapartition and Extrapartition TDQ.

DELETEQ TD: To delete an Intrapartition TDQ. Not valid for the Extrapartition TDQ.

It should be noted that TD represents Transient Data. If this is omitted, Temporary Storage (TS) will be assumed.

11.2   WRITEQ TD Command

Function

The WRITEQ TD command is used to write a record in a TDQ. This command is valid for both Intrapartition TDQ and Extrapartition TDQ.

Format

The format of the WRITEQ TD command is shown in the example below. QUEUE names the destination id (1 to 4 characters), which must be defined in DCT (see Section 11.5). FROM defines the name of the areas from which the data is to be written. LENGTH (halfword binary field, S9(4) COMP) indicates the length of the record.

Example

The following is an example of the WRITEQ TD command:

```
WORKING-STORAGE SECTION.
01   MSG-AREA.
     05   MSG-TO-LOC          PIC X(2) VALUE 'GE'.
     05   FILLER              PIC X    VALUE SPACE.
```

```
        05    MSG-OP-FROM           PIC X(5) VALUE 'JIM'.
        05    FILLER                PIC X     VALUE SPACE.
        05    MSG-OP-TO             PIC X(5).
        05    FILLER                PIC X     VALUE SPACE.
        05    MSG-MESSAGE           PIC X(40).
    77  MSG-LENGTH                  PIC S9(4) COMP.
        :
PROCEDURE DIVISION.
        :
        MOVE 'MARY' TO MSG-OP-TO.
        MOVE 'HELLO, THIS IS TEST FOR MESSAGE SWITCHING.'
             TO MSG-MESSAGE.
        MOVE 55 TO MSG-LENGTH.
        EXEC CICS WRITEQ TD
             QUEUE('MSGS')                <== Destination-id
             FROM(MSG-AREA)
             LENGTH(MSG-LENGTH)
        END-EXEC.
```

Execution Results   Data of MSG-AREA will be written in the TDQ 'MSGS' (either Intrapartition or Extrapartition TDQ, depending on the 'MSGS' entry in DCT).

Common Exceptional conditions

The following are the exceptional conditions common to the WRITEQ TD command:

QIDERR: The destination id specified cannot be found in DCT.

LENGERR: The length specified is greater than the maximum record length specified in DCT.

NOSPACE: No space is available in the TDQ.

11.3   READQ TD Command

Function

The READQ TD command is used to read a record of a TDQ. This command is valid for both Intrapartition TDQ and Extrapartition TDQ.

Format

The format of the READQ TD command is shown in the example below. QUEUE names the destination id (1 to 4 characters). INTO defines the area in the Working Storage Section where the data is to be placed. LENGTH (halfword binary field, S9(4) COMP) indicates the length of the record.

Alternative to the INTO option, the SET option can be used in the similar manner to the READ command with the SET option.

Example

The following is an example of the READQ TD command:

```
WORKING-STORAGE SECTION.
01   MSG-AREA.
        05   AREA1              PIC X(10).
        05   AREA2              PIC X(20).
77   MSG-LENGTH                 PIC S9(4) COMP.
        :
PROCEDURE DIVISION.
        :
     MOVE 30 TO MSG-LENGTH.
     EXEC CICS READQ TD
          QUEUE('MSGS')         <== Destination-id
          INTO(MSG-AREA)
          LENGTH(MSG-LENGTH)
     EXD-EXEC.
```

Execution Results A record of the TDQ 'MSGS' will be read into MSG-AREA. The actual length of the record will be placed in MSG-LENGTH.

Common Exceptional Conditions

The following are the exceptional conditions common to the READQ TD command:

QIDERR: The destination id specified cannot be found in DCT.

LENGERR: The length specified is shorter than the actual record length. The record will be truncated at the length specified, while the actual length will be placed in the LENGTH field.

QZERO: The queue is empty. This often means the
                          end of the file.

Sequential Read Technique

If you wish to read the entire queue, repeat the READQ TD command until the QZERO condition occurs. The following is an example
of sequential read of TDQ:

```
        EXEC CICS HANDLE CONDITION
            QZERO(EOF-RTN)
        END-EXEC.
READQ-LOOP.
        EXEC CICS READQ TD --------
        END-EXEC.
            :
        (process a record)
            :
        GO TO READ-LOOP.
EOF-RTN.
            :
        (EOF processing)
```

Execution Results   During the execution of this program logic, the following activities will occur:

• At the completion of each READQ TD command, the TDQ record
  will be read sequentially.
• When no more record exists, the QZERO condition will be detected
  through the HANDLE CONDITION command and control will be
  passed to EOF-RTN.

11.4   DELETEQ TD Command

Function

The DELETEQ TD command is used to delete an Intrapartition TDQ
entirely. This command is not valid for the Extrapartition TDQ.

Format

The format of the DELETEQ TD command is shown in the example below. QUEUE names the Intrapartition TDQ you wish to delete.

Example

The following is an example of the DELETEQ TD command:

```
CICS EXEC DELETEQ TD
     QUEUE('MSGS')
END-EXEC.
```

Execution Result All records in the queue 'MSGS' will be deleted.

Common Exceptional Condition

The following is the exceptional condition common to the DELETEQ TD command:

QIDERR: The destination id specified cannot be found in DCT.

11.5 Destination Control Table (DCT)

Function

The primary function of the Destination Control Table (DCT) is to register control information of all TDQs. The CICS Destination Control Program (DCP) uses this table for identifying all TDQs and performing input/output operations against them.

DCT Entry Definition

DCT entries can be defined using an Assembler macro DFHDCT. But the options and parameters are quite different between defining Intrapartition TDQ and defining the Extrapartition TDQ.

Intrapartition TDQ The following are the commonly used options and parameters of the DFHDCT macro for defining the Intrapartitioned TDQ:

```
DFHDCT    TYPE=INTRA,
          DESTID=name,
          [TRANSID=name,],
          [TRIGLEV=number,],
          [REUSE=YES|NO]]
```

TYPE=INTRA indicates that TDQ is the Intrapartition TDQ. DESTID defines the destination id (1 to 4 characters). REUSE option defines space availability after a TDQ record has been read (see Technical Notes below). This is useful for better disk space management. For the Automatic Task Initiation (ATI: see the next section), TRANSID and TRIGLEV must be specified. TRANSID names the transaction id of the transaction to be initiated. TRIGLEV indicates the number of the records in TDQ which triggers the transaction to be initiated.

Extrapartition TDQ The following are the commonly used options and parameters of the DFHDCT macro for defining the Extrapartitioned TDQ:

```
DFHDCT    TYPE=EXTRA,
          DESTID=name,
          DSCNAME=name,
          [OPEN=INITIAL | DEFERED]


DFHDCT    TYPE=SDSCI,
          DSCNAME=name,
          [TYPEFILE=INPUT | OUTPUT | RDBACK]
```

TYPE=EXTRA indicates that this is the Extrapartition TDQ. DESTID names the destination id (1 to 4 characters). OPEN defines the initial file status. If INITIAL is specified, the file will be open at the CICS start-up time. If DEFERED is specified, the file will be closed until it is specifically opened by the Master Terminal transaction (CEMT: see Section 16.10). DSCNAME defines the data control block name (1 to 8 characters). For one DSCNAME, a corresponding DFHDCT entry must be made with TYPE=SDSCI and the same DSCNAME, which in effect indicates DDNAME of the Extrapartition dataset in JCL of CICS job itself. TYPEFILE indicates the file to be input, output or input (read backward).

Examples

The following are examples of DCT entry definition for the Intrapartition TDQ and Extrapartition TDQ:

1. Intrapartition TDQ (without ATI):

```
DFHDCT      TYPE=INTRA,
            DESTID=MSGS
```

2. Extrapartition TDQ:

```
DFHDCT      TYPE=EXTRA,
            DESTID=DST1,
            DSCNAME=DDNDST1,
            OPEN=DEFERED


DFHDCT      TYPE=SDSCI,
            DSCNAME=DDNDST1,
            TYPEFILE=OUTPUT
```

Technical Notes

Once a record of Intrapartition TDQ is read by a transaction, the record is logically removed, but it still occupies the space. If REUSE=YES is specified, this space for the logically deleted record will be used for other TDQ records. But, in this case, records are not recoverable. If REUSE=NO is specified, the logically deleted records are recoverable. Although it is up to you and your installation's policy, REUSE=YES is recommended for the better spacing purpose.

11.6 Automatic Task Initiation (ATI)

The Automatic Task Initiation (ATI) is a facility through which a CICS transaction can be initiated automatically. The number of the records in an Intrapartition TDQ triggers the transaction initiation.

The transaction id (task) must be defined in the DCT entry of the Intrapartition TDQ, with nonzero trigger level. If the number of records in the Intrapartition TDQ reaches the trigger level, the task specified will be initiated automatically by CICS.

Example

Let us suppose that we accumulate message switching records in the Intrapartition TDQ "MSGS." If the number of records reaches 1,000, we wish to start transaction MSW1 to actually deliver the messages accumulated in MSGS. In this case, the DCT entry should be defined as follows:

```
DFHDCT    TYPE=INTRA,
          DESTID=MSGS,
          TRANSID=MSW1,
          TRIGLEV=1000
```

Once this DCT entry is defined, when the number of TDQ record reaches 1,000 in Intrapartition TDQ "MSGS," CICS will automatically start transaction MSW1.

Applications

ATI can be very useful if the application is carefully chosen. The following are some of the practical applications of ATI:

- *Message switching:* As in the example above, messages can be accumulated in an Intrapartition TDQ, and at a certain level, a transaction can be initiated automatically through ATI in order to route the messages.
- *Report print:* Reports can be accumulated in an Intrapartition TDQ, and at a certain level, a transaction can be automatically initiated through ATI in order to print the reports.

11.7 Design Considerations for TDQ

In the early days of CICS, TDQ was required as the means of data passing among CICS transactions (through Intrapartition TDQ) or between CICS application program and batch program (through Extrapartition TDQ). However, the current CICS provides other better means of data passing without TDQ.

For example, VSAM/ESDS through the File Control can be used for data passing between the CICS application program and batch program. Therefore, the QSAM file as Extrapartition TDQ dataset can be substituted by the VSAM/ESDS file. Since VSAM/ESDS is much more reliable than QSAM especially in the case of system down, this approach would be better.

Another example could be a Temporary Storage Queue (TSQ: see the next chapter) for data passing among CICS transactions. If TSQ is placed in the main storage, retrieving is much faster. Therefore, the Intrapartition TDQ can be substituted by TSQ.

The further example could be the COMMAREA option in LINK, XCTL, or RETURN command, through which data can be easily passed to another program or task. This could replace the Intrapartition or Extrapartition TDQ.

Suggestions

You should take advantage of the enhanced facilities of the current CICS such as the examples above. Then, at the present time, there is not much strong need for TDQ (either Extrapartition or Intrapartition).

You should try to use TDQ only when it is definitely advantageous. The following are some advantageous applications of TDQ:

- Any applications suitable to the Automatic Task Initiation function (ATI) through the Intrapartition TDQ.
- Data passing to the personal computers from the CICS transaction through the Extrapartition TDQ.

12

Temporary Storage Control

12.1 Introduction

The CICS Temporary Storage Control Program (TSP) provides the application programs with an ability to store and retrieve the data in a Temporary Storage Queue (TSQ).

Characteristics of TSQ

A Temporary Storage Queue (TSQ) is a queue of stored records (data). It is created and deleted dynamically by an application program without specifying anything in the CICS control tables, as long as data recovery is not intended. Therefore, the application program can use TSQ as a scratch pad memory facility for any purposes.

A TSQ is identified by the queue id (1 to 8 bytes), and a record within a TSQ is identified by the relative position number called item number, as shown below:

```
A TSQ (Queue-id = xxxxxxxx)

Item = 1      2          3          4

I  rec1  I  rec2  I  rec3  I  rec4  I  .......I
```

The records in TSQ, once written, remain accessible until the entire TDQ is explicitly deleted. The records in TSQ can be read sequentially or directly. Further, the records in TSQ can be read, re-read, and even updated.

TSQ may be written in the main storage or the auxiliary storage in the direct access device (see the further discussion below). Regardless of where TSQ resides, TSQ can be accessed by any transactions in the same CICS region.

The characteristics of TSQ described above are unique to TSQ in comparison to the Transient Data Queue (TDQ).

Naming Convention for TSQ Queue Id

A TSQ identified by the queue id (QID: 1 to 8 bytes) can be accessed by any transactions in the same CICS region. This means that TSQ could be accessed by any of following transactions:

• Same transaction:
  — From same terminal
  — From different terminal
• Different transaction:
  — From same terminal
  — From different terminal

In order to avoid confusion and to maintain data security, a strict naming convention for QID will be required in the installation. The following is an example of a QID naming convention:

Format: dttttann

where,

d:	Division id (e.g., A for Account, B for Budget)
tttt:	Terminal id (EIBTRMID)
a:	Application code (A, B, C, ...)
nn:	Queue number (1, 2, ...).

Terminal ID in QID For a terminal-dependent task (e.g., pseudo-conversational task), the terminal id should be included in QID in order to ensure the uniqueness of TSQ to the task.

If TSQ is to be shared commonly with other tasks, place 'COMM', for example, in the terminal id field. Then the TSQ can be accessed by all transactions in the division.

TSQ in MAIN Storage or AUXILIARY Storage

As mentioned briefly before, TSQ can be written in the main storage. In this case, accessing TSQ is a fast and convenient operation. But TSQ in this mode is not recoverable.

Mutually exclusive to the TSQ in the main storage, TSQ can be written in the auxiliary storage. The auxiliary storage is an external VSAM file (DFHTEMP) established by the system programmer. It is always available to application programs, which implies that no file open/close is required. TSQ in this mode is recoverable. If you wish to recover TSQ in this mode, you must specify so in the Temporary Storage Table (TST). In some installations, the AUXILIARY option is encouraged because the data is recoverable and because this option does not cause main storage contention.

Available Commands

The following commands are available for the Temporary Storage Control:

WRITEQ TS: To write or rewrite a record in a TSQ.
READQ TS: To read a record in a TSQ.
DELETEQ TS: To delete a TSQ. All records in the TSQ will be deleted.

It should be noted that TS represents Temporary Storage. Since TS is default in the command format, TS can be omitted.

12.2 WRITEQ Command (No Update)

Function

The WRITEQ command is used to write a record (item) in a TSQ. In this section, we will discuss the basic WRITEQ command without the option for update.

Format

The format of the WRITEQ command is shown in the example below. QUEUE names the queue id (QID). FROM defines the area from which data is to be written. LENGTH (halfword binary field, S9(4) COMP) indicates the length of the record. A halfword binary field (S9(4) COMP) should be provided to the ITEM parameter, to which CICS places the actual item number of the record written. MAIN indicates TSQ to be written in the main storage (not auxiliary storage).

Example

The following is an example of the WRITEQ command without update:

```
WORKING-STORAGE SECTION.
01    TSQ-QID.
       05    TSQ-QID-DIV        PIC X VALUE 'A'.     <== e.g., Acc. div.
       05    TSQ-QID-TERM       PIC X(4).
       05    TSQ-QID-APPL       PIC X.
       05    TSQ-QID-NUM        PIC 99.
01    TSQ-DATA.
       05    TSQ-FIELD1         PIC X(50).
       05    TSQ-FIELD2         PIC X(150).
77    TSQ-LENGTH               PIC S9(4) COMP.
77    TSQ-ITEM                 PIC S9(4) COMP.
       :

PROCEDURE DIVISION.
       :
*
* CONSTRUCT QID.
*
       MOVE EIBTRMID TO TSQ-QID-TERM.     <== To include terminal-id.
       MOVE 'I'      TO TSQ-QID-APPL.     <== e.g. Inquiry application.
       MOVE 1        TO TSQ-QID-NUM.
       :
       (Edit TSQ data)
       :
       MOVE 200 TO TSQ-LENGTH.            <== Establish the length.
*
* WRITE A QUEUE.
*
       EXEC CICS WRITEQ
            QUEUE(TSQ-QID)
            FROM(TSQ-DATA)
```

```
      LENGTH(TSQ-LENGTH)
      ITEM(TSQ-ITEM)              <== Should be always specified.
      MAIN
   END-EXEC.
```

Execution Results During the execution of this program logic, the following activities will occur:

- If TSQ with this QID does not exist, a TSQ will be created with QID = AttttI01, where tttt is the terminal id. CICS will write a record in the TSQ identified by the QID. CICS will place the actual relative record number (i.e., item number) of the TSQ into TSQ-ITEM. You may have to remember this for later use if more than one record is in the TSQ.
- If TSQ with this QID already exists, CICS will simply write a record in the existing TSQ at the next to the last existing record, and place the relative number of the record into TSQ-ITEM.

Common Options

The following are the common options of the WRITEQ command without update:

NOSUSPEND: Even if the NOSPACE condition is detected, instead of suspending the task, CICS will return control to the next statement after the WRITEQ command.

AUXILIARY: Mutually exclusive to the MAIN option. If the AUXILIARY option is specified, the TSQ will be written in the external VSAM file.

Common Exceptional Conditions

The following is the exceptional condition common to the WRITEQ command without update:

NOSPACE: Sufficient space is not available. The default action is to suspend the task until space becomes available.

12.3   READQ Command (Direct Read)

Function

The READQ command is used to read a particular record (item) of a particular TSQ. In this section, we will discuss the direct read of a particular record.

Format

The format of the READQ command is shown in the example below. QUEUE names the queue id (QID). INTO defines the area to which the record data is to be placed. LENGTH (halfword binary field, S9(4) COMP) indicates the length of the record to be read. ITEM (halfword binary field, S9(4) COMP) indicates the item number of the record to be read.

Alternative to the INTO option, the SET option can be used in the similar manner to the READ command with the SET option.

Example

Using the same Working Storage Section of Section 12.2, the following is an example of the READQ command for the direct read:

```
PROCEDURE DIVISION.
      :
*
* CONSTRUCT QID.
*
      MOVE EIBTRMID TO TSQ-QID-TERM.     )    <== Establish QID.
      MOVE 'I'      TO TSQ-QID-APPL.     )
      MOVE 1        TO TSQ-QID-NUM.      )
      MOVE 4        TO TSQ-ITEM.    <== Assume: to read 4th record.
      MOVE 200      TO TSQ-LENGTH.  <== Specify the record length.
*
* READ A QUEUE.
*
      EXEC CICS READQ
           QUEUE(TSQ-QID)
           INTO(TSQ-DATA)
           LENGTH(TSQ-LENGTH)
           ITEM(TSQ-ITEM)              <== Required.
      END-EXEC.
```

Execution Results The 4th record of the TSQ identified by TSQ-QID will be read into TSQ-DATA. The actual length of the record will be placed in TSQ-LENGTH.

Commonly Used Options

The following are the commonly used options of the READQ command for the direct read:

NUMITEMS: If you wish to know the number of items in the TSQ, specify NUMITEMS (data-area), where the data-area is defined as PIC S9(4) COMP. At the completion of the READ command, CICS will place the actual number of the records in the TSQ specified.

NEXT: Mutually exclusive to the ITEM option, if the NEXT option is specified, the task will read the next sequential logical record in the TSQ specified. See the technical note in the next section.

Common Exceptional Conditions

The following are some exceptional conditions common to the READQ command for the direct read:

QIDERR: The specified QID is not found.
ITEMERR: The specified item number is not found. If you are reading TSQ sequentially, this condition occurs at the end of the records of the TSQ.

12.4 READQ Command (Sequential Read)

Function

The READQ command can be used also for reading all records (i.e., items) sequentially in the queue. But the sequential read of TSQ should be performed based on the programming techniques described in this section, instead of the NEXT option of the READ command.

Format

The format of the READQ command for the sequential read is the same as the case of the direct read.

Example

Using the same Working Storage Section of Section 12.2, the following is an example of the READQ command for the sequential read of TSQ:

```
PROCEDURE DIVISION.
      :
*
* CONSTRUCT QID.
*
      MOVE EIBTRMID TO TSQ-QID-TERM.
      MOVE 'I'      TO TSQ-QID-APPL.
      MOVE 1        TO TSQ-QID-NUM.
      MOVE 0        TO TSQ-ITEM.        <== Initialize item number.
      MOVE 200      TO TSQ-LENGTH.      <== Specify record length.
*
* ESTABLISH HANDLE CONDITION.
*
      EXEC CICS HANDLE CONDITION
           ITEMERR(TSQ-EOF)            <== Attention.
           ERROR(TSQ-ERROR)
      END-EXEC.
 LOOP.
      ADD 1 TO TSQ-ITEM.
      MOVE 200 TO TSQ-LENGTH.
*
* READ A QUEUE.
*
      EXEC CICS READQ
           QUEUE(TSQ-QID)
           INTO(TSQ-DATA)
           LENGTH(TSQ-LENGTH)
           ITEM(TSQ-ITEM)              <== Required.
      END-EXEC.
      :
      (Process a record.)
```

```
   :
   GO TO LOOP.
TSQ-EOF.
   (EOF Processing)
   :
```

Execution Results   During the execution of this program logic, the following activities will occur:

- At the completion of each READQ command, the record will be sequentially read one by one based on the value in TSQ-ITEM.
- When there are no more records to read, the ITEMERR condition (implying the end of TSQ) will be detected through the HANDLE CONDITION command, and control will be passed to TSQ-EOF.

Technical Notes

The sequential read of TSQ should be done through this approach. This approach is better than specifying the NEXT option in the READQ command, which gives the application program the next record to the current record (i.e., item) read by any CICS transaction.

This means that if the NEXT option is specified in the READQ command instead of the ITEM option for a TSQ, and if other tasks have read several records of the same TSQ after the last read by this task, then this task would read a skipped record (i.e., not next to the record this task read last). Therefore, the NEXT option should be used very carefully, if you have to use it.

12.5   WRITEQ Command with REWRITE Option

Function

The WRITEQ command with the REWRITE option is used to rewrite a record (item) of a TSQ, which has been read.

Format

The format of the WRITEQ command with the REWRITE option is shown in the example below. REWRITE must be explicitly specified as the option. Other options and parameters are the same as the case of the WRITEQ command without update (Section 12.2).

Example

Let us suppose that you wish to update the fourth record (item) read in Section 12.3. The following is an example of the WRITEQ command with the REWRITE option for TSQ record update:

```
PROCEDURE DIVISION.
    :
    (READQ as per Section 12.3)
    :
    (Process data in TSQ-DATA)
    :
    EXEC CICS WRITEQ
        QUEUE(TSQ-QID)
        FROM(TSQ-DATA)
        LENGTH(TSQ-DATA)
        ITEM(TSQ-ITEM)
        REWRITE
        MAIN
    END-EXEC.
```

Execution Results   The fourth record (item) of the TSQ will be updated.

Technical Notes

The READQ command does not hold exclusive control over TSQ, as you note that there is no UPDATE option in the READQ command. Therefore, if a TSQ is shared by other transactions, it is the application program's responsibility to establish exclusive control over the TSQ during update. In this case, you must use the ENQ command before the READQ command and the DEQ command after the WRITEQ command with the REWRITE option (see Section 13.11).

However, if the QID of the TSQ includes the terminal id, then the queue is unique to the terminal. Therefore, most of the time, the ENQ/DEQ commands would not be required. This is one of the reasons why QID should include the terminal id.

12.6   DELETEQ Command

Function

The DELETEQ command is used to delete a TSQ entirely.

Format

The format is shown in the example below. QUEUE names the queue id of TSQ you wish to delete.

Example

The following is an example of the DELETEQ command:

```
:
(Establish QID)
:
EXEC CICS DELETEQ
     QUEUE(TSQ-QID)
END-EXEC.
```

Execution Results   The specified TSQ will be deleted; that is, all records (items) in the TSQ will be deleted.

Common Exceptional Condition

The following is the exceptional condition common to the DELETEQ command:

  QIDERR: The queue id specified is not found.

12.7   Design Considerations for TSQ

The Temporary Storage Queue (TSQ) placed in the main storage has many advantages over the Transient Data Queue (TDQ). Some of these advantages are:

• TSQ is efficient.

• TSQ is convenient.

Therefore, you should use TSQ as a "scratch pad" whenever it is applicable. Then, practically, you would not need TDQ. The only drawback of TSQ is that the records in TSQ with the MAIN option are nonrecoverable after a system crash or transaction ABEND. But, if you use TSQ as a "scratch pad," the loss would be really minimal even in such cases. You could restart the same transaction or reenter the same transaction for retry.

Applications of TSQ

TSQ can be used as a "scratch pad" for any application. Following are some typical applications:

• *Data passing among transactions:* This is especially useful in the pseudo-conversational mode, because data can be passed from one transaction to the other transactions, all of which are related as the pseudo-conversational transactions for one function.
• *Review mode in the multiple screens:* Review and correction of multiple order entry screens (for example) can be accomplished by saving the screen data in TSQ, and later retrieving them for review and correction.
• *Report Printing:* One transaction accumulates report data in TSQ. Then it initiates another transaction to print the report.

Exercise

Develop the Personnel Evaluation Report (PER1) transaction based on the following specifications:

1. Transaction id is PER1 and Program id is TXTCPER1.
2. The program uses the Personnel Master File (PERVSPMS) described in the Exercise for Chapter 4.
3. Code two maps MPBPER2/MSBPER2 and MPBPER3/MSBPER3 as follows:

Mapname = MPBPER2, Mapset name = MSBPER2

```
I      PERSONNEL EVALUATION REPORT DATA ENTRY              PER2 I
I                                                               I
I          EMP-NO       COMMENTS                                I
I  1.      nnnnn        xxxxxxxxxxxxxxxxxxxx                     I
I  2.      nnnnn        xxxxxxxxxxxxxxxxxxxx                     I
I  3.      nnnnn        xxxxxxxxxxxxxxxxxxxx                     I
I                                                               I
I          MORE DATA (Y/N): x                                   I
I yyyyyyyyyyyyyyyyyyyyyyyyyyyyyyyyyyyyyyyyyyyyyyyyyyyyyyyyyyyyy I
I yyyyyyyyyyyyyyyyyyyyyyyyyyyyyyyyyyyyyyyyyyyyyyyyyyyyyyyyyyyyy I
I yyyyyyyyyyyyyyyyyyyyyyyyyyyyyyyyyyyyyyyyyyyyyyyyyyyyyyyyyyyyy I
I yyyyyyyyyyyyyyyyyyyyyyyyyyyyyyyyyyyyyyyyyyyyyyyyyyyyyyyyyyyyy I
```

Mapname = MPBPER3, Mapset name = MSBPER3

```
I                PERSONNEL EVALUATION REPORT            PER3  I
I                                               PAGE: zz      I
I       EMP-NO  NAME                         COMMENTS         I
I  1. 99999  yyyyyyyyyyyyyyyyyyyyyyyyy   yyyyyyyyyyyyyyyyyyyy I
I  2. 99999  yyyyyyyyyyyyyyyyyyyyyyyyy   yyyyyyyyyyyyyyyyyyyy I
I  3. 99999  yyyyyyyyyyyyyyyyyyyyyyyyy   yyyyyyyyyyyyyyyyyyyy I
I  4. 99999  yyyyyyyyyyyyyyyyyyyyyyyyy   yyyyyyyyyyyyyyyyyyyy I
I  5. 99999  yyyyyyyyyyyyyyyyyyyyyyyyy   yyyyyyyyyyyyyyyyyyyy I
I                                                             I
I       END OF DISPLAY                                        I
I       ENTER PAGING COMMAND (EG. P/N, P/P, ETC): xxxxxxx     I
```

                where,

                     n: Unprotected numeric field
                     x: Unprotected alphanumeric field
                z or 9:   Autoskipped, edited numeric filed
                     y: Autoskipped alphanumeric field
                     _: Initial cursor position

Technical Notes:

- Above screen layouts should be considered as a guideline. The actual field position can be a little shifted. Try to code user-friendly maps.
- All title fields are autoskipped fields.

- The cursor must be skipped automatically to the next unprotected field.
- The "END OF DISPLAY" field is initially invisible.

4. The program starts with sending map MPBPER2/ MSBPER2. Return with the external transaction id = PER1 and the internal transaction id = PER2.

5. Upon receiving control again, receive the map PER2. Verify the input data. The employee numbers received must exist in the PMS file. The comment must be entered. The "MORE DATA (Y/N)" field must be "Y" or "N." If the data is invalid, highlight the field, position the cursor, send proper error message(s) and return with the external transaction id = PER1 and the internal transaction id = PER2, so that the user can correct and reenter.

5. If the data is valid, and if the "MORE DATA" filed is "Y," write record(s), with the employee number, name, and comment, into a TSQ whose QID is:

```
"T" + EIBTRMID + "PER"
```

Send a fresh map PER2. Return with the external transaction id = PER1 and the internal transaction id = PER2.

6. Let us assume that the terminal user enters data in the PER2 screen several times, then types "N" to the "MORE DATA" field.

7. If the data in the map PER2 is valid and if the "MORE DATA" field is "N," read all records sequentially in the TSQ. Edit the data onto map MPBPER3/MSBPER3. If the screen becomes full, send it as the multipage message. The page number on the top of the screen must be incremented properly. Repeat until EOF in the TSQ. The last PER3 screen must have "END OF DISPLAY" visible. Send the page. Delete the TSQ and terminate the task.

13

Interval Control and Task Control

13.1 Introduction

Interval Control

The CICS Interval Control Program (ICP) provides application programs with time-controlled functions, such as the time-oriented task synchronization, providing current date and time, and the automatic initiation of the time-ordered tasks.

Available Commands The following commands are available for the Interval Control:

ASKTIME:	To request the current date and time.
FORMATTIME:	To select a format of date and time.
DELAY:	To delay the processing of a task.
POST:	To request notification of when the specified time has expired.
WAIT EVENT:	To wait for an event to occur.
START:	To start a transaction and store data for the task.
RETRIEVE:	To retrieve the data stored by the START command for a transaction.
CANCEL:	To cancel the effect of the previous interval control command.

Task Control

The CICS Task Control Program (KCP) provides functions of synchronization of task activities and exclusive control of resources.

Available Commands   The following commands are available for the Task Control:

SUSPEND: To suspend a task.
ENQ: To gain exclusive control over a resource.
DEQ: To release exclusive control from a resource.

13.2   ASKTIME Command

Function

The ASKTIME command is used to request the current date and time. The EIBDATE and EIBTIME fields have the values at the task initiation time. Upon the completion of this command, these fields will be updated to have the current date and time.

Format .

The format of the ASKTIME is as follows:

```
EXEC CICS ASKTIME
END-EXEC.
```

This command can be placed in any place of the Procedure Division of the application program, where very accurate information of time and date is required.

13.3   FORMATTIME Command

Function

The FORMATTIME command is used to receive the information of date and time in various formats.

Format

The format of the FORMATTIME command with the commonly used options is as follows:

```
EXEC CICS FORMATTIME
      [YYDDD(data-area)]
      [YYMMDD(data-area)]
      [YYDDMM(data-area)]
      [MMDDYY(data-area)]
      [DDMMYY(data-area)]
      [DATESEP(data-value)]
      [DAYOFWEEK(data-area)]
      [DAYOFMONTH(data-area)]
      [MONTHOFYEAR(data-area)]
      [YEAR(data-area)]
      [TIME(data-area)
          [TIMESEP(data-value)]]
END-EXEC.
```

YYDDD, YYMMDD, YYDDMM, DDMMYY are used to receive the date in the form yy/ddd, yy/mm/dd, yy/dd/mm, mm/dd/yy, respectively, where "/" is the date separator. DATESEP indicates the date separator (default is "/"). If DATESEP is omitted, no data separator will be provided. DAYOFWEEK, DAYOFMONTH, MONTHOFYEAR, YEAR are used to receive the day of week (0 to 6), day of month (1 to 31), the month of year (1 to 12), and year, respectively. TIME is used to receive the time in the form of hh:mm:ss, where ":" is the time separater. TIMESEP indicates the time separator (default is ":"). If TIMESEP is omitted, no time separator will be provided.

Example

The following is an example of the FORMATTME command with the MMDDYY and TIME options:

```
WORKING-STORAGE SECTION.
01    WK-DATE.
         05    WK-D-MM    PIC 99.
         05    FILLER     PIC X.
         05    WK-D-DD    PIC 99.
         05    FILLER     PIC X.
         05    WK-D-YY    PIC 99.
```

```
01   WK-TIME.
     05   WK-T-HH   PIC 99.
     05   FILLER    PIC X.
     05   WK-T-MM   PIC 99.
     05   FILLER    PIC X.
     05   WK-T-SS   PIC 99.
     :
     :
PROCEDURE DIVISION.
     :
     :
     EXEC CICS FORMATTIME
          MMDDYY(WK-DATE)
          DATESEP
          TIME(WK-TIME)
          TIMESEP
     END-EXEC.
```

Execution Results   At the completion of this program logic, the following activities will occur:

- WK-DATE will contain the current date in the form of mm/dd/yy.
- WK-TIME will contain the current time in the form of hh:mm:ss.
- "/" and ":" are default separators for the date and time, respectively. You can change these separators by specifying other characters in the DATESEP and TIMESEP parameter, respectively.

13.4   DELAY Command

Function

The DELAY command is used to delay the processing of a task for the specified time interval or until the specified time.

Format

The format of the DELAY command is shown in the example below. INTERVAL defines the delay interval in the form of hhmmss. TIME defines the time in the form of hhmmss until when the task is to be delayed.

Example

The following is an example of the DELAY command:

```
EXEC CICS DELAY
     INTERVAL(001500)              <==  or TIME(163000)
END-EXEC.
```

Execution Results   The task will be suspended for 15 minutes if IN-TERVAL is specified, or until 16:30:00 if TIME is specified.

Application

If a heavy CPU bound calculation is performed in a task, it is a good practice to place the DELAY command in order to allow other tasks to proceed, because of the nature of the quasi-reentrancy of CICS task. For further discussion, see Section 13.10.

13.5   POST and WAIT EVENT Commands

Function

The POST command is used to request notification when the specified time has expired. The WAIT EVENT command is used to wait for an event to occur. Usually these two commands are used with a pair, as an alternative to the DELAY command.

Format

The format of the POST and WAIT EVENT commands are shown in the example below. The BLL cell must be prepared for these commands. The fullword field (S9(8) COMP) must be defined as the event control block (ECB) for the POST command. SET of the POST command and ECADDR of the WAIT EVENT command names the pointer-reference in the BLL cell. INTERVAL or TIME of the POST command defines the task suspension interval or the time until when the task is to be suspended, respectively, in the form of hhmmss.

Example

The following is an example of the POST and WAIT EVENT commands:

```
LINKAGE SECTION.
01    PARM-LIST.
      02    FILLER          PIC S9(8) COMP.
      02    POST-PTR        PIC S9(8) COMP.
01    POST-ECB.
      02    FILLER          PIC S9(8) COMP.
PROCEDURE DIVISION.
      :
      EXEC CICS POST
            INTERVAL(000010)                <==  or TIME(163000)
            SET(POST-PTR)
      END-EXEC.
*
      EXEC CICS WAIT EVENT
            ECADDR(POST-PTR)
      END-EXEC.
      :
      :
```

Execution Results During the execution of this program logic, the following activities will occur:

- The POST command will suspend the task for 10 seconds if INTERVAL is specified, or until 16:30:00 if TIME is specified.
- The WAIT EVENT command checks ECB set by the POST command for time expiration. When the time has expired, control will be given to the statement after the WAIT EVENT command.

Improvements by VS COBOL II

If the application program is written in VS COBOL II, the above example becomes simpler. The differences are as follows:

1. PARM-LIST as the BLL cell in the Linkage Section is not required.
2. The SET option of the POST command must use the special word ADDRESS for address pointer to the 01 area defined in the Linkage Section, as follows:

```
EXEC CICS POST
     INTERVAL(000010)                            or    TIME(163000)
     SET(ADDRESS OF POST-ECB)
END-EXEC.
```

13.6 START Command

Function

The START command is used to start a transaction at the specified terminal and at the specified time or interval. Optionally, data can be passed to the to-be-initiated transaction.

Format

The basic format of the START command is shown in the example below. TRANSID defines the transaction id of a transaction which you wish to initiate. TERMID defines the terminal id of a terminal (display terminal or printer) against which you intitiate the transaction. If TERMID is omitted, the specified transaction will be initiated against the terminal with which the current transaction is associated. TIME or INTERVAL indicates the time or the time interval of the transaction initiation, respectively, in the form of hhmmss.

Example

The following is an example of the basic START command:

```
EXEC CICS START
     TRANSID('REP1')
     TERMID('PRT1')
     TIME(083000)                 <==   or    INTERVAL(001500)
END-EXEC.
```

Execution Results   Transaction 'REP1' will be started on terminal (or printer) 'PRT1' at 8:30 (if TIME is specified) or 15 minutes later (if INTERVAL is specified).

Commonly Used Options

The data can be passed to the to-be-started transaction by specifying the following options:

FROM: To pass a field in the Working Storage Section.
LENGTH: To specify the length of the FROM field.
RTRANSID: To pass the transaction id (4 bytes) of the return transaction which initiates the new transaction.
RTERMID: To pass the terminal id (4 bytes) of the return terminal where the current transaction is being executed.
QUEUE: To pass the queue id (8 bytes) of a TSQ.

These data must be retrieved by the RETRIEVE command in the to-be-initiated transaction (see Section 13.8).

Applications

A typical application example of the START command is the following: One transaction prepares the TSQ records for report printing, and at the end, it starts the transaction REP1. Upon the initiation, the transaction REP1 reads the TSQ and simply prints onto the local printer by issuing the SEND MAP PRINT command.

Also, the START command is often used with the RETRIEVE command for initiating transactions in the remote CICS systems in the multisystem environment. We will discuss this topic in detail in Chapter 17.

13.7 Scheduled Transaction Initiation (STI)

Function

A special application of the START command is the Scheduled Transaction Initiation (STI), by which certain CICS transactions can be initiated automatically at the scheduled time or interval.

Program List Table (PLT)

STI is achieved in conjunction with the Program List Table (PLT). The Post-Initialization (PI) entry of PLT specifies a list of programs which are to be automatically executed by CICS immediately after CICS start-up. This table entry is usually referred to as PLTPI.

In order to achieve STI, an STI program (let us call STIPROG, for example) must be registered in the PLTPI entry, as well as the ordinary PPT entry. The requirements are the following:

In the System Intialization Table (SIT), specify:

```
PLTPI=xx        where xx is the PLT suffix.
```

In PLT, specify:

```
DFHPLT    TYPE=INITIAL,
          SUFFIX=xx
DFHPLT    TYPE=ENTRY,
          PROGRAM=(program[,program, ... ])
```

Example The following are examples of SIT entry and PLTPI entry:

```
In SIT,          PLTPI=I1


In PLT,          DFHPLT           TYPE=INITIAL,
                                  SUFFIX=I1
                 DFHPLT           TYPE=ENTRY,
                                  PROGRAM=(STIPROG)
```

Results Immediately after CICS comes up, program STIPROG will be executed automatically by CICS.

Technical Note The programs to be registered in PLT must also be registered in PPT as usual, since they are the application programs under CICS.

STI at Scheduled Time

If you wish to initiate a CICS transaction automatically at the scheduled time, you can achieve this by specifying the START command with the TIME option in the STI program registered in PLTPI.

Example In program STIPROG, specify:

```
EXEC CICS START
     TRANSID('ADI1')
     TERMID('ACC1')
     TIME(090000)
END-EXEC.
```

Execution Results For this program logic, the following activities will occur:

* Immediately after CICS comes up (for example, at 7:00 A.M.), CICS will automatically execute program STIPROG.
* Program STIPROG will issue the START command with the TIME option.
* As specified in the START command, transaction ADI1 will be automatically initiated by CICS at terminal ACC1 at 9:00 A.M.

STI at Scheduled Interval

If you wish to initiate a CICS transaction automatically and repeatedly at the scheduled interval (for example, every hour), you can achieve this by specifying the START command with the INTERVAL option in the STI program registered in PLTPI, as well as in the program associated with the transaction to be initiated.

Example In program STIPROG, specify:

```
EXEC CICS START
     TRANSID('MSG1')
     TERMID('CTR1')
     INTERVAL(010000)
END-EXEC.
```

The same START command must be specified at the end of the program (for example, PROGMSG1) associated with the MSG1 transaction.

Execution Results For this program logic, the following activities will occur:

* Immediately after CICS comes up (for example, at 7:00 A.M.), CICS will automatically execute program STIPROG.

• Program STIPROG will issue the START command with the IN-TERVAL option.
• One hour later, as specified in the START command, transaction MSG1 will be initiated automatically by CICS at terminal CTR1.
• Right before completing processing, MSG1 transaction (or program PROGMSG1) will issue the same START command with the IN-TERVAL option.
• One hour later, as specified in the START command, the same MSG1 transaction will be automatically initiated again by CICS at terminal CTR1.
• This will be repeated until CICS comes down. In effect, the MSG1 transaction will be automatically and repeatedly executed at the one-hour interval.

Applications

You could find many useful applications of STI in the actual business environment. For example, the day initialization transaction (ADI1) for the accounting system could be automatically initiated at 9:00 a.m. by CICS every day without any manual intervention. This is a good example of STI at the scheduled time.

Another example is that the message switching transaction (MSG1) could be automatically and repeatedly initiated at the one-hour interval by CICS without any manual intervention. This is a good example of STI at the schedule interval.

13.8   RETRIEVE Command

Function

The RETRIEVE command is used to retrieve the data passed by the START command which was issued in the other transaction in order to initiate this transaction.

Format

The format of the RETRIEVE command is shown in the example below. INTO defines the field in the Working Storage Section to which the data field passed by the FROM option of the START command is to be placed. LENGTH indicates the length of the INTO field. RTRANSID (4 bytes), RTERMID (4 bytes), and QUEUE (8 bytes) define the fields to which the transaction id, terminal id, and QID passed by the START command are to be placed, respectively.

Example

Let us assume that a transaction initiates a new transaction (INQ1) by issuing the START command with accompanying data. The following is an example of the START command in the original transaction and the RETREIVE command in the new (i.e., to be initiated) transaction:

1. In the transaction which is to initiate a new transaction (INQ1):

```
WORKING-STORAGE SECTION.
77    DATAFLD        PIC X(100).
77    QNAME          PIC X(8).
      :
PROCEDURE DIVISION.
      :
    (establish data in DATAFLD.)
    (establish QID in QNAME.)
      :
    EXEC CICS START
        INTERVAL(001500)
        TRANSID('INQ1')
        TERMID('TRM1')
        FROM(DATAFLD)                )  )
        LENGTH(100)                  )  )
        RTRANSID(EIBTRNID)           )  )  Optional.
        RTERMID(EIBTRMID)            )  )
        QUEUE(QNAME)                 )  )
    END-EXEC.
```

2. In the transaction (INQ1) which is to be initiated by the START command:

```
WORKING-STORAGE SECTION.
77    DATAFLD        PIC X(100).
77    RETTRN         PIC X(4).
```

```
77    RETTRM          PIC X(4).
77    RETQID          PIC X(8).
      :
PROCEDURE DIVISION.
      :
      EXEC CICS RETRIEVE
           INTO(DATAFLD)             ))
           LENGTH(100)               ))  Corresponds to options
           RTRANSID(RETTRN)          ))  in the START command.
           RTERMID(RETTRM)           ))
           QUEUE(RETQID)             ))
      END-EXEC.
```

Execution Results During the execution of these program logics, the following activities will occur:

- At the completion of the START command, the original transaction will initiate the new transaction (INQ1) based on the time specification (15 minutes later, in this case), and the data DATAFLD (100 bytes), transaction id, terminal id, and QID will be passed to the new transaction (INQ1).
- 15 minutes later, CICS will actually initiate the INQ1 transaction.
- At the completion of the RETRIEVE command, the INQ1 transaction will receive all specified data passed from the original transaction which has initiated this INQ1 transaction.

13.9 CANCEL Command

Function

The CANCEL command is used to cancel the Interval Control commands, such as DELAY, POST, and START, which have been issued. The Interval Control commands to be cancelled are identified by the REQID parameter of these commands.

Format

The format of the CANCEL command is shown in the example below. REQID defines the request id (up to 8 characters) which identifies the interval control command to be cancelled.

Example

Let us assume that you wish to cancel the START and DELAY commands which have been issued. The following is an example of the CANCEL command to cancel these commands:

```
EXEC CICS START
     REQID('START1')              <=== Specify Request-Id.
     --------                          (1 to 8 characters)
END-EXEC.
     :
     :
EXEC CICS DELAY
     REQID('DELAY1')
     --------
END-EXEC.
     :
     :
EXEC CICS CANCEL
     REQID('START1')         <=== Identifies which command to be
END-EXEC.                          canceled.
EXEC CICS CANCEL
     REQID('DELAY1')
END-EXEC.
```

Execution Results At the completion of the CANCEL command, the START and DELAY commands identified by START1 and DELAY1, respectively, will be cancelled.

13.10 SUSPEND Command

Function

The SUSPEND command is used to suspend a task. During the execution of this command, the task will be suspended, and control will be given to other tasks with higher priority. As soon as all higher-priority tasks have been executed, control will be returned to the suspended task.

Format

The format of the SUSPEND command is as follows:

```
EXEC CICS SUSPEND
END-EXEC.
```

Applications

Because of the quasi-reentrancy of the CICS programs, if a CPU intensive processing is performed in a program, it is a good practice to issue the SUSPEND command from time to time in the program in order to allow other tasks to proceed, similar to the case of the DELAY command. This practice will improve the transaction throughput of the CICS region as a whole.

For example, if a program has a repetitive processing of a CPU intensive subroutine 1,000 times, the program should issue the SUSPEND command at every 100 repetitions of this subroutine.

13.11 ENQ and DEQ Commands

Function

The ENQ command is used to gain exclusive control over a resource. The DEQ command is used to free the exclusive control from the resource. However, it should be noted that specifying the ENQ and DEQ commands under CICS is a convention, and unless all tasks (programs) use the ENQ and DEQ commands against the resource, exclusive control will not be maintained.

Format

The formats of the ENQ and DEQ are shown in the example below. RESOURCE defines the name of the resource to be ENQ'ed or DEQ'ed.

Example

Let us suppose that we wish to update a TSQ securely by reserving the exclusive control over the TSQ during the update. The following is an example of the ENQ and DEQ commands:

```
(Establish QID in TSQ-QID.)
    :
```

```
EXEC CICS ENQ                          <== The resource is reserved.
     RESOURCE(TSQ-QID)
     END-EXEC.
EXEC CICS READQ                        <== TSQ is read for update.
     QUEUE(TSQ-QID)--------
END-EXEC.
     :
(update the contents of TSQ)
     :
EXEC CICS WRITEQ                       <== TSQ is rewritten.
     QUEUE(TSQ-QID)--------
     REWRITE
END-EXEC.
EXEC CICS DEQ
     RESOURCE(TSQ-QID)                 <== The resource is freed.
END-EXEC.
```

Execution Results   During the execution of this program logic, the following activities will occur:

- At the completion of the ENQ command, TSQ specified by TSQ-QID will be exclusively controlled by this task.
- Therefore, this transaction can maintain data integrity during updating the TSQ by the READQ and WRITEQ/REWRITE commands.
- At the completion of the DEQ command, exclusive control over the TSQ will be released.

Common Options

The following are some of the commonly used options of the ENQ and/or DEQ commands:

LENGTH: If the resource is a character string, the LENGTH parameter must be specified in both ENQ/DEQ commands. The halfword binary (PIC S9(4) COMP) must have the length of the character string.

NOSUSPEND: If this is specified, even if the ENQBUSY condition occurs, control will be returned to the statement after the ENQ command.

Common Exceptional Condition

The following is the exceptional condition common to the ENQ command:

ENQBUSY: The resource specified is reserved to another task. The task will be suspended until the resource is freed by the other task.

Design Considerations

CICS automatically provides exclusive control over resources to a task in most cases (the above case of TSQ is only one of few exceptions). Therefore, a CICS application system should be developed in such a way that an application program does not have to issue the ENQ and DEQ commands. In other words, if an application program has to use the ENQ and DEQ commands, probably there could be some problem in the application system design.

However, for certain sharable resources, the ENQ and DEQ commands must be used for maintaining data integrity. Two typical examples are TSQ and printer. For updating TSQ among transactions, QID of the TSQ must be ENQ'ed and DEQ'ed. Similarly, the printer id must be ENQ'ed and DEQ'ed for printing into a printer which is shared among transactions.

Comments on Coding Example Above

If you wish to update a TSQ shared among other tasks, you must use the ENQ and DEQ commands as in the coding example above. However, TSQ should be used for a scratch pad purpose within a task itself. In this case, since only one task is using the TSQ, update can be done without the ENQ and DEQ commands. If TSQ is shared among tasks, this TSQ should be the read-only TSQ. Then, the tasks which use this TSQ do not have to issue the ENQ and DEQ commands.

Therefore, a design strategy for the coding example above should have been that the information in the TSQ be placed in a record of a VSAM file instead of TSQ. Then tasks can update the record using the File Control commands without issuing the ENQ and DEQ commands because CICS automatically takes care of exclusive control over the record in the file during update. This illustrates that use of the ENQ and DEQ commands can be avoided by the application system design.

Chapter

14

System Security

14.1 Introduction

In a DB/DC system environment, anybody who has authority to access the system can access other resources under the same DB/DC system. For example, if someone has CICS user id, he/she can access any transaction, and consequently files. The data in the file may be confidential, or some data must be updated based on strict conventions. Therefore, in order to prevent leak of information or loss (a damage) of data, the security of the system is a crucial issue.

CICS Security Facilities

As the DB/DC system becomes more complex, the issue of system security becomes more important. Therefore, usually the DB/DC software provides its own security facilities, and CICS offers some built-in security control facilities in order to protect not only an application system but also the CICS system as a whole.

The following are some of the CICS security control facilities which are related to application programming:

- Sign-on Table (SNT)
- Transaction Security
- Resource Security
- Resource Access Control Facility (RACF)
- Other Security Management Techniques

14.2 Sign-on Table (SNT)

Function

The primary function of the Sign-on Table (SNT) is to register the security information of all CICS users. Therefore, all CICS users must be registered in SNT.

SNT offers the following security mechanism to the users:

- Name or user id
- Password
- Resource security (optional)
- Transaction security (optional)
- Time out (optional)

In order to use the CICS system, each user has to sign on to the terminal using the sign-on transaction (CESN or CSSN). CESN requests the user id and password, based on which the user must type his/her own user id and password. Only if both user id and password entered are valid will CICS complete sign-on. Unless sign-on is successfully completed, the user cannot initiate a protected transaction and/or the user cannot use protected resources.

Alternatively, sign-on can be accomplished through the conventional CSSN transaction. We will discuss the differences between CESN and CSSN transactions shortly.

SNT Entry Definition

One SNT entry can be defined using an Assembler macro DFHSNT. The following are commonly used options and parameters of the DFHSNT macro:

```
DFHSNT    TYPE=ENTRY,
          [EXTSEC=NO | YES],
          [OPCLASS=1 | (n1,n2,....)],
          [OPIDENT=op-id],
          [OPNAME='name'],
          [OPPRTY=0 | number],
          [PASSWORD=name],
          [RSLKEY=(n1,n2,....)],
          [SCTYKEY=1 | n1,n2,...)],
          [TIMEOUT=number],
          [USERID=user-id]
```

EXTSEC=YES must be specified if an External Security Manager (ESM) such as RACF is to be accessed from CICS. OPCLASS defines the operator class (1 to 24). OPIDENT defines the operator group identifier (1 to 3 characters). OPNAME and PASSWORD define the name of the operator (1 to 20 characters) and his/her password (1 to 8 characters), respectively. IF EXTSEC=YES is specified, USERID must be specified, instead of OPNAME and PASSWORD. OPPRTY indicates the priority (0 to 255) to be given to the operator. RSLKEY and SCTYKEY define the resource level key (1 to 24) and transaction security key (1 to 64), respectively, discussed further in Sections 14.4 and 14.3, respectively. TIMEOUT is the timeout length in minutes between transactions. If this timeout length is expired, CICS will cancel the operator's CICS session. USERID defines the user id (1 to 7 characters) of the system defined by ESM. This must be specified if EXTSEC=YES is specified.

Example

The following example is a typical definition of one SNT entry for one terminal user:

```
DFHSNT     TYPE=ENTRY,
           EXTSEC=YES,
           OPIDENT=ACC,
           OPPRTY=3,
           SCTYKEY=7,
           TIMEOUT=30,
           USERID=ACC01S1
```

Sign-on Transactions

There are two sign-on transactions available: CESN and CSSN. CESN is the sign-on transaction with the External Security Manager (ESM) such as RACF. The ESM user id defined in SNT and the associated password must be provided for the CESN transaction.

On the other hand, the conventional CSSN is for the sign-on transaction without ESM. The OPNAME and PASSWORD defined in SNT must be provided for the transaction.

For further discussion, refer to Section 14.5.

14.3   Transaction Security

CICS transaction security function allows only the authorized user to be able to initiate a protected transaction. Proper use of this function protects the high-security transaction very effectively.

Procedures

The following is a set of procedures for using the transaction security function to protect the transaction:

1. In the SNT of the operator (i.e., terminal user) whom you wish to allow to access the protected transactions, specify SCTYKEY=n.
2. In PCT entry of transactions which you wish to protect, specify security key in the TRANSEC parameter as follows:

```
DFHPCT    TYPE=ENTRY,
          TRANSID=xxxx,
          PROGRAM=yyyyyyyy,
          :
          TRANSEC=1 | n
```

Effects

In order for a CICS user id to be able to initiate this transaction, the number in TRANSEC must be specified with the value of SCTYKEY=n in the SNT entry for the CICS user id. Only when SCTYKEY=n and TRANSSEC=n match, does CICS initiate the transaction. Otherwise, CICS rejects the transaction when the unauthorized CICS user tries to activate it. Thereby, the transaction is secured.

Example

The following is an example of SNT and PCT entries for using the transaction security function:

SNT Entry Definition

```
DFHSNT      TYPE=ENTRY,
            USERID=TESTUSR,
            SCTYKEY=7,                          <== Attention.
            :
```

PCT Entry Definition

```
DFHPCT      TYPE=ENTRY,
            TRANSID=TSK1,
            PROGRAM=PROG1,
            TRANSEC=7,                          <== Attention.
            :
```

Results These entry definitions will achieve the following:

- Transaction TSK1 will be protected by TRANSEC=7.
- If user TESTUSR signs on to a terminal and tries to start transaction TSK1, TSK1 will be initiated, since this user is authorized to use TSK1 by SCTYKEY=7 in his/her SNT entry.
- If other users, who do not have SCTYKEY=7 in SNT, try to initiate TSK1 even after a successful completion of the sign on, there will be a security violation and the task will not be initiated.

14.4 Resource Security

CICS Resource Security function allows only authorized users and transactions to access the protected resources. This is an advanced way of protecting the resources.

Procedures

The following is a set of the procedures for using the resource security function to protect the resources:

1. In the SNT entry of the operator (i.e., terminal user) you wish to allow to access the protected resourecs, specify RSLKEY=n.
2. Depending on which resources you wish to protect, specify RSL=n in:

FCT   for protecting files.
JCT   for protecting journals.
PCT   for protecting transactions.
PPT   for protecting programs.
DCT   for protecting transient data.
TST   for protecting TSQs in the auxiliary file.

3. In PCT entry of all transactions in which you wish the resource security level check to be mandated, specify RSLC=YES.

Effects

If a terminal user initiates a transaction with RSLC=YES, the transaction can access only those resources with RSL=n in the corresponding control table whose n matches that of RSLKEY=n in the SNT entry of the user, or resources without RSL=n in corresponding control table. If this condition is not met, the application program could not access the resource. CICS will return the NOTAUTH condition to the command which accessed the resource.

Example

Let us suppose that we wish to protect a file (FILEAAA), which is accessed by the transaction TSK1. The following is an example of the SNT, FCT, and PCT entry coding for the resource security function:

SNT Entry Definition

```
DFHSNT    TYPE=ENTRY,
          USERID=TESTUSR,
          RSLKEY=3,              <== Attention.
          :
```

FCT Entry Definition

```
DFHFCT    TYPE=DATASET,
          DATASET=FILEAAA,
          RSL=3,                 <== Attention.
          :
```

PCT Entry Definition

```
DFHPCT     TYPE=ENTRY,
           TRANSID=TSK1,
           PROGRAM=PROG1,
           RSLC=YES,                        <== Attention.
           :
```

Results   These entry definitions will achieve the following:

* File FILEAAA will be protected by RSL=3 of its FCT entry.
* Let us suppose that TSK1 (PROG1) uses FILEAAA. If the user TESTUSR logs on and tries to start the transaction TSK1, TSK1 (PROG1) will be able to access file FILEAAA, since this user is authorized to access the resource by RSLKEY=3 in his/her SNT entry.
* If other users, who do not have RSLKEY=3 in SNT, try to start TSK1 even after successful sign on, TSK1 (PROG1) will encounter the NOTAUTH condition (i.e., security authorization failed).

14.5   Resource Access Control Facility (RACF)

The Resource Access Control Facility (RACF) is an IBM resource security software product which protects a wide variety of resources. CICS has an interface to RACF as an External Security Manager (ESM). Therefore, even within the CICS region, you can use RACF functions against resources you wish to protect.

The following are some examples of resources you can protect through RACF under CICS:

* User id and password
* Files
* Transactions
* Programs
* Journals
* Temporary Storage
* Transient Data

Procedures

As long as the interface is fully established by the system programmer, you can use RACF in a normal manner. For the details of

RACF functions, refer to the Help function of RACF option in TSO/ISPF or equivalent.

User Id and Password Protection

If RACF is specified as ESM to CICS, RACF takes over the password assignment from SNT. For this, in SNT, EXTRSEC=YES and USERID=user id must be specified. The user id to be specified in SNT must be RACF user id. For the sign-on transaction (CESN), RACF user id and password must be provided (i.e., not OPNAME and PASSWORD in SNT).

RACF expires the password after the specified interval. Then the new password must be supplied, as the normal procedures for RACF. Since the password specified in SNT by the PASSWORD parameter is fixed (i.e., never automatically changed, unless manually changed), RACF provides much better security for the sign-on procedure.

File Protection

You can protect your files under CICS through RACF by using the following procedures:

1. Define datasets you wish to protect under RACF.
2. Define RACF user id for the CICS job itself, and specify it as USER=xxxxxxx in the JOB card of CICS job.
3. Define the access authority level (READ, UPDATE, CONNECT, CONTROL) for the CICS job (USER=xxxxxxx) for all datasets to be protected under RACF.

The effects of these procedures are the following: The CICS application programs can access only those files to which CICS has access authority. If a CICS application program tries to access a file to which CICS does not have access authority, CICS will encounter the RACF violation, and the entire CICS system will be abnormally terminated.

If other non-CICS users (e.g., batch jobs, TSO operations) try to access these files, unless they have proper access authority, they encounter RACF violation, and these jobs will be abnormally terminated.

14.6   Other Security Management Techniques

There are some other security management techniques under CICS, which can be easily applied in the application programs.

FCT SERVREQ Option

In the FCT definition macro (DFHFCT), there is one option called SERVREQ, through which you can restrict the type of accesses by CICS to the file on subject. Therefore, you should specify service requests only for required services to the file on subject, as follows:

```
DFHFCT     TYPE=DATASET,
           DATASET=name,
           :
           [SERVREQ=(--,--,--,--)],
               ADD          )
               BROWSE       )     Code only as required.
               DELETE       )
               READ         )
               UPDATE       )
```

CICS grants only specified services in the FCT entry of the file. If an application program issues unauthorized services to the file, CICS will reject it, returning the INVREQ condition.

One application is the following: If the file is a read-only file, specify READ, BROWSE only in the SERVREQ option of the DFHFCT macro for this file. Then, CICS will never write, update, or delete records onto/from the file. In this way, you can conveniently protect your file.

EIBTRMID

EIBTRMID contains the four-character terminal id defined in TCT for the terminal which the current transaction is associated. It is useful to check this EIBTRMID whether this terminal is authorized for this transaction or application.

One application is the following: You create in the application program a Terminal Table which lists only terminal ids which are authorized for the application. Then the program checks EIBTRMID in the beginning of the program whether this is registered in the Terminal Table. If it is not registered, the program terminates the task immediately with a warning message. In this way, you can easily protect your transaction from being accessed by unauthorized terminals.

15

Recovery and Restart

15.1 Introduction

Online systems tend to use significant amounts of resources including a large database. Also, as the nature of online system, at one time many transactions may be concurrently updating the database. Or, if we look at it differently, many terminal users may be using the system at the same time. Therefore, if one transaction encounters an ABEND or the entire online system crashes, it is crucial to recover the resources involved and to restart the transactions or the entire system as quickly as possible. Therefore, a large DB/DC system usually offers useful recovery/restart facilities.

Terminology

When discussing recovery/restart facilities, we are actually discussing two independent concepts: one is "recovery" and the other is "restart." The recovery facilities and restart facilities are independent of each other, although they are closely related to each other. Therefore, let us define these concepts separately, as follows:

Recovery Recovery is an attempt to come back to where the CICS system or the transaction was when the failure occurred, by recovering all recoverable resources relevant to the system or the transaction.

Restart   Restart is to resume the operations of the CICS system or the transaction when recovery is completed, by restarting the system or the transaction based on the recovered resources.

CICS Recovery/Restart Facilities

The objective of recovery/restart facilities is to minimize and, if possible, to eliminate the damage done to the online system when a failure occurs, so that the system integrity and data integrity can be maintained.

CICS offers extensive recovery/restart facilities for users to establish their own recovery/restart capability in their CICS system. The following are commonly used CICS recovery/restart facilities:

- Dynamic Transaction Backout (DTB)
- Automatic Transaction Restart
- Resource Recovery Using System Log
- Resource Recovery Using Journal
- System Restart
- Extended Recovery Facility (XRF)

Recoverable Resources

The recovery of a CICS system or a transaction can be accomplished by recovering all individual resources which have been used by the system or the transaction, respectively, until the time of the system failure or the transaction failure. Under CICS, the following are some of the resources which are considered "recoverable" and could be recoverd:

- VSAM files
- Intrapartition TDQ
- Temporary Storage Queue (TSQ) in the auxiliary storage, noting that TSQ in the main storage is not recoverable
- Input/output messages from/to transactions in a VTAM network

If you wish these resources to be recoverable, special options must be specified in the relevant CICS control tables. We will discuss this subject in detail in Section 15.9.

15.2   Dynamic Transaction Backout (DTB)

As we discussed, the HANDLE CONDITION command detects only abnormal status during the CICS command execution. If an abnormal status occurs outside CICS commands, since it cannot be detected by the HANDLE CONDITION command, the task usually will be abnormally terminated (ABEND). For this, some recovery mechanism is required.

In case a transaction ABEND occurs, CICS can automatically recover recoverable resources using information in the special data pool called "dynamic log." This is called "Dynamic Transaction Backout" (DTB), and it is managed by the CICS Dynamic Backout Program (DBP).

The objective of DTB is to restore automatically the recoverable resources after a transaction encounters an ABEND to the state where they were when everything was good. If this is successfully achieved, the transaction can be restarted from that point.

Sync Point and Logical Unit of Work (LUW)

In order to discuss DTB further, the concepts of "sync point" and "Logical Unit of Work" (LUW) must be introduced.

The sync point is a point in time at which the resources such as files are good. The beginning of a task is a sync point while the end of the task is another sync point. LUW is the activity which a task performs between two sync points. CICS maintains exclusive control over the recoverable resources for the duration of a LUW for the task. If an ABEND occurs, CICS recovers the recoverable resources over the current LUW up to the last sync point.

Between the beginning and end of a task, another sync point may be declared. This is called "intermediate sync point." Declaring the intermediate sync point has following advantages:

* It reduces the amount of resource to be maintained in the dynamic log (see below).
* It reduces the duration of exclusive control over a LUW.
* It prevents successful record updates from being backed out needlessly.

Dynamic Log

A CICS region has a special system area in the main memory called "dynamic log." Whenever a record of a recoverable resource such as a

VSAM file is changed during the execution of a transaction, CICS automatically writes the "before image" information of the record into the dynamic log for the duration of one LUW (i.e., between two consecutive sync points) of the transaction. The information in the dynamic log is the basis for the resource recovery.

Concept of DTB

If an ABEND occurs in the transaction, CICS applies the records ("before image") in the dynamic log backward one by one until all records in the dynamic log related to the transaction have been exhausted. Then, all recoverable resources are restored to the state where the transaction started or the last sync point of the transaction.

Since the recovery by DTB is achieved by reading the dynamic log backward, DTB is called "backward recovery."

Example Let us suppose that a task (transaction) added, deleted and read for update records 1, 2, and 3, respectively, into or from a recoverable file in this order, as illustrated in Figure 15-1.

As the task proceeds to its processing, the "before image" information of records 1, 2, 3 are written into the dynamic log at the time of the file activities by CICS. Note that for adding a record, only the key of the record is logged.

Let us suppose that after rewriting record 3, an ABEND occurs in this task. Then, CICS will automatically activate DTB, and read the dynamic log backward.

First, record 3 (before image) in the dynamic log will be copied back to the file, replacing the existing record in the file, so that the original record (i.e., before updating) will be restored in the file. Next, record 2 (before image) in the dynamic log will be copied back (added, in this case) to the file, so that the deleted recored will be recovered in the file. Lastly, using record 1 (key only) in the dynamic log, the existing record 1 will be deleted from the file. Then, the original state would have been recovered.

Requirements for Dynamic Log

The dynamic log will be automatically taken by CICS once a resource is defined as recoverable. Therefore, if you wish to apply DTB for a transaction, you must define all resources which the transac-

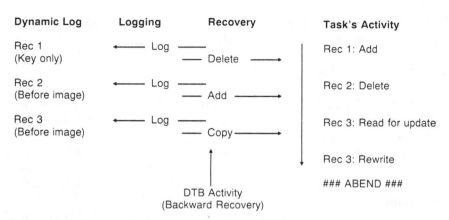

Figure 15-1 Dynamic Transaction Backout (DTB).

tion uses as recoverable. The requirements for defining the recoverable resources depend on the type of resources. We will discuss this subject in detail in Section 15.9.

Requirements for DTB

In order to apply DTB, you have to specify the special option in the PCT entry of all transactions to which you wish to apply DTB as follows:

```
DTB=YES
```

Once this is done, DTB will be performed automatically by CICS at the failure of this transaction.

15.3   Automatic Transaction Restart

The automatic transaction restart is a CICS capability to automatically restart a transaction after all recoverable resources have been recovered through DTB. Therefore, you can recover and restart the transaction automatically by using both DTB and the automatic transaction restart function, in the event of transaction failure.

Requirements

For the automatic transaction restart, DTB is a prerequisite. Another requirement is that you must specify a special option in the

PCT entry of all transactions to which you wish to apply the automatic transaction restart, as follows:

```
RESTART=YES    (default=NO)
```

If RESTART=YES is specified in the PCT entry of a transaction, DTB=YES is automatically assumed, so that DTB=YES may not be specified in the same PCT entry.

If these requirements are satisfied, when the task abnormally terminates, CICS will automatically activate DTB. Then, after the completion of DTB, CICS will automatically restart the task from the beginning.

Benefits

The automatic transaction restart is useful when a transaction is abnormally terminated, not because of a program bug or data exception, but because of a problem unique to the online system, such as the timeout after a transaction deadlock, no storage available at the TSQ writing or GETMAIN time, or storage violation. In these cases, the likelihood will be very high for the transaction to go through successfully after DTB and the transaction restart.

If the transaction encounters an ABEND because of a program bug or data exception, DTB and restart functions would not be helpful because even after DTB and transaction restart the task would encounter the same ABEND again by the same cause.

Drawbacks of Intermediate Sync Point

DTB recovers resources up to the last sync point within the transaction. If there is no intermediate sync point, when the transaction encounters an ABEND, CICS will recover related recoverable resources through DTB, to the state before executing this transaction. If DTB is successful, therefore, the same transaction could be restarted again from the beginning. If RESTART=YES is specified in PCT, CICS will automatically restart the transaction after DTB from the very beginning of the transaction through the automatic transaction restart.

However, if intermediate sync points are taken in the transaction, DTB would recover the recoverable resources up to the last sync point. That is, DTB would not recover recoverable resources at the state before executing this transaction.

In this case, if RESTART=YES is specified, since CICS restarts the transaction from the beginning, there may be a situation of double updating, record not found or duplicate key, between the beginning of the transaction and the last intermediate sync point before the ABEND. Therefore, in this case, restarting the task at the point where DTB completes (i.e., not from the beginning) becomes the user's responsibility.

Therefore, the intermediate sync points should be taken with great care and only when they are definitely required.

15.4 SYNCPOINT Command

Function

The SYNCPOINT command is used to define an intermediate sync point. This excludes the beginning and the end of a task, which are automatically taken by CICS. Otherwise, the SYNCPOINT command can be placed anywhere in the application program. At the completion of the SYNCPOINT command, CICS defines a sync point. However, on issuing the SYNCPOINT command, you should be aware of the drawbacks of the intermediate sync points described in the previous section.

Command Format

The format of the SYNCPOINT is as follows:

```
EXEC CICS SYNCPOINT
END-EXEC.
```

ROLLBACK Option

The SYNCPOINT command with the ROLLBACK option is used to make CICS perform DTB up to the last sync point and return control to the instruction following the SYNCPOINT/ROLLBACK command.

This option is very useful when you wish to automatically terminate the task for some reason (e.g., unusual exceptional conditions). Before terminating the task, you can issue the SYNCPOINT/ROLLBACK command. Then, the recoverable resources would be recovered to the last sync point.

Format   The format of the SYNCPOINT command with the ROLL-BACK option is as follows:

```
EXEC CICS SYNCPOINT
     ROLLBACK
END-EXEC.
```

Example   The following is an example of the SYNCPOINT command with the ROLLBACK option:

```
    EXEC CICS HANDLE CONDITION
         NOTFND(NOTFND-RTN)
         ERROR(ERROR-RTN)
    END-EXEC.
    :
    :
ERROR-RTN.
    EXEC CICS SYNCPOINT
         ROLLBACK
    END-EXEC.
    :
    (Send a message "General error condition occurred.   Resource
    recovered. Task canceled.")
    :
    EXEC CICS RETURN
    END-EXEC.
```

Execution Results   During the execution of this program logic, the following activities will occur:

- If a general error condition occurs, control will be passed to ERROR-RTN through the HANDLE CONDITION command.
- At the completion of the SYNCPOINT/ROLLBACK command, the recoverable resources will be recovered.
- At the completion of the RETURN command, the task will be terminated.

15.5   Resource Recovery Using System Log

Let us suppose that an entire CICS system crashed and you wish to recover the entire CICS system as soon as possible to the state where all recoverable resources were good. In this case, DTB does not work, because the dynamic log in the main storage is lost. Therefore, another approach must be sought for recovering the entire CICS system. The resource recovery using system log offers a solution to this kind of case.

System Log

The system log is similar to the dynamic log, except that the system log is kept in the external device, such as tape, recording the "before image" information of all records which are affected by the tasks in the CICS region. This recording process is called "automatic logging."

After a system failure, this system log will be used for recovering the recoverable resources by the CICS recovery control program.

Requirements

The system log must be defined in the Journal Control Table (JCT) with JFILEID=01 (see Section 15.8). Once it is defined, CICS automatically performs the automatic logging right before every activity occurs against the resources which are defined as recoverable (see Section 15.9).

Concept of Resource Recovery

After a system crash, the CICS recovery control program reads the system log backward. The tasks active at the time of crash are called "inflight tasks." The recovery program recovers records of "inflight tasks" one by one until it reaches a sync point for the task. Then, the task is considered "not inflight," and recovery will not be applied after that point for the task.

This process is very similar to the mechanism of DTB, except that the recovery is performed task by task until all "inflight tasks" become "not inflight," reading the system log backward. In this way, all resources associated to all transactions in the CICS region at the system crash will be recovered.

Since the recovery by the system log is achieved by reading the system log backward, this recovery is also called "backward recovery."

15.6 Resource Recovery using Journal

Instead of recovering the entire CICS system, if you are interested in recovering only certain recoverable resources, using the system log would not be practical, because the system log contains the information of all recoverable resources associated with the CICS system. The resource recovery using a special file called "journal," which is managed by the CICS Journal Control Program (JCP), offers a solution to this kind of case.

Journal

A journal is similar to the system log, but each journal is taken for only one resource (or a group of resources). As CICS processes the transactions, CICS writes the "after image" record onto the journal right after each activity in order to keep the activities of the recoverable resources. This is called "automatic journaling."

However, unlike the system log, how to use this journal is left to the installation (i.e., the CICS user's task, not CICS's task). That is, the CICS users must develop the recovery program based on the specifications unique to the installation. After a system crash, this user-written recovery program will be run for recovering the file on subject using this journal.

Requirements

A journal is identified by the journal identifier (2 to 99), and it must be defined in JCT. Once JCT is defined, CICS automatically performs automatic journalizing into the journal for the recoverable resources.

Concept of Resource Recovery

This recovery method requires a backup copy of the file which contains data at the time when CICS started. After a system crash, the recoverable file on subject is recovered to the starting state using the backup copy of the file. Then, the recovery program (user developed) reads the corresponding journal forward. Then, it replaces the record in the file with the corresponding record in the journal. This process will be repeated until the file has been fully recovered.

Since the file recovery using the journal is achieved by reading the journal forward, this recovery is called "forward recovery."

15.7   JOURNAL Command

Function

The automatic journaling is performed automatically by CICS for the recoverable resources, if JCT is specified as such. In addition to automatic journaling, an application program may write its own type of journal record using the JOURNAL command. That is, the JOURNAL command is used to write a user-defined journal record onto a journal file. This is called "explicit journaling." However, how to use these explicit journal records are left to the users, just as in the case of automatic journaling.

Command Format

The format of the JOURNAL command is as follows:

```
EXEC CICS JOURNAL
     JFILEID(data-value)
     JTYPEID(data-value)
     FROM(data-area)
     [LENGTH(data-value)]
     [PREFIX(data-value)
        [PFXLENG(data-value)]]
     [WAIT]
END-EXEC.
```

JFILEID defines the journal id (2-99) of the journal file. JTYPEID defines the 2-byte user id. FROM defines the area name from which the data (record) is to be written. LENGTH indicates the length of the data area to be journaled. PREFIX defines the user prefix. PFXLENG indicates the length of the user prefix. If WAIT is specified, CICS waits until the completion of the journaling before resuming the excution of the application program after the JOURNAL command. This is useful to secure that the journal has been taken before proceeding to the further processing.

Example

The following is an example of the JOURNAL command:

```
WORKING-STORAGE SECTION.
01    TSQ-RECORD.
      05    TSQ-FLD1        PIC X(10).
      05    TSQ-FLD2        PIC X(20).
77    WK-LEN                PIC S9(4) COMP.
77    WK-JUID               PIC XX VALUE 'U1'.
77    WK-UPREFIX            PIC X(8) VALUE 'TSQ00001'.
77    WK-UPLEN              PIC S9(4) COMP VALUE 8.
      :
PROCEDURE DIVISION.
      :
      :
      MOVE 30 TO WK-LEN.
      EXEC CICS JOURNAL
           JFILEID(2)
           JTYPEID(WK-JUID)
           FROM(TSQ-RECORD)
           LENGTH(WK-LEN)
           PREFIX(WK-UPREFIX)
           PFXLENG(WK-UPLEN)
           WAIT
      END-EXEC.
```

Execution Results   A TSQ record will be written as an explicit journal record with the user id (U1) and user prefix (TSQ00001) in journal file 2. The task will wait until the journaling has been completed,

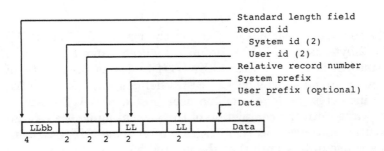

Figure 15-2 Format of journal record.

after which the control will be returned to the next statement after this command.

Journal Record Format

The format of the journal record is prefixed, regardless of whether the journal was taken by the automatic journaling or by the JOURNAL command, as shown in Figure 15-2. Based on this journal record format, the system programmers (or application programmers) have to develop the file recovery program.

15.8 Journal Control Table (JCT)

Function

The primary function of the Journal Control Table (JCT) is to register the control information of the system log and journal files. The CICS Journal Control Program (JCP) uses this table for identifying the system log and journal file and performing automatic logging and automatic journaling.

JCT Entry Definition

One JCT entry for one journal file or system log can be defined using the Assembler macro DFHJCT. The following are the commonly used options and parameters of the DFHJCT macro:

```
DFHJCT     TYPE=ENTRY,
           JFILEID=nn,
           BUFSIZE=mmmm,
           :
           (other parameters)
           :
```

JFILEID defines the journal id (1 to 99). 1 is reserved for the system log, and 2 to 99 is available for the journal files. BUFSIZE indicates the buffer size of the journal file. There are other options and parameters which are more related to the system programmer. Therefore, you should complete the specifications of the JCT entry with your system programmer.

15.9   Requirements for Recoverable Resources

In the past several sections, we have discussed the concepts and mechanisms of recovering recoverable resources. For the sake of simplicity, however, we have not really discussed how the resources can be defined as "recoverable" in CICS. Now that we know how the resources can be recovered in CICS, let us discuss the ways of defining resources as "recoverable."

Recoverable Resources

Figure 15-3 summarizes the requirements for defining resources as "recoverable" under CICS. As shown, CICS considers only certain resources as recoverable. These recoverable resources are: VSAM files, Intrapartition Transient Data Queue (TDQ), Temporary Storage Queue (TSQ) in the auxiliary storage, and input/output messages to/from the VTAM network. These resources can be made recoverable through automatic logging in the dynamic log or system log or through automatic journaling, except Intrapartition TDQ and TSQ in

Recoverable Resources	Relevant CICS Control Tables	Automatic Logging (Dynamic Log, System Log)	Automatic Journaling (Journal)
VSAM Files	File Control Table (FCT)	DFHFCT TYPE=ENTRY, DATASET=name, LOG=YES, :	DFHFCT TYPE=ENTRY, DATASET=name JID=nn :
Intrapartition TDQ	Destination Control Table (DCT)	DFHDCT TYPE=INTRA, DESTID=name, DESTRCV=LG, :	(n/a)
TSQ in Auxiliary Storage	Temporary Storage Table (TST)	DFHTST TYPE=RECOVERY, DATAID=(character string), :	(n/a)
I/O Message to/from VTAM Network	Processing Control Table (PCT)	DFHPCT TYPE=ENTRY, TRANSID=name, PROGRAM=name, JFILEID=SYSTEM, MSGJRNL=INPUT | OUTPUT | (INPUT,OUTPUT), :	DFHPCT TYPE=ENTRY TRANSID=name, PROGRAM=name JFILEID=nn, MSGJRNL= (same as left), :

Figure 15-3 Requirements for recoverable resources.

the auxiliary storage, which can be made recoverable only through automatic logging.

If you wish to recover resources other than these listed in Figure 15-3, you would have to use the implicit journaling. That is, you would have to journal a record of the resource which you wish to recover, using the JOURNAL command by yourself. In this case, it would be completely your responsibility to recover the resource properly based on the explicit journal record. You would have to develop your own program to do so.

Through Automatic Logging

If you wish to recover resources through the automatic logging, this means that you would use the dynamic log for the Dynamic Transaction Backout (DTB) or the system log for the entire system resource recovery. In either case, you have to define each resource as recoverable in the following way:

VSAM Files LOG=YES must be specified in the File Control Table (FCT) entry of each file which you wish to define as recoverable. In addition, you could specify the JREQ parameter for what kind of file control request should be logged. The default is JREQ=(WU,WN), where WU and WN indicates WRITE/UPDATE and WRITE/NEW, respectively. Usually, this default is good enough.

Intrapartition TDQ DESTRCV=LG must be specified in the Destination Control Table (DCT) entry of each Intrapartition TDQ (TYPE=INTRA) identified by the destination id (DESTID) which you wish to make recoverable. DESTRCV=LG means that this destination (Intrapartition TDQ) is logically recoverable, and this will ensure recovery of TDQ.

TSQ in Auxiliary Storage One entry in the Temporary Storage Table (TST) must be created with TYPE=RECOVERY, which indicates the recovery of TSQ. In this entry, the high order of QID string (8 bytes) must be specified in the DATAID parameter in order to identify TSQ's to be made recoverable. For example DATAID=(A,B) means that TSQ's whose QID start with "A" or "B" will be made recoverable. Note that TSQ can be recoverable only when it is placed in the auxiliary file and that TSQ placed in the main storage is not recoverable.

I/O Messages to/from VTAM Network   JFILEID=SYSTEM   must   be specified in the Program Control Table (PCT) entry of each transaction whose input/output messages from/to the VTAM network you wish to make recoverable. In addition, the MSGJRNL parameter must be specified with either INPUT for input message only, OUTPUT for output message only, or (INPUT,OUTPUT) for both input and output messages to be recovered.

Once CICS control table entries are specified in the above way, CICS will automatically activate automatic logging onto both the dynamic log and system log (if it is defined) whenever these resources are modified. The information in the dynamic log or system log will be used by DTB or the entire system resource recovery, respectively.

Through Automatic Journaling

If you wish to recover resources through automatic journaling, this means that you would use the journal for recovering a particular resource or a group of resources. In this case, you have to define each resource as recoverable in the following way:

VSAM Files   JID=nn (where nn is from 2 to 99) must be specified in the FCT entry of each dataset which you wish to define as recoverable. JID is the journal identifier defined in JCT, to which the journal records are to be written. In addition, the JREQ parameter can be specified as the case of automatic logging.

I/O Messages to/from VTAM Network   JFILEID=nn (where nn is from 2 to 99) must be specified in the PCT entry of each transaction whose input/output messages from/to the VTAM Network you wish to make recoverable. JFILEID is the journal identifier defined in JCT to which the journal records are to be written. In addition, the MSGJRNL parameter must be specified as the case of automatic logging.

Once CICS control table entries are specified in this way, CICS automatically activates automatic journaling into the journal(s) whenever these resources are modified. However, how to use these journal(s) is left to the installation.

15.10   System Restart

The previous sections discussed the procedures for system resource recovery after a system failure or a system crash. Once system resources have been fully recovered, the system can be restarted. Since CICS is equipped with both recovery and restart facilities, the system resource recovery and system restart occurs simultaneously. Or, more accurately, the system resource recovery occurs in the early part of system restart procedures.

Modes of System Start

The CICS system can be started in one of following three modes, depending on the specifications in the System Initialization Table (SIT):

Resources/ Activities	Cold Start	Warm Start	Emergency Restart
Information in System Log	Not used.	Not used.	Used.
TSQ in Auxiliary Storage	All data lost.	All data retained.	Only recoverable TSQ retained. Backout applied.
Intrapartition TDQ	All data lost.	All data retained.	Only recoverable intrapartition TDQ retained. Backout applied.
File	Not recovered.	Not recovered.	Backout applied only to recoverable files.
VTAM Message	Not recovered.	Not recovered.	Only recoverable message recovered.
Transaction Backout	Not performed.	Not performed.	Backout performed only for recoverable transactions.
Transaction Restart	Not performed.	Not performed.	Restart tried only for restartable transactions.

Figure 15-4 System restart and status of resources.

- Cold Start
- Warm Start
- Emergency System Restart

If START=COLD is specified in SIT, the CICS system will be always completely initialized for a fresh start (i.e., cold start).

If START=AUTO is specified in SIT, the CICS system will be started based on the situation of previous CICS termination. If it was a normal termination, a warm start will be applied. If it is an abnormal termination, an emergency system restart will be applied. If this is the first CICS start-up after the entire system initialization, a cold start will be applied.

Characteristics of these three types of system start are summarized in Figure 15-4. Let us discuss each type of system start further.

Cold Start

In the cold start, CICS and system control tables will be completely initialized irrespective of the previous system activities. Therefore, the system log, which may have been taken by the previous CICS execution, will not be used for the start-up. Since both Temporary Storage Queue (TSQ) in the auxiliary storage and Intrapartition Transient Data Queue (TDQ) will be initialized, TSQ and TDQ used in the previous CICS execution will be wiped out. As a result, CICS will start with the cleanest resources.

Warm Start

In the warm start, CICS will start itself with certain system information and resources carried over from the previous CICS execution which has been completed normally.

For example, if the contents in the CICS control tables were updated during previous CICS execution, the warm start will honor these updates; TSQ in the auxiliary storage and Intrapartition TDQ will be retained for new CICS execution; certain information in Common System Area (CSA), such as counters and storage cushion size, will be carried over to new CICS execution.

This information is kept in the special system file called "warm keypoints." Since the warm start uses the information of warm keypoints without completely reinitializing the system areas and tasks, system start-up is much faster than the cold start.

Emergency System Restart

If the previous CICS execution has been abnormally terminated, an emergency system restart will take place. The emergency system restart will reposition the system log at the very last recond, read the system log backward, and copy the log records of all "inflight tasks" into a restart dataset (or recovery dataset). Then, the recovery control program will perform backout of recoverable resources based on the restart dataset, as explained in Section 15.5. Through this backout process, all recoverable resources will be recovered.

Other CICS system areas and control table information will be also reconstructed using the warm keypoints at the state where the previous CICS abnormally terminated. Therefore, if updates had been applied to the CICS control tables, these updates will also be honored.

Since transactions are fully backed out by DTB, the CICS will restart those transactions to which RESTART=YES is specified in PCT.

These restart activities will occur automatically within a relatively short duration during the system recovery/restart process. As a result, the installation could continue operating the CICS system with a minimal interruption after the abnormal termination.

15.11 Extended Recovery Facility (XRF)

Extended Recovery Facility (XRF) is a new recovery/restart facility introduced in CICS/MVS Version 2.1. XRF offers a significantly improved capability of recovering and restarting the CICS system.

Objective

The primary objective of XRF is to increase availability of CICS to the extent of the fault-tolerant system. XRF achieves this objective by automating the fast recovery of the system components after failure. As a result, even after the system failure, CICS can automatically resume its production operation with a minimal interruption.

Concept

Figure 15-5 illustrates the concept of XRF. As shown, XRF is based on the dual system approach. The currently running system is called

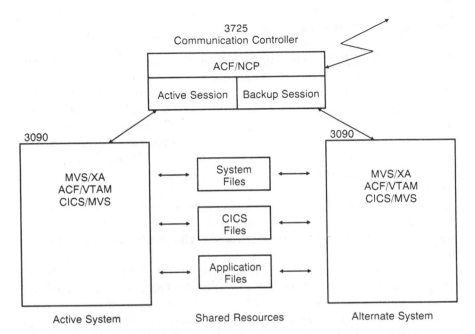

Figure 15-5 Concept of Extended Recovery Facility (XRF).

the "active system," while the to-be-switched system is called the "alternate system." The alternate system monitors the active system. At the failure of the active system, the alternate system takes over the operations from the active system.

In this example, the active system consists of Multiple Virtual Storage/Extended Architecture (MVS/XA) Operating System, Advanced Communication Function/Virtual Telecommunication Access Method (ACF/VTAM), CICS/MVS in the 3090 computer system. Whereas, the alternate system has the same system configuration in the independent 3090 system.

The 3725 Communication Controller is shared by both the active and alternate systems, but ACF/Network Control Program (ACF/NCP) has the active session for the active system, and independently the back-up session for the alternate system. The system files, CICS files and application files are shared by both the active and alternate system.

Under the normal circumstances, the active system performs normal processing, taking care of all CICS operations. The active system updates the system files and CICS files accordingly, maintaining recovery information. The active system normally updates the application files, taking into accounts sync points.

The alternate CICS system is partially initialized in the alternate system. But it performs nothing but monitoring the active system through the shared system files, CICS files, and application files. Since the alternate CICS system does not perform normal processing other than monitoring the active system, it does not require much system resources. Therefore, meantime, the alternate system could be used as the primary batch processor.

A failure in the active system could occur in the processor itself (hardware), MVS/XA, CICS/MVS, or ACF/VTAM. If this happens, the active system goes down entirely or partially. The alternate CICS system automatically detects the failure of the active system and immediately takes over the CICS operations from the active system. Using the information stored in the system files, CICS files, and application files, the alternate CICS system automatically recovers the resources and restarts the system.

The process of failure detection, system switch-over, recovery, and restart is automatically performed by the alternate CICS system. Therefore, XRF can achieve system restart much faster (as much as 90 percent faster according to a benchmark test) than the ordinary recovery/restart facility.

Applications

In the large CICS installations such as international airline companies, it is not unusual that several thousand terminal users are accessing the system concurrently for 24 hours a day. In this kind of environment, it is essential to run CICS continuously without interruption even in case of system failures. If the CICS system fails, and the services are interrupted for even 30 minutes, the business operations would be fatally damaged.

XRF offers a relief to this kind of situation. If XRF is effectively implemented, the system downtime could be reduced to only a few minutes. Since this is automatically done, from the terminal user's point of view, the CICS system looks as if it never failed. Therefore, many applications of XRF can be found in the large CICS installations.

Exercise

Modify Approach 3 (i.e., program TXTAIPRC) of the Exercise for Chapter 10 to include the SYNCPOINT command with the ROLLBACK option for backing out the resources in case of a general error condition (ERROR).

16

Tests and Debugging

16.1 Introduction

For an effective debugging and/or better management of abnormal termination of a program, CICS provides useful control functions over these areas. The Abnormal Termination Recovery function (ABEND Control) manages an abnormal termination (ABEND) of a task. The CICS Dump Control Program (DCP) manages dumping the main storage areas. The CICS Trace Control Program makes use of the Trace Table for debugging aid purposes.

For these functions, CICS provides a set of commands. However, utilizing these functions fully requires more than just issuing commands in the application programs, as we will discuss later.

Available Commands

The following commands are available for these control functions:

- Abend Control Commands:
  - — HANDLE ABEND: To detect an ABEND.
  - — ABEND: To force an ABEND.
- Dump Control Command:
  - — DUMP: To dump the main storage area.
- Trace Control Commands:
  - — ENTER: To create a user-entry to the Trace Table.
  - — TRACE: To control the Trace Control function.

Other Facilities

In addition, in order to facilitate effective tests and production operations, CICS provides the following facilities:

• Transaction Dump
• Execution Diagnostic Facility (EDF)
• Command Level Interpreter (CECI)
• Temporary Storage Browse (CEBR)
• Master Terminal Transaction (CEMT)
• Dynamic File Open/Close (DFOC)

16.2   HANDLE ABEND Command

Function

The HANDLE ABEND command is used to intercept an abnormal termination (ABEND) within a program, and to activate, cancel, or reactivate an exit for the ABEND processing. The HANDLE ABEND command is similar to, but different from, the HANDLE CONDITION command which intercepts only the abnormal conditions of the CICS command execution.

Format

The format of the HANDLE ABEND is as follows:

```
EXEC CICS HANDLE ABEND
     [PROGRAM(name) |
          LABEL(label) |
          CANCEL |
          RESET]
END-EXEC.
```

PROGRAM or LABEL is used to activate an exit (i.e., to pass control) to a program or a paragraph, respectively, for the ABEND processing. CANCEL is used to cancel the previously established HANDLE ABEND request. RESET is to reactivate the previously cancelled HANDLE ABEND request.

Example

The following is an example of the HANDLE ABEND command:

```
WORKING-STORAGE SECTION.
77    MSG-LEN              PIC S9(4) COMP.
01    MSG-DATA.
      05    MSG-DATA1      PIC X(15).
      05    MSG-DATA2      PIC X(50).
      :
PROCEDURE DIVISION.
      :
      EXEC CICS HANDLE ABEND
           LABEL(ABEND-ROUTINE)
      END-EXEC.
      :
      (some processing logic)
      :
ABEND-ROUTINE SECTION.
*
* ABEND HAS OCCURRED.
* TERMINATE THE TASK.
*
      EXEC CICS SYNCPOINT
           ROLLBACK
      END-EXEC.
      MOVE 'ABEND OCCURRED.'
           TO MSG-DATA1.
      MOVE 'TASK CANCELED WITH ABCODE 9999.'
           TO MSG-DATA2.
      MOVE 65 TO MSG-LEN.
      EXEC CICS SEND
           FROM(MSG-DATA)
           LENGTH(MSG-LEN)
           NOHANDLE
      END-EXEC.
      EXEC CICS HANDLE ABEND
           CANCEL                               <== Attention.
      END-EXEC.
      EXEC CICS ABEND
           ABCODE('9999')
      END-EXEC.
      EXEC CICS RETURN
```

```
        END-EXEC.
ABEND-EXIT.
        Exit.
```

Execution Results   During the execution of this program logic, the following activities will occur:

- If an ABEND occurs in this program, it will be intercepted through the HANDLE ABEND command, and control will be passed to ABEND-ROUTINE.
- At the completion of the SYNCPOINT/ROLLBACK command, the recoverable resources will be recovered.
- At the completion of the HANDLE ABEND/CANCEL command, the previous HANDLE ABEND request will be canceled. If the HANDLE ABEND/CANCEL command is not specified before the ABEND command, a loop on the HANDLE ABEND request will occur (similar to a loop in the HANDLE CONDITION request).
- At the completion of the ABEND command (see the next section), the task will be forcefully terminated with the user-code '9999'.

Programming Considerations

The HANDLE ABEND command is very useful in order to intercept an ABEND in the program, but care must be taken in the ABEND handling logic as to what you do then.

In the above example, the ABEND handling routine is a little meaningless, because if the recoverable resources are specified for DTB, DTB will be performed anyway by the ABEND triggered by the ABEND command, even without issuing the SYNCPOINT/ROLLBACK command.

16.3   ABEND Command

Function

The ABEND command is used to terminate a task intentionally, causing an ABEND.

Format

The format of the ABEND command is as follows:

```
EXEC CICS ABEND
     [ABCODE(name)]
END-EXEC.
```

ABCODE is used to specify the user abend code (1 to 4 characters).

Example

The following is an example of the ABEND command:

```
EXEC CICS HANDLE CONDITION
     ERROR(ERROR-RTN)
END-EXEC.
     :
     :
ERROR-RTN.
     EXEC CICS ABEND
          ABCODE('1234')
     END-EXEC.
```

Execution Results During the execution of this program logic, the following activities will occur:

• If a general error condition occurs, control will be passed to ERROR-RTN through the HANDLE CONDITION command.
• At the completion of the ABEND command, the task will be forcefully terminated with the user ABEND code 1234.

16.4 DUMP Command

Function

The DUMP command is used to dump the main storage areas related to the task.

Format

The format of the DUMP command with the commonly used options is as follows:

```
EXEC CICS DUMP
     DUMPCODE(name)
     [FROM(data-area)
          LENGTH(data-value)]
     [TASK]
     :
     (Other options)
     :
END-EXEC.
```

DUMPCODE names the user dump code (1 to 4 characters). FROM and LENGTH are used to define the name of a particular area of the program which you wish to dump and the length of the area, respectively. TASK indicates that the task-related system areas are to be dumped. There are other options for dumping system areas (see Appendix B for the full options). If no option is specified, the option TASK is assumed, in which case the following areas will be normally dumped:

> TCA, CSA, Trace Table
> Program Storage
> General Registers

Example

The following is an example of the DUMP command:

```
     EXEC CICS HANDLE ABEND
          LABEL(DUMP-RTN)
     END-EXEC.
          :
          :
DUMP-RTN.
     EXEC CICS DUMP
          DUMPCODE('ABCD')
          TASK
     END-EXEC.
     EXEC CICS RETURN
     END-EXEC.
```

Execution Results   During the execution of this program logic, the following activities will occur:

- If an ABEND occurs, control will be passed to DUMP-RTN through the HANDLE ABEND command.
- At the completion of the DUMP command, the TASK dump will be taken with user dump code ABCD.

Programming Considerations

The DUMP command is very useful for a difficult debugging. But the CICS report which contains your dump usually contains the dump of other users. This implies that an application programmer must share the dump list with other programmers, which is very inconvenient. Therefore, the use of this command should be restricted.

16.5 Trace Control

Function

The CICS Trace Control Program is a debugging aid. It provides information in the Trace Table in response to CICS or trace control commands during the execution of the CICS transactions. The Trace Table appears in the CICS dump in the edited form, which we will discuss later. The Trace Table can be used for program tracing or problem determination.

Trace Entry Point

The trace information is taken by CICS at each trace entry point. There are two types of trace entries:

1. *System Trace Entry Points:* These are automatically taken by the system at a command start time and at the command completion time.
2. *User Trace Entry Points:* These are taken by the application program through the ENTER command.

ENTER Command

Function The ENTER command is used to create a user entry to the Trace Table.

Format The format of the ENTER command is as follows:

```
EXEC CICS ENTER
     TRACEID(data-value)
     [FROM(data-area)]
     [RESOURCE(name)]
END-EXEC.
```

TRACEID defines the user trace id (0 to 99). FROM and RE-
SOURCE define the identification field (8 bytes) of the program and
the name (1 to 8 bytes) of the resource, respectively, which would
appear in the Trace Table.

TRACE Command

Function   The TRACE command is used to activate and deactivate
the CICS trace control facility.

Format   The format of the TRACE command is as follows:

```
EXEC CICS TRACE
     ON  |  OFF
END-EXEC.
```

Similar to the trace facility in the batch system, ON or OFF indicates activating or inactivating the trace facility, respectively. CICS
takes system trace entries during the period between TRACE ON
and TRACE OFF specified in the application program.

Example

The following is an example of the TRACE and ENTER commands:

```
WORKING-STORAGE SECTION.
          :
77    TRACE-INF      PIC X(8) VALUE 'BADLOGIC'.
77    PROG-ID        PIX X(8) VALUE 'PROGXXXX'.
          :
PROCEDURE DIVISION.
          :
      EXEC CICS TRACE ON
      END-EXEC.
          :
```

```
       :
EXEC CICS ENTER
     TRACEID(1)
     FROM(TRACE-INF)
     RESOURCE(PROG-ID)
END-EXEC.
       :
       :
EXEC CICS TRACE OFF
END-EXEC.
       :
       :
```

Execution Results   During the execution of this program logic, the following activities will occur:

- Between the TRACE/ON and OFF commands, the system trace entries will be written in the Trace Table.
- At the completion of the ENTER command, a user trace entry will be written in the Trace Table.

16.6   Analysis of CICS Transaction Dump

Let us suppose that a CICS application program has been coded, compiled, and successfully linkedited, and that the relevant CICS control tables such as PPT, PCT, and FCT have been prepared for this program. Then, try to execute this program by typing the associated transaction id into the terminal, and press the ENTER key. But, it would not be likely that the program functions properly the first time.

It is very common, as you know from your other programming experience, that the program often abnormally terminates (ABEND) in the middle of the processing, causing an ABEND dump, which contains useful information presenting the status of the program at the time of the ABEND.

Therefore, it would be very advantageous if you could analyze the ABEND dump, in order to determine the cause of the ABEND as fast as possible, and fix the problem. In this section, let us discuss how to analyze the ABEND dump.

For the ABEND dump analysis, a sample program (TXTSPNC1) is shown in Appendix A. This program is a simple program for the employee name change using the BMS map (MPBPNC2/MSBPNC2) prepared in Section 8.11. However, the program has an intentional bug in it, so that it caused an ABEND at the execution time. Appendix A shows the source list, compile list, linkedit list, and ABEND dump. Now, let us analyze this ABEND dump.

Dump Header Area

At the top of the ABEND dump (see page 1 of the dump list in Appendix A), there is a dump header area which provides mainly the following information:

CODE: This shows the ABEND code. This could be the system code which the system provides (refer to Appendix E), or the user code from the ABEND command in the application program. In our example, the ABEND code is ASRA.

TASK: This shows the transaction id of the task which ABENDed. In our example, the transaction id is PNC1.

PSW: This shows the Program Status Word (PSW) of the task at the time of the ABEND.

Registers: This shows the contents of the general registers at the time of the ABEND.

Storage Area Dump

After the header, various storage area dumps are printed depending on the installation default. If the DUMP command was issued in the application program, the user dump also appears with the dump-code specified by the application program. Typically, the following areas are printed:

TCA (User Area)
TCA (System Area)
Trace Table
Transaction Storage
Program Storage

Trace Table

Among the storage area dumps, the Trace Table is printed. The Trace Table shows the trace entries in the edited form, which were taken by the CICS at each trace entry point during the execution of the task. The table entries are printed in the FIFO base; that is, the oldest entry first and the most recent entry last.

Addressing Mode

In order to analyze the dump, it is essential to understand how the storage area is addressed. This used to be very simple because the address was always expressed in 24 bits. However, since the MVS/XA operating system came out, the address can be expressed in 31 bits. Therefore, there are presently two modes of addressing as follows:

Addressing Modes	Address Space
24-bit addressing	16 megabytes (16 million bytes)
31-bit addressing	2 gigabytes (2 billion bytes)

PSW is a double word (64 bits) field containing the status information at the interruption. One bit in PSW represents the addressing mode in which the program on subject is being executed. This bit is called "Addressing Mode Bit" (AMB), and it is at the bit position 32 (relative to zero) of PSW, as shown below.

If AMB is off (0), the program is being executed in the 24-bit addressing mode, so that the last 24 bits (from bit 40 to bit 63) of PSW represent the address of the next sequential instruction (NSI). If AMB is on (1), the program is being executed in the 31-bit addressing mode, so that the last 31 bits (form bit 33 to bit 63) represent the address of NSI.

```
Program Status Word (PSW)
```

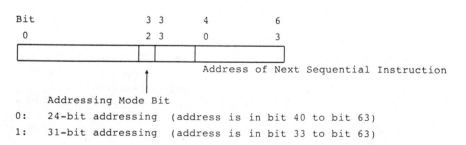

```
Bit                3 3    4       6
0                  2 3    0       3

                                      Address of Next Sequential Instruction

                  ↑
        Addressing Mode Bit
0:    24-bit addressing  (address is in bit 40 to bit 63)
1:    31-bit addressing  (address is in bit 33 to bit 63)
```

If VS COBOL II is used for the CICS application programs, you may be seeing the dump which is expressed in the 31-bit addressing mode, in which case you would have to interpretate the address of NSI based on the convention described above.

For simplicity, the sample program TXTSPNC1 in Appendix A was executed in the 24-bit addressing mode. Therefore, the following dump analysis assumes 24-bit addressing. However, you can verify the addressing convention mentioned above in the dump list of TXTSPNC1 in Appendix A. That is, AMB of PSW shows the off (0) state.

Finding Working Storage Field

Now, let us try to analyze the ABEND dump of sample program TXTSPNC1 in Appendix A. First, let us try to find from the ABEND dump a field defined in the Working Storage Section of the application program. Taking an example in the WK-ERR-CNT field of the sample program TXTSPNC1 (see page 3 of the compile list in Appendix A), the following is a set of procedures:

1. Find the Base Locator (BL), displacement and length of the field on subject from DMAP (or MAP if VS COBOL II is used) of the application program on subject. In our example, see page 16 of the compile list in Appendix A.

   WK-ERR-CNT: BL = 1, Disp = 25F, Length = 3

2. Find the corresponding register number from the Register Assignment in the compile list. In our example, see page 23 of the compile list in Appendix A.

   For BL = 1:   Register = 6

3. Find the value (address) of the register from the dump. Note that the values of the registers are printed in the order of the register 14, 15, 16, 1, 2, . . . to 11, excluding the registers 12 and 13, which are used for the special system purpose. In our example, see page 1 of the dump list in Appendix A.

   For Register = 6:   X'00021B2C'

4. Calculate the absolute address of the field by adding the value of the displacement to the value of the register. This is the starting address of the field on subject.

```
   21B2C
     25F (+
   21D8B
```

5. Locate the absolute address. Check the length. The area is the field on subject. In our example, see page 14 of the dump list in Appendix A.

> WK-ERR-CNT: The 3-byte area starting at X'00021D8B', which contains X'F0F0C0'.

Finding the Failed Instruction

Next, let us try to find from the ABEND dump the instruction which failed, causing the ABEND. Using the same ABEND dump of the sample program TXTSPNC1 in Appendix A of this book again, the following is a set of procedures:

1. Check PSW in the dump. The second fullword (Bit 32 to 63) of PSW (a double word field) contains the address of the next sequential instruction (NSI) which would have been executed if the ABEND had not occurred, based on the AMB convention mentioned before. Therefore, the location preceding this instruction contains the instruction which caused the ABEND. Note that the dump shows PSW in the double word accompanied by another double word field which contains condition codes. For the dump analysis purpose, this condition code field can be ignored. In our example, see page 1 of the dump list in Appendix A.

The second fullword of PSW: X'00225FBC'

Note that AMB is off, indicating the 24-bit addressing mode.

2. Find the starting address of the program storage (or load module) on subject. In our example, see page 16 of the dump list in Appendix A.

X'00225008'

3. Calculate the offset (displacement) of the NSI address from the beginning of the program storage.

225FBC
225008 (-
  FB4

4. Refer to the linkedit list, and find the displacement of the application program on subject from the beginning of the load module. In our example, see the linkedit list in Appendix A.

For the program TXTSPNC1:   X'48'

5. Calculate the real displacement of the NSI address in the application program from the beginning of the program storage.

FB4
  48 (-
F6C

6. Refer to CLIST (OFFSET if VS COBOL II is used) to find the COBOL statement number which falls into this address. If the calculated address falls between two COBOL statements, take the first. In our example, see page 25 of the compile list in Appendix A.

Statement 422 (ADD)

7. Analyze the cause.

Let us analyze the cause of the ABEND in our example. In this example, statement 422 of the source program is (see page 8 of the compile list in Appendix A):

```
ADD 1 to WK-LINE-CNT.
```

If you check the content of WK-LINE-CNT in the dump using the technique described before, it is X'000000' starting the address X'0021D88' (see page 14 of the dump list in Appendix A).

Since WK-LINE-CNT is defined as S999 (see page 3 of the compile list in Appendix A), the system expects a decimal value for the arithmetic calculation. But the field actually contains the null value (i.e., binary zero), which is illegal. Therefore, the system terminated the task with the ABEND code ASRA (i.e., a general ABEND in other than CICS commands), as the dump header shows. The WK-LINE-CNT should have been initialized in the Working Storage Section as follows:

```
05 WK-LINE-CNT    PIC S999 VALUE ZEROS.
```

Technical Notes PSW shows the address of the next sequential instruction (NSI) after the instruction which failed, causing the ABEND. Therefore, in precise terms, the above procedures are for finding NSI, not the instruction which caused the ABEND.

However, one COBOL statement usually consists of more than one Assembler instruction. Therefore, the above procedures approximate the COBOL statement which caused the ABEND. This is usually good enough. But, to be safe, you should also check the COBOL statement prior to the COBOL statement found through the above procedures. One of these two COBOL statements is definitely the cause of the ABEND.

If you wish to be very precise, you must refer to PMAP (or LIST if VS COBOL II is used) instead of CLIST (or OFFSET) of the compile list in order to locate the exact COBOL statement which caused the ABEND.

Finding the Last CICS Command Executed

Lastly, let us find from the Trace Table in the ABEND dump the last CICS command which the application program executed. Using the same ABEND dump of the sample program (TXTSPNC1) in Appendix A, the following is a set of procedures:

1. Refer the offset X'0011' of TCA (System Area). This is the 3-byte task sequence number field in a form of the packed decimal, which is placed in EIBTASKN by the system. In our example, see page 2 of the dump list in Appendix A.

    X'00059C' (implies task number 59)

2. Refer to the Trace Table backward; that is, from the bottom or from the most recent entry to the top or the oldest entry. In our example, see page 13 of the dump list in Appendix A, and read backward to page 12, and further to page 4, noting that pages 5 to 11 are omitted in Appendix A.

3. Pay attention only to your task number (59 in our case). TRACE TYPE in the Trace Table represents the CICS control program, and TYPE=EIP is for a CICS command. Referring backward, the first command in the EIP entry is the last CICS command executed for this task.
4. The EIP entries appear in the pair of ENTER (to be executed) and RESPONSE (executed). If the pair appears for a command, then the command has been normally completed. If there is only an ENTER entry for a command without RESPONSE, then this implies that the command has been abnormally terminated before the completion.
5. Check register 14 of the EIP/ENTER entry, which contains the return address after the command execution. Find the COBOL statement at this address using the procedures described above. The CICS command prior to this COBOL statement is the command which the task executed last.

Technical Notes

In our example (page 13 of the dump list in Appendix A), the Trace Table shows a pair of ENTRY and RESPONSE for the command RECEIVE-MAP, immediately after which it shows the PCP ABEND. Therefore, it can be concluded that after the normal completion of the RECEIVE command and before executing any other CICS commands, the task (program) encountered the ABEND. This conclusion is consistent with the conclusion drawn from the previous discussion of finding the instruction which caused the ABEND.

Formatted Dump from VS COBOL II

If the application program is written in VS COBOL II with the compiler option FDUMP (Formatted Dump), CICS produces a formatted dump at the abnormal termination of the program. This formatted dump has the program debugging information already interpreted from the raw ABEND dump, such as the line number of the most recently executed statement, fieldname and its data content at the ABEND time. Therefore, the formatted dump will make debugging of the application program significantly easier.

In addition, the formatted dump will be placed in the Temporary Storage Queue (TSQ) with the following naming convention for QID:

```
QID = CEBRxxxx
```

where xxxx is the terminal id of the terminal to which the transaction abnormally terminated was associated. This TSQ can be displayed by the TSQ browse transaction (CEBR) for the interactive debugging (see Section 16.9).

16.7   Execution Diagnostic Facility (EDF)

The Execution Diagnostic Facility (EDF) is a CICS-supplied transaction which monitors the execution of an application program as an interactive debugging aid. Therefore, you can execute EDF at any time with your own transaction for the debugging purposes.

Functions

EDF monitors an application program by executing and suspending an application program and displaying the status at the following points:

* At the transation initiation
* At the start of each CICS command
* At the completion of each CICS command
* At the program termination
* At the normal task termination
* At the abnormal task termination (ABEND)

At any points of interruption, the following information can be displayed:

* Values of EIB
* Program's Working Storage area in the hexadecimal or character mode
* Last 10 commands executed
* Contents of any address location within the CICS region
* Current, next, or previous application screen
* Content of Temporary Storage Queue (TSQ)

At any point of interruption, you can interact with the application program in the following ways:

* At "About to execute command":
  — By modifying argument values

— By suppressing the command itself
- At "Command completion time":
  — By modifying argument values
  — By modifying return code
- At any time:
  — By modifying the content of the Working Storage
  — By modifying the content of the most of EIB fields

At any time, EDF mode can be canceled and normal transaction processing can be resumed. Also, a specific STOP CONDITION can be requested to suspend the task at the specific condition.

Through EDF, you can perform all of these functions for monitoring the execution of the application program. However, a limitation of EDF is that EDF cannot suspend the execution between CICS commands unless an ABEND occurs. That is, you may wish to stop the execution at a specific COBOL paragraph or statement, but you cannot do so under EDF.

Two Modes of EDF Operations

There are two modes of EDF operations, depending on the type of telecommunication access method (VTAM or TCAM) associated with CICS, as follows:

Single screen mode (through VTAM) In this mode, an application transaction and EDF monitoring are executed on the same terminal. For initiating EDF, you type:

```
CEDF
```

and press the ENTER key. The CEDF mode message will be displayed. Then, you type the application transaction id. EDF will start monitoring the transaction on the same terminal.

Dual screen mode (through TCAM) In this mode, an application transaction and EDF monitoring are executed on the two different terminals. For intiating EDF, you type:

```
CEDF tttt
```

where tttt is the terminal id of the terminal to which the application transaction is to be excuted. After you press the ENTER key, the

EDF mode message will be displayed. Then, you type application transaction-id in the terminal tttt and press the ENTER key. The application transaction will be executed on the terminal tttt, while the original terminal will monitor the transaction execution.

EDF Operations and Associated Screens

Using the sample program TXTPNC1 in Appendix A, and using the single screen mode, the following are the highlights of the EDF operations and the associated EDF screens:

EDF Initiation Type "CEDF" and press the ENTER key. The system will display the response: "This terminal is under EDF mode."

Program Initiation Type the transaction id (PNC1) and press the ENTER key. The system will display the program initiation screen (Figure 16-1), which shows the initial status of the transaction PNC1 and the program TXTSPNC1. After the program initiation screen, every time the ENTER key is pressed, EDF executes the program on subject until the next CICS command or the program end.

```
TRANSACTION: PNC1   PROGRAM: TXTSPNC1   TASK NUMBER: 0003181   DISPLAY: 00
STATUS:   PROGRAM INITIATION

     EIBTIME     = 133927
     EIBDATE     = 89116
     EIBTRNID    = 'PNC1'
     EIBTASKN    = 3181
     EIBTRMID    = 'PNAR'

     EIBCPOSN    = 4
     EIBCALEN    = 0
     EIBAID      = X'7D'                          AT X'000F2442'
     EIBFN       = X'0000'                         AT X'000F2443'
     EIBRCODE    = X'000000000000'                 AT X'000F2445'
     EIBDS       = '.........'
  +  EIBREQID    = '.........'


ENTER:  CONTINUE
PF1 : UNDEFINED            PF2 : SWITCH HEX/CHAR     PF3 : END EDF SESSION
PF4 : SUPPRESS DISPLAYS    PF5 : WORKING STORAGE     PF6 : USER DISPLAY
PF7 : SCROLL BACK          PF8 : SCROLL FORWARD      PF9 : STOP CONDITIONS
PF10: PREVIOUS DISPLAY     PF11: UNDEFINED           PF12: UNDEFINED
```

Figure 16-1 EDF: Program initiation screen.

```
TRANSACTION: PNC1    PROGRAM: TXTSPNC1    TASK NUMBER: 0003203    DISPLAY:  00
STATUS:  ABOUT TO EXECUTE COMMAND
EXEC CICS RECEIVE MAP
 MAP ('MPBPNC2')
 INTO ('.................................................................'...)
 MAPSET ('MSBPNC2')
 TERMINAL




  OFFSET:X'001470'    LINE:00267           EIBFN=X'1802'


ENTER:  CONTINUE
PF1 : UNDEFINED                                        PF3 : UNDEFINED
PF4 : SUPPRESS DISPLAYS    PF5 : WORKING STORAGE       PF6 : USER DISPLAY
PF7 : SCROLL BACK          PF8 : SCROLL FORWARD        PF9 : STOP CONDITIONS
PF10: PREVIOUS DISPLAY     PF11: UNDEFINED             PF12: ABEND USER TASK
```

Figure 16-2 EDF: About to execute command screen.

```
TRANSACTION: PNC1    PROGRAM: TXTSPNC1    TASK NUMBER: 0003203    DISPLAY:  00
STATUS:  COMMAND EXECUTION COMPLETE
EXEC CICS RECEIVE MAP
 MAP ('MPBPNC2')
 INTO ('..............11111...AAAAAAAAAAAAAAAAAAAAAAAAAA...22222...BBBBB'...)
 MAPSET ('MSBPNC2')
 TERMINAL




  OFFSET:X'001470'    LINE:00267           EIBFN=X'1802'
  RESPONSE: NORMAL                          EIBRESP=0

ENTER:  CONTINUE
PF1 : UNDEFINED            PF2 : SWITCH HEX/CHAR       PF3 : END EDF SESSION
PF4 : SUPPRESS DISPLAYS    PF5 : WORKING STORAGE       PF6 : USER DISPLAY
PF7 : SCROLL BACK          PF8 : SCROLL FORWARD        PF9 : STOP CONDITIONS
PF10: PREVIOUS DISPLAY     PF11: UNDEFINED             PF12: ABEND USER TASK
```

Figure 16-3 EDF: Command execution completion screen.

About to Execute a Command Before executing one CICS command, EDF interrupts the execution and displays the screen (Figure 16-2), which shows the prestatus of the command execution (RECEIVE command, in this case). At this point, if you wish, the argument values may be modified.

Command Execution Completion At the completion of the command, EDF interrupts the execution and displays the screen (Figure 16-3), which shows the poststatus of the command execution (RECEIVE command, in this case).

Stop Condition By establishing the stop condition, you can execute the program on subject until the condition specified occurs without being interrupted at each command. The procedures for establishing the stop condition are as follows:

1. Press the PF4 (SUPRESS DISPLAYS) key. This will suppress EDF monitoring until the stop condition specified occurs.
2. Press the PF9 (STOP CONDITION) key. This will display the stop condition setting menu screen (Figure 16-4).
3. Specify the stop conditions on the menu with the following options:

```
TRANSACTION: PNC1   PROGRAM: TXTSPNC1   TASK NUMBER: 0003203   DISPLAY:  00
DISPLAY ON CONDITION:-

     COMMAND:              EXEC CICS
     OFFSET:                        X'......'
     LINE NUMBER:                   ........
     CICS EXCEPTIONAL CONDITION:
     ANY CICS ERROR CONDITION       YES
     TRANSACTION ABEND              YES
     NORMAL TASK TERMINATION        YES
     ABNORMAL TASK TERMINATION      YES




 ENTER:  CURRENT DISPLAY
 PF1 : UNDEFINED         PF2 : UNDEFINED          PF3 : UNDEFINED
 PF4 : SUPPRESS DISPLAYS PF5 : WORKING STORAGE    PF6 : USER DISPLAY
 PF7 : UNDEFINED         PF8 : UNDEFINED          PF9 : UNDEFINED
 PF10: UNDEFINED         PF11: UNDEFINED          PF12: REMEMBER DISPLAY
```

Figure 16-4 EDF: Stop condition screen.

- At the specific command
- At the specific offset of the command
- At the specific line number of the command
- At any CICS exceptional condition
- At any CICS error
- At the transaction ABEND
- At the normal task completion
- At the abnormal task completion

4. Press the ENTER key. The result will be that CICS will execute the program until the condition specified occurs.

Skipping a Command You may bypass (skip) a command to be executed by typing NOP in the "About to Execute" screen. For example, overtype NOP on RECEIVE in Figure 16-2.

Modifying Values on Screen You may change any value shown in the unprotected area of the screen by just overtyping on the field. For example, you can change the following fields:

- The values in the INTO field or FROM field
- The response code (EIBRCODE)
- The value of the LENGTH field

```
TRANSACTION: PNC1    PROGRAM: TXTSPNC1    TASK NUMBER: 0003203    DISPLAY:  00
STATUS:  COMMAND EXECUTION COMPLETE
EXEC CICS RECEIVE MAP
  MAP (X'D4D7C2D7D5C3F2')                                        AT X'000F962D'
  INTO (X'00000000000000000000000000000500F1F1F1F1F1001900C1'...)  AT X'000F2D3C'
  MAPSET (X'D4E2C2D7D5C3F2')                                     AT X'000F963B'
  TERMINAL




  OFFSET:X'001470'    LINE:00267          EIBFN=X'1802'
  RESPONSE: NORMAL                         EIBRESP=X'00000000'

ENTER:  CONTINUE
PF1 : UNDEFINED              PF2 : SWITCH HEX/CHAR      PF3 : END EDF SESSION
PF4 : SUPPRESS DISPLAYS      PF5 : WORKING STORAGE      PF6 : USER DISPLAY
PF7 : SCROLL BACK            PF8 : SCROLL FORWARD       PF9 : STOP CONDITIONS
PF10: PREVIOUS DISPLAY       PF11: UNDEFINED            PF12: ABEND USER TASK
```

Figure 16-5 EDF: HEX mode display.

```
TRANSACTION: PNC1    PROGRAM: TXTSPNC1    TASK NUMBER: 0003203   DISPLAY:  00
ADDRESS: 000F2D3C                         WORKING STORAGE
000F2D30   000000                                    00000000    ................
000F2D40   000004    00000000 00000000 000500F1 F1F1F1F1    ..........11111
000F2D50   000014    001900C1 C1C1C1C1 C1C1C1C1 C1C1C1C1    ...AAAAAAAAAAAAA
000F2D60   000024    C1C1C1C1 C1C1C1C1 C1C1C1C1 000500F2    AAAAAAAAAAAA...2
000F2D70   000034    F2F2F2F2 001900C2 C2C2C2C2 C2C2C2C2    2222...BBBBBBBBB
000F2D80   000044    C2C2C2C2 C2C2C2C2 C2C2C2C2 C2C2C2C2    BBBBBBBBBBBBBBBB
000F2D90   000054    00000000 00000000 00000000 00000000    ................
000F2DA0   000064    00000000 00000000 00000000 00000000    ................
000F2DB0   000074    00000000 00000000 00000000 00000000    ................
000F2DC0   000084    00000000 00000000 00000000 00000000    ................
000F2DD0   000094    00000000 00000000 00000000 00000000    ................
000F2DE0   0000A4    00000000 00000000 00000000 00000000    ................
000F2DF0   0000B4    00000000 00000000 00000000 00000000    ................
000F2E00   0000C4    00000000 00000000 00000000 00000000    ................
000F2E10   0000D4    00000000 00000000 00000000 00000000    ................
000F2E20   0000E4    00000000 00000000 00000000 00000000    ................

ENTER:   CURRENT DISPLAY
PF1  : UNDEFINED           PF2 : BROWSE TEMP STORAGE PF3  : UNDEFINED
PF4  : EIB DISPLAY         PF5 : WORKING STORAGE      PF6  : USER DISPLAY
PF7  : SCROLL BACK HALF    PF8 : SCROLL FORWARD HALF PF9  : UNDEFINED
PF10: SCROLL BACK FULL     PF11: SCROLL FORWARD FULL PF12: REMEMBER DISPLAY
```

Figure 16-6 EDF: Working storage display.

Displaying and Modifying Working Storage Area   You can display any part of the Working Storage area of the application program on subject, and modify any part of it. The procedures for this are the following:

1. Press the PF3 key to switch to the hexadecimal (HEX) mode.
2. At the command completion screen expressed in the hexadecimal mode (Figure 16-5), the Working Storage address is shown. Take note of the address on subject (for example, X'000F2D3C' for the INTO field).
3. Press the PF5 key to display the Working Storage. It will display from the beginning of the Working Storage (Figure 16-6).
4. You may use the PF8/7 keys for scrolling forward/backward.
5. You may type the address on subject (e.g., X'000F2D3C') in ADDRESS field in the hexadecimal mode. Press the ENTER key. The Working Storage starting from the fullword boundary of that address will be displayed.
6. If you wish to modify the content, just overtype the field in the character mode or in the hexadecimal mode.

Intercepting an ABEND   If the program encounters an ABEND, EDF will intercept it and display the status of the program at the ABEND

```
TRANSACTION: PNC1   PROGRAM: TXTSPNC1   TASK NUMBER: 0003203   DISPLAY:  00
STATUS:  AN ABEND HAS OCCURRED
    COMMAREA    = 'PNC2'
    EIBTIME     = 134342
    EIBDATE     = 89116
    EIBTRNID    = 'PNC1'
    EIBTASKN    = 3203
    EIBTRMID    = 'PNAR'

    EIBCPOSN    = 246
    EIBCALEN    = 4
    EIBAID      = X'7D'                                  AT X'000F2442'
    EIBFN       = X'1802'  RECEIVE                       AT X'000F2443'
    EIBRCODE    = X'000000000000'                        AT X'000F2445'
    EIBDS       = '........'
 +  EIBREQID    = '........'
  OFFSET:X'2A7FEA'                     INTERRUPT: DATA EXCEPTION
  ABEND :  ASRA                        PSW: X'078D2000 002A7FF0 00060007'

ENTER:  CONTINUE
PF1 : UNDEFINED           PF2 : SWITCH HEX/CHAR      PF3 : END EDF SESSION
PF4 : SUPPRESS DISPLAYS   PF5 : WORKING STORAGE      PF6 : USER DISPLAY
PF7 : SCROLL BACK         PF8 : SCROLL FORWARD       PF9 : STOP CONDITIONS
PF10: PREVIOUS DISPLAY    PF11: UNDEFINED            PF12: REGISTERS AT ABEND
```

Figure 16-7 EDF: ABEND status display.

```
TRANSACTION: PNC1   PROGRAM: TXTSPNC1   TASK NUMBER: 0003236   DISPLAY:  00
STATUS:  PROGRAM TERMINATION




















ENTER:  CONTINUE
PF1 : UNDEFINED           PF2 : SWITCH HEX/CHAR      PF3 : UNDEFINED
PF4 : SUPPRESS DISPLAYS   PF5 : WORKING STORAGE      PF6 : USER DISPLAY
PF7 : SCROLL BACK         PF8 : SCROLL FORWARD       PF9 : STOP CONDITIONS
PF10: PREVIOUS DISPLAY    PF11: UNDEFINED            PF12: ABEND USER TASK
```

Figure 16-8 EDF: Program termination screen.

(Figure 16-7). This screen shows useful information for debugging, such as EIB, PSW, program offset address of the ABEND point, ABEND code, and interruption code. Using this information, you can find the instruction which caused the ABEND and analyze the cause. All of this can be done interactively. Here, you would find the power and convenience of EDF.

Program Completion   At the end of the program execution, EDF displays the program termination screen (Figure 16-8).

For Pseudo-Conversational Program   At the end of one task, EDF displays the transaction termination screen (Figure 16-9). Specify "YES" for continuing the pseudo-conversational processing, and press the ENTER key. Then, EDF will continue to monitor the next iteration of the pseudo-conversation. In this way, you can monitor the complete series of pseudo-conversations no matter how many iterations the one transaction has.

Transaction Completion   If "NO" is specified in the task termination screen (Figure 16-9), EDF will end the EDF session.

```
TRANSACTION: PNC1                     TASK NUMBER: 0003236   DISPLAY:  00
STATUS:   TASK TERMINATION




















TO CONTINUE EDF SESSION REPLY YES                             REPLY: NO
ENTER:   CONTINUE
PF1  : UNDEFINED          PF2 : SWITCH HEX/CHAR    PF3  : END EDF SESSION
PF4  : SUPPRESS DISPLAYS  PF5 : WORKING STORAGE    PF6  : USER DISPLAY
PF7  : SCROLL BACK        PF8 : SCROLL FORWARD     PF9  : STOP CONDITIONS
PF10: PREVIOUS DISPLAY    PF11: UNDEFINED          PF12: UNDEFINED
```

Figure 16-9 EDF: Task termination screen.

16.8   Command Level Interpreter (CECI)

The Command Level Interpreter (CECI) is a CICS-supplied transaction which performs syntax checking of a CICS command. If the syntax is satisfied, it will actually execute the command. This may be useful for interactive patching into the application system.

Invoking CECI

For invoking CECI, you type CECI with the CICS command to be interpreted, as in the following example:

```
CECI READ DATASET ('FILEAAA')
```

After pressing the ENTER key, the syntax check will be provided by CEDI.

Definition of Variables

For certain commands, the variable name and data must be defined, especially for the write commands. The variable name must have the & sign as the first character (e.g., &FIELDA).

For checking the characteristics of a variable, do the following:

1. Type the variable name in the NAME field which appears at the upper right of the screen, and press the ENTER key. The variable list will be shown.
2. Press the PF3 key to return to the original screen.

To define, modify, or add the variables, do the following:

1. Press the PF5 key for the variable list.
2. Modify, if required, the existing variables by simply typing over them.
3. Add, if required, the new variables.

To delete a variable, do the following in the variable list screen:

1. Place a cursor on the & sign of the variable to be deleted.
2. Press the ERASE EOF key.

An Application

Suppose that you have coded a BMS map (e.g., MPBINQ2/ MSBINQ2). Assembling and linkediting have been successfully completed and the mapset name has been registered in PPT. However, the program which uses this map has not been coded yet. You could see how this map looks by using the CECI transaction as the following example:

```
CECI SEND MAP('MPBINQ2') MAPSET('MSBINQ2') ERASE
```

Then, the map will be displayed into your terminal.

16.9 Temporary Storage Browse (CEBR)

The Temporary Storage Browse (CEBR) is a CICS-supplied transaction which browses Temporary Storage Queue (TSQ). It is a very convenient tool if you wish to display the content of TSQ when you are monitoring an application program through EDF. Also, if the application program is written in VS COBOL II with the FDUMP option, since the formatted dump is to be stored in TSQ in case of ABEND, CEBR through EDF will facilitate the interactive debugging.

Invoking CEBR Directly

Invoking CEBR is simple. You type CEBR and press the ENTER key. The CEBR initial screen will be displayed. Then, you type:

```
QUEUE xxxxxxxx
```

where xxxxxxxx is the queue id of TSQ to be browsed. After pressing the ENTER key, the content of the TSQ will be displayed.

Invoking CEBR through EDF

CEBR can be invoked while you are already in the EDF mode. Press the PF5 key to display the Working Storage Section (see Section 16.7 and Figure 16-6). Then, press the PF12 key to invoke CEBR. The system will display the CEBR initial screen. Then, type the QUEUE command as described above.

When you complete the CEBR operations, press the PF3 key. The Working Storage display screen will reappear. From here, you can resume the normal EDF operations.

16.10   Master Terminal Transaction (CEMT)

The CEMT (Enhanced Master Terminal) transaction is a CICS-supplied transaction which manipulates the CICS environment, such as transactions, programs, files, TSQs, and tasks. It is a menu-driven and easy-to-use transaction, but due to its nature of manipulating the CICS environment, it is usually a restricted transaction which an application programmer or the end-users cannot use freely. But it helps application programmers for program testing, monitoring, and/or trouble shooting.

Major Functions

The CEMT transaction performs the following major functions:

INQUIRE: To inquire about the status of CICS environments

SET: To update the status of CICS environments
PERFORM: For further system operations

CEMT Operations

You can operate the CEMT transaction very easily by responding to a series of instruction screen CEMT displays. The following are the highlights of the CEMT operations:

CEMT Initiation In order to initiate the CEMT transaction, you type CEMT and press the ENTER key. The following response screen will appear:

```
STATUS     :   ENTER ONE OF FOLLOWING
INQUIRE
PERFORM
SET
```

You select a function by typing INQ, PER, or SET and press the ENTER key.

INQ/SET Functions   If you have selected the INQ or SET option, the response screen shows the options as follows:

```
STATUS    :    ENTER ONE OF FOLLOWING
TRANSACTION       TRA
PROGRAM           PRO
  :
```

Then you type one of the options you wish to use, and press the ENTER key.

TRANsaction Option   The TRANsaction option is used to deal with the information from PCT. If this option is selected, the system will display the transaction id, priority, and status in the format below. If you wish to change the status from ENA(abled) to DIS(abled), or vice versa, just overtype the column with the new status you wish.

```
TRAN(xxxx)     PRI(nnn)   ENA
                          (or DIS)
```

PRogram Option   The PRogram option is used to deal with the information from PPT. If this option is selected, the system will display the program-related information in the format below. If you wish to change the status from ENA(abled) or to DIS(abled), or vice versa, just overtype the column with the new status you wish. If you wish to refresh an old load module with the new module during the CICS session, type 'NEW' at the right. This is useful for testing.

```
PRO(xxxxxxx)   LEN(nnnn) RES(nnn) USE(nnn) ASM     ENA
                                           (COB)   (DIS)
                                           (PLI)
```

DAtaset (or FILE) Option   The DAtaset (or FILE) option is used to deal with the information from FCT. If this option is selected, the system will display the dataset-related information in the format below. You can change OPEn/CLOse, DISable/ENAble, or Access Service Requests (REA, BRO, UPD, ADD, DEL) as you wish, by overtyping appropriate column with the new status or service you wish.

FILE is the preferred name under CICS/MVS, but it performs the same function as DAtaset.

```
DAT(xxxxxxx)  VSA  CLO   DIS  REA  UPD  ADD ... EXEC
              (OPE) (ENA)
```

TAsk Option The TAsk option is used to see the status of the currently running tasks. If this option is selected, the system will display the task-related information in the format below. TAS, TRA, and FAC show the task number, transaction id, facility (usually terminal id), respectively. If you wish to purge a task because of looping or task hang-up, type PURGE at the right of the task line on subject.

```
TAS(nnnnn) TRA(xxxx) FAC(tttt) ACT TER
```

PERFORM Function If you have selected the PERFORM function in the initial menu screen, the system will display the prompt screen with the following options, which you can select as you wish by typing these options on the screen:

RESET:	To synchronize CICS date and time with the Operating System
SNAP:	To take a snap dump
SHUTDOWN:	To shut down the entire CICS system

Technical Notes

The CEMT transaction affects not only your transaction or other resources you are interested in, but also the CICS system as a whole. For example, if you execute the PERFORM function with the SHUTDOWN option carelessly, the entire CICS system will go down, while other users might wish to continue the CICS operations.

Therefore, in some installations, ordinary CICS users are not permitted to use the CEMT transaction. When you use it, careful attention must be paid.

16.11 Dynamic File Open/Close (DFOC)

Initial File Status

As we discussed in Section 6.6, when CICS comes up, the initial status of a file is determined by the FILESTAT parameter in the FCT entry for the file, as follows:

```
DFHFCT     TYPE=DATASET,
           DATASET=name,
           FILESTAT=(ENABLED | DISABLED,
                     OPENED  | CLOSED),
           :
```

In order for a CICS transaction to be able to access a file, the file must be opened and enabled. Otherwise, the transaction will encounter the exceptional condition for the file not open (NOTOPEN). Therefore, if the file is closed or disabled, the file must be opened and enabled before the transaction which uses the file starts. On the other hand, keeping a file with the open status requires a large amount of resources. Therefore, as soon as the file is no longer required, the file should be closed.

Improvements by CICS Ver. 1.7 (or later)

CICS Ver. 1.7 (or later) provides an improvement on the file open/close status. That is, at the time of file access by an application program, if the file is not open, CICS automatically opens the file and executes the file access command such as READ or WRITE. In effect, the exceptional condition NOTOPEN has been removed. Therefore, the application program can issue freely any input/output commands against the file irrespective of the open/close status of the file.

This function for automatic file open by CICS Ver. 1.7 (or later) gives some convenience in application programming. However, from the point of view of system resource consumption, a file should be open only while it is required by the application system and the file should be closed as soon as the file is no longer required.

For the efficiency of not only the application system, but also the CICS system as a whole, therefore, it is required to establish some way of opening/closing the file(s) dynamically.

File Open/Close Through CEMT Transaction

As we discussed before, a file can be opened or closed through the Master Terminal (CEMT) transaction. You can use the conventional procedures described in Section 16.10. Or, you can use the shortcut procedures for the CEMT transaction by typing:

```
CEMT INQ DA(filename).
```

Then, on the prompt screen which shows the file status in the format described in Section 16.10, you type either CLO or OPE on the file open/close status column for closing or opening the file, respectively. In this way, regardless of the initial staus of the file, you can open/close the file as many times as you wish in either direction (i.e., from "open" to "close," or from "close" to "open").

Needs for Dynamic File Open/Close (DFOC)

Changing the file open/close status through the CEMT transaction involves a human intervention. Therefore, under this approach, an automatic switch-over from a CICS session to a batch session, and vice versa, is not possible, as far as the files under CICS are concerned.

For a certain CICS application system, however, it is more desirable if a CICS application program automatically switches the session from CICS to batch and vice versa, by dynamically closing or opening the files under CICS.

Let us call this "Dynamic File Open/Close" (DFOC). DFOC can be accomplished by the special techniques in the CICS application programs or the batch jobs. The following are three alternative approaches currently available to DFOC:

• DFOC by LINK command
• DFOC by SET command
• DFOC by batch job

We will discuss these approaches one by one in the next three sections.

VSAM File Requirements for DFOC

When a VSAM file is closed under the CICS system, this file could be accessed (including update) by other batch systems or TSO jobs, even while CICS itself is up. In order to make this possible, the following two requirements must be satisfied:

Requirement for VSAM Definition When a VSAM cluster is defined through the VSAM Access Method Service (IDCAMS) program, the SHAREOPTION option must be specified, as follows:

```
SHAREOPTION(2,3)
```

The SHAREOPTION option indicates how the VSAM file is to be shared among regions or systems. The first parameter is the cross-region parameter, and value 2 means that one user can write onto the file while other users can read from it. Other values can be specified in the cross-region parameter, but value 2 is the safest. The second parameter is the cross-system parameter, and value 3 means that the file can be fully shared among the systems.

JCL Requirement   In addition, in the JCL of the CICS job itself, DISP=SHR must be specified for the DD card of this file, as follows:

```
//ddname   DD DSN=dataset-name,DISP=SHR
```

where,

ddname:	The file name registered in FCT.
dataset-name:	The VSAM cluster name.

DISP=SHR allows more than one job (including CICS, TSO, and batch jobs) to share the file simultaneously.

16.12   DFOC by LINK Command

The Dynamic File Open/Close (DFOC) can be achieved from a CICS application program by conceptually executing the Master Terminal (CEMT) transaction through the LINK command.

Approach

For this, the application program links (through the LINK command) the Master Terminal Program (DFHEMTP) and passes the CEMT parameter data required for the file open/close through COMMAREA. Receiving the data, the DFHEMTP program opens/closes the files specified, after which control is returned to the application program. In effect, the application program appears to be opening/closing the files although the actual file open/close is done by the DFHEMTP program.

Issuing the LINK command to the DFHEMTP program, the data in the COMMAREA fileld must be the exact data for executing the CEMT transaction for the file open/close, as follows:

```
SET DATASET(name1, name2,.....) OPENED
                                (or CLOSED)
```

where name1, name2, so on, are the names of the files to be opened or closed. Also the LENGTH field of the LINK command must contain the exact length of the COMMAREA field.

Example

The following is an example of DFOC by the LINK command to the DFHEMTP program:

```
WORKING-STORAGE SECTION.
      :
01    WS-CEMT-WORKAREA.
      05    WS-CEMT-LENGTH            PIC S9(4) COMP VALUE 35.
      05    WS-CEMT-COMMAREA.
            10    WS-CEMT-SERVICE     PIC X(04) VALUE
                  'SET '.
            10    WS-CEMT-DATASET     PIC X(25) VALUE
                  'DATASET(FILEAAA,FILEBBB) '.
            10    WS-CEMT-ACTION      PIC X(06) VALUE
                  'OPENED'.
      :
      :
PROCEDURE DIVISION.
      :
      :
*
* INVOKE CEMT COMMAND FOR DYNAMIC FILE OPEN/CLOSE.
*
      EXEC CICS LINK
            PROGRAM('DFHEMTP')
            COMMAREA(WS-CEMT-COMMAREA)
            LENGTH(WS-CEMT-LENGTH)
      EXD-EXEC.
```

Execution Results   The files specified (FILEAAA and FILEBBB) will be dynamically opened (in this case), and control will be returned to the statement after the LINK command of the application program.

16.13   DFOC by SET Command

The SET command is an advanced CICS command which virtually performs all functions of the SET option of the Master Terminal (CEMT) transaction. Therefore, DFOC can be achieved from a CICS application program simply by issuing the SET command for file open/close.

Format

The format of the SET command for the file open/close purpose is as follows:

```
EXEC CICS SET
     DATASET(name)  |  FILE(name)
     OPEN | CLOSED
END-EXEC.
```

DATASET (or FILE) names the name of the file you wish to dynamically open or close. One name can be specified at a time. OPEN or CLOSED indicates the file to be opened or closed, respectively.

FILE is the preferred name under CICS/MVS, but it performs the same function as DATASET.

Example

The following is an example of DFOC by the SET command:

```
EXEC CICS SET
     DATASET('FILEAAA')
     OPEN
END-EXEC.
```

Execution Results   File FILEAAA will be opened.

16.14   DFOC by Batch Job

The Dynamic File Open/Close (DFOC) can be also achieved from a
batch job which issues the MASTER Terminal (CEMT) transaction
as the data for the JES Modify (F) command against the system
console terminal.

Prerequisite

There is one prerequisite to this approach, and you should clarify
with your system programmer whether your installation satisfies
this prerequisite. The prerequisite is that the MVS system console
must be defined in TCT as the system console for CICS, by specifying TRMTYP=CONSOLE and CONSLID=00, as follows:

```
DFHTCT    TYPE=TERMINAL,
          TRMTYP=CONSOLE,
          CONSLID=00,        <== Required.
          TRMIDNT=name,
          :
```

Approach

Once the prerequisite is satisfied, a batch job must be created. This
batch job uses a dummy program (IEFBR14), which does nothing.
JCL of this job, however, contains JES Modify (F) command against
the system console terminal, which is defined as the CICS terminal
by the prerequisite. The accompanying data to the F command is
data for the master terminal transaction (CEMT), as follows:

```
// F cicsjob,'CEMT SET DATASET(name1,name2,..) OPENED'
//                                              (or CLOSED)
```

where,

F:	JES command for modify
cicsjob:	Jobname of CICS job itself
name1,name2, . . :	DDNAME of one or more files
OPENED:	To open the file(s)
CLOSED:	To close the file(s)

In effect, the CEMT transaction will be executed for file open/close through the system consol.

Example

The following is an example of DFOC by a batch job:

```
//-------- JOB ----------
//CEMT    EXEC PGM=IEFBR14
// F cicsjob,'CEMT SET DATASET(FILEAAA,FILEBBB) OPENED'
//
```

Execution Results   The files (FILEAAA and FILEBBB) will be opened for the CICS region (i.e., not for the batch job), and the message will be displayed on the system console.

16.15   Applications of DFOC

Under the production environment, it is not desirable that the Data Processing (DP) personnel open or close production files everyday for the end users, because production operations should be taken care of entirely by the users. However, at the same time, since the Master Terminal (CEMT) transaction is a restricted transaction, it should not be given to the users (non-DP personnel) for file opening and closing. The Dynamic File Open/Close (DFOC) approach is conveniently suited to resolve this difficult situation.

You can easily imbed the DFOC logic in the user's online transaction and/or batch jobs. Then, users can open/close files as a part of their daily operations without knowing about file open/close. This frees the DP personnel from opening/closing files for users every day.

Case

Let us make a case study. You have developed an Accounting System using CICS for the Accounts Division of your company. Your users are accounting professionals and clerks without any knowledge of DP. They enter online transactions during the day and run batch jobs in the evening.

Your DP Division runs the computer for 24 hours a day, and CICS is up for 24 hours a day. Since there are many CICS users other

Time	Events	CICS File Status	Online Op.	Batch Op.
8:55	Run Batch job. (File initialization)	Close	No	Ok
9:00	Online Day Initialize (ADI1)	Open	Ok	No
:	(Other normal online operations) :	:	:	:
:	:	:	:	:
:	:	:	:	:
17:00	Online Day Close (ADC1)	Close	No	Ok
17:05	Batch Job Processing	:	:	:
:		:	:	:

Figure 16-10 Application of Dynamic File Open/Close (DFOC).

than the Accounts Division, you cannot bring down CICS for batch job processing by your users (the Accounts Division).

You do not wish to give the CEMT transaction to the users (non-DP personnel), but you do not wish to open/close the files for the users every day either. How should you resolve this situation?

A Solution

In this situation, you can apply the DFOC approach in the following way: Usually, there are both an initial housekeeping transaction and final housekeeping transaction in an online system. Let us call these "Day Initialize Transaction" (ADI1) and "Day Close Transaction" (ADC1), respectively. In the program for ADI1, you imbed the DFOC logic for file opening after its own processing. In the program for ADC1, you embed the DFOC logic for file closing after its own processing.

As illustrated in Figure 16-10, you instruct the users in the Accounts Division to run the ADI1 transaction in the morning once before any other transactions are entered, for example, at 9:00. You also instruct the users to run the ADC1 transaction after all Accounts transactions have been entered for the day, for example, at 17:00.

Between the ADI1 and ADC1 transaction executions, the files for the Accounts Division are open under CICS, so that the users can enter its online transactions. After the ADC1 transaction execution and before the next ADI1 transaction execution (next day), the files are closed, so that the users can run the batch jobs.

In this way, the users do not have to use the CEMT transaction for opening/closing the files, which is automatically done during the execution of the ADI1 and ADC1 transactions, respectively. Therefore, you do not have to be involved in opening/closing the files for the users.

You might find many similar situations in actual business applications. DFOC will offer a very effective solution to them.

Exercise

Modify Approach 4 (i.e., program TXTAIPRD) of the Exercise for Chapter 10 to intercept an ABEND within the program. Then, intentionally dump the task areas and terminate the task with a proper message.

Intercommunication

17.1 Introduction

CICS intercommunication is a general concept of communications by CICS with other systems in the multisystem environment. The other systems to be communicated may be CICSs in the same processor, CICSs in the different processors, or even non-CICS systems.

Forms of Intercommunication

CICS intercommunication can be achieved in one of the following two forms:

• Multi-Region Operation (MRO)
• Intersystem Commnication (ISC)

Once the link among the participating systems has been established, however, the actual communications among these participating systems will be performed in a similar manner regardless of whether MRO or ISC is used for intercommunication. Therefore, for the purpose of application programming, it is quasi-transparent whether MRO or ISC is used for intercommunication. We will discuss MRO and ISC further in subsequent sections of this chapter.

Facilities for Intercommunication

Intercommunication involves resources of the participating systems. These resources can be exchanged or distributed among the participating systems through the following facilities:

- Function Request Shipping
- Asynchronous Processing
- Transaction Routing
- Distributed Transaction Processing (DTP)

These facilities are available for both MRO and ISC, but the degree of availability is different. Some facilities are more available to MRO, while other facilities are more available to ISC. We will discuss these facilities individually in the later sections of this chapter.

Terminology

In discussion of intercommunication, the terms "local" and "remote" are often used to describe the participating systems and their resources. Let us define these terms clearly here, so that the discussions in the following sections will be clearer.

Local The term "local" is used for the initiating side of intercommunication. Therefore, "local system" means the system which initiates intercommunication, and "local resources" means the resources of the local system.

Remote The term "remote" is used for the to-be-initiated side of intercommunication. Therefore, "remote system" means the system which is initiated as the result of the intercommunication request by the local system, and "remote resources" means the resources of the remote system.

17.2   Multi-Region Operation (MRO)

Within one processor, there could be more than one CICS, each of which runs independently under the same operating system (e.g., MVS/XA). In this environment, one CICS can communicate with the other CICSs. This form of intercommunication is called Multi-Region Operation (MRO).

Example

One of the typical applications of MRO is a multidepartmental system. In this system, one CICS region is responsible for the applications of one department, and major departments of a firm or an organization have their own CICS region. If the resources must be shared among the departments, it would be done so through MRO.

Figure 17-1 illustrates one example of such multidepartmental system based on MRO. In this example, all information processing of the firm is centralized in the Headquarters Office. There are three major departments — Accounts, Sales, and Warehouse — each of which is the principal owner of the Accounting System, Sales System, and Inventory System, respectively. Each department (e.g., Accounts Dept.) is responsible for updating the database of its own system (e.g., Accounting System) but is not allowed to update other systems (e.g., Sales System or Inventory System) owned by the other departments. However, if one department (e.g., Accounts Dept.) requires information from the other departments (e.g., Sales Dept.), it

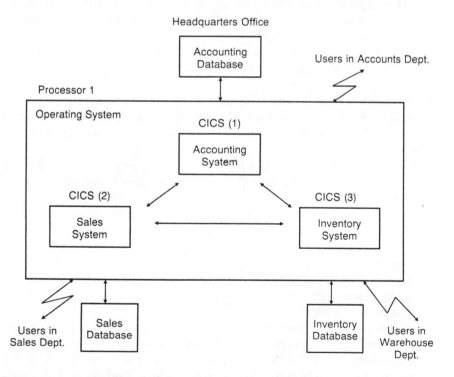

Figure 17-1 Multidepartmental system based on MRO.

is allowed to access (read only) the database of other systems (e.g., Sales System).

All three systems are CICS systems running under one operating system (e.g., MVS/XA). Each system runs independently while the resources can be effectively shared among three CICS systems.

Facilities

As mentioned in the previous section, the actual intercommunication among CICS systems through MRO is achieved by the four intercommunication facilities: Function Request Shipping, Asynchronous Processing, Transaction Routing, and Distributed Transaction Processing (DTP). We will discuss these facilities in detail in the later sections.

Benefits

Since each CICS communicates with other CICSs under the same operating system (e.g. MVS/XA), MRO does not require the sophisticated communication networking facilities. Therefore, MRO can be implemented relatively easily.

Further, a proper implementation of MRO brings many benefits, some of which are summarized as follows:

- *Operation Independence:* The operations of the systems are independent among CICS systems. Therefore, the principal owner of one CICS system can have the complete control over its own system.
- *Reliability:* Even if one CICS system goes down, other CICS systems will still be operational. This will improve the reliability of the system as a whole.
- *Security:* Since the principal owner of one CICS system has complete control over its own system, security of the system can be well established.
- *Performance:* System performance can be tuned independently for each CICS system based on its own requirements and priority relative to other systems. This would improve the performance of the systems as a whole.
- *No Redundancy:* Since resources can be shared among CICS systems, each CICS system does not need in its system any information which can be obtained from other CICS systems. This will reduce or eliminate the resource redundancy among the CICS systems. Consequently, the systems will be much more efficient as a whole.

• *Project Phasing:* Instead of developing one big comprehensive system which includes all functional components, the system can be divided into several functional subsystems, each of which performs the specialized functions. In this way, each subsystem can be developed in phases, each of which concentrates on one subsystem based on the functional priority and requirements. At the end of each phase, the subsystem becomes operational one by one independently. At the completion of all phases, the total system becomes operational. This is an efficient and practical way to develop a complex online system.

However, one drawback of MRO is that all operations must be centralized in one main office (more specifically, in one processor). Therefore, MRO may not be suitable if operations are distributed among several regional offices.

17.3   Intersystem Communication (ISC)

One CICS in one processor can communicate with other CICSs in other processors or other non-CICS systems, regardless of where the other processors or non-CICS systems are physically located. This form of intercommunication is called Intersystem Communication (ISC).

ISC requires sophisticated communication networks based on the System Network Architecture (SNA) which defines protocols, standards, and data formats of communiations by different hardware and software in the multisystem environment. The concept of ISC is thus best described, if it is discussed in conjunction with SNA, especially a special protocol called LU6.2.

LU6.2

A SNA network defines special points called "Logical Units" (LUs), which are used by the end users to access the network. There are several types of LUs, among which LU6.2 is the most commonly used LU with the most advanced capabilities. LU6.2 provides a comprehensive set of transmission capabilities and services. A general term for ISC based on the LU6.2 protocol is called "Advanced Program to Program Communication" (APPC).

One CICS in one processor participating in a SNA network can be defined as a LU. Then, this CICS can establish Intersystem Communication (ISC) with other LUs based on the LU6.2 protocol. The other LUs could be other CICSs in the same processor, other CICSs in the different processor (physically in the same location or in the distant location), other non-CICS systems (e.g., AS/400 midrange systems or PS/2 personal computers), or even other device-level products (i.e., terminals), as long as the other LUs are linked to SNA based on the LU6.2 protocol.

This concept of ISC makes CICS able to communicate with the other systems in the standardized way irrespective of the physical distance, difference in hardware, or difference in software.

CICS can achieve ISC based on not only the LU6.2 protocol, but also other LU protocols. However, since LU6.2 is the most widely used LU protocol, and for the sake of simplicity let us limit our discussion of ISC only based on the LU6.2 protocol.

Example

One of the typical applications of ISC is a distributed corporate system. In this system, computers (processors) are independently installed in the geographically distant locations based on the corporate office structure. Each office has its own CICS system for its functionally responsible operations. If resources must be shared among offices, it would be done so through ISC.

Figure 17-2 illustrates one example of distributed corporate system based on ISC. In this example, all information processing is decentralized to the regional corporate offices. The Headquarters Office in City 1 processes all accounting information, so that the Accounting System (CICS system) is installed in its computer (processor 1). The Central Sales Office in City 2 is responsible for all sales information, so that the Sales System (CICS system) is installed in its computer (processor 2). Likewise, the Central Warehouse in City 3 takes care of all inventory information, so that the Inventory System (CICS system) is installed in its computer (processor 3).

These three systems are linked to each other based on ISC. Operations are carried out similarly to those of the multidepartmental system based on MRO, except that each CICS system resides in the physically distant computer (processor).

Facilities

The actual intercommunication among systems through ISC is achieved by the four facilities: Function Request Shipping, Asynchronous Processing, Transaction Routing, and Distributed Transaction Processing (DTP). Among these, DTP based on LU6.2 has the most powerful potential for future applications.

Benefits

Since ISC requires sophisticated SNA networks, it may not be easy to implement. However, once ISC is implemented, we can develop a complex but effective distributed system relatively easily.

Implementing ISC will bring the same benefits as MRO described in the previous section. In addition, ISC will bring the following benefits unique to ISC:

- *Hardware/Software Independence:* As long as the intercommunication session is established based on LU6.2, it is transparent to the local CICS what kind of hardware and software the remote system consists of. This advantage is so significant that the future applications of ISC based on LU6.2 may be limitless.
- *Transparency of Physical Distance:* Since physically distant resources can be shared through ISC, it would be easy to integrate the corporate operations even if operations are scattered among regional offices.

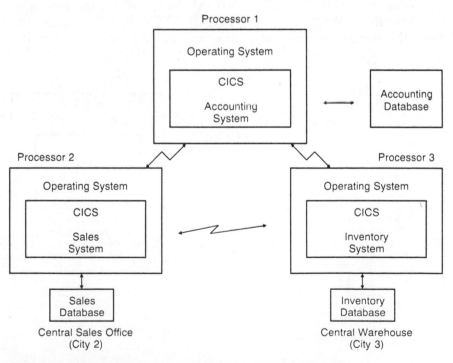

Figure 17-2 Distributed corporate system based on ISC.

17.4   Links to Remote Systems

Defining links to the remote systems is a system programmer's task, since it requires understanding of SNA networks and the Advanced Communication Function/Virtual Telecommunication Access Method (ACF/VTAM). However, it would be useful to discuss the basic concept for linking the remote systems. If application programmers (or systems analysts) understand the basic concept, it would be much easier to follow the discussion of intercommunication facilities in the subsequent sections.

Figure 17-3 illustrates an example of an intercommunication network. This example shows three commonly used links: a link for MRO between CIC1 and CIC2 in processor 1, a link for CICS LU6.2 ISC between CIC1 in processor 1 and CIC3 in processor 2, a link for LU6.2 APPC between CIC1 in processor 1, and PS2A which is an intelligent workstation (PS/2 personal computer).

TCT Definition

The links for intercommunication are defined in the Terminal Control Table (TCT) of each CICS system (CIC1, CIC2, and CIC3, in this example). The DFHTCT TYPE=INITIAL entry defines the local system identifier (SYSIDNT), the DFHTCT TYPE=SYSTEM entry defines the remote system and characteristics of intercommunication

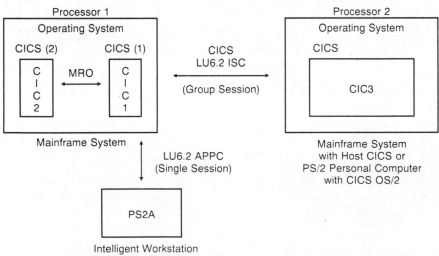

Figure 17-3 Example of intercommunication network.

(e.g., MRO, CICS LU6.2 ISC, or LU6.2 APPC), and the DFHTCT TYPE=MODESET entry defines a group of sessions for ISC.

Taking the example of Figure 17-3, in TCT of the CIC1 system, the local system identifier (SYSIDNT) is defined as CIC1. For the remote system, CIC2 is defined as the remote CICS system based on MRO. CIC3 is defined as the remote CICS system based on LU6.2 ISC. PS2A is defined as the remote LU6.2 APPC intelligent workstation (PS/2 personal computer). In addition, since CIC3 is a CICS system creating multiple ISC sessions concurrently, a group session code is defined for CIC3. However, since PS2A is an intelligent workstation working with only one session at a time, it is defined as a single session station.

Similarly, in TCT of the CIC2 system, the local system identifier (SYSIDNT) is defined as CIC2. For the remote system, CIC1 is defined as the remote CICS system based on MRO.

In TCT of the CIC3 system, the local system identifier (SYSIDNT) is defined as CIC3. For the remote system, CIC1 is defined as the remote CICS system based on LU6.2 ISC. In addition, since CIC1 is a CICS system creating multiple ISC sessions concurrently, a group session code is defined for CIC1, corresponding to the group session code defined in the CIC3 entry of the CIC1 system's TCT.

It should be noted that Processor 2 in Figure 17-3 could be a mainframe system with the host CICS, or it could be a PS/2 personal computer with CICS OS/2. TCT definition for Processor 2 is virtually the same regardless of whether Processor 2 is the mainframe system with the host CICS or the PS/2 personal computer with CICS OS/2.

System Identifier

Once these links have been established, each system (CIC1, CIC2, CIC3, and PS2A in this example) can communicate with other remote system(s) identified by the system identifier (SYSIDNT) defined in its TCT.

From application programming's point of view, once SYSIDNT of the remote systems are known, intercommunication can be accomplished in a similar manner, irrespective of MRO, CICS LU6.2 ISC, or LU6.2 APPC.

17.5   Function Request Shipping

The Function Request Shipping facility allows a CICS application program in the local CICS system to access the resources owned by another remote CICS system, regardless of whether the remote CICS system is within the same processor (MRO case) or in a different processor (ISC case). The CICS application program can be written without knowing where the requested resources locate.

Available Remote Resources

The Function Request Shipping facility makes only limited remote resources available to the application program in the local CICS system. These available remote resources are:

- VSAM files
- DL/I database
- Transient Data Queue (TDQ)
- Temporary Storage Queue (TSQ)

Mirror Transactions

The mirror transactions are the CICS-supplied transactions for administrating Function Request Shipping, and they reside in the remote system. When a remote system receives a function request shipped by a local system, it initiates a corresponding mirror transaction for the function requested. The mirror transaction in turn decodes the function request, and issues the actual CICS command against the resource owned by the remote system. After the completion of the command, the mirror transaction formats the reply data and transmits to the requestor in the local system.

In effect, a transaction in the local system can execute CICS commands against the remote resources through the mirror transactions in the remote system, as if these remote resources belonged to the local system.

Concept of Function Request Shipping

Figure 17-4 illustrates the concept of Function Request Shipping. There are two CICS systems. In this case, CIC1 is the local CICS system, and CIC2 is the remote CICS system. Let us suppose that an application program in local system CIC1 wishes to read a remote file FILEAAA owned by the remote system CIC2.

Since local system CIC1 does not own file FILEAAA, this file must be defined as the remote file in the File Control Table (FCT) of CIC1. The DFHFCT TYPE=REMOTE entry defines a remote file. SYS-IDNT must name the system identifier of the remote system (CIC2,

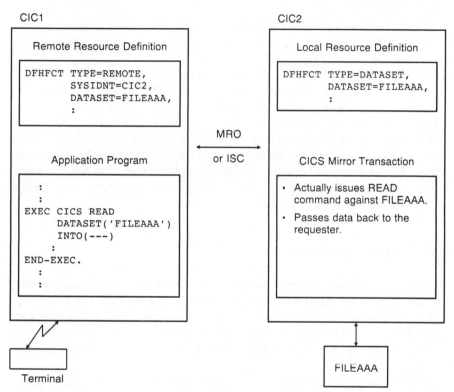

Figure 17-4 Concept of Function Request Shipping.

in this case) which owns file FILEAAA. DATASET should name the dataset name of the remote file (FILEAAA, in this case). Since remote system CIC2 owns file FILEAAA, this file must be defined in FCT of CIC2 in the normal manner as the local resource of CIC2. Now, the link between local system CIC1 and remote system CIC2 has been established with respect to the resource FILEAAA.

In local system CIC1 the application program issues the READ command against FILEAAA. The application program does not have to know where this file exists. Therefore, the application program can issue the READ command in a normal manner without any special considerations for the remote file.

Local system CIC1 intercepts this READ command and looks up FCT, which indicates that FILEAAA is owned by remote system CIC2. Therefore, CIC1 ships this READ request to CIC2 through the intercommunication link between CIC1 and CIC2, which could be MRO or ISC.

When remote system CIC2 receives the function request from CIC1, CIC2 activates a proper mirror transaction, which actually issues the READ command against file FILEAAA which CIC2 owns. After the completion of the READ command, the mirror transaction formats the reply data containing the record of FILEAAA and transmits to CIC1. When CIC1 receives the reply data from CIC2, it places the data in the INTO parameter of the READ command.

This process is performed automatically by CICS (i.e., both CIC1 and CIC2), and it is completely transparent to the application program in local system CIC1. At the completion of the READ command, the application program in CIC1 can continue processing using the data from FILEAAA.

Remote Resource Definition

As briefly explained in the concept of Function Request Shipping, the remote resources must be defined in the corresponding CICS control tables of the local system. Once the remote resources are defined in the CICS control tables, the application programs can freely use the remote resources as if the remote resources were owned by the local system.

The following summarizes the CICS table entries for defining remote resources:

Remote File

```
DFHFCT      TYPE=REMOTE,
            SYSIDNT=name,
            DATASET=name | FILE=name,
            [RMTNAME=name],
            :
```

Remote TDQ

```
DFHDCT      TYPE=REMOTE,
            SYSIDNT=name,
            DESTID=name,
            [RMTNAME=name],
            :
```

Remote TSQ

```
DFHTST     TYPE=REMOTE,
           SYSIDNT=name,
           DATAID=character-string,
           [RMTNAME=character-string],
           :
```

TYPE=REMOTE identifies the table entry defining the remote resource. SYSIDNT defines the system identifier of the remote system
which owns the resource. DATASET, DESTID, and DATAID define
the name of file, destination-id, and generic QID of TSQ, respectively. These names should correspond to the names defined in the
remote system. If these names are different from the remote resource name, the exact remote resource name defined in the remote
system must be specified in RMTNAME.

For the remote DL/I database, there are no special resource definition requirements. This is because DL/I by itself decides the access
request to be done in the local system or the remote system.

Design Considerations

The Function Request Shipping facility is easy to implement. Once
the remote resources are defined in the CICS control tables of the
local system, the application programs in the local system can freely
use these remote resources without considering which system owns
these resources. Therefore, many applications can be found in the
multisystem environment involving intercommunication, regardless
of whether it is MRO or ISC. However, for implementing the Function Request Shipping facility, the following points should be taken
into account.

Security   Since application programs in the local system can freely
access the remote resources in the remote system, the remote system
does not have complete control over the security of its resources.
Some unauthorized application programs in the local system may
perform unauthorized access to the remote resources. Therefore, the
resources must be well protected by the security facilities.

Performance   Function Request Shipping transfers an execution of
CICS command from the local system to the remote system. This will
create a series of activities through the intercommunication link be-

tween two systems, resulting in an increase of data traffic in the communication link. Therefore, the application program in the local system should issue CICS commands against the remote resources only when it is necessary. Otherwise, Function Request Shipping will decrease the performance of the program (or transaction). For example, unnecessary browsing commands should not be issued against a remote file in order to read a particular record. In this case, a direct READ command should be issued for the particular record.

17.6   Asynchronous Processing

The Asynchronous Processing facility allows a CICS application program in the local CICS system to initiate remote transactions, which are owned by the remote system, in the remote CICS system, regardless of whether the remote CICS system is in the same processor (MRO case) or in the different processor (ISC case). The CICS application program in the local system can be written without knowing to which remote CICS system this remote transaction belongs.

Once a remote transaction is initiated in the remote system, the local application program has no control over the remote transaction. That is, there is no synchronized conversation between the local application program (or transaction) and the remote transaction. This is the reason why the term "asynchronous" is used.

If Asynchronous Processing is performed in the proper order, an application in the local system can achieve a distributed processing with the remote system.

Initiation of Remote Transaction

START Command   The application program in the local system initiates a remote transaction in the remote system by issuing the START command with the transaction id of the remote transaction. The START command can be issued without knowing where the remote transaction will actually be executed. The local application program can pass various data to the remote transaction through the START command using appropriate options. For a detailed description of the START command, see Section 13.6.

The NOCHECK option could be specified in the START command. If specified, no error checking will be done in the remote system side. This will improve the performance.

RETRIEVE Command If some data is passed by the START command in the local application program, the remote transaction initiated by the START command can receive the data through the RETRIEVE command. The remote transaction can issue the RETRIEVE command without knowing which local system passed the data. For a detailed description of the RETRIEVE command, see Section 13.8.

Concept of Asynchronous Processing

Asynchronous Processing is one form of Function Request Shipping, if we consider a remote transaction as a remote resource. Therefore, the Asynchronous Processing is achieved in a way very similar to that of Function Request Shipping.

Figure 17-5 illustrates the concept of Asynchronous Processing, based on the similar multisystem environment used for describing Function Request Shipping (Figure 17-4). CIC1 is the local CICS system and CIC2 is the remote CICS system. Let us suppose that application program ASPTRA1 (transaction TRA1) wishes to pass some data to remote transaction TRA2 in remote system CIC2 for some distributed processing. Remote transaction TRA2 processes the data and sends the results back to the local system by initiating a new transaction TRA3 in CIC1.

Since local system CIC1 does not own the transaction TRA2, TRA2 must be defined as the remote transaction in the Program Control Table (PCT) of CIC1 with the remote system identifier CIC2. The application program ASPTRA1 in the local system CIC1 issues the START command to initiate transaction TRA2 (specified in the TRANSID parameter) with accompanying data. RTRANSID specifies the returning transaction (TRA3 in this case). RTERMID specifies the returning terminal (EIBTRMID containing 'TRM1' in this case). FROM and LENGTH specify the data area and its length, respectively. After this, program ASPTRA1 terminates.

The local system CIC1 intercepts this START command and looks up PCT, which indicates transaction TRA2 is owned by remote system CIC2. Therefore, CIC1 ships this START request to CIC2 through the intercommunication link between CIC1 and CIC2, which could be MRO or ISC.

When remote system CIC2 receives the function request, the mirror transaction decodes the request and executes the START command for this transaction TRA2. Since transaction TRA2 is owned by CIC2, CIC2 looks up its PCT, finds the entry of this TRA2 transac-

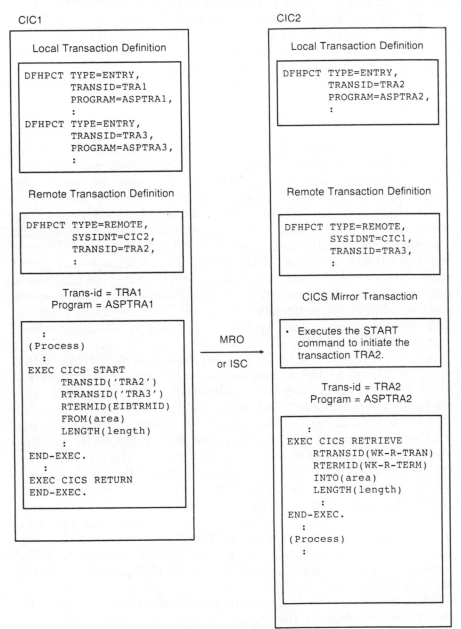

Figure 17-5 Concept of asynchronous processing.

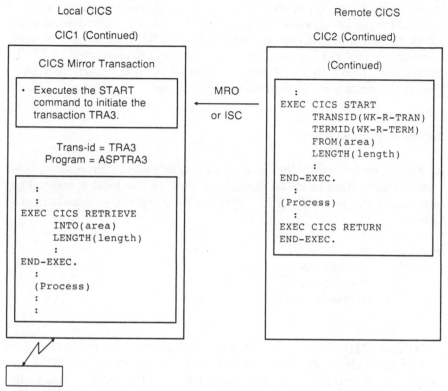

Local CICS

CIC1 (Continued)

CICS Mirror Transaction

• Executes the START
  command to initiate the
  transaction TRA3.

Trans-id = TRA3
Program = ASPTRA3

```
      :
      :
EXEC CICS RETRIEVE
     INTO(area)
     LENGTH(length)
     :
END-EXEC.
      :
   (Process)
      :
      :
```

MRO

or ISC

Remote CICS

CIC2 (Continued)

(Continued)

```
   :
EXEC CICS START
     TRANSID(WK-R-TRAN)
     TERMID(WK-R-TERM)
     FROM(area)
     LENGTH(length)
   :
END-EXEC.
   :
(Process)
   :
EXEC CICS RETURN
END-EXEC.
```

Terminal

Figure 17-5 (continued) Concept of Function Request Shipping.

tion, and initiates the corresponding program ASPTRA2. Program
ASPTRA2 issues the RETRIEVE command to receive the data sent
by program ASPTRA1. WK-R-TRAN has the value 'TRA3' for the
returning transaction. WK-R-TERM has the value 'TRM1' for the returning terminal. Also, other data is received. Program ASPTRA2
then performs processing based on the specifications. At the end,
program ASPTRA2 issues the START command to initiate transaction TRA3 obtained from WK-R-TRAN at terminal TRM1 obtained
from WK-R-TERM. It also passes data from the processing results.

In CIC2, transaction TRA3 is defined as a remote transaction in
the system CIC1. Following the similar process, transaction TRA3 is
initiated in CIC1 at the same terminal TRM1, which previously executed transaction TRA2.

This process is automatically performed by CICS, so that none of
the application programs have to know which system owns the

transaction. However, it should be noted that the execution of each transaction is completely independent. That is, once transaction TRA2 started in CIC2, transaction TRA1 in CIC1 has no control over transaction TRA2. Likewise, once transaction TRA3 started in CIC1, transaction TRA2 in CIC2 has no control over transaction TRA3. This is the nature of Asynchronous Processing.

Remote Resource Definition

As briefly explained in the concept of Asynchronous Processing, the remote transaction must be defined in PCT of the local system. The following summarizes the PCT entry for defining the remote transaction:

```
DFHPCT     TYPE=REMOTE,
           SYSIDNT=name,
           TRANSID=name,
           [RMTNAME=name],
           :
```

TYPE=REMOTE identifies that the table entry is for defining a remote transaction. SYSIDNT defines the system identifier of the remote system which owns the transaction. TRANSID defines the transaction identifier. If this name is different from the transaction id defined in the remote system, the exact remote transaction id must be defined in RMTNAME.

Asynchronous Conversation

In Figure 17-5, when transaction TRA2 returns the data to CIC1, it initiates transaction TRA3, which is associated with the program ASPTRA3. If we use a technique similar to the pseudo-coversational technique 3 (see Section 3.14), transaction TRA2 can initiate the transaction TRA1, which is associated with program ASPTRA1. In this case, transaction TRA1 in local system CIC1 can achieve a conversation with transaction TRA2 in remote system CIC2.

This conversation is not synchronized as the nature of Asynchronous Processing. Let us call this "Asynchronous Conversation" in order to distinguish this from the synchronous conversation, which will be discussed in Section 17.8.

Design Considerations

Asynchronous Processing (Conversation) is one way of achieving distributed processing between two or more systems in the intercommunication environment. It is relatively easy to implement, and it has some advantages over Function Request Shipping. These advantages should be taken into account when an application is designed. Some of these advantages are:

• *More Security:* Since the remote system owns the remote transaction, the remote system can control the security over the remote resources better. If caution is taken to giving the transaction only to authorized systems, security of resources and system will be much better.
• *Better Performance:* Since Asynchronous Processing is primarily executed in both the local system itself and remote system itself, the intercommunication link will be used only for transaction initiation and data transfer. Therefore, it does not increase the data traffic in the link. Consequently, it produces better performance.

The disadvantage of Asynchronous Processing (Conversation) is that the local transaction does not have control over the remote transaction while the remote transaction is being executed because of its asynchronous nature. However, if an application is carefully chosen, Asynchronous Processing (Conversation) may be adequate for distributed processing.

Therefore, if there is no need for synchronous conversation between two transactions, particularly when no updates are involved in the remote system, Asynchronous Processing (Conversation) should be used for distributed processing.

17.7 Transaction Routing

The Transaction Routing facility allows a terminal connected to the local CICS system to run remote transactions which are owned by the remote CICS system in the remote CICS system, regardless of whether the remote CICS system is within the same processor (MRO case) or in the different processor (ISC case).

Both conversational and pseudo-conversational transactions are supported. Even BMS paging operations are supported. Therefore, the user of the terminal can operate a transaction normally without knowing in which remote system this transaction is actually executed.

Relay Program

The relay program is the CICS-supplied program for administrating Transaction Routing, and it resides in the local system. When a transaction is entered in the terminal of the local system, if the transaction is owned by the remote system, this relay program in the local system sends a request to the remote system to execute the transaction in the remote system, receives all responses from the remote transaction, and communicates with the terminal.

In effect, this relay program acts as if it were executing the remote transaction in the local system.

Concept of Transaction Routing

Figure 17-6 illustrates the concept of Transaction Routing, based on the similar multisystem environment used before. Let us assume that the user at terminal TRM1 owned by the local CICS system CIC1 wishes to operate transaction TRA2, which is owned by the remote CICS system CIC2. In this environment, local system CIC1 is the terminal-owning system and remote system CIC2 is the transaction-owning system.

Since local system CIC1 does not own transaction TRA2, TRA2 must be defined as the remote transaction in the Program Control Table (PCT) of CIC1 with remote system identifier CIC2. Since remote system CIC2 does not own terminal TRM1, TRM1 must be defined as the remote terminal in the Terminal Control Table (TCT) of CIC2 with remote system identifier CIC1, noting that CIC1 is a remote system from the CIC2's point of view.

When transaction TRA2 is entered from terminal TRM1 owned by local system CIC1, CIC1 recognizes from PCT that this is a remote transaction owned by remote system CIC2. CIC1 activates the relay program, which requests CIC2 to execute transaction TRA2 owned by CIC2 through the intercommunication link. CIC2 executes transaction TRA2. In CIC2, terminal TRM1 is defined as the remote terminal owned by CIC1. Therefore, CIC2 routes all data, which transaction TRA2 produces for the terminal conversation, to the relay program in CIC1 through the intercommunication link. The relay program in turn communicates with terminal TRM1.

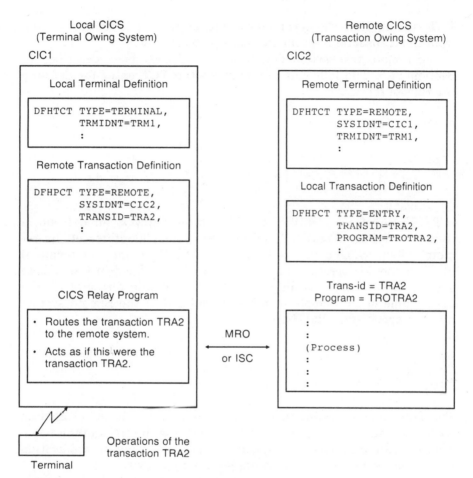

Figure 17-6 Concept of Transaction Routing.

This process is automatically done by CICS. In effect, the terminal user at TRM1 can run transaction TRA2 as if TRA2 were owned by the local system CIC1.

Remote Resource Definition

The local system (terminal-owning system) must define the transaction owned by the remote system as the remote transaction in its PCT. The remote system (transaction-owning system) must define the terminal owned by the local system as the remote terminal in its

TCT, noting that the terminal-owning system is a remote system from the transaction-owning system's point of view.

The remote transaction definition has already been described in Section 17.6. The following summarizes the TCT entry for defining the remote terminal:

```
DFHTCT    TYPE=REMOTE,
          SYSIDNT=name,
          TRMIDNT=name,
          [RMTNAME=name],
          :
```

TYPE=REMOTE identifies that the table entry is for defining a remote terminal. SYSIDNT defines the system identifier of the remote system which owns the termial. TRMIDNT names the terminal id. This should correspond to the terminal id defined in the remote system. If this name is different from the remote terminal id, the exact name of the remote terminal id defined in the remote system must be specified in RMTNAME.

Design Considerations

The Transaction Routing facility offers many advantages for dealing with the multisystem environment involving intercommunication. These advantages should be taken into account when an application is designed. Some of these advantages are as follows:

- *Easy Implementation:* Any transactions which run in the single CICS system environment can be used without modification for Transaction Routing, once the remote transactions and remote terminals are properly defined in PCT and TCT, respectively. Therefore, implementing the Transaction Routing facility is easy.
- *Operational Transparency:* The terminal user of the local system can run the transaction as if the transaction were owned by the local system.
- *Less Communication Traffic:* Since the transaction is executed in the remote system which owns the transaction, and since only data for terminal conversation are sent back to the terminal owned by the local system, the data traffic in the intercommunication link is much less.

• *Better Security:* Since the remote transaction executed in the remote system has control over processing and its resources, system security is much better in both the local system and remote system. The transaction must, however, be given only to the authorized personnel.

Applications

The Transaction Routing facility can be effectively used in an environment such as the distributed corporate system illustrated in Figure 17-2.

For example, let us suppose that the account receivable inquiry transaction is owned by the Accounting System in the Headquarters Office (City 1). This transaction is primarily used by the Headquarters personnel. However, a sales manager in the Central Sales Office (City 2) might wish to inquire about the status of account receivables of his clients.

If the Transaction Routing facility is implemented for this account receivable transaction and a terminal in the Central Sales Office, the sales manager can operate the account receivable transaction through the terminal in the Central Sales Office, while the transaction is executed in the Accounting System in the Headquarters Office. Since the transaction is a read-only transaction (for inquiry), the Headquarters Office would not have to worry about intentional or accidental updates against the database of the Accounting System by the sales manager in the Central Sales Office.

Figure 17-2 applies to ISC. Similar application can be effectively implemented for the case of MRO illustrated in Figure 17-1. Likewise, the Transaction Routing facility can be used in many other applications in the intercommunication environment.

17.8   Distributed Transaction Processing (DTP)

The Distributed Transaction Processing (DTP) facility allows a CICS application program (or transaction) in one CICS system to perform synchronous communication (or conversation) with another program (or transaction) in the other system. In case of DTP, the other system could be another CICS system within the same processor (MRO case), another CICS system in the other processor (CICS LU6.2 ISC case), another non-CICS system or even another intelligent workstation (LU6.2 APPC case).

Since the DTP facility makes possible synchronous conversation between two application programs in different systems, an effective use of the DTP facility can achieve the most flexible and productive distributed processing.

CICS is now installed in many firms or other organizations. It is not unusual that one organization has more than one CICS installed in different places. Further, many midrange systems and personal computers are coming on the market based on the LU6.2 protocol. Eventually, these systems would have to be connected and intercommunicated. Therefore, the DTP facility would play an increasingly important role in the future.

As an introduction to the DTP facility in this section, let us discuss the basic concept of DTP and how it can be used.

Terminology

In the DTP environment, two systems carry out a synchronous conversation with each other. In a sense, each system has the same right to each other. Therefore, the terms "local" and "remote" are a little misleading. For this reason, in the DTP environment, different terms are used, as follows:

Front-End The term "front-end" is used for the initiating side of the conversation. Therefore, front-end transaction means the transaction which initiates a conversation, and the front-end system means the system which owns the front-end transaction.

Back-End Conversely, the term "back-end" is used for the to-be-initiated side of the conversation. Therefore, back-end transaction means the transaction which is initiated as a result of the request by the front-end transaction, and the back-end system is the system which owns the back-end transaction.

Basic Concept of DTP

Figure 17-7 illustrates the basic concept of Distributed Transaction Processing (DTP). Transaction TRA1 in system SYS1 is to initiate a conversation with transaction TRA2 in system SYS2. Therefore,

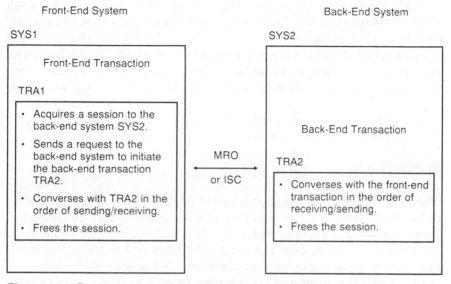

Figure 17-7 Basic concept of Distributed Transaction Processing.

TRA1 is the front-end transaction and SYS1 is the front-end system, while TRA2 is the back-end transaction and SYS2 is the back-end system.

A conversation is performed in the following manner: First, front-end transaction TRA1 acquires a conversation session to back-end system SYS2. The front-end system SYS1 establishes the session with back-end system SYS2 through the intercommunication link (MRO or ISC), and grants the session by passing the session identifier to TRA1. This session identifier is to be used throughout the conversation.

Once a session is established, the front-end transaction is eligible for initiating a back-end transaction, so that TRA1 sends a request to back-end system SYS2 to initiate transaction TRA2. Receiving the request, back-end system SYS2 initiates back-end transaction TRA2.

At this point, TRA1 is in the send state, while TRA2 is in the receive state. TRA1 can proceed to a series of conversations by sending and receiving data to/from TRA2, in that order. Being synchronized with TRA1's activities, TRA2 can proceed to a series of conversations by receiving and sending data from/to TRA1, in that order.

When the conversation is no longer required, either transaction (i.e., front-end or back-end) in the send state frees (i.e., terminates) the conversation session.

This is the basic concept of DTP. A primary difference between DTP and Asynchronous Processing (Conversation) is that the conversation in DTP is synchronous. That is, in DTP both the front-end transaction and the back-end transaction are active in the front-end system and the back-end system, respectively, during the conversation, and the conversation is carried synchronously by both transactions.

We will discuss more details of the synchronous conversation process of DTP in the later sections of this chapter.

Session Identifier

The session identifier (or conversation identifier) is a four-character code identifying the conversation session established between the front-end and back-end transactions. When the front-end transaction acquires the conversation session to the back-end system, the front-end system assigns this session identifier and passes to the front-end transaction. The front-end transaction must use this session identifier in the subsequent commands for the conversation with the back-end transaction.

When the front-end transaction requests the back-end system to initiate the back-end transaction, the front-end transaction passes this session identifier to the back-end system. When the back-end system initiates the back-end transaction, the back-end system passes the session identifier to the back-end transaction. The back-end transaction must use this session identifier in the subsequent commands for the conversation with the front-end transaction.

DTP is characterized by the synchronous conversation. The session identifier is the principal information for synchronizing the conversation by both front-end and back-end transactions. Therefore, both transactions must use the session identifier properly in every command for the conversation during the conversation.

Application Programming Interface (API)

Since we are discussing CICS intercommunication, we assume that front-end system SYS1 in Figure 17-7 is a CICS system. In the DTP environment, however, back-end system SYS2 could be another CICS (MRO case or CICS LU6.2 ISC case) or non-CICS system (LU6.2 APPC case).

In the front-end system, all front-end transactions can achieve DTP by issuing CICS commands for DTP based on the MRO protocol or LU6.2 protocol depending on the intercommunication link to the back-end system. If the LU6.2 protocol is used, it is transparent to the front-end transaction whether the back-end system is based on CICS LU6.2 ISC or LU6.2 APPC. This means that the same transaction (program) for DTP against one CICS system based on CICS LU6.2 ISC can be used for another PS/2 personal computer (for example) based on LU6.2 APPC.

If the back-end system is another CICS system, the back-end transaction can achieve DTP using CICS commands for DTP based on the MRO protocol or CICS LU6.2 ISC protocol depending on the intercommunication link to the front-end system.

If the back-end system is a non-CICS system based on the LU6.2 APPC protocol (e.g., PS/2 personal computer with the OS/2 Extended Edition operating system), obviously the back-end transaction cannot use the CICS commands. However, the back-end system has the Application Programming Interface (API), so that the back-end transaction can issue its own commands (called "verbs"), which are equivalent to CICS commands for DTP.

Therefore, once you learn CICS application programming for DTP using CICS commands, you can apply the same concept to any other non-CICS systems based on the LU6.2 APPC protocol.

17.9   CICS Commands and EIB for DTP

Before discussing actual CICS application programming for Distributed Transaction Processing (DTP), let us discuss first the basic CICS commands and EIB information relevant to DTP.

ALLOCATE Command

Function   The ALLOCATE command is used by the front-end transaction (or program) to acquire an intercommunication session to the back-end system, which could be based on the MRO or LU6.2 protocol. At the normal completion of this command, a conversation session will be allocated. The front-end system will make the session (or conversation) identifier (4-character code) available to the front-end transaction in the EIBRSRCE field. This value must be immediately saved for later use, because all subsequent conversations will be done based on this session (or conversation) identifier.

Format   The format of the ALLOCATE command is as follows:

```
EXEC CICS ALLOCATE
     SYSID(name)
     [NOQUEUE]
END-EXEC.
```

SYSID defines the system identifier of the back-end system. If NOQUEUE is specified, and if the session is not available, the control will be returned to the next statement after the ALLOCATE command. If NOQUEUE is not specified, and if the session is not available, the session will be queued until the session becomes available.

Common Exceptional Conditions The following are some of the exceptional conditions common to the ALLOCATE command:

SYSIDERR: The system identifier specified in SYSID cannot be recognized by CICS, or it is out of service. The default action: the task will be abnormally terminated.

SYSBUSY: All sessions assigned to the specified system are in use. The default action depends on whether the NOQUEUE option is specified. See the description of the command format.

SEND Command

Function In DTP, the SEND command is used to send data to the other partner transaction during the conversation. The session (or conversation) identifier must be specified to identify the conversation session. The SEND command can be issued only when the transaction is in the send state. Since the basic use of this command has been described in Section 7.4, this section describes only topics related to DTP.

Format The format of the SEND command is as follows:

```
EXEC CICS SEND
     SESSION(name)  |  CONVID(name)
     FROM(data-area)
     LENGTH(data-value)
     [INVITE | LAST]
     [WAIT]
END-EXEC.
```

Either SESSION (for MRO) or CONVID (for LU6.2) must be specified to define the session (or conversation) identifier. If INVITE is not specified, the send state remains in effect, even after the completion of the SEND command. If INVITE is specified, the transaction's communication state will be switched from the send state to the receive state after the completion of the SEND command, allowing the other partner transaction to send data to this transaction. LAST indicates that this is the last data transmission from this transaction. If WAIT is specified, the data will be sent immediately. For the parameters FROM and LENGTH, see Section 7.4.

RECEIVE Command

Function In DTP, the RECEIVE command is used to receive data from the other partner transaction during the conversation. The session (or conversation) identifier must be specified to identify the conversation session. The RECEIVE command can be issued only when the transaction is in the receive state. The receive state remains the same even after the completion of this command. Since the basic use of this command has been described in Section 7.2, this section describes only topics related to DTP.

Format The format of the RECEIVE command is as follows:

```
EXEC CICS RECEIVE
     SESSION(name)     |   CONVID(name)
     INTO(data-area)   |   SET(ptr-ref)
     LENGTH(data-value)
END-EXEC.
```

Either SESSION (for MRO) or CONVID (for LU6.2) must be specified to define the session (or conversation) identifier. For other parameters, see Section 7.2.

CONVERSE Command

Function In DTP, the CONVERSE command performs the combined functions of the SEND command with the INVITE option and the RECEIVE command. That is, the CONVERSE command sends data to the other partner transaction during the conversation, automatically switches the communication state from the send state to the receive state, inviting the other partner transaction to send the data, and then receives data from the other partner transaction. The CONVERSE command can be issued only when the transaction is in the send state.

Format The format of the CONVERSE command is as follows:

```
EXEC CICS CONVERSE
     SESSION(name)    |    CONVID(name)
     FROM(data-area)
     FROMLENGTH(data-value)
     INTO(data-area)  |    SET(ptr-ref)
     TOLENGTH(data-value)
END-EXEC.
```

Either SESSION (for MRO) or CONVID (for LU6.2) must be specified to define the session (or conversation) identifier. Other parameters are the same as those in the SEND command and RECEIVE command.

FREE Command

Function The FREE command is used to free (i.e., terminate) the conversation session. The session (or conversation) identifier must be specified to identify the conversation session to be freed. The FREE command can be specified in the front-end transaction or the back-end transaction, as long as the transaction is in the send state. If the transaction is in the receive state, the transaction could issue the FREE command only if the EIBFREE field is on.

Format The format of the FREE command is as follows:

```
EXEC CICS FREE
     SESSION(name)    |    CONVID(name)
END-EXEC.
```

Either SESSION (for MRO) or CONVID (for LU6.2) must be specified to define the session (or conversation) identifier.

CONNECT PROCESS Command

Function The CONNECT PROCESS command is used only for the LU6.2 link, and it is not used for the MRO link. This command is used by the front-end transaction to request the back-end system to initiate a "process" in the back-end system. After the normal completion of the command, the front-end transaction will be in the send state, and it can proceed to the conversation with the process in the back-end system. For the concept of "process," see Section 17.11.

Format The format of the CONNECT PROCESS command is as follows:

```
EXEC CICS CONNECT PROCESS
     CONVID(name)
     PROCNAME(name)
     PROCLENGTH(data-value)
     SYNCLEVEL(data-value)
END-EXEC.
```

CONVID must be specified to define the conversation identifier. PROCNAME defines the name of "process" in the back-end system. PROCLENGTH defines the length (as the halfword binary value) of the process name defined in PROCNAME. SYNCLEVEL is the level of synchronization for resource recovery. The available levels are: 0 (none), 1 (commit only), and 2 (all). For the details of the synchronization level, see Section 17.11.

Other Commands

There are a number of other CICS commands specifically related to DTP. These commands are the advanced commands for syncpoint handling or abnormal status handling. For the sake of simplicity, these commands are not described here. If these commands are required, see the proper IBM manuals.

EIB Information for DTP

During the DTP conversation between the front-end and back-end transactions, both the front-end CICS system and back-end CICS system (if CICS is used) provide conversation control information in the EXEC Interface Block (EIB) of the front-end and back-end transactions, respectively. Based on the EIB information, each transaction can control the flow of conversation smoothly. The following is some of this EIB information for DTP.

EIBRSRCE   Eight-character field. For DTP conversation, this field is used by the front-end transaction to identify the session (or conversation) identifier (4 characters). At the completion of the ALLOCATE command by the front-end transaction, this field contains the session identifier. The front-end transaction must save this value immediately and use it in the SESSION (in case of MRO) or CONVID (in case of LU6.2) parameter of the subsequent commands for the conversation during the conversation with the back-end transaction.

EIBTRMID   Four-character field. For DTP conversation, this field is used by the back-end transaction to identify the session (or conversation) identifier (4 characters). The back-end transaction must save this value at the beginning of the processing and use it in the SESSION (in case of MRO) or CONVID (in case of LU6.2) parameter of the subsequent commands for the conversation during the conversation with the front-end transaction.

EIBFREE   One-character field. This represents the status of the conversation session. If this is off (X'00'), the session is still on by the partner transaction. If this is on (X'FF'), the session has been freed (i.e., terminated) by the partner transaction, so that this transaction must free the session.

EIBRECV   One-character field. This field represents the communication state. If this is off (X'00'), this transaction is in the send state, so that this transaction can send data to the partner transaction. If this is on (X'FF'), this transaction is in the receive state, so that this transaction can receive data from the partner transaction.

Other EIB Information   There is other EIB information relevant to DTP — related to syncpoint handling or abnormal status handling. For the sake of simplicity, these are not described here. If this EIB information is required, the proper IBM manuals should be referred to.

17.10   DTP in MRO Environment

In the previous section, we discussed the CICS commands and EIB information relevant to Distributed Transaction Processing (DTP). Now, let us discuss how the CICS application programs for DTP look. First, in this section, let us discuss DTP in the MRO environment; that is, DTP between two CICS systems in the same processor.

Front-End System (CIC1)   Back-End System (CIC2)

Front-End Transaction (TRA1)   Back-End Transaction (TRA2)

```
                          State                                            State
Commands                  C  A              Commands                       C  A

ALLOCATE                  SN S
SYSID('CIC2')

(Save EIBRSRCE for                          (Save EIBTRMID for
 session-id.)                                session-id.)
                                  Data
CONVERSE                  S       ----->    RECEIVE                         R  S
SESSION(---)                                SESSION(---)
'TRA2,--------'
                          R       Data      CONVERSE                        S
                                  <-----     SESSION(---)
CONVERSE                  S       Data
SESSION(---)                      ----->                                       R
                          R       Data      CONVERSE                        S
:                                 <-----     SESSION(---)
:
:                                           :
FREE                      S       ----->    :                                  R
SESSION(---)                 SN             (EIBFREE on)

                                            FREE                            R
                                            SESSION(---)                       SN
```

Abbreviations:

C: Current communication state
A: Communication state after the command execution
SN: Session not allocated
S: Send state
R: Receive state

Figure 17-8 Command sequence of DTP for MRO.

In this case, since no sophisticated SNA network is involved, the DTP conversation is relatively simple.

Command Sequence

Figure 17-8 illustrates the command sequence of two CICS transactions conversing each other for DTP in the MRO environment. In this example, the front-end CICS system is CIC1 and the back-end CICS system is CIC2. The front-end transaction is TRA1 and the back-end transaction is TRA2.

Since only the front-end transaction can initiate a conversation session, TRA1 issues the ALLOCATE command with SYSID('CIC2') to acquire a conversation session to back-end system CIC2. At the completion of the ALLOCATE command, the session identifier is available in EIBRSRCE, so that TRA1 saves the value of EIBRSRCE. Front-end transaction TRA1 must use this saved value (i.e., session identifier) in the SESSION parameter of all subsequent commands for conversing with back-end transaction TRA2.

Then, front-end transaction TRA1 initiates back-end transaction TRA2 in the front-end system. This is achieved by sending transaction id TRA2 as the first part of the output data stream in the FROM parameter of the SEND command or CONVERSE command. Since the CONVERSE command automatically switches the communication state from the send state to the receive state, it is more convenient for the continuous conversation. Thus, TRA1 issues the CONVERSE command to send transaction id TRA2 and accompanying data. At this point, TRA1 turns to the receive state, inviting the back-end transaction to send data.

Back-end system CIC2 detects the incoming data, and initiates back-end transaction TRA2 using the first 4 characters of the incoming data. When back-end transaction TRA2 is initiated, it is in the receive state. TRA2 saves the value of EIBTRMID which contains the session identifier, which must be used in the SESSION parameter of the subsequent commands for the conversation. Then, TRA2 issues the RECEIVE command and receive the data from TRA1. After the completion of the RECEIVE command, TRA2 turns to the send state because TRA1 issued the CONVERSE command. Now, TRA2 can send data to TRA1, so that TRA2 issues the CONVERSE command to send data to TRA1, then turns into the receive state, inviting TRA1 to send data.

TRA1 receives data as a part of the CONVERSE function. At the completion of the CONVERSE command, TRA1 turns into the send state because TRA2 issued the CONVERSE command. Therefore, TRA1 now can send data to TRA2, so that TRA1 issues another CONVERSE command. Here, another iteration of conversation starts in TRA1.

TRA2 then receives data from TRA1 as a part of the CONVERSE function. At the completion of the CONVERSE command, TRA2 turns into the send state because TRA1 issued the CONVERSE command. Therefore, TRA2 now can send data to TRA1, so that TRA2 issues another CONVERSE command. Here, another iteration of conversation starts in TRA2.

This conversation will be repeated until all data have been exchanged. When the conversation is no longer required, the transaction in the send state (TRA1 in this case) can issue the FREE command to free the conversation, after which TRA1 can no longer converse with TRA2.

Meantime, TRA2 checks EIBFREE, which tells whether the session has been freed by the partner transaction. In this case, the session has been freed by TRA1 (i.e., EIBFREE is on), so that TRA2 issues the FREE command. This completes the conversation session in the TRA2 side.

This is a typical command sequence to achieve a DTP conversation session in the MRO environment. This example is a simple one. Additionally, as the advanced application, you could implement a syncpoint handling for resource recovery and abnormal condition handling using the advanced commands.

Conversation Control

Figure 17-8 illustrates a basic flow of conversation. However, actually both the front-end and back-end transactions can control the flow of conversation more flexibly using the EIB information discussed in the previous section.

Current State	Commands Allowed	EIB after Command Exec	New State	Next Commands Allowed
Send	SEND	-	Send	Any commands allowed for the send state
	SEND/ INVITE	-	Receive	RECEIVE
	CONVERSE	EIBFREE (on)	-	FREE
		EIBRECV (on)	Receive	RECEIVE
		EIBRECV (off)	Send	Any commands allowed for the send state
	FREE	-	Session not allocated	No conversation allowed
Receive	RECEIVE	EIBFREE (on)	-	FREE
		EIBRECV (on)	Recieve	RECEIVE
		EIBRECV (off)	Send	Any commands allowed for the send state

Figure 17-9 Summary of conversation control.

In order to control the flow of the conversation, both front-end and back-end transactions must follow a rule based on their current communication state. This rule is summarized in Figure 17-9.

When a transaction is in the send state, it is allowed to issue the SEND, SEND/INVITE, CONVERSE or FREE command. If the transaction issues the SEND command, the send state will remain, and the transaction can issue any commands allowed for the send state. If the transaction issues the SEND command with the INVITE option, the state will be switched to the receive state inviting the partner transaction to send data, so that this transaction can issue the RECEIVE command. If the transaction issues the FREE command, the state will be switched to the session-not-allocated state, so that the conversation will no longer be allowed.

When the transaction is in the send state, and if it issues the CONVERSE command, the next action will depend on the value of the EIB information. At the completion of the CONVERSE command, if EIBFREE is on (X'FF'), this means that the partner transaction freed the conversation session, so that this transaction must issue the FREE command to free the session. If EIBRECV is on (X'FF'), this means that the state is now switched to the receive state, so that the transaction must issue the RECEIVE command. If EIBRECV is off (X'00'), this means that the transaction is still in the send state, so that it can issue any commands allowed for the send state.

When the transaction is in the receive state, it is allowed to issue the RECEIVE command. The next action will depend on the EIB information. If EIBFREE is on (X'FF'), this means that the partner transaction freed the conversation session, so that this transaction must issue the FREE command to free the session. If EIBRECV is on (X'FF'), this means that the transaction is still in the receive state, so that it must issue the RECEIVE command again. If EIBRECV is off (X'00'), this means that the state is now switched to the send state, so that the transaction can issue any commands allowed for the send state.

This rule is necessary because a transaction cannot predict the next command which the partner transaction might issue. The partner transaction might issue a command which does not change the communication state, it might issue a command which switches the communication state from send to receive or vice versa, or it might issue the FREE command. Based on this rule, each transaction can control the flow of conversation flexibility to meet the unpredictable change of the communication state.

17.11   DTP in ISC Environment

In the previous section, we discussed Distributed Transaction Processing (DTP) in the MRO environment. Now, let us discuss DTP in the ISC environment.

In the ISC environment, the front-end system resides in a processor while the back-end system resides independently in another processor. Since two independent processors are involved, both processors must be linked through a sophisticated communication network based on the Systems Network Architecture (SNA).

Two Types of DTP in ISC Environment

Depending on the type of the system in the front-end and back-end, DTP in the ISC environment can be achieved in the following two ways:

DTP for CICS LU6.2 ISC   A CICS system in a processor can achieve DTP with another CICS system in another processor based on the LU6.2 protocol. Let us call this "DTP for CICS LU6.2 ISC."

LU6.2 APPC   A CICS system in a processor can achieve DTP with another non-CICS system in another processor based on the LU6.2 protocol. Another non-CICS system is usually a program (called "Transaction Program") in a personal computer, but it could be any other program in any other system which conforms to the LU6.2 protocol. The general term used for this type of DTP is LU6.2 Advanced Program-to-Program Communications (APPC).

If the front-end system is a CICS system, since both DTP for CICS LU6.2 ISC and LU6.2 APPC use the same LU6.2 protocol, DTP programming in the front-end system is the same, regardless of the type of back-end system. Further, as far as application programming is concerned, DTP programming for CICS LU6.2 ISC is very similar to that for MRO, with only few exceptions.

Unique Concepts for ISC

DTP in the ISC LU6.2 environment has a few unique concepts which are different from MRO. If these unique concepts are understood clearly, then it will be much easier to understand DTP programming for ISC LU6.2 in conjunction with DTP Programming for MRO. The following are some of these unique concepts:

Process   "Process" is a general term for an entity which performs processing in the back-end system. If the back-end system is based on CICS LU6.2 ISC, "process" simply means a CICS transaction. If the back-end system is based on LU6.2 APPC, "process" usually means a program (called "transaction program") or any other entity depending on the type of back-end system. Therefore, unlike DTP in the MRO environment, the front-end transaction cannot simply send a transaction id to the back-end system to initiate the "process." The front-end transaction must issue a special command (CONNECT PROCESS) to request the back-end system to initiate the "process" in the back-end system.

Conversation Identifier   The conversation identifier is the identifier of the conversation session between the front-end and back-end systems. It is the same as the session identifier in the MRO environment, and only the naming convention is different. Therefore, it is the same as the MRO case in how the conversation identifier is created, how it can be obtained by the front-end transaction and the back-end transaction (or process). This conversation identifier must be used in the CONVID parameter (equivalent to the SESSION parameter for the MRO case) in the commands for the conversation.

Synchronization Levels   In order to protect the resources used by both front-end transaction and back-end transaction (or process), LU6.2 offers three levels of resource synchronization as follows:

Level 0:   None
Level 1:   Commit only
Level 2:   All

Level 0 (none) means that no synchronization can take place. Level 1 (commit only) means that the conversation partners handle all synchronization by themselves. Level 2 (all) means that complete synchronization will take place through normal CICS syncpoint handling. This synchronization level must be specified in the CONNECT PROCESS command.

If level 1 or 2 is specified, the program logic becomes complex but resources could be recovered. If level 0 is specified, the program logic may be simple, but resources could not be recovered. For the sake of simplicity, the following discussion assumes level 0 (none).

Front-End System (CIC1)   Back-End System (CIC2)

Front-End Transaction (TRA1)   Back-End Transaction (TRA2)

```
                        State                                    State
Commands                C  A          Commands                   C  A

ALLOCATE                SN SA
 SYSID('CIC2')

(Save EIBRSRCE for
 conv-id.)

CONECT PROCESS          SA S           (Save EIBTRMID for
 CONVID(---)                            conv-id.)
 PROCNAME('TRA2')
 PROCLENGTH(4)
 SYNCLEVEL(0)
                              Data
CONVERSE                S      ──────▶ RECEIVE                    R   S
 CONVID(---)                            CONVID(---)
                              Data
                        R     ◀────── CONVERSE                    S
                                        CONVID(---)
                              Data
CONVERSE                S      ──────▶                                R
 CONVID(---)                   Data
                        R     ◀────── CONVERSE                    S
                                        CONVID(---)
  :                                      :
  :                                      :
  :                                      :

FREE                    S     ──────▶
 CONVID(---)            SN              (EIBFREE on)                  R

                                       FREE                      R
                                        CONVID(---)                  SN
```

Mainframe System   Mainframe System

Abbreviations:

C: Current communication state
A: Communication state after the command execution
SN: Session not allocated
S: Send state
R: Receive state

Figure 17-10 Command sequence of DTP for CICS LU6.2 ISC.

17.12   DTP for CICS LU6.2 ISC

Let us first discuss the case of DTP for CICS LU6.2 ISC. In this case, both front-end and back-end systems are CICS, but they reside independently in the different processors. Since both front-end and back-end systems are CICS, the DTP conversation in this mode is relatively simple and very similar to that for MRO.

Command Sequence

Figure 17-10 illustrates the command sequence of a front-end transaction and a back-end transaction (or process), which are conversing with each other for DTP in the CICS LU6.2 ISC environment. It is very similar to the case of DTP in the MRO environment (Figure 17-8), with a few exceptions because of the unique concepts of ISC described before.

In this example, the front-end system (CICS) is CIC1, and the back-end system (CICS) is CIC2. The front-end transaction is TRA1, and the back-end transaction (or process) is TRA2.

The command sequence is very similar to that of DTP in the MRO environment, with the following exceptions:

1.   The conversation identifier must be specified in the CONVID (instead of SESSION) parameter of all commands involved in conversation during the conversation.
2.   After the ALLOCATE command, the front-end transaction must issue the CONNECT PROCESS command for requesting the back-end system to initiate the process. Therefore, in this case, transaction id (or process name) TRA2 and its length (4) are specified in the PROCNAME and PROCLENGTH parameters, respectively. Also, the synchronization level must be specified (level 0, in this case).
3.   After the CONNECT PROCESS command, the front-end transaction can send data to the back-end transaction. The data stream in the first SEND command or CONVERSE command does not require to include the transaction id of the back-end transaction.

The rest of the command sequence is identical to the case of MRO. All discussions of the conversation control in the MRO case are also applicable here.

As can be seen, the command sequence of DTP for CICS LU6.2 ISC is not much different from MRO. However, if you wish, you could additionally implement syncpoint handling and abnormal status handling using the advanced commands for DTP. In this case, the resource updates could be synchronized between the front-end and back-end transactions. If an abnormal situation arises, the resources could be backed out. This will increase reliability of DTP in both the front-end and back-end systems.

17.13 LU6.2 APPC

Now, let us extend the discussion into LU6.2 APPC. In this environment, both the front-end and back-end systems reside independently in the different processors, and they could be CICS or non-CICS. The possible combination of the systems could be as follows:

Case	Front-End System	Back-End System
1	CICS	CICS
2	CICS	Non-CICS
3	Non-CICS	CICS
4	Non-CICS	Non-CICS

Case 1 (CICS to CICS) is the case of CICS LU6.2 ISC, which we discussed in the previous section. Since we are discussing CICS intercommunication, let us exclude Case 4 (non-CICS to non-CICS). This leaves us Case 2 (CICS to non-CICS) and Case 3 (non-CICS to CICS). Actually, both Cases 2 and 3 are similar to each other because the common Application Programming Interface (API) is established between CICS and non-CICS. Therefore, for the sake of simplicity, let us take Case 2 (CICS to non-CICS) for explaining the concept of LU6.2 APPC.

Non-CICS System

In the LU6.2 APPC environment, the non-CICS system is usually a program (called "transaction program") in a personal computer or any other processor which conforms to the LU6.2 protocol. In this discussion, let us assume that the non-CICS system is a transaction program in an IBM PS/2 personal computer with the OS/2 Extended Edition (E.E.) operating system.

APPC Verbs

OS/2 E.E. has the common Application Programming Interface (API) for LU6.2 APPC. That is, a set of common verbs are created in OS/2

E.E. for LU6.2 APPC, and they can be used by such programming languages as Macro Assembler/2, C/2, Pascal/2, and COBOL/2. Therefore, a transaction program written by one of these languages under OS/2 E.E. can achieve APPC using these verbs.

The APPC verbs under OS/2 are created based on the same API for CICS intercommunication. This means that there is almost a one-to-one relationship between OS/2 LU6.2 APPC verbs and CICS commands with few exceptions.

Figure 17-11 summarizes the commonly used OS/2 LU6.2 APPC verbs, and they correspond to the equivalent CICS commands or sets of equivalent CICS commands. As can be seen, there is a close conceptual similarity between OS/2 LU6.2 APPC verbs and CICS commands.

In essence, therefore, LU6.2 APPC can be carried out by replacing CICS commands for DTP for CICS LU6.2 ISC with the corresponding APPC verbs.

Concept of LU6.2 APPC Conversation

Now, let us discuss more concretely how LU6.2 APPC conversation can be achieved. For this discussion, let the front-end system be a CICS system in a processor, and let the back-end system be a transaction program in a PS/2 personal computer with OS/2 E.E.

OS/2 LU6.2 APPC Verb	Function	Equivalent CICS Command (EXEC CICS)
TP_STARTED	To initiate a transaction program as a front-end program.	(n/a)
MC_ALLOCATE	To allocate a mapped conversation session.	ALLOCATE CONNECT PROCESS
RECEIVE_ALLOCATE	To initiate a transaction program as a back-end program.	(n/a)
MC_PREPARE_TO_RECEIVE	To send data and change the mapped conversation from send to receive state.	SEND/INVITE/WAIT
MC_RECEIVE_AND_WAIT	To wait and receive data.	RECEIVE
MC_PREPARE_TO_RECEIVE MC_RECEIVE_AND_WAIT	(Combination of two verbs)	CONVERSE
MC_DEALLOCATE	To deallocate a mapped conversation session.	SEND/LAST SYNCPOINT FREE
TP_ENDED	To end the transaction program.	(n/a)

Figure 17-11 Example of OS/2 LU6.2 APPC verbs.

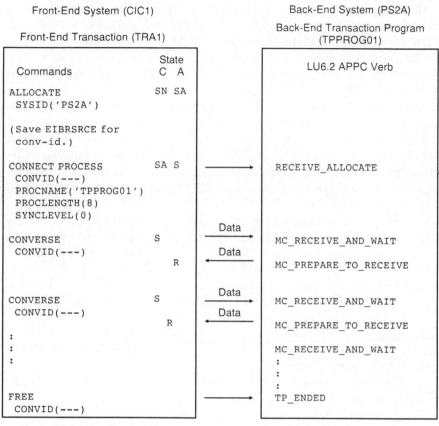

Figure 17-12 illustrates the CICS command sequence in the front-end system (CICS) and the APPC verb sequence in the back-end system (non-CICS) based on the same DTP conversation for CICS LU6.2 ISC in Figure 17-10. Therefore, in the front-end system, the command sequence is exactly the same as Figure 17-10 except the SYSID name, process name and process length. However, in the back-end system, since it is the non-CICS system, it uses a set of OS/2 LU6.2 APPC verbs. If you look closely at Figure 17-12 and compare it with Figure 17-10 and Figure 17-11, you will realize that the CICS commands in the back-end system in Figure 17-10 have been replaced by the corresponding OS/2 LU6.2 APPC verbs summarized in Figure 17-11.

The front-end transaction (CICS transaction TRA1) issues the AL-LOCATE command with SYSID ('PS2A'), which is the system id of Back-end system (PS/2 personal computer), to acquire a conversation session. It then issues the CONNECT PROCESS command to initiate a process (an OS/2 transaction program TPPROG01) in the back-end system, with the process name TPPROG01 and the length 8 in the PROCNAME and PROCLENGTH parameters, respectively. Back-end transaction program TPPROG01 issues the RECEIVE_AL-LOCATE verb to initiate itself as a back-end program. The front-end transaction issues the CONVERSE command (which is a combination of the SEND/INVITE/WAIT command and RECEIVE command) to send data to the back-end program and change the communication state to the receive state. The back-end program issues the MC_RE-CEIVE_AND_WAIT verb to receive the data from the front-end transaction, then issues the MC_PREPARE_TO_RECEIVE verb to send data to the front-end transaction and change the communication state to the receive state.

The front-end transaction receives data, and issues another CON-VERSE command to send and receive data to/from the back-end program. Here, another iteration of conversation starts in the front-end transaction. The back-end program issues a pair of MC_RE-CEIVE_AND_WAIT and MC_PREPARE_TO_RECEIVE verbs in that order to receive and send data from/to the front-end transaction. Here, another iteration of conversation starts in the back-end program.

This conversation will be repeated until all data have been exchanged. When the conversation is no longer required, the front-end transaction issues the FREE commands to free the conversation session. The back-end program also issues the TP_ENDED verb to end the back-end processing.

This is only one of the typical LU6.2 APPC conversations between a CICS transaction and an OS/2 transaction program. If more flexible control is required for conversation, a similar concept of conversation control of DTP for CICS LU6.2 ISC can also be applied here.

Figure 17-12 is a case of the front-end system being CICS and the back-end system being non-CICS (an OS/2 transaction program). Similarly, LU6.2 APPC can be achieved for the case of front-end system being non-CICS (an OS/2 transaction program) and the back-end system being CICS. This can be done by replacing CICS commands of front-end transaction in Figure 17-10 with the corresponding LU6.2 APPC verbs in Figure 17-11.

Advantage and Disadvantage

The primary advantage of LU6.2 APPC is that distributed processing is possible between two systems even without CICS. Further, if one of two systems is CICS, it can achieve distributed processing with other non-CICS systems relatively easily based on LU6.2 APPC, because the concept of LU6.2 APPC is very similar to that of distributed processing between CICS and CICS (MRO or DTP for CICS LU6.2 ISC). This is the significant advantage of LU6.2 APPC when one wishes to perform distributed processing among CICS and personal computers (PCs).

However, a disadvantage of LU6.2 APPC is that APPC programming tends to be complex and cumbersome. For example, OS/2 E.E. Version 1.1 allows only Macro Assembler/2, C/2, and Pascal/2 to use APPC verbs. Application development in these languages is very time-consuming. The new Version 1.2 of OS/2 E.E. allows COBOL/2 to use APPC verbs. Even so, APPC programming is difficult, especially if one wishes to control conversation more flexibly, taking into account abnormal conditions and resource recovery. Therefore, LU6.2 APPC has relatively low productivity in terms of application development. Some better way should be sought in order to improve application development productivity for distributed processing.

17.14   Intercommunication with CICS OS/2

In the previous section, we discussed LU6.2 APPC. It is technically possible to achieve distributed processing between CICS and non-CICS based on LU6.2 APPC. This is convenient because there are many applications for distributed processing between CICS in the mainframe system (host) and personal computers (PCs). However, since LU6.2 APPC has rather low productivity in terms of applications development, a better approach should be sought. CICS intercommunication with CICS OS/2 in PCs provides an excellent solution to this productivity problem.

CICS OS/2 is a new member of the CICS family, and it is particularly designed for the PS/2 personal computer with the OS/2 E.E.

operating system. It is compatible with other CICS members, such as CICS/MVS, CICS/OS/VS, CICS/DOS/VS and CICS/VM. Therefore, if a PS/2 personal computer is equipped with OS/2 E.E. and CICS OS/2, a CICS system in a mainframe system (host) can communicate freely with PS/2 based on CICS intercommunication facilities, instead of complex LU6.2 APPC.

CICS OS/2 System Configuration

In order to maximize the technological advantages, it is recommended that CICS OS/2 be used under the following system configuration:

Hardware:	PS/2
System Software:	OS/2 E.E.
Compiler:	COBOL/2
Communication Protocol:	LU6.2

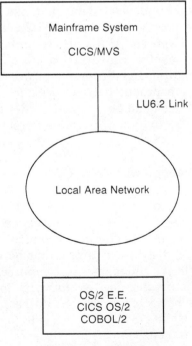

PS/2 Personal Computer

Figure 17-13 Typical CICS OS/2 system configuration.

Other hardware (PC-AT or XT), system software (PC-DOS), or communication protocol (LU2) may be used with CICS OS/2, in which case, however, the functionality of CICS OS/2 will be restricted.

Figure 17-13 illustrates a typical CICS OS/2 system configuration as an example. In this example, each PS/2 personal computer has OS/2 E.E., CICS OS/2, and COBOL/2. Each PS/2 is linked together through a Local Area Network (LAN), which is in turn linked to the mainframe system (host) based on the LU6.2 communication protocol. Each PS/2 in the LAN can communicate with CICS in the mainframe system (host CICS) using CICS intercommunication facilities.

Resource Definition

CICS OS/2 works with the following resources which must be defined in the corresponding CICS control tables:

Resource	CICS Control Table
Program (COBOL)	PPT
Transaction	PCT
File (VSAM)	FCT
Terminal	TCT
Transient Data Queue (TDQ)	DCT
Temporary Storage Queue (TSQ)	TST
User id	SNT
System entry	SIT
Workstation set-up characteristics	WSU

As can be seen, the resources of CICS OS/2 are basically the same as those of CICS in the mainframe system (e.g., CICS/MVS). It should be noted that CICS OS/2 can deal with VSAM files (KSDS, ESDS, RRDS, and Alternate key), TSQ as well as TDQ in the PS/2 personal computer, which are very convenient and useful in terms of compatibility with the host CICS.

Application Programming

All application programs are written in COBOL/2 with CICS commands. A minimum set of BMS functions are supported so that all screen handling is managed by BMS, except that BMS paging is not supported at the time of this book's publication. VSAM files are supported so that application programs can utilize VSAM/KSDS, ESDS, RRDS, as well as Alternate Index.

Command Format Most CICS commands of CICS/MVS are supported by CICS OS/2 with some exceptions. The format of CICS OS/2 commands is virtually identical to that of CICS/MVS, as each command starts with EXEC CICS and ends with END-EXEC. If there are some differences, they are primarily caused by the differences in the hardware and system software.

Taking the READ command as an example, let us compare the command format of CICS OS/2 with that of CICS/MVS. As can be seen below, both commands in this example are indeed identical.

CICS OS/2   **CICS/MVS**

```
EXEC CICS READ                   EXEC CICS READ
     DATASET(name) | FILE(name)       DATASET(name) | FILE(name)
     INTO(data-area) |                INTO(data-area) |
        SET(ptr-ref)                     SET(ptr-ref)
     [LENGTH(data-area)]              [LENGTH(data-area)]
     RIDFLD(data-area)                RIDFLD(data-area)
     [KEYLENGTH(data-value)           [KEYLENGTH(data-value)
        [GENERIC]]                       [GENERIC]]
     [GTEQ | EQUAL]                   [GTEQ | EQUAL]
     [RBA | RRN]                      [RBA | RRN]
     [UPDATE]                         [UPDATE]
END-EXEC.                        END-EXEC.
```

Commands Not Supported by CICS OS/2 Certain CICS/MVS commands are not supported by CICS OS/2. If these are coded in an application program, the translator will either ignore or generate error messages. The following are some notable CICS commands not supported by CICS OS/2:

ALLOCATE	POST
CONNECT PROCESS	PURGE MESSAGE
DELAY	RELEASE
DEQ	ROUTE
ENQ	SEND PAGE
FORMATTIME	SEND TEXT
FREE	SUSPEND
JOURNAL	TRACE
LOAD	

This is only a partial list. For the full list of CICS commands not supported by CICS OS/2, see the proper IBM CICS OS/2 manual.

In short, these are advanced CICS commands, so that even without these unsupported commands, CICS OS/2 application programs can perform basic CICS functions without any difficulties.

Exceptional Conditions As is the case for CICS/MVS, each CICS OS/2 command has the associated exceptional conditions, which can be detected by the HANDLE CONDITION command or the RESP option.

SQL Statements The Database Manager of the new OS/2 E.E. Ver. 1.2 has the precompiler support for SQL statements embedded in COBOL/2 programs. This means that if CICS OS/2 and COBOL/2 are used under OS/2 E.E. Ver. 1.2, CICS OS/2 application programs written in COBOL/2 can issue SQL statements freely in order to access a relational database under the OS/2 Database Manager.

The concept of accessing the relational database by a COBOL/2 program with SQL statements under CICS OS/2 and OS/2 E.E. Ver. 1.2 is very similar to the concept of accessing the DB/2 database by a COBOL program with SQL statements in the host CICS system, which has been discussed in Section 6.8.

Therefore, it is worth noting that, in terms of relational database access, the CICS OS/2 application programs written in COBOL/2 with SQL statements under OS/2 E.E. Ver. 1.2 are as powerful as the host CICS application programs written in COBOL with SQL statement in the mainframe system.

Procedures CICS OS/2 application programs are developed based on similar procedures for CICS/MVS. But, in the case of CICS OS/2, a batch command is prepared for each of these procedures. The following are the procedures and their associated batch commands (expressed in the parentheses):

1. Translating BMS maps (CICSMAP)
2. Translating programs (CICSTRAN)
3. Compiling programs   (CICSCOMP)
4. Linkediting programs (CICSLINK)

Program Portability

In essence, CICS OS/2 works just the same as the host CICS (e.g., CICS/MVS) in terms of application programming. The procedures for application development are also the same as the host CICS.

Therefore, if it is desirable, it is possible to bring a CICS application program written in VS COBOL II for the host CICS into the PC side. If the program is recompiled and relinkedited based on COBOL/2 and CICS OS/2, the program will successfully run in the PS/2 personal computer with virtually no modification, as long as the host program does not use the CICS commands not supported by CICS OS/2.

An implication of this program portability is that a CICS application program can be moved around from the host CICS to the PS/2 personal computer, and vice versa, depending on the situation.

For example, a CICS host application program can be brought down to a PC in order to reduce the system load in the host CICS. Or, a CICS application program can be developed in a PC, and after completion of the tests, it could be brought into the host CICS.

Therefore, this program portability between host CICS and CICS OS/2 makes CICS application systems much more flexible and dynamic. This is one significant advantage of CICS OS/2.

Intercommunication Facilities

One of the primary reasons why CICS OS/2 was developed is an ever-increasing demand for distributed processing between the host CICS and personal computers. Therefore, CICS OS/2 has a capability of distributed processing, which is achieved by the CICS intercommunication facilities.

Based on the LU6.2 protocol, CICS OS/2 supports the following CICS intercommunication facilities:

• Function Request Shipping
• Asynchronous Processing
• Transaction Routing

Each of these intercommunication facilities has been discussed in Sections 17.5, 17.6, 17.7, respectively. The same concepts can be applied to CICS OS/2. At the time of this book's publication, CICS OS/2 does not support Distributed Transaction Processing (DTP), which is one of CICS intercommunication facilities in the host CICS. But it will probably be only a matter of time until the future enhancement of CICS OS/2 will support DTP as well.

The host CICS supported by CICS OS/2 for these CICS intercommunication facilities are the following:

- CICS/MVS Ver. 2.1
- CICS/OS/VS Ver. 1.7
- CICS/DOS/VS Ver. 1.7
- CICS/VM Rel. 2 (No support for Transaction Routing)

This means that if a PS/2 personal computer has CICS OS/2, and if the host CICS system is one of CICS/MVS, CICS/OS/VS, or CICS/DOS/VS described above, then one can achieve distributed processing between the host CICS system and CICS OS/2 in the PS/2 personal computer, using Function Request Shipping, Asynchronous Processing, or Transaction Routing.

Implications for Distributed Processing

As stated earlier, CICS OS/2 works in the PS/2 personal computer just the same as the host CICS works in the mainframe system. Particularly, one should take advantage of CICS intercommunication facilities supported by CICS OS/2.

Function Request Shipping, Asynchronous Processing and Transaction Routing are convenient and easy-to-use facilities of CICS intercommunication. This means that application programming productivity will be significantly improved if one uses Function Request Shipping, Asynchronous Processing, or Transaction Routing for distributed processing between the host system and PS/2 personal computers. Then, a complex LU6.2 APPC will not be necessary in order to achieve distributed processing.

17.15 Systems Application Architecture (SAA)

As a future direction, the CICS intercommunication facilities, especially Intersystem Communication (ISC) based on the LU6.2 protocol, should be looked at in light of Systems Application Architecture (SAA). In this section, therefore, let us discuss the concept of SAA and the role of CICS in the future.

Objective

Systems Application Architecture is a set of interfaces, conventions, and protocols in order to establish an enhanced level of consistency, portability and connectivity of data, applications, and communications in the multisystem environment.

Each SAA participating system consists of the common user interface, common programming interface, and common communications support, in order to ensure consistency, portability, and connectivity, respectively, among other SAA participating systems.

The ultimate goal of SAA is that any data, applications, and communications can be ported or distributed to any SAA participating systems, regardless of the differences among the systems.

Concept

Figure 17-14 illustrates a simplified concept of SAA from the point of view of distributed processing. There are three typical systems: 3090 mainframe system with the MVS/XA operating system, AS/400 midrange system with the OS/400 operating system, and PS/2 personal computer with the OS/2 Extended Edition (E.E.) operating system. Each of them is a representative processor of its system size, while all of them are SAA participants.

As SAA participants, each of these three systems has three SAA dimensions which are designed for consistency, portability, and connectivity to other systems. Let us discuss each of these three dimensions of SAA a little further.

Data   Some of the SAA participants in the data dimension are Database 2 (DB2) in 3090 with Structured Query Language (SQL), the relational database in AS/400 with SQL/400, the relational database in PS/2 with the OS/2 E.E. Database Manager which has the SQL support. Therefore, these databases and SQL applications are consistent and portable across the SAA participating systems. This means that a portion of DB2 in 3090 could be ported to AS/400 or PS/2, which could process it and port back to 3090, for example.

Applications   Some of the SAA participants in the application dimension are VS COBOL II in 3090, COBOL/400 in AS/400, and COBOL/2 in PS/2. Therefore, applications written in these languages are consistent and portable across the SAA participating systems. This means that an application program written in VS COBOL II in 3090 could be used in AS/400 or PS/2 after recompiling it with COBOL/400 or COBOL/2, respectively, with virtually no modifications.

Communications   Some of the SAA participants in the communication dimension are LU6.2 APPC by CICS/MVS in 3090, LU6.2 APPC by OS/400 in AS/400, LU6.2 APPC by Communication Manager of OS/2

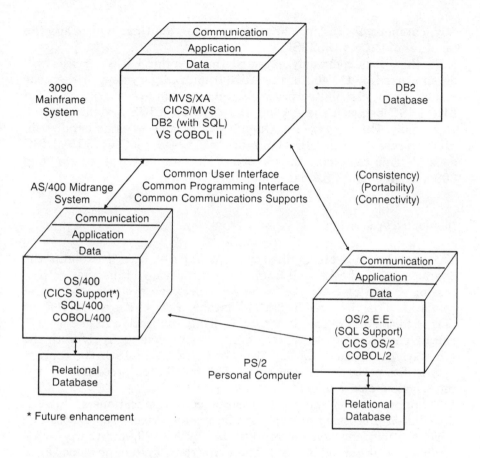

Figure 17-14 Concept of systems application architecture (SAA).

E.E. in PS/2. Therefore, all three systems can converse and exchange data with each other based on the same LU6.2 APPC protocol. This means that an application program in CICS/MVS in 3090 can freely converse with another application in AS/400 or PS/2 based on LU6.2 APPC. Since LU6.2 APPC commands or verbs are standardized, it is relatively easy to develop APPC programs.

In addition, the PS/2 personal computer can now run CICS OS/2 with OS/2 E.E. as discussed in the previous section. In this case, distributed processing between the host CICS system and PS/2 personal computer can be easily accomplished using Function Shipping,

Asynchronous Processing, and Transaction Routing, which are the facilities of CICS LU6.2 ISC.

Further, it is commonly expected that similar CICS services will be supported by OS/400 in the AS/400 midrange system in the near future. Then, distributed processing can be achieved based on CICS LU6.2 ISC between the AS/400 and the host CICS system in 3090. Eventually, CICS services of OS/400 will be able to establish distributed processing with CICS OS/2 in PS/2 based on CICS LU6.2 ISC as well. This completes the picture of distributed processing among 3090, AS/400, and PS/2 based on CICS LU6.2 ISC.

Distributed Processing

This may be an oversimplified concept of SAA. But, it explains the characteristics of SAA well from the point of view of distributed processing. Based on SAA, the boundaries between systems are almost removed. The SAA participating database in one system can be ported to the other. The SAA participating application in one system can be ported to the other. One system can converse freely with the other system based on LU6.2 APPC or CICS LU6.2 ISC. The concept of SAA fits perfectly into the picture of distributed processing in the multisystem environment.

Therefore, one of the most advantageous applications of SAA is distributed processing among the mainframe system represented by 3090, the midrange system represented by AS/400, and the personal computer represented by PS/2. The mainframe system gives powerful processing and fast access to the large database. The midrange system offers departmental independence in one organization. The personal computer offers attractive graphics, presentation manager, user-friendly menu operations with the mouse for the end users as the intelligent workstation. The SAA participating data (e.g., DB2 type relational database) can be freely ported and processed among systems through LU6.2 APPC or CICS LU6.2 ISC. This type of application will become increasingly more important and common in the future.

Role of CICS

In such SAA applications as distributed processing, all communications among systems will be based on LU6.2 APPC or CICS LU6.2 ISC, each of which is nothing but one form of CICS Intersystem Communication (ISC).

This implies that if CICS (a SAA participant) is used with a DB2 type relational database (another participant to SAA) with SAA participating COBOL, CICS will play a major role in the multisystem environment based on SAA, in order to establish distributed processing among systems. For this, CICS ISC based on the LU6.2 protocol will be the essential tool. CICS has a challenging future in this area.

18

System Design Considerations

18.1 Introduction

By this point, we have discussed virtually all of the individual CICS commands, their programming techniques and other relevant topics of CICS application development. The next step is to design an efficient and reliable CICS application system. In this chapter, therefore, let us discuss comprehensively some important considerations for designing better CICS application systems.

Design Considerations

There are many things to consider for the CICS application system design. The following are some important considerations, each of which will be discussed further in the coming sections of this chapter:

- *User Requirements:* What kind of information do users need? How should it be presented?
- *User-Friendliness:* Is the system friendly enough to the users?
- *Technology:* Is the system taking advantage of up-to-date CICS facilities?
- *Resource Usage:* Is the resource usage reasonable (disk space, CPU time, main storage size)?
- *Performance:* Is the response time acceptable? Is the online throughput under the transaction concurrency acceptable?

- *Security:* Is tight security required?
- *Reliability:* Is the application system reliable? Are the recovery/restart functions adequate?
- *Maintainability:* Is the application system easy to maintain?
- *Naming Convention:* What kind of naming convention should be established and enforced in the installation or an application system?
- *Menu-Driven System:* Is the system using the approach which is best suitable for an online system?
- *Intercommunication:* Is Multi-Region Operation (MRO) or Intersystem Communication (ISC) feasible? If so, what kind of intercommunication facilities should be used?
- *System Standards:* Is the system standard adequately established?

Rational Decision

Among these considerations, when you design an actual CICS application system, some considerations may have to be weighted more than others, depending on the situation. For example, sometimes reliability is the first priority, while other times performance is the first priority. At the same time, some considerations are completely contradictory. For example, if you try to emphasize system reliability, system performance tends to decrease.

Therefore, the final decision on the application system design should be made rationally based on the well-balanced priorities of these considerations, taking into account the individual situation. Your goal should be to maximize the total quality of the application system.

18.2   User's Requirements

To absorb the user's requirements and reflect them into the application system is one of the most important considerations for designing any application system. The considerations of this aspect are not limited to the CICS application system itself. Therefore, this section discusses the subject only briefly.

Requirements Definition

After the initial feasibility study, including interviews with personnel in the user's organization, the user's requirements should be clearly defined in the following fashion:

- Online system requirements
  - Processing requirements
  - Screen requirements
  - On-site printing requirements
- Batch system requirements
  - Processing requirements
  - Report requirements
- File requirements

Constraints

The user's requirements are always subject to certain constraints which the users must realize and face. The following are some of these constraints:

- Hardware availability
- Software availability
- Personnel availability
  - For operating the application system
  - For developing/maintaining the application system
- Fund availability
- Time availability

Finalization

The user's requirements must be finalized with the users' consent and approval taking these constraints into account, then they must be clearly documented for future reference.

18.3 User-Friendliness

Since an online system has direct contact with the end users through the terminals, user-friendliness is a significant factor for the application system to be well accepted by the users. Both the online side and batch side of the system must be considered.

Online System

Since the users are involved in the terminal operations, the screen layout and screen input/output operations must be friendly. We have already discussed this subject extensively (see Section 8.16).

Batch System

The batch job preparation and submission through TSO (or equivalent) should be done by some of the users' personnel who are reasonably familiar with data processing (DP). The intensive use of the Cataloged Procedure is recommended, so that users do not have to be concerned with the details of JCL. Also, if the parameters are provided through the Cataloged Procedures, it would lower the likelihood of JCL errors.

File Open/Close

Under the production operations, the user personnel should operate an application system for themselves. That is, the system development personnel should not be involved in the day-to-day production operations. However, at the same time, the users should not use the Master Terminal (CEMT) transaction for opening/closing the files of their system, because the CEMT transaction is a restricted transaction.

Therefore, the file open/close should be done dynamically by users' transactions in which the Dynamic File Open/Close (DFOC) techniques are imbedded. We have discussed this subject already (see Sections 16.11 through 16.15).

18.4 Technology

During the course of CICS's evolution from the early days in the late 1960s to the present time, CICS has been constantly improved and its functions have been enhanced. At the same time, in most of the cases, upward compatibility was maintained.

This implies that the current CICS/MVS Version 2.1 has many advanced functions, while keeping the old functions which have been already antiquated. This situation gives the systems analysts and application programmers too many choices in terms of technological availability for designing CICS application systems.

Strategies

You should take advantage of the enhanced functions of the current CICS. You should not use the outdated CICS functions, which are kept primarily for an upward compatibility purpose. At the same time, since the current CICS offers so much variety of advanced functions, you should try to avoid making the system (or program) too complicated. The system should be as simple as possible for the purposes of performance, reliability, and maintainability.

Suggestions

In the previous chapters, we have discussed the advantageous CICS functions over the outdated functions. The following is a summary of the suggestions in the area of technology:

- Instead of using CSA, CWA, TWA, TCTUA,
  - Use EIB information.
  - Use TSQ with the MAIN option.
  - Use the COMMAREA option in the RETURN, XCTL, and LINK commands.
- Instead of using the GETMAIN command,
  - Define simply the space in the Working Storage Section.
- Instead of using BDAM, ISAM, QSAM,
  - Take the advantage of VSAM, which is IBM's most reliable primary data access method.
  - Take the advantage of the VSAM Alternate Index function.
  - Replace BDAM with VSAM/RRDS.
  - Replace ISAM with VSAM/KSDS.
  - Replace QSAM with VSAM/ESDS.
- Instead of using the multimap panel approach (both single and multiple page),
  - Use the simple multipage message (with single map panel) approach.
  - Use the "free-format" map approach.
- Instead of using the Extrapartition TDQ,
  - Use VSAM/ESDS.
- Instead of using the Intrapartition TDQ,
  - Use TSQ with the MAIN option.

18.5 Resource Usage

The system resources are such objects as a record, disk space, storage space, CPU time, terminal buffer (TIOA), file control buffer, and VSAM string, which are ready to be used by the system control programs and application programs for performing their functions.

How the resources are used determines the performance of not only the transaction on subject, but also the entire CICS system. Since in the online environment, many tasks run concurrently, the efficient use of resources is very crucial to the efficiency of the transaction as well as the CICS system as a whole.

General Considerations

The following are general considerations for the effective use of the system resources:

- Be aware what resources the program requires, and try to use resources as little as possible. "Conservation" is the best strategy for dealing with the issue of resource usage.
- Use the pseudo-conversational mode, since resources are freed while the program is waiting for the response from the terminal.
- Minimize the size of Working Storage Section, since each task receives its own copy of the Working Storage.
- Ensure that when a program holds a resource, it uses and frees the resource as quickly as possible (e.g., during the file update operations).
- Be conscious of preventing the transaction deadlocks (see Section 4.13).
- Modularize programs based on the functional unit, since some modules can be shared by more than one program.

File Browse Operations

The file browse operation does not hold exclusive control over the file, since it is the read-only operation. But, it holds a VSAM string of the file during the browse operation. If all VSAM strings of the file have been reserved by the transactions, the newly arriving transactions which access this file will have to wait until the VSAM string of the file becomes available.

Therefore, for the browse operation, a limited file search should be enforced by the GENERIC key option, GTEQ option of the STARTBR command, or the skip sequential read technique. For the same reason, the multiple browse operation should be avoided if possible.

18.6   System Performance

Under the online system, the system performance is very visible. If the performance is good, the terminal users could operate transactions or the system as a whole with the good response time. Contrary to this, if the performance is poor, the response time will be poor. This section discusses the general considerations for improving performance of not only an application program, but also the CICS system as a whole.

Multithreading

As we discussed, under the CICS environment, a single program is to process several tasks concurrently. This concept is called "multithreading." In order to achieve multithreading, under the CICS command level, all COBOL application programs are automatically guaranteed to be quasi-reentrant. Because of this quasi-reentrancy, between two CICS commands in the application program, an exclusive control is given to a corresponding task which uses this program, as follows:

```
    :
Command
    :          )
    :          )      The task holds an exclusive control over
    :          )      the c.p.u. resource.
Command
    :
```

If there is a heavy CPU bound calculation between two consecutive CICS commands in the application program, the corresponding task would hold the CPU resource for the duration for the task itself, thereby degrading the throughput of the CICS system as a whole. In this respect, for improving the performance of the CICS system as a whole, there should not be the heavy CPU bound calculation between two consecutive CICS commands in the application program.

If the application program involves a lengthy calculation, it should issue the SUSPEND or DELAY command from time to time. For example, if 10,000 loops exist, the program should issue the SUSPEND command every 1000 loops.

The SUSPEND command suspends the task and gives control to higher-priority tasks. When no higher-priority task exists, the control will be returned to the original task. The DELAY command simply suspends the task until the specified time or for the specified interval. It may depend on the situation which command, SUSPEND or DELAY, should be issued. But, generally, the SUSPEND command will optimize the entire CICS system throughput.

Paging

Since CICS works under the virtual storage environment, each CICS application program is affected by paging. Therefore, in order to improve performance, each CICS application program must be coded in such a way that the number of page faults would be minimized during program execution.

The following are general guidelines for reducing number of page faults based on three paging concepts:

Locality of Reference   The locality of reference is the paging concept for the consistent reference to the instruction and data within a relatively small number of pages during execution of a program. If the locality of reference in an application program is improved, the number of page faults will be decreased, thereby improving the performance of the application program.

For improving the locality of reference, the following techniques should be used:

- The application program should execute itself sequentially without branches (or branches should be minimal).
- The subroutines should be placed near the caller.
- The subroutines should be embedded in the caller rather than calling the external subprograms, if possible.
- The XCTL command should be used to transfer control to other programs instead of the LINK command, which acquires an extra storage for itself.
- The data should be initialized as close as possible to its first use.
- The data structure should be defined in the order in which they are to be referred.
- The GETMAIN command should be avoided.

Working Set   The working set is the paging concept for the number and combination of pages a program needs in a given period. If the working set is stabilized in an application program, the number of page faults will be decreased, thereby improving the performance of the program.

For stabilizing the working set, the following techniques should be used:

- Write the modularized programs and structure the modules according to the frequency and anticipated time of reference.

- Do not tie up the main storage awaiting a reply from a terminal operator; that is, do not use the conversational mode. Instead, use the pseudo-conversational mode.
- Use the commands, such as READ, RECEIVE MAP, with the SET option rather than with the INTO option.
- Specify the constant directly in the application program, rather than as the data variable in the Working Storage Section.
- Avoid the LINK command which requests the main storage.
- Use the CICS command subroutine approach, since it stabilizes the working set as the number of concurrency of a transaction increases.

Validity of Reference   The validity of reference is the paging concept for the direct reference to the required page without intermediate references. If the validity of reference in an application program is improved, the number of page faults will be decreased, thereby improving the performance of the program.

For improving the validity of reference, the following techniques should be used:

- Avoid a long search for the data within the program.
- Avoid the indirect addressing or chains in a table in order to find the right entry of the table.

Pseudo-Conversational Program

The pseudo-conversational program is advantageous for reducing resource consumption as described before, since it releases resources while waiting for the response from the terminal. This has two implications in terms of improving performance.

- *Reduced Resource Contention:* The reduced resource consumption makes more resources available to other transactions, thereby lowering the likelihood of waiting for resources by resource contention. This improves performance of individual transactions.
- *Shortened Exclusive Control:* The pseudo-conversational program terminates the task itself while waiting for the response from the terminal. This means that exclusive control over resources will be terminated also. Therefore, the resources are freed and other tasks can use them. This improves performance of other tasks which access the same resources.

For these reasons, the pseudo-conversational program improves performance of the CICS system as a whole. Therefore, the pseudo-conversational approach is essential to the performance-oriented CICS application systems. This is the reason why the pseudo-conversational approach was chosen to be the programming standard in this book.

Input/Output Operations

In the present days, the CPU speed is so fast that the program logic, except input/output operations, does not make significant difference in terms of program performance. This means that in most cases the input/output operations are the bottle-neck for program performance. Therefore, reducing the number of input/output operations in the program provides the most visible performance improvement.

The following are some suggestions for improving program performance with respect to the input/output operations:

* Minimize the input/output operations for files, terminals, BMS, TSQ, TDQ, and main storage.
* Use the multipage message approach with single map panel. Do not use the multimap panel approach.
* Minimize logging for DTB or system log.
* Minimize journaling.
* Minimize the amount of sync points by avoiding the intermediate sync points as much as possible.
* Minimize the duration of the exclusive control over the resouce, especially the duration between the READ/UPDATE and RE-WRITE commands, and the duration between the ENQ and DEQ commands.

Data Traffic of Communication Line

If terminals are connected to CICS through communication lines, data traffic of the communication lines has a significant impact on the system performance, which is measured by the terminal users as the response time.

The communication line with the transmission speed 9,600 bits per second (b.p.s.) is considered as the fast line. Even in this case, suppose we wish to transmit the full screen data of a 3270 terminal (24 x 80 = 1,920 bytes), it would take approximately 2 seconds to transmit the data, not counting processing time. The response time over 2 seconds may be considered slow by many end users. If the line speed is less than 9,600 b.p.s. or the line is shared with multiple terminals, the response time would be worse. This illustrates how important the data traffic of the communication line is.

Therefore, data traffic of the communication line should be minimized by the following techniques:

* Use the MAPONLY and DATAONLY options effectively in the SEND MAP command. The MAPONLY option sends only the default value defined in the physical map, whereas the DATAONLY option sends only the data defined in the symbolic map in the application program.
* Use the ERASE and ERASEAUP options effectively in the SEND MAP command. The ERASE option simply erases the existing screen, so that the new screen must be sent entirely. The ERASEAUP option erases all unprotected fields, keeping the protected field unchanged, so that the new screen does not have to be sent.
* Always be conscious about MDT in order to minimize the data traffic in the communication line. Do not turn on MDT unnecessarily. Use the FRSET option effectively in the DFHMSD (mapset definition) or DFHMDI (map definition) macro. Use the FSET option effectively in the DFHMDF (field definition) macro. Use the FRSET option effectively in the SEND MAP command.
* Use the edit-error screen approach (see Section 9.10).
* Do not send space characters (X'40') unnecessarily. CICS considers space (X'40') as data, so that sending space to terminal unnecessarily increases the data traffic. If you wish to clear the field, simply move LOW-VALUES (X'00') to the field. Since CICS does not consider X'00' as data, it does not increase the data traffic, but it will clear the field.

18.7 System Security

Under the online system, any users can access the resources or information if they have proper user ids. Therefore, in order to protect the resources or confidentiality of the information, security of the system is a crucial issue.

CICS Security Control Facilities

CICS provides a variety of security control facilities which can be conveniently used in the application systems in order to protect the resources. This subject has been already discussed in detail in Chapter 14.

Audit Trail

In addition, as a general consideration, the CICS application system should provide the detailed audit trail information in order to keep a trace record of when and under what circumstances the protected resources were accessed. The audit trail information should include such information as the time, date, name of the user, terminal used, name of the program which requested the resource, type of resource requested, type of request (READ, WRITE, REWRITE, DELETE, so on).

If the audit trail information is thoroughly collected by the application system, when an intended or accidental access to the unauthorized resources occurs, one could easily trace back to find out what actually happened based on the audit trail information.

18.8 System Reliability

A perfectly reliable online system requires no system recovery. But, unfortunately, as you know well, there is no such thing as a "perfectly reliable" system. The system malfunctions or goes down due to even a small problem. Therefore, the online system must be equipped with an adequate recovery/restart capability for ensuring the system reliability.

Exceptional Condition Handling

The reliability of CICS application programs improves significantly if proper exceptional condition checking is thoroughly performed in the application programs. In this respect, the HANDLE CONDITION command (or alternative methods) should be used for every command you issue in order to check the exceptional conditions.

Nonrecovery/Restart Approach

Before trying to think of recovery/restart, you should consider the ways of designing an online system in such a way that the recovery/restart is not required.

One way to achieve this goal is to minimize (or to eliminate entirely if possible) online updates of files. You should try to update the files in the batch processing as much as possible. This can be accomplished by performing the online data collection and batch processing against the collected data. Then, even in case of an online system crash or transaction ABEND, the loss of data integrity of the files or other resources will be minimal. Therefore, such online systems can be recovered with the minimal recovery/restart functions.

This is a sort of common sense, but many people do not realize that this approach works very well for certain applications. Only after the considerations of the nonrecovery/restart approach should the recovery/restart approach be used.

Recovery/Restart Approach

The objectives of the recovery/restart are to minimize the damages done by the system or program failure, and to maintain data integrity and system integrity. Achieving these objectives is very costly especially in the online application system. Therefore, the recovery/restart functions in the online application system should be designed within the following constraints:

- *Time:* How much of time is allowed from system failure to restarting: 30 minutes, 1 hour, 1/2 day?
- *Hardware:* Is the same (or similar) hardware available for switchover as backups?
- *Personnel:* Who is to perform the recovery/restart?
- *Fund:* If additional hardware is required, how much can you afford?
- *Performance:* Usually, the recovery/restart functions slow down the system performance. To what extent is slowdown allowed?

The final decision for designing the recovery/restart functions for the online application system must be made based on well-balanced considerations for the objectives and the constraints you would face.

CICS Recovery/Restart Facilities

Since CICS has adequate built-in recovery/restart facilities, as discussed in Chapter 15, these facilities should be utilized as much as possible. Especially if you use CICS/MVS Extended Recovery Facility (XRF), you could achieve a fault-tolerant CICS system.

18.9   System Maintainability

As the system becomes more complex, system maintainability becomes the more critical factor to be considered. Since online programs tend to be more complex than batch programs, system maintainability must be well considered. Otherwise, soon after starting the production operations of an online system, the system will become unmaintainable. Eventually, the system will have to be either put to death or restructured for a new system life cycle at the significant costs. Therefore, the online system with good maintainability is most cost effective in the long run.

The following are some approaches to keeping good maintainability:

Modularized Program

Instead of developing one big program, the program should be modularized to smaller programs (i.e., functional modules). In this case, one functional module could be used by the other application programs (through the LINK command, for example). If some modifications are required, you can achieve the objective by modifying only this functional module. This will increase the maintainability significantly. The MACS system in Chapter 19 (Case Study) is the typical example of the modularized program approach.

Structured Coding

The program should have a well-organized structure by dividing itself into the structured paragraphs with the top-down concept. This approach might increase the page faults, but this increases maintainability. Also, you should keep in mind that visually neat programs are easy to maintain. For this, you should use the indentation, page EJECT statements and SPACE statements.

While the sample program in Appendix A shows a good example of structured coding, the following is another example:

```
MAIN-LINE SECTION.
      PERFORM HOUSE-KEEP-RTN.
      IF ------
            PERFORM A-RTN.
      IF ------
```

```
        PERFORM B-RTN.
    PERFORM EOJ-RTN.
    :
    :

HOUSE-KEEP-RTN SECTION.
    :
    :

A-RTN SECTION.
    PERFORM A-A-RTN.
    PERFORM A-B-RTN.
    :
    :

B-RTN SECTION.
    :
    :

ABNORMAL-END-RTN SECTION.
    :
    :
```

Comments in Source Program

The application program should have sufficient comments in such a way that if someone reads the comments only in the program, he should be able to understand what the program is doing. If you use this approach in a high-level language such as COBOL and PL/I, the program documentation required would be minimal, since the source code itself serves as the program documentation.

CICS Command Subroutines

All CICS commands can be coded in a form of subroutines and placed at the back of the application program. In this case, in the mainline logic of the program, only COBOL statements can be specified. This approach has many advantages over conventional programming, as we discussed in Section 10.16.

While the sample program in Appendix A uses the CICS command subroutine approach, the following is another example:

```
        :
    (prepare parameters)
    PERFORM FILEA-READ-WITH-FULLKEY.
```

```
        :
    (prepare parameters)
    PERFORM FILEB-WRITE.
        :
    (prepare parameters)
    PERFORM FILEC-DELETE.
        :
        :
FILEA-READ-WITH-FULLKEY SECTION.
    (prepare H/C)
    EXEC CICS READ
        FILE(-----)
        ----------
    END-EXEC.
    GO TO FILEA-READ-EXIT.
    (handle condition routines)
FILEA-READ-EXIT.
    EXIT.
```

Variables Instead of Constants

The variables should be used instead of the literal constants in an application program. That is, the variables should be defined in the Working Storage Section and used in the program, as the example below, because the cross-reference of the fields in the compile list can be used for program tracing.

Better:	MOVE TERMID TO XXXX.
Poor:	MOVE 'TRM1' TO XXXX.

18.10   Naming Convention

Since many CICS users are using the same CICS system, naming convention in some areas is the only way of avoiding confusion among application programs. Therefore, a strict naming convention should be established in the installation. The following are some examples:

Transaction-id:	dxxx,	
where	d:	Division code. e.g., 'P' for Personal.
	xxx:	User-defined detail-id.

Program name:	dddxxxxx,	
where	ddd:	Division code. e.g., 'ACC' for Accounts.
	xxxxx:	User-defined name.

BMS map:	Mxyzzzz,	
where	x:	S=Mapset, P=Map
	y:	I=Input, O=Output, B=I/O
	zzzz:	Transaction id or user-defined name

TSQ queue-id:	dyyyyyyy,	
where	d:	Division code
	yyyyyyy:	User-defined name (max. 7)

File name:	dddfffff,	
where	ddd:	Division code
	fffff:	User-defined file name

Field name prefix:

WK-:	Work fields
TSQ-:	TSQ fields
Mxxxxxx:	BMS map symbolic fields
fff-:	File record fields where fff is a file code
Rnn-:	Report fields where nn is a report number

18.11 Menu-Driven System

The menu-driven system or transaction is the most user-friendly and efficient way of conversing with the terminal users for the online system or transaction. It typically works in the following way:

The terminal user needs to know only one or a few transaction ids, each of which displays a primary menu screen. On the primary menu screen, the user can make a choice for processing options. Thereafter, the functional menu screen(s) automatically guide the order of a series of terminal conversations with the terminal user.

Advantages

The menu-driven system approach has many advantages over the conventional dialog between the system and the terminal user. Some advantages are the following:

- It is very user-friendly.
- It provides better performance if the program is coded in a pseudo-conversational mode.
- It makes the program easy to be modularized, thereby accomplishing high maintainability and low resource usage.

Design Considerations

The following are some design considerations for developing an effective menu-driven system:

- Design the options in the menu screen in the rational order.
  — The options should be grouped with functional order.
  — The options should be displayed in logical order.
  — The most frequently used option should be at the top.
  — The least frequently used option should be at the bottom.

- Always come back to the menu screen after the function(s) selected have been completed.
- Provide a mechanism of terminating processing and going back to the original menu screen, for example, by pressing the PF11 key.
- Provide a mechanism of canceling the entire transaction, for example, by pressing the PF12 key.

Example

The MACS system in Chapter 19 (Case Study) is a typical example of the menu-driven application system.

18.12   Intercommunication

CICS intercommunication allows one CICS region to communicate with the other CICS regions in the same processor (Multi-Region Operations: MRO), other CICSs in the other processor or other non-CICS systems (Intersystem Communication: ISC). MRO and ISC bring many benefits as discussed in Chapter 17. Therefore, CICS intercommunication is a powerful vehicle to integrate the multisystem environment into one strategic corporate system.

Facilities

CICS provides the following facilities for intercommunication:

- Function Request Shipping
- Asynchronous Processing
- Transaction Routing
- Distributed Transaction Processing (DTP)

These facilities are available for both MRO and ISC. Therefore, from application programming's point of view, it is almost transparent whether MRO or ISC is used. Some of these facilities are easy to implement for sharing resources among systems, while others serve as effective tools for distributed processing. We had extensive discussions on these topics in Chapter 17.

Corporate Strategy

Designing an application system based on CICS intercommunication should not be accomplished by a group of systems analysts and programmers. It should involve not only system programmers, system managers of computer installations, but also the corporate executive management. The reason is that the application system based on CICS intercommunication is effective and productive only if information and resources of individual systems are shared with each other based on the cohesive corporate strategies. Therefore, for designing such a system, the involvement of corporate executive management is essential as to how the information and resources are shared among departments and divisions.

Distributed Processing

In the early days of data processing, all data processing was centralized. As the computer systems became more powerful and more common, data processing tended to be gradually decentralized to several departmental systems. This trend was accelerated when personal computers came out. However, recently it was realized that the decentralized information and resources must be integrated. After all, the headquarters of a corporation must control the entire organization based on the corporate strategies. Here is a need for system integration, which can be achieved by distributed processing.

For distributed processing, CICS intercommunication will play an essential role. As discussed in Chapter 17, if CICS intercommunication is used in the context of Systems Application Architecture (SAA), we could build a highly integrated system where the boundaries among the mainframe systems, midrange systems, and personal computers are nearly transparent. In results, a large corporation could achieve a successful system integration of data processing in its corporate headquarters. This will make it possible for the corporate executive management to enforce the centralized management from top to bottom of the corporate structure, irrespective of the physical location of departments and divisions.

Designing such an integrated system by distributed processing based on CICS intercommunication would be one of the most rewarding experience for the data processing professional.

18.13   System Standards

The objective of system standards is to impose some discipline in developing and operating application systems in an installation. The system standards improve firm control over the application systems, consequently over the entire system as a whole. Therefore, the design considerations discussed in the previous sections can be standardized in the installation as a whole and/or in an individual application system.

Since this subject is much beyond the CICS application development, this section describes only brief guidelines on this subject.

Installation Standards

The installation can establish its own system standards and enforce the users to maintain them. The installation standards should not be defined too rigidly, because too rigid system standards only lower the productivity of application programmers. Instead, they should be the minimal guidelines which users must follow. The users of the installation (i.e., systems analysts and programmers) should be allowed a reasonable degree of freedom.

Application Standards

Within the constraints of the installation standards, an application system can establish its own system standards and enforce the systems analysts, programmers, and end users of the application system to maintain. The application standards also should not be defined too rigidly for the same reason mentioned above. Instead, they should be the minimal guidelines which systems analysts, programmers, and end users must follow. The systems analysts, programmers, and end users should be allowed a reasonable degree of freedom.

19

Case Study: MACS System

19.1 Introduction

Now that we have discussed all essential topics of CICS application development, we are ready for developing CICS application systems. In this last chapter, therefore, let us discuss a model case of CICS application development. The objective of this case study is to integrate all of the knowlege and skills you have gained from this book into the model case, which follows:

Computer Express Company

Computer Express Company is a fast-growing mail order company based in Manhattan, which sells personal computers, peripherals, boards, and supplies. The current president, Kenneth O. McMillan, founded the company seven years ago. Since then, the company has been growing continuously in terms of business revenues, profits, customer base, product base and number of employees.

As Mr. McMillan is very computer-minded, two years ago he decided to acquire an IBM 3090 mainframe computer with the MVS/XA operating system in order to handle the company's business activities more efficiently. The system has been used primarily in a batch mode with some Time Sharing Option (TSO) applications for accounting, payroll and personnel applications, as well as mail order applications.

Need for New System

To Mr. McMillan's delight and worry, the company's mail order business has expanded to the extent that the current batch mail order system can no longer handle the complexity and volume of mail orders which the company receives from the customers. In addition, there is a desperate need for a capability of online inquiry of the order status.

Therefore, Mr. McMillan hired a well-known professor of Information Systems at New York University, Professor Smart, as an independent consultant to investigate the current situation and to come up with a proposal for a new system which will solve the current problems.

Proposal for MACS

Professor Smart spent several weeks with Computer Express Co., reviewing the current system and interviewing order-entry personnel. The investigation has been completed, and Professor Smart submitted a report which served as a proposal for a new Marketing Activity Automated System (MACS) based on CICS/MVS in the mainframe system.

As Professor Smart's proposal states, the MACS system will eventually become a complex core system for all data processing activities of Computer Express Co. However, one fundamental requirement demanded by Mr. McMillan was that the new system must be operational as soon as possible. Therefore, as the first phase, the MACS system should be simple in order to be implemented quickly.

Mr. McMillan immediately approved Professor Smart's proposal, and requested the company's Information Systems Department to implement the MACS system as soon as possible.

19.2 System Overview

The proposed MACS system is very simple, but functional enough to deal with the current mail orders of Computer Express Co. The characteristics of the system are summarized as follows:

Application Functions

The Customer Information (CI) function is for creating a new customer profile or updating an existing customer's profile. The Remittance Entry (RE) function is for entering a remittance from the customer. The Order Entry (OE) function is for entering a new order from the customer. And the Activity Inquiry (AI) function is for inquiring into the customer's past activities.

System Support Functions

The MACS system is constructed in a form of a menu-driven multi-transaction system. Only the transaction id "MAC1" is used by the user, and this transaction id triggers the Menu screen. Based on the user's requests in the Menu screen, the system guides further processing for CI, RE, OE, and AI functions.

At the completion of all actions requested by the user for one customer, a fresh Menu screen will be displayed for the next customer session. This process will be repeated until the user specifically requests the end of the transaction.

At any point in time, if the PF12 key is pressed, the entire transaction will be forcefully cancelled. Similarly, at any point in time, if the PF11 key is pressed, the processing at the time will be cancelled and a fresh Menu screen will be displayed for a new entry.

Resources Involved

The MACS system simply consists only of five programs, five BMS maps, four CICS transactions, and three VSAM files. Therefore, the system can be easily developed, while it has promising expandability.

19.3 System Structure

Professor Smart insists in his proposal that the MACS system must be a menu-driven system because the menu-driven system improves the user-friendliness of the system. In addition, the menu-driven system makes the system more structured. Hence, the MACS system is designed based on the menu-driven system approach, and it has the following system structure:

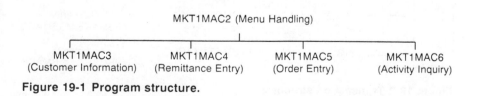

Figure 19-1 Program structure.

Program Structure

The MACS system consists of five programs. Taking advantage of the menu-driven system, the programs are modularized for their specialized functions. Each program passes control to another program based on the information in the Menu screen.

As shown in Figure 19-1, program MKT1MAC2 is the menu handling program which controls a flow of applications programs based on the actions requested in the Menu screen. The rest of the programs are the specialized functional programs: MKT1MAC3, MKT1MAC4, MKT1MAC5 and MKT1MAC6 for the activities of Customer Information (CI), Remittance Entry (RE), Order Entry (OE), and Activity Inquiry (AI), respectively.

Control is initially to be passed to these functional programs by either program MKT1MAC2 (Menu Handling) or other functional programs through the XCTL command.

Transaction Structure

Professor Smart also emphasizes in his proposal that each CICS application program must be coded as a pseudo-conversational program in order to maximize system efficiency of CICS as a whole. Therefore, each of five MACS programs are designed for pseudo-conversation, as shown in Figure 19-2.

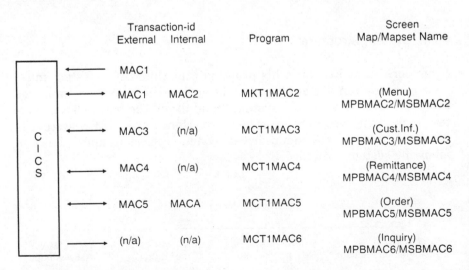

Figure 19-2 Transaction structure.

Programs   MKT1MAC2,   MKT1MAC3,   MKT1MAC4   and MKT1MAC5 use an external transaction id MAC1, MAC3, MAC4, and MAC5, respectively, but program MKT1MAC6 does not use any external transaction id at all. Further, in order to achieve pseudo-conversation, programs MKT1MAC2 and MKT1MAC5 use an internal transaction id MAC2 and MACA, respectively.

One BMS map is prepared for each program for conversing with the end users. Programs MKT1MAC2, 3, 4, 5 and 6 use map/mapset MPBMAC2/MSBMAC2, 3, 4, 5, and 6, respectively.

19.4   Design of Screens, Files and TSQ

Based on the system structure described in the previous section, screens, files, and TSQ are designed. The specifications of these resources are as follows:

Screens

According to Professor Smart, an effective design of screen layout is one of the most important considerations for a user-friendly CICS application system. Based on his suggestion, six screens are designed. A BMS mapname and mapset name are given to each screen.

As a standard, the Skippers are placed in such a way that the cursor moves automatically to the next unprotected field (i.e., input field). Also, as another standard, the bottom four lines of each screen are reserved for the data edit error message fields.

Menu Screen (MPBMAC2/MSBMAC2)   As shown in Figure 19-3, the Menu (MAC2) screen is the initial screen to be shown in the MACS system. It has the customer number field, action item fields, and error message fields. Information entered in the Menu screen will control one customer session.

Customer Information Screen (MPBMAC3/MSBMAC3)   As shown in Figure 19-4, the Customer Information (MAC3) screen is used for creating a profile of a new customer or updating the profile of an existing customer. The Document Control Number (DCN) is a control number which the program automatically assigns to the customer session. The fields of name, customer type, and discount (%) are initially defined as the autoskip fields. However, if the customer is new, these

```
┌─────────────────────────────────────────────────────────────┐
│                MARKETING ACTIVITY MENU                  MAC2  │
│                                                               │
│         CUSTOMER NUMBER:  nnnnn (SPACE FOR NEW CUSTOMER)       │
│                                                               │
│    ACTION ITEMS (ENTER X TO THE ACTIONS YOU WISH)             │
│                                                               │
│         CUSTOMER INFORMATION : x                              │
│         REMITTANCE ENTRY     : x                              │
│         ORDER ENTRY          : x                              │
│         ACTIVITY INQUIRY     : x                              │
│         END                  : x                              │
│                                                               │
│                                                               │
│                                                               │
│  yyyyyyyyyyyyyyyyyyyyyyyyyyyyyyyyyyyyyyyyyyyyyyyyyyyyyyyyyyyyy  │
│  yyyyyyyyyyyyyyyyyyyyyyyyyyyyyyyyyyyyyyyyyyyyyyyyyyyyyyyyyyyyy  │
│  yyyyyyyyyyyyyyyyyyyyyyyyyyyyyyyyyyyyyyyyyyyyyyyyyyyyyyyyyyyyy  │
│  yyyyyyyyyyyyyyyyyyyyyyyyyyyyyyyyyyyyyyyyyyyyyyyyyyyyyyyyyyyyy  │
└─────────────────────────────────────────────────────────────┘
```

```
where   n : Unprotected numeric fields
        x : Unprotected alphanumeric field
        y : Autoskipped alphanumeric field
 z or 9 : Autoskipped numeric edited field
        _ : Initial cursor position
```

The numeric fields must be defined as such. The cursor must automatically skip to the next unprotected field. The bottom four lines are reserved for the error messages. These general rules apply globally to all other screens as well.

Figure 19-3 Menu screen (MPBMAC2/MSBMAC2).

fields will be changed to the unprotected field dynamically by the program.

Remittance Entry Screen (MPBMAC4/MSBMAC4) As shown in Figure 19-5, the Remittance Entry (MAC4) screen is used for entering the remittance which the customer sent for purchasing the mail order products. This is the simplest screen layout, which has only two data entry fields: the remittance amount and its type.

Order Entry Screen (MPBMAC5/MSBMAC5) As shown in Figure 19-6, the Order Entry (MAC5) screen is used for entering the customer's order. The items and quantity are the only required items for entry. The item value, total value, discount, and net order value will be calculated by the program. The confirmation title must be initially invisible. If all data entered have been validated, and if there is no error, the program changes the item and quantity fields to the autoskip fields, makes the confirmation title visible, expecting the end

```
                    CUSTOMER INFORMATION                    MAC3

CUSTOMER NUMBER: yyyyy                    DCN: yyyyyyyyy
NAME:    yyyyyyyyyyyyyyyyyyyyyyyyyyyyyy
ADDRESS: xxxxxxxxxxxxxxxxxxxxxxxxxxxxxx
         xxxxxxxxxxxxxxxxxxxxxxxxxxxxxx


CUSTOMER TYPE:    y    (G=General, S=Special)
DISCOUNT %:       z9
CURRENT BALANCE: zz,zzz,zz9.99-



yyyyyyyyyyyyyyyyyyyyyyyyyyyyyyyyyyyyyyyyyyyyyyyyyyyyyyyyyyyyyy
yyyyyyyyyyyyyyyyyyyyyyyyyyyyyyyyyyyyyyyyyyyyyyyyyyyyyyyyyyyyyy
yyyyyyyyyyyyyyyyyyyyyyyyyyyyyyyyyyyyyyyyyyyyyyyyyyyyyyyyyyyyyy
yyyyyyyyyyyyyyyyyyyyyyyyyyyyyyyyyyyyyyyyyyyyyyyyyyyyyyyyyyyyyy
```

The address lines must be followed by Stopper and Skipper in that order. The current balance must be edited as the zero suppressed numeric value with the comma, decimal point, and sign.

Figure 19-4 Customer Information Screen (MPBMAC3/MSBMAC3).

user to type the confirmation response. Professor Smart strongly suggests using the occurrence-handling approach for dealing with five lines of the item, quantity, and value fields.

```
                    REMITTANCE ENTRY                       MAC4

CUSTOMER NUMBER: yyyyy                    DCN: yyyyyyyyy
NAME:    yyyyyyyyyyyyyyyyyyyyyyyyyyyyyy

REMITTANCE AMOUNT: nnnnnnnn
REMITTANCE TYPE:    x    WHERE  P: PERSONAL CHECK
                               C: CASH
                               R: RETURNED ORDER CREDIT

yyyyyyyyyyyyyyyyyyyyyyyyyyyyyyyyyyyyyyyyyyyyyyyyyyyyyyyyyyyyyy
yyyyyyyyyyyyyyyyyyyyyyyyyyyyyyyyyyyyyyyyyyyyyyyyyyyyyyyyyyyyyy
yyyyyyyyyyyyyyyyyyyyyyyyyyyyyyyyyyyyyyyyyyyyyyyyyyyyyyyyyyyyyy
yyyyyyyyyyyyyyyyyyyyyyyyyyyyyyyyyyyyyyyyyyyyyyyyyyyyyyyyyyyyyy
```

The remittance field should be defined as the numeric field, and value 9(6)V99 is assumed to be entered. That is, the decimal point handling in this map is primitive for the sake of the program simplicity.

Figure 19-5 Remittance Entry Screen (MPBMAC4/MSBMAC4).

```
                        ORDER ENTRY                        MAC5

   CUSTOMER NUMBER: yyyyy                   DCN: yyyyyyyyy
   NAME:     yyyyyyyyyyyyyyyyyyyyyyyyyyyyyy

        ITEM          QTY          VALUE
   1.   nnnn          nnnn        zzz,zz9.99
   2.   nnnn          nnnn        zzz,zz9.99
   3.   nnnn          nnnn        zzz,zz9.99
   4.   nnnn          nnnn        zzz,zz9.99
   5.   nnnn          nnnn        zzz,zz9.99

                     TOTAL:    z,zzz,zz9.99
                  DISCOUNT:    z,zzz,zz9.99-
         NET ORDER VALUE:      z,zzz,zz9.99-

   CONFIRM (Y/N): x
   yyyyyyyyyyyyyyyyyyyyyyyyyyyyyyyyyyyyyyyyyyyyyyyyyyyyyyyyyyyyyyyy
   yyyyyyyyyyyyyyyyyyyyyyyyyyyyyyyyyyyyyyyyyyyyyyyyyyyyyyyyyyyyyyyy
   yyyyyyyyyyyyyyyyyyyyyyyyyyyyyyyyyyyyyyyyyyyyyyyyyyyyyyyyyyyyyyyy
   yyyyyyyyyyyyyyyyyyyyyyyyyyyyyyyyyyyyyyyyyyyyyyyyyyyyyyyyyyyyyyyy
```

All monetary values should be edited as the zero suppressed numeric with comma, decimal point. The discount value must have the minus (-) sign. The confirmation title must be initially dark (i.e., invisible).

Figure 19-6 Order Entry Screen (MPBMAC5/MSBMAC5).

Activity Inquiry Screen (MPBMAC6/MSBMAC6) As shown in Figure 19-7, the Activity Inquiry (MAC6) screen is used to display the customer's past activities. This screen is used for the multipage message with single panel. Therefore, at the bottom, a paging command field must be provided. All fields except the paging command fields are defined as the autoskip fields. Professor Smart strongly recommends the use of the free format approach for dealing with five lines of DCN, activity, and amount fields.

Files

According to Professor Smart, VSAM is the only data access method which should be used under CICS/MVS because of its reliability and performance. Therefore, the MACS system uses three VSAM/KSDS files. They are Control file, Customer Master file and Product Master file, and their dataset names registered in FCT are MKTVSCTL, MKTVSCMA, and MKTVSPMS, respectively. These files are to be updated on a real-time basis.

Figure 19-8 shows the layout of records in these files.

```
                         ACTIVITY INQUIRY                      MAC6
                                                             PAGE z9


   CUSTOMER NUMBER: yyyyy          CURRENT BALANCE: z,zzz,zz9.99-
   NAME:      yyyyyyyyyyyyyyyyyyyyyyyyyyyyyyyyyyy

           DCN          ACTIVITY      AMOUNT
       1.  yyyyyyyyyy      yy         z,zzz,zz9.99-
       2.  yyyyyyyyyy      yy         z,zzz,zz9.99-
       3.  yyyyyyyyyy      yy         z,zzz,zz9.99-
       4.  yyyyyyyyyy      yy         z,zzz,zz9.99-
       5.  yyyyyyyyyy      yy         z,zzz,zz9.99-



       ENTER PAGING COMMAND (EG. P/N, P/P, P/L, ETC): xxxxx
```

All monetary values should be edited as the zero suppressed numeric with comma, decimal point with sign. The CI activity does not have the amount; RE has the positive amount, and OE has the negative sign.

Figure 19-7 Activity Inquiry Screen (MPBMAC6/MSBMAC6).

Control File (MKTVSCTL)   The Control (CTL) file is used for providing control number information for the MACS system. It contains only one record which provides the next customer number for the next customer and the next Document Control Number (DCN) for one customer session.

Customer Master File (MKTVSCMA)   The Customer Master (CMA) file contains customer profile and activity records of all customers. It consists of four record types. The CMA-A record is a header record of a customer and it contains the profile of the customer and his/her current balance. There is only one CMA-A record per customer.

The other three record types are the activity records, and they are created only when the customer has that activity. One customer can have many of these records depending on his/her activities. The CMA-B record is created when the customer is created or when he/she changes the profile. The CMA-C record is created when the customer sends a remittance for the order. The CMA-D record is created when the customer sends an order which may consist of several items.

Product Master File (MKTVSPMA)   The Product Master (PMA) file contains product information. Each record contains such information as product name, unit price, and available inventory of one product

```
CTL Next Number Record (CTL-A-RECORD)
          Record Key
               Record Type            PIC X          Constant 'A'
          Record Detail
               Next Customer Number   PIC 9(5)
               Next Doc. Control Num.  PIC 9(10)     yymmddnnnn

CMA Header Record (CMA-A-RECORD)
          Record Key
               Customer Number         PIC 9(5)
               Document Control Number  PIC 9(10)     Constant zero
               Record Type             PIC X          Constant 'A'
          Record Detail
               Customer Name           PIC X(30)
               Address 1               PIC X(30)
               Address 2               PIC X(30)
               Customer Type           PIC X          G=General
                                                      S=Special
               Discount %              PIC 99
               Current Balance         PIC S9(7)V99 COMP-3

CMA Customer Information Record (CMA-B-RECORD)
          Record Key
               Customer Number         PIC 9(5)
               Document Control Number  PIC 9(10)     yymmddnnnn
               Record Type             PIC X          Constant 'B'
          Record Detail
               Action Type             PIC X          N=New Customer
                                                      C=Address Change

CMA Remittance Record (CMA-C-RECORD)
          Record Key
               Customer Number         PIC 9(5)
               Document Control Number  PIC 9(10)     yymmddnnnn
               Record Type             PIC X          Constant 'C'
          Record Detail
               Remittance Amount       PIC 9(6)V99 COMP-3
               Remittance Type         PIC X          P=Personal Check
                                                      C=Cash
                                                      R=Returned Order

CMA Order Record (CMA-D-RECORD)
          Record Key
               Customer Number         PIC 9(5)
               Document Control Number  PIC 9(10)     yymmddnnnn
               Record Type             PIC X          Constant 'D'
          Record Detail
               Item Information (Occurs 5 times)
                    Item Number        PIC 9(4)
                    Quantity           PIC 9(4)
                    Item Value         PIC 9(7)V99 COMP-3
               Total Item Value        PIC 9(7)V99 COMP-3
               Discount                PIC 9(7)V99 COMP-3
               Net Order Value         PIC 9(7)V99 COMP-3
```

Figure 19-8 File record layout.

```
PMA Item Record (PMA-I-RECORD)
          Record Key
               Item Number          PIC 9(4)
          Record Detail
               Product Name         PIC X(30)
               Unit Price           PIC 9(4)V99 COMP-3
               Available Inventory  PIC 9(7) COMP-3
```

Figure 19-8 (continued) File record layout.

item which Computer Express Co. sells to the customers. The information is used to calculate order value and new inventory level.

Temporary Storage Queue (TSQ)

For programming convenience, a TSQ is used in the MACS system as a scratch pad. The TSQ is called TSQ Menu Information, and is used for passing the menu information among the MACS programs. It is created, updated and deleted dynamically by the programs during processing for one customer session. The QID and the record layout are shown below:

QID: 'M' + EIBTRMID + 'MEN'

Record Layout:

```
Customer Number    PIC 9(5)
New Customer Flag  PIC X        Y = New Customer
DCN                PIC 9(10)
CI Action          PIC X        X = Action requested
RE Action          PIC X        X = Action requested
OE Action          PIC X        X = Action requested
AI Action          PIC X        X = Action requested
```

19.5 CICS Control Tables

The CICS control tables are defined for the MACS system so as to maximize security, reliability, and performance of the system. Considered here are SNT, PPT, PCT, and FCT. Other CICS control tables (such as TCT and SIT) are prepared by system programmers, so that they are not listed here.

Sign-on Table (SNT)

A number of CICS user ids for the MACS system are prepared and registered in SNT. For better security management, RACF is used as the External Security Manager software. Each user has the security key to access the authorized MACS transactions.

One entry of SNT defines one CICS user id. Therefore, one SNT entry should look as follows:

```
DFHSNT    TYPE=ENTRY,
          EXTSEC=YES,
          OPIDENT=MKT,
          OPPRTY=3,
          SCTYKEY=7,
          TIMEOUT=30,
          USERID=MKTOE01
```

Processing Program Table (PPT)

Since the MACS system consists of five programs and five BMS maps, these programs and maps must be registered in PPT. Each entry defines one program or mapset. All five programs are to be written in COBOL. In order to improve virtual storage paging, programs and maps are grouped in accordance with their primary use.

The PPT entries for the MACS system, therefore, should look as follows:

```
DFHPPT    TYPE=ENTRY,PROGRAM=MKT1MAC2,PGMLANG=COBOL
DFHPPT    TYPE=ENTRY,PROGRAM=MSBMAC2
DFHPPT    TYPE=ENTRY,PROGRAM=MKT1MAC3,PGMLANG=COBOL
DFHPPT    TYPE=ENTRY,PROGRAM=MSBMAC3
DFHPPT    TYPE=ENTRY,PROGRAM=MKT1MAC4,PGMLANG=COBOL
DFHPPT    TYPE=ENTRY,PROGRAM=MSBMAC4
DFHPPT    TYPE=ENTRY,PROGRAM=MKT1MAC5,PGMLANG=COBOL
DFHPPT    TYPE=ENTRY,PROGRAM=MSBMAC5
DFHPPT    TYPE=ENTRY,PROGRAM=MKT1MAC6,PGMLANG=COBOL
DFHPPT    TYPE=ENTRY,PROGRAM=MSBMAC6
```

Program Control Table (PCT)

The MACS system uses four CICS transaction ids which are referred to as the external transaction ids. These transaction ids must be registered in PCT. Each entry defines a transaction id, associated program, and other information. In order to improve system security, reliability, and performance, Professor Smart recommends specifying parameters for time-out, automatic transaction restart, transaction security, and transaction priority.

The PCT entries for the MACS system, therefore, should look as follows:

```
DFHPCT      TYPE=ENTRY,
            TRANSID=MAC1,
            PROGRAM=MKT1MAC2,
            DTIMEOUT=15,
            RTIMEOUT=15,
            RESTART=YES,
            TRANSEC=7,
            DUMP=YES,
            TRNSPRTY=10
DFHPCT      TYPE=ENTRY,
            TRANSID=MAC3,
            PROGRAM=MKT1MAC3,
            :
            (Other parameters are the same as the first entry.)
            :
DFHPCT      TYPE=ENTRY,
            TRANSID=MAC4,
            PROGRAM=MKT1MAC4,
            :
            (Other parameters are the same as the first entry.)
            :
DFHPCT      TYPE=ENTRY,
            TRANSID=MAC5,
            PROGRAM=MKT1MAC5,
            :
            (Other parameters are the same as the first entry.)
            :
```

File Control Table (FCT)

The MACS system uses three VSAM/KSDS files. These files must be registered in FCT. In order to improve system reliability, Professor Smart strongly suggests applying Dynamic Transaction Backout (DTB) against these files. Therefore, the log parameter should be specified. Also, Professor Smart recommends specifying the parameters of number of buffers and strings with the reasonable value in order to optimize system performance. For security purposes, the service request parameter should be specified with valid options. Also, in order to save system resource consumption, the file status parameter should be specified with the recommended options.

Taking these into account, the FCT entries of the MACS system should look as follows:

```
DFHFCT    TYPE=DATASET,
          ACCMETH=VSAM,
          DATASET=MKTVSCTL,
          SERVREQ=(ADD,DELETE,READ,UPDATE),
          FILESTAT=(DISABLED,CLOSED),
          LOG=YES, BUFND=3, BUFNI=2, STRNO=2
DFHFCT    TYPE=DATASET,
          ACCMETH=VSAM,
          DATASET=MKTVSCMA,
          SERVREQ=(ADD,BROWSE,DELETE,READ,UPDATE),
          :
          (Other parameters are the same as the first entry.)
          :
DFHFCT    TYPE=DATASET,
          ACCMETH=VSAM,
          DATASET=MKTVSPMA,
          SERVREQ=(ADD,DELETE,READ,UPDATE),
          :
          (Other parameters are the same as the first entry.)
          :
```

19.6 Program Specifications

Now that all resources have been defined for the MACS system, the program specification for each of five programs must be defined. The specifications of one program differ from those of other programs, depending on the function of the program.

However, as the MACS system standards, Professor Smart strongly recommends the following two points:

1. All CICS commands (except the RETURN command) must be accompanied with proper HANDLE CONDITION commands (or the RESP option) for detecting significant exceptional conditions. This is required for improving system reliability.

2. All programs must be coded as the pseudo-conversational program using technique 3 described in Chapter 3. This is required for improving system efficiency and performance as a whole.

Taking into account these system standards, systems analysts and senior programmers of Computer Express Co. developed specifications of each of five MACS programs under the guidance of Professor Smart. These program specifications are described below.

Program MKT1MAC2 (Menu Handling)

1. The program begins with sending the Menu screen (MAC2) to the terminal. Return with the external transaction id = MAC1 and internal transaction id = MAC2. The user will type data in the unprotected fields and press the ENTER key.
2. The program will receive the Menu screen. Validate the data as follows:
   • For a new customer, the customer number must be null.
   • For an existing customer, the specified customer number must be in the CMA file.
   • At least one action item must be selected.
   • The END action must be selected alone.
   • The CI, RE, OE, and AI actions can be selected alone or together with any combination.
3. If errors are detected, edit error messages at the bottom of the Menu screen and send. Return with the external transaction id = MAC1 and internal transaction id = MAC2. Then the user will make corrections on the same screen and reenter.
4. If there is no error, process action items in the following manner:
5. If the END action is requested, delete the TSQ Menu Information, display a transaction completion message, and terminate the transaction.
6. Otherwise, read CTL-A-RECORD. Save the next DCN, increment the original value by 1. If the customer is new, also save the next customer number and increment the original value by 1. Update the record. Then, using the saved DCN, new customer number (if new customer) and information in the Menu screen, create TSQ Menu Information for subsequent programs. If there is existing TSQ Menu Information, it must be deleted before creating a new one. If the customer is new, the

Customer Number and New Customer Flag in the TSQ Menu Information must be set to the one from CTL-A-RECORD and "Y," respectively.

7. If the customer is a new customer, transfer control to MKT1MAC3. If the first action is CI, transfer control to MKT1MAC3. If the first action is RE, transfer control to MKT1MAC4. If the first action is OE, transfer control to MKT1MAC5. If the first action is AI, transfer control to MKT1MAC6.

8. At any point, if the PF12 key is pressed, display a transaction cancellation message and terminate the task. Similarly, if the PF11 key is pressed, display a fresh Menu screen for starting over again. Return with the external transaction id = MAC1 and internal transaction id = MAC2.

Program MKT1MAC3 (Customer Information)

1. The program begins with receiving control from another program. Read the TSQ Menu Information.

2. If the New Customer Flag is "Y," this means a new customer. Edit the Customer Information screen (MAC3) with the customer number. Make the Name, Customer type and Discount fields unprotected, so the user can type the data in these fields, too. The initial current balance should be zero. Go to step 4.

3. If the New Customer Flag is not "Y," this means that this is an existing customer. Read the customer's CMA-A-RECORD and edit the MAC3 screen.

4. Send the MAC3 screen. Return with the external transaction id = MAC3. The user will enter the necessary data in the unprotected fields and press the ENTER key.

5. The program will receive the MAC3 screen. Read the TSQ Menu Information and validate the screen data as follows:
   • If an existing customer, both address lines must have some data.
   • If a new customer, all unprotected fields must have proper data.

6. If errors are detected, edit error message(s) at the bottom of the MAC3 screen and send. Return with the external transaction id = MAC3. The user will make corrections on the same screen and reenter.

7. If there is no error, do the following:

8. If the customer is an existing one, read the customer's CMA-A-RECORD and compare the address with the one from the screen. If it is different, update the CMA-A-RECORD with the new address.

9. If the customer is a new customer, prepare a new CMA-A-RECORD using the data from the screen (the current balance must be zero), and add the record into CMA file.

10. For the new customer or existing customer whose address has been updated, prepare a new CMA-B-RECORD and add the record into the CMA file.

11. From the TSQ Menu Information, space out the CI action and update the TSQ. Then select the next action. If the next action is RE, OE or AI, transfer control to the appropriate program. Otherwise, send a fresh Menu screen (MAC2) for starting a new entry for another customer. Return with the external transaction id = MAC1 and internal transaction id = MAC2.

12. At any point, if the PF12 key is pressed, display a transaction cancellation message and terminate the task. Similarly, if the PF11 key is pressed, display a fresh Menu screen for starting over again. Return with the external transaction id = MAC1 and internal transaction id = MAC2.

Program MKT1MAC4 (Remittance Entry)

1. The program begins with receiving control from another program. Read the TSQ Menu Information.

2. Read the customer's CMA-A-RECORD. Edit the Remittance Entry screen (MAC4) and send it. Return with the external transaction id = MAC4. The user will type data in the unprotected fields and press the ENTER key.

3. The program will receive the MAC4 screen. Validate the data. All data must be proper. In this system, the input decimal point handling is primitive as it is ignored and the PIC 9(6)V99 entry is assumed.

4. If errors are detected, edit the error message at the bottom of the MAC4 screen, and send it. The user will make corrections on the same screen and reenter.

5. If there is no error, do the following: Prepare a new CMA-C-RECORD and add the record into the CMA file. Update CMA-A-RECORD to reflect the new balance (i.e., the remittance amount is to be added to the current balance).

6. From the TSQ Menu Information, space out the RE action, and update the TSQ. Then, select the next action. If the next action is OE or AI, transfer control to the appropriate program. Otherwise, send a fresh Menu screen (MAC2) to start a new entry for another customer. Return with the external transaction id = MAC1 and internal transaction id = MAC2.
7. At any point, if the PF12 key is pressed, display a transaction cancellation message and terminate the task. Similarly, if the PF11 key is pressed, display a fresh Menu screen for starting over again. Return with the external transaction id = MAC1 and internal transaction id = MAC2.

Program MKT1MAC5 (Order Entry)

1. The program begins with receiving control from another program. Read the TSQ Menu Information.
2. Read the customer's CMA-A-RECORD, edit the Order Entry screen (MAC5), and send it. Return with the external transaction id = MAC5. The user will type data in the unprotected fields and press the ENTER key.
3. The program will receive the MAC5 screen. Validate the data. All data must be proper. The item numbers typed must exist in the PMA file. One order consists of the maximum of five items, but not all five lines need to be filled.
4. If errors are detected, edit error message(s) at the bottom of the MAC5 screen and send it. Return with the external transaction id = MAC5. The user will make corrections on the same screen and reenter.
5. If no error is detected, do the following: Read PMA-I-RECORD for an item on the screen. Calculate the item value (i.e., unit value x quantity on the screen). Repeat for all items on the screen. Calculate the total item value. Read the customer's CMA-A-RECORD for the discount %. Calculate the discount amount (i.e., total item value x discount % / 100). Calculate the net order amount (i.e., total item value − discount). Prepare CMA-D-RECORD in COMMAREA based on the information at hand. Edit the MAC5 screen for the calculated values. Make all unprotected fields (except the confirmation field) autoskipped. Brighten the confirmation title field. Then send the screen. Return with the external transaction id = MAC5 and the internal transaction id = MACA. Also pass CMA-D-RECORD through COMMAREA.

6. The user will type the confirmation (Y or N). If the confirmation is 'N', make the item and quantity fields unprotected. Darken the confirmation title. Null out all value fields and confirmation field. Send the screen. Return with the external transaction id = MAC5. The user will make the necessary change and reenter.
7. If the confirmation is 'Y', do this: Prepare a new CMA-D-RECORD and add the record into the CMA file. Update CMA-A-RECORD to show a new balance (i.e., the net order amount is to be subtracted from the current balance). Also, update PMA-I-RECORD to reflect the order amount (i.e., the order quantity of the item is to be subtracted from the current inventory).
8. From the TSQ Menu Information, space out the OE action and update the TSQ. Then, select the next action. If the next action is AI, transfer control to the appropriate program. Otherwise, send a fresh Menu screen (MAC2) to start a new entry for another customer. Return with the external transaction id = MAC1 and internal transaction id = MAC2.
9. At any point, if the PF12 key is pressed, display a transaction cancellation message and terminate the task. Similarly, if the PF11 key is pressed, display a fresh Menu screen for starting over again. Return with the external transaction id = MAC1 and internal transaction id = MAC2.

Program MKT1MAC6 (Action Inquiry)

1. The program begins with receiving control from another program. Read the TSQ Menu Information.
2. Using the customer number given, read all records of the customer in the CMA file sequentially. Depending on the record type (A, B, C, or D), edit the Action Inquiry screen (MAC6), as follows:
3. The customer profile portion of MAC6 screen should be edited using the information from the CMA record type A. The activity field of the MAC6 screen should be CI, RE, or OE for the CMA record type B, C, or D, respectively. In the amount field, the CI activity should have no amount, the RE activity should have the positive amount, and OE activity should have the negative amount from the corresponding record.
4. One MAC6 screen can contain a maximum of five activities. If the screen becomes full, send it as a multipage message. Keep sending (accumulating) the MAC6 screen in the form of the

multipage message until EOF is detected or the next customer's record is read, whichever comes first. The page number on the MAC6 screen must be incremented accordingly.

5. Send (accumulate) the Menu screen (MAC2) as the last page of the logical message. Then send the entire logical message.

6. Terminate the task in such a way that after retrieving pages, the user can enter data in the fresh Menu screen for starting a new entry for another customer. That is, return with the external transaction id = MAC1 and internal transaction id = MAC2.

19.7 Psudo-Coding

As described in the previous section, the specifications of five MACS programs have been well-defined. Mr. McMillan himself reviewed and approved them as they satisfied the functional requirements for the mail order system of Computer Express Co.

However, Mr. McMillan realized that the MACS system is the first CICS application system for his company. Although he had great confidence in his systems analysts and programmers, in order to ensure a smooth system development, he asked Professor Smart to write pseudo-coding for each of five MACS programs based on the specifications.

Professor Smart kindly agreed and came up with the pseudo-coding. According to Professor Smart, the primary objective of his pseudo-coding is to guide the system analysts and programmers for developing the effective and productive MACS system. Therefore, the emphasis is given mainly on how tasks and programs are to be initiated and terminated. The other program logics are described very briefly because these systems analysts and programmers are adequately proficient in ordinary COBOL programming in the batch environment.

In addition, according to Professor Smart, his pseudo-coding should be considered as an example; as such it is not meant to be the only solution available. If there are better approaches, they should be taken as long as they are in accordance with the program specifications.

At this point, Professor Smart felt that his role as an independent consultant to Computer Express Co. has been completed. Therefore, he thanked Mr. McMillan for the challenging task given to him, and wished Mr. McMillan, systems analysts, and programmers good luck with a successful development of the MACS system. Then, Professor Smart left Computer Express Co. and returned to New York University, where he intends to write a case study for his CICS application development course based on his experience with Computer Express Co.

The following is the pseudo-coding of each of five MACS programs which Professor Smart provided to Computer Express Co.:

Program MKT1MAC2 (Menu Handling)

```
    If EIBAID = DFHPF12, go to CANC-RTN.
    If EIBAID = DFHPF11, go to MAC1-RTN.
    If EIBTRNID = 'MAC1' and EIBCALEN = 0, go to MAC1-RTN.
    If EIBTRNID = 'MAC1' and EIBCALEN > 0,
    and the internal transaction-id = 'MAC2', go to MAC2-RTN.
LOGIC-ERR.
    Send an error message and return.
MAC1-RTN.
    Send the map MPBMAC2/MSBMAC2.
    Prepare the internal transaction-id = 'MAC2' in COMMAREA.
    Return with the external transaction-id = 'MAC1' and COMMAREA.
MAC2-RTN.
    Receive the map MPBMAC2/MSBMAC2.
    Validate the data as per the program specifications.
    If there is no error, go to SEL-RTN.
    Prepare the edit error messages.
    Send the map MPBMAC2/MSBMAC2.
    Prepare the internal transaction-id = 'MAC2'.
    Return with the external transaction-id = 'MAC1' and COMMAREA.
SEL-RTN.
    If END is requested, go to END-RTN.
    If the customer is an existing customer, read/update CTL-A-
    RECORD and create the TSQ Menu Information as per the program
    specifications.
    If the customer is a new customer, XCTL to MKT1MAC3.
    If the first action is CI, XCTL to MKT1MAC3.
    If the first action is RE, XCTL to MKT1MAC4.
    If the first action is OE, XCTL to MKT1MAC5.
    If the first action is AI, XCTL to MKT1MAC6.
    Go to LOGIC-ERR.
END-RTN.
    Delete the TSQ Menu Information.
    Send a transaction completion message.
    Return.
CANC-RTN.
    Send a cancellation message.
    Return.
```

Program MKT1MAC3 (Customer Information)

```
        If EIBFN = X'0E04' (i.e., 3588), go to XCTL-RTN.
        If EIBAID = DFHPF12, go to CANC-RTN.
        If EIBAID = DFHPF11, go to NO-MORE-ACTION.
        If EIBTRNID = 'MAC3', go to MAC3-RTN.
LOGIC-ERR.
        Send an error message and return.
XCTL-RTN.
        Read TSQ Menu Information.
        If the new customer flag = 'Y', go to NEW-CUST.
        Do the existing customer logic as per the program specifica-
        tions.
        Go to SEND1-RTN.
NEW-CUST.
        Do the new customer logic as per the program specifications.
SEND1-RTN.
        Send the map MPBMAC3/MSBMAC3.
        Return with the external transaction-id = 'MAC3'.
MAC3-RTN.
        Read the TSQ Menu Information.
        Receive the map MPBMAC3/MSBMAC3.
        Validate the data as per the program specifications.
        If there is no error, go to UPDT1.
        Prepare the edit error messages.
        Send the map MPBMAC3/MSBMAC3.
        Return with the external transaction-id = 'MAC3'.
UPDT1.
        Do the CMA record update logic as per the program specifica-
        tions.
NEXT-ACTION.
        Read the TSQ Menu Information.
        Reset the CI action (i.e., space out).
        Update the TSQ.
        If the next action is RE, XCTL to MKT1MAC4.
        If the next action is OE, XCTL to MKT1MAC5.
        If the nect action is AI, XCTL to MKT1MAC6.
NO-MORE-ACTION.
        Send the map MPBMAC2/MSBMAC2.
        Prepare the internal transaction-id = 'MAC2' in COMMAREA.
        Return with the external transaction-id = 'MAC1' and COMMAREA.
CANC-RTN.
        Send a cancellation message and return.
```

Program MKT1MAC4 (Remmittance Entry)

```
       If EIBFN = X'0E04' (i.e., 3588), go to XCTL-RTN.
       If EIBAID = DFHPF12, go to CANC-RTN.
       If EIBAID = DFHPF11, go to NO-MORE-ACTION.
       If EIBTRNID = 'MAC4', go to MAC4-RTN.
LOGIC-ERR.
       Send an error message and return.
XCTL-RTN.
       Read the TSQ Menu Information.
       Prepare and send the map MPBMAC4/MSBMAC4.
       Return with the external transaction-id = 'MAC4'.
MAC4-RTN.
       Receive the map MPBMAC4/MSBMAC4.
       Validate the data as per the program specifications.
       If there is no error, go to UPDT1.
       Prepare the edit error messages.
       Send the map MPBMAC4/MSBMAC4.
       Return with the external transaction-id = 'MAC4'.
UPDT1.
       Do the CMA record update logic as per the program specifica-
       tions.
NEXT-ACTION.
       Read the TSQ Menu Information.
       Reset the RE action (i.e., space out).
       Update the TSQ.
       If the next action is OE, XCTL to MKT1MAC5.
       If the next action is AI, XCTL to MKT1MAC6.
NO-MORE-ACTION.
       Send the map MPBMAC2/MSBMAC2.
       Prepare the internal transaction-id = 'MAC2' in COMMAREA.
       Return with the external transaction-id = 'MAC1' and COMMAREA.
CANC-RTN.
       Send a cancellation message and return.
```

Program MKT1MAC5 (Order Entry)

```
       If EIBFN = X'0E04' (i.e., 3588), go to XCTL-RTN.
       If EIBAID = DFHPF12, go to CANC-RTN.
       If EIBAID = DFHPF11, go to NO-MORE-ACTION.
       If EIBTRNID = 'MAC5' and EIBCALEN = 0, go to MAC5-RTN.
       If EIBTRNID = 'MAC5' and EIBCALEN > 0, and
```

the internal transaction-id = 'MACA', go to MACA-RTN.

LOGIC-ERR.

Send an error message and return.

XCTL-RTN.

Read the TSQ Menu Information.

Prepare and send the map MPBMAC5/MSBMAC5.

Return with the external transaction-id = 'MAC5'.

MAC5-RTN.

Receive the map MPBMAC5/MSBMAC5.

Validate the data as per the program specifications.

If no error, go to CONF-RTN.

Prepare the edit error messages.

Send the map MPBMAC5/MSBMAC5.

Return with the external transaction-id = 'MAC5'.

CONF-RTN.

Calculate the net order amount as per the program specifications.

Edit the map MPBMAC5/MSBMAC5 for confirmation.

Brighten the "CONFIRM (Y/N)" title.

Place the cursor at the confirmation field.

Send the map.

Prepare the internal transaction-id = 'MACA' and CMA-D-RECORD
in COMMAREA.

Return with the external transaction-id = 'MAC5 and COMMAREA.

MACA-RTN.

If the confirmation is 'Y', go to UPDT1.

Make the item and quantity fields unprotected. Darken the
confirmation title. Null out all value fields and confirmation field.

Send the map.

Return with the external transaction-id = 'MAC5'.

UPDT1.

Do the CMA record update logic as per the program specifications.

Do the PMA record update logic as per the program specifications.

NEXT-ACTION.

Read the TSQ Menu Information.

Reset the OE action (i.e., space out).

Update the TSQ.

If the next action is AI, XCTL to MKT1MAC6.

NO-MORE-ACTION.

Send the map MPBMAC2/MSBMAC2.

Prepare the internal transaction-id = 'MAC2' in COMMAREA.

Return with the external transaction-id = 'MAC1' and COMMAREA.

CANC-RTN.

Send a cancellation message and return.

Program MKT1MAC6 (Activity Inquiry)

If EIBFN = X'0E04' (i.e., 3588), go to XCTL-RTN.

LOGIC-ERR.

Send an error message and return.

XCTL-RTN.

Read the TSQ Menu Information.

Given the customer number, start browsing the CMA file for the customer.

Read next to get the record of the customer.

Depending on the record type, prepare the map MPBMAC6/MSBMAC6 as per the program specifications.

If the map is full, send the map MPBMAC6/MSBMAC6 with ACCUM and PAGING.

Repeat until the end of file is reached or the record of another customer is read.

EOF-RTN.

Send the map MPBMAC6/MSBMAC6 with ACCUM and PAGING for the remaining lines.

Send the map MPBMAC2/MSBMAC2 with ACCUM and PAGING.

Send page.

Prepare the internal transaction-id = 'MAC2' in COMMAREA.

Return with the external transaction-id = 'MAC1' and COMMAREA.

Sample Program

Appendix A provides a complete CICS application program (command level) using COBOL as a sample program which is often referred to in this book. Since this program uses a reasonable variety of CICS commands and programming techniques, all of which have been discussed in this book, this program could be used as a prototype model for the typical CICS application program (command level).

Program Overview

The program name is TXTSPNC1 and the associated transaction id (external) is PNC1. The program uses a BMS map/mapset (MPBPNC2/MSBPNC2) which was coded in Chapter 8. It also uses a VSAM/KSDS file called Personnel Master File (PERVSPMS), which was used in the Exercises for Chapter 4 and other chapters of this book. The main functions of the program are documented in the source program itself.

Programming Techniques Used

The program TXTSPNC1 uses various programming techniques which are very useful for CICS application development. The notable programming techniques used are the following:

Pseudo-Conversation This program uses pseudo-conversational technique 3, which was discussed in Chapter 3. The external transaction id is PNC1 and the internal transaction id is PNC2. The MAINLINE section shows how the first iteration (PNC1 routine) and second iteration (PNC2 routine) are distinguished based on EIBTRNID, EIBCALEN, and data in DFHCOMMAREA. Since pseudo-conversation improves system efficiency, and since technique 3 is the best approach for pseudo-conversation, all CICS application programs should be written in this way.

PF Key This program interrupts processing if the PF12 is pressed by the terminal user. This is accomplished by checking EIBAID field, as shown in the MAINLINE section. A similar technique can be used for detecting other PF keys which could have other functions based on the system convention. This technique increases the user-friendliness and functionality of the program.

Command Subroutine In this program, every CICS command (except the HANDLE CONDITION command) is coded in a form of subroutine, placed in back of the program, and performed from the main body of the program. This is called the CICS command subroutine approach, as discussed in Chapter 10. The advantage of this approach is that each command is standardized and can be performed as many as required. This approach also makes the fact less disturbing that the command translator comments the CICS command, shifts to the left, and inserts COBOL statements. Therefore, this approach significantly increases program maintainability.

Occurrence Handling If a BMS map has repeated lines, each of which consists of more than one field, the symbolic map becomes very difficult to use because of the large number of unique field names. The occurrence handling approach solves this problem, as discussed in Chapter 10. In this program, the symbolic map MPBPNC2/MSBPNC2 is intentionally redefined so that the program can use a subscript representing the line counter for identifying the fields of the line. This technique is very convenient, practical and useful. It significantly improves the program maintainability.

Translation, Compile, and Linkedit

Translation The first list in this appendix is the source list of the program TXTSPNC1, which is produced by the command translator. The source list shows the original coding. The second list is the compile list produced by the COBOL compiler. There are significant differences between the source list and compile list. These differences are results of either translation by the command translator or COBOL COPY statements. As can be seen, the command translator automatically inserts certain CICS-related field definitions or COBOL statements. The most notable one is that every CICS command is commented, shifted to the left, and new COBOL statements are added.

Compile Once CICS command translation is completed by the command translator, the program becomes a pure COBOL program. Therefore, compiling is done the same as the batch program compile. The only exception is that CICS-related COPYLIB members are copied into. In this program, the copied members are symbolic map MPBPNC2/MSBPNC2, DFHAID, and DFHBMSCA. As to compiler options, CLIST (or OFFSET if COBOL II is used) should be specified for program debugging purposes.

Linkedit After the completion of program compile, the program is linkedited as usual. The third list of this appendix is the linkedit list. It should be noted that the first control section name is DFHECI, followed by program TXTSPNC1. DFHECI is the CICS application interface program, which interfaces between CICS and the application program (TXTSPNC1, in this case). The existence of DFHECI should be remembered, for it is used at dump analysis time.

Program Execution

PPT, PCT, and FCT were properly prepared for this transaction and program. Then the program was actually executed using transaction id PNC1.

However, one program bug, which was not related to CICS, was intentionally included in the program. Therefore, execution of this program was abnormally terminated with the ABEND dump. The fourth list of this appendix is the ABEND dump from CICS. The cause of this ABEND was analyzed in Chapter 16 based on the ABEND dump included in this appendix.

Attached Lists

Following is the complete set of source list, compile list, linkedit list, and ABEND dump list of the program TXTSPNC1, based on VS/COBOL (Release 2.4), CICS/MVS (Version 2.1), and MVS/XA (Version 2.2):

CICS/MVS COMMAND LANGUAGE TRANSLATOR VERSION 2.1   TIME 15.06 DATE 8 AUG 89   PAGE   1

OPTIONS SPECIFIED:-NOSEQ,LANGLVL(2)

OPTIONS IN EFFECT

```
     CICS
     DEBUG
NOFE
     SPIE
     EDF
     LINECOUNT(60)
     TABLE(DFHEITAB)
     SOURCE
NOVBREF
     OPTIONS
     FLAG(W)
NOSEQ
     APOST
NONUM
     OPT
     SPACE(1)
     LANGLVL(2)
```

LINE   SOURCE LISTING

```
00001   000700 IDENTIFICATION DIVISION.
00002   000100 ****************************************************************
00003   000200 *                                                            * *
00004   000300 *         SAMPLE CICS APPLICATION PROGRAM (COMMAND LEVEL)     * *
00005   000400 *                                                            * *
00006   000500 ****************************************************************
00007   000600 PROGRAM-ID.         TXTSPNC1.
00008   000800 AUTHOR.             Y.K.
00009   000900
00010   001000 ****************************************************************
00011   001100 *                                                              *
00012   001200 * PROGRAM TITLE:    PERSONNEL NAME CHANGE PROGRAM              *
00013   001300 *                                                              *
00014   001400 * TRANSACTION-ID:   EXTERNAL = PNC1                            *
00015   001500 *                   INTERNAL = PNC2                            *
00016   001600 *                                                              *
00017   001700 * MAP/MAPSET:       MPBPNC2/MSBPNC2                            *
00018   001710 *                                                              *
00019   001720 *                                                              *
00020   001730 *                                                              *
00021   001800 * OBJECTIVE:                                                   *
00022   001900 * ---------                                                    *
00023   002000 * THIS IS A SAMPLE CICS APPLICATION PROGRAM (COMMAND LEVEL) IN *
00024   002100 * ORDER TO SHOW THE PROGRAM STRUCTURE, BMS MAP, CICS COMMANDS. *
00025   002200 * AND VARIOUS PROGRAMMING TECHNIQUES.                          *
00026   002300 *                                                              *
00027   002400 * MAIN FUNCTIONS:                                              *
00028   002600 * --------------                                               *
00029   002700 * (1) UPON RECEIVING CONTROL, SEND MAP/MAPSET MPBPNC2/MSBPNC2, *
00030   002800 *     AND RETURN WITH EXTERNAL TRANS-ID=PNC1, INTERNAL TRANS-ID=*
00031   002900 *     PNC2.                                                     *
00032   003000 * (2) RECEIVING CONTROL NEXT, RECEIVE THE MAP AND VERIFY DATA. *
00033   003100 *     IF THERE ARE ERRORS, POSITION THE CURSOR AT THE FIELDS.  *
00034   003200 *     HIGHLIGHT THE FIELDS, SEND ERROR MESSAGES, AND RETURN    *
```

```
CICS/MVS COMMAND LANGUAGE TRANSLATOR VERSION 2.1                                TIME 15.06 DATE 8 AUG 89     PAGE 2

  LINE      SOURCE LISTING

00035   003300*
00036   003310*                 WITH EXTERNAL TRANS-ID=PNC1 AND INTERNAL TRANS-ID=PNC2,
00037   003500*            (3)  SO THAT THE USER COULD CORRECT AND REENTER.
00038   003510*                 IF NO ERROR EXISTS, UPDATE PMS FILE BASED ON THE DATA
00039   003600*                 RECEIVED.
00040   003700*            (4)  SEND A COMPLETION MESSAGE AND TERMINATE THE TASK.
00041   003800*            (5)  HANDLE CONDITION IS APPLIED TO INTERCEPT EXCEPTiONAL
00042   003900*                 CONDITIONS.
00043   004000*            (6)  PSEUDO-CONVERSATION IS MAINTAINED.
00044   004100*            (7)  THE SIMPLE CICS COMMAND SUBROUTINE APPROACH IS USED.
00045   004200*
00046   004300************************************************************
00047   004400  ENVIRONMENT DIVISION.
00048   004500  DATA DIVISION.
00049   004600*
00050   004700  WORKING-STORAGE SECTION.
00051   004800*
00052   004900  01  MAP I-O AREA
00053   005000      COPY MSBPNC2.
00054   005100*
00055   005200* MAP REDEFINITION FOR OCCURRENCE HANDLING.
00056   005300  01  MPBPNC2-REDEFINE REDEFINES MPBPNC2I.
00057   005400      05  FILLER                  PIC X(12).
00058   005500      05  FILLER OCCURS 2 TIMES.
00059   005600          10  M2EMPNNL            PIC S9(4) COMP.
00060   005700          10  M2EMPNNA            PIC X.
00061   005800          10  M2EMPNNI            PIC 9(5).
00062   005810          10  FILLER REDEFINES M2EMPNNI
00063   005820              15  M2EMPNNO        PIC 9(5).
00064   005900          10  M2NAMENL            PIC S9(4) COMP.
00065   006000          10  M2NAMENA            PIC X.
00066   006100          10  M2NAMENI            PIC X(25).
00067   006110          10  FILLER REDEFINES M2NAMENI
00068   006120              15  M2NAMENO        PIC X(25).
00069   006200      05  FILLER OCCURS 4 TIMES.
00070   006300          10  M2ERRNL             PIC S9(4) COMP.
00071   006400          10  M2ERRNA             PIC X.
00072   006500          10  M2ERRNO             PIC X(79).
00073   006600*
00074   006700  01  TC-O-AREA.
00075   006800      05  TC-O1-AREA.
00076   006900          10  FILLER              PIC X(80).
00077   007000*
00078   007100* PMS RECORD DEFINITION (RECORD LENGTH = 88 BYTES)
00079   007200  01  PMS-IOAREA.
00080   007300      05  PMS-RECORD-KEY.
00081   007400          10  PMS-EMPNO           PIC 9(5).
00082   007500      05  PMS-RECORD-DETAIL.
00083   007600          10  PMS-NAME            PIC X(25).
00084   007700          10  PMS-DEPT            PIC X(10).
00085   007800          10  PMS-ROOM            PIC X(10).
00086   007900          10  PMS-EXT             PIC 9(4).
00087   008000          10  PMS-RANK            PIC X(5).
00088   008100          10  PMS-TITLE           PIC X(10).
00089   008200          10  PMS-AGE             PIC 99.
00090   008300          10  PMS-SEX             PIC X.
```

```
LINE       SOURCE LISTING

00091  008400            10  PMS-SALARY      PIC S9(10)V99 COMP-3.
00092  008500            10  PMS-INSPOLICY   PIC S9(7) COMP-3.
00093  008600            10  PMS-INSPREM     PIC S9(7)V99 COMP-3.
00094  008700*
00095  008800  01  WK-COMMAREA.
00096  008900      05  WK-COM-INTTRAN        PIC X(4).
00097  009000*
00098  009100  01  WK-CICS-WORK.
00099  009200      05  CSCO-LENGTH           PIC S9(4) COMP.
00100  009300      05  CSFC-LENGTH           PIC S9(4) COMP.
00101  009400      05  CSHC-ALLOW            PIC X.
00102  009500      05  CSHC-NOTFND           PIC X.
00103  009600      05  CSPC-TRANSID          PIC X(4).
00104  009700      05  CSTC-LENGTH           PIC S9(4) COMP.
00105  009800*
00106  009900      05  WK-LINE-CNT           PIC S999.
00107  010000      05  WK-ERR-CNT            PIC S999 VALUE ZERO.
00108  010100*
00109  010200      COPY DFHAID.
00110  010300      COPY DFHBMSCA.
00111  010400*
00112  010500  LINKAGE SECTION.
00113  010600  01  DFHCOMMAREA.
00114  010700      05  LK-COM-INTTRAN        PIC X(4).
00115  010800*
00116  010900  PROCEDURE DIVISION.
00117  011000******************************************************
00118  011100* MAINLINE PROCESSING                                 *
00119  011200******************************************************
00120  011300******************************************************
00121  011400*
00122  011500  MAIN-0000-MAINLINE SECTION.
00123  011600*
00124  011700      IF EIBTRNID NOT = 'PNC1'
00125  011800         PERFORM X100-LOGICERR-ROUTINE
00126  011900         GO TO MAIN-9999-GOBACK.
00127  012000      IF EIBAID = DFHPF12
00128  012100         PERFORM X200-FORCE-CANCEL
00129  012200         GO TO MAIN-9999-GOBACK.
00130  012300      IF EIBCALEN = 0
00131  012400         PERFORM A000-PNC1-ROUTINE
00132  012500         GO TO MAIN-9999-GOBACK.
00133  012600      IF LK-COM-INTTRAN = 'PNC2'
00134  012700         PERFORM B000-PNC2-ROUTINE
00135  012800         GO TO MAIN-9999-GOBACK
00136  012900         PERFORM X100-LOGICERR-ROUTINE.
00137  013000*
00138  013100  MAIN-9999-GOBACK.
00139  013200      GOBACK.
00140  013300******************************************************
00141  013400* PNC1 PROCESSING                                     *
00142  013500******************************************************
00143  013600******************************************************
00144  013700  A000-PNC1-ROUTINE SECTION.
00145  013800*
00146  013900* SEND MAP PNC2.
```

```
LINE      SOURCE LISTING

00147     014000 A100-SEND-MAP.
00148     014100        MOVE LOW-VALUES TO MPBPNC20.
00149     014110        MOVE -1          TO M2EMPN1L.
00150     014200        PERFORM ZBM20-PNC2-SEND.
00151     014300*
00152     014400* RETURN WITH INTERNAL TRANSID = PNC2.
00153     014500 A200-RETURN-WITH-TRANSID.
00154     014600        MOVE 'PNC1' TO CSPC-TRANSID.
00155     014700        MOVE 'PNC2' TO WK-COM-INTTRAN.
00156     014800        MOVE 4 TO CSCO-LENGTH.
00157     014900        PERFORM ZPC20-PC-RETURN-TRANSID-COM.
00158     015000*
00159     015100 A999-EXIT.
00160     015200        EXIT.
00161     015300*
00162     015400* ***********************************************************
00163     015500* PNC2 PROCESSING                                           *
00164     015600* ***********************************************************
00165     015700*
00166     015800 B000-PNC2-ROUTINE SECTION.
00167     015900*
00168     016000* RECEIVE MAP.
00169     016100 B100-RECEIVE-MAP.
00170     016200        PERFORM ZBM10-PNC2-RECEIVE.
00171     016300*
00172     016400* VALIDATE INPUT DATA.
00173     016500        IF LOW-VALUE = M2EMPN1I AND M2EMPN2I
00174     016600           ADD 1 TO WK-ERR-CNT
00175     016700           MOVE ' AT LEAST ONE LINE MUST BE ENTERED.'
00176     016800                TO M2ERRNO (WK-ERR-CNT)
00177     016900           GO TO B120-CHECK-ERR.
00178     017000 B110-EDIT-LOOP.
00179     017100        ADD 1 TO WK-LINE-CNT.
00180     017200        IF M2EMPN1I (WK-LINE-CNT) = LOW-VALUES
00181     017300           GO TO B115-EDIT-SKIP.
00182     017400        MOVE M2EMPN1I (WK-LINE-CNT) TO PMS-EMPNO.
00183     017500        MOVE '1 TO CSHC-ALLOW.
00184     017600        MOVE 88 TO CSFC-LENGTH.
00185     017700        PERFORM ZFC10-PMS-READ-FULLKEY.
00186     017800        IF CSHC-NOTFND = '1'
00187     017900           ADD 1 TO WK-ERR-CNT
00188     018000           MOVE 'EMPLOYEE NUMBER NOT FOUND.' TO M2ERRNO (WK-ERR-CNT)
00189     018100           MOVE -1 TO M2EMPNNL (WK-LINE-CNT)
00190     018200           MOVE DFHUNINT TO M2EMPNNA (WK-LINE-CNT).
00191     018300        IF M2NAMENI (WK-LINE-CNT) = LOW-VALUES
00192     018400           ADD 1 TO WK-ERR-CNT
00193     018500           MOVE 'NEW NAME MUST BE ENTERED.' TO M2ERRNO (WK-ERR-CNT)
00194     018600           MOVE -1 TO M2NAMENL (WK-LINE-CNT)
00195     018700           MOVE DFHUNINT TO M2NAMENA (WK-LINE-CNT).
00196     018800 B115-EDIT-SKIP.
00197     018900        IF WK-LINE-CNT < 3
00198     019000           GO TO B110-EDIT-LOOP.
00199     019100 B120-CHECK-ERR.
00200     019200        IF WK-ERR-CNT = ZERO
00201     019300           GO TO B200-VALID-DATA.
00202     019400*
```

CICS/MVS COMMAND LANGUAGE TRANSLATOR VERSION 2.1   TIME 15.06 DATE 8 AUG 89   PAGE 5

LINE   SOURCE LISTING

```
00203  019500* DATA INVALID.  SEND ERR MSG AND RETURN FOR REENTRY.
00204  019600  B130-INVALID-DATA.
00205  019700     PERFORM ZBM20-PNC2-SEND.
00206  019800     MOVE 'PNC1' TO CSPC-TRANSID.
00207  019900     MOVE 'PNC2' TO WK-COM-INTTRAN.
00208  020000     MOVE 4 TO CSCO-LENGTH.
00209  020100     PERFORM ZPC20-PC-RETURN-TRANSID-COM.
00210  020200     GO TO B999-EXIT.
00211  020300*
00212  020400* DATA VALID.  UPDATE PMS FILE.
00213  020500  B200-VALID-DATA.
00214  020600     MOVE ZERO TO WK-LINE-CNT.
00215  020700  B210-UPDATE-LOOP.
00216  020800     IF M2EMPNNI (WK-LINE-CNT) = LOW-VALUES
00217  020900        GO TO B215-UPDATE-SKIP
00218  021000     MOVE M2EMPNNI (WK-LINE-CNT) TO PMS-EMPNO.
00219  021100     MOVE 88 TO CSFC-LENGTH.
00220  021200     MOVE '8' TO CSHC-ALLOW.
00221  021300     PERFORM ZFC20-PMS-READ-FULLKEY-UPDATE.
00222  021400     MOVE M2NAMENI (WK-LINE-CNT) TO PMS-NAME.
00223  021500     PERFORM ZFC30-PMS-REWRITE.
00224  021600  B215-UPDATE-SKIP.
00225  021700     IF WK-LINE-CNT < 3
00226  021800        GO TO B210-UPDATE-LOOP.
00227  021900*
00228  022000* SEND COMPLETION MESSAGE AND RETURN.
00229  022100     MOVE 'TRANSACTION PNC1 SUCCESSFULLY COMPLETED.' TO TC-O-AREA.
00230  022200     MOVE 40 TO CSTC-LENGTH.
00231  022300     PERFORM ZTC20-TC-SEND.
00232  022400     PERFORM ZPC10-PC-RETURN.
00233  022500*
00234  022600  B999-EXIT.
00235  022700     EXIT.
00236  022800*
00237  022900***********************************************
00238  023000*         APPLICATION SUBROUTINES             *
00239  023100***********************************************
00240  023200*
00241  023300  X100-LOGICERR-ROUTINE SECTION.
00242  023400     MOVE 'LOGIC ERROR.  TRANSACTION CANCELED.'
00243  023500        TO TC-O-AREA.
00244  023600     MOVE 35 TO CSTC-LENGTH.
00245  023700     PERFORM ZTC20-TC-SEND.
00246  023800     PERFORM ZPC10-PC-RETURN.
00247  023900  X199-EXIT.
00248  024000     EXIT.
00249  024100*
00250  024200  X200-FORCE-CANCEL SECTION.
00251  024300     MOVE 'TRANSACTION CANCELED BY OPERATOR REQUEST.'
00252  024400        TO TC-O-AREA.
00253  024500     MOVE 42 TO CSTC-LENGTH.
00254  024600     PERFORM ZTC20-TC-SEND.
00255  024700     PERFORM ZPC10-PC-RETURN.
00256  024800  X199-EXIT.
00257  024900     EXIT.
00258  025000*
```

```
LINE        SOURCE LISTING

00259   025100*****************************************************
00260   025200*          CICS COMMAND SUBROUTINES                 *
00261   025300*****************************************************
00262   025400*
00263   025500  ZBM10-PNC2-RECEIVE SECTION.
00264   025600      EXEC CICS HANDLE CONDITION
00265   025700          ERROR(ZBM1A-ERROR)
00266   025800      END-EXEC.
00267   025900      EXEC CICS RECEIVE
00268   026000          MAP('MPBPNC2')
00269   026100          MAPSET('MSBPNC2')
00270   026200      END-EXEC.
00271   026300      GO TO ZBM19-EXIT.
00272   026400*
00273   026500  ZBM1A-ERROR.
00274   026600      MOVE 'GEN ERROR OCCURRED AT PNC2 RECEIVE.   TRANS CANCELED.'
00275   026700          TO TC-O-AREA.
00276   026800      MOVE 49 TO CSTC-LENGTH.
00277   026900  ZBM1X-SEND-RETURN.
00278   027000      PERFORM ZTC30-TC-SEND-NOHANDLE.
00279   027100      PERFORM ZPC10-PC-RETURN.
00280   027200      GOBACK.
00281   027300*
00282   027400  ZBM19-EXIT.
00283   027500      EXIT.
00284   027600*
00285   027700*****************************************************
00286   027800*
00287   027900  ZBM20-PNC2-SEND SECTION.
00288   028000      EXEC CICS HANDLE CONDITION
00289   028100          ERROR(ZBM2A-ERROR)
00290   028200      END-EXEC.
00291   028300      EXEC CICS SEND
00292   028400          MAP('MPBPNC2')
00293   028500          MAPSET('MSBPNC2')
00294   028600          ERASE
00295   028700          CURSOR
00296   028800      END-EXEC.
00297   028900      GO TO ZBM29-EXIT.
00298   029000*
00299   029100  ZBM2A-ERROR.
00300   029200      MOVE 'GEN ERROR OCCURRED AT PNC2 SEND.   TRANS CANCELED.'
00301   029300          TO TC-O-AREA.
00302   029400      MOVE 49 TO CSTC-LENGTH.
00303   029500  ZBM2X-SEND-RETURN.
00304   029600      PERFORM ZTC30-TC-SEND-NOHANDLE.
00305   029700      PERFORM ZPC10-PC-RETURN.
00306   029800      GOBACK.
00307   029900*
00308   030000  ZBM29-EXIT.
00309   030100      EXIT.
00310   030200*
00311   030300*****************************************************
00312   030400*
00313   030500  ZFC10-PMS-READ-FULLKEY SECTION.
00314   030600      MOVE 'O' TO CSHC-NOTFND.
```

CICS/MVS COMMAND LANGUAGE TRANSLATOR VERSION 2.1

SOURCE LISTING

```
LINE

00315  030700       EXEC CICS HANDLE CONDITION
00316  030800            NOTFND(ZFC1A-NOTFND)
00317  030900            ERROR(ZFC1B-ERROR)
00318  031000       END-EXEC.
00319  031100       EXEC CICS READ
00320  031200            DATASET('PERVSPMS')
00321  031300            INTO(PMS-IOAREA)
00322  031400            RIDFLD(PMS-RECORD-KEY)
00323  031500            LENGTH(CSFC-LENGTH)
00324  031600       END-EXEC.
00325  031700       MOVE '0' TO CSHC-ALLOW
00326  031800       GO TO ZFC19-EXIT.
00327  031900*
00328  032000   ZFC1A-NOTFND.
00329  032100       IF CSHC-ALLOW = '1'
00330  032200           MOVE '0' TO CSHC-ALLOW
00331  032300           MOVE '1' TO CSHC-NOTFND
00332  032400           GO TO ZFC19-EXIT.
00333  032500       MOVE 'RECORD NOT FOUND AT READ-FK.  TRANS CANCELED.'
00334  032600           TO TC-O-AREA.
00335  032700       MOVE 46 TO CSTC-LENGTH.
00336  032800       GO TO ZFC1X-SEND-RETURN.
00337  032900*
00338  033000   ZFC1B-ERROR.
00339  033100       MOVE 'GEN ERROR OCCURRED AT READ-FK.  TRANS CANCELED.'
00340  033200           TO TC-O-AREA.
00341  033300       MOVE 47 TO CSTC-LENGTH.
00342  033400   ZFC1X-SEND-RETURN.
00343  033500       PERFORM ZTC30-TC-SEND-NOHANDLE.
00344  033600       PERFORM ZPC10-PC-RETURN.
00345  033700       GOBACK.
00346  033800*
00347  033900   ZFC19-EXIT.
00348  034000       EXIT.
00349  034100 ****************************************************
00350  034200 ****************************************************
00351  034300   ZFC20-PMS-READ-FULLKEY-UPDATE SECTION.
00352  034400       MOVE '0' TO CSHC-NOTFND.
00353  034500       EXEC CICS HANDLE CONDITION
00354  034600            NOTFND(ZFC2A-NOTFND)
00355  034700            ERROR(ZFC2B-ERROR)
00356  034800       END-EXEC.
00357  034900       EXEC CICS READ
00358  035000            DATASET('PERVSPMS')
00359  035100            INTO(PMS-IOAREA)
00360  035200            RIDFLD(PMS-RECORD-KEY)
00361  035300            LENGTH(CSFC-LENGTH)
00362  035400            UPDATE
00363  035500       END-EXEC.
00364  035600       MOVE '0' TO CSHC-ALLOW.
00365  035700       GO TO ZFC29-EXIT.
00366  035800*
00367  035900   ZFC2A-NOTFND.
00368  036000       IF CSHC-ALLOW = '1'
00369  036100           MOVE '0' TO CSHC-ALLOW
00370  036200           MOVE '0' TO CSHC-ALLOW
```

CICS/MVS COMMAND LANGUAGE TRANSLATOR VERSION 2.1   TIME 15.06 DATE 8 AUG 89   PAGE 8

LINE   SOURCE LISTING

```
00371    036300              MOVE '1' TO CSHC-NOTFND
00372    036400              GO TO ZFC19-EXIT.
00373    036600         MOVE RECORD NOT FOUND AT READ-FK-UPD.  TRANS CANCELED.'
00374    036600              TO TC-O-AREA.
00375    036700         MOVE 50 TO CSTC-LENGTH.
00376    036800         GO TO ZFC2X-SEND-RETURN.
00377    036900*
00378    037000    ZFC2B-ERROR.
00379    037100         MOVE 'GEN ERROR OCCURRED AT READ-FK-UPD.  TRANS CANCELED.'
00380    037200              TO TC-O-AREA.
00381    037300    ZFC2X-SEND-RETURN.
00382    037400         MOVE 51 TO CSTC-LENGTH.
00383    037500         PERFORM ZTC30-TC-SEND-NOHANDLE.
00384    037600         PERFORM ZPC10-PC-RETURN.
00385    037700         GOBACK.
00386    037800*
00387    037900    ZFC29-EXIT.
00388    038000         EXIT.
00389    038100*
00390    038200    ***************************************************************
00391    038300*
00392    038400    ZFC30-PMS-REWRITE SECTION.
00393    038500         EXEC CICS HANDLE CONDITION
00394    038600              ERROR(ZFC3A-ERROR)
00395    038700         END-EXEC.
00396    038800         EXEC CICS REWRITE
00397    038900              DATASET('PERVSPMS')
00398    039000              FROM(PMS-IOAREA)
00399    039100              LENGTH(CSFC-LENGTH)
00400    039200         END-EXEC.
00401    039300         GO TO ZFC29-EXIT.
00402    039400*
00403    039500    ZFC3A-ERROR.
00404    039600         MOVE 'GEN ERROR OCCURRED AT REWRITE.  TRANS CANCELED.'
00405    039700              TO TC-O-AREA.
00406    039800         MOVE 47 TO CSTC-LENGTH.
00407    039900    ZFC3X-SEND-RETURN.
00408    040000         PERFORM ZTC30-TC-SEND-NOHANDLE.
00409    040100         PERFORM ZPC10-PC-RETURN.
00410    040200         GOBACK.
00411    040300*
00412    040400    ZFC39-EXIT.
00413    040500         EXIT.
00414    040600*
00415    040700    ***************************************************************
00416    040800*
00417    040900    ZPC10-PC-RETURN SECTION.
00418    041000         EXEC CICS RETURN
00419    041100         END-EXEC.
00420    041200    ZPC19-EXIT.
00421    041300         EXIT.
00422    041400*
00423    041500*
00424    041600    ZPC20-PC-RETURN-TRANSID-COM SECTION.
00425    041700         EXEC CICS RETURN
00426    041800
```

```
CICS/MVS COMMAND LANGUAGE TRANSLATOR VERSION 2.1                                          TIME 15.06 DATE 8 AUG 89      PAGE 9

LINE        SOURCE LISTING

00427       041900          TRANSID(CSPC-TRANSID)
00428       042000          COMMAREA(WK-COMMAREA)
00429       042100          LENGTH(CSCO-LENGTH)
00430       042200      END-EXEC.
00431       042300  ZPC29-EXIT.
00432       042400      EXIT.
00433       042500*********************************************************
00434       042600*********************************************************
00435       042700
00436       042800  ZTC20-TC-SEND SECTION.
00437       042900      EXEC CICS HANDLE CONDITION
00438       043000          LENGERR(ZTC2A-LENGERR)
00439       043100          ERROR(ZTC2B-ERROR)
00440       043200      END-EXEC.
00441       043300      EXEC CICS SEND
00442       043400          FROM(TC-O-AREA)
00443       043500          LENGTH(CSTC-LENGTH)
00444       043600          ERASE
00445       043700      END-EXEC.
00446       043800      GO TO ZTC29-EXIT.
00447       043900
00448       044000  ZTC2A-LENGERR.
00449       044100      MOVE 'LENGERR OCCURRED AT SEND.  TRANS CANCELED.'
00450       044200          TO TC-O-AREA.
00451       044300      MOVE 42 TO CSTC-LENGTH.
00452       044400      GO TO ZTC2X-SEND-RETURN.
00453       044500
00454       044600  ZTC2B-ERROR.
00455       044700      MOVE 'GENERAL ERROR OCCURRED AT SEND.  TRANS CANCELED.'
00456       044800          TO TC-O-AREA.
00457       044900      MOVE 48 TO CSTC-LENGTH.
00458       045000  ZTC2X-SEND-RETURN.
00459       045100      PERFORM ZTC30-TC-SEND-NOHANDLE.
00460       045200      PERFORM ZPC10-PC-RETURN.
00461       045300      GOBACK.
00462       045400
00463       045500  ZTC29-EXIT
00464       045600      EXIT.
00465       045700*********************************************************
00466       045800*********************************************************
00467       045900
00468       046000  ZTC30-TC-SEND-NOHANDLE SECTION.
00469       046100      EXEC CICS SEND
00470       046200          FROM(TC-O-AREA)
00471       046300          LENGTH(CSTC-LENGTH)
00472       046400          ERASE
00473       046500          NOHANDLE
00474       046600      END-EXEC.
00475       046700  ZTC39-EXIT
00476       046800      EXIT.

NO MESSAGES PRODUCED BY TRANSLATOR.

TRANSLATION TIME:-   0.00 MINS.
```

```
00001  000700 IDENTIFICATION DIVISION.
00002  000100*****************************************************************
00003  000200*                                                               *
00004  000300*         SAMPLE CICS APPLICATION PROGRAM (COMMAND LEVEL)        *
00005  000400*                                                               *
00006  000500*****************************************************************
00007  000600*
00008  000800 PROGRAM-ID.            TXTSPNC1.
00009  000900 AUTHOR.               Y.K.
00010  001000*
00011  001100*****************************************************************
00012  001200*
00013  001300 PROGRAM TITLE:      PERSONNEL NAME CHANGE PROGRAM
00014  001400*
00015  001500 TRANSACTION-ID:      EXTERNAL = PNC1
00016  001600*                     INTERNAL = PNC2
00017  001700*
00018  001710 MAP/MAPSET:         MPBPNC2/MSBPNC2
00019  001720*
00020  001730*
00021  001800 OBJECTIVE:
00022  001900*-----------
00023  002000*    THIS IS A SAMPLE CICS APPLICATION PROGRAM (COMMAND LEVEL) IN
00024  002100*    ORDER TO SHOW THE PROGRAM STRUCTURE, BMS MAP, CICS COMMANDS,
00025  002200*    AND VARIOUS PROGRAMMING TECHNIQUES.
00026  002300*
00027  002400 MAIN FUNCTIONS:
00028  002500*---------------
00029  002700*  (1)  UPON RECEIVING CONTROL, SEND MAP/MAPSET MPBPNC2/MSBPNC2,
00030  002800*       AND RETURN WITH EXTERNAL TRANS-ID=PNC1, INTERNAL TRANS-ID=
00031  002900*       PNC2.
00032  003000*  (2)  RECEIVING CONTROL NEXT, RECEIVE THE MAP AND VERIFY DATA.
00033  003100*       IF THERE ARE ERRORS, POSITION THE CURSOR AT THE FIELDS,
00034  003200*       HIGHLIGHT THE FIELDS, SEND ERROR MESSAGES, AND RETURN
00035  003300*       WITH EXTERNAL TRANS-ID=PNC1 AND INTERNAL TRANS-ID=PNC2.
00036  003310*       SO THAT THE USER COULD CORRECT AND REENTER.
00037  003500*  (3)  IF NO ERROR EXISTS, UPDATE PMS FILE BASED ON THE DATA
00038  003510*       RECEIVED.
00039  003600*  (4)  SEND A COMPLETION MESSAGE AND TERMINATE THE TASK.
00040  003700*  (5)  HANDLE CONDITION IS APPLIED TO INTERCEPT EXCEPTIONAL
00041  003800*       CONDITIONS.
00042  003900*  (6)  PSEUDO-CONVERSATION IS MAINTAINED.
00043  004000*  (7)  THE SIMPLE CICS COMMAND SUBROUTINE APPROACH IS USED.
00044  004100*
00045  004200*****************************************************************
00046  004300*
00047  004400 ENVIRONMENT DIVISION.
00048  004500 DATA DIVISION.
00049  004600*
00050  004700 WORKING-STORAGE SECTION.
00051  004800*
00052  004900*    MAP I-O AREA
00053  005000     COPY MSBPNC2.
00054 C          01  MPBPNC2I.
```

```
2   TXTSPNC1          15.06.28        AUG  8.1989

00055 C        02  FILLER PIC X(12).
00056 C        02  M2EMPN1L COMP  PIC  S9(4).
00057 C        02  M2EMPN1F PICTURE X.
00058 C        02  FILLER REDEFINES M2EMPN1F.
00059 C          03  M2EMPN1A PICTURE X.
00060 C        02  M2EMPN1I PIC 9(5).
00061 C        02  M2NAME1L COMP  PIC  S9(4).
00062 C        02  M2NAME1F PICTURE X.
00063 C        02  FILLER REDEFINES M2NAME1F.
00064 C          03  M2NAME1A PICTURE X.
00065 C        02  M2NAME1I PIC X(25).
00066 C        02  M2EMPN2L COMP  PIC  S9(4).
00067 C        02  M2EMPN2F PICTURE X.
00068 C        02  FILLER REDEFINES M2EMPN2F.
00069 C          03  M2EMPN2A PICTURE X.
00070 C        02  M2EMPN2I PIC 9(5).
00071 C        02  M2NAME2L COMP  PIC  S9(4).
00072 C        02  M2NAME2F PICTURE X.
00073 C        02  FILLER REDEFINES M2NAME2F.
00074 C          03  M2NAME2A PICTURE X.
00075 C        02  M2NAME2I PIC X(25).
00076 C        02  M2ERR1L COMP  PIC  S9(4).
00077 C        02  M2ERR1F PICTURE X.
00078 C        02  FILLER REDEFINES M2ERR1F.
00079 C          03  M2ERR1A PICTURE X.
00080 C        02  M2ERR1I PIC X(79).
00081 C        02  M2ERR2L COMP  PIC  S9(4).
00082 C        02  M2ERR2F PICTURE X.
00083 C        02  FILLER REDEFINES M2ERR2F.
00084 C          03  M2ERR2A PICTURE X.
00085 C        02  M2ERR2I PIC X(79).
00086 C        02  M2ERR3L COMP  PIC  S9(4).
00087 C        02  M2ERR3F PICTURE X.
00088 C        02  FILLER REDEFINES M2ERR3F.
00089 C          03  M2ERR3A PICTURE X.
00090 C        02  M2ERR3I PIC X(79).
00091 C        02  M2ERR4L COMP  PIC  S9(4).
00092 C        02  M2ERR4F PICTURE X.
00093 C        02  FILLER REDEFINES M2ERR4F.
00094 C          03  M2ERR4A PICTURE X.
00095 C        02  M2ERR4I PIC X(79).
00096 C    01  MPBPNC2O REDEFINES MPBPNC2I.
00097 C        02  FILLER PIC X(12).
00098 C        02  FILLER PICTURE X(3).
00099 C        02  M2EMPN1O PIC 9(5).
00100 C        02  FILLER PICTURE X(3).
00101 C        02  M2NAME1O PIC X(25).
00102 C        02  FILLER PICTURE X(3).
00103 C        02  M2EMPN2O PIC 9(5).
00104 C        02  FILLER PICTURE X(3).
00105 C        02  M2NAME2O PIC X(25).
00106 C        02  FILLER PICTURE X(3).
00107 C        02  M2ERR1O PIC X(79).
00108 C        02  FILLER PICTURE X(3).
00109 C        02  M2ERR2O PIC X(79).
00110 C        02  FILLER PICTURE X(3).
00111 C        02  M2ERR3O PIC X(79).
```

```
3        TXTSPNC1           15.06.28      AUG  8,1989

00112 C
00113 C
00114    005100*
00115    005200*   MAP REDEFINITION FOR OCCURRENCE HANDLING.
00116    005300  01   MPBPNC2-REDEFINE REDEFINES MPBPNC21.
00117    005400       05   FILLER                      PIC X(12).
00118    005500       05   FILLER OCCURS 2 TIMES.
00119    005600            10   M2EMPNNL               PIC S9(4) COMP.
00120    005700            10   M2EMPNNA               PIC X.
00121    005800            10   M2EMPNNI               PIC 9(5).
00122    005810            10   FILLER REDEFINES M2EMPNNI
00123    005820                 15   M2EMPNNO          PIC 9(5).
00124    005900            10   M2NAMENL               PIC S9(4) COMP.
00125    006000            10   M2NAMENA               PIC X.
00126    006100            10   M2NAMENI               PIC X(25).
00127    006110            10   FILLER REDEFINES M2NAMENI
00128    006120                 15   M2NAMENO          PIC X(25).
00129    006200       05   FILLER OCCURS 4 TIMES.
00130    006300            10   M2ERRNL                PIC S9(4) COMP.
00131    006400            10   M2ERRNA                PIC X.
00132    006500            10   M2ERRNO                PIC X(79).
00133    006600*
00134    006700  01   TC-O-AREA.
00135    006800       05   TC-O1-AREA                  PIC X(80).
00136    006900       10   FILLER
00137    007000*
00138    007100   PMS RECORD DEFINITION (RECORD LENGTH = 88 BYTES)
00139    007200   PMS-IOAREA.
00140    007300  01   PMS-RECORD-KEY.
00141    007400       05   PMS-EMPNO                   PIC 9(5).
00142    007500       05   PMS-RECORD-DETAIL.
00143    007600            10   PMS-NAME               PIC X(25).
00144    007700            10   PMS-DEPT               PIC X(10).
00145    007800            10   PMS-ROOM               PIC X(10).
00146    007900            10   PMS-EXT                PIC 9(4).
00147    008000            10   PMS-RANK               PIC X(5).
00148    008100            10   PMS-TITLE              PIC X(10).
00149    008200            10   PMS-AGE                PIC 99.
00150    008300            10   PMS-SEX                PIC X.
00151    008400            10   PMS-SALARY             PIC S9(10)V99 COMP-3.
00152    008500            10   PMS-INSPOLICY          PIC 9(7) COMP-3.
00153    008600            10   PMS-INSPREM            PIC S9(7)V99 COMP-3.
00154    008700*
00155    008800  01   WK-COMMAREA.
00156    008900       05   WK-COM-INTTRAN             PIC X(4).
00157    009000*
00158    009100  01   WK-CICS-WORK.
00159    009200       05   CSCO-LENGTH                PIC S9(4) COMP.
00160    009300       05   CSFC-LENGTH                PIC S9(4) COMP.
00161    009400       05   CSHC-ALLOW                 PIC X.
00162    009500       05   CSHC-NOTFND                PIC X.
00163    009600       05   CSPC-TRANSID               PIC X(4).
00164    009700       05   CSTC-LENGTH                PIC S9(4) COMP.
00165    009800*
00166    009900       05   WK-LINE-CNT                PIC S999.
00167    010000       05   WK-ERR-CNT                 PIC S999 VALUE ZERO.
00168    010100*
```

```
4        TXTSPNC1        15.06.28        AUG  8,1989

00169
00170   010200 C       01  COPY DFHAID.
               C          01  DFHAID.
00171          C             02  DFHNULL   PIC X   VALUE IS ' '.      02000000
00172          C             02  DFHENTER  PIC X   VALUE IS QUOTE.    04000000
00173          C             02  DFHCLEAR  PIC X   VALUE IS '_'.      06000000
00174          C             02  DFHCLRP   PIC X   VALUE IS 'T'.      08000000
00175          C             02  DFHPEN    PIC X   VALUE IS '='.      09000000
00176          C             02  DFHOPID   PIC X   VALUE IS 'W'.      10000000
00177          C             02  DFHMSRE   PIC X   VALUE IS 'X'.      12000000
00178          C             02  DFHSTRF   PIC X   VALUE IS 'h'.      14000000
00179          C             02  DFHTRIG   PIC X   VALUE IS '"'.      16000000
00180          C             02  DFHPA1    PIC X   VALUE IS '%'.      18000000
00181          C             02  DFHPA2    PIC X   VALUE IS '>'.      20000000
00182          C             02  DFHPA3    PIC X   VALUE IS ','.      22000000
00183          C             02  DFHPF1    PIC X   VALUE IS '1'.      25000000
00184          C             02  DFHPF2    PIC X   VALUE IS '2'.      28000000
00185          C             02  DFHPF3    PIC X   VALUE IS '3'.      31000000
00186          C             02  DFHPF4    PIC X   VALUE IS '4'.      34000000
00187          C             02  DFHPF5    PIC X   VALUE IS '5'.      37000000
00188          C             02  DFHPF6    PIC X   VALUE IS '6'.      40000000
00189          C             02  DFHPF7    PIC X   VALUE IS '7'.      43000000
00190          C             02  DFHPF8    PIC X   VALUE IS '8'.      46000000
00191          C             02  DFHPF9    PIC X   VALUE IS '9'.      49000000
00192          C             02  DFHPF10   PIC X   VALUE IS ':'.      52000000
00193          C             02  DFHPF11   PIC X   VALUE IS '#'.      55000000
00194          C             02  DFHPF12   PIC X   VALUE IS '@'.      58000000
00195          C             02  DFHPF13   PIC X   VALUE IS 'A'.      61000000
00196          C             02  DFHPF14   PIC X   VALUE IS 'B'.      64000000
00197          C             02  DFHPF15   PIC X   VALUE IS 'C'.      67000000
00198          C             02  DFHPF16   PIC X   VALUE IS 'D'.      70000000
00199          C             02  DFHPF17   PIC X   VALUE IS 'E'.      73000000
00200          C             02  DFHPF18   PIC X   VALUE IS 'F'.      76000000
00201          C             02  DFHPF19   PIC X   VALUE IS 'G'.      79000000
00202          C             02  DFHPF20   PIC X   VALUE IS 'H'.      82000000
00203          C             02  DFHPF21   PIC X   VALUE IS 'I'.      85000000
00204          C             02  DFHPF22   PIC X   VALUE IS '¢'.      88000000
00205          C             02  DFHPF23   PIC X   VALUE IS '.'.      91000000
00206          C             02  DFHPF24   PIC X   VALUE IS '<'.      94000000
00207   010300 C       01  COPY DFHBMSCA.                            97000000
00208          C          01  DFHBMSCA.
00209          C             02  DFHBMPEM  PICTURE X   VALUE IS ';'.  02000000
00210          C             02  DFHBMPNL  PICTURE X   VALUE IS ' '.  04000000
00211          C             02  DFHBMASK  PICTURE X   VALUE IS '0'.  06000000
00212          C             02  DFHBMUNP  PICTURE X   VALUE IS '&'.  08000000
00213          C             02  DFHBMUNN  PICTURE X   VALUE IS 'H'.  10000000
00214          C             02  DFHBMPRO  PICTURE X   VALUE IS '<'.  12000000
00215          C             02  DFHBMBRY  PICTURE X   VALUE IS 'A'.  14000000
00216          C             02  DFHBMDAR  PICTURE X   VALUE IS '/'.  16000000
00217          C             02  DFHBMFSE  PICTURE X   VALUE IS '1'.  18000000
00218          C             02  DFHBMPRF  PICTURE X   VALUE IS '8'.  20000000
00219          C             02  DFHBMASB  PICTURE X   VALUE IS ' '.  22000000
00220          C             02  DFHBMEOF  PICTURE X   VALUE IS ' '.  24000000
00221          C             02  DFHBMDET  PICTURE X   VALUE IS ' '.  26000000
00222          C             02  DFHBMPSO  PICTURE X   VALUE IS ' '.  26600000
00223          C             02  DFHBMPSI  PICTURE X   VALUE IS ' '.  27300000
00224          C             02  DFHSA     PICTURE X   VALUE IS ' '.  27700000
00225          C                                                     28000000
```

```
5     TXTSPNC1                    15.06.28      AUG  8,1989

00226 C    02  DFHCOLOR  PICTURE X   VALUE IS 'è'        30000000
00227 C    02  DFHPS     PICTURE X   VALUE IS 'é'        33000000
00228 C    02  DFHHLT    PICTURE X   VALUE IS 'ê'        34000000
00229 C    02  DFH3270   PICTURE X   VALUE IS ' '        37000000
00230 C    02  DFHVAL    PICTURE X   VALUE IS 'A'        40000000
00231 C    02  DFHOUTLN  PICTURE X   VALUE IS 'B'        41000000
00232 C    02  DFHBKTRN  PICTURE X   VALUE IS 'A'        42000000
00233 C    02  DFHALL    PICTURE X   VALUE IS 'â'        43000000
00234 C    02  DFHERROR  PICTURE X   VALUE IS 'é'        46000000
00235 C    02  DFHDFT    PICTURE X   VALUE IS ' '        49000000
00236 C    02  DFHDFCOL  PICTURE X   VALUE IS '1'        52000000
00237 C    02  DFHBLUE   PICTURE X   VALUE IS '1'        55000000
00238 C    02  DFHRED    PICTURE X   VALUE IS '2'        58000000
00239 C    02  DFHPINK   PICTURE X   VALUE IS '3'        61000000
00240 C    02  DFHGREEN  PICTURE X   VALUE IS '4'        64000000
00241 C    02  DFHTURQ   PICTURE X   VALUE IS '5'        67000000
00242 C    02  DFHYELLO  PICTURE X   VALUE IS '6'        70000000
00243 C    02  DFHNEUTR  PICTURE X   VALUE IS '7'        73000000
00244 C    02  DFHBASE   PICTURE X   VALUE IS ' '        76000000
00245 C    02  DFHDFHI   PICTURE X   VALUE IS '1'        79000000
00246 C    02  DFHBLINK  PICTURE X   VALUE IS '2'        82000000
00247 C    02  DFHREVRS  PICTURE X   VALUE IS '4'        85000000
00248 C    02  DFHUNDLN  PICTURE X   VALUE IS ' '        88000000
00249 C    02  DFHMFIL   PICTURE X   VALUE IS ' '        91000000
00250 C    02  DFHMENT   PICTURE X   VALUE IS ' '        94000000
00251 C    02  DFHMFE    PICTURE X   VALUE IS ' '        97000000
00252 C    02  DFHUNNOD  PICTURE X   VALUE IS '('        97050000
00253 C    02  DFHUNIMD  PICTURE X   VALUE IS 'I'        97070000
00254 C    02  DFHUNNUM  PICTURE X   VALUE IS 'J'        97090000
00255 C    02  DFHUNINT  PICTURE X   VALUE IS 'R'        97110000
00256 C    02  DFHUNNON  PICTURE X   VALUE IS ' '        97130000
00257 C    02  DFHPROTI  PICTURE X   VALUE IS 'Y'        97150000
00258 C    02  DFHPROTN  PICTURE X   VALUE IS 'Z'        97170000
00259 C    02  DFHMT     PICTURE X   VALUE IS '%'        97600000
00260 C    02  DFHMFT    PICTURE X   VALUE IS ' '        98000000
00261 C    02  DFHMET    PICTURE X   VALUE IS ' '        98200000
00262 C    02  DFHMFET   PICTURE X   VALUE IS ' '        99400000
00263 C    02  DFHDFFR   PICTURE X   VALUE IS ' '        99540000
00264 C    02  DFHLEFT   PICTURE X   VALUE IS ' '        99610000
00265 C    02  DFHOVER   PICTURE X   VALUE IS ' '        99680000
00266 C    02  DFHRIGHT  PICTURE X   VALUE IS ' '        99760000
00267 C    02  DFHUNDER  PICTURE X   VALUE IS ' '        99840000
00268 C    02  DFHBOX    PICTURE X   VALUE IS ' '        99920000
00269 C    02  DFHSOSI   PICTURE X   VALUE IS ' '        99940000
00270 C    02  DFHTRANS  PICTURE X   VALUE IS 'O'        99960000
00271 C    02  DFHOPAQ   PICTURE X   VALUE IS ' '        99980000
00272 C  010400*
00273 C    01  DFHLDVER PIC X(22) VALUE 'LD TABLE DFHEITAB 210.'
00274 C    01  DFHEIDO PICTURE S9(7) COMPUTATIONAL-3 VALUE ZERO.
00275 C    01  DFHEIBO PICTURE S9(4) COMPUTATIONAL VALUE ZERO.
00276 C    01  DFHEICB PICTURE X(8) VALUE IS COMPUTATIONAL VALUE ZERO.
00277 C
00278 C    01  DFHEIV16 COMP PIC S9(8).
00279 C    01  DFHB0041 COMP PIC S9(8).
00280 C    01  DFHB0042 COMP PIC S9(8).
00281 C    01  DFHB0043 COMP PIC S9(8).
00282 C    01  DFHB0044 COMP PIC S9(8).
```

```
6       TXTSPNC1        15.06.28        AUG  8,1989

00283   01  DFHB0045  COMP PIC S9(8).
00284   01  DFHB0046  COMP PIC S9(8).
00285   01  DFHB0047  COMP PIC S9(8).
00286   01  DFHB0048  COMP PIC S9(4).
00287   01  DFHEIV11  COMP PIC S9(4).
00288   01  DFHEIV12  COMP PIC S9(4).
00289   01  DFHEIV13  COMP PIC S9(4).
00290   01  DFHEIV14  COMP PIC S9(4).
00291   01  DFHB0025  COMP PIC S9(4).
00292   01  DFHEIV5   PIC X(4).
00293   01  DFHEIV6   PIC X(4).
00294   01  DFHEIV17  PIC X(4).
00295   01  DFHEIV18  PIC X(4).
00296   01  DFHEIV19  PIC X(4).
00297   01  DFHEIV1   PIC X(8).
00298   01  DFHEIV2   PIC X(8).
00299   01  DFHEIV3   PIC X(8).
00300   01  DFHEIV20  PIC X(8).
00301   01  DFHC0084  PIC X(8).
00302   01  DFHC0085  PIC X(8).
00303   01  DFHC0320  PIC X(32).
00304   01  DFHEIV7   PIC X(2).
00305   01  DFHEIV8   PIC X(2).
00306   01  DFHC0022  PIC X(2).
00307   01  DFHC0023  PIC X(2).
00308   01  DFHEIV10  PIC S9(7) COMP-3.
00309   01  DFHEIV9   PIC X(1).
00310   01  DFHC0011  PIC X(1).
00311   01  DFHEIV4   PIC X(6).
00312   01  DFHC0070  PIC X(7).
00313   01  DFHC0071  PIC X(7).
00314   01  DFHC0440  PIC X(44).
00315   01  DFHDUMMY  COMP PIC S9(4).
00316   01  DFHEIV0   PICTURE X(29).
00318   010500 LINKAGE SECTION.
00319   01  DFHEIBLK.
00320   02  EIBTIME   PIC S9(7) COMP-3.
00321   02  EIBDATE   PIC S9(7) COMP-3.
00322   02  EIBTRNID  PIC X(4).
00323   02  EIBTASKN  PIC S9(7) COMP-3.
00324   02  EIBTRMID  PIC X(4).
00325   02  DFHEIGDI  COMP PIC S9(4).
00326   02  EIBCPOSN  COMP PIC S9(4).
00327   02  EIBCALEN  COMP PIC S9(4).
00328   02  EIBAID    PIC X(1).
00329   02  EIBFN     PIC X(2).
00330   02  EIBRCODE  PIC X(6).
00331   02  EIBDS     PIC X(8).
00332   02  EIBREQID  PIC X(8).
00333   02  EIBRSRCE  PIC X(8).
00334   02  EIBSYNC   PIC X(1).
00335   02  EIBFREE   PIC X(1).
00336   02  EIBRECV   PIC X(1).
00337   02  EIBFIL01  PIC X(1).
00338   02  EIBATT    PIC X(1).
00339   02  EIBEOC    PIC X(1).
```

TXTSPNC1   15.06.28   AUG 8,1989

```
00340          02  EIBFMH     PIC X(1).
00341          02  EIBCOMPL   PIC X(1).
00342          02  EIBSIG     PIC X(1).
00343          02  EIBCONF    PIC X(1).
00344          02  EIBERR     PIC X(1).
00345          02  EIBERRCD   PIC X(4).
00346          02  EIBSYNRB   PIC X(1).
00347          02  EIBNODAT   PIC X(1).
00348          02  EIBRESP    COMP PIC S9(8).
00349          02  EIBRESP2   COMP PIC S9(8).
00350          02  EIBRLDBK   PIC X(1).
00351   010600 01  DFHCOMMAREA.
00352   010700     05  LK-COM-INTTRAN         PIC X(4).
00353   010800*
00354          01  DFHBLLSLOT1 PICTURE X(1).
00355          01  DFHBLLSLOT2 PICTURE X(1).
00356   010900 PROCEDURE DIVISION USING DFHEIBLK DFHCOMMAREA.
00357   011000*****************************************************
00358   011100*
00359   011200*                MAINLINE PROCESSING
00360   011300*
00361   011400*****************************************************
00362
00363          CALL 'DFHEI1'.
00364          SERVICE RELOAD DFHEIBLK.
00365          SERVICE RELOAD DFHCOMMAREA.
00366   011500 MAIN-0000-MAINLINE SECTION.
00367   011600
00368   011700     IF EIBTRNID NOT = 'PNC1'
00369   011800         PERFORM X100-LOGICERR-ROUTINE
00370   011900         GO TO MAIN-9999-GOBACK.
00371   012000     IF EIBAID = DFHPF12
00372   012100         PERFORM X200-FORCE-CANCEL
00373   012200         GO TO MAIN-9999-GOBACK.
00374   012300     IF EIBCALEN = 0
00375   012400         PERFORM A000-PNC1-ROUTINE
00376   012500         GO TO MAIN-9999-GOBACK.
00377   012600     IF LK-COM-INTTRAN = 'PNC2'
00378   012700         PERFORM B000-PNC2-ROUTINE
00379   012800         GO TO MAIN-9999-GOBACK.
00380   012900     PERFORM X100-LOGICERR-ROUTINE.
00381   013000
00382   013100 MAIN-9999-GOBACK.
00383   013200     GOBACK.
00384   013300
00385   013400*****************************************************
00386   013500*                PNC1 PROCESSING
00387   013600*****************************************************
00388   013700 A000-PNC1-ROUTINE SECTION.
00389   013800*
00390   013900 A100-SEND-MAP.
00391   014000     SEND MAP PNC2.
00392   014100     MOVE LOW-VALUES TO MPBPNC2O.
00393   014110     MOVE -1          TO M2EMPN1L.
00394   014200     PERFORM ZBM2O-PNC2-SEND.
00395   014300
00396   014400* RETURN WITH INTERNAL TRANSID = PNC2.
        014500 A2OO-RETURN-WITH-TRANSID.
```

8   TXTSPNC1   15.06.28   AUG 8.1989

```
00397  014600         MOVE 'PNC1' TO CSPC-TRANSID.
00398  014700         MOVE 'PNC2' TO WK-COM-INTTRAN.
00399  014800         MOVE 4 TO CSCO-LENGTH.
00400  014900         PERFORM ZPC20-PC-RETURN-TRANSID-COM.
00401  015000*    A999-EXIT.
00402  015100     A999-EXIT.
00403  015200         EXIT.
00404  015300*
00405  015400*    PNC2 PROCESSING                                     *
00406  015500*                                                        *
00407  015600****************************************************
00408  015700****************************************************
00409  015800 B000-PNC2-ROUTINE SECTION.
00410  015900*
00411  016000*    RECEIVE MAP.
00412  016100     B100-RECEIVE-MAP.
00413  016200         PERFORM ZBM10-PNC2-RECEIVE.
00414  016300*
00415  016400*    VALIDATE INPUT DATA.
00416  016500         IF LOW-VALUE = M2EMPN1I AND M2EMPN2I
00417  016600             ADD 1 TO WK-ERR-CNT
00418  016700             MOVE ' AT LEAST ONE LINE MUST BE ENTERED.'
00419  016800                 TO M2ERRNO (WK-ERR-CNT)
00420  016900             GO TO B120-CHECK-ERR.
00421  017000     B110-EDIT-LOOP.
00422  017100         ADD 1 TO WK-LINE-CNT.
00423  017200         IF M2EMPNNI (WK-LINE-CNT) = LOW-VALUES
00424  017300             GO TO B115-EDIT-SKIP.
00425  017400         MOVE M2EMPNNI (WK-LINE-CNT) TO PMS-EMPNO.
00426  017500         MOVE '1' TO CSHC-ALLOW.
00427  017600         MOVE 88 TO CSFC-LENGTH.
00428  017700         PERFORM ZFC10-PMS-READ-FULLKEY.
00429  017800         IF CSHC-NOTFND = '1'
00430  017900             ADD 1 TO WK-ERR-CNT
00431  018000             MOVE 'EMPLOYEE NUMBER NOT FOUND ' TO M2ERRNO (WK-ERR-CNT)
00432  018100             MOVE -1 TO M2EMPNNL (WK-LINE-CNT)
00433  018200             MOVE DFHUNINT TO M2EMPNNA (WK-LINE-CNT).
00434  018300         IF M2NAMENI (WK-LINE-CNT) = LOW-VALUES
00435  018400             ADD 1 TO WK-ERR-CNT
00436  018500             MOVE 'NEW NAME MUST BE ENTERED.' TO M2ERRNO (WK-ERR-CNT)
00437  018600             MOVE -1 TO M2NAMENL (WK-LINE-CNT)
00438  018700             MOVE DFHUNINT TO M2NAMENA (WK-LINE-CNT).
00439  018800     B115-EDIT-SKIP.
00440  018900         IF WK-LINE-CNT < 3
00441  019000             GO TO B110-EDIT-LOOP.
00442  019100     B120-CHECK-ERR.
00443  019200         IF WK-ERR-CNT = ZERO
00444  019300             GO TO B200-VALID-DATA.
00445  019400*
00446  019500*    DATA INVALID.  SEND ERR MSG AND RETURN FOR REENTRY.
00447  019600     B130-INVALID-DATA.
00448  019700         PERFORM ZBM20-PNC2-SEND.
00449  019800         MOVE 'PNC1' TO CSPC-TRANSID.
00450  019900         MOVE 'PNC2' TO WK-COM-INTTRAN.
00451  020000         MOVE 4 TO CSCO-LENGTH.
00452  020100         PERFORM ZPC20-PC-RETURN-TRANSID-COM.
00453  020200         GO TO B999-EXIT.
```

```
00454   020300*
00455   020400* DATA VALID. UPDATE PMS FILE.
00456   020500 B200-VALID-DATA.
00457   020600     MOVE ZERO TO WK-LINE-CNT.
00458   020700 B210-UPDATE-LOOP.
00459   020800     IF M2EMPNNI (WK-LINE-CNT) = LOW-VALUES
00460   020900         GO TO B215-UPDATE-SKIP.
00461   021000     MOVE M2EMPNNI (WK-LINE-CNT) TO PMS-EMPNO.
00462   021100     MOVE 88 TO CSFC-LENGTH.
00463   021200     MOVE 'O' TO CSHC-ALLOW.
00464   021300     PERFORM ZFC20-PMS-READ-FULLKEY-UPDATE.
00465   021400     MOVE M2NAMENI (WK-LINE-CNT) TO PMS-NAME.
00466   021500     PERFORM ZFC30-PMS-REWRITE.
00467   021600 B215-UPDATE-SKIP.
00468   021700     IF WK-LINE-CNT < 3
00469   021800         GO TO B210-UPDATE-LOOP.
00470   021900*
00471   022000* SEND COMPLETION MESSAGE AND RETURN.
00472   022100     MOVE 'TRANSACTION PNC1 SUCCESSFULLY COMPLETED.' TO TC-O-AREA.
00473   022200     MOVE 40 TO CSTC-LENGTH.
00474   022300     PERFORM ZTC20-TC-SEND.
00475   022400     PERFORM ZPC10-PC-RETURN.
00476   022500*
00477   022600 B999-EXIT.
00478   022700     EXIT.
00479   022800*
00480   022900*************************************************************
00481   023000* APPLICATION SUBROUTINES                                  *
00482   023100*************************************************************
00483   023200*
00484   023300 X100-LOGICERR-ROUTINE SECTION.
00485   023400     MOVE 'LOGIC ERROR. TRANSACTION CANCELED.'
00486   023500         TO TC-O-AREA.
00487   023600     MOVE 35 TO CSTC-LENGTH.
00488   023700     PERFORM ZTC20-TC-SEND.
00489   023800     PERFORM ZPC10-PC-RETURN.
00490   023900 X199-EXIT.
00491   024000     EXIT.
00492   024100*
00493   024200 X200-FORCE-CANCEL SECTION.
00494   024300     MOVE 'TRANSACTION CANCELED BY OPERATOR REQUEST.'
00495   024400         TO TC-O-AREA.
00496   024500     MOVE 42 TO CSTC-LENGTH.
00497   024600     PERFORM ZTC20-TC-SEND.
00498   024700     PERFORM ZPC10-PC-RETURN.
00499   024800 X199-EXIT.
00500   024900     EXIT.
00501   025000*
00502   025100*************************************************************
00503   025200* CICS COMMAND SUBROUTINES                                 *
00504   025300*************************************************************
00505   025400*
00506   025500 ZBM10-PNC2-RECEIVE SECTION.
00507   *EXEC CICS HANDLE CONDITION
00508           ERROR(ZBM1A-ERROR)
00509   *END-EXEC.
00510   025600     MOVE '                    00264 ' TO DFHEIVO
```

```
10        TXTSPNC1          15.06.28        AUG  8.1989

                CALL 'DFHEI1' USING DFHEIVO
                GO TO ZBM1A-ERROR DEPENDING ON DFHEIGDI.
           *EXEC CICS RECEIVE
           *     MAP('MPBPNC2')
           *     MAPSET('MSBPNC2')
           *END-EXEC.
025900          MOVE '...)              00267    ' TO DFHEIVO
                MOVE 'MPBPNC2' TO DFHC0070
                MOVE 'MSBPNC2' TO DFHC0071
                CALL 'DFHEI1' USING DFHEIVO   DFHC0070 MPBPNC21 DFHDUMMY
                DFHC0071.
                GO TO ZBM19-EXIT.
026300 *
026400 * ZBM1A-ERROR.
026500     MOVE 'GEN ERROR OCCURRED AT PNC2 RECEIVE.  TRANS CANCELED.'
026600          TO TC-0-AREA.
026700     MOVE 49 TO CSTC-LENGTH.
026800 ZBM1X-SEND-RETURN.
026900     PERFORM ZTC30-TC-SEND-NOHANDLE.
027100     PERFORM ZPC10-PC-RETURN.
027200     GOBACK.
027300 *
027400 ZBM19-EXIT.
027500     EXIT.
027600 *
027700 *
027800 * ZBM20-PNC2-SEND SECTION.
027900 *EXEC CICS HANDLE CONDITION
           *     ERROR(ZBM2A-ERROR)
           *END-EXEC.
                MOVE ,                  00288    ' TO DFHEIVO
028000          CALL 'DFHEI1' USING DFHEIVO
                GO TO ZBM2A-ERROR DEPENDING ON DFHEIGDI.
           *EXEC CICS SEND
           *     MAP('MPBPNC2')
           *     MAPSET('MSBPNC2')
           *     ERASE
           *     CURSOR
           *END-EXEC.
028300          MOVE ',J        ,S      00291    ' TO DFHEIVO
                MOVE 'MPBPNC2' TO DFHC0070
                MOVE 'MSBPNC2' TO DFHC0071
                MOVE -1 TO DFHEIV11
                CALL 'DFHEI1' USING DFHEIVO   DFHC0070 MPBPNC20 DFHDUMMY
                DFHC0071 DFHDUMMY DFHDUMMY DFHEIV11.
                GO TO ZBM29-EXIT.
028900 *
029000 * ZBM2A-ERROR.
029100     MOVE 'GEN ERROR OCCURRED AT PNC2 SEND.  TRANS CANCELED.'
029200          TO TC-0-AREA.
029300     MOVE 49 TO CSTC-LENGTH.
029400 ZBM2X-SEND-RETURN.
029500     PERFORM ZTC30-TC-SEND-NOHANDLE.
029600     PERFORM ZPC10-PC-RETURN.
029700     GOBACK.
029800 *
```

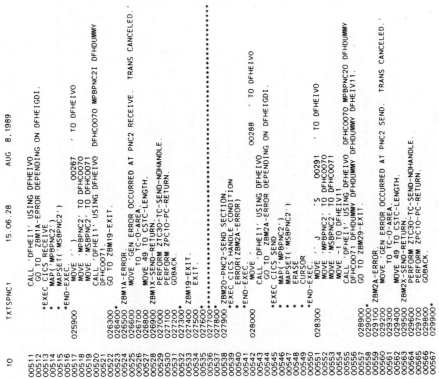

```
11        TXTSPNC1        15.06.28      AUG  8.1989

00568  030000  ZBM29-EXIT.
00569  030100      EXIT.
00570  030200* ****************************************************
00571  030300* ****************************************************
00572  030400  ZFC10-PMS-READ-FULLKEY SECTION.
00573  030500      MOVE 'O' TO CSHC-NOTFND.
00574  030600* EXEC CICS HANDLE CONDITION
00575               NOTFND(ZFC1A-NOTFND)
00576               ERROR(ZFC1B-ERROR)
00577  *     *
00578  *END-EXEC.
00579           MOVE '   (               00315   ' TO DFHEIVO
00580           CALL 'DFHEI1' USING DFHEIVO      00315    ' TO DFHEIVO
00581           GO TO ZFC1A-NOTFND ZFC1B-ERROR DEPENDING ON DFHEIGDI.
00582
00583  *EXEC CICS READ
00584               DATASET('PERVSPMS')
00585               INTO(PMS-IOAREA)
00586               RIDFLD(PMS-RECORD-KEY)
00587               LENGTH(CSFC-LENGTH)
00588  *END-EXEC.
00589  031100      MOVE '   O           00319   ' TO DFHEIVO
00590           MOVE 'PERVSPMS' TO DFHEIV1
00591           CALL 'DFHEI1' USING DFHEIVO    DFHEIV1    PMS-IOAREA CSFC-LENGTH
00592           PMS-RECORD-KEY.
00593
00594
00595  031700      MOVE 'O' TO CSHC-ALLOW.
00596  031800      GO TO ZFC19-EXIT.
00597  031900*
00598  032000  ZFC1A-NOTFND.
00599  032100      IF CSHC-ALLOW = '1'
00600  032200          MOVE 'O' TO CSHC-ALLOW
00601  032300          MOVE 'O' TO CSHC-NOTFND
00602  032400          GO TO ZFC19-EXIT.
00603  032500      MOVE 'RECORD NOT FOUND AT READ-FK.   TRANS CANCELED.'
00604  032600          TO TC-O-AREA.
00605  032700      MOVE 46 TO CSTC-LENGTH.
00606  032800      GO TO ZFC1X-SEND-RETURN.
00607  032900*
00608  033000  ZFC1B-ERROR.
00609  033100      MOVE 'GEN ERROR OCCURRED AT READ-FK.   TRANS CANCELED.'
00610  033200          TO TC-O-AREA.
00611  033300      MOVE 47 TO CSTC-LENGTH.
00612  033400  ZFC1X-SEND-RETURN.
00613  033500      PERFORM ZTC30-TC-SEND-NOHANDLE.
00614  033600      PERFORM ZPC10-PC-RETURN.
00615  033700      GOBACK.
00616  033800*
00617  033900  ZFC19-EXIT.
00618  034000      EXIT.
00619  034100*
00620  034200* ****************************************************
00621  034300* ****************************************************
00622  034400  ZFC20-PMS-READ-FULLKEY-UPDATE SECTION.
00623  034400      MOVE 'O' TO CSHC-NOTFND.
00624  034500* EXEC CICS HANDLE CONDITION
```

12   TXTSPNC1   15.06.28   AUG 8,1989

```
00625                       NOTFND(ZFC2A-NOTFND)
00626                       ERROR(ZFC2B-ERROR)
00627           *END-EXEC.
00628  034600           MOVE '(              00354    ' TO DFHEIVO
00629                    CALL 'DFHEI1' USING DFHEIVO
00630                    GO TO ZFC2A-NOTFND ZFC2B-ERROR DEPENDING ON DFHEIGD1.
00631
00632           *EXEC CICS READ
00633                    DATASET('PERVSPMS')
00634                    INTO(PMS-IOAREA)
00635                    RIDFLD(PMS-RECORD-KEY)
00636                    LENGTH(CSFC-LENGTH)
00637                    UPDATE
00638           *END-EXEC.
00639  035000           MOVE ' O       d 00358   ' TO DFHEIV1
00640                    MOVE 'PERVSPMS' TO DFHEIV1
00641                    CALL 'DFHEI1' USING DFHEIVO DFHEIV1 PMS-IOAREA CSFC-LENGTH
00642                    PMS-RECORD-KEY.
00643
00644
00645
00646  035700           MOVE 'O' TO CSHC-ALLOW.
00647  035800           GO TO ZFC29-EXIT.
00648  035900  *
00649  036000  ZFC2A-NOTFND.
00650  036100           IF CSHC-ALLOW = '1'
00651  036200           MOVE 'O' TO CSHC-ALLOW
00652  036300           MOVE '1' TO CSHC-NOTFND
00653  036400           GO TO ZFC19-EXIT.
00654  036500           MOVE 'RECORD NOT FOUND AT READ-FK-UPD.  TRANS CANCELED.'
00655  036600           MOVE TO TC-O-AREA.
00656  036700           MOVE 50 TO CSTC-LENGTH.
00657  036800           GO TO ZFC2X-SEND-RETURN.
00658  036900  *
00659  037000  ZFC2B-ERROR.
00660  037100           MOVE 'GEN ERROR OCCURRED AT READ-FK-UPD.  TRANS CANCELED '
00661  037200           MOVE TO TC-O-AREA.
00662  037300           MOVE 51 TO CSTC-LENGTH.
00663  037400  ZFC2X-SEND-RETURN.
00664  037500           PERFORM ZFC30-TC-SEND-NOHANDLE.
00665  037600           PERFORM ZPC10-PC-RETURN.
00666  037700           GOBACK.
00667  037800  *
00668  037900  ZFC29-EXIT.
00669  038000           EXIT.
00670  038100  *
00671  038200  *********************************************
00672  038300  ZFC30-PMS-REWRITE SECTION.
00673  038400  *EXEC CICS HANDLE CONDITION
00674                    ERROR(ZFC3A-ERROR)
00675           *END-EXEC.
00676  038500           MOVE '(              00393    ' TO DFHEIVO
00677                    CALL 'DFHEI1' USING DFHEIVO
00678                    GO TO ZFC3A-ERROR DEPENDING ON DFHEIGD1.
00679
00680           *EXEC CICS REWRITE
00681                    DATASET('PERVSPMS')
```

```
00682                     *       FROM(PMS-IOAREA)
00683                     *       LENGTH(CSFC-LENGTH)
00684                     *END-EXEC.
00685   038800                MOVE '        00396 ' TO DFHEIVO
00686                         MOVE 'PERVSPMS' TO DFHEIV1
00687                         CALL 'DFHEI1' USING DFHEIVO DFHEIV1 PMS-IOAREA CSFC-LENGTH.
00688
00689
00690                         GO TO ZFC29-EXIT.
00691   039300
00692   039400*  ZFC3A-ERROR.
00693   039500                MOVE 'GEN ERROR OCCURRED AT REWRITE.  TRANS CANCELED.'
00694   039600                    TO TC-0-AREA.
00695   039700                MOVE 47 TO CSTC-LENGTH.
00696   039800*  ZFC3X-SEND-RETURN.
00697   039900                PERFORM ZTC30-TC-SEND-NOHANDLE.
00698   040000                PERFORM ZPC10-PC-RETURN.
00699   040100                GOBACK.
00700   040200
00701   040300*  ZFC39-EXIT.
00702   040400                EXIT.
00703   040500
00704   040600
00705   040700
00706   040800***************************************************
00707   040900   ZPC10-PC-RETURN SECTION.
00708                         *EXEC CICS RETURN
00709                         *END-EXEC.
00710   041000                MOVE '        00418 ' TO DFHEIVO
00711                         CALL 'DFHEI1' USING DFHEIVO.
00712   041200 ZPC19-EXIT.
00713   041300                EXIT.
00714   041400*
00715   041500
00716   041600   ZPC20-PC-RETURN-TRANSID-COM SECTION.
00717   041700              *EXEC CICS RETURN
00718                       *  TRANSID(CSPC-TRANSID)
00719                       *  COMMAREA(WK-COMMAREA)
00720                       *  LENGTH(CSCO-LENGTH)
00721                       *END-EXEC.
00722   041800                MOVE '        00426 ' TO DFHEIVO
00723                         CALL 'DFHEI1' USING DFHEIVO CSPC-TRANSID WK-COMMAREA
00724                             CSCO-LENGTH.
00725
00726
00727   042300 ZPC29-EXIT.
00728   042400                EXIT.
00729   042500*
00730   042600**************************************************
00731   042700   ZTC20-TC-SEND SECTION.
00732   042800              *EXEC CICS HANDLE CONDITION
00733                       *  LENGERR(ZTC2A-LENGERR)
00734                       *  ERROR(ZTC2B-ERROR)
00735                       *END-EXEC.
00736
00737   042900                MOVE '        00437 ' TO DFHEIVO
00738                         CALL 'DFHEI1' USING DFHEIVO
```

```
14       TXTSPNC1        15.06.28        AUG  8.1989

00739               GO TO ZTC2A-LENGERR ZTC2B-ERROR DEPENDING ON DFHEIGDI.
00740
00741        *EXEC CICS SEND
00742        *    FROM(TC-O-AREA)
00743        *    LENGTH(CSTC-LENGTH)
00744        *    ERASE
00745        *END-EXEC.
00746 043300      MOVE ' ß      a    00441   ' TO DFHEIVO
00747              CALL 'DFHEI1' USING DFHEIVO DFHDUMMY TC-O-AREA
00748              CSTC-LENGTH.
00749
00750
00751              GO TO ZTC29-EXIT.
00752
00753 043800
00754 043900* ZTC2A-LENGERR.
00755 044000      MOVE 'LENGERR OCCURRED AT SEND.  TRANS CANCELED.'
00756 044100        TO TC-O-AREA.
00757 044200      MOVE 42 TO CSTC-LENGTH.
00758 044300      GO TO ZTC2X-SEND-RETURN.
00759 044400
00760 044500*
00761 044600 ZTC2B-ERROR.
00762 044700      MOVE 'GENERAL ERROR OCCURRED AT SEND.  TRANS CANCELED.'
00763 044800        TO TC-O-AREA.
00764 044900      MOVE 48 TO CSTC-LENGTH.
00765 045000 ZTC2X-SEND-RETURN.
00766 045100      PERFORM ZTC30-TC-SEND-NOHANDLE.
00767 045200      PERFORM ZPC10-PC-RETURN.
00768 045300      GOBACK.
00769 045400*
00770 045500 ZTC29-EXIT.
00771 045600      EXIT.
00772 045700*
00773 045800*********************************************
00774 045900*
00775 046000 ZTC30-TC-SEND-NOHANDLE SECTION.
00776        *EXEC CICS SEND
00777        *    FROM(TC-O-AREA)
00778        *    LENGTH(CSTC-LENGTH)
00779        *    ERASE
00780        *    NOHANDLE
00781        *END-EXEC.
00782 046100      MOVE ' ß      a    00469   ' TO DFHEIVO
00783              CALL 'DFHEI1' USING DFHEIVO DFHDUMMY TC-O-AREA
00784              CSTC-LENGTH.
00785
00786 046700 ZTC39-EXIT.
00787 046800      EXIT.
```

INTRNL NAME	LVL	SOURCE NAME	BASE	DISPL	INTRNL NAME	DEFINITION	USAGE	R O Q M
DNM=3-275	01	MP8PNC21	BL=1	000	DNM=3-275	DS 0CL412	GROUP	
DNM=3-296	02	FILLER	BL=1	000	DNM=3-296	DS 12C	DISP	
DNM=3-307	02	M2EMPN1L	BL=1	00C	DNM=3-307	DS 2C	COMP	R
DNM=3-325	02	M2EMPN1F	BL=1	00E	DNM=3-325	DS 1C	DISP	
DNM=3-343	02	FILLER	BL=1	00E	DNM=3-343	DS 1C	GROUP	
DNM=3-360	03	M2EMPN1A	BL=1	00F	DNM=3-360	DS 1C	DISP-NM	
DNM=3-378	02	M2EMPN1I	BL=1	00F	DNM=3-378	DS 5C	COMP	R
DNM=3-396	02	M2NAME1L	BL=1	014	DNM=3-396	DS 2C	DISP	
DNM=3-414	02	M2NAME1F	BL=1	016	DNM=3-414	DS 1C	DISP	
DNM=3-432	02	FILLER	BL=1	016	DNM=3-432	DS 1C	GROUP	R
DNM=3-449	03	M2NAME1A	BL=1	017	DNM=3-449	DS 1C	DISP	
DNM=3-470	02	M2NAME1I	BL=1	030	DNM=3-470	DS 25C	COMP	
DNM=3-488	02	M2EMPN2L	BL=1	032	DNM=3-488	DS 1C	DISP	R
DNM=4-000	02	M2EMPN2F	BL=1	032	DNM=4-000	DS 1C	GROUP	
DNM=4-018	02	FILLER	BL=1	033	DNM=4-018	DS 1C	DISP-NM	
DNM=4-035	03	M2EMPN2A	BL=1	038	DNM=4-035	DS 5C	COMP	R
DNM=4-053	02	M2EMPN2I	BL=1	03A	DNM=4-053	DS 2C	DISP	
DNM=4-071	02	M2NAME2L	BL=1	03A	DNM=4-071	DS 1C	GROUP	
DNM=4-089	02	M2NAME2F	BL=1	03B	DNM=4-089	DS 1C	DISP	R
DNM=4-107	02	FILLER	BL=1	054	DNM=4-107	DS 25C	COMP	
DNM=4-124	03	M2NAME2A	BL=1	056	DNM=4-124	DS 1C	DISP	
DNM=4-145	02	M2NAME2I	BL=1	056	DNM=4-145	DS 1C	GROUP	R
DNM=4-163	02	M2ERR1L	BL=1	057	DNM=4-163	DS 0CL1	DISP	
DNM=4-180	02	M2ERR1F	BL=1	0A6	DNM=4-180	DS 79C	DISP	
DNM=4-197	02	FILLER	BL=1	0A8	DNM=4-197	DS 2C	COMP	R
DNM=4-214	03	M2ERR1A	BL=1	0A8	DNM=4-214	DS 1C	GROUP	
DNM=4-231	02	M2ERR1I	BL=1	0A9	DNM=4-231	DS 1C	DISP	
DNM=4-251	02	M2ERR2L	BL=1	0F8	DNM=4-251	DS 79C	DISP	
DNM=4-268	02	M2ERR2F	BL=1	0FA	DNM=4-268	DS 1C	COMP	R
DNM=4-285	02	FILLER	BL=1	0FA	DNM=4-285	DS 1C	GROUP	
DNM=4-302	03	M2ERR2A	BL=1	0FB	DNM=4-302	DS 1C	DISP	
DNM=4-319	02	M2ERR2I	BL=1	14A	DNM=4-319	DS 79C	DISP	
DNM=4-336	02	M2ERR3L	BL=1	14C	DNM=4-336	DS 2C	COMP	R
DNM=4-353	02	M2ERR3F	BL=1	14C	DNM=4-353	DS 1C	GROUP	
DNM=4-370	02	FILLER	BL=1	14D	DNM=4-370	DS 1C	DISP	
DNM=4-387	03	M2ERR3A	BL=1	000	DNM=4-387	DS 79C	DISP	
DNM=4-404	02	M2ERR3I	BL=1	00C	DNM=4-404	DS 1C	DISP	
DNM=4-421	02	M2ERR4L	BL=1	00F	DNM=4-421	DS 2C	COMP	R
DNM=4-438	02	M2ERR4F	BL=1	014	DNM=4-438	DS 1C	DISP	
DNM=4-455	02	FILLER	BL=1	017	DNM=4-455	DS 1C	GROUP	
DNM=4-472	03	M2ERR4A	BL=1	030	DNM=4-472	DS 1C	DISP	
DNM=4-489	02	M2ERR4I	BL=1	033	DNM=4-489	DS 79C	DISP	
DNM=5-000	01	MP8PNC20	BL=1	000	DNM=5-000	DS 0CL412	GROUP	
DNM=5-024	02	FILLER	BL=1	000	DNM=5-024	DS 12C	DISP	
DNM=5-038	02	M2EMPN10	BL=1	00C	DNM=5-038	DS 3C	DISP	
DNM=5-052	02	FILLER	BL=1	00F	DNM=5-052	DS 5C	DISP-NM	
DNM=5-070	02	M2NAME10	BL=1	014	DNM=5-070	DS 3C	DISP	
DNM=5-084	02	FILLER	BL=1	017	DNM=5-084	DS 25C	DISP	
DNM=5-102	02	M2EMPN20	BL=1	030	DNM=5-102	DS 3C	DISP	
DNM=5-116	02	FILLER	BL=1	033	DNM=5-116	DS 5C	DISP-NM	
DNM=5-134	02	M2NAME20	BL=1	038	DNM=5-134	DS 3C	DISP	
DNM=5-148	02	FILLER	BL=1	054	DNM=5-148	DS 25C	DISP	
DNM=5-166	02	M2ERR10	BL=1	057	DNM=5-166	DS 3C	DISP	
DNM=5-180	02	FILLER	BL=1	0A6	DNM=5-180	DS 79C	DISP	
DNM=5-197	02	FILLER	BL=1	0A6	DNM=5-197	DS 3C	DISP	

16   TXTSPNC1   15.06.28   AUG   8.1989

Base	Lvl	Name	DS	Length	Category	Flag	Internal Name	Offset
BL=1	02	M2ERR2O	DS	79C	DISP		DNM=5-211	OA9
BL=1	02	FILLER	DS	3C	DISP		DNM=5-228	OFB
BL=1	02	M2ERR3O	DS	79C	DISP		DNM=5-242	OFB
BL=1	02	FILLER	DS	3C	DISP		DNM=5-259	14A
BL=1	02	M2ERR4O	DS	79C	DISP		DNM=5-273	14D
BL=1	01	MPBPNC2-REDEFINE	DS	OCL412	GROUP	R	DNM=5-290	000
BL=1	02	FILLER	DS	12C	DISP		DNM=5-319	00C
BL=1	02	FILLER	DS	OCL36	GROUP		DNM=5-333	00C
BL=1	03	M2EMPNNL	DS	2C	COMP		DNM=5-350	00F
BL=1	03	M2EMPNNA	DS	1C	DISP		DNM=5-374	00F
BL=1	03	M2EMPNNI	DS	5C	DISP-NM		DNM=5-395	00F
BL=1	03	FILLER	DS	OCL5	GROUP		DNM=5-416	014
BL=1	03	M2EMPNNO	DS	5C	DISP-NM		DNM=5-436	016
BL=1	03	M2NAMENL	DS	2C	COMP		DNM=5-460	017
BL=1	03	M2NAMENA	DS	1C	DISP		DNM=5-484	017
BL=1	03	M2NAMENI	DS	25C	DISP		DNM=6-000	017
BL=1	03	FILLER	DS	OCL25	GROUP		DNM=6-021	054
BL=1	04	M2NAMENO	DS	25C	DISP		DNM=6-041	054
BL=1	03	FILLER	DS	OCL82	GROUP	R	DNM=6-062	056
BL=1	03	M2ERRNL	DS	2C	COMP		DNM=6-079	057
BL=1	03	M2ERRNA	DS	1C	DISP		DNM=6-099	
BL=1	03	M2ERRNO	DS	79C	DISP		DNM=6-119	
BL=1	01	TC-O-AREA	DS	OCL80	GROUP		DNM=6-139	1A0
BL=1	01	TC-O1-AREA	DS	OCL80	GROUP		DNM=6-161	1A0
BL=1	02	FILLER	DS	80C	DISP		DNM=6-184	1A0
BL=1	01	PMS-IOAREA	DS	OCL88	GROUP		DNM=6-198	1F0
BL=1	03	PMS-RECORD-KEY	DS	OCL5	GROUP		DNM=6-221	1F0
BL=1	03	PMS-EMPNO	DS	5C	DISP-NM		DNM=6-248	1F0
BL=1	03	PMS-RECORD-DETAIL	DS	OCL83	GROUP		DNM=6-267	1F5
BL=1	03	PMS-NAME	DS	25C	DISP		DNM=6-297	20E
BL=1	03	PMS-DEPT	DS	10C	DISP		DNM=6-315	218
BL=1	03	PMS-ROOM	DS	10C	DISP-NM		DNM=6-333	222
BL=1	03	PMS-EXT	DS	4C	DISP		DNM=6-351	226
BL=1	03	PMS-RANK	DS	5C	DISP-NM		DNM=6-368	228
BL=1	03	PMS-TITLE	DS	10C	DISP		DNM=6-386	235
BL=1	03	PMS-AGE	DS	2C	DISP-NM		DNM=6-408	237
BL=1	03	PMS-SEX	DS	2C	DISP		DNM=6-425	23F
BL=1	03	PMS-SALARY	DS	7P	COMP-3		DNM=6-442	243
BL=1	03	PMS-INSPOLICY	DS	4P	COMP-3		DNM=6-462	248
BL=1	03	PMS-INSPREM	DS	5P	COMP-3		DNM=6-485	248
BL=1	01	WK-COMMAREA	DS	OCL4	GROUP		DNM=7-000	250
BL=1	01	WK-COM-INITTRAN	DS	4C	DISP		DNM=7-027	250
BL=1	01	WK-CICS-WORK	DS	OCL18	GROUP		DNM=7-051	252
BL=1	02	CSCO-LENGTH	DS	2C	COMP		DNM=7-076	254
BL=1	02	CSFC-LENGTH	DS	2C	COMP		DNM=7-097	255
BL=1	02	CSHC-ALLOW	DS	1C	DISP		DNM=7-118	256
BL=1	02	CSHC-NOTFND	DS	1C	DISP		DNM=7-141	25C
BL=1	02	CSPC-TRANSID	DS	2C	DISP		DNM=7-162	25F
BL=1	02	CSTC-LENGTH	DS	2C	COMP		DNM=7-184	268
BL=1	02	WK-LINE-CNT	DS	3C	DISP-NM		DNM=7-205	268
BL=1	02	WK-ERR-CNT	DS	3C	DISP-NM		DNM=7-226	269
BL=1	01	DFHATD	DS	OCL36	GROUP		DNM=7-246	26A
BL=1	02	DFHNULL	DS	1C	DISP		DNM=7-265	26B
BL=1	02	DFHENTER	DS	1C	DISP		DNM=7-282	26C
BL=1	02	DFHCLEAR	DS	1C	DISP		DNM=7-300	
BL=1	02	DFHCLRP	DS	1C	DISP		DNM=7-318	
BL=1	02	DFHPEN	DS	1C	DISP		DNM=7-335	

17   TXTSPNC1   15.06.28   AUG 8.1989

DNM	Lvl	Name	Addr		DNM		Type	Storage
DNM=7-354	02	DFHOPID	26D	BL=1	DNM=7-354	DS	1C	DISP
DNM=7-371	02	DFHMSRE	26E	BL=1	DNM=7-371	DS	1C	DISP
DNM=7-388	02	DFHSIRF	26F	BL=1	DNM=7-388	DS	1C	DISP
DNM=7-405	02	DFHTRIG	270	BL=1	DNM=7-405	DS	1C	DISP
DNM=7-422	02	DFHPA1	271	BL=1	DNM=7-422	DS	1C	DISP
DNM=7-438	02	DFHPA2	272	BL=1	DNM=7-438	DS	1C	DISP
DNM=7-457	02	DFHPA3	273	BL=1	DNM=7-457	DS	1C	DISP
DNM=7-473	02	DFHPF1	274	BL=1	DNM=7-473	DS	1C	DISP
DNM=7-489	02	DFHPF2	275	BL=1	DNM=7-489	DS	1C	DISP
DNM=8-000	02	DFHPF3	276	BL=1	DNM=8-000	DS	1C	DISP
DNM=8-016	02	DFHPF4	277	BL=1	DNM=8-016	DS	1C	DISP
DNM=8-032	02	DFHPF5	278	BL=1	DNM=8-032	DS	1C	DISP
DNM=8-048	02	DFHPF6	279	BL=1	DNM=8-048	DS	1C	DISP
DNM=8-067	02	DFHPF7	27A	BL=1	DNM=8-067	DS	1C	DISP
DNM=8-086	02	DFHPF8	27B	BL=1	DNM=8-086	DS	1C	DISP
DNM=8-102	02	DFHPF9	27C	BL=1	DNM=8-102	DS	1C	DISP
DNM=8-118	02	DFHPF10	27D	BL=1	DNM=8-118	DS	1C	DISP
DNM=8-138	02	DFHPF11	27E	BL=1	DNM=8-138	DS	1C	DISP
DNM=8-155	02	DFHPF12	27F	BL=1	DNM=8-155	DS	1C	DISP
DNM=8-172	02	DFHPF13	280	BL=1	DNM=8-172	DS	1C	DISP
DNM=8-192	02	DFHPF14	281	BL=1	DNM=8-192	DS	1C	DISP
DNM=8-212	02	DFHPF15	282	BL=1	DNM=8-212	DS	1C	DISP
DNM=8-229	02	DFHPF16	283	BL=1	DNM=8-229	DS	1C	DISP
DNM=8-246	02	DFHPF17	284	BL=1	DNM=8-246	DS	1C	DISP
DNM=8-263	02	DFHPF18	285	BL=1	DNM=8-263	DS	1C	DISP
DNM=8-280	02	DFHPF19	286	BL=1	DNM=8-280	DS	1C	DISP
DNM=8-300	02	DFHPF20	287	BL=1	DNM=8-300	DS	1C	DISP
DNM=8-317	02	DFHPF21	288	BL=1	DNM=8-317	DS	1C	DISP
DNM=8-337	02	DFHPF22	289	BL=1	DNM=8-337	DS	1C	DISP
DNM=8-357	02	DFHPF23	28A	BL=1	DNM=8-357	DS	1C	DISP
DNM=8-374	02	DFHPF24	28B	BL=1	DNM=8-374	DS	1C	DISP
DNM=8-391	01	DFHBMSCA	28B	BL=1	DNM=8-391	DS	OCL63	GROUP
DNM=8-412	02	DFHBMPEM	290	BL=1	DNM=8-412	DS	1C	DISP
DNM=8-430	02	DFHBMPNL	291	BL=1	DNM=8-430	DS	1C	DISP
DNM=8-448	02	DFHBMASK	292	BL=1	DNM=8-448	DS	1C	DISP
DNM=8-466	02	DFHBMUNP	293	BL=1	DNM=8-466	DS	1C	DISP
DNM=8-484	02	DFHBMUNN	294	BL=1	DNM=8-484	DS	1C	DISP
DNM=9-000	02	DFHBMPRO	295	BL=1	DNM=9-000	DS	1C	DISP
DNM=9-018	02	DFHBMBRY	296	BL=1	DNM=9-018	DS	1C	DISP
DNM=9-036	02	DFHBMDAR	297	BL=1	DNM=9-036	DS	1C	DISP
DNM=9-054	02	DFHBMFSE	298	BL=1	DNM=9-054	DS	1C	DISP
DNM=9-075	02	DFHBMPRF	299	BL=1	DNM=9-075	DS	1C	DISP
DNM=9-093	02	DFHBMASF	29A	BL=1	DNM=9-093	DS	1C	DISP
DNM=9-114	02	DFHBMASB	29B	BL=1	DNM=9-114	DS	1C	DISP
DNM=9-135	02	DFHBMEOF	29C	BL=1	DNM=9-135	DS	1C	DISP
DNM=9-153	02	DFHBMDET	29D	BL=1	DNM=9-153	DS	1C	DISP
DNM=9-171	02	DFHBMPSO	29E	BL=1	DNM=9-171	DS	1C	DISP
DNM=9-192	02	DFHBMPSI	29F	BL=1	DNM=9-192	DS	1C	DISP
DNM=9-210	02	DFHSA	2A0	BL=1	DNM=9-210	DS	1C	DISP
DNM=9-225	02	DFHCOLOR	2A1	BL=1	DNM=9-225	DS	1C	DISP
DNM=9-246	02	DFHPS	2A2	BL=1	DNM=9-246	DS	1C	DISP
DNM=9-261	02	DFHHLT	2A3	BL=1	DNM=9-261	DS	1C	DISP
DNM=9-277	02	DFH3270	2A4	BL=1	DNM=9-277	DS	1C	DISP
DNM=9-297	02	DFHVAL	2A5	BL=1	DNM=9-297	DS	1C	DISP
DNM=9-313	02	DFHOUTLN	2A6	BL=1	DNM=9-313	DS	1C	DISP
DNM=9-331	02	DFHBKTRN	2A7	BL=1	DNM=9-331	DS	1C	DISP
DNM=9-349	02	DFHALL	2A8	BL=1	DNM=9-349	DS	1C	DISP

18   TXTSPNC1   15.06.28   AUG 8, 1989

DNM	Level	Name	DNM	Addr	BL	DS	Usage
DNM=9-365	02	DFHERROR	DNM=9-365	2A9	BL=1	DS 1C	DISP
DNM=9-383	02	DFHDFT	DNM=9-383	2AA	BL=1	DS 1C	DISP
DNM=9-399	02	DFHDFCOL	DNM=9-399	2AB	BL=1	DS 1C	DISP
DNM=9-420	02	DFHBLUE	DNM=9-420	2AC	BL=1	DS 1C	DISP
DNM=9-440	02	DFHRED	DNM=9-440	2AD	BL=1	DS 1C	DISP
DNM=9-459	02	DFHPINK	DNM=9-459	2AE	BL=1	DS 1C	DISP
DNM=9-476	02	DFHGREEN	DNM=9-476	2AF	BL=1	DS 1C	DISP
DNM=9-494	02	DFHTURQ	DNM=9-494	2B0	BL=1	DS 1C	DISP
DNM=10-000	02	DFHYELLO	DNM=10-000	2B1	BL=1	DS 1C	DISP
DNM=10-018	02	DFHNEUTR	DNM=10-018	2B2	BL=1	DS 1C	DISP
DNM=10-039	02	DFHBASE	DNM=10-039	2B3	BL=1	DS 1C	DISP
DNM=10-056	02	DFHDFHI	DNM=10-056	2B4	BL=1	DS 1C	DISP
DNM=10-076	02	DFHBLINK	DNM=10-076	2B5	BL=1	DS 1C	DISP
DNM=10-094	02	DFHREVRS	DNM=10-094	2B6	BL=1	DS 1C	DISP
DNM=10-112	02	DFHUNDLN	DNM=10-112	2B7	BL=1	DS 1C	DISP
DNM=10-130	02	DFHMFIL	DNM=10-130	2B8	BL=1	DS 1C	DISP
DNM=10-150	02	DFHMENT	DNM=10-150	2B9	BL=1	DS 1C	DISP
DNM=10-167	02	DFHMFE	DNM=10-167	2BA	BL=1	DS 1C	DISP
DNM=10-183	02	DFHUNNOD	DNM=10-183	2BB	BL=1	DS 1C	DISP
DNM=10-201	02	DFHUNIMD	DNM=10-201	2BC	BL=1	DS 1C	DISP
DNM=10-219	02	DFHUNNUM	DNM=10-219	2BD	BL=1	DS 1C	DISP
DNM=10-240	02	DFHUNINT	DNM=10-240	2BE	BL=1	DS 1C	DISP
DNM=10-258	02	DFHUNNON	DNM=10-258	2BF	BL=1	DS 1C	DISP
DNM=10-276	02	DFHPROTI	DNM=10-276	2C0	BL=1	DS 1C	DISP
DNM=10-294	02	DFHPROTN	DNM=10-294	2C1	BL=1	DS 1C	DISP
DNM=10-312	02	DFHMT	DNM=10-312	2C2	BL=1	DS 1C	DISP
DNM=10-327	02	DFHMFT	DNM=10-327	2C3	BL=1	DS 1C	DISP
DNM=10-346	02	DFHMET	DNM=10-346	2C4	BL=1	DS 1C	DISP
DNM=10-365	02	DFHMFET	DNM=10-365	2C5	BL=1	DS 1C	DISP
DNM=10-382	02	DFHDFFR	DNM=10-382	2C6	BL=1	DS 1C	DISP
DNM=10-399	02	DFHLEFT	DNM=10-399	2C7	BL=1	DS 1C	DISP
DNM=10-416	02	DFHOVER	DNM=10-416	2C8	BL=1	DS 1C	DISP
DNM=10-433	02	DFHRIGHT	DNM=10-433	2C9	BL=1	DS 1C	DISP
DNM=10-451	02	DFHUNDER	DNM=10-451	2CA	BL=1	DS 1C	DISP
DNM=10-472	02	DFHBOX	DNM=10-472	2CB	BL=1	DS 1C	DISP
DNM=10-491	02	DFHSOSI	DNM=10-491	2CC	BL=1	DS 1C	DISP
DNM=11-000	02	DFHTRANS	DNM=11-000	2CD	BL=1	DS 1C	DISP
DNM=11-021	02	DFHOPAQ	DNM=11-021	2CE	BL=1	DS 1C	DISP
DNM=11-038	01	DFHLDVER	DNM=11-038	2D0	BL=1	DS 22C	COMP-3
DNM=11-056	01	DFHEIDO	DNM=11-056	2E8	BL=1	DS 4P	DISP
DNM=11-073	01	DFHEICB	DNM=11-073	2F0	BL=1	DS 2C	COMP
DNM=11-090	01	DFHEIV16	DNM=11-090	2F8	BL=1	DS 8C	COMP
DNM=11-110	01	DFHB0041	DNM=11-110	300	BL=1	DS 4C	COMP
DNM=11-128	01	DFHB0042	DNM=11-128	308	BL=1	DS 4C	COMP
DNM=11-146	01	DFHB0043	DNM=11-146	310	BL=1	DS 4C	COMP
DNM=11-167	01	DFHB0044	DNM=11-167	318	BL=1	DS 4C	COMP
DNM=11-188	01	DFHB0045	DNM=11-188	320	BL=1	DS 4C	COMP
DNM=11-206	01	DFHB0046	DNM=11-206	328	BL=1	DS 4C	COMP
DNM=11-224	01	DFHB0047	DNM=11-224	330	BL=1	DS 4C	COMP
DNM=11-242	01	DFHB0048	DNM=11-242	338	BL=1	DS 4C	COMP
DNM=11-260	01	DFHEIV11	DNM=11-260	340	BL=1	DS 2C	COMP
DNM=11-281	01	DFHEIV12	DNM=11-281	348	BL=1	DS 2C	COMP
DNM=11-302	01	DFHEIV13	DNM=11-302	350	BL=1	DS 2C	COMP
DNM=11-320	01	DFHEIV14	DNM=11-320	358	BL=1	DS 2C	COMP
DNM=11-341	01	DFHEIV15	DNM=11-341	360	BL=1	DS 2C	COMP
DNM=11-359	01	DFHB0025	DNM=11-359	368	BL=1	DS 2C	COMP
DNM=11-380	01	DFHB0025	DNM=11-380	370	BL=1	DS 2C	COMP

DNM	Lvl	Name	DNM	Base	Displ	Def	Usage
DNM=11-401	01	DFHEIV5	DNM=11-401	BLL=1	378	DS 4C	DISP
DNM=11-418	01	DFHEIV6	DNM=11-418	BLL=1	380	DS 4C	DISP
DNM=11-438	01	DFHEIV17	DNM=11-438	BLL=1	388	DS 4C	DISP
DNM=11-456	01	DFHEIV18	DNM=11-456	BLL=1	390	DS 4C	DISP
DNM=11-474	01	DFHEIV19	DNM=11-474	BLL=1	398	DS 4C	DISP
DNM=11-492	01	DFHEIV1	DNM=11-492	BLL=1	3A0	DS 4C	DISP
DNM=12-000	01	DFHEIV2	DNM=12-000	BLL=1	3A8	DS 8C	DISP
DNM=12-017	01	DFHEIV3	DNM=12-017	BLL=1	3B0	DS 8C	DISP
DNM=12-034	01	DFHEIV20	DNM=12-034	BLL=1	3B8	DS 8C	DISP
DNM=12-052	01	DFHCOO84	DNM=12-052	BLL=1	3C0	DS 8C	DISP
DNM=12-070	01	DFHCOO85	DNM=12-070	BLL=1	3C8	DS 8C	DISP
DNM=12-091	01	DFHCO0320	DNM=12-091	BLL=1	3D0	DS 32C	DISP
DNM=12-109	01	DFHEIV7	DNM=12-109	BLL=1	3F0	DS 2C	DISP
DNM=12-126	01	DFHEIV8	DNM=12-126	BLL=1	3F8	DS 2C	DISP
DNM=12-143	01	DFHCOO22	DNM=12-143	BLL=1	400	DS 2C	DISP
DNM=12-164	01	DFHCOO23	DNM=12-164	BLL=1	408	DS 2C	DISP
DNM=12-182	01	DFHEIV10	DNM=12-182	BLL=1	410	DS 4P	COMP-3
DNM=12-203	01	DFHCOO11	DNM=12-203	BLL=1	418	DS 1C	DISP
DNM=12-220	01	DFHEIV4	DNM=12-220	BLL=1	420	DS 6C	DISP
DNM=12-238	01	DFHCOO70	DNM=12-238	BLL=1	428	DS 7C	DISP
DNM=12-255	01	DFHCOO71	DNM=12-255	BLL=1	430	DS 7C	DISP
DNM=12-276	01	DFHCOO440	DNM=12-276	BLL=1	438	DS 44C	DISP
DNM=12-294	01	DFHDUMMY	DNM=12-294	BLL=1	440	DS 2C	COMP
DNM=12-312	01	DFHEIV0	DNM=12-312	BLL=1	470	DS 2C	DISP
DNM=12-330	01	DFHEIBLK	DNM=12-330	BLL=3	478	DS 29C	GROUP
DNM=12-350	02	EIBTIME	DNM=12-350	BLL=3	000	DS OCL85	OCL85
DNM=12-374	02	EIBDATE	DNM=12-374	BLL=3	004	DS 4P	COMP-3
DNM=12-394	02	EIBTRNID	DNM=12-394	BLL=3	008	DS 4C	COMP-3
DNM=12-411	02	EIBTASKN	DNM=12-411	BLL=3	00C	DS 4P	DISP
DNM=12-432	02	EIBTRMID	DNM=12-432	BLL=3	010	DS 4C	COMP-3
DNM=12-453	02	DFHEIGDI	DNM=12-453	BLL=3	014	DS 2C	DISP
DNM=12-474	02	EIBCPOSN	DNM=12-474	BLL=3	016	DS 2C	COMP
DNM=13-000	02	EIBCALEN	DNM=13-000	BLL=3	018	DS 2C	COMP
DNM=13-018	02	EIBAID	DNM=13-018	BLL=3	01A	DS 1C	COMP
DNM=13-039	02	EIBFN	DNM=13-039	BLL=3	01B	DS 1C	DISP
DNM=13-055	02	EIBRCODE	DNM=13-055	BLL=3	01D	DS 6C	DISP
DNM=13-073	02	EIBDS	DNM=13-073	BLL=3	023	DS 8C	DISP
DNM=13-091	02	EIBREQID	DNM=13-091	BLL=3	02B	DS 8C	DISP
DNM=13-109	02	EIBRSRCE	DNM=13-109	BLL=3	033	DS 8C	DISP
DNM=13-127	02	EIBSYNC	DNM=13-127	BLL=3	03B	DS 1C	DISP
DNM=13-145	02	EIBFREE	DNM=13-145	BLL=3	03C	DS 1C	DISP
DNM=13-162	02	EIBRECV	DNM=13-162	BLL=3	03D	DS 1C	DISP
DNM=13-182	02	EIBFILO1	DNM=13-182	BLL=3	03E	DS 1C	DISP
DNM=13-199	02	EIBATT	DNM=13-199	BLL=3	03F	DS 1C	DISP
DNM=13-217	02	EIBEOC	DNM=13-217	BLL=3	040	DS 1C	DISP
DNM=13-233	02	EIBFMH	DNM=13-233	BLL=3	041	DS 1C	DISP
DNM=13-249	02	EIBCOMPL	DNM=13-249	BLL=3	042	DS 1C	DISP
DNM=13-265	02	EIBSIG	DNM=13-265	BLL=3	043	DS 1C	DISP
DNM=13-286	02	EIBCONF	DNM=13-286	BLL=3	044	DS 1C	DISP
DNM=13-302	02	EIBERR	DNM=13-302	BLL=3	045	DS 1C	DISP
DNM=13-322	02	EIBERRCD	DNM=13-322	BLL=3	046	DS 4C	DISP
DNM=13-338	02	EIBSYNRB	DNM=13-338	BLL=3	04A	DS 1C	DISP
DNM=13-359	02	EIBNODAT	DNM=13-359	BLL=3	04B	DS 1C	DISP
DNM=13-377	02	EIBRESP	DNM=13-377	BLL=3	04C	DS 4C	COMP
DNM=13-398	02	EIBRESP2	DNM=13-398	BLL=3	050	DS 4C	COMP
DNM=13-418	02	EIBRLDBK	DNM=13-418	BLL=3	054	DS 1C	DISP
DNM=13-436	02	EIBRLDBK	DNM=13-436	BLL=3	054	DS 1C	DISP

```
20     TXTSPNC1        15.06.28          AUG  8.1989

DNM=13-457   01  DFHCOMMAREA        BLL=4   000   DNM=13-457   DS OCL4   GROUP
DNM=13-481   02  LK-COM-INITTRAN    BLL=4   000   DNM=13-481   DS 4C     DISP
DNM=14-000   01  DFHBLLSLOT1        BLL=5   000   DNM=14-000   DS 1C     DISP
DNM=14-024   01  DFHBLLSLOT2        BLL=6         DNM=14-024   DS 1C     DISP
```

MEMORY MAP

TGT   00538

SAVE AREA	00538
SWITCH	00580
TALLY	00584
SORT SAVE	00588
ENTRY-SAVE	0058C
SORT CORE SIZE	00590
RET CODE	00594
SORT RET	00596
WORKING CELLS	00598
SORT FILE SIZE	006C8
SORT MODE SIZE	006CC
PGT-VN TBL	00600
TGT-VN TBL	00604
RESERVED	00608
LENGTH OF VN TBL	0060C
LABEL RET	0060E
RESERVED	0060F
DBG R14SAVE	006E0
COBOL INDICATOR	006E4
A(INIT1)	006E8
DEBUG TABLE PTR	006EC
SUBCOM PTR	006F0
SORT-MESSAGE	006F4
SYSOUT DDNAME	006FC
RESERVED	006FD
COBOL ID	006FE
COMPILED POINTER	00700
COUNT TABLE ADDRESS	00704
RESERVED	00708
DBG R11SAVE	00710
COUNT CHAIN ADDRESS	00714
PRBL1 CELL PTR	00718
RESERVED	0071C
TA LENGTH	00721
RESERVED	00724
PCS LIT PTR	0072C
DEBUGGING	00730
CD FOR INITIAL INPUT	00734
OVERFLOW CELLS	00738
BL CELLS	00738
DECBADR CELLS	0073C
FIB CELLS	0073C
TEMP STORAGE	00740
TEMP STORAGE-2	00748
TEMP STORAGE-3	00748
TEMP STORAGE-4	00748
BLL CELLS	00748
VLC CELLS	00764
SBL CELLS	00764
INDEX CELLS	00764
SUBADR CELLS	00764

```
22     TXTSPNC1          15.06.28       AUG  8.1989

               ONCTL CELLS      00774
               PFMCTL CELLS     00774
               PFMSAV CELLS     00774
               VN CELLS         007F0
               SAVE AREA =2     00858
               SAVE AREA =3     00858
               XSASW CELLS      00858
               XSA CELLS        00858
               PARAM CELLS      00858
               RPTSAV AREA      0087C
               CHECKPT CTR      0087C

LITERAL POOL (HEX)

00900 (LIT+0)      0000FFFF  00041C40  00000052  00000024  00583C0F  F0F0C000
00918 (LIT+24)     28002300  2A003100  2E002F00  32003300  30D705C3  F1D705C3
00930 (LIT+48)     F240C1E3  4003C5C1  E2E34006  D5C540D3  C905C540  D4E4E2E3
00948 (LIT+72)     40C2C540  C505E3C5  D9C5C44B  C5D040D3  D6E8C5C5  40D5E4D4
00960 (LIT+96)     C2C5D940  D5D6E340  C6D6E4D5  C44B05C5  E64005C1  D4C540D4
00978 (LIT+120)    E4E2E340  C2C540C3  D5E3C5D9  C5E3C3C3  09C105E2  C1C3E3C9
00990 (LIT+144)    D6D540D7  D5C3F140  E2E4C3C3  C5E2E2C6  E4D3D3E8  40C3D6D4
009A8 (LIT+168)    D7D3C5E3  C5C44BD3  D6C7C9C3  40C559D9  D9C5C440  40E3D9C1
009C0 (LIT+192)    D5E2C1C3  E3C9D6D5  40C3C1D5  C3C5D3C5  C44BE3D9  C1D5E2C1
009D8 (LIT+216)    C3E3C9D6  D540C3C1  D5C3C5D3  C5C44BC2  E840D6D7  C5D9C1E3
009F0 (LIT+240)    D6D94DD9  C5D8E4C5  E2E34BD2  04B00005  01000000  1802D000
00A08 (LIT+264)    00000000  00000000  00F0F0F2  F0F2FFF7  40400001  D7D2D705
00A20 (LIT+288)    05000000  00500000  2FC7C5D5  40C5D9D9  40400004  D6D94006
00A38 (LIT+312)    C3F7D4E2  C1E34007  F2C7C5D5  40C5D9D9  09E5C548  C3C3E4D9
00A50 (LIT+336)    D9C5C240  C1D705C3  D5C3F240  D5C3F540  00050100  4040E309
00A68 (LIT+360)    C1D5C240  C3C1D5C3  C5D3C5C4  4B020480  40404018  00D10005
00A80 (LIT+384)    00000000  00000000  000000F0  F2F2F8F8  4040C7C5  04D10005
00A98 (LIT+408)    D9D6E940  00020F00  0909C5C4  F2F9F140  D7D5C3F2  40E2C5D5
00AB0 (LIT+432)    D9D6C940  06D3C3E4  E240C3C1  40C1E340  C5C44B02  04C0C5D5
00AC8 (LIT+456)    C44B4040  E3D9C105  E240C3C1  D5C3C5D3  C5C44B02  F1F54040
00AE0 (LIT+480)    00D10005  00D10000  00000080  000000F3  00FC0F03  C440C1E3
00AF8 (LIT+504)    40400002  0607F000  05000000  04B00005  F1F94040  40D7C509
00B10 (LIT+528)    E5E2D7D4  E209C5C3  D609C440  D6D9C440  C606E405  C440C1E3
00B28 (LIT+552)    40D9C5C1  C460C6D2  4B040040  D9C105E2  40C3C105  C3C5D3C5
00B40 (LIT+576)    C440C7C5  D540C5D9  D9D6D940  D6C3C3E4  D9D9C5C4  40C1E340
00B58 (LIT+600)    D9C5C1C4  60C6D24B  C105C605  C105E240  C3C1D5C3  C5D3C5C4
00B70 (LIT+624)    4B020400  00050D01  40404006  D6D9C440  00000000  000000F0
00B88 (LIT+648)    F0F3F5F4  02F00005  D6E340C6  D6E4D5C4  F0F0F3F5  F8404040
00BA0 (LIT+672)    D9C5C3D6  D9C44005  D9D6D940  D9C5C1C4  40C1E340  D9C5C1C4
00BB8 (LIT+696)    60C6D260  E4D7C44B  4040E309  C1D5E240  C3C1D5C3  C5D3C5C4
00BD0 (LIT+720)    4B07C5D5  40C5D909  D6094006  D6E4D5C4  D9C5C440  C1E34009
00BE8 (LIT+744)    C5C1C460  C6D260E4  D7C44B40  40E309C1  D5E24009  C1D5C3C5
00C00 (LIT+768)    0000F000  02048000  05010000  40404006  00000000  00000000
00C18 (LIT+792)    F3F9F340  C5C50000  D9D9C5C4  40C1E340  04D10000  F0F3F9F6
00C30 (LIT+816)    40404007  C5D540C6  D9D6E340  D9C5C440  E4D909C5  D9D6F3F6
00C48 (LIT+840)    4009E5C1  D9C5E2C5  4BD9C505  D9C5C440  40C9D5C5  C3C3C3C5
00C60 (LIT+864)    C44BE4D6  00010000  00100000  D9C5C440  40403C05  08E00005
00C78 (LIT+888)    4B040040  05000000  F6404040  40C3C1C5  05160100  0000000F
00C90 (LIT+912)    00010000  00000000  00000000  0000000F  40404040  30000500
00CA8 (LIT+936)    00008100  40400000  0000000F  00FC0F04  40D3C5D5  C7C5D9D9
00CC0 (LIT+960)    40D6C3C3  40E2C5D5  C4C1D5C3  C5D3C5C4  40D3C5D5  E309C9D5
00CD8 (LIT+984)    E240C6C7  05D3C3E4  E240C3C1  C44B4040  C1D3C0C5  D9D9C6D5
00CF0 (LIT+1008)   40D6C3C3  E4D9D9C5  E4D9D9C5  40E2C5D5  C44B4040  E3D9C1D5
```

23   TXTSPNC1   15.06.28   AUG 8,1989

```
00008 (LIT+1032)  E240C3C1  D5C3C5D3  C5C44B04  04300025  00000081  00004000
00020 (LIT+1056)  0000F0F0  F4F6F940  4040
```

PGT   00880

```
DEBUG LINKAGE AREA        00880
OVERFLOW CELLS            00880
VIRTUAL CELLS             00884
PROCEDURE NAME CELLS      00898
GENERATED NAME CELLS      00898
DCB ADDRESS CELLS         00898
VNI CELLS                 00898
LITERALS                  00900
DISPLAY LITERALS          00D2A
PROCEDURE BLOCK CELLS     00D2C
```

REGISTER ASSIGNMENT

```
REG 6    BLL =1
REG 7    BLL =3
REG 8    BLL =4
```

WORKING-STORAGE STARTS AT LOCATION 000A0 FOR A LENGTH OF 00498.

24   TXTSPNC1   15.06.28   AUG   8.1989

PROCEDURE BLOCK ASSIGNMENT

PBL = REG 11

PBL =1   STARTS AT LOCATION 000D34   STATEMENT 356
PBL =2   STARTS AT LOCATION 001A5C   STATEMENT 716

25   TXTSPNC1   15.06.28   AUG 8,1989

CONDENSED LISTING

Line	Verb	Address	Line	Verb	Address	Line	Verb	Address
356	ENTRY	000D34	362	CALL	000D54	363	SERVICE	000D70
364	SERVICE	000D74	367	IF	000D78	368	PERFORM	000D86
369	GO	000DA2	370	IF	000DAA	371	PERFORM	000DB4
372	GO	000DCC	373	IF	000DD4	377	PERFORM	000DE0
375	GO	000DF8	376	IF	000E00	382	PERFORM	000E0A
378	MOVE	000E22	379	PERFORM	000E2A	393	GOBACK	000E42
391	MOVE	000E6C	392	MOVE	000E7C	399	PERFORM	000E82
397	PERFORM	000E9E	398	MOVE	000EA4			000EAA
400	PERFORM	000EB0	403	EXIT	000ED0	413	PERFORM	000EDA
416	IF	000EF2	417	ADD	000F1A	418	MOVE	000F2C
420	GO	000F5C	422	MOVE	000F60	423	IF	000F72
424	GO	000FA4	425	MOVE	000FA8	426	MOVE	000FCA
427	MOVE	000FD2	428	PERFORM	000FD8	429	IF	000FF0
430	ADD	000FFC	431	MOVE	00100E	432	MOVE	00103E
433	MOVE	00105C	434	IF	001086	435	ADD	001088
436	MOVE	00105A	437	MOVE	0010FA	438	MOVE	001118
440	IF	001142	441	GO	001152	443	IF	001156
444	GO	001166	448	PERFORM	00116A	449	MOVE	001182
450	MOVE	001188	451	MOVE	00118C	452	PERFORM	001194
453	MOVE	0011B4	457	MOVE	0011BC	459	IF	0011C2
460	GO	0011F4	461	PERFORM	0011F8	462	MOVE	00121A
463	GO	001220	464	IF	001228	465	MOVE	001240
466	PERFORM	001266	468	IF	001282	469	GO	001296
472	PERFORM	00129A	473	MOVE	0012AA	474	PERFORM	0012B0
475	PERFORM	0012CC	478	EXIT	0012E8	485	PERFORM	0012F2
487	MOVE	001302	488	PERFORM	001308	489	MOVE	001324
491	EXIT	001340	494	MOVE	00134A	496	EXIT	001398
497	PERFORM	001360	498	PERFORM	00137C	500	GO	0013D2
510	MOVE	0013A2	511	CALL	0013A8	512	MOVE	0013FE
517	MOVE	0013E8	518	MOVE	0013F8	519	MOVE	001452
520	CALL	001404	522	GO	00144E	525	PERFORM	001484
527	MOVE	001462	529	PERFORM	001468	530	MOVE	0014D4
531	GOBACK	0014A0	534	EXIT	0014CA	542	MOVE	00151A
543	CALL	0014DA	544	GO	001504	551	MOVE	001536
552	MOVE	00152A	553	MOVE	001530	554	MOVE	00155A
555	CALL	00153C	557	GO	0015A6	560	MOVE	0015DC
562	MOVE	0015BA	564	PERFORM	0015C0	565	MOVE	00162C
566	GOBACK	0015F8	569	EXIT	001622	574	CALL	001660
579	MOVE	001630	580	CALL	001636	581	IF	001690
589	MOVE	00167A	590	MOVE	00168A	591	GO	0016F2
595	MOVE	00169A	596	GO	0016DE	599	PERFORM	00172C
600	MOVE	0016EA	601	MOVE	0016EE	602	EXIT	001788
603	MOVE	0016F6	605	MOVE	001706	606	CALL	001798
609	MOVE	001710	611	MOVE	001720	613	GO	0017F0
614	PERFORM	001742	615	GOBACK	00175E	618	MOVE	001844
623	MOVE	001792	628	MOVE	001796	629	CALL	00185C
630	GO	0017C6	639	MOVE	0017E0	640	MOVE	001850
641	CALL	0017F6	646	MOVE	001840	647	GO	00185C
650	IF	001848	651	MOVE	00185C	652	MOVE	00186C
653	GO	001858	654	MOVE	001876	656	MOVE	001886
657	GO	001872	665	PERFORM	0018A8	662	MOVE	0018B8
664	PERFORM	00188C	677	MOVE	0018F8	666	GOBACK	0018C4
669	EXIT	0018EE	685	MOVE	00193E	678	CALL	0018FE
679	GO	001928	690	GO	001996	686	MOVE	00194E
687	CALL	001954				693	MOVE	00199A

```
26     TXTSPNC1     15.06.28     AUG  8,1989

695  MOVE     0019AA      697  PERFORM  0019B0      698  PERFORM  0019CC
699  GOBACK   0019E8      702  EXIT     001A12      709  MOVE     001A1C
710  CALL     001A2C      712  EXIT     001A56      722  MOVE     001A5C
723  CALL     001A6C      728  EXIT     001AAE      737  MOVE     001AB4
738  CALL     001ABA      739  GO       001AE4      746  MOVE     001AFE
747  CALL     001B0E      751  GO       001B58      754  MOVE     001B60
756  MOVE     001B70      757  GO       001B76      760  MOVE     001B7A
762  MOVE     001B8A      764  PERFORM  001B90      765  PERFORM  001BA8
766  GOBACK   001BC8      769  EXIT     001BF2      780  MOVE     001BFC
781  CALL     001C0C      787  EXIT     001C56
```

27   TXTSPNC1   15.06.28   AUG 8.1989

STATISTICS SOURCE   RECORDS =   787   DATA DIVISION STATEMENTS =   287   PROCEDURE DIVISION STATEMENTS =   193
                       SIZE = 593920   BUF = 40960   LINECNT = 57   SPACE1, FLAGW, NOSEQ, SOURCE
OPTIONS IN EFFECT   DMAP, NOPMAP, CLIST, NOSUPMAP, NOXREF, SXREF, LOAD, NODECK, APOST, NOTRUNC, NOFLOW
OPTIONS IN EFFECT   NOTERM, NONUM, NOBATCH, NONAME, COMPILE=01, NOSTATE, NORESIDENT, NODYNAM, LIB, NOSYNTAX
OPTIONS IN EFFECT   OPTIMIZE, NOSYMDMP, NOTEST, VERB, ZWB, SYST, NOENDJOB, NOMIGR, NOLVL
OPTIONS IN EFFECT   NOLST, NOFDECK, NOCDECK, LCOL2, L120, DUMP, NOADV, NOPRINT,
OPTIONS IN EFFECT   NOCOUNT, NOVBSUM, NOVBREF, LANGLVL(2)

```
28    TXTSPNC1        15.06.28        AUG  8,1989

                      CROSS-REFERENCE DICTIONARY

DATA NAMES      DEFN      REFERENCE

CSCO-LENGTH     000159    000399 000451 000723 000641 000687 000646 000650 000651
CSFC-LENGTH     000160    000427 000462 000591 000599 000600
CSHC-ALLOW      000161    000426 000463 000595 000601 000623 000652
CSHC-NOTFND     000162    000429 000574
CSPC-TRANSID    000163    000397 000449 000723 000496 000527 000562 000605 000611 000656 000662 000695
CSTC-LENGTH     000164    000473 000487 000756 000762 000781

DFHAID          000170
DFHALL          000233
DFHBASE         000244
DFHBKTRN        000232
DFHBLINK        000246
DFHBLLSLOT1     000354
DFHBLLSLOT2     000355
DFHBLUE         000357
DFHBMASB        000220
DFHBMASF        000219
DFHBMASK        000211
DFHBMBRY        000215
DFHBMDAR        000216
DFHBMDET        000222
DFHBMEOF        000221
DFHBMFSE        000217
DFHBMPEM        000209
DFHBMPNL        000210
DFHBMPRF        000218
DFHBMPRO        000214
DFHBMPSI        000224
DFHBMPSO        000223
DFHBMSCA        000208
DFHBMUNN        000213
DFHBMUNP        000212
DFHBOX          000268
DFHBOO25        000292
DFHBOO41        000279
DFHBOO42        000280
DFHBOO43        000281
DFHBOO44        000282
DFHBOO45        000283
DFHBOO46        000284
DFHBOO47        000285
DFHBOO48        000286
DFHCLEAR        000173
DFHCLRP         000174
DFHCOLOR        000226
DFHCOMMAREA     000351
DFHCOO11        000311
DFHCOO22        000308
DFHCOO23        000313
DFHCOO70        000313    000518 000520 000552 000555
DFHCOO71        000314    000519 000520 000553 000555
```

29   TXTSPNC1   15.06.28   AUG 8.1989

Symbol	Defn
DFHCO084	000302
DFHCO085	000303
DFHCO320	000304
DFHCO440	000315
DFHDFCOL	000236
DFHDFFR	000263
DFHDFHI	000245
DFHDFT	000235
DFHDUMMY	000316
DFHEIBLK	000319
DFHEIBO	000275
DFHEICB	000276
DFHEIDO	000274
DFHEIGDI	000325
DFHEIVO	000317

Symbol	Defn
DFHEIV1	000298
DFHEIV10	000309
DFHEIV11	000287
DFHEIV12	000288
DFHEIV13	000289
DFHEIV14	000290
DFHEIV15	000291
DFHEIV16	000278
DFHEIV17	000295
DFHEIV18	000296
DFHEIV19	000297
DFHEIV2	000299
DFHEIV20	000301
DFHEIV3	000300
DFHEIV4	000312
DFHEIV5	000293
DFHEIV6	000294
DFHEIV7	000305
DFHEIV8	000306
DFHEIV9	000310
DFHENTER	000172
DFHERROR	000234
DFHGREEN	000240
DFHHLT	000228
DFHLDVER	000273
DFHLEFT	000264
DFHMENT	000250
DFHMET	000251
DFHMFE	000262
DFHMFET	000249
DFHMFIL	000260
DFHMFT	000177
DFHMSRE	000259
DFHMT	000243
DFHNEUTR	000171
DFHNULL	000271
DFHOPAQ	000176
DFHOPID	000231
DFHOUTLN	000265
DFHOVER	

Reference line numbers (as printed):

```
000520   000555   000747   000781

000554   000555

000512   000544   000581   000630   000679   000739
000510   000511   000517   000520   000542   000543
000589   000591   000628   000629   000639   000641
000709   000710   000722   000723   000737   000738
000590   000591   000640   000641   000686   000687

000551   000555   000579   000580
000677   000678   000685   000687
000746   000747   000780   000781
```

30   TXTSPNC1   15.06.28   AUG 8.1989

DFHPA1	000180		
DFHPA2	000181		
DFHPA3	000182		
DFHPEN	000175		
DFHPF1	000183		
DFHPF10	000192		
DFHPF11	000193	000370	
DFHPF12	000194		
DFHPF13	000195		
DFHPF14	000196		
DFHPF15	000197		
DFHPF16	000198		
DFHPF17	000199		
DFHPF18	000200		
DFHPF19	000201		
DFHPF2	000184		
DFHPF20	000202		
DFHPF21	000203		
DFHPF22	000204		
DFHPF23	000205		
DFHPF24	000206		
DFHPF3	000185		
DFHPF4	000186		
DFHPF5	000187		
DFHPF6	000188		
DFHPF7	000189		
DFHPF8	000190		
DFHPF9	000191		
DFHP1NK	000239		
DFHPROTI	000257		
DFHPROTN	000258		
DFHPS	000227		
DFHRED	000238		
DFHREVRS	000247		
DFHRIGHT	000266		
DFHSA	000225		
DFHSOSI	000269		
DFHSTRF	000178		
DFHTRANS	000270		
DFHTRIG	000179		
DFHTURQ	000241		
DFHUNDER	000267		
DFHUNDLN	000248		
DFHUNIMD	000255	000433	000438
DFHUNINT	000256		
DFHUNNON	000252		
DFHUNNUM	000254		
DFHVAL	000230		
DFHYELLO	000242		
DFH3270	000229		
EIBAID	000328	000370	
EIBATT	000338		
EIBCALEN	000327	000373	
EIBCOMPL	000341		
EIBCPOSN	000326		

```
EIBDATE           000321
EIBDS             000331
EIBEOC            000339
EIBERR            000344
EIBERRCD          000345
EIBFILO1          000337
EIBFMH            000340
EIBFN             000329
EIBFREE           000335
EIBNODAT          000347
EIBRCODE          000330
EIBRECV           000336
EIBREQID          000332
EIBRESP           000348
EIBRESP2          000349
EIBRLDBK          000350
EIBRSRCE          000333
EIBSIG            000342
EIBSYNC           000334
EIBSYNRB          000346
EIBTASKN          000323
EIBTIME           000320
EIBTRMID          000324    000367
EIBTRNID          000322
LK-COM-INTTRAN    000352    000376
MPBPNC2-REDEFINE  000116
MPBPNC2I          000054    000520
MPBPNC20          000120    000391    000555
M2EMPNNA          000096    000433
M2EMPNNI          000121    000423    000425    000459    000461
M2EMPNNL          000119    000432
M2EMPNNO          000123
M2EMPN1A          000057
M2EMPN1F          000060    000416
M2EMPN1I          000056    000392
M2EMPN1L          000099
M2EMPN10          000069
M2EMPN2A          000067    000416
M2EMPN2F          000070
M2EMPN2I          000066
M2EMPN2L          000103
M2EMPN20          000131
M2ERRNA           000130
M2ERRNL           000132    000418    000431    000436
M2ERRNO           000079
M2ERR1A           000080
M2ERR1F           000077
M2ERR1I           000076
M2ERR10           000107
M2ERR2A           000084
M2ERR2F           000082
M2ERR2I           000085
M2ERR2L           000081
M2ERR20           000109
M2ERR3A           000089
M2ERR3F           000087
```

```
32      TXTSPNC1          15.06.28          AUG   8,1989

M2ERR3I            000090
M2ERR3L            000086
M2ERR3O            000111
M2ERR4A            000094
M2ERR4F            000092
M2ERR4I            000095
M2ERR4L            000091
M2ERR4O            000113
M2NAMENA           000125  000438
M2NAMENI           000126  000434
M2NAMENL           000124  000437
M2NAMENO           000128
M2NAME1A           000064
M2NAME1F           000062
M2NAME1I           000065
M2NAME1L           000061
M2NAME1O           000101
M2NAME2A           000074
M2NAME2F           000072
M2NAME2I           000075
M2NAME2L           000071
M2NAME2O           000105
PMS-AGE            000149
PMS-DEPT           000144  000425  000461
PMS-EMPNO          000141
PMS-EXT            000146
PMS-INSPOLICY      000152
PMS-INSPREM        000139  000591  000641  000687
PMS-IOAREA         000143  000465
PMS-NAME           000147
PMS-RANK           000142  000591  000641
PMS-RECORD-DETAIL  000140
PMS-RECORD-KEY     000145
PMS-ROOM           000151
PMS-SALARY         000150
PMS-SEX            000148
PMS-TITLE          000134  000472  000485  000494  000525  000560  000603  000609  000654  000660  000693
TC-O-AREA          000747  000754  000760  000781

TC-01-AREA         000135  000398  000450
WK-CICS-WORK       000158  000723
WK-COM-INTTRAN     000156
WK-COMMAREA        000155  000417  000418  000430  000431  000435  000436  000443
WK-ERR-CNT         000167  000422  000423  000432  000433  000434  000438  000440  000457
WK-LINE-CNT        000166  000459  000461  000465  000468  000437
```

33   TXTSPNC1   15.06.28   AUG 8,1989

PROCEDURE NAMES	DEFN	REFERENCE
A000-PNC1-ROUTINE	000387	000374
A100-SEND-MAP	000390	
A200-RETURN-WITH-TRANSID	000396	
A999-EXIT	000402	
B000-PNC2-ROUTINE	000409	000377
B100-RECEIVE-MAP	000412	
B110-EDIT-LOOP	000421	000441
B115-EDIT-SKIP	000439	000424
B120-CHECK-ERR	000442	000420
B130-INVALID-DATA	000447	
B200-VALID-DATA	000456	000444
B210-UPDATE-LOOP	000458	000469
B215-UPDATE-SKIP	000467	000460
B999-EXIT	000477	000453
MAIN-0000-MAINLINE	000365	
MAIN-9999-GOBACK	000381	000369 000372 000375
X100-LOGICERR-ROUTINE	000484	000368 000379 000378
X199-EXIT	000490	
X200-FORCE-CANCEL	000499	
ZBM1A-ERROR	000493	000371
ZBM1X-SEND-RETURN	000524	000512
ZBM10-PNC2-RECEIVE	000528	
ZBM19-EXIT	000533	000413
ZBM2A-ERROR	000559	000522
ZBM2X-SEND-RETURN	000563	000544
ZBM20-PNC2-SEND	000538	000393
ZBM29-EXIT	000598	000557
ZFC1A-NOTFND	000608	000581
ZFC1B-ERROR	000573	000606
ZFC1X-SEND-RETURN	000617	000596
ZFC10-PMS-READ-FULLKEY	000649	000602 000653
ZFC19-EXIT	000659	
ZFC2A-NOTFND	000663	000630
ZFC2B-ERROR	000622	000657
ZFC2X-SEND-RETURN	000668	000464
ZFC20-PMS-READ-FULLKEY-UPDATE	000692	000647 000690
ZFC29-EXIT	000696	
ZFC3A-ERROR	000673	000679
ZFC3X-SEND-RETURN	000701	
ZFC30-PMS-REWRITE	000706	000466
ZFC39-EXIT	000711	
ZPC10-PC-RETURN	000716	000475 000489 000498 000530 000565 000614 000665 000698 000765
ZPC19-EXIT	000727	
ZPC20-PC-RETURN-TRANSID-COM	000753	000400 000452
ZPC29-EXIT	000759	
ZTC2A-LENGERR	000763	000739
ZTC2B-ERROR	000732	000739
ZTC2X-SEND-RETURN	000768	000757 000488 000497
ZTC20-TC-SEND	000786	000474 000564 000613 000664 000697 000764
ZTC29-EXIT		000751
ZTC30-TC-SEND-NOHANDLE		000529
ZTC39-EXIT		

541

```
MVS/XA DFP VER 2 LINKAGE EDITOR    15:07:08  TUE  AUG 08, 1989
JOB PSTSAO1F  STEP COBUCL    PROCEDURE LKED
INVOCATION PARAMETERS - XREF
ACTUAL SIZE=(317440,86016)
OUTPUT DATA SET PSTSAO1.TEXT.LOADLIB IS ON VOLUME PSTXXX
```

CROSS REFERENCE TABLE

CONTROL SECTION			ENTRY									
NAME	ORIGIN	LENGTH	NAME	LOCATION	NAME	LOCATION	NAME	LOCATION	NAME	LOCATION	NAME	LOCATION
DFHECI	00	48	DFHEI1	8	DFHEI11	8	DLZEIO1	8	DLZEIO2	8	DLZEIO3	8
			DLZEIO4	8	DFHCBLI	26						
TXISPNC1	48	1D42										
ILBOCOMO*	1D90	173	ILBOCOM	1D90								
ILBOGDO0	1F08	120	ILBOGDO0	1FOA	ILBOGDO1	1FOE	ILBOGDO2	1F12				
ILBOSRV*	2028	4D4	ILBOSRVO	2032	ILBOSR5	2032	ILBOSR3	2032	ILBOSR	2032		
			ILBOSRV1	2036	ILBOSTP1	2036	ILBOST	203A	ILBOSTPO	203A		
ILBOBEG*	2500	1DC	ILBOBEGO	2502								
ILBOMSG*	26E0	100	ILBOMSGO	26E2								

LOCATION	REFERS TO SYMBOL	IN CONTROL SECTION	LOCATION	REFERS TO SYMBOL	IN CONTROL SECTION
8CC	ILBOSRVO	ILBOSRV	8D0	ILBOSR5	ILBOSRV
8D4	DFHEI1	DFHECI	8D8	ILBOSRV1	ILBOSRV
8DC	ILBOGDO	ILBOGDO0	738	ILBOCOMO	ILBOCOMO
23BC	ILBOCMMO	$UNRESOLVED(W)	2300	ILBOSTTO	$UNRESOLVED(W)
23C0	ILBOMSGO	ILBOMSG	23C4	ILBOBEGO	ILBOBEG
2640	ILBOPRMO	$UNRESOLVED(W)	23CC	ILBOSND2	$UNRESOLVED(W)

```
ENTRY ADDRESS       48

TOTAL LENGTH      27E0
*** TXISPNC1 REPLACED AND HAS AMODE 24
*** LOAD MODULE HAS RMODE 24
*** AUTHORIZATION CODE IS    0.
```

```
ACBCICSE   --- CICS TRANSACTION DUMP ---      CODE=ASRA      TASK=PNC1                    DATE=08/08/89      TIME=15:10:49      PAGE   1

SYMPTOMS= AB/UASRA PIDS/566540300 FLDS/FOOOKC RIDS/TXTSPNC1

CICS/VS LEVEL = 0210

PSW         078D2000   00225FBC   00060007   00000000
REGS 14-4   503A0A42   00226098   00000000   00225F3C   A03A2412   00000001   00221374
REGS 5-11   8001D018   0002182C   00021428   8001D018   00226004   00225050   00225D84

TASK CONTROL AREA (USER AREA)      ADDRESS 00021190 TO 00021A3F      LENGTH 0008B0

00000000   00021000  0035B69C  01056814  003F6AD0   00021580  00000000  2000FF00  44310A00   *....................................*   00021190
00000020   003F3532  00021378  0035EAB8  00000000   00225090  00021AF0  00225098  003A2280   *....................................*   000211B0
00000040   00021000  00225050  U03F346C  000221DC   003A4FF0  00212C0  503A0A42  00224440    *.......................ASRA.........*   000211C0
00000060   403A0B08  C1E2D9C1  00000000  00060000   003A1AA0  00000001  035EAA0  003A03EC    *....ASRA............................*   000211F0
00000080   FE000000  00000000  C1E2D9C1  00000000   07802000  00225FBC  00060007  00000000    *........ASRA.......NC2 ASRA.........*   00021230
000000A0   503A0A42  00226098  00000000  00225F3C   A03A2412  00221374  00021374  8001D018    *..........................jd........*   00021250
000000C0   0002182C  00021428  8001D018  00226D04   00225050  00225D84  00000000  800014F    *.................................*      00021270
000000E0   00000000  00021290  00000000  0039D4E8   00021AD0  00000000  00000000  00000000    *..................MY................*   00021290
00000100   00000028  00000000  24000000  00000000   0000025C  00000000  00021428  00000000    *....................................*   000212B0
00000120   00000000  00000000  00000000  40404040   00056814  00021AF0  00021428  00000000    *....................................*   000212D0
00000140   00000000  00000000  00000000  40404040   00000000  00000000  00212C0  00000000     *....................................*   00021310
00000160   00000000  00000000  00000000  00000000   00000000  00000000  00000000  00000000    *..................................o.*   00021330
00000180   00000000  00000000  00000000  00000000   00021480  00000000  00000000  000223F0    *..............................b.*      00021350
000001A0   00000000  00000000  00000000  00000000   00000000  00000004  00000000  00008200    *....................................*   00021370
000001C0   00000000  00000000  00222320  00000000   0002182C  00000000  0035EABB  00040000    *.....................D..............*   00021390
000001E0   003F3700  00225050  8001D018  00021FC4   00225090  00021AF0  00225098  003A2280    *...................D...o.q..........*   000213C0
00000200   00021000  003F66D0  003F346C  00225084   0039D4B4  00021378  00021190  00000000    *.................jd..M...o.q........*   000213F0
00000220   00200000  00000000  00000000  00000000   00021374  8002130  00000000  00000000      *....................................*   00021410
00000240   00000000  00000000  00000000  00000000   40C4C6C8  C5C9C240  00021428  00222E4     *..........................DFHEIB....*   00021430
00000260   D7D5C3F1  00000059C  00000000  F000000    4CC4C6C8  C5C9C240  01510490  0092220F    *..PNAR...6...DFHEIB.....j............*  00021450
00000280   0002182C  00000040  D705C1D9  00000F6    00047D18  02000000  00000000  00000000    *....................................*   00021470
000002A0   00000000  00000000  40404040  00000000   40404040  00000000  00000000  00000000    *....................................*   00021490
000002C0   00000000  00000000  00000000  00000000   00000000  00000000  00000000  00000000    *..............................U.....*   000214B0
000002E0   LINES TO  00000360  SAME AS ABOVE
00000300   00000001  0032310C  00000001  00000000   00000000  00000000  00000000  00230EC     *....................................*  00021510
00000320   00000001  0035F26C  00000000  00000000   42000068  00021B2C  00000000  00000000    *....................................*   00021530
00000340   003A03EC  00000000  D3C9C6D6  E2E3D609   00021F5C  00021B2C  FF021F8E8  00384712    *.............LIFOSTOR...............*   00021550
00000360   90384890  00225008  00000000  00384638   42000050  00021190  003F6600  0001C940    *...........U..u..*...........Y.i....*   00021570
00000380   00000002  003F439C  00021F44  00056814   00212C0  00021190  003F6600  FE0215E8     *...................................*    00021590
000003A0   F0002C3  003F08F4  50381F68  0000005C    00000000  00000000  48000060  00021580     *O.KC...4..................*.........*   000215B0
000003C0   00021648  4038208C  48000060  003F439C   00000000  00021F5C  00021F5C  00021590    *...................................*    000215D0
000003E0   00021F9C  00021000  00000000  003F439C   00056814  01056814  48000050  00021F5C    *................................Y...*   000215F0
00000400   003F66D0  FE021648  FA00D4C3  00021000   01000000  48000250  003A186A  0002152F8    *............MC............q..MC.....*  00021610
00000420   FF021898  403A1904  00365F0C  C0000200   00021130  003A14A0  B03A196C  00021190     *............q..M...M................*  00021630
00000440   003A03EC  00021000  48000250  00021000   003A2098  003A2C50  803A196C  00021190     *...........M.......q..MC.*..........*  00021650
00000460   003F66D0  FE021898  FA00D4C3  00385C6    01026814  0035AE24  0035AE24  00000706      *............MC*.MPBPNC2 MSBPNC2.....*  00021670
00000480   D7D5C3F1  00056814  D407C2D7  D5C3F240   D4E2C2D7  D5C3F240  0001C060  00000000     *.PNC1...MPBPNC2 MSBPNC2............*    00021690
000004A0   803B0BCE  0001C060  000230F8  07800000   00000000  001C060  00000000  00000000      *...........8......Q...q..8..........*  000216F0
00000580   0035EE70  00021130  00000000  00000000   00000000  00000000  00000000  11000000     *....................................*  00021710
```

```
ACBCICSE    --- CICS TRANSACTION DUMP ---    CODE=ASRA    TASK=PNC1    DATE=08/08/89    TIME=15:10:49    PAGE  2

TASK CONTROL AREA (USER AREA)        ADDRESS 00021190 TO 00021A3F    LENGTH 0008B0

000005A0  00000000 00000000 00000000 00000000  *................*  00021730
000005C0  LINES TO 00000660 SAME AS ABOVE                          00021750
00000680  00000000 0000004D 00000000 00000000  *................*  00021810
000006A0  00000000 000000E0 00000000 00000000  *................*  00021830
000006C0  LINES TO 000006E0 SAME AS ABOVE                          00021850
00000700  00000000 48000190 00021648  00000000 *................*  00021890
00000720  00000000 00000000 FE021A28 E4OOE3O4  *...........h....* 000218B0
00000740  00000000 803BC77C EAOOE304 0O38C6D4  *......G....TM.FM*  000218D0
00000760  00000000 8O3BC8FC 8O3BC84E 00000000  *......H....H+...*  000218F0
00000780  00000000 803BECOC 00021908 00000000  *......H....H....*  00021910
000007A0  LINES TO 000007E0 SAME AS ABOVE                          00021930
00000800  803BD8CE 00023118 00021908 00219C8   *...Q...........*  00021950
00000820  0035EE70 00021130 00018138 00021980   *...a...........*  00021980
00000840  00000020 0039D4E8 00000000 0001E184   *...MY......d...*  000219D0
00000860  00021524 00021310C 00000000 00000000  *................*  000219F0
00000880  03030000 00000000 00000000 00000000   *................*  00021A10
000008A0  8A040A38 00022440                      *................*  00021A30

TASK CONTROL AREA (SYSTEM AREA)      ADDRESS 00021000 TO 000211BF    LENGTH 000190

00000000  8A040A38 00022440 000224F0 0003A59C  *................O.O*  00021000
00000020  00000000 00021290 FE3904B4 00021FC4  *...............D*   00021020
00000040  00021AEO 00000000 00000000 000212CO  *................*   00021040
00000060  BOOOOOOO 80000000 36O04800 00021580   *.........ASRA...*   00021060
00000080  FE021A28 FE021570 003F8E28 00021580   *................*   00021080
000000A0  00056814 00022440 D7D5C3F1 12COOOOO   *........PNC1....*   000210A0
000000C0  C1E2D9C1 00000005 D4E2C207 00022400B  *ASRA....MSBPNC2.*  000210C0
000000E0  00000000 00022400B D5C3F240 50180101  *..........TXTSPNC1.* 000210E0
00000100  00000000 00224008 E3E7E3E2 D7D5C3F1   *...........-....*   00021100
00000120  00000000 106000000 00021214 0O3994E8  *................*   00021120
00000140  00000000 00021518 01000300 C3E2D5C5   *.........NYCSNET ACBCIC*  00021140
00000160  E2C5B8O8 B78751C 19100SE8 E34BC1C3     *SE..g....ACBCIC*   00021160
00000180  07D7E2E3 E2C1FOF1 00000000 C2C3C9C3    *.PSTSA01........*   00021180

LIFO STACK ENTRY OWNED BY DFHKCP

00000000  42000068 FF0215E8 00384712 90384890  *..........Y.....*   00021580
00000020  00021F5C 00021B2C 0001C940 00225008   *......I.........*   000215A0
00000040  000212CO 0002119O 003F66DO 003F439C   *......YO.KC...4.*   000215C0
00000060  00000000 FE0215E8 F00002C3 003F0BF4   *................*   000215E0

PROGRAM COMMUNICATION AREA           ADDRESS 0001D018 TO 0001D01B    LENGTH 000004

00000000  D7D5C3F2                              *PNC2            *   0001D018
```

```
ACBCICSE    --- CICS TRANSACTION DUMP ---    CODE=ASRA    TASK=PNC1              DATE=08/08/89    TIME=15:10:49    PAGE    3

     REGS  0 THRU 15                          ADDRESS 0035B700 TO 0035B73F    LENGTH 000040

00000000  00000000 00225F3C A03A2412 00000001   00021374 8001D018 00021B2C 00021428  *........................jd......* 0035B700
00000020  8001D018 00226004 00225050 00225084   00225800 00021FC4 5022648E 00226D98  *.............D....q*             0035B720

COMMON SYSTEM AREA                              ADDRESS 003F66D0 TO 003F6ACF    LENGTH 000400

00000000  00005FA8 00021374 0000570C 70371384   00226D98 00000000 00225F3C A03A2412  *.........................y......* 003F6600
00000020  00000001 00021374 8001D018 00021B2C   00021428 8001D018 00226004 00225050  *.................................* 003F66F0
00000040  00225084 00372306 00101000 00002119   1510495F 00018650 07000100 00000000  *jd..F...o..k.........f........* 003F6710
00000060  0053637C 00012C00 007FB0F0 0000001E   0000A000 00006000 00405000 0089220F  *............o..........* 003F6730
00000080  003F8130 E0FFFFFE 0000001E 00018000   00000004 00000000 00017030 E738E721  *a........c......d..Q..E.* 003F6750
000000A0  00000000 00018380 003F6AD0 003A14A0   000184A0 003F6ED8 007FB0F0 00000000  *.............X..O.* 003F6770
000000C0  403EF94C 003A77E8 0003CE3C 003B6858   0037138C 003AA938 00395FEC 00389108  *.9......y.....z..j.* 003F6790
000000E0  0038CE3C 0037698A 00365F0C 00392228   00000000 003EB60C 0130EB50 0035E960  *......$......z...Z.* 003F67B0
00000100  00000000 003AA368 00000000 00000000   00385F08 00285F08 0023FA00 003F8C28  *......$...$...Q.* 003F67D0
00000120  00000000 0035B680 00000000 00000000   0035AEA0 00000000 00000000 00000000  *.......t.......Q.* 003F67F0
00000140  00000000 00000000 00000000 BB058075   00F63713 02000100 00000000 00000000  *.........6.........* 003F6810
00000160  00000000 00000000 00000000 00007228   00000000 00000100 00000000 003F6668  *...............6.* 003F6830
00000180  070E58F0 D19C07FF 00F42A76 00FA2B0A   00096000 000C0000 E6D6D902 C1D9C5C1  *...0...........OJ......WORKAREA* 003F6850
000001A0  00000000 000C0000 0022C003C 000C0000   00588C00 00539F00 00000000 C1D9C5C1  *...............$....* 003F6870
000001C0  03000300 000C0000 0000000C 00059C00   00000000 00000000 0000000C 00000000  *............* 003F6890
000001E0  00000000 0000003E0 SAME AS ABOVE                                          003F68B0
00000200  LINES TO                                                                   003F68D0
00000220                                                                             003F68F0

CSA OPTIONAL FEATURE LIST                       ADDRESS 003F6AD0 TO 003F6DF7    LENGTH 000328

00000000  00000000 0035A130 003790F8 0038IF92   00000000 003A7290 003A7290 003A730C  *...............8.* 003F6AD0
00000020  0036FA8C 0036F438 0000FE00 0036694    00000000 00000000 00000000 00000000  *........8...k.* 003F6AF0
00000040  803F8084 01F4F15B A0B80580 0000FE00   0036694 0089220F 00395028 003F8D4B   *...D..4.......D..* 003F6B10
00000060  003F8D84 003A7B18 00731A8 82304CC0    0038CC8 0089220F 00395028 003F6600  *d.41$.....h..j..)* 003F6B30
00000080  003F8E28 00000000 003F346C 003F57C8    003E43C8 00000000 0038C878 00391B0B  *.........yb..H..H..q* 003F6B50
000000A0  003A9E88 003F92C8 003E69E8 003F2E88    003A73C8 00000000 0038463B 00365028  *h..2H..y..H..FQ.* 003F6B70
000000C0  003730F8 00388038 003888398 00000000   003F6078 003F6078 003F86C8 00000000  *..8...x8..cQ...Q...fH* 003F6B90
000000E0  003D5128 003A7948 003A7638 003D06BF8   003D6BF8 00000000 003DESCC 00000000  *....x8...M...8....* 003F6BB0
00000100  0003CE778 003C4458 0037CA12 0037DB02    00386752 0038520B 003851C2 003811C2  *.M..Q..v..Q...B* 003F6BD0
00000120  00387892 0038D052 0037F8E2 00375CE8    00375CE8 003A03EC 000077D4 00000000  *.........8S..BH..H..*Y..M* 003F6BF0
00000140  00000000 0038C69C 003638CC 003ECB88    00000000 00000000 00000000 00000000  *.k...85..BH...H...*Y..* 003F6C10
00000160  00363A28 003A28B0 00000000 00037A8CC   0037A8CC 0036D62C 0036CBAC 00000000  *.F...8S..BH...H...* 003F6C30
00000180  003C1828 003BC69C 00000000 00000000    003C0CC8 0035AE00 003F60F8 00000000  *..........y...H.* 003F6C50
000001A0  0035EFB0 0001D394 00000000 003E904C    0035B268 00000000 00000000 00000000  *.....Lm...........8* 003F6C70
000001C0  00000000 00000000 00000000 00000000    40000000 00000000 00000000 00000000  *.* 003F6C90
000001E0  00000000 00005858 00000000 00000000    C0000000 D7E2E3E2 C1F0F240 00000000  *......PSTSAO2.* 003F6CB0
00000200  00000000 80000000 00008000 00000000    00000000 035FE60 00000000 00000000  *.......R.P,* 003F6CD0
00000220  0AD90AD7 00000000 00000000 12AE3B00    00000000 035FE60 00360000 00000000  *R.P,........SO* 003F6CF0
00000240  A0BB057D 12AE3B00 12AE3B00 00000000    00006020 0036D62C 0001E2FO 00000000  *.........SO* 003F6D10
00000260  00000000 00000000 003C0E38 00000000    00000000 00000000 00000000 00000000  *............* 003F6D30
00000280  00000000 00000000 00000000 00000000    00000000 00000000 00000000 00000000  *............* 003F6D50
000002A0  00000000 00000000 00000000 00000000    00000000 00000000 00000000 00000000  *............* 003F6D70
000002C0  00000000 00000000 00000000 00000000    00000000 00000000 00000000 00000000  *............* 003F6D90
000002E0  00000000 00000000 00000000 00000000    00000000 00000000 00000000 00000000  *............* 003F6DB0
00000300  00000000 00000000 00000000 00000000    00000000 00000000 00000000 003BEC9C  *............* 003F6DD0
00000320  00000000 00000000 00000000 00000000                                         003F6DF0
```

```
ACBCICSE   --- CICS TRANSACTION DUMP ---   CODE=ASRA   ADDRESS 02300020 TO 02303FFF   TASK=PNC1          DATE=08/08/89   TIME=15:10:49   PAGE   4

TRACE TABLE
TRACE HDR   02302CE0   02300020   ADDRESS 02300020 TO 02303FFF   LENGTH 003FE0
            02303FE0   800001FF   00535710   1E90D200   00000000   00000000
```

TIME OF DAY	ID	REG 14	REQD	TASK	FIELD A	FIELD B	CHARS	RESOURCE	TRACE TYPE	INTERVAL
15:10:13.520224	F1	803A9F28	0004	00056	800C2B00	650229FC	....		SCP GETMAIN	00 000032
15:10:13.520256	C8	503A8828	0004	00056	00022BF0	8C2B0078	.0..		SCP ACQUIRED USER STORAGE	00 000000
15:10:13.520256	E1	8021470C	00F4	00056	00000000	00000C02	....		EIP GETMAIN RESPONSE	00 000000
15:10:13.520288	E1	802147C6	8E04	00056	00007010	00000A02	....		EIP WRITEQ-TS ENTRY	00 000032
15:10:13.520288	F1	803F474E	8E04	00056	0002005B	01056814	...$		SCP GETMAIN	00 000000
15:10:13.520320	C8	503A8828	4503	00056	00022C70	8E020068	....		SCP ACQUIRED TEMPSTRG STORAGE	00 000064
15:10:13.520384	F7	8039C8E	0005	00056	F000C5C4	D7D5C1D9	EDPNAR		TSP APPL REQ PUTQ-REPLACE	00 000032
15:10:13.520416	F7	803F474E	4004	00056	00022C70	01056814	....		TSP RETN APPL RESP NORMAL	00 000000
15:10:13.520416	C9	503A8864	0005	00056	8E020068	8E020068	....		SCP FREEMAIN	00 000032
15:10:13.520416	E1	8021470C	00F4	00056	00022C70	00000A02	....		SCP RELEASED TEMPSTRG STORAGE	00 000000
15:10:13.520448	E1	802147C6	0004	00056	00070010	00000C04	.0..		EIP WRITEQ-TS RESPONSE	00 000032
15:10:13.520448	F1	803A9FD0	00F4	00056	40002BF0	650229FC	....		EIP FREEMAIN ENTRY	00 000032
15:10:13.520480	C9	503A8864	0004	00056	00022BF0	8C2B0078	.0..		SCP FREEMAIN	00 000032
15:10:13.520480	E1	8021470C	00F4	00056	00070010	00000C04	....		SCP RELEASED USER STORAGE	00 000032
15:10:13.520480	E1	802147EC	0004	00056	000706E0	00000C02	....		EIP FREEMAIN RESPONSE	00 000032
15:10:13.520512	E1	803A9F28	0004	00056	00070010	650229FC	....		EIP GETMAIN ENTRY	00 000032
15:10:13.520512	C8	8021CAB0	0004	00056	C00C0000	00000C04	....		SCP GETMAIN INITIMG	00 000128
15:10:13.520640	E1	8021CAB0	00F4	00056	00032000	00000C02	....		SCP ACQUIRED USER STORAGE	00 000864
15:10:13.520640	FA	802136EA	0004	00056	0000150E	650229FC	....		EIP GETMAIN RESPONSE	00 000032
15:10:13.521504	E1	803B4712	0003	00056	00015E2	04000020	....		EIP SEND-MAP ENTRY	00 000032
15:10:13.521536	FA	803B209C	0003	00056	00000400	04000020	..S		BMS SEND-OUT CURSOR MAP MAPSET SAVE ERASE	00 000032
15:10:13.521536	F2	503B5492	8404	00056	00022BF0	01056814	..S		BMS SEND-OUT CURSOR MAP MAPSET SAVE ERASE	00 000032
15:10:13.521568	C8	503A7C60	CC04	00056	01000304	00001804	....		PCP LOAD-CONDITIONAL	00 000032
15:10:13.521568	FA	503A8904	0003	00056	01000300	00022214	.0.	DFHEDFMM	SCP GETMAIN INITIMG	00 000032
15:10:13.521600	EA	403BD8AC	0405	00056	01000304	00000000	....		SCP ACQUIRED USER STORAGE	00 000032
15:10:13.521600	EA	403BD8AC	0404	00056	01000300	00022214	....	DFHEDFMM	TMP PPT LOCATE	00 000032
15:10:13.521632	F2	5038 5E2	0404	00056	01000300	0390F0C	....		TMP RETN NOT FOUND	00 000032
15:10:13.521632	EA	403A19D4	0004	00056	00028440	8502089B	....	DFHEDFMM	PCP LOAD	00 000032
15:10:13.521664	EA	403BD8AC	0004	00056	00028440	01056814	....	DFHEDFMM	TMP PPT LOCATE	00 000032
15:10:13.521664	EA	403BD8AC	8504	00056	00000017	00056814	....		TMP RETN NORMAL	00 000032
15:10:13.521696	C8	503A80EA	0004	00056	00810000	00056814	....		SCP GETMAIN	00 000032
15:10:13.521728	FC	503A8828	EE03	00056	00810400	00028440	....		SCP ACQUIRED TERMINAL STORAGE	00 000320
15:10:13.522048	C8	5038648E	0103	00056	00000000	00000000	....		ZCP EXIT TRACE ZRVX	00 000000
15:10:13.522048	FC	5038648E	0105	00056	00000000	00001804	....		ZCP ZARQ APPL REQ ERASE WRITE	00 000032
15:10:13.522048	FC	403DEF74	CC04	00056	00000400	00001802	....		ZCP RETN ZARQ APPL REQ ERASE WRITE DEFER	00 000032
15:10:13.522080	FA	403B5C8A	0005	00056	00000000	01056814	....		BMS RETN	00 000032
15:10:13.522080	FA	403B20AA	00F4	00056	00327B0	00022214	....	DFHEDFMM	EIP SEND-MAP RESPONSE	00 000032
15:10:13.522112	E1	8021376C	4004	00056	01000304	00000000	....		EIP RECEIVE-MAP ENTRY	00 000032
15:10:13.522112	E1	803F474E	00F4	00056	00000000	00001802	....		SCP FREEMAIN	00 000032
15:10:13.522112	F1	503A8864	0004	00056	00070010	01056814	....		SCP RELEASED TERMINAL STORAGE	00 000128
15:10:13.522144	C9	803B4712	0003	00056	0007F000	00000020	.0.		BMS MAP MAPSET WAIT IN	00 000032
15:10:13.522144	FA	503B5492	8404	00056	00020509	00056814	....		BMS MAP MAPSET WAIT IN	00 000000
15:10:13.522272	FA	503A8828	CC04	00056	00000400	01056814	....		PCP LOAD-CONDITIONAL	00 000000
15:10:13.522304	F1	503A8828	0004	00056	01000304	00327B0	....	DFHEDFMM	SCP GETMAIN INITIMG	00 000032
15:10:13.522304	F2	403BD8AC	0405	00056	01000304	00022214	....		SCP ACQUIRED USER STORAGE	00 000000
15:10:13.522336	C8	403A1904	0004	00056	00564880	00056814	....		TMP PPT LOCATE	00 000032
15:10:13.522336	EA	403BD8AC	0004	00056	00000000	00056814	....		TMP RETN NOT FOUND	00 000000
15:10:13.522368	EA	503B57F8	0103	00056	00564880	00056814	....		ZCP ZARQ APPL REQ READ WAIT	00 000032
15:10:13.522400	FC	7030B758	1804	00056	00564880	00056814	....		ZCP ZSDS SEND	00 000032
15:10:13.522432	FC	503DB818	1D04	00056	0664A880	00056814	....		ZCP ZSDR SEND RESPONSE	00 000032

ACBC1CSE   --- CICS TRANSACTION DUMP ---   CODE=ASRA   TASK=PNC1   DATE=08/08/89   TIME=15:10:49   PAGE 12

TIME OF DAY	ID	REG 14	REQD	TASK	FIELD A	FIELD B	CHARS	RESOURCE	TRACE TYPE	INTERVAL
15:10:34.362848	F0	502619E0	4004	00015	80000000	0026195C	·······*		KCP WAIT DCI=SINGLE	00 000224
15:10:34.370944	F3	50260SA4	2403	00015	0000010C	00000000	········		ICP WAIT	00 008096
15:10:34.370976	F1	403E632C	604	00015	00000044	00000000	········		SCP GETMAIN INITIMG	00 000032
15:10:34.370976	C8	503A8828	0004	00015	00018650	86000050	·····&·		SCP ACQUIRED ICE STORAGE	00 000032
15:10:35.024896	F0	403DE790	4004	00015	19000000	00000000	········		KCP SUSPEND ICP DELAY	00 000032
15:10:36.025440	FD	0000009C	0104	TCP	40000000	00359860	·······/		KCP WAIT DCI=LIST	*01 653888
15:10:44.371104	F3	603F1962	C003	TCP	00535E32	00536154	········		REPEAT 00009 TIMES	*08 345664
15:10:44.371136	F3	603E60DA	0804	KCP	00019190	0100015C	········		ICP ICE EXPIRY ANALYSIS	*01 000544
15:10:44.371168	F3	403E5EAC	0005	KCP	00000000	00000000	········		KCP RESUME	00 000032
15:10:44.371232	C9	503E6682	4004	00015	00018650	86000050	·····&·		ICP RETN NORMAL	00 000064
15:10:44.371232	F3	503E8864	0005	00015	00000000	00000000	········		SCP FREEMAIN	00 000032
15:10:44.371456	F3	403E5EAC	4004	00015	00018650	86000050	·····&·		SCP RELEASED ICE STORAGE	00 000032
15:10:44.371456	F3	502619E0	2403	00015	80000000	0026195C	·······*		ICP RETN NORMAL	00 000192
15:10:44.381984	F3	50260SA4	2403	00015	0000010C	00000000	········		KCP WAIT DCI=SINGLE	00 010528
15:10:44.381984	C8	503A8828	0004	00015	00018650	86000050	·····&·		ICP WAIT	00 000032
15:10:44.382016	F0	403DE790	4004	00015	19000000	00000000	········		SCP GETMAIN INITIMG	00 000032
15:10:44.382048	FD	403E632C	604	00015	00000044	00000000	········		SCP ACQUIRED ICE STORAGE	00 000032
15:10:45.049280	F0	403E632C	604	00015	00000044	00000000	········		KCP SUSPEND ICP DELAY	00 000032
15:10:46.053504	FD	0000004C	0104	TCP	00010400	01056814	········		KCP WAIT DCI=LIST	00 667232
15:10:49.565792	FC	403DE6EE	1404	TCP	0068B1A6	00056814	········		REPEAT 00004 TIMES	*01 004224
15:10:49.565824	FC	503D909C	1304	TCP	00284880	8501041B	······I		ZCP ZRAC RECEIVE ANY	*03 512288
15:10:49.565856	EE	703D80C0	0024	TCP	F611C3F6	F111C3F6	·C6·C6		ZCP ZGET GETMAIN	00 000032
15:10:49.565856	EE	703D80C0	0024	TCP	F1F1F1F1	F111C440	11111·C6	1D000090	VIO RECEIVE BB CD OIC DATA RQE 1	00 000032
15:10:49.565888	EE	703D80C0	1125	TCP	00010400	01056814	········	1D000090	VIO DATA	00 000032
15:10:49.565888	F1	503D844A	A504	TCP	0068B1A6	00056814	········	1D000090	VIO DATA	00 000000
15:10:49.565920	C8	503A8828	0004	TCP	00010940	00056814	········		VIO DATA	00 000224
15:10:49.566144	FC	403DD7AC	1103	TCP	00284880	00056814	········		SCP GETMAIN CONDITIONAL	00 000032
15:10:49.566176	F0	503E0A12	9304	TCP	D7D5C109	D7D5C3F1	·PNARPNC1		SCP ACQUIRED TERMINAL STORAGE	00 000000
15:10:49.566176	EA	503F0384	0003	TCP	01040100	003F71E0	········		ZCP ZATT ATTACH	00 000000
15:10:49.566208	EA	403B08AC	0025	TCP	01040100	003A4FD0	········	PNC1	KCP ATTACH-CONDITIONAL	00 000032
15:10:49.566240	EA	403F0AD8	0025	TCP	0C000100	003A4FD0	········		TMP PCT LOCATE	00 000032
15:10:49.566240	EA	403B08AC	0025	TCP	00000100	00000000	········		TMP RETN NORMAL	00 000000
15:10:49.566272	FC	403E0B10	1125	TCP	00000000	00359860	········		TMP PCT TRANSFER	00 000032
15:10:49.566304	F0	403DE790	4004	TCP	40000000	00000000	········		TMP RETN NORMAL	00 000000
15:10:49.566304	F1	403F1EE4	EA04	KCP	00010940	85010418	········		ZCP RETN ZATT ATTACH	00 000000
15:10:49.566432	C8	503A8828	0004	KCP	00020100	8A040A38	········		KCP WAIT DCI=LIST	00 000128
15:10:49.566464	FC	503F21CC	0004	00059	D7D5C109	D7D5C3F1	·PNARPNC1		SCP GETMAIN CONDITIONAL INITIMG	00 000032
15:10:49.566464	DO	503E12B0	0503	00059	00284880	00056814	········		SCP ACQUIRED TCA STORAGE	00 000032
15:10:49.566496	E5	503E1454	0C03	00059	00021688	01056814	········	PNC1	KCP CREATE	00 000000
15:10:49.566528	E5	403E8282	0005	00059	00000000	00056814	········		ZCP ZSUP START UP TASK	00 000032
15:10:49.566528	F1	503A77E0	DB04	00059	00000086	98000098	········		XSP SECURITY CHECK	00 000032
15:10:49.566560	C8	503A8828	0004	00059	00021A40	00000000	········		XSP SECURITY RETN	00 000032
15:10:49.566560	F2	503E25A6	8B04	00059	00000000	00021214	········		SCP GETMAIN INITIMG	00 000000
15:10:49.566592	EA	403A19D4	0003	00059	01000300	00390484	········		SCP ACQUIRED JCA STORAGE	00 000032
15:10:49.566624	EA	403B08AC	0005	00059	01000300	01056814	········		TMP PCT-CONDITIONAL	00 000032
15:10:49.566624	F1	603A26DA	8C04	00059	00020824	BC020838	········M		TMP PCT LOCATE	00 000032
15:10:49.566624	C8	503A8828	0004	00059	00021AE0	01056814	········		TMP RETN NORMAL	00 000064
15:10:49.566688	E1	50226412	2004	00059	FF000000	BC020838	········	TXTSPNC1	SCP GETMAIN	00 000000
15:10:49.566688	F1	003F3532	2004	00059	00021B2C	00000204	········	TXTSPNC1	SCP ACQUIRED USER STORAGE	00 000064
15:10:49.566752	E1	003F474E	CC04	00059	00000000	01056814	········		KCP CHAP	00 000064
15:10:49.566816	C8	503A8828	0004	00059	00022320	8C0000C8	········H		EIP HANDLE-CONDITION ENTRY	00 000032
15:10:49.566848	E1	003F474E	CC04	00059	00000000	01056814	········		SCP GETMAIN INITIMG	00 000032
15:10:49.566848	F1	003F474E	CC04	00059	00000000	00000204	········		SCP ACQUIRED USER STORAGE	00 000032
15:10:49.566880	C8	503A8828	0004	00059	00223F0	8C000048	········		SCP GETMAIN INITIMG	00 000032
15:10:49.566880	E1	50226412	00F4	00059	00000204	00000204	········O		SCP ACQUIRED USER STORAGE	00 000064
15:10:49.566912									EIP HANDLE-CONDITION RESPONSE	00 000032

ACBCICSE   --- CICS TRANSACTION DUMP ---   CODE=ASRA   TASK=PNC1   DATE=08/08/89   TIME=15:10:49   PAGE 13

TIME OF DAY	ID	REG 14	REQD TASK	FIELD A	FIELD B	CHARS	RESOURCE	TRACE TYPE	INTERVAL
15:10:49.566912	E1	5022648E	0004	00059	00021B2C	00021802	....		EIP RECEIVE-MAP ENTRY	00.000000
15:10:49.566944	FA	50382012	0003	00059	00020505	00000020	....		BMS MAP MAPSET MAP-FROM IN	00.000032
15:10:49.566944	FA	4038208C	0003	00059	00020505	00000000	....		BMS MAP MAPSET MAP-FROM IN	00.000032
15:10:49.566944	F2	50385AB2	8404	00059	00000000	00021214	....		PCP LOAD-CONDITIONAL	00.000032
15:10:49.566976	F2	403A19D4	0003	00059	01000304	00021214	....		TMP PPT LOCATE	00.000032
15:10:49.566976	EA	403BD8AC	0405	00059	01000304	00000000	....		TMP RETN NOT FOUND	00.000032
15:10:49.567008	EA	50385AE2	0404	00059	01000300	00021214	....		PCP LOAD	00.000032
15:10:49.567008	F2	403A19D4	0003	00059	01000300	0039D4E8	....		TMP PPT LOCATE	00.000032
15:10:49.567040	EA	403BD8AC	0095	00059	00000197	0039D4E8	..MY	MSBPNC2M	TMP RETN NORMAL	00.000032
15:10:49.567072	F1	5038583C	C504	00059	0001CD60	01056814	....	MSBPNC2M	TMP RETN NORMAL	00.000032
15:10:49.567072	F1	503A8828	0004	00059	0001CD60	850001A8	....		SCP GETMAIN INITIMG	00.000032
15:10:49.567104	C8	50385C4E	4004	00059	0001C940	85010418	..I		SCP ACQUIRED TERMINAL STORAGE	00.000032
15:10:49.567136	C9	503A8864	0004	00059	0001C940	85010418	..I		SCP FREEMAIN	00.000000
15:10:49.567136	FA	40385C8A	0005	00059	0001CD60	01056814	....	MSBPNC2	SCP RELEASED TERMINAL STORAGE	00.000032
15:10:49.567136	FA	403B20AA	0004	00059	0001CD60	01056814	....	MSBPNC2	BMS RETN	00.000032
15:10:49.567168	C9	003F474E	4004	00059	0001C060	850001A8	....		BMS RETN	00.000032
15:10:49.567168	C9	503A8864	0004	00059	0001CD60	850001A8	....		SCP FREEMAIN	00.000000
15:10:49.567200	E1	5022648E	Q0F4	00059	00021802	....		SCP RELEASED TERMINAL STORAGE	00.000032
15:10:49.567200	F2	80370A44	6004	00059	C1E2D9C1	00000000	ASRA..		EIP RECEIVE-MAP RESPONSE	*04.009696
15:10:53.576896	F1	403A0B08	CC04	00059	000000A0	01056814	....		PCP ABEND	00.000032
15:10:53.576928	C8	503A8828	0004	00059	00022440	8C0000A8	....		SCP GETMAIN INITIMG	00.000032
15:10:53.576960	F4	503A0A42	FE04	00059	00022440	C1E2D9C1	.ASRA		SCP ACQUIRED USER STORAGE	
15:10:53.576960									DCP TRANSACTION	

TRANSACTION STORAGE -USER   ADDRESS 00022440 TO 000224EF   LENGTH 0000B0

00000000	8C0000A8	000223F0	00001840	C4C6C8E3	C1C3C240 80600010 C1E209C1	*...y..0....DFHTACB -..ASRA*
00000020	E3E7E3E2	D7D5C3F1	00000000	00000000	00225F3C A03A2412 00000001	*TXTSPNC1.........REGS.PSW ..*
00000040	00000000	00000000	D9C5C7E2	50D7E2E6	00000000 00000000 00000000	*........REGS.PSW....*
00000060	00021374	00021190	003F660D	0021B2C	80010018 00226D04 00225084	*.......q........ .d*
00000080	00000000	00000000	5022648E	00226098	07802D000 00225FBC 00060007	*.......y..O..*
000000A0	00000000	00000000	8C0000A8	000223F0		

TRANSACTION STORAGE -USER   ADDRESS 000223F0 TO 0002243F   LENGTH 000050

00000000	8C000048	00022320	00000000	00000000	00225F3C 000222E4 A03A2412 00000004	*........U.......*
00000020	00021374	80010018	00000000	00021428	80010018 00226D04 00225050 00225084	*............ ..d*
00000040	00225BD0	00021FC4	8C000048	00022320		

TRANSACTION STORAGE -USER   ADDRESS 00022320 TO 0002236F   LENGTH 000050

00000000	8C0000C8	00021AE0	00023389	00B60201	00000000 00000000 00000000 00000000	*...H........*
00000020	00000000	00000000	00000000	00000000	00000000 00000000 00000000 00000000	*...........*
00000040	00000000	00000000	00000000	00000000	00000000 00000000 00010420 00000223	*.......O...*
00000060	C4000000	00000000	00000000	00000000	00000000 00000000 00000223 F000021F	*D.........*
00000080	00000000	00000000	00000000	00000000	00000000 00000000 00000000 00FF0000	*...H...*
000000C0	00000000	00000000	8C0000C8	00021AE0		

```
ACBCICSE    --- CICS TRANSACTION DUMP ---    CODE=ASRA   TASK=PNC1          DATE=08/08/89    TIME=15:10:49    PAGE   14

TRANSACTION STORAGE -USER     ADDRESS 00021AEO TO 0002231F   LENGTH 000840

00000000  8C020838 00021A40 00000000 00000000  50226066 A0342412 003F6AD0  *................*  00021AEO
00000020  00226CAC 5022604A 00225FO0 00000000  00226D04 00225050 00225050  *................*  00021B00
00000040  00225B80 003A267C 00000000 00000000  00050OF1 F1F1F1F1 F1F1F1F1  *.........O......1111*  00021B20
00000060  0019900C1 C1C1C1C1 C1C1C1C1 C1C1C1C1  C1C1C1C1 00500OF2 C2C2C2C2  *........AAAAAAAAAAAAAAAAAA*  00021B40
00000080  F2F2F2F2 0019900C2 C2C2C2C2 C2C2C2C2  C2C2C2C2 C2C2C2C2 C2C2C2C2  *.2222....BBBBBBBBBBBBBBBBBB.2*  00021B60
000000A0  00000000 00000280 00000000 00000000  00000000 00000000 00000000  *................*  00021B80
000000C0  LINES TO 00000280  SAME AS ABOVE
000000A0  00000000 00000000 0070606A 7E6EE788  7F6C6E6B  *.........h....=wXh.*  00021BA0
000000C0  F1F2F3F4 F5F6F7F8 F9FACOOO C94A4B4C  919F5F040  *123456789..OO.ABCDEFGHI*  00021D80
000000E0  5060C84C C161F1F8 80FFOEOF 2842434A  F1F2F3F4 F5F6F700  *-H.A/18....AB....123456.O*  00021DA0
00000300  00F1F2F4 04020640 D01D95D C0C1C246  003FFF00 0402010F  *.124.(IJR)Y.......O.LD.T*  00021DC0
00000320  C1C2D3C5 40C4C6C8 C5C9E3C1 C240F2F1  0402010F D3C440E3  *ABLE.DFHEITAB.210*  00021DE0
00000340  F0480000 40404040 40404040 00000000  00000000 00000000 00000000  *................*  00021E00
00000360  00000000 00000440  SAME AS ABOVE
00000460  D5C3F200 D4E2C2D7 00000000 00000000  D4D7C2D7  *.NC2.MSBPNC2.....MPBP*  00021E20 / 00021F40
00000480  D5C3F200 D5C3F200 00000000 00000000  00000000  *................*  00021F60
000004A0  00000000 1802D000 05000000 00050900  40404040  *................*  00021F80
000004C0  40000000 00300000 0020F0F0 F0F2F6F7  40404040  *.........00267*  00021FA0
000004E0  00000001 00021384 5022648E 00021428  00022E4  *................U*  00021FC0
00000500  A03A2412 00021374 0021B2C 00021428  00226D04  *.........d*  00021FE0
00000520  00225050 00225800 2102A04B 00021F44  003F3668  *.......)d*  00022000
00000540  00000000 00000580  SAME AS ABOVE
00000560  LINES TO 00000580  SAME AS ABOVE
00000580  00000000 00000660  SAME AS ABOVE
000005A0  LINES TO 00000660  SAME AS ABOVE
00000680  00000000 C105E2C3 00225050 00000000  00226098  *................q*  00022160
000006A0  E2E8E2D6 E4E34040 E3800000 00000000  002250D8  *SVSOUT.T....Q.....ANSC.*  00022180
000006C0  00000000 00225070 00000000 00000000  00021428  *.....)......Q*  000221A0
000006E0  00000000 00021B2C 00000000 00000000  00021428  *.......U*  000221C0
00000700  80010018 00000000 00000000 003F66D0  00226524  *................*  000221E0
00000720  00000000 00000000 00000000 00226342  00226342  *................*  00022200
00000740  00000000 00000000 00000000 00000000  0022639A  *.....2*  00022220
00000760  00000000 00000000 00000000 00000000  002266F2  *................*  00022240
00000780  00000000 002263F2 00000000 0022556C  0022567C  *................*  00022260
000007A0  00000000 00226B04 00000000 002267E2  00226948  *.........S*  00022280
000007C0  00000000 00226A6C 00000000 00226CAC  00226CAC  *................*  000222A0
000007E0  00000000 00021FA4 00000000 00021F9C  00021A40  *.......u..*  000222C0
00000800  00000000 00021F5C 00021F8C 8C020838  00021A40  *................*  000222E0
00000820  00000000 00000000 00000000 00000000  00021000  *................q*  00022300

TRANSACTION STORAGE -JCA     ADDRESS 00021A40 TO 00021ADF   LENGTH 0000A0

00000000  9B000098 00021000 00000000 00000000  00000000 00000000 00000000  *.........q*  00021A40
00000020  03B00100 00000000 00000000 00080000  0001D014 00000000 00000000  *................*  00021A60
00000040  8A10FF00 00000000 00000000 00800000  00000098 9B000098 00021100  *.........q*  00021A80
00000060  00000000 00000000 00000000 00000000  00000000                    *................*  00021AA0
00000080  00000000 00000000 00000000 00000000  00000000                    *................*  00021ACO
```

```
ACBCICSE     --- CICS TRANSACTION DUMP ---     CODE=ASRA     TASK=PNC1          DATE=08/08/89     TIME=15:10:49     PAGE  15

TERMINAL CONTROL TABLE               ADDRESS 00056814 TO 000569CB     LENGTH 0001B8

00000000  D7D5C1D9 91F20006 00056818 00000000  00021190 0000000 D4E2C2D7 00000000   *PNARj2.........6' MSBPNC2*  00056814
00000020  00000000 0CD7E2E3 0000430A 00000910  00F67034 D4E2C2D7 D5C3F240 00000000   *....PST.........6' MSBPNC2*  00056834
00000040  00000000 2000B0E0 07B01B50 018B0000  01BB0000 00000002 0001B6F4 000186F4   *..................f4...f4*  00056854
00000060  00000000 0B000000 00200001 000569D4  0001F004 00056A54 00000000 00000000   *..........M.O............*  00056874
00000080  0001D000 0001D000 00000000 00840040  0001D394 6B000000 00000000 00001900   *.............d..Lm.......*  00056894
000000A0  00340BA6 00B00000 00000000 00000000  01000000 00000100 49000000 04000020   *...........................*  000568B4
000000E0  08240BA6 00800000 00000000 00840040  00000000 0C000000 0C000000 08008400   *.......d.............d...*  000568D4
00000120  06B005C 00000000 1D000090 00000000  00000000 00000000 00000000 00000000   *............M............*  000568F4
00000140  01000000 00000000 00000000 00000000  FFFF5040 00550000 00000000 06001000   *.........&.........*  00056914
00000160  00000000 00000000 00000000 000000E0  00000000 00000000 00000000 00000000   *........................*  00056934
00000180  28A14800 00400000 000186CC 00056A35  28A14800 00440000 000016CC D4000000   *........f4.......M....*  00056954
000001A0  00000000 00000000 00565A4 00000000   00000000 00000014 00000000 00000000   *.........u...............*  00056974
                                                                                      00056994
                                                                                      000569B4

UNIDENTIFIABLE RECORD AT OFFSET 0538: BUFFER FLUSHED.

00000000  00420000 02840000 04020008 00021AE0  00000840 000005A0 00000000 00000000   *...d...............*  00000000
00000020  00000000 00000000 000000E0 00000000  00000000 00000000 00000000 00000000   *......................*  00000020
00000040  00000000 SAME AS ABOVE                                                                                   00000040
00000100  E380000C C10SE2C3 C10SE2050 00000000  00226D98 E2E8E206 E4E34040 00000000   *T....ANSC....@SYSOUT )..*  00000100
00000120  00000000 00225D08 00000000 00000000   00000000 00000000 0225D7C 00000000   *........Q........U*  00000120
00000140  003F66D0 00000000 00000000 00000000  00021428 8001D018 00221B2C 00000000   *..........U...*  00000140
00000160  00000000 00000000 00000000 00000000  00226524 00000000 000221E4 00000000   *...........U*  00000160
00000180  00000000 00226342 00000000 00000000  00000000 00000000 00000000 00000000   *........*  00000180
000001A0  00000000 00000000 00000000 000000A0  00226524 00000000 00000000 00000000   *........*  000001A0
000001C0  00000000 00000000 00000000 00000000  0022639A 00000000 00000000 00000000   *........*  000001C0
000001E0  00000000 0225F2A 00000000 00000000   0022667C 02263F2 00000000 00000000   *.......2...*  000001E0
00000200  00000000 00226524 00000000 00000000  0022694B 0226B04 00000000 00000000   *.......S.*  00000200
00000220  00000000 00226C4C 00000000 00000000  00226CAC 00226A6C 00000000 00000000   *.......*  00000220
00000240  00021F5C 00021B2C 00000000 80021F64  00000000 0021FA4 00000000 00000000   *.......u.*  00000240
00000260  00021A40 00000000 00000000 80040000  00021A40 00B40000 04000008 00000000   *.....a..........*  00000260
00000280  00000000 00000000 9B000098 00021000  8C020838 00000000 00B40000 00000000   *...........*  00000280
000002A0  00000000 00000000 00000000 03800100  8A10FF00 00000000 00000000 00000000   *........*  000002A0
000002E0  00000000 0001D014 00000000 00000000  00180000 00000000 00000000 00000000   *........*  000002E0
00000300  00080000 9B000098 00021000 01CC0000  A000008 00000000 00000000 00000000   *........*  00000300
00000320  00000000 00000000 00210000 00000910  00021190 00000000 0000018B 00000000   *........*  00000320
00000360  D7D5C1D9 91F20006 00056818 00000000  00F67034 D4E2C2D7 D5C3F240 00000000   *PNARj2.........6' MSBPNC2*  00000360
00000380  00000000 0CD7E2E3 0000430A 00000910  00021190 D4E2C2D7 D5C3F240 00000000   *....PST.........6' MSBPNC2*  00000380
000003A0  00000000 2000B0E0 07B01B50 018B0000  01BB0000 00000002 0001B6F4 000186F4   *..................f4...f4*  000003A0
000003C0  00000000 0B000000 00200001 000569D4  0001F004 00056A54 00000000 00000000   *..........M.O............*  000003E0
000003E0  0001D000 0001D000 00000000 00840040  0001D394 6B000000 00000000 00001900   *.............d..Lm.......*  00000420
00000420  00300000 00800000 00000000 00000000  01000000 00000100 49000000 04000020   *........*  00000440
00000440  08240BA6 00800000 00000000 00840040  00000000 0C000000 0C000000 08008400   *.......d.............d...*  00000460
00000460  06B005C 00000000 1D000090 00000000   00000000 00000000 00000000 00000000   *............M............*  00000480
00000480  01000000 00000000 00000000 00000000  FFFF5040 00550000 00000000 06001000   *.........&.........*  000004A0
000004A0  00000000 00000000 00000000 000000E0  00000000 00000000 00000000 00000000   *........................*  000004C0
000004E0  28A14800 00400000 000186CC 00056A35  28A14800 00440000 000016CC D4000000   *........f4.......M....*  000004E0
00000500  00000000 00000000 00565A4 00000000   00000000 00000014 00000000 00340000   *.........u...............*  00000500
00000520                                                                              16000008                     00000520
```

```
ACBCICSE        --- CICS TRANSACTION DUMP ---        CODE=ASRA        TASK=PNC1                    DATE=08/08/89        TIME=15:10:49        PAGE   16

00000540  00056454 00000020 00000020 20000000  50185082 00000004 D4000600                   *..........&.........&.........MM.*
00000560  00000000 00000000 00056814 00420000  3C000008 00186F4  000186F4  00000002E                   *....................b...?4.......b..*
00000580  002EC000 D7E2E3E2 C1F0F140 7FFF2F70  00000022 00000043 000001D7                   *....PSTSA01 "........*.........P.*
000005A0  E2E30007 C8E8C3F2 F1F05BF0 00000794  00080022 50080000  27E00000                   *ST.PSTSA01 ...m.............*
000005C0  0000C4C6 C8E8C3F2 F1F05BF0 001058F0  F0045BF0 F0D05BF0 F01458F0                   *..DFHYC210.0..00..00..00..00..00.0.*
000005E0  F00C58FF 000C07FF 58FF0010 58FF0004  58FF0004 F010E3F7 C3F1E5E2                   *.O...........H..d....).O..O.TXTSPNC1VS*
00000600  58FF00C8 58FF0184 07FF90EC D00C185D  41F00001 07FFE022 2412003F                   *...H..d.......).O...TXTSPNC1VS*
00000620  D9F10700 989FF024 07FFE024 103407FE  6CC40022 6066A03A 50500022                   *R1..q.o...D..)d...D...........*
00000640  50500022 58D00002 1FC40022 50840022  00005022 60040022 2412003F                   *.....D.......D........*
00000660  6AD00022 6CAC5022 604A0022 50F00000  00000022 60040022 50500022                   *.....h..O..D..D.......*
00000680  50500022 58D00022 5580003A 267C0022  57A0F1F4 4BF2F14B F4F1C1E4                   *...h..O..D...........14.21.41AUG..*
000006A0  6840F1F9 F8F90000 00000000 00000000  00000000 00000000 C74040F8                   *.1989.........14.21.41AUG..8.*
000006C0  00000000 00000000 00000000 00000000  00000000 00000000 00000000                   *.........*
000006E0  LINES TO 00000000 SAME AS ABOVE

00000900  00000000 00000000 00000000 0F0F0FC0  0000007D 606A7EE6 E7887F6C 6E6BF1F2                   *.............=wXh..12*
00000920  F3F4F5F6 F7F8F97A F7B7C1C2 C3C4C5C6  C7C8C94A 4B4C0000 00001915 F0405060                   *3456789.:.ABCDEFGHI.........0.-*
00000940  C84CC161 F1F880FF 0E0F2842 4341C0C1  C246003F FF0F1F2 F3F4F5F6 F7000000                   *H.A/18......AB....1234567.1*
00000960  F2F40402 064DC901 D950E86C 01050307  00080402 010F01F0 FF00D3C4 40E3C1C2                   *24.(IJR)V....0..LD TAB*
00000980  D3C540C4 C6C8C5C9 E3C1C240 F2F1F000  00000000 00000000 00000000                   *LE DFHEITAB 210.*

PSEUDO SIGN-ON TABLE ENTRY                    ADDRESS 000186F4 TO 00018721   LENGTH 0002E

00000000  002EC000 00000000 00000000 00000000  00000000 00000043 0000000A 000001D7                   *.................P.*
00000020  E2E30007 D7E2E3E2 C1F0F140 7FFF2F70  0000                   *ST.PSTSA01 "...*

PROGRAM STORAGE                               ADDRESS 00225008 TO 002277E7   LENGTH 0027E0

00000000  C4C6C8E8 C3F2F1F0 5BF0F004 58FF0010  58FF0004 F0045BF0 58F0F00C                   *DFHYC210.0..00..00..00..00..00.*
00000020  58FF000C 07FFE000 001058F0 F0D05BF0  F0045BF0 F01458F0 F00858FF                   *.H..d...)..0.TXTSPNC1VSR1*
00000040  00C85FF  018407FF 90EC07FE 4580F010  E3F7E3E2 D7D5C3F1 E5E209F1                   *..q.o...D..O.TXTSPNC1VSR1*
00000060  0709989F F02407FF 96021034 07FE41F0  00226D04 A03A2412 003F6AD0                   *..q.o...D..)d...D...........*
00000080  00225800 00021FC4 00225084 00226CC4  50226D66 00225050 003A267C                   *..D.......D........*
000000A0  00226CAC 50226D0A 00226D04 00225050  F14BF4F1 C1E4C740 40F86B40                   *...14.41AUG..8..*
000000C0  00225800 00225588 003A267C 002257A0  F14BF4F1 C1E4C740 F86B40                   *..h....h..O.14.41AUG..8.*
000000E0  F1F9F8F9 00000000 00000320 00000000  7EE6E788 7F6C6E6B F1F2F3F4                   *1989.........=wXh..1234*
00000100  LINES TO 00000000 SAME AS ABOVE
00000340  00000000 FOC00000 7EE6E788 7F6C6E6B  0070606A C944B4C  1915F040 5060C84C                   *........=wXh...-.H*
00000360  F5F6F7F8 F97A7B7C C1C2C3C4 C5C6C7C8  C944B4C 5C6C7C8 0FF1F2F4 0FF1F2F4                   *56789.:.ABCDEFGHI...-H*
00000380  C161F1F8 80FF0E0F 28424341 C1C2C3C4  003FFF00 F1F3F4 F5F6F700 00F1F2F4                   *A/18......AB....1234567.124*
000003A0  04020640 C9D1D95D E8C0105 03070008  04020010 F1F0FF00 D3C440E3 C1C2D3C5                   *..(IJR)V....0..LD TABLE*
```

00186F4
00018714

00225008
00225028
00225048
00225068
00225088
002250A8
002250C8
002250E8
00225108
00225128
00225348
00225368
00225388
002253A8

```
ACBCICSE    ---  CICS TRANSACTION DUMP  ---    CODE=ASRA    TASK=PNC1                    DATE=08/08/89    TIME=15:10:49    PAGE   17

PROGRAM STORAGE                      ADDRESS  00225008 TO 002277E7    LENGTH 0027E0

000003C0  40C4C6C8 C5C9E3C1 C240F2F1 F04B0000  00000000 00000000 00000000 00000000  * DFHEITAB 210.                  *  002253C8
000003E0  40404040 40404040 00000000 00000000  00000000 00000000 00000000 00000000  *                                *  002253E8
00000400  00000000 00000000 00000560 00000000  00000000 00000000 00000000 00000000  *                                *  00225408
00000420  LINES            TO     00000560     SAME AS ABOVE                                                               00225428
00000580  00300000 0035EABB 00000000 00000000  00000000 00000000 00000000 00000000  *                  )d            *  00225588
000005A0  00000000 00000000 00000000 00000000  00000000 00000000 00000000 00000000  *                                *  002555A8
000005C0  00000000 00000000 00000000 00000000  00000000 00000000 00000000 00000000  *                                *  00225568
000005E0  00000000 2102A04B 00000000 00000000  00000000 00000000 00000000 00000000  *                                *  00225588
00000600  00000000 00000000 00000000 00000000  00000000 00000000 00000000 00000000  *                                *  00225608
          LINES            TO     00000700     SAME AS ABOVE
00000740  E4E34040 E3800000 C1D5E2C3 00000000  00225050 00000000 E2E8E2D6 00000000  *UT  T     ANSC      .QSYSO      *  00225728
00000760  0022507C E3800000 C1D5E2C3 00225000  00226342 00000000 00226098 00000000  *          .Q                    *  00225748
00000780  00225FFC00000000 00000000 00000000  00000000 00000000 00000000 00000000  * )  .O                          *  00225768
000007A0  00000000 00000000 00000000 00000000  00000000 00000000 00000000 00000000  *                                *  00225788
000007C0  00000800 SAME AS ABOVE                                                                                           002257A8
          LINES            TO     000007C0
00000820  00000000 00226F2 00226524 00225010  0022703A 0022703E 0022639A 00000000  *  .2                             *  00225828
00000840  0022639A 00226F2A 00226524 00225000  00226342 00226342 00226670 00000000  * .2       .S                    *  00225848
00000860  0022667C 00226B04 00226C4C 00000000  00226AAC 00226E2 00226948 00000000  *          .S                    *  00225868
00000880  00226CAC 00000000 0041C40 00000052  00000000 00000000 00226CAC 00000000  *                                *  00225888
000008A0  28002300 2E000FFF 30D705C3 F1D705C3  F240C1E3 00583C0F F0F0C000 00000000  *         .PNC1PNC2 AT LEA..   00*  002558A8
000008C0  2A003100 C9D5C540 40CC2C540 C5D5E3C5  F240C1E3 C5D407D3 C5D407D3 00000000  *DYEE NUMBER NOT FOUND NEW NAME M*  002558C8
000008E0  D6E8C5C5 40D5E4D4 C2C540C5 C6D64D05  C4AB05C5 E6405C1 D4C54D04 00000000  *UST BE ENTERED TRANSACTION PNC1 *  002558E8
00000900  E4E2E340 C2C540C5 D5E3C5D9 07D3C5E3  C3C5D3C5 E6405D9 D5C3F140 00000000  *SUCCESSFULLY COMPLETED LOGIC ERR*  00225908
00000920  D6D94B40 E3C5D9C1 C4B04840 D9D94D00  07405C3 C3C5D309 00226342 00000000  *OR TRANSACTION CANCELED TRANSA  *  00225928
00000940  C3E3C9D6 D5400000 C1C3C5D3 C5C4C4B0  40440018 F6F44040 D7C20705 00000000  *CTION CANCELED BY OPERATOR REQUE*  00225948
00000960  E2E3400B C9D5C540 D4E4E2E3 40C2C540  C5D5E3C5 D9C5C44B F240C1E3 00000000  *ST         .PNC1PNC2 AT  00267  *  00225968
00000980  D6EBC5C5 40D5E4D4 C2C5C540 C5C6D640  05583C5 D9C5C44B D4E207B0 00000000  *C2MSBPNC2GEN ERROR OCCURRED AT P*  00225988
000009A0  E4E2E340 C2C5C540 C5D5E3C5 D9C5C44B  F240C1E3 C5D407D3 D5C3F140 00000000  *NC2 RECEIVE. TRANS CANCELED.  J *  002559A8
000009C0  D6D94B40 E3C5D9C1 C4B04840 D9D94D00  D9609940 D8C3C5E4 D9C3C5C4 00000000  *RRED AT PNC2 SEND. TRANS CANCEL *  002559C8
000009E0  E4E2C3C3 C5E22C6 C5A0C5 D9C5C44B  E240C1E3 C5E207D4 F1F54040 00000000  *ED.          00315              *  002559E8
00000A00  D6D94B40 40E3D9C1 E3C90605 D9C5C44B  00F0F0F3 E240C1E3 D9C1D5E2 00000000  *         .O     00319  PERVSPMSREC*  00225A09
00000A20  C3E3C9D6 40C5D9C1 D5C3C5D9 D9C5C44B  C4AB05E3 D9C1D5E2 C9C5E340 00000000  *ORD NOT FOUND AT READ-FK. TRANS *  00225A28
00000A40  40400001 1802D000 00405900 00005001  07F00940 40C5D340 40C1D540 00000000  *CANCELED.GEN ERROR OCCURRED AT  *  00225A48
00000A60  C3F2DAE2 C2D705C3 D9C5C44B 01000000  00509900 D9C3C5C4 07C20705 00000000  *READ-FK. TRANS CANCELED.    00354*  00225A68
00000A80  D5C3F240 D9C5C544 C9E5C54B 40C509D9  D6E8C540 40405900 C1E34D09 00000000  *   0     .d   RECORD NOT FOUND AT*  00225A88
00000AA0  00050100 C4C00005 00000000 00000000  40405900 D7C30E4 4B020480 00000000  *-FK-UPD. TRANS CANCELED.GEN ERR *  00225AA8
00000AC0  00000000 1E204000 0020F0F0 F2F9F140  05D4C7C5 D9C3E4 04D10005 00000000  *OR OCCURRED AT READ-FK-UPD. TRA *  00225AC8
00000AE0  D9D9C5C4 40C1E340 D7D5C3F2 40E2C5D5  E4B04040 E240C1C1 D6C3C3E4 00000000  *NS CANCELED.    00291  GEN ERROR OCCU*  00225AE8
00000B00  C5C44B40 04C00005 00100000 00F0F0F3  E3D9C1D5 E340C1E3 F1F54040 00000000  *RRED AT PNC2 SEND.  TRANS CANCEL*  00225B08
00000B20  40400002 0607F0F0 00F0F0F3 F1F94040  E5E207D4 E24060D5 E2D9C5C3 00000000  *ED.     00315   PERVSPMSREC     *  00225B28
00000B40  D6D9C440 D5D6E340 C6D6E4D5 C44040C1  4B400E3 D9C1D5E2 40C1E340 00000000  *ORD NOT FOUND AT READ-FK. TRANS *  00225B48
00000B60  C3C1D5C3 C5D3C5C4 4B47C5 C5D5C5D9  D6D9C3E4 D9D9C5C4 40C1E340 00000000  *CANCELED.GEN ERROR OCCURRED AT  *  00225B68
00000B80  D9C5C1C4 60C6D240 D9C5C44B 40E3D9C1  4B020400 D9C1D5E2 40C1E340 00000000  *READ-FK. TRANS CANCELED.        *  00225B88
00000BA0  F0F3F5F5 D6E340C6 F0F4F1F8 40C1E340  02F00005 40C509D9 40C1E340 00000000  *   00358   RECORD NOT FOUND AT RE*  00225BA8
00000BC0  F0F0F3F5 40C5D3C5 D9C3E4 D6E4405C5  40C6D240 4BC7C5D5 D9C3C5C4 00000000  *-FK-UPD. TRANS CANCELED.GEN ERR *  00225BC8
00000BE0  60C6D240 40E3D9C1 D5E2407C5 D6D5E340  E240D7C1 4BC7C5D5 40E3D9C1 00000000  *OR OCCURRED AT READ-FK-UPD. TRA *  00225BE8
00000C00  60C6D260 E4D7C44B 40E3D9C1 D5E24D07  C7C5D540 4BC7C5D5 40E309C1 00000000  *NS CANCELED.    00396  GEN E    *  00225C08
00000C20  D5E240C3 C1D5C3C5 D3C5C44B 40400000  4B400D3 C3C5D3C5 40E3D9C1 00000000  *            00418               *  00225C28
00000C40  00010000 04C00606 C5E2400A 40404000  F0F9F6F6 4BA0040E3 0BE0005 00000000  *NS CANCELED.                    *  00225C48
00000C60  0F0F0F4 F3F9F340 4BD6C6C3 C3C4D9C5  C4404040 4B400D3 D9C105C5 00000000  *   00393         .GEN.E  TRANS  *  00225C68
00000C80  D9D9D609 40D6C3C3 E4D9D9C5 C4405C1  09C5D9D9 C5C4400F OBE0005 00000000  *RROR OCCURRED AT REWRITE. TRANS *  00225C88
00000CA0  40C3C1D5 C3C5D3C5 C4405C7 C5D5400E3  4B400D3 0F0F0F4 FF140040 00000000  *CANCELED.      00426            *  00225CA8
00000CC0  00010000 F6404040 4040C000 05160100  00000000 0BE0005 0BE0005 00000000  *        00437   a      00441    *  00225CC8
00000CE0  0F0F0F40 F4F3F740 40404000 00409000  00400000 F0F0F4 F4F14040 00000000  *                                *  00225CE8
00000D00  4003C5D5 C7C5D909 40D6C3C3 E4D9D9C5  C4405C1 40E2C5D5 C4D5E3C4 00000000  *LENGERR OCCURRED AT SEND. TRAN  *  00225D08
```

ACBCICSE   --- CICS TRANSACTION DUMP ---   CODE=ASRA   TASK=PNC1   DATE=08/08/89   TIME=15:10:49   PAGE   18

PROGRAM STORAGE

ADDRESS 00225008 TO 0027277E7   LENGTH 0027E0

ACBCICSE   --- CICS TRANSACTION DUMP ---   CODE=ASRA   TASK=PNC1   DATE=08/08/89   TIME=15:10:49   PAGE   19

PROGRAM STORAGE   ADDRESS 00225008 TO 002277E7   LENGTH 0027E0

00001400 96400D049 58F0C0C0C 05EF94BF D04940F0 D05C58F0 D1B85000 F0B04810 70144100 *..........O.*.OJ..O....* 00226408
00001420 00004830 C19A58F0 C0140E5F 0001071E D2166478 C19C9240 648FD204 6490648F *...A.0........K..A..K..A.* 00226428
00001440 D2066430 C1B3D206 643BC1BA 41106478 50100320 41106000 96800330 41106400 *K...A.K...A...........L..* 00226448
...
(hexadecimal program storage dump continues through)
...
00001AC0 50100324 41106248 50100328 41106250   *..........L..O...*   00226CC8

```
ACBCICSE     --- CICS TRANSACTION DUMP ---     CODE=ASRA   TASK=PNC1                        DATE=08/08/89   TIME=15:10:49   PAGE  20

PROGRAM STORAGE                              ADDRESS 0225008 TO 002277E7   LENGTH 0027E0

00000 1AE0   58FOCOOC  05EF94BF  D0049AF0  D05C58FO  D1885D00  F0805810  D2E007F1  D2106478   *.0....m...0.*.O.J.].O...K..1K....*   00226AE8
00000 1B00   C4044110  64785010  D3204110  D3209640  D04958FO  4830C27A  C00C55EF  94BF0049   *D.........L...L..O.O...B...m.....*   00226B08
00000 1B20   40F0C005C  58FOD188  5000F080  48107014  41000000  D2046490  62450010  05EF0002   *.0...0.h..O.....B.O...K.........*   00226B28
00000 1B40   01040002  011ED216  C478C422  9240640F  D3284110  02046490  64785010  03204110   *......K.D.D...O.L...B..K....*   00226B48
00000 1B60   64705010  D3244110  64705010  D3209640  61A05010  61A05010  6245A010  05EF0000   *..L.....L..O.../...../.K.....O..*   00226B68
00000 1B80   D3304110  D3209640  D04958F0  94BF0049  94BF0D05C  58F0D188  58F00188  5000D980   *L..L.O.O..m..m.*.O.h.O....D.O.*   00226B88
00000 1BA0   5B8OC4BO  47FOB196  D3209640  94BF0D049  61CAD224  61CB61CA  D2016254  C09847F0   *$.D..O.o.L.O...m.../.K../../.K...0*   00226BA8
00000 1BC0   B134D22F  61AOC463  92406100  D21E61D1  61DD0201  625ACOA7  D203D280  D3184100   *..K../.D..../.K../../...$...D.K.D..*   00226BC8
00000 1BE0   B1465000  D3184FO  B1A0D203  D318D2B0  D203D2B4  D3105880  C4B04100  B1665000   *..O....O..K..L.K..K.K.L...D..O.*   00226BE8
00000 1C00   D3105BB0  C4AC47FO  BCEAD203  D3100294  58FOD1B0  625ACOA7  05F09110  D04847EO   *L..$.D..O..K.L..m.O....$...0.O..O*   00226C08
00000 1C20   FOOE5BFO  C01007FF  4BF0D05C  58D00004  980C0014  58E0D00C  07FE58B0  C4B05810   *0..$.0..O..K.O.O...O...O.$.....*   00226C28
00000 1C40   D308O7F1  D2166478  C439924O  648FD204  649064BF  4110D03C  50100330  41106470   *L..1.K..D...D...d..K.O.O...*   00226C48
00000 1C60   50100324  41106478  50100328  58FOC10C  980C0000  4110625A  50100330  96800330   *O...O...O.O.A...O...Z.O.O..m.O.*   00226C68
00000 1C80   41100320  9640D049  58FOC10C  980C0000  16100AOD  D05C58F0  D18B58FO  F0040200   *...m.O.O.A...O...O.*.O..O.O.0..K*   00226C88
00000 1CA0   D31807F1  41100207  980C0018  8900D04F  94BF0049  5BBOC4AC  47FOB10E  96100048   *L..1..K..O.....O.m.O.$.D..O..m..H*   00226CA8
00000 1CC0   50500054  50ED0054  9120D048  47E0F02E  D04B58FO  41600D04  4160D018  96040000   *P.P....K.O..O..K.O.....m..*   00226CC8
00000 1CE0   58F02038  41F0F004  07F7F94BF  D04B58FO  C0407FE  58B00200  4170C207  05F09120   *.O..0..O.*.O..O.O...O...B.O...*   00226CE8
00000 1D20   05805840  10001E4B  50401000  87165000  9140D049  4160000B  41700207  05105800   *...........P.....O...B..K.O.*   00226D28
00000 1D40   D2BBC018  58E0D054  07FE0000  87165000  00000000  D2005870  02188880  D21C0267   *K......O..K...K.h..K..g*   00226D48
00000 1D60   00000000  00000000  00000000  00000000  80000000  00255588  C9D3C206  D5E309F0   *........h.ILBON.RO*   00226D68
00000 1D80   00000000  00000000  0022703A  07FE0000  00000000  00000000  00000000  00000000   *K...................*   00226D88
00000 1DA0   00000000  00000000  00000000  00000000  00000000  00000000  00000000  00000000   *...................*   00226DA8
00000 1DC0   00000000  00000000  00000000  00000000  00000000  00000000  00000000  00000000   *...................*   00226DC8
00000 1DE0   00000000  00000000  00000000  00000000  00000000  00000000  00000000  00000000   *...................*   00226DE8
00000 1E00   00000000  00000000  00000000  00000000  00000000  0022F1C4  00000000  00000000   *.............D...*   00226E08
00000 1E20   00000000  00000000  00000000  00000000  40404040  40404040  00000000  00000000   *...................*   00226E28
00000 1E40   00000000  00000000  00000000  00000000  40404040  40404040  00000000  FOFOFOFO   *...............0000*   00226E48
00000 1E60   FOFOFOFO  00000000  00000000  00000000  00000000  00000000  FOFOF0F0  D4400000   *0000..............0000.D..*   00226E68
00000 1E80   00000000  6003D4F1  40C0C35D  40C30607  00C90C3  C2DC6306  C2DC6306  D4000000   *....M1.(.C)..I..B..B..D.*   00226E88
00000 1EA0   F5F74FO  6B40F1F9  F7F66B40  40C5D5E2  E809C9C7  C805E2C9  C2D404C1  D609D740   * 5740-LM1 (C) COPYRIGHT IBM CORP*   00226EA8
00000 1EC0   F1F9F7F2  F6B40F1F9  F7F668B40  4003C9C3  C5D5E2C5  E840D6C6  C440D4C1  E3C5D9C9   * 1972, 1976, 1983 LICENSED MATERI*   00226EC8
00000 1EE0   C1034060  D31A4860  00031266  48100018  C1D34060  D7D60640  C5D9E3E8  69BF2F4F0   *AL - PROGRAM PROPERTY OF IBM.240*   00226EE8
00000 1F00   F3F7F700  000047FO  47F0F010  F0084740  F6F44F4  F6F4F00  C0DC589F  0026C0599   *377......0...00..00.00...*   00226F08
00000 1F20   C903C206  C7C6D640  E5E209C5  E4D3C5F2  4040F4E4  D7F24F46  F4F8F40C  0026C0FC8   *ILBOGO0 VSREL2 4UP27604...H*   00226F28
00000 1F40   0226CFCC  41EE0000  20000061  01C7950C  47290094  06108910  0021A1E1  92000061   *.........n....K...*   00226F48
00000 1F60   9102D004  82000061  D1C795D6  06147890  9669500  E0004780  E0004780  90669800C   *....B...J.Gn.......h*   00226F68
00000 1F80   D01418F2  07FF5840  D1E01B55  4350E001  0650B950  0021A145  5BB4C000  1B11410    *.....2....J.......$...*   00226F88
00000 1FA0   E0004BE0  E0021AEB  950C0061  47B090B0  47F090FC  89300002  1AE398FC  D01007FE   *.......o...........Ta.*   00226FA8
00000 1FC0   47F090B0  41E10000  88100018  47F090B0  49109106  47409FC  19014780  90FC4210   *..........B...../.Jqj...*   00226FC8
00000 1FE0   D0604860  D1A48B60  00031266  40800203  47800FC  58800198  91800000  9B0AD014   *...J..........j...h.....*   00226FE8
00000 2000   D5000060  80044770  90F00203  70008000  41880000  4660900B  4669008  F08A50F0   *N....h.j..O...N.....0.0.*   00227008
00000 2020   58C00044  07FE0032  00000000  00202450  53B24780  5AED0503  F0CA47F0  F08A50F0   *.....h.......S...0.0.0.*   00227028
00000 2040   F30690E7  F3AE185F  D503E000  50935306  53B4A58F0  E0005A03  5392056F  0203538C   *3..X3..N..O.S.....Qq...*   00227048
00000 2060   4BE053A6  D503E000  50624770  50935306  538FE5840  89300198  1AE398FC  D203S038C   *.......N..j.S...h..Ta.K...*   00227068
00000 20A0   F8BA07FE  50F0F3CE  4BFOF3A0  00037805  47F0F070  501053B8  140094780  01100188   *..h.0.O.0..../...O.0N.....*   00227088
00000 20C0   5088C903  C2DC6306  D4F0F811  OAOB1810  5010538A  180498EF  53AE9827  F3BE5810   *..I.B..M08.....O.....a.3...*   002270C8
00000 20E0   90ECF306  184F5820  D1B99140  20024710  5010538A  96801000  50C24100  47F050F2   *..3..O..J...O..m..B..O.02*   002270E8
00000 2100   439212F1  47800408  056F4FF1  41204100  11404780  20044780  41504780  415058F0   *.....K.../..@........O*   00227108
00000 2120   0000AA08  18F0056F  4500411E  C9D3C206  D4E2C7D6  A0A91255  4774412C  98EC4306   *.....O..K.ILBOMSGO..Q...a.*   00227128
00000 2140   07FE58E0  43A448EE  000040E0  D05C12EE  07B80703  4774414A  80000127  000040E0   *.........O.*....w.J.....*   00227148
00000 2180   58104146  OAOD4580  40E89180  20024780  418A58E0  20384BF0  43A448EE  000040E0   *.....m..Yj.......0.....*   00227188
00000 21A0   D05C12EE  47404140  58F0202C  12FF4780  418A4943E  200241FF  001C05EF  47F041A8   *.*....O......*.....O.y*   002271A8
```

```
ACBCICSE    --- CICS TRANSACTION DUMP ---    CODE=ASRA    TASK=PNC1                    DATE=08/08/89    TIME=15:10:49    PAGE   21

PROGRAM STORAGE

                                ADDRESS 00225008 TO 0027277E7    LENGTH 0027E0

000021C0  58F0208C 12FF4780 41AB189D 410D00A8 50090008 509D0004 1B1105EF 18090502  *................y.....y.R.*  002271C8
000021E0  439E205D 478041CE 4110205C 18744580 432C0502 439E3065 478041CE 41130064  *................P.....N.*    002271E8
00002200  47F04188 D502439E 20594780 41E24110 20581874 4580432C D7072058 2058D502  *ILBOSND2.O...S.......N.*     00227208
00002220  439E2055 4780423E 58F04396 12FF4780 420205EF 47F04228 4100420A 47F04212  *.O.O.........ILBOSND2.kj*    00227228
00002240  C9D3C206 E2D5C4F2 1B110A08 1BF005EF 45004226 C9D3C206 E2D5C4F2 0A099140  *..................N.....k*   00227248
00002260  20024780 42344580 40E84110 20541877 4580432C D502439E 20514780 4929108   *.................N.....e..k* 00227268
00002280  20504780 425C4500 425C9D03 C2D60BE2 E2F00A09 4322C9D3 439E3075 47645000  *IEDQB1..ILBOQSSO.N...e...k*  00227288
000022A0  4274C9C5 C4D8C2F1 40404003 41102050 1B744580 42D85850 40963075 47804292  *.O.N../.....j............*   002272A8
000022C0  41130074 47F0427C D502439E 4580432C 42DE5850 20604135 20854780 30304780  *.......Q......j.......*      002272C8
000022E0  42BA5035 02141415 02141874 41102050 20134780 12334780 420E4133 05A09110  *.........m...j..w..j.*       002272E8
00002300  30304780 42DE5035 02149280 52144115 58350850 9477C9D3 439A12FF 478042F4  *.............j.w...4*        00227308
00002320  D7034386 43869400 02141280 43A69101 2015D014 47F042FF 94742040 4310F9F3  *.P.f.m..wj..........IL*      00227328
00002340  C206E2E3 438694FF 4100431A 2007C9D3 436C58F0 E93E12FF 07FF45A6 0A181BF7  *BOSTTO.j....hk.ILBOSTTO.*    00227348
00002360  07FF5831 00099110 30300788 40004322 F0047EC0 E93E1813 07881813 96010B17  *.........O.j.....O.*         00227368
00002380  1BEE43E0 F0054CE0 E0090140 92801000 400206EF F0047EE0 4364410F F000A0A0   *8.O..j.O.....q.*             00227388
000023A0  07F84AF0 D055800F 00045800 D0045800 00098DEC E0104110 00066008 00226098   *.............q.*             002273A8
000023C0  00000000 00227030A 00276CF0 00003103E 00021374 00021AF0 00066008 00021384 *...........q.*               002273C8
000023E0  50226CFC 00227030A 00356AB8 00022703A 00000000 00225098 00225098 00000000 *........d.*                  002273E8
00002400  00021000 0036660D 00022703A 00000000 00000000 00000000 00000000 00000000  *...*                         00227408
00002420  00002460  00000000 00000000 00000000 00000000 00000000 00000000 00000000  *...*                         00227428
00002440  LINES 00002440 TO 00002460 SAME AS ABOVE                                  *                             00227448
00002460  00000000 00000000 00000000 00000000 00000000 00000000 00000000 00000000  *                             00227468
00002480  00000000 00000000 00000000 00000000 47F0445E 00000000 00000000 00000000  *......O.;..*                 00227488
000024A0  00000000 00000000 00000000 00000000 00000000 00000000 00000000 00000000  *                             002274A8
000024C0  00000000 C9D3C206 E2D9E540 E5E209C5 D3F24BF4 E407F2F7 F6F0F440 70249204  *.ILBOSRV.VSREL2.4UP27604*    002274C8
000024E0  00000000 F004187F 92020049 D05D3014 71640770 E407F440 D4F04110 70249204  *.ILBOSRV.VSREL2.4UP27604.k*  002274E8
00002500  000047F0 F004187F 91020049 58300180 703C9D03 703C9D03 C206C3D6 D4F04110  *..O..ILBOCOMO.k.*            00227508
00002520  D1C7947F D1C51834 12444770 70484100 30AC1222 4770707A 58203010 12224780  *JGm.JE..O..N.*               00227528
00002540  00000A08 50000188 18305050 30385020 D4F04110 00000A08 500030AC 91803000  *.........ILBOCMMO.j.wN.*     00227548
00002560  707A4100 706847F0 7070C9D3 58100018 58201018 12224780 71189103 101B4770  *.........O.......j.*         00227568
00002580  47107122 96803004 71189101 50D03004 58201004 12224780 70A60523 71424700  *.........j.j.j.*             00227588
000025A0  714A101C 47707118 91030007 4770707A 71185B10 00004920 47F07102 C903C2D6  *............j...ILBO*        002275A8
000025C0  71189180 20004780 71189101 4770711C 410070FA 10004920 47F07102 71380SEF  *PRMO.O......ILBOPRMO.O.ILBO* 002275C8
000025E0  D7D904F0 20004780 71185BF0 C903C2D6 D4F00A09 0A094FF0 18441813 07F60000  *PRMO.O......ILBOCOMO..6*     002275E8
00002600  47F07138 12444770 7134C903 C206C3D6 C206C3D6 D4F00A09 18441813 70760000  *......ILBOCOMO..*            00227608
00002620  00000000 C3D4E240 C1D5E2F4 E3C8C9E2 40C9E240 C140E2C1 E5C540C1 D9C5C140  *FOR.CMS.ANS4THIS.IS.A.SAVE.AREA* 00227628
00002640  C606D940 C3D4E240 E3D64040 C3D6C2D6 D3401C40 E5C2D6D3 40C1D9C5 C1400000  *FOR.CMS.TO.COBOL.O*          00227648
00002660  00000000 00000000 00000000 00000000 00000000 00000000 00000000 00000000  *                             00227668
00002680  00000000 00000000 00000000 00000000 00000000 00000000 00000000 00000000  *                             00227688
000026A0  00000000 00000000 C9D3C206 E5E209C5 D3F24BF4 E407F2F7 F6F0F440 00000000  *.ILBOBEG.VSREL2.4UP27604*    002276A8
000026C0  000047F0 F004187F 91042000 4780705C D276010F D10ED224 D10ED709 4770704C  *.OO..J.K.J..*k.J.K.C.J.K.J*  002276C8
000026E0  58300180 D207D133 300C020C D13B70C3 18105800 2000470B D0070DDB 4770704C  *.J.K.J.O.J.K..Jm.j*          002276E8
00002700  58300180 D207114B 300C47F0 7052020A 11487000 18D194F8 2000470E 70700104  *SK.J.O.J.K..=*               00227708
00002720  20024780 707094FB 20025810 D10847F0 70741110 20024780 9434200F D203107E  *IKF9921..RECURSIVE.CALL.TO.MO* 00227728
00002740  70E2D201 10047009 0A234150 D9C5C3E4 D9E2C9E5 70941B55 9434200F 07F64040  *DULE.FROM.MODULE.(NOT.COBOL)* 00227748
00002760  C9D2C6F9 F9F2C940 40404040 40404040 40404040 D8C3D0E3 06A000A6 00000000  *..ILBOMSG.VSREL2.4UP27604*   00227768
00002780  C4E4D3C5 40404040 06D44004 D8C2D6D3 C940E34F 5404D005 D8E340C9 D9C1B5C5  *..ILBOMSG.VSREL2.4UP27604*   00227788
000027C0  00F78000 02004020 C9D3C2D6 D4E2C740 E5E209C5 E5E209C5 F6F0F440 00000000  *=..ILBOMSG.VSREL2.4UP27604*  002277C8
```

```
ACBCICSE    --- CICS TRANSACTION DUMP ---    CODE=ASRA    TASK=PNC1                    DATE=08/08/89    TIME=15:10:49    PAGE    22

PROGRAM STORAGE              ADDRESS 00224008 TO 0022411F    LENGTH 000118

00000000  D4E2C2D7 D5C3F240 00704040 004F0000  00000000 D4D7C2D7 D5C3F240 010300AA  *MSBPNC2........MPBPNC2   *  00224008
00000020  01970221 C04B00F6 00185001 01100000  00000000 00000000 40404000 00000000  *.p......6.........       *  00224028
00000040  00000000 00000000 00000000 00000000  00000000 00000040 40404000 00001402  *.................        *  00224048
00000060  F80007C5 D4D7D3D6 E8C5C540 D5C1D4C5  40C3C8C1 D5C7C500 00000402 F0004D5D7  *8..EMPLOYEE NAME CHANGE...0..P*  00224068
00000080  D5C3F200 00000E02 F000A5C5 D4D76D05  D6404040 40D5C1D4 C5000000 0202F000  *NC2......0.VEMP-NO   NAME....0.*  00224088
000000A0  F0F14B00 00000050D D100F500 D100FB00  00001901 C100FF00 00000100 00000100  *01...J.5....A........*  002240A8
000000C0  F0011900 00002202 F00140F2 48000000  0500D101 45000000 0100FF01 4B000000  *0....0. 2...J....0...*  002240C8
000000E0  1901C101 4F000000 69000000 4F01F006  40000000 4F01F006 90000000            *.A.O....O.0. .O.0...*  002240E8
00000100  4F01F006 E0000000 4F01F007 30FFFFFF  FFFFFF00 00000000                      *.O.0....O.0.........*  00224108
```

B

CICS Commands

Appendix B summarizes all CICS commands discussed in this book. Each command is listed with the full options and associated exceptional conditions unless otherwise noted. Some of the options or conditions may not be discussed in this book because they are rarely used. The number in parentheses indicates the chapter(s) of this book in which the command is discussed.

Although virtually all available CICS commands are discussed in this book, some CICS commands which are rarely used are not included here, because use of these commands is limited to special applications only. Therefore, these rarely used commands are not included in this appendix. However, most CICS application programs for general business applications can be developed using the commands discussed in this book, which follow:

ABEND   To terminate a task abnormally.   (16)

```
EXEC CICS ABEND
     [ABCODE(name)]
     [CANCEL]
```

ADDRESS   To access CICS system area.   (2)

```
EXEC CICS ADDRESS
     option(ptr-ref)
```

```
CSA                  Common system area
CWA                  Common work area
EIB                  EXEC interface block
TCTUA                Terminal control table user area
TWA                  Transaction work area
```

ALLOCATE   To acquire a session.   (17)

```
EXEC CICS ALLOCATE
     SYSID(name)
     [PROFILE(name)]
     [NOQUEUE | NOSUSPEND]
```

Conditions: CBIDEER, EOC, INVREQ, SESSBUSY, SESSIONERR, SYSBUSY, SYSIDERR

ASKTIME   To request the current time of the day.   (13)

```
EXEC CICS ASKTIME
     [ABSTIME(data-area)]
```

ASSIGN   To obtain CICS system values.   (2)

```
EXEC CICS ASSIGN
     option(data-area)
```

```
ABCODE               Current value of ABEND code
APPLID               VTAM application identification
CWALENG              Length of CWA
OPCLASS              Operator class
OPID                 Operator identifier
SYSID                Local CICS system identifier
TCTUALENG            Length of TCTUA
TERMCODE             Terminal type and model number
TWALENG              Length of TWA
USERID               User identifier
(Others)
```

Condition: INVREQ

CANCEL   To cancel previous interval control command.   (13)

```
EXEC CICS CANCEL
     [REQID(name)
      [TRANSID(name)][SYSID(name)]]
```

Conditions: INVREQ, ISCINVREQ, NOTAUTH, NOTFND, SYS-IDERR

CONNECT PROCESS   To initiate a process.   (17)

```
EXEC CICS CONNECT PROCESS
    [CONVID(name)]
    PROCNAME(data-area)
    PROCLENGTH(data-value)
    SYNCLEVEL(data-value)
    [PIPLIST(data-area)
      PIPLENGTH(data-value)]
```

Conditions: INVREQ, NOTALLOC, LENGERR

CONVERSE   To converse (send and receive) with terminal or LU.   (17)

```
EXEC CICS CONVERSE
    [FROM(data-area)
      [FROMLENGTH(data-value) |
        FROMFLENGTH(data-value)] [FMH]]
    [INTO(data-area) | SET(ptr-ref)]
    [TOLENGTH(data-area) | TOFLENGTH(data-area)]
    [ASIS]
    [SESSION(name) | CONVID(name)]
    (Others)
```

Conditions: CBIDERR, EOC, EODS, EOF, IGREQCD, INBFMH, LENGERR, NOTALLOC, RDATT, SIGNAL, TERMERR, WRBRK

DELAY   To suspend processing of task.   (13)

```
EXEC CICS DELAY
    [INTERVAL(hhmmss) | TIME(hhmmss)]
    [REQID(name)]
```

Conditions: EXPIRED, INVREQ

DELETE   To delete record(s).   (4)

```
EXEC CICS DELETE
    DATASET(name) | FILE(name)
    [RIDFLD(data-area)
      [KEYLENGTH(data-value)
        [GENERIC [NUMERIC(data-area)]]]]
    [SYSID(name)]
    [RBA | RRN]
```

Conditions: DISABLED, DSIDERR, DUPKEY, ILLOGIC, INVREQ, IOERR, ISCINVREQ, NOTAUTH, NOTFND, SYSIDERR

DELETEQ TD   To delete a record from intrapartition queue.   (11)

```
EXEC CICS DELETEQ TD
     QUEUE(name)
     [SYSID(name)]
```

Conditions: ISCINVREQ, NOTAUTH, QIDERR, SYSIDERR

DELETEQ TS   To delete a record from temporary storage queue.   (12)

```
EXEC CICS DELETEQ TS
     QUEUE(name)
     [SYSID(name)]
```

Conditions: ISCINVREQ, NOTAUTH, QIDERR, SYSIDERR

DEQ   To release exclusive control from a resource.   (13)

```
EXEC CICS DEQ
     RESOURCE(data-area)
     [LENGTH(data-value)]
```

DUMP   To dump main storage area(s).   (16)

```
EXEC CICS DUMP
     DUMPCODE(name)
     [FROM(data-area)
       LENGTH(data-value) | FLENGTH(data-value)]
     [COMPLETE]
     [TASK]
     [STORAGE]
     [PROGRAM]
     [TERMINAL]
     [TABLES]
     (Others)
```

ENDBR   To end a browse operation.   (5)

```
EXEC CICS ENDBR
     DATASET(name) | FILE(name)
     [REQID(data-value)]
     [SYSID(name)]
```

Conditions: DISABLED, DSIDERR, ILLOGIC, INVREQ, ISCINVREQ, NOTAUTH, SYSIDERR

ENQ   To acquire exclusive control over a resource.   (13)

```
EXEC CICS ENQ
     RESOURCE(data-area)
     [LENGTH(data-value)]
     [NOSUSPEND]
```

Condition: ENQBUSY

ENTER   To create a user trace entry.   (16)

```
EXEC CICS ENTER
     TRACEID(data-value)
     [FROM(data-area)]
     [RESOURCE(name)]
     (Others)
```

Condition: INVREQ

FORMATTIME   To select format of time and date.   (13)

```
EXEC CICS FORMATTIME
     ABSTIME(data-value)
     [YYDDD(data-area)]
     [YYMMDD(data-area)]
     [YYDDMM(data-area)]
     [DDMMYY(data-area)]
     [MMDDYY(data-area)]
     [DATE(data-area)]
     [DATEFORM(data-area)]
     [DATESEP(data-value)]
     [DAYCOUNT(data-area)]
     [DAYOFWEEK(data-area)]
     [DAYOFMONTH(data-area)]
     [MONTHOFYEAR(data-area)]
     [YEAR(data-area)]
     [TIME(data-area)
       [TIMESEP(data-value)]]
```

FREE   To free a session.   (17)

```
EXEC CICS FREE
     [SESSION(name)  |  CONVID(name)]
```

Conditions: INVREQ, NOTALLOC, SYSIDERR

FREEMAIN   To release main storage.   (2)

```
EXEC CICS FREEMAIN
     DATA(data-area)
```

GETMAIN   To acquire main storage.   (2)

```
EXEC CICS GETMAIN
     SET(ptr-ref)
     LENGTH(data-value) | FLENGTH(data-value)
     [INITIMG(data-value)]
     [NOSUSPEND]
```

Conditions: LENGERR, NOSTG

HANDLE ABEND   To intercept an abnormal termination of task.   (16)

```
EXEC CICS HANDLE ABEND
     [LABEL(label) | PROGRAM(name) | CANCEL | RESET]
```

Condition: PGMIDERR

HANDLE AID   To intercept attention identifier key(s).   (7)

```
EXEC CICS HANDLE AID
     option(label)
```

```
ANYKEY               Any PA keys, any PF keys or CLEAR key
CLEAR                Clear key
ENTER                Enter key
PA1 - PA3            Program attention keys
PF1 - PF24           Program function keys
LIGHTPEN             Light pen
OPERID               Operator id card reader
(Others)
```

HANDLE CONDITION   To intercept exceptional condition(s).   (2)

```
EXEC CICS HANDLE CONDITION
     condition(label)
```

IGNORE CONDITION   To ignore exceptional condition(s)   (2)

```
EXEC CICS IGNORE CONDITION
     condition
```

ISSUE COPY   To copy screen image.   (7)

```
EXEC CICS ISSUE COPY
     TERMID(name)
     [CTLCHAR(data-value)]
     [WAIT]
```

Conditions: TERMERR, TERMIDERR

ISSUE PRINT To print a hard copy of screen image.   (7)

```
EXEC CICS ISSUE PRINT
```

Condition: TERMERR

JOURNAL   To create a journal record.   (15)

```
EXEC CICS JOURNAL
     JFILEID(data-value)
     JTYPEID(data-value)
     FROM(data-area)
     [LENGTH(data-value)]
     [REQID(data-area)]
     [PREFIX(data-value)
       [PFXLENG(data-value)]]
     [STARTIO]
     [WAIT]
     [NOSUSPEND]
```

Conditions: IOERR, JIDERR, LENGERR, NOJBUFSP, NOTAUTH, NOTOPEN

LINK   To pass control to a program, expecting return.   (3)

```
EXEC CICS LINK
     PROGRAM(name)
     [COMMAREA(data-area)
       [LENGTH(data-value)]]
```

Conditions: NOTAUTH, PGMIDERR

LOAD   To load a program, table, or mapset.   (3)

```
EXEC CICS LOAD
     PROGRAM(name)
     [SET(ptr-ref)]
```

```
        [LENGTH(data-area) | FLENGTH(data-area)]
        [ENTRY(ptr-ref)]
        [HOLD]
```

   Conditions: NOTAUTH, PGMIDERR

POP   To reinstate HANDLE commands.   (2)

```
    EXEC CICS POP HANDLE
```

POST   To post time expiration.   (13)

```
    EXEC CICS POST
        [INTERVAL(hhmmss) | TIME(hhmmss)]
        SET(ptr-ref)
        [REQID(name)]
```

   Conditions: EXPIRED, INVREQ

PURGE MESSAGE   To delete a logical message.   (10)

```
    EXEC CICS PURGE MESSAGE
```

   Condition: TSIOERR

PUSH   To suspend HANDLE commands.   (2)

```
    EXEC CICS PUSH HANDLE
```

READ   To read a record.   (4, 6)

```
    EXEC CICS READ
        DATASET(name) | FILE(name)
        INTO(data-area) | SET(ptr-ref)
        [LENGTH(data-area)]
        RIDFLD(data-area)
        [KEYLENGTH(data-value) [GENERIC]]
        [SYSID(name)]
        [RBA | RRN]
        [GTEQ | EQUAL]
        [UPDATE]
```

   Conditions: DISABLED, DSIDERR, DUPKEY, ILLOGIC, INVREQ,
   IOERR, ISCINVREQ, LENGERR, NOTAUTH, NOTFND, SYSIDERR

READNEXT   To read a record sequentially forward.   (5, 6)

```
EXEC CICS READNEXT
     DATASET(name) | FILE(name)
     INTO(data-area) | SET(ptr-ref)
     [LENGTH(data-area)]
     RIDFLD(data-area)
     [KEYLENGTH(data-value)]
     [REQID(data-value)]
     [SYSID(name)]
     [RBA | RRN]
```

Conditions: DISABLED, DSIDERR, DUPKEY, ENDFILE, ILLOGIC, INVREQ, IOERR, ISCINVREQ, LENGERR, NOTAUTH, NOTFND, SYSIDERR

READPREV   To read a record sequentially backward.   (5)

```
EXEC CICS READPREV
```

(Options and conditions are the same as READNEXT.)

READQ TD   To read a record from transient data queue.   (11)

```
EXEC CICS READQ TD
     QUEUE(name)
     INTO(data-area) | SET(ptr-ref)
     [LENGTH(data-area)]
     [SYSID(name)]
     [NOSUSPEND]
```

Conditions: IOERR, ISCINVREQ, LENGERR, NOTAUTH, NOTOPEN, QBUSY, QIDERR, QZERO, SYSIDERR

READQ TS   To read a record from temporary storage queue.   (12)

```
EXEC CICS READQ TS
     QUEUE(name)
     INTO(data-area) | SET(ptr-ref)
     [LENGTH(data-area)]
     [NUMITEMS(data-area)]
     [ITEM(data-value) | NEXT]
     [SYSID(name)]
```

Conditions: INVREQ, IOERR, ISCINVREQ, ITEMERR, LENGERR, NOTAUTH, QIDERR, SYSIDERR

RECEIVE   To receive data from terminal or LU.   (7, 17)

```
EXEC CICS RECEIVE
     [SESSION(name) | CONVID(name)]
     [INTO(data-area) | SET(ptr-ref)]
     [LENGTH(data-area) | FLENGTH(data-area)]
     [ASIS]
     (Others)
```

Conditions: ENDINPT, EOC, EODS, EOF, INBFMH, INVREQ, LENGERR, NOPASSBKRD, NOTALLOC, RDATT, SIGNAL, TER-MERR

RECEIVE MAP   To receive mapped input data.   (9)

```
EXEC CICS RECEIVE
     MAP(name)
     [MAPSET(name)]
     [INTO(data-area) | SET(ptr-ref)]
     [FROM(data-area) LENGTH(data-value) |
        TERMINAL [ASIS] [INPARTN(name)]]
```

Conditions: EOC, EODS, INVMPSZ, INVPARTN, MAPFAIL, NOTAUTH, PARTNFAIL, RDATT, UNEXPIN

RELEASE   To delete a loaded program.   (3)

```
EXEC CICS RELEASE
   PROGRAM(name)
```

Conditions: NOTAUTH, PGMIDERR

RESETBR   To reset a start of browse operation.   (5)

```
EXEC CICS RESETBR
     DATASET(name) | FILE(name)
     RIDFLD(data-area)
     [KEYLENGTH(data-value) [GENERIC]]
     [REQID(data-value)]
     [SYSID(name)]
     [GTEQ | EQUAL]
     [RBA | RRN]
```

Conditions: DISABLED, DSIDERR, ILLOGIC, INVREQ, IOERR, ISCINVREQ, NOTAUTH, NOTFND, SYSIDERR

RETRIEVE   To retrieve data passed by START command.   (13)

```
EXEC CICS RETRIEVE
     [INTO(data-area) | SET(ptr-ref)]
     [LENGTH(data-area)]
     [RTRANSID(data-area)]
     [RTERMID(data-area)]
     [QUEUE(data-area)]
     [WAIT]
```

Conditions: ENDDATA, ENVDEFERR, INVREQ, INVTSREQ, IOERR, LENGERR, NOTAUTH, NOTFND

RETURN   To return control.   (3)

```
EXEC CICS RETURN
     [TRANSID(name)
       [COMMAREA(data-area)
         [LENGTH(data-value)]]]
```

Conditions: INVREQ, NOTAUTH

REWRITE   To rewite a record.   (4)

```
EXEC CICS REWRITE
     DATASET(name) | FILE(name)
     FROM(data-area)
     [LENGTH(data-value)]
     [SYSID(name)]
```

Conditions: DISABLED, DSIDERR, DUPREC, ILLOGIC, INVREQ, IOERR, ISCINVREQ, LENGERR, NOSPACE, NOTAUTH, SYSIDERR

ROUTE   To route message to terminals.   (10)

```
EXEC CICS ROUTE
     [INTERVAL(hhmmss) | TIME(hhmmss)]
     [ERRTERM(name)]
     [TITLE(data-area)]
     [LIST(data-area)]
     [OPCLASS(data-area)]
     [REQID(name)]
     [LDC(name)]
     [NLEOM]
```

Conditions: INVERRTERM, INVLDC, INVREQ, RTEFAIL, RTE-SOME

SEND   To send data to terminal or LU.   (7, 17)

```
EXEC CICS SEND
     [FROM(data-area)
       [LENGTH(data-value) | FLENGTH(data-value)][FMH]]
     [INVITE | LAST]
     [WAIT | CONFIRM]
     [SESSION(name) | CONVID(name)]
     (Others)
```

Conditions: CBIDERR,   IGREQCD,   INVREQ,   LENGERR,
NOPASSBKWR, NOTALLOC, SIGNAL, TERMERR, WRBRK

SEND CONTROL   To send terminal control orders.   (9)

```
EXEC CICS SEND CONTROL
     [ERASEAUP | ERASE]
     [ALARM]
     [FREEKB]
     [FRSET]
     [CURSOR(data-value)]
     [PRINT]
     [ACCUM]
     (Other)
```

Conditions: IGREQCD, IGREQID, INVLDC, INVPARTN, INVREQ,
RETPAGE, TSIOERR, WRBRK

SEND MAP   To send mapped output data.   (9, 10)

```
EXEC CICS SEND
     MAP(name)
     [MAPSET(name)]
     [[FROM(data-area)][DATAONLY] | MAPONLY]
     [LENGTH(data-value)]
     [CURSOR[(data-value)]]
     [ACCUM]
     [ERASE | ERASEAUP]
     [PRINT]
     [FREEKB]
     [ALARM]
     [FRSET]
     [L40 | L64 | L80 | HONEOM]
     [NLEOM]
     [FORMFEED]
     (Others)
```

Conditions: IGREQCD, IGREQID, INVLDC, INVMPSZ, INVPARTN, INVREQ, OVERFLOW, RETPAGE, TSIOERR, WRBRK

SEND PAGE   To send a logical message.   (9, 10)

```
EXEC CICS SEND PAGE
     [[TRANSID(name)] RELEASE | RETAIN]
     [TRAILER(data-area)]
     [AUTOPAGE | NOAUTOPAGE [CURRENT | ALL]]
     [OPERPURGE]
     (Others)
```

Conditions: IGREQCD, INVREQ, RETPAGE, TSIOERR, WRBRK

SEND TEXT   To send text without mapping.   (9, 10)

```
EXEC CICS SEND TEXT
     FROM(data-area)
     LENGTH(data-value)
     [CURSOR(data-value)]
     [FORMFEED]
     [ERASE]
     [PRINT]
     [ALARM]
     [FREEKB]
     [NLEOM]
     [HEADER(data-area)]
     [TRAILER(data-area)]
     [ACCUM]
     [L40 | L64 | L80 | HONEOM]
     (Others)
```

Conditions: IGREQCD, IGREQID, INVLDC, INVREQ, RETPAGE, TSIOERR, WRBRK, INVPARTN

SET DATASET   To open or close a dataset (or file).   (16)

```
EXEC CICS SET
         DATASET(name) | FILE(name)
         OPEN | CLOSED
```

START   To initiate a transaction.   (13)

```
EXEC CICS START
     TRANSID(name)
     [INTERVAL(hhmmss) | TIME(hhmmss)]
     [REQID(name)]
```

```
[FROM(data-area)
  [LENGTH(data-value) [FMH]]]
[TERMID(name)]
[SYSID(name)]
[RTRANSID(name)]
[RTERMID(name)]
[QUEUE(name)]
[NOCHECK]
[PROTECT]
```

Conditions: INVREQ, IOERR, ISCINVREQ, NOTAUTH, SYSIDERR, TERMIDERR, TRANSIDERR

STARTBR   To start a browse operation.   (5, 6)

```
EXEC CICS STARTBR
    DATASET(name) | FILE(name)
    RIDFLD(data-area)
    [KEYLENGTH(data-value) [GENERIC]]
    [REQID(data-value)]
    [SYSID(name)]
    [RBA | RRN | DEBKEY | DEBREC]
    [GTEQ | EQUAL]
    [UPDATE]
```

Conditions: DISABLED, DSIDERR, ILLOGIC, INVREQ, IOERR, ISCINVREQ, NOTAITH, NOTFND, SYSIDERR

SUSPEND   To suspend execution of the task.   (13)

```
EXEC CICS SUSPEND
```

SYNCPOINT   To establish a sync point.   (15)

```
EXEC CICS SYNCPOINT
    [ROLLBACK]
```

Condition: ROLLEDBACK

TRACE   To start or stop trace.   (16)

```
EXEC CICS TRACE
    ON | OFF
    [ALL]
    [SYSTEM]
    [EI]
    [USER]
    (Others)
```

UNLOCK   To release exclusive control.   (4)

```
EXEC CICS UNLOCK
      DATASET(name) | FILE(name)
      [SYSID(name)]
```

Conditions: DISABLED, DSIDERR, ILLOGIC, IOERR, ISCINVREQ, NOTAUTH, SYSIDERR

WAIT EVENT   To wait for event to occur.   (13)

```
EXEC CICS WAIT EVENT
      ECADDR(ptr-ref)
```

Condition: INVREQ

WRITE   To write a record.   (4, 6)

```
EXEC CICS WRITE
      DATASET(name) | FILE(name)
      FROM(data-area)
      RIDFLD(data-area)
      [LENGTH(data-value)]
      [KEYLENGTH(data-value]
      [SYSID(name)]
      [RBA | RRN]
      [MASSINSERT]
```

Conditions: DISABLED, DSIDERR, DUPREC, ILLOGIC, INVREQ, IOERR, ISCINVREQ, LENGERR, NOTAUTH, NOSPACE, SYSIDERR

WRITEQ TD   To write a record to a transient data queue.   (11)

```
EXEC CICS WRITEQ TD
      QUEUE(name)
      FROM(data-area)
      [LENGTH(data-value)]
      [SYSID(name)]
```

Conditions: IOERR,   ISCINVREQ,   LENGERR,   NOSPACE, NOTAUTH, NOTOPEN, QIDERR, SYSIDERR

WRITEQ TS   To write a record to a temporary storage queue.   (12)

```
EXEC CICS WRITEQ TS
      QUEUE(name)
```

```
FROM(data-area)
[LENGTH(data-value)]
[ITEM(data-area) [REWRITE]]
[SYSID(name)]
[MAIN | AUXILIARY]
[NOSUSPEND]
```

Conditions: INVREQ, IOERR, ISCINVREQ, ITEMERR, NOSPACE, NOTAUTH, QIDERR, SYSIDERR

XCTL   To transfer control to another program.   (3)

```
EXEC CICS XCTL
     PROGRAM(name)
     [COMMAREA(data-area)
       [LENGTH(data-value)]]
```

Conditions: NOTAUTH, PGMIDERR

C

BMS Map Definition Macros

Appendix C summarizes BMS macros discussed in this book. There are three sets of BMS: Minimum, Standard and Full. This appendix is based on the Full BMS, which is used in this book. Each BMS macro is listed with the full options. Some of the options may not be discussed in this book because their use is limited to special BMS applications. For detailed discussion, see Chapter 8.

DFHMSD Macro To define a mapset or to conclude a mapset definition.

```
[mapset]  DFHMSD    TYPE=DSECT | MAP | &SYSPARM | FINAL
                    [,MODE=IN | OUT | INOUT]
                    [,LANG=ASM | COBOL | PLI | RPG]
                    [,STORAGE=AUTO | BASE=name]
                    [,CTRL=([PRINT][,[length]
                      [,FREEKB][,ALARM][,FRSET])]
                    [,EXTATT=NO | MAPONLY | YES]
                    [,COLOR=DEFAULT | color]
                    [,HIGHLIGHT=OFF | BLINK | REVERSE | UNDERLINE]
                    [,PS=BASE | psid]
                    [,VALIDN=([MUSTFILL][,MUSTENTER][,TRIGGER])]
                    [,TERM=type | ,SUFFIX=n]
                    [,TIOAPFX=YES | NO]
                    [,MAPATTS=(attr1,attr2, ...)]
                    [,DSATTS=(attr1,attr2, ...)]
                    [,OUTLINE=BOX |
```

```
               ([LEFT][,RIGHT][,OVER][,UNDER])])
       [,SOSI=NO | YES]
       [,TRANSP=YES | NO]
       [,PARTN=(name[,ACTIVATE])]
       [,LDC=mnemonic]
       [,OBFMT=YES | NO]
       [,HTAB=tab[,tab] ...]
       [,VTAB=tab[,tab] ...]
       [,DATA=FIELD | BLOCK]
       [,FLDSEP=char | X'hex-char']]
```

DFHMDI Macro   To define a map within a mapset.

```
mapname   DFHMDI    [,SIZE=(line,column)]
                    [,CTRL=([PRINT][,length]
                      [,FREEKB][,ALARM][,FRSET])]
                    [,EXTATT=NO | MAPONLY | YES]
                    [,COLOR=DEFAULT | color]
                    [,HIGHLIGHT=OFF | BLINK | REVERSE | UNDERLINE]
                    [,PS=BASE | psid]
                    [,VALIDN=([MUSTFILL][,MUSTENTER][,TRIGGER])]
                    [,COLUMN=number | NEXT | SAME]
                    [,LINE=number | NEXT | SAME]
                    [,FIELDS=NO]
                    [,MAPATTS=(attr1,attr2, ...)]
                    [,DSATTS=(attr1,attr2, ...)]
                    [,OUTLINE=BOX |
                      ([LEFT][,RIGHT][,OVER][,UNDER])]
                    [,SOSI=NO | YES]
                    [,TRANSP=YES | NO]
                    [,JUSTIFY=([LEFT | RIGHT][,FIRST | LAST])]
                    [,PARTN=(name[,ACTIVATE])]
                    [,OBFMT=YES | NO]
                    [,DATA=FIELD | BLOCK]
                    [,FLDSEP=char | X'hex-char']]
                    [,TIOAPFX=YES | NO]
                    [,HEADER=YES]
                    [,TRAILER=YES]
```

DFHMDF Macro To define a field within a map.

```
[field]    DFHMDF    [,POS=number  |  (line,column)]
                     [,LENGTH=number]
                     [,JUSTIFY=([LEFT  |  RIGHT][,BLANK  |  ZERO])]
                     [,INITIAL='char data'  |  XINIT=hex data]
                     [,ATTRB=([ASKIP  |  PROT  |  UNPROT[,NUM]]
                      [,BRT  |  NORM  |  DRK]
                       [,DET][,IC][,FSET])]
                     [,COLOR=DEFAULT  |  color]
                     [,PS=BASE  |  psid]
                     [,HILIGHT=OFF  |  BLINK  |  REVERSE  |  UNDERLINE]
                     [,VALIDN=([MUSTFILL][,MUSTENTER][,TRIGGER])]
                     [,GRPNAME=group-name]
                     [,OCCURS=number]
                     [,PICIN='value']
                     [,PICOUT='value']
                     [,OUTLINE=BOX  |
                       ([LEFT][,RIGHT][,OVER][,UNDER])]
                     [,SOSI=NO  |  YES]
                     [,TRANSP=YES  |  NO]
                     [CASE=MIXED]
```

D

Common CICS COPYLIB Members

Appendix D lists two CICS COPYLIB members which are very commonly copied into the CICS application programs. They are DFHEIBLK and DFHBMSCA, which contain the Execute Interface Block fields and the attribute characters, respectively, as follows:

DFHEIBLK Member

The DFHEIBLK member is a set of field definitions of the Execute Interface Block (EIB), and it is automatically copied into a CICS application program by the CICS command translator and COBOL compiler. When CICS activates the application program, it places the proper value into the corresponding EIB fields, and the values will be continuously updated as the program is executed. Therefore, the application program can use these fields freely for the application purposes. For the detailed discussions, see Chapter 2.

The following is the full list of EIB fields included in the DFHEIBLK member and their characteristics:

Field	Function	Length	Picture
EIBTIME	Time (0HHMMSS)	4	S9(7) COMP-3
EIBDATE	Day (00YYDDD)	4	S9(7) COMP-3
EIBTRNID	Transaction Identifier	4	X(4)
EIBTASKN	Task Number	4	S9(7) COMP-3
EIBTRMID	Terminal Identifier	4	X(4)
DFHEIGDI	(Reserved)	2	S9(4) COMP
EIBCPOSN	Cursor Position	2	S9(4) COMP
EIBCALEN	COMMAREA Length	2	S9(4) COMP
EIBAID	Attention Identifier	1	X(1)
EIBFN	Function Code	2	X(2)
EIBRCODE	Response Code	6	X(6)
EIBDS	Dataset Name	8	X(8)
EIBREQID	Request Identifier	8	X(8)
EIBRSRCE	Resource Name	8	X(8)
EIBSYNC	Syncpoint Request Flag	1	X(1)
EIBFREE	Free Request Flag	1	X(1)
EIBRECV	Receive Request Flag	1	X(1)
EIBFIL01	(Reserved)	1	X(1)
EIBATT	Attach Data Receive Flag	1	X(1)
EIBEOC	End of Chain Receive Flag	1	X(1)
EIBFMH	FMHS Receive Flag	1	X(1)
EIBCOMPL	Data Complete Flag	1	X(1)
EIBSIG	Signal Receive Flag	1	X(1)
EIBCONF	Confirm Receive Flag	1	X(1)
EIBERR	Error Receive Flag	1	X(1)
EIBERRCD	Error Code Received	4	X(4)
EIBSYNRB	Sync/Rollback Request Flag	1	X(1)
EIBNODAT	No Application Data Receive Flag	1	X(1)
EIBRESP	Internal Condition Number	4	S9(8) COMP
EIBRESP2	Supplementary Information to EIBRESP	4	S9(8) COMP
EIBRLDBK	Rolled-back Flag	1	X(1)

DFHBMSCA Member

The DFHBMSCA member is a standard list of field attributes and printer control characters which are commonly used in CICS application programs. An application program must issue the COPY statement in order to include this member in the program since this member is not automatically included by the CICS translator and COBOL compiler. For detailed discussions, see Chapter 9.

The following is the full list of character definitions included in the DFHBMSCA member and their characteristics:

Name	Function	Value Chr	Hex
DFHBMPEM	Printer, end of message		19
DFHBMPNL	Printer, new line		15
DFHBMASK	Autoskip	'0'	F0
DFHBMUNP	Unprotected		40
DFHBMUNN	Unprotected, numeric	'&'	50
DFHBMPRO	Protected	'-'	60
DFHBMBRY	Bright	'H'	C8
DFHBMDAR	Dark	'<'	4C
DFHBMFSE	MDT on	'A'	C1
DFHBMPRF	Protected, MDT on	'/'	61
DFHBMASF	Autoskip, MDT on	'1'	F1
DFHBMASB	Autoskip, bright	'8'	F8
DFHBMEOF	Field erased		80
DFHBMDET	Field detected		FF
DFHBMPSO	Shift out value X'0E'		0E
DFHBMPSI	Shift in value X'0F'		0F
DFHSA	Set attribute order		28
DFHCOLOR	Color		42
DFHPS	PS		43
DFHHLT	Highlight		41
DFH3270	Base 3270 field attribute		C0
DFHVAL	Validation	'A'	C1
DFHOUTLN	Field outlining attribute code	'B'	C2
DFHBKTRN	Background transparency attribute code		46
DFHALL	Reset all to default		00
DFHERROR	Error code		3F
DFHDFT	Default		FF
DFHDFCOL	Default color		00
DFHBLUE	Blue	'1'	F1
DFHRED	Red	'2'	F2
DFHPINK	Pink	'3'	F3
DFHGREEN	Green	'4'	F4
DFHTURQ	Turquoise	'5'	F5
DFHYELLO	Yellow	'6'	F6
DFHNEUTR	Neutral	'7'	F7
DFHBASE	Base PS		00
DFHDFHI	Normal		00

Name	Function	Value Chr	Hex
DFHBLINK	Blink	'1'	F1
DFHREVRS	Reverse video	'2'	F2
DFHUNDLN	Underscore	'4'	F4
DFHMFIL	Mandatory fill		04
DFHMENT	Mandatory enter		02
DFHMFE	Mandatory fill, mandatory enter		06
DFHUNNOD	Unprotected, nondisplay, nonprint, nondetectable, MDT on	'('	4D
DFHUNIMD	Unprotected, intensify, light pen detectable, MDT on	'I'	C9
DFHUNNUM	Unprotected, numeric, MDT on	'J'	D1
DFHUNINT	Unprotected, numeric, intensify, light pen detectable, MDT on	'R'	D9
DFHUNNON	Unprotected, numeric, nondisplay, nonprint, nondetectable, MDT on	')'	5D
DFHPROTI	Protected, intensify, light pen detectable	'Y'	E8
DFHPROTN	Protected, nondisplay, nonprint, nondetectable	'%'	6C
DFHMT	Trigger		01
DFHMFT	Mandatory fill, trigger		05
DFHMET	Mandatory enter, trigger		03
DFHMFET	Mandatory fill, mandatory enter, trigger		07
DFHDFFR	Default outline		00
DFHLEFT	Left		08
DFHOVER	Overline		04
DFHRIGHT	Right		02
DFHUNDER	Under		01
DFHBOX	Box (left+right+over+under)		0F
DFHSOSI	SOSI=yes		01
DFHTRANS	Background transparency	'0'	F0
DFHOPAQ	No background transparency		FF

E

Common Response and ABEND Codes

Appendix E lists the common response codes in EIBRCODE and ABEND codes, which are very useful for program debugging.

EIBRCODE

The EIBRCODE field is a 6-byte field containing the response code of the last CICS command excution. It must be interpretated in conjunction with the value of the EIBFN field, which is a 2-byte field containing the function code of the last command excuted. The interpretation of EIBRCODE in this way represents exceptional conditions of that command. Therefore, it is very useful to analyze the value of both EIBRCODE and EIBFN fields for effective debugging. For detailed discussion, see Chapters 2 and 16.

The following table summarizes the values of EIBRCODE with respect to CICS commands which are discussed in this book and their associated exceptional conditions summarized in Appendix B. The table should be read as follows: The value in byte 0 of EIBFN represents a CICS control group. The value in byte 1 of EIBFN represents a CICS command of that control group. In general, a combination of byte 0 of EIBFN and byte 0 of EIBRCODE determines an exceptional condition associated with CICS commands of that control group. Bytes 1, 2, and 3 of EIBRCODE provide further detailed description of the condition. Bytes 4 and 5 of EIBRCODE are used for other purposes, so they are not listed here.

EIBFN 0	1	Control Group/ Command	EIBRCODE 0	1	2	3	Exceptional Condition	Further Description
02	02	ADDRESS	E0				INVREQ	
	04	HANDLE CONDITION						
	06	HANDLE AID						
	08	ASSIGN						
	0A	IGNORE CONDITION						
	0C	PUSH HANDLE						
	0E	POP HANDLE						
		Terminal Control						
04	02	RECEIVE	04				EOF	
	04	SEND	10				EODS	
	06	CONVERSE	C1				EOF	
	0A	ISSUE COPY	C2				ENDINPT	
	1C	ISSUE PRINT	D0	04			SYSIDERR	Name not valid.
	20	ALLOCATE	D0	08			SYSIDERR	Link out of service.
	22	FREE	D0	0C			SYSIDERR	Name unknown.
	32	CONNECT PROCESS	D2	04			SESSIONERR	Name not valid.
			D2	08			SESSIONERR	Link out of service.
			D2	0C			SESSIONERR	Name not known.
			D3				SYSBUSY	
			D4				SESSBUSY	
			D5				NOTALLOC	
			E0		04		INVREQ	Already allocated.
			E0		08		INVREQ	Wrong state.
			E0		0C		INVREQ	Invalid SYNCLVL.
			E0		10		INVREQ	Invalid data.
			E0		14		INVREQ	Invalid CONFIRM.
			E0		18		INVREQ	Invalid netname.
			E0		1C		INVREQ	Invalid command.
			E0		20		INVREQ	Invalid command.
			E1	00			LENGERR	Input data truncated.
			E1	04			LENGERR	Wrong output length.
			E1	08			LENGERR	Wrong input length.
			E3				WRBRK	
			E4				RDATT	
			E5				SIGNAL	
			E6				TERMIDERR	
			E7				NOPASSBKRD	
			E8				NOPASSBKWR	
			EA				IGREQCD	
			EB				CBIDERR	
			F1				TERMERR	
				20			EOC	
				40			INBFMH	
					F6		NOSTART	
					F7		NONVAL	

EIBFN 0 1		Control Group/ Command	EIBRCODE 0 1 2 3	Exceptional Condition	Further Description
		File Control			
06	02	READ	01	DSIDERR	
	04	WRITE	02	ILLOGIC	
	06	REWRITE	08	INVREQ	
	08	DELETE	0C	NOTOPEN	
	0A	UNLOCK	0D	DISABLED	
	0C	STARTBR	0F	ENDFILE	
	0E	READNEXT	80	IOERR	
	10	READPREV	81	NOTFND	
	12	ENDBR	82	DUPREC	
	14	RESETBR	83	NOSPACE	
			84	DUPKEY	
			D0 04	SYSIDERR	Name not valid.
			D0 08	SYSIDERR	Link out of service.
			D0 0C	SYSIDERR	Name unknown.
			D1	ISCINVREQ	
			D6	NOTAUTH	
			E1	LENGERR	
		Transient Data Control			
08	02	WRITEQ TD	01	QZERO	
	04	READQ TD	02	QIDERR	
	06	DELETEQ TD	04	IOERR	
			08	NOTOPEN	
			10	NOSPACE	
			C0	QBUSY	
			D0 04	SYSIDERR	Name not valid.
			D0 08	SYSIDERR	Link out of service.
			D0 0C	SYSIDERR	Name unknown.
			D1	ISCINVREQ	
			D6	NOTAUTH	
			E1	LENGERR	
		Temporary Storage Control			
0A	02	WRITEQ TS	01	ITEMERR	
	04	READQ TS	02	QIDERR	
	06	DELETEQ TS	04	IOERR	
			08	NOSPACE	
			20	INVREQ	
			D0 04	SYSIDERR	Name not valid.
			D0 08	SYSIDERR	Link out of service.
			D0 0C	SYSIDERR	Name unknown.
			D1	ISCINVREQ	
			D6	NOTAUTH	
			E1	LENGERR	

EIBFN 0 1		Control Group/ Command	EIBRCODE 0 1 2 3	Exceptional Condition	Further Description
		Storage Control			
0C	02	GETMAIN	E1	LENGERR	
	04	FREEMAIN	E2	NOSTG	
		Program Control			
0E	02	LINK	01	PGMIDERR	
	04	XCTL	D6	NOTAUTH	
	06	LOAD	E0	INVREQ	
	08	RETURN			
	0A	RELEASE			
	0C	ABEND			
	0E	HANDLE ABEND			
		Interval Control			
10	02	ASKTIME	01	ENDDATA	
	04	DELAY	04	IOERR	
	06	POST	11	TRANSIDERR	
	08	START	12	TERMIDERR	
	0A	RETRIEVE	14	INVTSREQ	
	0C	CANCEL	20	EXPIRED	
			81	NOTFND	
			D0 04	SYSIDERR	Name not valid.
			D0 08	SYSIDERR	Link out of service.
			D0 0C	SYSIDERR	Name unknown.
			D1	ISCINVREQ	
			D6	NOTAUTH	
			E1	LENGERR	
			E9	ENVDEFERR	
			FF	INVREQ	
		Task Control			
12	02	WAIT EVENT	32	ENQBUSY	
	04	ENQ	E0	INVREQ	
	06	DEQ			
	08	SUSPEND			
		Journal Control			
14	02	JOURNAL	01	JIDERR	
			02	INVREQ	
			05	NOTOPEN	
			06	LENGERR	
			07	IOERR	
			09	NOJBUFSP	
			D6	NOTAUTH	

EIBFN 0 1		Control Group/ Command	EIBRCODE 0 1 2 3				Exceptional Condition	Further Description
		Syncpoint Control						
16	02	SYNCPOINT	01				ROLLEDBACK	
		Basic Mapping Support						
18	02	RECEIVE MAP	01				INVREQ	
	04	SEND MAP	02				RETPAGE	
	06	SEND TEXT	04				MAPFAIL	
	08	SEND PAGE	08				INVMPSZ	
	0A	PURGE MESSAGE	20				INVERRTERM	
	0C	ROUTE	40				RTESOME	
	12	SEND CONTROL	80				RTEFAIL	
			E1				LENGERR	
			E3				WRBRK	
			E4				RDATT	
				02			PARTNFAIL	
				04			INVPARTN	
				08			INVPARTNSET	
				10			INVLDC	
				20			UNEXPIN	
				40			IGREQCD	
				80			TSIOERR	
					01		OVERFLOW	
					04		EODS	
					08		EOC	
					10		IGREQID	
		Trace Control						
1A	02	TRACE	E0				INVREQ	
	04	ENTER						
		Dump Control						
1C	02	DUMP						
		Interval Control						
4A	02	ASKTIME ABSTIME			01		ERROR	
	04	FORMATTIME						

Common ABEND Codes

When a CICS task is terminated abnormally, an ABEND code will be shown with the abnormal termination message. This code also appears in the ABEND dump of the task. Analyzing this ABEND code will greatly facilitate problem determination and program debugging, as discussed in Chapter 16. There are many ABEND codes associated with CICS, but they can be grouped into the following two categories:

ABEND Codes Related to Exceptional Conditions   As discussed in Chapter 2, the likelihood of abnormal termination (ABEND) of task will be significantly reduced if exceptional conditions are checked after every command execution by means of the HANDLE CONDITION command or the RESP option. If the exceptional conditions are not checked at all, the following exceptional conditions will cause the task to be terminated abnormally with the following ABEND codes:

Code	Condition	Code	Condition
AEIA	ERROR	AEI8	TSIOERR
AEID	EOF	AEI9	MAPFAIL
AEIE	EODS	AEXL	DISABLED
AEIG	INBFMH	AEYA	INVERRTERM
AEIH	ENDINPT	AEYB	INVMPSZ
AEII	NONVAL	AEYC	IGREQID
AEIJ	NOSTART	AEYE	INVLDC
AEIK	TERMIDERR	AEYG	JIDERR
AEIL	DSIDERR	AEYH	QIDERR
AEIM	NOTFND	AEYJ	DSSTAT
AEIN	DUPREC	AEYK	SELNERR
AEIO	DUPKEY	AEYL	FUNCERR
AEIP	INVREQ	AEYM	UNEXPIN
AEIQ	IOERR	AEYN	NOPASSBKRD
AEIR	NOSPACE	AEYO	NOPASSBKWR
AEIS	NOTOPEN	AEYQ	SYSIDERR
AEIT	ENDFILE	AEYR	ISCINVREQ
AEIU	ILLOGIC	AEYT	ENVDEFERR
AEIV	LENGERR	AEYU	IGREQCD
AEIW	QZERO	AEYV	SESSIONERR
AEIZ	ITEMERR	AEYY	NOTALLOC
AEI0	PGMIDERR	AEYZ	CBIDERR
AEI1	TRANSIDERR	AEY1	INVPARTNSET
AEI2	ENDDATA	AEY2	INVPARTN
AEI3	INVTSREQ	AEY3	PARTNFAIL

Other Common ABEND Codes If an ABEND occurred is not related to exceptional conditions, CICS will provide another set of ABEND codes. The following are some of the most commonly observed such ABEND codes:

ABMG	Requested BMS service not included at system generation
ABMP	PA/PF key not defined for page retrieval
AEY7	Resource security check failed
AEY9	Unsupported command issued
AICA	Transaction abended as a runaway task
AKCS	Deadlock time-out encountered
AKCT	Read time-out encountered
ASRA	ABEND due to program interruption
ASRB	ABEND due to OS ABEND intercepted by CICS

This is only a partial list. For the full list of ABEND codes, see the proper IBM CICS manual.

Glossary

ABEND. Abnormal end of online task or batch job.

ACF. Advanced Communication Function. It is used in conjunction with VTAM, TCAM, and NCP to identify the advanced version.

AID. Attention Identifier. Terminal key which causes device interrupt to transmit data to the host computer.

AIX. Alternate Index. A VSAM file's unique feature by which records of the same file can be accessed by the different key configuration (Alternate Key).

Alternate Key. A key of an Alternate Index (AIX) file. It is used in contrast to Prime Key, which is a key of the original VSAM file (Base Cluster).

AMB. Addressing Mode Bit. Bit 32 (relative to zero) of the Program Status Word (PSW), indicating whether addressing is based on the 24 bit mode (in case of 0) or the 31-bit mode (in case of 1).

API. Application Programming Interface. A standardized programming interface between the system control program and the application program, through which the application program can utilize the services of the system control program.

APPC. Advanced Program-to-Program Communications. A general term for a program in a system communicating with another program in another system based on the LU6.2 communication protocol.

AS/400. Application System/400. An IBM product family of advanced midrange computer systems.

Asynchronous Processing. One mode of CICS intercommunication, which allows a CICS application program in a local system to initiate a remote transaction owned by the remote CICS system.

ATI. Automatic Task Initiation. Based on the trigger level of a Transient Data Oueue (TDQ), CICS automatically initiates a CICS task.

Attribute Character. One-byte control character which precedes a field of a terminal screen. It defines characteristics of the field.

Auxiliary Storage. Data storage external to the main storage, such as disk and tape.

Back-End. The term used for the to-be-initiated side of Distributed Transaction Processing (DTP) conversation. The back-end system, therefore, means the system in which a transaction (back-end transaction) is initiated by the partner system (front-end system).

Backward Recovery. One mode of resource recovery, by which recoverable resources are recovered based on reading Dynamic Log or System Log backward.

Base Cluster. The original VSAM/ESDS or KSDS file against which an Alternate Index (AIX) can be created.

BDAM. Basic Direct Access Method. A data access method which is effective for random access.

BLL. Base Locator for Linkage. A group of address pointers to be used for accessing areas outside of a program.

BMS. Basic Mapping Support. A CICS facility for terminal screen operations with device and format independence.

BTAM. Basic Telecommunication Access Method. The most basic access control software for telecommunication.

CA. Control Area. A group of Control Intervals (CIs) representing a component of VSAM file data area.

CEBR. CICS-supplied Temporary Storage Browse transaction. It displays the content of Temporary Storage Queue (TSQ).

CECI. CICS-supplied Command Interpreter transaction. It verifies the syntax of a CICS command and executes the command.

CEDF. CICS-supplied Execution Diagnostic Facility transaction. It provides interactive program execution and debugging functions of a CICS program.

CEMT. CICS-supplied Extended Master Terminal transaction. It displays or manipulates CICS control environment interactively.

CESN. CICS-supplied Extended Sign-on transaction. It allows a user to start a CICS session.

Command. An instruction similar to a high-level language statement. It has more functional capability than macro.

Command Subroutine Approach. A technique by which each CICS command is coded in a form of subroutine, placed back of an CICS application program, and performed from the main body of the program. Since the main body of the program can be coded using only COBOL statements with no CICS commands, this approach increases program maintainability significantly.

COMMAREA. Communication Area. It is used for passing data among programs or transactions under CICS.

Conversation Identifier. Four-character code which identifies a conversation session of CICS Intersystem Communication (ISC).

Conversational. A mode of dialog between program and terminal based on a combination of sending message and receiving message within the same task.

CI. Control Interval. The smallest physical component of VSAM file, based on which all physical input/output operations are performed.

CICS. Customer Information Control System. IBM's most popular DB/DC control system.

CSA. Common System Area. One of the major CICS system control areas.

CSMT. CICS-supplied Master Terminal transaction. This is an older version of the CEMT transaction.

CSSF. CICS-supplied Sign-off transaction. This terminates a CICS session.

CSSN. CICS-supplied Sign-on transaction. This is an old version of the CESN transaction.

CWA. Common Work Area. A common user work area in CICS, whose size is defined in the System Intialization Table (SIT).

Data Integrity. The state of data quality where data is good and ready to be used.

DB/DC. Database/Data Communication. A general term expressing a complex online/real-time system involving large database.

DB2. IBM DATABASE 2. IBM's relational database management system.

DBD. DL/I Database Description. It defines a physical structure of DL/I database.

DBP. Dynamic Backout Program. It performs Dynamic Transaction Backout (DTB) for a CICS task.

DCP. Dump Control Program. This manages dump requests from CICS itself as well as CICS application programs.

DCT. Destination Control Table. This registers all Transient Data Queues (TSQs).

DFOC. Dynamic File Open/Close. A technique by which files in a CICS region can be dynamically opened or closed from a CICS application program or a batch job.

DL/I. Data Language/I. Originally developed as the database access method for IBM IMS database. Now, it is also used to express the database itself.

DOS/VS. Disk Operating System/Virtual Storage. An operating system based on the virtual storage concept which is suitable for small-scale mainframe system configuration.

DTB. Dynamic Transaction Backout. A process to recover recoverable resources based on information stored in the Dynamic Log.

DTP. Distributed Transaction Processing. One mode of CICS intercommunication, which allows a CICS application program (or transaction) in one CICS system to perform a synchronous communication (or conversation) with other programs in the partner system.

Dynamic Log. A main storage area of a CICS region where all changes made to recoverable resources are stored.

EDF. Execution Diagnostic Facility. An IBM program product, which works under CICS, for interactive execution and debugging of CICS application programs.

EIB. Execute Interface Block. A CICS control block containing useful CICS system information. It is automatically given to each CICS application program.

EIP. Execution Interface Program. This interfaces between CICS control programs and application programs.

ESDS. Entry Sequenced Dataset. One type of VSAM file.

Exceptional Condition. An abnormal condition occurred during execution of a CICS command.

FCP. File Control Program. Manages all input/output operations of files under CICS.

FCT. File Control Table. Registers all files to be used in the CICS region.

Forward Recovery. One mode of resource recovery, by which recoverable resources are recovered based on reading journal(s) forward.

Free-Format Map. A plain full-screen map (for example, 24 lines x 80 columns) whose entire space is defined as the free space. It facilitates complex screen layout handling.

Front-End. A term used for the initiating side of Distributed Transaction Processing (DTP) conversation. The front-end system, therefore, means the system which initiates a DTP conversation with a partner system (back-end system).

Function Request Shipping. One mode of CICS intercommunication, which allows a CICS application program in the local system to access resources in the remote system.

Generic Key. A higher part of a record key. It is used to identify a group of records generically or a record which belongs to that generic group.

ICP. Interval Control Program. Provides all time-related services under CICS.

IMS. Information Management System. IBM's popular DB/DC control system similar to CICS. It has a unique database access method called DL/I.

Intercommunication. A general term for a CICS system to communicate with other systems.

Inflight Task. A task which has not completed resource updates within a Logical Unit of Work (LUW) at the time of abnormal termination of the system.

ISAM. Indexed Sequential Access Method. One type of data access method, which is effective for both random access and sequential access.

ISC. Intersystem Communication. Communication between a CICS system and other non-CICS system or between a CICS system and other CICS system in the other processor.

JCL. Job Control Language.

JCP. Journal Control Program. Performs logging (journaling) of data onto external files called journals.

JCT. Journal Control Table. Registers the system log file and all user journal files.

Journal. A chronological record of changes made to recoverable resources.

KCP. Task Control Program. It controls a flow of CICS tasks.

KSDS. Key Sequenced Dataset. One type of VSAM file.

LUW. Logical Unit of Work. A sequence of processing between two sync points. Resource recovery is to be applied for one LUW.

Local. A term used for the initiating side of intercommunication. The local system, therefore, means the system which initiates an intercommunication session.

Locality of Reference. A virtual storage paging concept for the consistent reference to the instructions and data within a relatively small number of pages during execution of a program.

Logical Level. Level at which a CICS application program is to be placed when control is passed from CICS or other CICS application program. The highest level is 0, at which CICS itself locates.

LU2. Logical Unit 2. A commonly used communication protocol based on the 3270 type terminal data stream, by which a user can access a network.

LU6.2. Logical Unit 6.2. The most advanced and commonly used communication protocol, by which a user can access a network.

Macro. An instruction similar to the Assembler macros, which is a group of Assembler instructions for a specific function.

Main Storage. A storage area which can be addressed by a program.

Map. A format to create a screen layout based on BMS.

Mapset. A group of BMS maps linkedited together.

MDT. Modified Data Tag. One bit of an attribute character, which indicates whether the screen field has been modified (in case of 1) or not (in case of 0).

Message Routing. One function of BMS, by which a message can be routed to more than one terminal or printer simultaneously.

Mirror Transaction. A CICS-supplied transaction to administrate Function Request Shipping of CICS intercommunication.

MRO. Multi-Region Operation. Communication between a CICS system and other CICS systems in the same processor.

Multitasking. Execution of more than one task concurrently within the same region.

Multithreading. Execution of more than one task concurrently initiated by the same program within the same region.

MVS. Multiple Virtual Storage. An advanced version of OS/VS operating system.

MVS/XA. MVS/Extended Architecture. An advanced version of MVS operating system, which provides address space of 2,000 million bytes.

NCP. Network Control Program. System software residing in the communications controller to manage communications network.

Nonreentrant. A concept that a program modifies itself during its execution, so that it cannot reenter into itself after an interruption by the operating system. A batch program is an example of a nonreentrant program.

NMDS. Native Mode Data Stream. The data stream which terminal hardware sends/receives to/from the host computer.

NSI. Next Sequential Instruction. The program instruction which would have been executed next if an interruption had not occurred.

OS. Operating System.

OS/2. Operating System/2. An advanced operating system for PCs, particularly for the higher end of the PS/2 personal computers.

OS/2 E.E. OS/2 Extended Edition. One member of OS/2 family. It includes a number of extended functions in addition to the basic functions.

OS/400. Operating System/400. An advanced operating system for AS/400 family of midrange systems.

OS/VS. Operating System/Virtual Storage. An operating system which is suitable for a large-scale mainframe system configuration.

PA Key. Program Attention (or Access) key. It is used for triggering attention to the associated program.

Page (BMS). BMS makes it possible to send a series of screen panels to a terminal as one logical message. In such a case, one screen panel of this logical message is called a page.

Page (VS). One unit (usually 4,000 bytes) of virtual storage (VS), which is to be brought in or out from the real storage.

Path. A special VSAM pointer by which a record in the original VSAM file (Base Cluster) can be read based on the Alternate Key in the Alternate Index (AIX) Cluster.

PC. Personal Computer. A general term for microcomputer systems.

PF Key. Program Function Key. It is used for performing a special function assigned to that key.

PBS. DL/I Program Specification Block. The logical database structure of DL/I database to be used by an application program.

PCP. Program Control Program. It manages a flow of CICS application programs.

PCT. Program Control Table. It registers all CICS transactions with various options such as security, priority, recovery.

PLT. Program List Table. It registers a set of programs to be automatically executed at the CICS start-up time or the CICS shutdown time.

PPT. Processing Program Table. It registers all CICS application programs.

Process. An entity to perform processing. Usually, it means program or CICS transaction, but it could be any other entity depending on the hardware or software on subject.

Program. A set of instructions to achieve some unit of work in a computer system.

Pseudo-Conversational. A mode of dialog between program and terminal which appears to the operator as a continuous conversation, but which is actually carried by a series of separate tasks.

PS/2. Personal System/2. An IBM product group of advanced personal computers.

PSW. Program Status Word. It contains program status information at the time of interruption, which is useful for program debugging.

QID. Queue Identifier. One- to eight-character code which identifies a Temporary Storage Queue (TSQ).

QSAM. Queued Access Method. A data access method for sequential files.

Quasi-Reentrant. A concept that a program does not modify itself during its execution under CICS, so that it can reenter into itself after an interruption by CICS at a CICS command.

RACF. Resource Access Control Facility. An IBM program product for resource security management.

RBA. Relative Byte Address. The record's address within a file relative to the first byte of the file. It identifies a record of VSAM/ESDS file.

Real Storage. The memory which exists physically in a processor. It is usually used in contrast to Virtual Storage (VS).

Reentrant. A concept that a program does not modify itself during its execution under the operating system (OS), so that it can reenter into itself after an interruption by OS. An online program under OS must be reentrant.

Relay Program. A CICS-supplied program to administrate Transaction Routing of CICS intercommunication.

Remote. A term used for the to-be-initiated side of CICS intercommunication. The remote system, therefore, means the system which is initiated as the results from the CICS intercommunication request by the partner system (local system).

Rollback. Recovery of the recoverable resources to the last sync point.

RRDS. Relative Record Dataset. One type of VSAM file.

RRN. Relative Record Number. The record number of a file relative to the first record. It identifies a record of VSAM/RRDS.

SAA. Systems Application Architecture. A set of interfaces, conventions, and protocols in order to establish an enhanced level of consistency, portability, and connectivity of data, applications, and communications in the multisystem environment.

SCP. Storage Control Program. It manages requests of dynamic storage by CICS control programs and application programs.

SDF. Screen Definition Facility. An IBM program product which runs under CICS or TSO. It enables users to define screen layout interactively facing directly to the terminal.

Session-Id. Four-character code which identifies a conversation session of CICS Multi-Region Operation (MRO).

SIT. System Initialization Table. It contains control information for CICS initialization.

Skipper. An unlabeled 1-byte field in a BMS map with the autoskip attribute. It makes the cursor automatically skip to the next unprotected field.

SNA. Systems Network Architecture. The description of a set of protocols and procedures for controlling operations of sophisticated communications networks.

SNT. Sign-on Table. It registers all CICS users and their profile with respect to operating CICS, such as security and priority.

SQL. Structured Query Language. A database access method for the DB2 database.

STI. Scheduled Transaction Initiation. A technique by which CICS transactions can be automatically initiated at the scheduled time or interval.

Stopper. An unlabeled 1-byte field with the protect attribute. It makes the cursor stop forcefully at its position.

SVC. Supervisor Call.

Sync Point. Synchronization Point. A point during processing activities of a program where all resource updates are complete and the resources are in good condition.

System Identifier. One- to four-character code which identifies a system participating to CICS intercommunication.

System Log. A special journal reserved for storing all changes made to the recoverable resources of the entire CICS system

Task. A basic unit of work which is scheduled by the operating system or CICS.

TCA. Task Control Area. A CICS control block for goverming execution of a CICS task.

TCAM. Telecommunications Access Method. A high-level access method for telecommunication.

TCP. Terminal Control Program. Manages data exchange between terminals and CICS application programs.

TCT. Terminal Control Table. Registers all terminals used under CICS.

TCTTE. Terminal Control Table Terminal Entry. A system area of the TCT entry for a terminal.

TCTUA. Terminal Control Table User Extention. A user area of the TCT entry for a terminal.

TDP. Transient Data Program. It manages input/output operations of Transient Data Queue (TDQ).

TDQ. Transient Data Queue. A group of sequential data placed in the external dataset under CICS.

TGT. Task Global Table. A COBOL program control table which contains such information as address pointers and program alteration information during execution.

TIOA. Terminal Input/Output Area. A buffer for terminal input/output operations.

Transaction. An entity which initiates execution of a task. In CICS, transaction is identified by the transaction identifier.

Transaction Deadlock. An infinite wait state where two tasks are waiting for each other to release resources which are held by the other.

Transaction Identifier. One- to four-character code which identifies a CICS transaction.

Transaction Routing. One mode of CICS intercommunication, which allows a terminal connected to a local CICS system to run a remote transaction owned by the remote CICS system.

TSP. Temporary Storage Program. It manages input/output operations of Temporary Storage Queue (TSQ).

TSQ. Temporary Storage Queue. A group of sequential data used for scratchpad purposes under CICS.

TST. Temporary Storage Table. Registers all Temporary Storage Queues (TSQs) which requires recovery or security check.

TWA. Transaction Work Area. A user work area for a CICS task, whose size is defined in Program Control Table.

Validity of Reference. A virtual storage paging concept for the direct reference to the required page without intermediate references.

VM. Virtual Machine. An operating system for mainframe system which can define more than one logical computer system (virtual machine), each of which can run its own operating system independently.

VS. Virtual Storage. The logical space which can be accessed by application program. It is mapped into the real storage address by the operating system.

VSE. Virtual Storage Extended. An operating system which is an advanced version of DOS/VS.

VSAM. Virtual Storage Access Method. The most effective data access method currently available in the IBM mainframe system.

VTAM. Virtual Telecommunications Access Method. The most advanced access method for telecommunication.

Working Set. A virtual storage paging concept for the number and combination of virtual storage pages which a program needs at a given time.

XRF. Extended Recovery Facility. An advanced CICS recovery facility by which CICS system can be recovered and restarted automatically very quickly.

Index